*Art Nouveau in
Fin-de-Siècle France*

STUDIES ON THE HISTORY OF SOCIETY AND CULTURE
Victoria E. Bonnell and Lynn Hunt, Editors

DEBORA L. SILVERMAN

Art Nouveau in Fin-de-Siècle France

POLITICS, PSYCHOLOGY, AND STYLE

UNIVERSITY OF CALIFORNIA PRESS

Berkeley   Los Angeles   London

The publisher acknowledges
with gratitude the generous support
given this book from the
ART BOOK FUND
of the Associates of the
University of California Press,
which is supported by a major gift
from The Ahmanson Foundation.

The publisher gratefully acknowledges
the Division of Research Programs, National Endowment for the Humanities,
an independent federal agency, for their generous support.

University of California Press
Berkeley and Los Angeles, California
University of California Press, Ltd.
London, England
© 1989 by
The Regents of the University of California
Printed in the United States of America
1   2   3   4   5   6   7   8   9

Library of Congress Cataloging-in-Publication Data

Silverman, Debora Leah.
    Art nouveau in fin-de-siècle France: politics, psychology, and style.
        p.   cm.—(Studies on the history of society and culture)
    Bibliography: p.
    ISBN 0-520-06322-8
    1. Art nouveau—France.   2. Art, Modern—19th century—France.
I. Title. II. Series.
N6847.5.A78S55 1989
709'.44—dc19   88-14409

For Carl Schorske

CONTENTS

ILLUSTRATIONS

Plates
Following Page 158

Figures

ACKNOWLEDGMENTS

THIS BOOK BEGAN as a dissertation, which was inspired by the interdisciplinary teaching and writings of Professor Carl E. Schorske. He introduced me to the historical study of cultural forms, guided by a rigorous respect for the internal coherence of the object. Professor Schorske's advice, encouragement, and example influenced the project at every stage. I hope the book also reflects the independence he always granted me and the autonomy he made me cherish as his student.

During the formative phases of the project, I was fortunate to have the benefit of working with four other historians. Professor Jerrold Seigel suggested ways of thinking about the role of the artist in nineteenth-century French society and a compelling and original method for tracking the convergence of personal and social history. Professor Arno Mayer guided me through the bibliography of Third Republic France and alerted me to the tensions between bourgeois and aristocratic cultures in nineteenth-century Europe that have their resonance here. Professor Natalie Zemon Davis stimulated my interest in cultural symbolism and in the importance of gender in public discourse and private artistic creation. Professor Lynn Hunt provided new interpretations of French history and coaxed me to reconsider and sharpen my conceptions of the theory and method underlying cultural analysis.

In my effort to explore the connections between visual form and historical change, I immersed myself in art historical scholarship and methods and encountered a vital corpus of work in a newly consolidated substratum of the field: the social history of art. The writings of five individuals were particularly important to the development of my thinking. Professor T. J. Clark's books on artists and politics in 1848 had just been published when I was beginning my training in interdisciplinary cultural history; they revealed to me the social meaning carried in images. And Professor Clark's keen interest in my work from its very early stages has buoyed and fortified me at critical moments. Professor Eugenia Herbert's book *The Artist and Social Reform: France and Belgium, 1885–1898* had a long-lasting effect on my approach to fin-de-siècle art and politics, and her book still offers a point of departure for any study of this period. The writings of Professor Albert Boime isolated the significance of the institutional settings in which nineteenth-century French art was produced and alerted me to the points of intersection—stylistic and social—between official and avant-garde art. Professor Robert Herbert's work illuminated the special contribution of urban, suburban, and rural change in the evolution of nineteenth-century French painting and suggested the distinct resonance of the ideas of nature and artifice in nineteenth-century French artistic innovation. Professor Svetlana Alpers trained me to think visually, and her writings on the relationship between art and craft in the seventeenth-century Netherlands informed my interpretation of a later period and another context.

As the book evolved, I benefited greatly from the reactions and support of a number of other art historians, whose receptivity to my work gave me confidence that a historian could have something to contribute to visual interpretation: My thanks to Thomas Crow, Celeste Brusati, Carol Armstrong, Marion Burleigh-Motley, Linda Nochlin, James Rubin, Aaron Sheon, Kirk Varnedoe, Ken Silver, Paul Tucker, Nancy Troy, and Robin Middleton.

Research in France was made possible by grants from the Social Science Research Council and French-American Foundation, and later by the Academic Senate of the University of California at Los Angeles and the American Council of Learned Societies. During my initial stay in France from 1979–1980, a number of friends provided sustaining emotional and intellectual support that I have never forgotten: Lizabeth Cohen, Cheryl Gould, Edward Berenson, Francesco Passanti, Mirka Beneš, and Molly Nesbit. Professors Michelle Perrot and Madeleine Rébérioux gave me the valuable opportunity to test out some of my ideas among French colleagues.

I am indebted to the staffs of several libraries for their assistance, particularly those of the Cabinet des Estampes at the Paris Bibliothèque Nationale, the Paris Musée Rodin, and the Bibliothèque des Arts Décoratifs, with special thanks to Madame Geneviève Bonté. In this country, I used the collections of Princeton University, the University of California at Berkeley and Los Angeles, and the Philadelphia Museum of Art. UCLA's Art Librarian, Dr. Joyce Ludmer, was especially gracious and helpful throughout the project. The Inter-Library Loan Services of Princeton University, the Institute for Advanced Study, and UCLA provided crucial research materials with exemplary efficiency.

I wrote much of the book when I was a visitor at the Institute for Advanced Study in 1984–1985. While my husband was a member, the Social Science faculty also generously provided me with research facilities and support, as well as the opportunity to participate in an unusual scholarly environment. My deep thanks to Professors Clifford Geertz, Albert Hirschman, and Michael Walzer for making this possible. In addition, I am grateful to Professor Irving Lavin of the School of Historical Studies for enabling me to attend his weekly art history seminar at the Institute. I benefited considerably from the reactions of this group to my work.

I would like to thank Mrs. Lucille Allsen for her splendid work typing and retyping the manuscript, for the time she took perfecting technical and stylistic matters, and for her encouragement. Mrs. Peggy Clarke and Lynda Emery also patiently typed parts of the manuscript, offering gracious assistance with good humor. The women at UCLA's Central Word Processing, guided by Ms. Jane Bitar, shepherded the manuscript through its final phases with unusual speed and precision.

I am indebted to James Clark of the University of California Press, who initially acquired the manuscript. I have been fortunate to have worked at the Press with

Sheila Levine, who was involved in every phase of the manuscript's preparation and production and attended to the book with enthusiasm and efficiency. Stephanie Fay provided expert editorial assistance and helped make the book's final form both sharper and more accessible.

Many friends and colleagues have read the manuscript or have helped in ways that I cannot detail here but deeply appreciate: Sherrill Cohen, Joyce Appleby, Ruth Bloch, Robert Westman, Norton Wise, Margaret Rustin, Michael Rustin, Bert Hansen, Ann Koblitz, Philip Nord, Deborah Nord, David Abraham, Michael Hui, Hans Rogger, Robert Wohl, Ron Mellor, Ann Mellor, Sarah Melzer, Robert Nye, Peter Reill, Miriam Levin, Rachel Klein, Dora Weiner, Herbert Weiner, Peter Loewenberg, Mark Phillips, Ruth Phillips, Barbara Schneider, Mary Yeager, Susanna Barrows, Sarah Hirschman, Paul Rabinow, Peter Paret, Elizabeth Schorske, and Patricia O'Brien.

Six loyal friends encouraged me to pursue this work at a crucial early stage and continued to contribute the ideas, advice, energy, and support that enabled me to complete the book. I express my gratitude to Mary McLoed, Leila Kinney, Michael Rogin, Temma Kaplan, Dina Copelman, and Sarah Maza.

My parents, David and Ziona Silverman, have been steadfast in their love and their commitment to my work. Their presence in my life is rich and sustaining.

Finally, I want to thank my husband, Jeffrey Prager, for accepting this work as part of our life together. His ideas and suggestions indelibly shaped and strengthened the manuscript. Part way through the project our son, Daniel, was born, a perpetual source of wonder and joy for his parents. Only with Jeff's deep commitment to partnership have I been able to balance, albeit delicately, the challenges and pleasures of mothering Daniel with the demands and satisfactions of sustained intellectual work.

INTRODUCTION

The Transformation of Art Nouveau, 1889–1900

THE TERM "art nouveau" conjures up images of a European-wide invasion by the restless dynamism of organic form. The tremulous whiplash of Van de Velde rooms; the mushroom lamps of Emile Gallé; the giant plant-orb sprouting from the top of Joseph Olbrich's Secession Palace; the dripping plasticity of Emilio Gaudi; the germinating lilies of Guimard's métros—all contribute to a composite picture of a fin-de-siècle design movement dedicated to vitalizing all recesses of the urban artifice with the evocations of metamorphic growth.

Art nouveau did indeed transcend national boundaries. European art nouveau artists shared not only a propensity for effervescent linearity and highly worked surfaces but also three goals. First, they wanted to disrupt the hierarchy of media and to reunite art and craft. Second, they sought to discover a new and distinctively modern design style, liberated from the conventions of historical eclecticism. In the return to nature's forms they found a powerful antidote to the moribund formulas of the period styles. Third, they wished to assert the primacy of individual vision over the function of materials. For art nouveau artists, materials were vessels; design substances, no matter how durable and intractable, were destined to yield, bend, and rend according to the dictates of the imagination.[1]

This book examines the origins of art nouveau in one specific national and historical context: late nineteenth-century France. The premise is that the European-wide search for the unity of the arts and the shared preoccupation with nature had very different sources, forms, meanings, and functions in particular national settings. Rather than evaluate art nouveau as a divination or disruption of a stylistic progress, the book treats art nouveau as a historical phenomenon that is part of the broader cultural and political history of fin-de-siècle France. It aims to reconstruct as precisely as possible the motives and meanings associated with a particular development: the definition of modern style as a nature style of interior decoration. What kinds of assumptions about modernity were expressed in an art of organic retreat and irrepressible curvature? And why then?

The term "art nouveau" was not always associated in France with plantlike forms used in interior decoration. Indeed, in 1889 the term heralded a new world of public

1

technology and advanced industrial production. At the Paris World Exhibition of 1889, officials of the Third Republic inaugurated a monumental wrought-iron architecture. Prime Minister Jules Ferry had conceived of the fair to celebrate the achievements of French liberalism under the Third Republic. As he envisioned it, the exhibition, marking the centennial of the French Revolution, would be a bold statement of confidence: a confirmation of the consolidation of the Third Republic after its uncertain beginnings; a glorification of the Third Republic as the guardian and heir of the French Revolution; and an affirmation of the promises of liberal republicanism in the decades to come.[2]

The architectural symbols of this liberal republican apotheosis were two unprecedented structures: the Gallery of Machines and the Eiffel Tower. The Gallery of Machines, composed entirely of wrought-iron beams and glass panes, resembled a huge shed or hangar. Never had the roof of a single building spanned so great a space. The Eiffel Tower (Fig. 1) rose as the vertical complement to the horizontal mass of the Gallery of Machines (Fig. 2) directly opposite it on the Champ-de-Mars. Gustave Eiffel's thousand-foot tower, a synthesis of new materials and new methods of engineering construction, boldly proclaimed the triumph of engineering aesthetics over architectural tradition. Its form and its assemblage from prefabricated parts riveted at the site derived from Eiffel's experience as an engineer. The tower was actually a

Fig. 1. Eiffel Tower, 1889, Paris Exhibition.

Fig. 2. Gallery of Machines, 1889, Paris Exhibition.

giant iron pylon, a structural support Eiffel had devised as a technical solution to problems of wind, water, and weather. The Eiffel Tower, the new master of the Parisian skyline, invaded the sacred domain of culture with a feat of engineering construction, divested of all functional utility.[3]

The state planners of 1889, inspired by Ferry, commissioned the Gallery of Machines and the Eiffel Tower to embody their vision of a new public environment, constructed in accord with modern science and advanced industry. The colossal iron architecture of 1889 actualized a decade-long discussion within official circles about the need to find new modes of representation, new forms of beauty that would correspond to novel elements of the republican program: the expansion of heavy industry; the pursuit of laissez-faire economic policies; and the assault on religious mentalities by the inculcation of civic morality and secular science. Progress through the union of science, industry, and technology was the constant theme of the planners' 1889 reports; the two wrought-iron structures prefigured the new world.

Although there were many proposals for the gateway to the 1889 fair, the republican committee selected Eiffel's tower unanimously. The chairman, Edouard Lockroy, explained that the committee sought "an original masterpiece of the metals industry"; a stone monument would not do, and "only the Eiffel tower fit these requirements."[4] Georges Berger, director of works for the exhibition, identified the tower as a metaphor for the liberal credo of progress; it would testify to the audacious ascent of man:

We shall show our sons what their fathers have accomplished in the space of a
century through progress in knowledge, love of work, and respect for liberty.
We shall give them a view from the summit of the steep slope that has been
climbed since the dark ages. . . . For the law of progress is immortal, just as
progress itself is infinite.[5]

In 1889 planners and commentators alike designated the new iron monuments as
the forms of an "art nouveau," a "modern style," terms associated with the values of
youth, virility, production, and democracy. Vicomte Melchior de Vogüé, for example, a regular contributor to the *Revue des deux mondes,* enthusiastically welcomed
the two structures as the spectacular shapes of a *"monde nouveau"* made possible by
advanced technology and scientific rationalism.[6] He declared the art nouveau of
wrought-iron architecture appropriate to an emerging technological civilization.[7]
Glorifying their precision, prefabrication, and graceful geometry, he construed the
two structures as symbolic "bridges" between European nations united by free
trade, standardized technology, and industrial advance. The Eiffel Tower was, to de
Vogüé, a giant "crucifix," the wrought-iron steeple in a new universalist church of
technological progress.[8]

Gustave Eiffel himself identified the iron monuments as art nouveau. His tower
was not merely a feat of engineering wizardry but a statement of a new aesthetic.
"The tower will have its own beauty," he claimed; it is "imposing in its own way."[9]
Construction in stone had reached the limits of its usefulness; "new materials" enabled an unprecedented colossus to grip the imagination in the same way that the
pyramids did in their time.[10]

Eiffel emphasized that his tower would focus international attention on France as
a center of technological strength. "The Eiffel Tower . . . will show that we are . . .
a country of engineers and builders who are called upon all over the world to construct bridges, viaducts, trains, and the great monuments of modern industry."[11] He
wanted "to raise to the glory of modern science, and to the greater honor of French
industry, an arch of triumph as striking as those that previous generations had raised
to conquerors."[12]

Republican officials too defined and celebrated an art nouveau in 1889. Alfred
Picard, deputy director of planning for the fair, praised the new beauty inherent in
modern materials. He glorified the Eiffel Tower "as a brilliant manifestation of the
industrial strength of our country," which "attests to the immense progress realized
in the art of metal structures."[13] Edouard Lockroy, who worked with Minister
Charles de Freycinet to promote iron architecture at the 1889 fair, defined the modern style as one of public monumentality, based on the inventions of the engineer:

The centuries preceding us—religious, military, authoritarian, and aristocratic—discovered their architectural formulas in temples, palaces, châteaux,
and churches; our industrial and democratic era must definitively discover its
own. . . . Slowly, however, the modern style emerges, and it takes shape as

industry and science put new materials and new techniques at our disposal. The more wrought iron and steel play a role in our construction, the more we will achieve our own distinctive effects. Their lines will combine differently from before; this is the art of the nineteenth century, of the twentieth century. . . . The 1889 exhibition has accelerated its birth.[14]

By the 1900 exhibition, a significant shift had occurred: the terms "art nouveau" and "modern style" were used to identify architectural forms and meanings antithetical to those they had signified in 1889. In 1900, traditional stone facades enclosed the giant shedlike iron frames. Monuments to industrial technology were replaced by monuments to cultural tradition, such as the Grand and Petit Palais. The massive Gallery of Machines was enveloped in a bristling masonry shell, replete with terraced grottoes and fountains. The entryway for the fair was redirected from the Eiffel Tower on the Champ-de-Mars to an elegant hundred-foot stone statue on the Champs-Elysées called *La Parisienne*. Perched on rounded, heavily ornamented arches, *La Parisienne* wore elaborate robes designed by the couturier Paquin. In 1900 this queen of the decorative arts was described as the art nouveau; this statue was "supple and vital," in stark contrast to the denuded "carcass" of the Eiffel Tower.[15]

If the 1889 exhibition glorified the wrought-iron column, the 1900 exhibition signaled the reinvocation of conventional overwrought masonry structures in the public domain and the retreat to an ornamental fantasy in the organicized private interior. In 1889 art nouveau welcomed a new world of public technology and the potential for a collective existence; in 1900 art nouveau miniaturized iron materials, recast into organic and feminine forms (Fig. 3). Replacing the public iron monument with the private iron ornament, art nouveau celebrated modernity in domestic ensembles of nature and interiority. The artisan of visionary irregularity, not the engineer of standardized rational plans, was now the carrier of modern expression.

The shift from public technology to private organicism embodied in the two exhibitions echoed in the thinking of republican officials and commentators. Many of those who had affirmed the art nouveau of technological possibility in 1889 embraced the art nouveau of organic interior crafts in 1900. Vicomte de Vogüé, for example, repudiated his faith in the universal technological civilization prefigured in the Eiffel Tower. He explained in 1900 that the promises of 1889 were not to be realized. Rather than a "point of departure on an ever-ascending ladder," the "iron architecture of 1889 was more like the culminating point of a descending curve."[16] Alfred Picard, official planner for both the 1889 and 1900 exhibitions, had a similar change of heart. In 1900 Picard located art nouveau, or the modern style, in the home, in the elegant adornment of the private domain. The pace of modern urban life had to be offset by the soothing envelopment of modern interiors.[17]

Deputy Georges Berger and the museum administrator Roger Marx also redefined art nouveau between 1889 and 1900. Berger, who in 1889 construed the Eiffel Tower as a metaphor for the spectacular ascent of man, in 1900 felt that man had descended from "the summit of the steep slope" to two structures at the base

Fig. 3. Pendant in gold and copper, by Marcel Bing, 1900. Courtesy of the Musée des Arts Décoratifs, Paris.

of the Eiffel Tower: the Palace of Woman and the Pavilion of the Decorative Arts. Berger claimed by 1900 that France's greatest contributions to the world were not her scientists and engineers but her artists and artisans.[18]

Roger Marx, inspector-general of French provincial museums, had glorified the massive Gallery of Machines in 1889 as the essence of a new aesthetic. He applauded the exposed wrought-iron construction and praised the airy, floating sensibility created by the interpenetration of light and air through the glass panels of the gallery's roof. Asserting that this was a public collective architecture, an architecture to "serve the worker," he called the gallery a place of "soaring grace," which evoked the feeling of "a bird in flight."[19] In 1900, Roger Marx no longer praised wrought-iron architecture as the essence of French modernity. As a central defender of organic craft arts, the inspector-general now affirmed the feminine, interior world. The "soaring grace" of the latticed beams and glass panels of 1889 had given way to the "soaring grace" and fluidity of a woman dancer emulating a "bird in flight"—Loïe Fuller.[20]

The architect Eugène Hénard and the writer Emile Zola expressed the same shift. As director of works in 1889 for the Gallery of Machines, Hénard had idealized iron architecture as a new style befitting an industrial era.[21] A decade later he was responsible for constructing the tripartite ensemble of permanent buildings for the 1900 fair—the sweeping vista uniting the Invalides with the Champs-Elysées and the Grand Palais and Petit Palais. By 1900, Hénard had redirected his energies from technology to culture, from a new industrial architecture to traditional monument building. His plan for the two palaces was modeled on a similar vista at Versailles and the twin palaces of the Grand and Petit Trianon.[22]

During the 1880s Emile Zola had been a technological optimist, anticipating a world re-created by science, industry, and engineering. In his 1888 novel, *L'Oeuvre,* the hero, Claude Lantier, envisioned a new architecture:

> If there ever was a century in which architecture should have a style of its own, it was the century about to begin. . . . Down with Greek temples, there was no use for them in modern society! Down with Gothic cathedrals—belief in legends was dead! Down with the Renaissance . . . it would never house modern democracy! What was wanted was an architectural formula to fit that democracy, . . . something big and strong and simple, the sort of thing that was already asserting itself in railroad stations and market halls, the solid elegance of metal girders.[23]

Soon Zola too would change his mind about the architecture appropriate to modernity. In 1896 he revealed his reevaluation in answering a survey question, "What is modern architecture?" "Some years ago," he noted, "I believed absolutely that a new material, iron, would create the basis for a new and modern style." "Now it seems that we shall have to wait a long time for such a style."[24] That same year Zola commented further: "Modern society is racked without end by a nervous irritability. We are sick and tired of progress, industry, and science."[25]

The transformation of the thinking of these six figures was indicative of a broader

cultural and historical change between the two world's fairs. The ideas of these individuals, and the transfer of "art nouveau" from wrought-iron monuments to decorative interiors, expressed a fundamental change in the conception of modern urban
life and its promises in the ten-year period between the two exhibitions.

This book explores the origins and meanings of this shift in the locus of modernity in late nineteenth-century France. The contrasting world's fairs provide the
structural and chronological frames. The explanations for this retreat to the interior
are many and emerge from the interaction between artistic producers and political,
social, and intellectual factors specific to the 1890s. The analysis combines two levels
of explanation: both long-term artistic traditions and short-term historical conditions contributed to the formulation of a modern style as a nature style of interior
decoration.

The term art nouveau and the goals associated with it are usually assigned to a
purely artistic group in France, which coalesced in 1895 under the direction of the art
dealer and connoisseur Siegfried Bing. In the decade preceding the 1900 exhibition,
however, a much broader institutional craft initiative existed, directed by an organization called the Central Union of the Decorative Arts. After the exhibition of 1889,
a coalition of prominent politicians and cultural administrators became affiliated
with the Central Union's efforts to promote the reform of design in France. Key state
officials and the Central Union organizers pursued a common program of craft revitalization in the 1890s, calling their efforts to create a modern style based on reintegrating art and craft the quest for an art nouveau. Before 1895 both Siegfried Bing
and the French artists associated with him participated directly in this broader official
movement to rehabilitate the applied arts. Many of Bing's art nouveau artists were
long-standing members of the Central Union as well as the beneficiaries, as of 1890,
of state Salon reforms to include the exhibition of artistic crafts. Bing himself functioned as a central figure—consultant, emissary, and middleman—in the network of
Central Union and state officials endorsing craft modernism. The 1895 Art Nouveau
Bing thus marks not the inception of French art nouveau but one of the final stages
of a craft initiative articulated within the institutions of official culture.

A major part of the book traces the interlocking political and cultural elites who
promoted French art nouveau as craft luxury in the 1890s. I examine the personnel,
policies, and programs of two overlapping institutional centers of the craft modern
style: the Central Union of the Decorative Arts and the state beaux-arts ministry.
And I identify the political, economic, and social changes of the 1890s underlying
the transfer of official attention to the decorative arts as a source of national integration and international preeminence.

The French design reformers seeking to reunite art and craft knew of the English
arts and craft movement and the guiding ideas of John Ruskin and William Morris.
Although they praised some of the English ideals, they also departed from their English predecessors. First, they deradicalized the critique of the division of labor at the
heart of Ruskin and Morris's conception of craft, focusing on the comfort and stimulation of the beholder rather than the imperative of joy in the work process.[26] Sec-

ond, they were immersed in a profoundly nationalist discourse. They repudiated English medievalism and criticized the archaism, inelegance, and ponderousness of the English applied arts. Affirming that each country must return to the best of its own traditions, the French isolated a distinctively national model for their unity of artist and artisan: not the artisan of medieval faith but the artisan of rococo grace. This artisan represented to the late nineteenth-century French craft reformers the "essential" and "superior" qualities of their "race."[27]

This book examines the centrality of the rococo as a privileged national tradition in the attitudes and programs of the 1890s craft art nouveau. It emphasizes how the rococo in particular represented a French tradition linking the notion of modernity with the notion of privacy and interiority. In the period of Louis XV modernity became associated with the nature style; by the mid-eighteenth century, the term "modern style" described the retreat to an organic, feminine, and intimate interior. The promoters and producers of French art nouveau were explicitly inspired by the principles of the rococo style. The institutional sponsors of French craft unity undertook the restoration of a series of rococo building interiors and campaigned successfully to incorporate rococo applied arts into French museums. They redefined the national self-image by officially recognizing the rococo as part of the cultural patrimony. At the same time, art nouveau artists immersed themselves in the rococo precedent and discovered in the period of Louis XV a legacy that matched their own stylistic goals: a unity of all the arts and an organic ensemble of interior decoration.

French art nouveau was not, however, a derivative neo-rococo. Artists and their institutional sponsors shared a contemporary nationalist ideal: to renew French craft forms based on an inspiration from, rather than an imitation of, French rococo organic elegance. More important, one source of this artistic renewal was clearly unprecedented: the meaning of the 1890s craft modern style was inextricably linked to a new French medical psychology that identified the interior of the human organism as a sensitive nervous mechanism. The language of art criticism, the ideas expressed by artists themselves, and the statements of some promoters of art nouveau form a consistent pattern: an appeal to concepts absorbed from late nineteenth-century French neuropsychiatry. The diffusion of a specific body of knowledge, originating with Doctor Jean-Martin Charcot of the Paris Salpêtrière and his rival Doctor Hippolyte Bernheim of Nancy, stimulated a discourse in the artistic world connecting the organic curvature of modern craft arts to nervous palpitation, hypnotic suggestibility, and the inducement of dream states. The writings and activities of Charcot and Bernheim make it clear that pre-Freudian French psychiatry was charged with implications for the artistic community. Both doctors were immersed in aesthetic concepts and practices, and their redefinition of rational consciousness was generated in part by their experiments with the fluid, dynamic power of images to release unconscious forces. Neuropsychiatric medicine was not simply a new source for, or an influence upon, art nouveau. Rather, the interaction between art and neuropsychiatry in the 1890s was complex and reciprocal, with influence flowing in both directions. At the center is the case of Jean-Martin Charcot, the clinical proponent of unconscious "ideodynamism" and a lifelong practitioner of applied arts and drawing. The interdependence of art and medicine comes full circle in the Charcot family's participation as producers of modern crafts in the Central Union of the Decorative Arts and in their patronage of one art nouveau artist clearly affected by the fin-de-siècle neuropsychiatry of the unconscious, Emile Gallé.

Four issues underlie my analysis of the institutional and intellectual origins of French art nouveau. First, the shift from an art nouveau of technological monumentality to an art nouveau of organic interiority is not an antimodernist reaction. Rather, modernity, privacy, and interiority were deeply linked in France, informed both by an aristocratic tradition that had joined modern style to private retreat in the eighteenth century and by the new knowledge of the psychological interior in the late nineteenth century. The redefinition of the interior world by psychological categories transposed the meaning of private space in an unprecedented and quintessentially modern way. For if the late nineteenth century produced the possibilities for a dynamic and collective existence, the space and setting of mass man, it also gave birth to the triumph of psychological man, whose liberty and isolation were heightened by the monumental configuration emerging in the metropolis. French art nouveau provided a visual language for this modern psychological discovery, as modern in its way as the Eiffel Tower.

A second, related, point is that the modernism of the Eiffel Tower was not suddenly and abruptly replaced by the modernism of craft luxury. Each conception of style and society had its history in France, and each continued to play a role in the twentieth century. The two types of modernism formed coexisting currents, corresponding to the enduring character of France's dual economy, which could be tapped and emphasized in particular contexts. The call for the unity of the arts and the renewal of the crafts developed in a series of stages and found an institutional home in the Central Union of the Decorative Arts before 1889. My analysis isolates the distinctive conjuncture of factors in the 1890s—political, economic, social, and cultural—that enabled the definition and program of craft interior modernism to crystallize and become the focus of official and artistic attention.

Third, I confine my study to the origins of French art nouveau as an interior design style. Earlier accounts have treated art nouveau as a unitary, multimedia style, and writers have surveyed art nouveau tendencies in painting, sculpture, graphic arts, architecture, decorative arts, and so forth. New scholars are intensively examining art nouveau in separate media of expression. My own work parallels the recent effort of art historians to redirect attention to art nouveau as an initiative in interior design, with a history separate from that of architecture.[28]

A fourth and final point about method. The book seeks to balance institutional history with the history of style. Part of the account reconstructs the personnel and programs of the official centers of art nouveau and suggests that many French artists functioned comfortably within these institutions. I do not, however, want to reduce the art to its institutional context. Indeed, sections of the book are devoted to a close formal analysis of art nouveau art and emphasize that visual forms sometimes carried meaning that transcended their institutional boundaries and functions. The artists who absorbed the neuropsychiatric theories of fluidity, indeterminacy, and internal tension created art forms more complex, dynamic, and unstable than any institutional framework containing them.

With these issues in mind, I have divided my analysis into three parts. Part 1 examines the formative influence of an artistic tradition particularly important to the craft art nouveau of the 1890s: the rococo style of the mid-eighteenth century. This tradition was rediscovered in the mid-nineteenth century by the brothers de Goncourt, from whom the champions of art nouveau absorbed directly the principles both of rococo art and craft and of organic intimism. The brothers were the mediators of the rococo style to the craft reformers of the late nineteenth century. Part 1 thus explores the forms and principles of eighteenth-century art as they were recovered and interpreted by the Goncourts. Part 2 analyzes four short-term historical conditions of the 1890s that contributed directly to the formulation of the French modern style as interior nature style: (1) the political realignment of the liberal Third Republic, including its reconciliation with aristocratic elites and the search for an antisocialist national solidarity; (2) the economic reorientation of the governing elites from advanced industrial technology to luxury crafts as the presumed source of French market preeminence in a period of intensified international competition; (3) the social problem of the New Woman, who threatened to disrupt the boundaries between public and private domains; and (4) the association between modernity and a new French medical psychology, which had profound implications for the conception of visual form. Part 3 discusses the institutions and artistic practitioners of craft modernism and the program of rococo rediscovery and nationally inspired stylistic innovation that united their efforts.

*

I hope the book will contribute to historical interpretations of fin-de-siècle France as well as to broader comparative discussions of the period. Characterizations of late nineteenth-century France emphasize either the period's meliorist, progressive tendencies or its dissension, conflict, and degeneration.[29] I find evidence for both interpretive choices, though from different sources. As an intellectual historian, I take seriously the articulations of anguish, anxiety, subversion, and disorder expressed in the high culture of the period and the particularly perplexing problems posed by the new medical psychiatry to the inherited assumptions of the rational mind. I have found corroboration for some historians' emphasis on the widespread preoccupation with neurasthenia and social pathology. I was also struck, however, by a number of shared and integrative discourses protecting intellectuals from their sense of discordance and decline. Nationalism and Cartesian rationalism were still vital in this period, offsetting the potential disintegration of language and social unity. Furthermore, elements of structural solidification continued to be strong. Despite significant political conflicts between 1889 and 1898, the republican liberal core of the French state remained intact. And some practitioners of cultural innovation, rather than separating themselves in defiant communities, attached and accommodated themselves to official institutions. Such findings support the meliorist interpretation, though I want to emphasize the durability of liberalism and the resilience of institutions in mediating conflict and absorbing change rather than the gap between the misperception of crisis by the elite and the popular experience of progress.

Elsewhere in fin-de-siècle Europe separatist artistic communities proliferated; artists in Brussels, Vienna, Munich, and Berlin staged radical defections from inflexible official cultures to search for a modern style and ways to integrate all the arts. In France this search flourished within the official culture and in fact marked a lull in avant-garde secessions. While other European countries were experiencing in the 1890s the first shock waves of avant-garde negation, the French modern style marked a domestication of the artistic elite, which had had its strident polarization from official culture earlier. In inverted phasing with Belgium, Austria-Hungary, and Germany, France's movement for a craft modern style represented artistic innovators' reconciliation with, and reattachment to, an official culture that, unlike others in Europe, proved remarkably resilient and absorptive. After the rupture between artists and society of 1848, the aesthetic withdrawal of the Symbolists, and the radical political engagement of the Neo-Impressionists, French artists in the 1890s realigned themselves with an officially sponsored modernist cause and joined with bureaucrats, curators, and collectors in a campaign for national solidarity and an exclusively French variety of artisanal supremacy.[30] Further, the French movement for the renovation of the decorative arts was strikingly depoliticized and divested of a critical social vision. In England and Belgium the unity of the arts and the integration of artist and artisan had been goals of left-wing political and egalitarian social movements. In France, the goal of reuniting artist and artisan was pursued in the inverse direction. Rather than seek to democratize art and to recover it for the people, French art nouveau sought to aristocratize the crafts, to extend the hierarchy of the arts to include the artisan. Finally, in the French art nouveau movement a shared nationalist ethos superseded anti-traditionalism and generational conflict. In Belgium, Austria-Hungary, and Germany, the quest for modernity meant negating and repudiating history and tradition; the only way out of the prison house of bourgeois petrification was the totalistic embrace of the new. In France the search for the new was itself defined as *renouveau,* "renewal," a confirmation and regeneration of elemental national endowments; and the search for craft modernity was not articulated as a youth movement, pitting creative and rebellious sons against their conventional and suffocating fathers. The antihistoricism of German *Jugendstil,* Belgian *Jeune Belgique,* and Austrian *Ver Sacrum* contrasted with the French modernist call for a "solidarity" of young and old, who "reattached themselves to the tradition of the race" and rallied in an affirmation of national vitality and revitalizing continuity.[31]

The interaction of art, politics, and neuropsychiatry in France has implications for the most general and compelling issue in late nineteenth-century comparative history: the fin de siècle as a period of crisis. H. Stuart Hughes characterized the fin de siècle as a period of a European-wide "reaction against positivism," as the crucible of new forms of twentieth-century social theory.[32] Carl Schorske identified the conditions distinctive to late-century Austria-Hungary—a small and cohesive intellectual elite, a weak bourgeoisie, a short-lived liberal triumph, and a devastating liberal debacle—that facilitated a multiplicity of radical cultural innovations amid the crisis of liberalism.[33] The variation of forms, meanings, and functions of fin-de-siècle antiliberalism, antirationalism, and avant-gardism in different national environments demands much further exploration. The chapters that follow suggest that France may have differed from her European counterparts in experiencing a more muted version of both the crisis of liberalism and the reaction against positivism.

PART ONE

The Goncourts' Legacy

CHAPTER ONE

The Brothers de Goncourt
between History and the Psyche

A GENERATION BEFORE the Eiffel Tower arrived on the Paris skyline as a powerful symbol of public, collective existence, urban invasiveness had been experienced and overcome in an elaborately crafted retreat to the interior. The architects of this retreat were the brothers de Goncourt; its component parts were aristocratic: the rococo arts of the eighteenth century. Although the political, social, and psychological conditions initiating the Goncourts' retreat to the interior differed from those of the fin-de-siècle modernists, the results of their work played a direct and formative role in the development of a modern style as interior nature style in the 1890s.

Edmond de Huot de Goncourt (Fig. 4), born in 1822, and his brother Jules, born in 1830, were half-aristocratic, half-bourgeois. Their father was an army officer who died in 1834, their mother a descendant of Old Regime nobility whose own father had been guillotined in 1793. A modest inheritance allowed the brothers to devote their energies to art; they decided first to become painters and later settled on a collaborative career as writers and art critics.[1]

The brothers were deeply attached to an idealized image of the social hierarchy and cultural grace of Old Regime France, whose culmination they assigned to the epoch of Louis XV (1715–1774). Resentful and bitter children of the nineteenth century, the Goncourts considered themselves born too late to enjoy the effervescent leisure and languorous sensuality that noble elites had enjoyed during the era of the *fêtes galantes*.

Edmond and Jules reached adulthood in the wake of the bloody fratricidal violence of 1848 and the coup d'état of Louis-Napoléon. They assimilated the new realities of the Second Empire to the pre-1848 ideology that equated laboring classes with dangerous classes. The Goncourts' contempt for and terror of the masses were unrelenting; they defined the lower classes as the "dissolute *canaille*" and as the destructive and barbarian mob.[2] Their abhorrence of the lower orders was matched only by their vindictive indictment of the philistine bourgeois, whose corrupt materialism and corrosive individualism instilled greed and envy in the people and eliminated the refinements of hierarchical culture. To them the French Revolution was the first enemy, nineteenth-century democratic individualism the second. For them the

Fig. 4. Edmond de Goncourt, by Félix Bracquemond. Courtesy of the Bibliothèque Nationale, Paris.

taste, politesse, and cultivation of the Old Regime nobility had been replaced during the Second Empire by the bourgeoisie's crude leveling pursuit of Mammon.[3]

Fated to live in a world without legal aristocracy and gracious sociability, the brothers de Goncourt translated their anger and resentment toward the nineteenth century into the creation of an alternative world of eighteenth-century arts. There they found compensatory association with the dead generations of the Old Regime. Scorning the lower classes as vile animals and the bourgeois as vulgar philistines, they dedicated their lives to reconstituting the aristocratic art, manners, customs, and objects of the era of Louis XV.

The cultural treasures of the mid-eighteenth century had attracted a series of nineteenth-century enthusiasts, both official and avant-garde. Like the successive waves of Japonism, the rococo revival served different purposes for its various proponents. The first official champion of the era of the *fêtes galantes* was Louis XVIII, who believed that with the restoration of the monarchy, the cultural vestiges of Napoleonic rule had to be obliterated; the resuscitated extravagances of the mid-eighteenth-century nobility replaced Egyptian enigma and the sober linearity of the First Empire style.[4] Disaffected literati during the Restoration were also entranced by the rococo, for reasons that differed from those of their counterparts at court. Gérard de Nerval celebrated eighteenth-century dalliance as part of his cult of art for art's sake.[5] During the bourgeois monarchy of Louis Philippe, the literary devotees of the *fêtes galantes* included Théophile Gautier and Arsène Houssaye.[6] Gautier expressed his rococo passions by glorifying woman as a natural artificer and by celebrating fashion as art. The playful sensuality of the first *style moderne* fueled Gautier's affirmation of modernity, of the enthralling spectacle of contemporaneity.[7] Arsène Houssaye, a less marginal man of letters than the romantic bohemian Gautier, began in the 1840s a lifelong apotheosis of the "etiquette," "passion," and "elegance" of the "century dominated by Woman." Houssaye's own writings consciously emulated the preciosity and punning of the rococo *saloniers*.[8]

The Second Empire witnessed rococo revivals in both official and avant-garde circles. Empress Eugénie's infatuation with the eighteenth century resulted in the court craze for the *fêtes galantes* and led her to appear at masked balls as Marie Antoinette or Madame de Pompadour.[9] Moreover, because of her enthusiasms, eighteenth-century furniture was brought to the imperial dwellings at Saint-Cloud, Malmaison, and the newly erected Tuileries Palace. The Garde-Meuble National, originally the Garde-Meuble Royal, built by Louis XV, provided her with a storehouse of royal furniture.[10] Louis-Napoléon's support for the industrial arts during the 1860s contributed to the reemergence of eighteenth-century forms of craft embellishment.[11] Yet this official endorsement of rococo styles yielded inconsistent pastiches and gaudy composites; eighteenth-century rockwork and vines commingled, in effusive ostentation, with quintessentially Second Empire inventions.[12]

Aesthetes, collectors, and art dealers of the 1860s countered the bastardized rococo revival favored by the emperor with accurate artistic restoration, especially in painting. By 1870 the wealthy collectors Doctor La Caze and Walferdin donated their holdings of Fragonard, Watteau, Nattier, Boucher, Van Loo, and Lancret to the Louvre, establishing the first galleries devoted to the "lesser masters" of the *fêtes galantes*.[13] Simultaneously, the art dealer Martinet organized a large exhibition of these same eighteenth-century painters, stimulating the enthusiasm of Manet, Duret, Baudelaire, and Arsène Houssaye.[14]

The Goncourts were unique, during the Second Empire, in pursuing a historical and cultural reconstitution of the eighteenth century and in documenting the integration of all the rococo arts. Their interests ranged beyond painting to the fashion, applied arts, and interior design christened by the refined elites of the epoch of Louis XV.

After writing a series of scholarly books on the art of the *fêtes galantes* of the mid-eighteenth century, the brothers began to collect the objets d'art and drawings themselves.[15] Their consuming fever of identification with the elite of the Old Regime compelled them to assemble relics of the nobility's daily life: fashion manuals, address cards, signs, invitations to masked balls, memoirs of the mistresses of Louis XV, furniture, fire screens, jewelry, picture frames, porcelain bowls, vases, boxes of all shapes and sizes, tapestries, candelabra, and many etchings, engravings, and pastels. Complementing these French rococo objects were the Japanese products that eighteenth-century French elites had sought out enthusiastically: lacquer screens, ebony and onyx small furnishings, ivory carved boxes and miniatures, and painted porcelains.[16]

The Goncourts' identification with the dead aristocratic generations culminated in 1869 when they installed their vast collection in a spacious mansion in Auteuil, on the outskirts of Paris, arranging the objects to create an authentic ensemble of eighteenth-century interiors. At once the place of work and rest for the brothers, the house was conceived as a sealed fortress where the Goncourts could live completely surrounded by vestiges of a lost aristocratic culture.[17]

The impetus to create this home as aristocratic fortress was the new invasive metropolis. The house in Auteuil was a response to the experience of menacing Haussmannization, which Edmond described in 1860:

> My Paris, the Paris where I grew up is disappearing. Social life is undergoing a vast evolution. I see women, children, households, and families in the cafés. The interior is dying. Life threatens to become public . . . I am a stranger to what is coming, to what is there, like these new boulevards, lacking in all curves, implacable axes of the straight line. It makes me think of some American Babylon of the future.[18]

To struggle against this menace of invasive public life, the Goncourts enclosed themselves in a world of private interiors. To counter the oppressive boulevard, "lacking in all curves, implacable axes of the straight line," the Goncourts celebrated in their aristocratic retreat the epitome of an art that defied regularity and uniformity. In their house, every object was unique, glorifying nature's undulating, curvaceous, and irregular rhythms. Every raw material, from gold to bronze to iron and ceramic, was stamped by the hand of a distinctive artisan. Edmond described his objets d'art as examples of the "*tour de force*" and "*tour de main*" of each individual creator; even bronze and metal assumed the "supple," "pliant," and "molded character of melted wax." In their house, claimed Edmond, "all harsh and rebellious matter was subordinated to the supple caress of the artisan." [19]

The Goncourts' house was recorded in photographs that Edmond commissioned. Detailed descriptions of every object in the house and the arrangement of objects in suites of interiors are contained in his two-volume work *La Maison d'un artiste,* first published in 1881.

Figure 5 documents the outside of the house, whose facade proudly proclaimed the tone of the interior. Incised in the iron balcony over the entrance was a medallion with a portrait of Louis XV, "signaling the richest and most complete container of the eighteenth century that exists in Paris." [20] Figures 6 and 7 present two views of the grand salon. Figure 6 shows an elegant *canapé,* "sofa," "elongated to hold the hooped skirts fashionable at the time," according to Edmond. [21] It was embroidered with scenes from a fable by La Fontaine, interpreted by the rococo artist Oudry. On the walls hung framed drawings and engravings (Gravelot's *L'Entretien Galant* is at the lower right). At the far right corner stands a lacquer corner table, called an *encoignure,* on which rests a Sèvres porcelain vase; Edmond imagined Madame de Pom-

Fig. 5. The Goncourts' house in Auteuil, external view. Courtesy of the Bibliothèque Nationale, Paris.

Fig. 6. The Goncourts' house in Auteuil, grand salon. Courtesy of the Bibliothèque Nationale, Paris.

Fig. 7. The Goncourts' house in Auteuil, grand salon with fireplace. Courtesy of the Bibliothèque Nationale, Paris.

Fig. 8. The Goncourts' house in Auteuil, bedroom. Courtesy of the Bibliothèque Nationale, Paris.

padour touching the vase before adjusting her skirts to seat herself on the sofa. Figure 7 shows two Oudry chairs, matching the sofa with their embroidered fables; the frames for the Boucher and Fragonard drawings are of gilded wood, shaped at the top into a fanning scroll or shell. The same form graced the backs of the Oudry chairs and sofa.

A final photograph and description captured the tone of the Goncourts' interiors. On the bedroom walls (Fig. 8) are cascading floral garlands and cameos of lovers romping in pastoral settings. The canopy over the bed, visible in the mirror at the left, had a crown sculpted of wood and adorned with a gilded floral wreath. This bed, Edmond explained, had originally been part of the château at Rambouillet, a prime example of rococo decoration. The bed had been made for and used by the chatelaine, the princesse de Lamballe. Lying in bed, with Boucher's scenes of amorous country romps on the walls, Edmond could "open his eyes not on the era I abhor but on the era that is the object of my studies and the love of my life." "My bedroom," he continued, "is an authentic room of a château, where I become a sleeping beauty from the era of Louis XV."[22]

From this citadel of aristocratic reaction came the theoretical and visual bases for the *style moderne* of the 1890s. The Goncourts' house, collection, and writings reconstituted systematically for the first time the splendor of mid-eighteenth-century craft arts. Through their scholarship and their model home, the Goncourts offered primers of rococo design principles to the nineteenth century.

With their knowledge of the technical skills that had allowed eighteenth-century artisans to infuse the objects of daily aristocratic life with beauty and sensuality, the Goncourts launched a critique of the ugliness and bad taste of contemporary industrial society. They operated in France as John Ruskin did in England, using an aes-

thetic measure from the past to judge the deformations of the industrial and commercial present. Ruskin's vision was medieval and social, the Goncourts' rococo and
elite. Ruskin's main targets were the industrial revolution and the division of labor;
the Goncourts' were the French Revolution and the leveling of taste. The power of the
Goncourts' critique and their impact on the producers and promoters of art nouveau
in France were as decisive as Ruskin's effect on the generation of William Morris in
England.

The Goncourts' recovery of eighteenth-century arts clarified three precedents that
would shape the assumptions of fin-de-siècle craft reformers. The first was the unity
of the arts as an aristocratic patrimony. Until the end of the eighteenth century, the
word *art* signified technical skill, the capacity for masterful execution, not visionary
talent or the capacity for originality.[23] This tradition flourished under a noble elite.
Beginning with the establishment of the privileged métiers by King Henri IV at the
Gobelins, the *arts somptuaires,* subsidized by Louis XIV, continued as an appendage
of autocratic power.[24] But the reign of the Regency and Louis XV from 1715 to 1774
witnessed a golden age when all the arts were unified, for the expansion and dis-
placement of the aristocratic elite in these years gave an unparalleled stimulus to artisans. Liberated from the restrictive court life at Versailles after the death of Louis
XIV, the nobles transplanted themselves to Paris. There they avidly consumed the
elegant accoutrements provided by all the craft guilds.[25] The court of Louis XV encouraged an increase in the number of artisans and in the refinement of their work.
In the Royal Academy of Painting, for example, the preference of Louis XIV for
large-scale history paintings gave way to one for diminutive decorative panels of nature. Watteau began a fashion for an antihistorical and non-narrative painting of the
fêtes galantes, which triumphed in the Academy under Boucher and Fragonard.[26]
These artists were all artisans, the producers of street signs, drawings of all types, and
decorative wall panels. Their work, with its naturist subjects and serpentine forms,
was often commissioned for installation in interior spaces.[27] Boucher and Falconet, a
favored sculptor of the period, were also the directors of the Royal Porcelain Manufacture at Sèvres, founded by Madame de Pompadour in 1756. There these artists
transferred to porcelain and terra-cotta the same forms and themes they executed in
their paintings and sculptures.[28]

Thus for such artist-artisans of the eighteenth century as Watteau, Boucher,
Fragonard, and Falconet and for their elite patrons, all the concrete media—furniture, picture frames, precious stones, fans, umbrellas, porcelain—were considered
art, which was defined as a technical wizardry for fashioning surfaces.

The character of the eighteenth-century elite and the practical, craft-centered definition of art may be seen in a number of examples. Edmond de Goncourt's *Maison
d'un artiste* included lengthy descriptions of the manuals and memoirs in his collection that catalogued the "art collections" of mid-eighteenth-century nobles. Edmond provided detailed inventories of these eighteenth-century collections, which
comprised a mélange of precious stones, shells, porcelains, Japanese ivory sculptures, and lacquer boxes.[29] An image engraved by Boucher in 1758 illustrates the

contents of such a collection (Fig. 9). The image itself is not an art object but a sign
advertising the shop of Boucher's friend Gersaint. a merchant. According to the
sign, Gersaint, in his shop "A la Pagode," sold all types of "novelties of taste," including "jewelry, mirrors, small paintings, glazed pagodas, shells, and Japanese porcelains." Boucher illustrated this potpourri below this list of offerings. Other examples of this elite eighteenth-century mixture of arts and crafts celebrated by the
Goncourts were shop signs executed by Watteau and Chardin. The Goncourts' collection included a barber's sign by Chardin, depicting fashionable ladies and gentle-
men stepping out of their carriages into elegant chairs for grooming by the barbers.

Artisans like Boucher, Watteau, and Fragonard shaped the image of the artist-
artisan in the mind of the Goncourts. The brothers glorified the eighteenth century
as one "qui a l'ambition de joli en tout" ("which quested for Beauty in all things").[30]
Beauty in all things, integrating useful objects and art—these goals were also Ruskin's. Yet for the Goncourts "all things" hardly meant the simple and rough fashion-
ings of medieval craft culture, indivisible from a community of faith; it meant instead splendid and luxurious embellishments for an aristocracy of taste: secular, elite,
and socially insulated (Fig. 10).

If the Goncourts recovered the mid-eighteenth century as the golden age of art
and craft, they also rediscovered the birth of private space, and of private space conceived as an *ensemble,* during the era of Louis XV. The unity and equality of the
rococo arts found their principal expression in intimate interior installations created
for an aristocratic elite. This elite, fleeing from politics and social conflict, discovered
the interior as a sanctuary of nature and the female form, where monumentality was
rejected for grace, rational symmetry for sensual irregularity. The architecture of
these intimate ensembles was called after 1720 *le style moderne.*[31] The *style moderne* of
the late nineteenth century would develop striking affinities with this intimate,
organic, and artisanal modern style of the eighteenth century. The Goncourts formed
the bridge between them.

The Goncourts celebrated the epoch of Louis XV as "almost a century of grace,
the century of woman and her caressing domination over manners and customs."[32]
They described the elite as insulated in a "closed, gilded world" where politics was
replaced by "a government of manners."[33] These phrases evoke the political and cultural transformation that conditioned the emergence of the *style moderne* of the eighteenth century. The nobles who dispersed and sought a decentralized life in the city
of Paris after the death of Louis XIV reacted against the restrictive solemnity of Versailles and pursued private pleasures. They replaced the ritualized ceremonies of the
court with spirited, comfortable conversations among small groups of aristocrats
(Fig. 11). Madame du Châtelet explained that "we now live only for agreeable and
charming sensations";[34] another chronicler of the time noted the beginning in the
1720s of a "quintessence of the agreeable, the complexion of grace and charm, the
adornments of pleasure and love."[35]

After 1720 the political and cultural liberation from the court to the city, from
pomp and ceremony to intimate play, found architectural expression. The construc-

Fig. 9. *A La Pagode,* by François Boucher. Courtesy of the Bibliothèque Nationale, Paris.

Fig. 10. Porcelain and gilded bronze perfume fountain with gilded bronze base, mid-eighteenth century.

Fig. 11. *The Reading of Molière,* by François De Troy.

tion of both private residential mansions in the city and luxurious *maisons de plai-sance*—pleasure palaces—in the countryside increased. Inside these new dwellings a new kind of spatial arrangement and decoration was born, called the *style moderne*.[36]

The three characteristics of this style were reassembled in the Goncourts' own collection. First, private space was differentiated. Repudiating the vast monumentality of the open galleries at Versailles, the elite of the 1720s and 1730s created intimate, compartmentalized spaces. The modern style of the eighteenth century was launched with a celebration of the *petit appartement,* "the small apartment," which subdivided and dismantled the huge open antechambers favored by the period preceding it. The epoch of Louis XV witnessed the invention of the interior, a spatial celebration of a newly liberated aristocratic dalliance.[37]

Second, aristocratic women played a central role in the practice of the decorative arts and in the definition of interior space. The Goncourts' writings revealed the participation of noble women in various crafts, from the embroidery circles of Saint-Cyr to Madame de Pompadour's engravings.[38] More important, the Goncourts clarified how the rococo interior was inseparable from its female identity, for the Louis XV *style moderne* was initiated to oppose the *grand goût* of Louis XIV with the ethos of *la grâce,* a petite, amorous, and explicitly female form. Seeking to replace heavy

LE MATIN

Fig. 12. Le Matin, by François Boucher:
the new ritual of *la toilette.* Courtesy of
the Bibliothèque Nationale, Paris.

sumptuosity with capricious sensuality, the *style moderne* of the eighteenth century
filled the new private aristocratic spaces with diminutive objects and furnishings,
vested with forms and functions that were conceived as explicitly feminine. After
1725, a new arsenal of furniture appeared, accompanying the discovery of private
space. It facilitated the *douceur de vivre*—long hours of leisure, pleasure, and languor.
First there came the *canapé,* made, as Edmond de Goncourt explained, "for the flowing skirts of the period."[39] Furniture with anthropomorphic female names multiplied:
la causeuse, "the chatterer"; *la bergère,* "the shepherdess"; *la chiffonnière,* "the dresser";
la marquise brisée, "the divided marquise" (Pl. 1); *la chaise à la reine; la chaise longue;*
and especially *la toilette.*[40] The feminization of rococo furnishings culminated here, as
toilette named both the small dressing table for women and the art of women's prepa-
rations of their bodies and clothes for display (Fig. 12). If nobles at the court of Louis
XIV participated in the domesticating ritual of dressing the king, after 1720 an elegant woman would receive her amorous court as she finished her own embellishment. Seductive play replaced the politics of taming the nobility.

The third feature of the eighteenth-century *style moderne* reconstituted by the
Goncourts' house and writings was the discovery of the interior as an organic ensemble. The eighteenth-century *style moderne* unified the diverse media of painting,
sculpture, woodwork, and paneling in a single repertoire of subjects and a single
vocabulary of forms. The rococo modern style glorified nature as its subject and
fashioned all the elements of interior space into animated, undulating, and asymmetrical forms derived from the flowing trellises of plants and the scroll and serpentine fan shapes of grottoes and shells (Fig. 13).[41]

Fig. 13. Boudoir of the marquise de Pompadour at the château of Bellevue.

The rococo ensemble extended not only to the walls but to every interior element. The diminutive female furnishings echoed in their curves and color schemes the wall-paneling motifs and the garlanded tapestries. The *canapés* and *chaises longues,* inserted into alcoves, complemented the designs of the woodwork. The furnishings were framed by the same gilded woodwork of shells, flowers, and garlanded roses that danced across the walls and ceilings. The shepherd scenes represented in the uphol-stery of the furniture were the same as those that decorative painters like Boucher installed in panels along the walls (Fig. 14).[42]

The ensemble of the eighteenth-century *style moderne* was completed by the aris-tocratic woman as an objet d'art (Fig. 15), fashioned as an integral part of the inte-rior. The shapes and accessories sprouting from the dresses and hair of the women harmonized with the plant trellises and undulating grotto-work along the walls, ceil-ings, and furniture. The Goncourts explained that an important change in fashion accompanied the discovery of private space and the creation of the organic, feminine furnishings. When the monumentality of public architecture was replaced by gra-cious intimacy, heavy sumptuous costume also gave way to lighter, more delicate clothes. Women's dresses were made of the same cloth that draped the walls and the furniture, with its scenes of shepherdesses and country romps. Louis XV period dresses were distinguished by their floral patterns, according to the *manuels de la mode* in the Goncourts' possession. Artificial flowers were sewn on and embroidered into the fabric, and real flowers and vines adorned the hair, changing according to the season. In the middle of the eighteenth century this fashion was called *la mode ondoyante et serpentée,* "the undulating and serpentine fashion."[43]

When the aristocratic woman thus became a central element in interior decora-tion, a special artisan appeared to unify all the elements of the scheme: the *marchande des modes,* depicted in a Boucher engraving in the Goncourts' collection. The *mar-chande* provided the trimmings and accessories for the dresses *and* the furniture, co-ordinating woman's dress with the other curvaceous and meandering surfaces of the interior.[44]

Nature against History, private intimacy against public monumentality, feminine caprice against male rationality, the integration of all the arts in an interior ensemble where the woman herself was a principal part of the organic rhythms: these were some of the characteristics of the eighteenth-century *style moderne* rediscovered by the brothers de Goncourt and reassembled in their remarkable Maison d'Auteuil.

The resonance of these characteristics would have been less important for late nineteenth-century craft reformers had not the Goncourts transposed their efforts from historicist revival into an aesthetic model. Indeed, the power and centrality of their rediscovery for the next generation lay in their capacity to infuse the rococo model with new meaning. Whatever their lament for a vanished Old Regime, the Goncourts were very much mid-nineteenth-century artists. They performed an al-chemical transformation of the eighteenth-century model reassembled in their home, adapting the tradition to express new meanings and functions. Let us look briefly at the important ways the Goncourts recast the eighteenth-century legacy of

Fig. 14. Rococo chair, with Boucher shepherd scene.

Fig. 15. Lounging *à la rocaille*. Courtesy of the Bibliothèque Nationale, Paris.

the aristocratization of the decorative arts, the feminization of the decorative arts, and the notion of the interior as an organic ensemble.

Although they were deeply immersed in the historical tradition that posited the unity of all the arts as an aristocratic patrimony, the Goncourts promoted the aristocratization of the decorative arts on a new basis. Their attitude toward their eighteenth-century artifacts was tinctured by two contemporary values wholly unavailable to eighteenth-century producers and patrons, for whom art had been a matter of technical mastery, not individual genius. First, the Goncourts measured the quality of applied art by the Romantic criteria of individualism and the proximity of the objects to the immaterial refinements of painting.

The Goncourts clearly valued their eighteenth-century collection for its noble social origins. Edmond sometimes described the cherished objects in his *Maison d'un artiste* by categorizing them socially, assigning to them the titles of their aristocratic provenance. Throughout his book, Edmond impresses the reader with detailed accounts of the nobles to whom the objects in the collection originally belonged, relishing an aristocratic status by association. Thus, for example, he notes that the vestibule porcelains resemble those of Madame de Pompadour; that his book collection includes the leather-bound volumes that had belonged to Louis XV's four daughters; that a Japanese embroidered silk screen, called a *kakemono,* had been used by the Japanese emperor himself to wrap royal gifts.[45]

Yet the Goncourts subordinated the aristocratic lineage of an object to their individualist criteria as bourgeois aristocrats of the spirit. Although the historical information about original noble owners offered the Goncourts nostalgic memories, it was new aesthetic criteria that confirmed their own living artistic identities. Indeed, the highest praise that Edmond lavished on his vast array of applied arts centered on their uniqueness, on their expression of exceptional vision and individual genius. *La Maison d'un artiste* glorifies each splendid object for its "rarity," affirmed in the signature of the individual master who produced it. Edmond catalogued in intricate detail the signatures on his Japanese and Chinese bowls, swords, penholders, tapestries, and screens and those incised on his eighteenth-century French furniture, engravings, and porcelains.[46] He zealously chronicled the uniqueness of his objects, recording when the lost-wax process was used for bronze and iron ornaments, assuring that only one copy could be cast.[47]

Edmond not only celebrated the unique individual qualities of his applied arts but also glorified the individual creator of the objects in nineteenth-century terms. If the sculpted furniture, delicately shaped boxes, molded iron belt buckles, and painted porcelains were prized in the eighteenth century for the manipulation of their surfaces, Edmond applauded them for the breadth of creative vision *preceding* the material execution. Attributing Romantic abstract intellectual powers to eighteenth-century artisans, he interpreted the intricate handiwork of his objets d'art as tours de force of artistic vision. He praised the eighteenth-century rococo and Oriental artists who bent, shaped, contorted, and dominated all materials according to the subtle commands of creative inspiration; all "harsh and rebellious matter" had to yield to the fires of artistic imagination.[48]

As he appreciated the decorative arts not for the execution of their surfaces but for the creative process preceding it, so too Edmond de Goncourt emphasized the immaterial appeal of his applied arts. He repeatedly identified in them the same high quality of artistry found in painting. He said of a Satsuma pot that its "delicate nuances in relief seem to have been created for the joy of painters; it appears as a playful sketch on canvas."[49] "Immaterial," "impalpable," and "pure" were adjectives he used to characterize his Japanese lacquers, Sèvres bowls, and embroidered screens.[50] The "artistic imagination" emanating from his lacquer screen gave it the "immaterial lightness" of "small paintings."[51] And the silk embroidered squares, called *fukasa*s, were like "*le grand art du dessin*"; the embroiderers used a "colorist's palette like painters" and "vied with painters in the nuanced effects of light and contrasting colors across a surface."[52]

This evaluation of the applied arts according to nineteenth-century criteria of individualism and a dematerialized painterly vision derived not only from Romantic assumptions but from more recent developments. The Goncourts' attitudes toward eighteenth-century objects were also shaped by their post-1848 stance of aesthetic withdrawal and self-cultivation. Thus they measured the quality of the art by its nourishment of a hyperrefined visual sensibility.

The Goncourts were part of a literary generation for whom the bonds between artistic ideals, political action, and shared social values were irrevocably shattered on the barricades of the June Days. As the Romantic assumption of art for society's sake was exposed as a tawdry illusion in the events of the revolution of 1848, the Goncourts bitterly replaced it with art for art's sake. They defined art as the creation of complicated sensory impressions for a refined and exclusive elite.

In their literary work, the Goncourts were engaged in transforming language from narrative description to suggestive evocation. Erich Auerbach, among others, has indicated the heightened artifice and aestheticism emerging from the chrysalis of realism in the Goncourts' novels.[53] The Goncourts effected an elaborate distance from and transformation of the external world by their concentration on language itself and the formal qualities of words. The Goncourts achieved this distancing process by emphasizing the analysis of sensory impressions, in which visual modes were indispensable. In their novels, they infused language with pictorial properties, evoking the intangible refractions of light and shade and the mobility of visual sensations.[54] This visual attentiveness derived from the Goncourts' early practice and training as draftsmen and sketchers. Contemporary admirers described their work as "plastic prose," "the literal rendering of perceptions," a style "molded in forms and colors."[55] Like Impressionism, with its dialectic of observation and temperament, the Goncourts' writings began in realism and evolved toward subjective expression. Within a realist framework their novels concentrated on the complex subtleties of visual appearances and on painstaking, nuanced accounts of visual impressions registered on individual sensibilities.

This aestheticized, visually oriented literary practice shaped the Goncourts' appraisal of the applied arts as bearers of intangible, painterly effects, of rarified and complex visual sensations. Paul Bourget, in an article on the Goncourts' house in

1883, commented that the brothers ascribed the same character to their private sanctuary of aristocratic art as to the external world: each realm was a "clinic" of sensory analysis.[56] Both the beloved decorative arts and the abhorred metropolis were, ironically, to be valued for the range and quality of sensory stimuli they offered the sensitive aesthete. In the artificial world of the isolated artist, the rule of life was the expansion of sensibility. Visual sensations, detached from the objects that gave rise to them, were to be analyzed and evoked in a nuanced visual vocabulary, such as that employed by Edmond in the *Maison d'un artiste*.[57]

The complex painterly effects Edmond glorified in his eighteenth-century arts were also those the Goncourts orchestrated for their entire interior design. A consistent aesthetic program informed their arrangement of objects. Despite the historical character of these objects, the Goncourts turned their house into a monument against bourgeois eclecticism. They adhered to a ruthless unity of periods, negating eclecticism by composing spaces with objects solely from eighteenth-century France and from the Orient. They also superimposed over the historical objects an aesthetic program, what they called their *harmonie artiste*.[58] They employed a nonhistorical criterion for this program, juxtaposing objects for the variety and subtlety of their *visual* properties. In his journal, Edmond noted that it took him years to arrive at the "assembled nuances" of an "artistic harmony" for "a single wall" in the entryway.[59] Earlier he had described the pleasures of his aesthetic interior coordination, which he compared to the creation of a great painting: "One will never know the pleasure gained by an impassioned decorator as he composes panel walls of an apartment, on which materials and colors harmonize or contrast. It is like creating a great painting when he combines bronze, porcelain, lacquer, jade, and embroidery. This can satisfy one completely."[60]

Edmond's aesthetic and personal coordination of the objects in the house culminated in the installation of a vast collection of eighteenth-century prints in the living room. Edmond and Jules painted the lower walls of the room black, with a veneer paint used for Parisian omnibuses. Only this paint had a sheen bright enough to enhance the visual forms hung on the walls above. Along the ceiling the brothers spread red silk matting to provide a bold contrast to the black. The combination of red matting, black veneer, and rococo prints seemed to offer a pure visual harmony. When he completed the design, Edmond described a decorator's principle for aesthetic integration:

> To *create* a room in my house; that was my goal. . . . After long meditation, akin to the meditation for a chapter of a book, I was convinced that only a bright black and dull red would do for the drawings. . . . A uniform and warm color had to envelop them. Only this could bring out the whites and the milky bright spots that a plaster ceiling kills. Let us posit, in principle, that there are no harmonious apartments unless the objects within stand out because of the contrast and the opposition of two largely dominant tones. Red and black is one of the best such combinations a decorator can use; they highlight and enhance that which furnishes a room.[61]

If the brothers de Goncourt elevated the applied arts on a new basis, they also reinterpreted feminization in the rococo arts. As historians and collectors they chronicled the important tradition of noble women as practitioners of the applied arts. And they also reconstituted the explicitly feminine meaning of interior space in the rococo model, which compared women to svelte Sèvres porcelains and assigned to diminutive furnishings the qualities of delicate women. But as aesthetes and misogynists, the Goncourts also pressed their feminized objets d'art into the service of their erotic needs. The new meaning the Goncourts attributed to the rococo feminization of the applied arts derived from the convergence of their social critique and their psychological perversion.

The Goncourts identified their rococo objects as erotic substitutes for real women—in a tract of 1856, *La Révolution dans les moeurs;* in their journal; and in the *Maison d'un artiste*. In the early tract, Edmond registered his hatred of bourgeois women as an extension of his critique of post–French Revolution society. The argument was tightly knit: the end of absolutist monarchy undermined patriarchy, unleashing greedy and envious drives among the lower orders. These drives were particularly intense in women, who became the engines of unbridled egotism in modern society. Not knowing their proper social station, all women imagined themselves educated, piano-playing matrons, and they would drive their men to money, ambition, and greed. The true elegance and intelligence of women, available only in a hierarchical system, were eradicated forever by the insatiable striving of the bourgeoise.[62]

If the Goncourts propounded their hatred for modern women as part of their critique of bourgeois society, the sources for their venom were deep-rooted and psychological. I will discuss them here only as they relate to the Goncourts' peculiar attitude toward their decorative arts.

Neither Edmond nor Jules ever married, though each occasionally procured a mistress, and they often shared one between them.[63] There is some evidence of fused selves in the two brothers, who lived together, worked together, and even spoke of their love as a bond superseding all others.[64] Both brothers channeled powerful eroticism into their applied arts, abandoning the playful sensuality originally attributed to rococo forms to pursue a more tormented and perverse relation. Jules recorded in his journal dreams of raping a delicate young woman who resembled one of his rococo porcelain figurines.[65] Edmond wrote of caressing his Clodion statuette as if her stomach and neck had the touch of real skin.[66] The theme of the objets d'art as surrogate sexual companions and as vehicles of vicarious union emerged as Edmond described sleeping in the bed occupied by the princesse de Lamballe, drinking from porcelain cups molded from the breasts of Marie Antoinette, and returning from a long day of foraging for eighteenth-century art objects exhausted, "as if from a night of sexual debauchery."[67] Finally, at the beginning of the *Maison d'un artiste,* Edmond explained how his objets d'art functioned for him as a form of sexual sublimation; unable to sustain ties to real women, he found in objets d'art a compensatory erotic energy:

Contemporary life is a life of struggle; it demands in all professions a concentration, a striving, an effort in an enclosed private world. Our existence is
no longer exterior as in the eighteenth century; it is no longer played out amid
society from the age of seventeen until one's death. . . . These less worldly habits have led to a contraction of the role of woman in male thinking; she is no
longer the gallant occupation of our whole existence, which hitherto was the
career of many. . . . Because of this transformation of values, we have arrived
thus: that men's interests have shifted from the charming beings to pretty, inanimate objects, with a passion charged with the nature and character of erotic
love. There were no *young* collectors in the eighteenth century: this captures
the difference between our two centuries. For our generation, art collecting is
only the index of how women no longer possess the male imagination. I must
admit here that when by chance my heart has been given, I have had no interest
in the objet d'art. . . . This passion . . . gives immediate gratification from all
the objects that tempt, charm, seduce: they provide a momentary abandon in
aesthetic debauchery. . . . These are some of the causes that invest an almost
human tenderness in objects; they have made me in particular the most passionate of collectors.[68]

The last element of the Goncourts' modern transformation of the rococo tradition
is their redefinition of the eighteenth-century ensemble. As historians, the Goncourts
had reconstituted the way all of the components of eighteenth-century interior design cohered in an ensemble composed of the subjects and forms of nature. As psychological beings, the Goncourts projected into the rococo space the vibrations and
complications of the interior life of the nerves. We have seen how the Goncourts
installed their collection by subordinating the historical nature of the objects to a
nuanced aesthetic program. Their absorption of a particular kind of psychology
radically altered the meaning of their ensemble.

The Goncourts' literary cult of visual sensations was linked to the cultivation of
their nerves. Like many of their fellow artists, they had absorbed from medical psychology ideas concerning the human organism as a sensitive nervous mechanism.
Two clinicians, Doctors Moreau de Tours and Jean-Martin Charcot, were particularly influential in shaping the Goncourts' thinking. The two doctors related the
psyche to an interior life regulated by the palpitations of the nervous system. They
defined the human being as suspended between stimulus and response; the external
world acted directly upon the internal world of the nerves. If there was too much
stimulation, the nervous system would become overworked, and the subject would
lapse into a state of mental fatigue and physical inactivity.

Both Jules and Edmond de Goncourt read Moreau de Tours's work on nervous
tension and degeneration, which predated the period of Charcot's major achievements.[69] In the decades after Jules's death, Charcot became both an intellectual influence on Edmond and a figure in his social circles. In the fall of 1878 Edmond recorded
in his journal attending a small dinner with Charcot, given by the commissioner-

general of the Japanese exhibit at the 1878 Paris World's Fair.[70] In 1879 Edmond went to the Charcots' home for a drink after a lecture by their common friend Philippe Burty, the art critic and connoisseur.[71] Edmond de Goncourt and the Charcots were frequent guests of the Alphonse Daudets in 1882 and 1883. Edmond recorded that at one of the Daudet soirées Charcot described an interesting case.[72] Alphonse Daudet, one of Edmond's closest friends, was treated by Doctor Charcot throughout the 1880s.[73] By 1883 and in the years following, Edmond's entries in his journal indicate his fluency with clinical terminology and familiarity with Charcot's methods and therapies.[74]

The Goncourts considered themselves "clinical writers of the nerves" and fastidiously attended to the clinical analysis of their sensations.[75] They cultivated the relation between the arduousness of artistic work and nervous degeneration. Medical psychologists warned that continuous mental effort, unrelieved by physical action, could yield a state of physical exhaustion and mental hypersensitivity, called neurasthenia. The Goncourts perceived the neurasthenic state as the ground of existence for the modern artist. They defined themselves as aristocrats of the spirit precisely because of the extreme refinement of their nerves.[76] The modern artist, with his overdeveloped nervous sensibilities, could invest the clinical analysis of impressions and sensations with literary form. In 1870 one of the brothers wrote to Zola that "the originality of our work rests on an understanding of nervous disorders."[77] Edmond even developed a special clinical file for the documentation of neuropsychiatric cases, which he would refer to in developing his literary projects.[78]

If a literature of the nerves brought new insight, the artist was also bound to live out the painful consequences of this expansion of inner experience. When Edmond de Goncourt stated, in 1888, that Charcot did not have a "monopoly on nervous diseases" and that he and his brother had cast "nervous diseases into literature,"[79] he also accounted for the torment this attentiveness unleashed. For a clinical analyst of sensibility and a hypersensitive neurasthenic, there was no rest; the slightest tremor in the sensory world registered its effects on the nerves. The brothers wrote in *Germinie Lacerteux* that "the normal effect of nervous disorders of the body is to destroy all sense of proportion in human joys and sorrows so that they are only experienced in their extreme forms."[80] In 1866 the brothers characterized their neurasthenic state as one of mutilation, in which they made forays into the world as raw, exposed cords of vibrations:

> I have come to the sad conclusion that observation, instead of blunting my sensibilities, has extended them, developed them; it has left me laid bare. This type of incessant working on oneself, on one's sensations, on the movements of one's heart, this perpetual and daily autopsy of one's being, results in the discovery of the most delicate fibers; one can manipulate these fibers in the most throbbing, quivering ways. One can thereby discover a thousand sources for making one suffer. One becomes, as a result of this constant self-analysis, the opposite of inured: a kind of skinned and chafed moral and sensitive being,

wounded by the minutest impression, defenseless, without a casing, all bloody
and raw.[81]

The perpetual exercise of their nervous sensibilities had important consequences
for the Goncourts' conception of rococo ensemble. With their particular form of
self-analysis, they transformed the eighteenth-century ensemble from organic oasis
to a source of nervous palpitation. The objects in their eighteenth-century rooms
were not soothing and stable reminders of a historical past; they shifted according to
the brothers' superaesthetic eyes and played inner chords of nervous vibrations.
Throughout the *Maison d'un artiste,* Edmond engaged in detailed analyses of the
varied and continuously changing subtleties of color dancing across the walls and
objects of his rooms, offering him an ever-refined awareness of nuance and a corresponding nervous tremor.[82] In other passages, he discussed how the wall patterns,
engraving lines, and furniture forms in his boudoir stimulated him to a "feverish,"
palpitating, and heightened state necessarily preceding his writing.[83] Two of the
Goncourts' friends, Paul Bourget and Roger Marx, noted how the rococo arts fed
the brothers' nervous excitation. Both remarked that the eighteenth-century arts assembled in the Goncourts' house were objects neither of pleasure nor of leisure for
the brothers. The rococo relics were the indispensable and "invincible need of their
entire beings,"[84] the vehicles of creativity for men who equated art with nervous
vibration and physical degeneration.[85]

   "Defenseless," and *"sans enveloppe"* ("without a casing"); this was how the
Goncourts portrayed themselves as psychological beings. Ironically, the elaborate,
plush, and rare spatial casings the brothers built in their house offered them no protection from the ravages of an acutely developed inner tension. If they retreated to an
aristocratic interior at Auteuil to evade the menacing boulevards and crowds, the
Goncourts' psychological knowledge, projected inside, brought with it another
form of suffering. External invasion was replaced by internal explosion.

                                         *

The Goncourts' writings and model home would have a formative impact on the
artistic producers and official promoters of a modern style in the 1890s. As historians
and archaeologists, the Goncourts concretized the three elements of the rococo interior model, identified in the eighteenth century as a new, modern, style that rejected
history for nature. The unity of all the arts; the particularly feminine identity of intimate space; and the interdependence of all rooms in an organic ensemble—these elements of the mid-eighteenth-century legacy were reconstituted in the Goncourts'
Auteuil mansion.

   If the Maison d'Auteuil concentrated these elements of the rococo modern style in
one place, it also projected to the next generation a set of meanings that transcended
historical lessons. I have analyzed how the Goncourts' own post-1848 stance of aestheticism and self-cultivation shaped their redefinition of the quality of the applied
arts. The Goncourts glorified their applied arts not as gracious useful objects origi-

nally created for the eighteenth-century nobility but as vessels of nuanced, immaterial visual impressions and as the products of inspired artists. Moreover, their own troubled misogyny led them to eroticize their objets d'art in a way that was very different from the original caprices of rococo sensuality. Finally, they infused new psychological meaning into their enveloping rococo ensemble; rather than provide stable historical anchors, the eighteenth-century objects were made to throb and vibrate by the interminable exercise of neurasthenic sensibility.

Some of the Goncourts' transformations of the rococo legacy were peculiar and inimitable; others would resonate clearly in the art nouveau of the 1890s. The elevation of the decorative arts for their uniqueness and their approximation of the imaginative effects of painting would reappear in the 1890s; so too would the relation between the interior ensemble and the vibration of the nerves.

In many ways, the Goncourts stood as intermediate figures, offering the generation of the 1890s the first major reassessment of the rococo design legacy and transforming it in accord with new and unprecedented needs. In the 1890s, the invocation and transformation of the rococo model would also provide the theoretical underpinnings for a French modern style. This revival and adaptation differed from that of the Goncourts; its rationale was elaborated by a broader official group and expressed the meanings and functions peculiar to the fin de siècle. I turn now to these special political, social, and intellectual conditions of the 1890s.

PART TWO

Fluctuat nec Mergitur:
Belle Epoque and Fin de Siècle

CHAPTER TWO

Aristocratic *Ralliement*
and Social *Solidarité*

The most incredible thing we have seen since 1870 is not the telephone, the auto-
mobile, radium, or the wireless telegraph; it is that the Republic has endured! . . .
The Republic is a regime . . . that can defend itself and bear up.
Arthur Meyer, 1911[1]

As in other European countries, the program of economic and political liberalism
in France was subjected to wide-ranging attack during the 1880s. By 1889, when its
official sponsors organized the Paris Exhibition to apotheosize the aggressive sec-
tarian liberalism of the Republic's founding fathers, Gambetta and Ferry, a reaction
against that tradition had already been unleashed. Internally, laissez-faire orthodoxy
was challenged by important French economists such as Paul Cauwès and Charles
Gide. In 1886 Cauwès became the first professor of law and political economy
to identify the market chaos and social costs of the unregulated economic competition at the heart of Ferry's policies. Gide's writings demanded that laissez-faire be
"openly and officially abandoned."[2] Both thinkers denounced economic liberalism
in the context of France's worst economic recession since the 1840s, which the Ferry
governments failed to offset.[3]

Responding to the retrenchment of a laissez-faire world market, France moved
toward economic nationalism in the late 1880s, repudiating international free trade
and adopting tariff protection for native industry.[4] Ferry's political system suffered
from the unanticipated consequences of its own program, universal suffrage and nationalism. Although the liberals assumed that the ballot was a tool of responsible
citizenship, they confronted the reality that it could be pressed into the service of
anti-parliamentarism. Liberal policies were further subverted by the rise of a bellig-
erent mass nationalism. Whereas Ferry's policies incorporated nationalist ideology as
a rationale for imperialist campaigns, conservatives mobilized around a banner of
virulent chauvinist nationalism. The meteoric rise of General Boulanger from popular demagogue to political threat between 1888 and 1889 revealed to the republicans
the power of nationalism and anti-parliamentarism to rally a variety of social groups
against the Republic.[5]

Rather than capitulate to new antiliberal forces, the French Third Republic dem-onstrated a durability and capacity for internal metamorphosis that surprised and shocked many of her enemies at home and rescued France from the calamitous fate of other liberal political systems on the Continent. Indeed, 1889 marked a watershed in the history of French republicanism, and the initiation of the transformation of French liberalism in the face of new realities. Between 1889 and 1898, beginning with the aftermath of the Boulanger crisis and ending before the full-scale eruption of the Dreyfus affair, a new form of liberal republicanism emerged as the regnant force in French politics. It was fundamentally different from the combative en-lightenment liberalism of the founding fathers, for it was based on forging political alliances and economic compromises with the very forces that had been the target of Gambetta's and Ferry's anticlerical and individualist crusade. From 1889 to 1898 the goal of the Third Republic was political consolidation. The realignment of political forces in this period made possible a fundamental stability that persisted despite the superficial changes of ministers and cabinets.[6]

Instead of christening the glorious new decade of liberal ascendancy prescribed by Ferry, the Paris Exhibition of 1889 marked the end of an era of aggressive secular individualism and laissez-faire capitalism. As the new republican synthesis unfolded, the Eiffel Tower became transformed into a monumental tombstone for the liber-alism it had been designed to celebrate. In its place, a less imposing and more accom-modating symbol emerged in the official architectural forms of the 1890s (Fig. 16). *Fluctuat nec mergitur,* a banderole inserted into the frame of a royal coat of arms, was incised after 1889 as the seal of the Third Republic on a series of public build-ings, including the new Sorbonne, the reconstructed Hôtel de Ville, and the Pont Alexandre III, Grand Palais, and Petit Palais completed in 1898 for the 1900 exposi-tion. The seal consisted of a cartouche with a ship, atop which was a panel of royal fleur-de-lis and a crown. Beneath the ship unfolded the scroll with the motto, sig-nifying that the ship of state might be tossed about by the ocean waves, but it would not capsize.

The use of this seal after 1889 symbolically attached the Third Republic to a mo-narchical and imperial tradition. Originally the arms of the medieval water carriers, the seal had been appropriated by Louis XIV in the seventeenth century and invested with the royal fleur-de-lis. Rejected during the French Revolution and replaced with the seals of the liberty tree and liberty cap, the seal of royal arms was reinvoked by Baron Haussmann in 1853. It was Haussmann himself who added the banderole to the royal seal to express his hopes, in the aftermath of 1848, that the empire would not founder. But the Third Republic in the last decade of the nineteenth century would be better equipped to realize the dreams of its imperial predecessor.[7]

This peculiar amalgam of an Old Regime seal and a Haussmann inscription trans-posed into stone the shift from Ferry's uncompromising liberal crusade to the more tempered accommodation of the 1890s Third Republic. On the one hand, the official reinvocation of the seal affirmed the continuity of the Republic with previous re-gimes. After the ruptures of the Commune and the divisive anticlerical zeal of the Opportunism in the 1880s, the republicans of the 1890s launched a decade of recon-

Fig. 16. Fluctuat nec mergitur device,
Paris. Courtesy of the Bibliothèque
Nationale, Paris.

ciliation, concretized in a symbol which recapitulated various French regimes, and
asserted the Republic as their durable descendant. On the other hand, the image and
legend of the ship of state skillfully navigating the rough waters was appropriate for
a Republic whose strength in this decade lay in its very resiliency, its capacity to
chart a fluid course, shifting and gliding according to the changing conditions of
political winds and weather.

The elections of 1889 and 1893 catapulted what historians have called a new generation of political leadership to the forefront of republican statecraft.[8] Although
older politicians shaped by Gambettism in their youth, such as Eugène Spuller and
Réné Waldeck-Rousseau, would play a prominent part in government between 1889
and 1898, they did so in a new context. The primary architects of state policies were
no longer those who had dominated the political scene since the founding of the Republic. The combined effects of Boulangism and the Panama scandals of 1892 depleted the ranks of the opportunist followers of Gambetta and Ferry.[9] Among the
signal victims of the Panama crisis was Charles de Freycinet, the engineer-politician
who in the 1880s championed France's heavy industrial development, coordinated
massive railroad programs, and sought a monumental architecture to celebrate new
technology.[10] In the place of the discredited opportunists, a new group of republicans arrived. They were all young and had made their political debuts within the
preceding ten years. Called the youths by their contemporaries, these new republican leaders included Léon Bourgeois, Paul Deschanel, Georges Leygues, Léon
Barthou and Raymond Poincaré.[11] André Siegfried described them as "another gen-

eration, distinct from the great republican ancestors. They were too young to have suffered the Republic's founding."[12]

The new generation of republican leadership articulated a new political doctrine, *progressisme,* which was to underlie state policy and shape unprecedented factional alliances between 1893 and 1898.[13] *Progressisme* had little to do with the critical anticlericalism and the cult of secular and technological progress promoted by Ferry. Its linchpin was the reclassification of political divisions, the attempt to restructure the political landscape to forge a new moderate republican unity based on realignments with right and left.[14] In part, the search for political realignment reflected the end of the heated divisiveness between the Republic and the right. After 1889 the monarchist right was resigned to the constitution and acknowledged it would be "more profitable to use their political weight within the republican system."[15] The republicans, however, having implemented their major programs of extended universal suffrage and compulsory secular education, were in a position to consider reconciliation and to offer their former enemies the opportunity to join the ranks of a regenerated, inclusive, and more tolerant republican order.[16]

A common fear brought about the political realignment, and *progressisme* provided a negative and defensive strategy against a common enemy—socialism. Divergent elements of the political spectrum, perceiving an escalating and imminent collectivist challenge, formed a common front.[17] One of the leaders of the new republicans, Paul Deschanel, who articulated the doctrine of *progressisme* in 1893, posited the "*République nouvelle*" as the new unity of political elites, who transcended their differences in the fight against a greater enemy: "The surest way to save France from the perils of revolutionary socialism is by a politics that is purely, highly *progressiste.*"[18]

Between 1889 and 1894 a series of radical social movements were suddenly consolidated, erupting with a vociferousness and public identifiability that belied their numerical strength and ability to coordinate their tactics. Internally divided and organizationally weak, the movements that appeared simultaneously—socialism, anarchist terrorism, syndicalism, and Christian associationalism—were construed by the elite as a single block of marauders against property. Although the fear of these movements was unwarranted by their actual size and power as well as by the moderate goals of some of them, the accelerated pace of social agitation during the five-year period explains why the social question monopolized the political scene.[19]

Workers began in the late 1880s to reactivate their own forms of resistance after a decade of withdrawal and resignation in response to post-Commune repression and recession. The number of strikes doubled between 1890 and 1893, particularly among miners.[20] Workers' visibility was enhanced not only by strikes but by the new organization of public demonstrations. In 1889 workers in sixty towns coordinated a march for an eight-hour work day. In 1890 the first May Day celebration was held in France, detaching workers as a group from the official republican holiday of Bastille Day. The "panic" of overreaction against the May Day parades in Paris was repeated in another town, Fourmies, with more lethal consequences: the peaceful procession of workers was met by the town troops, who killed ten marchers by firing into the crowd.[21]

Organized socialism made significant national breakthroughs from 1889 to 1896. After the International of 1889, French socialists were inspired to join forces to create a single newspaper, *La Petite Républicaine,* and to define a minimum program. Most important, socialists entered official political life in 1893, when the first deputies on the extreme left were elected to the Chamber. Representatives of *progressiste* republicanism won three hundred seats and the socialists fifty, effecting what one historian has called a "profound modification of the political equilibrium."[22] Jules Guesde's radical anti-parliamentarist campaigns were most successful in the areas of industrial concentration. Between 1890 and 1893 Guesde's Parti Ouvrier expanded from two thousand to ten thousand members, most of them textile and metallurgical workers in the North.[23]

Syndicalism joined socialism as a vigorous political force during the 1890s. Encompassing both revolutionary syndicalism and more moderate forms of anti-political mutualism, the *syndicats* between 1890 and 1895 increased their membership from 5 to 15 percent of the labor force.[24] In 1892 the first of a series of attempts was made to consolidate a Fédération nationale des Syndicats. Members of the *syndicats* were drawn primarily from the heavy industrial sector. Among skilled artisans membership increased minimally between 1890 and 1895, but during the same period the number of *syndiqués* in the new chemical industries expanded fivefold and *syndicat* membership in both mining and metallurgy doubled.[25]

A third form of radical working-class organization was also consolidated between 1890 and 1895. This was the proliferation of local workers' *bourses du travail,* which initiated a national federation in 1892. Under the leadership of Fernand Pelloutier, the *bourses du travail* included skilled independent workers, particularly from the construction and metallurgical sectors. Tending toward anarchism, Pelloutier joined with non-Guesdists in forming a Confédération générale du travail in 1895.[26]

Two developments between 1890 and 1895, which intensified the sense of beleaguerment among the republican elite, ensured that the social question would move to the forefront of national politics. The first was a series of violent acts that lent urgency and intensity to the need for social defense. From 1892 to 1894 anarchist bombs exploded in the center of the Chamber of Deputies and in fashionable cafés and hotels. Although the perpetrators of what anarchists called this propaganda by the deed were not political conspirators, the bourgeoisie was shocked into confronting some of the signal victims of the social order. Three of the bombers, Ravachol, Henri, and Vaillant, were impoverished and marginal figures, seen by some as catalysts for revenge by the oppressed. The violence escalated in 1894 when the president of the Republic, Sadi Carnot, was assassinated.[27]

Not only anarchist violence but a traditional and respectable institution, the Catholic church, assured the entry of the social question onto the political stage of the 1890s. The papal encyclical *Rerum Novarum* of 1891 chastised republicans for the social injustices unchecked by economic liberalism while condemning the socialist alternative. In a double coup, Leo XIII proclaimed that Catholics should embrace the "godless" Republic and work within the state system in a conservative block; at the same time, he launched the church as a competitor for working-class allegiance, urging that the workers' plight be met not only by traditional Christian charity but by an active campaign for Catholic labor associations. The papal encyclical also included an unprecedented claim for state assistance to the poor and underprivileged. At the very time that radical demands for social legislation were being defined, the pope announced that "the secular power had a duty, not only to keep order but also to insure distributive justice and to protect the weak." By demanding active state sponsorship of social improvement, the church helped to make the social question central to the republican politics of the 1890s.[28]

Thus the synchronized appearance of a variety of movements championing social and economic justice and the overestimation of their tactical force and numerical strength shaped the political alliances of the new republican *progressistes* in the 1890s. The counter-socialist impulse guiding the *progressiste* republic was channeled into three political phases, each of which would have important consequences for the officially sponsored craft modern style.

Between 1893 and 1895, *progressisme* turned its conciliatory and absorptive powers toward the right. Republicans concentrated on a realignment with clerical and aristocratic elites, hoping to defuse the socialist menace with the unifying, coercive bond of an *esprit nouveau*. Eugène Spuller, Gambetta's close collaborator through the early 1880s, formulated the theory of the *esprit nouveau* in 1894, as minister of public instruction and beaux-arts under Prime Minister Casimir Perier: "'*L'esprit nouveau*' is the spirit that tends, in a society as profoundly troubled as ours, to draw all Frenchmen together around the ideas of good sense, justice, and charity. These ideas are necessary for any society that wants to endure. It is a spirit that aspires to reconcile all citizens."[29] The practical extension of the *esprit nouveau* was the political program called the *ralliement*. Specifically aimed at the church and the monarchist right associated with it, the *ralliement* was made possible by the papal recognition of the Republic and the tempering of liberal anticlericalism. Led by Jacques Piou and Etienne Lamy, part of the Catholic and conservative right offered themselves as candidates labeled *ralliés,* signifying the new cooperation with republicans to establish a homogeneous party of "order."[30] Although only thirty-four were elected in 1893, the *ralliés* continued to play an important part in republican government throughout the 1890s.

The significance of the *ralliement* extended beyond the specific episode of the 1893 elections, and beyond the specific group of Catholic-affiliated politicians, and should be seen as a particular manifestation of a more general effort by bourgeois republicans to find a basis for unity with the older aristocratic forces, an ongoing quest to solidify the ranks of one elite. This conception of the *ralliement* as a broader process of aristocratic rapprochement had an international dimension: the Franco-Russian alliance. Before 1889 French republicans refused to consider solving the problem of France's diplomatic isolation by allying with an absolutist religious power, and Czar Alexander III was equally distrustful of the nation spawned by revolution and regicide. Between 1890 and 1898, the Third French Republic prepared and sealed an alliance with the czar that synchronized exactly with the internal *esprit nouveau*. Thus the welding with aristocratic forces at home was replicated at the international level by the conciliation between the French Republic and the Russian autocracy.[31]

During the second phase of republican *progressisme,* in 1895 and 1896, the Republic moved to the left, attempting to undermine the socialist challenge by incorporating some of its theoretical assumptions and practical programs into the mainstream of a revitalized liberalism. The architect of this social republicanism was Prime Minister Léon Bourgeois, whose limited practical success and short term in office were outweighed by his major theoretical contribution, the formulation of the doctrine of organic solidarity as a liberal route to "outbid the socialists."[32] Bourgeois's solidarism, as it was called, effected what amounted to an ideological revolution, which left the principles of liberal individualism intact while adjusting them in response to the radical communitarian critiques of republican egoism. At the same time, Bourgeois recuperated for the liberals a theoretical model that had long been the monopoly of the right—organicism.

Historians have only recently begun to assess the meaning and impact of solidarism, which they have designated the official creed of the Third Republic in the fin de siècle.[33] It is clear that Bourgeois did not originate the liberal version of organic solidarity but synthesized efforts by progressive thinkers to come to terms with the vociferous challenges to agonistic individualism.[34] Aided by the social theorist Emile Durkheim and the philosopher Alfred Fouillée, Bourgeois assimilated the findings of biologists and zoologists who countered Social Darwinism with evidence of cooperation and interdependence in nature. Not only was mutual aid a characteristic of species, but each individual organism was made up of cells working together.[35] Both Durkheim and Fouillée, dissatisfied with the normative liberal tradition of negative freedom, discovered in these scientific findings a rational basis for a positive social doctrine.[36] Léon Bourgeois pressed their formulations into the service of a rejuvenated republicanism, developing an organic model of unity in diversity. He discovered a compelling compromise between individualism and community, analogous to the relations of cells and of species: each element was irreplaceable, but all individual elements worked interdependently for the sake of the whole.[37]

Thus at a moment of heightened perception of class conflict, of what contemporaries called the distension and dismemberment of the social body[38] by anarchist bombs and of what Durkheim identified as the acceleration of individualism into a frenzied social *"dérèglement,"*[39] Léon Bourgeois posited a theory of fundamental order and unity, social solidarity. Like Saint-Simon after the French Revolution and Taine after the Commune, Bourgeois discovered in organicism the most profound and indisputable vision of harmony with which to negate and neutralize his particular experience of a discordant social reality. Unlike Saint-Simon and Taine,

Bourgeois's liberal version of organic solidarity sidestepped the issue of hierarchy and emphasized the structural differentiation of function and coordination of parts as the exemplary natural imperative for social cooperation.

As a political doctrine, Bourgeois's solidarity subordinated individual freedom to membership in a family and nation and emphasized a shift from "The Declaration of the Rights of Man" to the "Declaration of Men's Duties" as the basis for a social republicanism. Bourgeois claimed that those who were born came into society as "debtors"—they were not free but encumbered with obligations to their fellows.[40] The state regulated the reciprocal duties among men and itself incurred a "duty" to "discharge the debt" of the whole society by active sponsorship of the poor.[41] Both the conception of the citizen as predestined to carry a burden of social debt and the theory that the state had a "duty" to protect the poor and redress social injustices evoked the papal alternatives to economic and political liberalism. Léon Bourgeois absorbed the message of the *Rerum Novarum* and pressed it into the service of the internal transformation of the secular liberal legacy.[42]

The doctrine of organic solidarity contributed to the resiliency and adaptiveness of the Third French Republic in the fin de siècle, as it attempted in this second phase of *progressisme* to forge a middle way between liberal individualism, which was under attack, and social collectivism, by which it perceived itself to be menaced.

When Léon Bourgeois's ministry was overturned after the defeat of a graduated income tax, the third and final phase of republican *progressisme* was initiated by Jules Méline. Between 1896 and 1898, Méline administered one of the longest lasting cabinets in the Republic's history by synthesizing the two earlier phases of *progressisme,* the *ralliement* and solidarism. Méline is credited with reconsolidating the *ralliement* by offering important cabinet positions to clerical and aristocratic conservatives under a broad antisocialist program of "protectionism, patriotism and social defense."[43] At the same time, Méline retained and celebrated the revised liberal principles of social solidarity, particularly evident in his government's support for mutual aid societies as a compromise between state intervention and unregulated individual competition.[44] Méline summarized the three phases of the *progressiste* countersocialist Republic in the fin de siècle with his slogan "Neither revolution nor reaction."[45]

*

The major characteristic of political life in the 1890s, post-Boulanger and pre-Dreyfus, was the reclassification of the old factional divisions, and the solidification of one elite against a common enemy—socialism. The forms of this consolidation shifted between the republicans' reattachment to the old clerical and monarchist right and their quest to modernize their individualist heritage with a social vision derived from an organicist model. Thus the Third Republic in the 1890s was peculiarly conservative and progressive at the same time, responsive to external challengers and able to defuse their critical power by absorbing them.

The officially sponsored movement to regenerate the crafts would extend the two elements of the political realignment to the less volatile domain of culture. Replicating the simultaneous conservatism and modernism of political *progressisme,* the agents of that *progressisme* in official culture formulated a dual program with striking theoretical affinity to the *ralliement* and organic solidarism. At the center of the craft movement lay a rapprochement with the aristocracy, realized when the artisanal splendors of the eighteenth century were institutionalized and when artists were encouraged to draw inspiration from the elegant interpenetration of all the arts in the rococo nature style. To this aristocratic artistic revival the official craft sponsors joined a quest for the modern unity of all the arts based on new organic forms, balancing individual artistic creation with a social ideal of collaboration for coordinated design ensembles.

If the ideals of the *ralliement* and organic solidarity were constrained by the fractious necessities of real politics, they would blossom more freely in the noncontingent realm of art. In the craft movement, the political architects of the *ralliement* and solidarism would participate in a social form that lay behind their realignment efforts—the solidified ranks of one elite. Politicians and cultural officials would converge in promoting the artistic equivalents of aristocratic affirmation and bourgeois solidarism, an apotheosis of republicanism in transformation.

CHAPTER THREE

The Abdication of Technology and the Elevation of the Crafts

THE POLITICAL PROJECT of republican consolidation during the 1890s would facilitate official sponsorship of a craft modern style. But the problem of the French economy and its relation to the world market between 1889 and 1896 propelled the crafts into the center of government concern. This chapter will discuss two economic factors that helped to redirect the republican elite from technological monumentality to artisanal work of high quality as the source of French modernity: intensified international competition in the heavy industrial sector and the advent of protectionism. It will go on to examine how the craft sector itself was beset by external challenges and internal crises in the 1890s, thus suggesting the defensiveness that underlay the republican celebration of French craft preeminence and the selectivity of official policy.

Although the heavy industrial sector expanded and consolidated in the 1890s, France was unable to compete successfully in an international market suddenly transformed by the meteoric rise of German and American industrial power. If the concentration of the socialist menace in the advanced sectors of metallurgy, mining, and chemicals turned some among the republican elite against technological modernism, the possibility of French industrial stagnation shattered the illusion that heavy industry and technology would provide the basis for French national ascendancy and economic vitality as the twentieth century beckoned.

The "tendency toward industrial stagnation" crystallized between 1889 and 1896.[1] By 1896, France had descended from the 1885 rank of the second most powerful industrial producer to that of the fourth.[2] Developments in mining failed to offset the chronic shortage of raw materials; in 1894 France still produced less than one-third of the coal it consumed and was the only industrial country that had to import coal regularly to meet national demand.[3] The traditional impoverishment in natural resources, however, was easier to accept than the unexpected explosion in productivity of France's economic rivals. Between 1885 and 1895, heavy industrial production quadrupled in the United States and tripled in Germany while France's output increased by only one-fourth. At the same time, industrial production in Britain continued to outpace that in France by a multiple of four.[4] One result of this rapid new expansion of international heavy industry was that French exports diminished.

In 1895 France alone among the major European nations had fewer industrial exports than in 1875 and 1883.[5]

The French government's response to this decline in industrial competitiveness was protectionism. Méline's tariff of 1892 imposed duties on foreign imports; its aim was to temper industrial expansion and to favor the existing agricultural and artisanal sectors. Believing that "French taste conflicted with mass production," Méline sought in protectionism a means through which France could remain a country of "a multitude of small workshops, best suited to making varied and individual goods."[6]

If France had to acknowledge other nations as the champions of heavy industrial output and if French exports were burdened with tariffs, how was France to maintain its position as a healthy competitor in the world market? Some members of the republican elite responded: by countering industrial rivalry with traditions of quality. Affirming the goals of Méline's protectionist policies, political officials celebrated the *artisan d'art* as the new source of French supremacy in an altered international economy. With its national resources of elegance and its reputation as the mecca of taste, fashion, and luxury, France would compensate for industrial deceleration with civilizing graces. In a decade of protectionist contractions, the *objet bien fait* would assure for France an exclusive and profitable corner of the competitive world market.

The republican deputy Georges Berger identified artisans as indispensable in the protectionist period. Prior to 1892, Berger had been one of the most irrepressible supporters of advanced technology and heavy industry. An engineer by training, he participated in planning the Paris Exhibitions of 1867 and 1878 and served as deputy commissioner of the Paris Exhibition of 1889. Berger edited the official reports of the exhibition of 1889, lending his voice to a chorus of politicians praising a nascent technological universe and the monumental iron architecture appropriate to it.[7]

After 1889, Berger was forced to temper his enthusiasm for technology and to take into account, like his colleagues, the rapid ascendancy of German and American industrial power. Berger reconsidered the capacity of France to realize the massive industrialization prefigured at the exhibition of 1889 and turned elsewhere for the forms of a distinctively French response to modernity. With the advent of protectionism, Berger definitively altered his position and claimed that the quality of French artisans' work, not industrial technology, would provide the basis for French economic invincibility. In a speech of 1892, Berger explained how French luxury articles could triumph in the international market, despite high duties. Before the superior artistry and unparalleled grace of French crafts, the walls of protectionism erected by other nations would tumble:

> The recent revision of international tariff policy has altered the economic situation of the entire world. Many European nations . . . now boast that they can be self-sufficient and will no longer need to import foreign products. . . . It is possible, even certain, that many nations continue to dominate us from a purely industrial point of view. . . . But none is likely to give its consumer goods and its luxury articles—fashion, clothing, ornaments, furniture, and in-

terior decoration—that French-styled imprint that no civilized country has ever ceased to favor. The authentic French trademark is a passport that opens all borders and overturns all tariff barriers, when it is stamped on those thousands of products in which form and decor play the leading role, in which they are essential qualities.[8]

As members of the political elite turned toward the artisanal sector in the 1890s, they discovered that the reputation of the "French trademark" was seriously undermined by new realities. Indeed, the crafts, the supposed reservoir of inimitable French grace and exceptional quality, were beleaguered as much as the industrial sector by intensified international rivalry. By the 1890s France was no longer the incontestable champion of elegant and artistic consumer goods. Other countries, no longer willing to yield automatically to superior renderings of the *goût français,* attempted through extensive educational programs to compensate for their lack of hereditary French taste.

After 1870 France's competitiveness in craft production began to decline. Exports of French jewelry, ceramics, and furniture, which increased rapidly between 1867 and 1873, began to contract sharply after 1873.[9] At the Paris Exhibition of 1878, official reports indicated for the first time the powerful potential of international rivalry in craft production.[10] Between 1873 and 1889, exports of furniture from France as a whole dropped by one-third, those from Paris by two-thirds.[11] Imports of furniture, in contrast, increased sharply. Between 1873 and 1889, the volume of European furniture entering the French market as a whole increased fivefold, from one to five million pieces.[12] The Gallic regime of international consumer elegance was threatened.

The Paris Exhibition of 1889 culminated a decade of French anxiety over European competition in craft production. Official reports were no longer marked by absolute confidence that France would keep its monopoly of "*le bon goût*" and "*l'originalité.*"[13] America, the country without a history, and Germany, the leviathan of blood and iron, particularly alarmed French officials by demonstrating unanticipated agility in creating useful objects tastefully and elegantly embellished.[14] In 1889 a chorus of voices rose in unison for the first time to complain of French beleaguerment and to urge the defense of Gallic artisanal exceptionalism.

A series of articles published in French periodicals in 1889 explored the various contributions in tapestry, porcelain, bronze, jewelry, goldsmithery, glasswork, and bookbinding. The articles developed a common theme: the work of French artisans had lost its vitality and was superseded by foreign artisans' work. One writer, Henri Béraldi, claimed that "among all of us there is a mounting horror of the sterility of French imitation and copying."[15] In 1892 Georges Berger qualified his statement that French grace would automatically dissolve the barriers of tariff duties. He argued, alarmingly, that France needed a movement of "national defense" to combat the menace of international rivalry and the loss of its own vitality in craft production. "We must fortify and reinvigorate our national reputation for craft excellence," he insisted, lamenting that foreign governments were taking more initiative than the French to foster craft production of high quality.[16]

One result of the 1889 exhibition was the proliferation of official delegations to study the artistic institutions and the artisanal reforms of France's new rivals. French delegates were sent to Russia, Portugal, Austria, England, Belgium, Italy, and Germany. In 1895 Siegfried Bing, a merchant-importer of Oriental arts, was asked to report on the state of the arts in America. His report, presented to the director of beaux-arts, Henri Roujon, in November 1895, was published in 1896 under the title *La Culture artistique en Amérique*. Marius Vachon, however, compiled the most extensive official report on the applied arts institutions of France's rivals. Vachon traveled around Europe, chronicling non-French experiments in design education and the opening of various industrial arts museums. His vast study, *Les Musées et les écoles d'art industrielle en Europe,* which appeared in 1890, received heightened public attention after the revelations of the 1889 exhibition.[17] After 1890, through the personal sponsorship of Jules Méline, Vachon continued his surveys and recommendations to revitalize the crafts, and in 1898 he presented to the protectionist and solidarist government a program for sustaining French artisanal supremacy, elaborated in a work entitled *Pour la défense de nos industries d'art.*[18]

The German menace was a continual source of alarm to Vachon. France must prepare to wage an "industrial war," he argued, transposing the arena of confrontation from the military battlefield to the consumer market.[19] Vachon was particularly concerned about the proliferation of decorative arts museums throughout the new German state, and lamented that French-trained skilled artisans had emigrated to Germany after the annexations of 1870.[20] The remarks of Prince Wilhelm upon the establishment of the Berlin museum in 1881, quoted by Vachon, set the tone for French apprehension during the 1890s: "War, but an industrial war, is what the imperial prince of Germany declared to us in 1881 when he inaugurated a museum of industrial art in Berlin and spoke these words: 'We defeated France on the battlefields in 1870. Now we want to defeat her in commerce and industry.'"[21]

Besides identifying Germany as a powerful rival to French craft production, Vachon developed a second, more general, theme: the unanticipated consequences of protectionism for French artisanal supremacy. With other commentators in the 1890s, Vachon recognized that the economic vitality of the French luxury sector was conditioned by the deference of an international elite to France as the center of fashion, taste, and manners.[22] Protectionism undermined this deference by expressing and intensifying national differences and traditions. A cosmopolitan transnational community dominated by Gallic elegance was destroyed by the quest for national distinctiveness and the new focus on native production. Although Georges Berger was confident that protective barriers would yield to the power of French refinements, Vachon's evidence suggested more formidable obstacles: aggressive nationalisms.

> Every country in Europe wants to . . . break out of a boring uniformity, a collective flatness. This is no longer the fusion economists and philosophers

predicted, the fusion toward which our trains and steamships would have pushed us. No, particularism triumphs instead, and the most inveterate nationalism is expressed through art. . . . It seems that each country can now fight only via the special character of its productions, its indigenous art, and its particular oh-so-original industry.[23]

The republicans who confronted the problem of international rivalry in craft production were presented with a second problem in the 1890s: the internal crisis of the artisanate. This crisis had both technological and commercial sources. It derived to a limited extent from the elimination of traditional skills by mechanization and to a large extent from the protracted subversion of traditional skills by new market pressures. By the 1890s the traditional conditions in which artisans operated were altered irrevocably by department stores, which transformed the market. Behind the facade of the unchanging atelier, artisans worked under new constraints; from glove makers to jewelers and from furniture makers to porcelain painters, artisans were mobilized into an army to supply the department stores. Although the tools and the methods of production largely continued preindustrial patterns, the context in which they were enacted absorbed them into an uncompromisingly modern "sweating system."[24]

Pierre Du Maroussem, a professor of law at the University of Paris, documented with extraordinary richness and sophistication the work structure and family relations among Parisian carpenters, cabinetmakers of the Faubourg Saint-Antoine, the food suppliers of Les Halles, and the toy makers of the Palais-Royal in a series of monographs between 1891 and 1894. It was he who characterized the artisans' conditions of work as a "sweating system" and vividly described how the finest artisans were shackled to supply the needs of the department stores.[25]

Du Maroussem was a devoted follower of Le Play and approached his working-class subjects with the tools of the social scientist.[26] From Le Play, Du Maroussem derived the method of the family monograph, melding an extensive description of the daily work process of specific trades with a detailed rendering of the laborers' activities, budgets, and interests outside the workplace. Du Maroussem's "objective" social science was tempered, however, by moral fervor and ideological allegiance. A vehement antisocialist, he celebrated the corporate and familial traditions of Parisian artisans, attributing their dissolution and the emergence of labor radicalism to the greed and corruption of merchant elites. His analysis was stamped by a particularly French strain of conservative thought, from Balzac to Drumont, that focused on the corrosive pathology of money and diagnosed its carrier as the Jew. In one passage, for example, Du Maroussem characterized the rapacious merchant representative of the *grands magasins* as the "Israelite tradesman" and suggested that Drumont include this type in his portrait of *La France juive*.[27]

Despite its manifest biases, Du Maroussem's work remains indispensable to the historian. Although he filtered his descriptions through ideological prisms, the data

Du Maroussem amassed in the second volume of his survey, *Les Ebénistes du Fau-bourg Saint-Antoine: Grands magasins, "Sweating system"* (1892), are extremely valu-able. He provides one of the only sources that documents the specific structure of the furniture trade in the very decade of the officially sponsored arts and crafts movement.[28]

The Faubourg Saint-Antoine persisted in the 1890s as the "furniture city," where wood craftsmen had been concentrated since the eighteenth century. The creation of individual pieces for Parisian Old Regime clients gave way in the nineteenth century to the new demands of mass consumption and large-scale retail marketing. The end of corporate regulation and the expanded urban market powerfully altered the struc-ture of the Parisian furniture sector.

By the late nineteenth century, the Faubourg Saint-Antoine replicated in one ar-tisanal trade the hierarchy of aristocratic, bourgeois, and working-class elements that marked Paris as a whole. This vertical stratification was complicated by a horizontal form of division in the faubourg: national differences. Concentrated in the lower two tiers were the craftsmen from Italy, Belgium, Germany, and Luxembourg who had flooded the faubourg after 1870, transforming it into an "almost alien city."[29]

By the 1890s the three tiers of the furniture trade had become spatially distinct, inhabiting three concentric geographical circles. The outermost was the zone of the proletarians among the furniture trade, called the *trôleurs*. Because of the misery and deprivation he observed there, Du Maroussem designated it as "Dante's third circle of hell in Paris."[30] Of the almost twenty thousand *ébénistes* in the Faubourg Saint-Antoine in 1892, nine thousand were producers of *meubles de trôle*.[31] Most of them were Italian, from the Piedmont region.[32] These *trôleurs* (from the verb *trôler*, "to stroll") were furniture hawkers; they carried their wares strapped to their backs or in crude rolling wagons, walking the streets in search of a buyer.[33] Usually specialists in a particular genre of furniture, the *trôleurs* were the only *ébénistes* who worked alone and fashioned the entire product. The *trôleur*, without a workshop, apprentices, and family support, was an important part of the vast putting-out system organized by the *grands magasins* in the Faubourg Saint-Antoine.[34] The department stores did not order his merchandise directly; instead, the *trôleur* usually found customers in the weekly furniture fairs in the outlying zone of the faubourg, which were attended by the merchant representatives of the various commercial emporia. These middlemen would bid at the lowest possible price, and the *trôleur*, desperate, would have no choice but to take it, often accepting for a table or chest of drawers less than what it cost to make. The shoddy, lightweight *meubles de trôle* were then shellacked or var-nished and put up for sale in the display rooms of the *grands magasins*, retailing at prices much higher than those the *trôleur* could command. Thus were the nomadic *trôleurs* enslaved.[35]

In the second ring of the Faubourg Saint-Antoine were the artisans of the *meubles courants*, the furniture trade. There were seven thousand of them; one-half were for-eign, largely from Belgium, Luxembourg, and Germany.[36] This sector's cabinetmakers were organized into small workshops, each with a *petit patron,* who usually owned his tools; between one and three journeymen under the master's supervision; and an apprentice, boarding with the family. Until the Second Empire, these small ateliers of the *meubles courants* sector supplied solid and comfortable furniture for the burgeoning middle classes of the city. With the consolidation of the *grands magasins* between 1865 and 1890, the *petit patron* kept his atelier but lost his independence, and his relations with his fellow workers changed irrevocably. For it was the scattered ranks of the *petits patrons* that the department store coordinated into an army of suppliers.

Du Maroussem isolated three crucial changes in the period between 1865 and 1890 that altered the position of the middle ranks of the *ébénistes.* First, the *petit patron* gradually lost his individual clients and no longer had personal relations with his customers. The small showroom that had been an essential part of the workshop disappeared, and few items were sold to individual buyers who came to the faubourg to order furniture for their homes. Rather than a producer-merchandiser, the *petit patron* became exclusively a producer, who contracted on a monthly basis to furnish a vast supply of objects for a single anonymous client, the *grand magasin.*[37]

Accompanying this change to an impersonal single client was a system of extensive specialization. The department store would order a large number of a particular type of furniture from each individual workshop, forcing on the *petit patron* extreme specialization and repetitive work patterns. Some *petits patrons* would be responsible for the "small English dressing table," others for entire rooms in a single genre: "old oak or old walnut dining room, walnut or mahogany bedroom, etc."[38]

The new volume of orders and the intense specialization demanded by the department stores contributed to yet another change in the traditional organization of the *petit patron* workshop. The speeded-up pace of work and the longer hours necessary to complete the monthly deadlines turned the atelier of the independent artisan into a sweatshop, and leveled the relations between master craftsmen and journeymen and between journeymen and apprentices so that all workers became "human machines."[39] Divested of responsibility for the showroom and clients, the head of the workshop was relegated to the ranks of his employees, entrapped in the service of the department store. All faced a threat: if monthly orders were not adequately filled and the *petit patron* lost his supplier contract, he and his artisans would sink to the degradation of the *trôleur,* consigned to a nomadic quest for customers at a miserable price.[40]

The erosion of corporate solidarity wrought by unprecedented commercial pressures took its greatest toll, according to Du Maroussem, on the most junior member of the small workshop, the apprentice. When the hierarchy of relations between the patron and his employees had been intact, it was the apprentice who had epitomized the union of practical skill and moral fiber sustaining the corporate structure. The dual role of the apprentice as technical novice and moral fledgling was expressed by his membership in the family of the *patron* who trained him. This integration of family relations and work patterns created the reciprocal obligations binding the apprentice and his master and made the small atelier a place of both shared values and the transmission of skills.

By 1890 the technical, moral, and familial continuum embodied in the institution of apprenticeship was severed. The middle ranks of the tripartite community of artisans in the Faubourg Saint-Antoine were no longer characterized by the small workshop whose *patron* accommodated his apprentice as a member of his own family. Unable to afford to clothe and house a surrogate son, the *patron* paid his apprentice a low hourly wage; the position of the apprentice came to resemble that of a menial day laborer rather than that of the recipient of technical and moral education.[41] The teaching of the craft no longer went on inside the workshop but unfolded in large institutions, some municipal, some private, where young trainees were concentrated, schooled, and hired out to individual workshops. The traditional functions of the *patron* were wrested from him and assigned to large organizations, disrupting the family unit that had hitherto been the essential counterpart to the craft production process.[42]

If the multiple strains on the producers of the *meubles courants*—the inhabitants of the middle circle of the Faubourg Saint-Antoine—threatened them with the fate of the disinherited *trôleurs,* there was little chance that they could ever gain entry to the exclusive world in the center of the furniture district. The innermost core of the Faubourg Saint-Antoine belonged to the aristocracy of the furniture trade, the sector of *haut luxe* production.[43] Insulated from both foreign labor and commercial denigration, the *haut luxe* sector was marked by national purity and aristocratic traditions. According to Du Maroussem, there were still four thousand members of this elite corps in 1892; their distinctively French character had been ensured by the generational continuity of the craft since the eighteenth century.[44]

Unlike the degraded *trôleur* and the sweatshops of the small producers, the artisans of the *haut luxe* sector maintained relations with individual clients, who custom-ordered their objects, giving explicit instructions. Further, the *haut luxe* sector of furniture making was organized into a few large groups of artisans, who assembled under a single roof to collaborate in creating complicated and extensively finished objects. The workshops of *haut luxe* usually contained between sixty and three hundred individuals, each of whom performed a specialized task on a single item.[45]

The specialization operative in the *haut luxe* atelier was qualitatively different from that of the small workshop of the *meubles courants*. The department stores had forced their *petit patron* suppliers to produce repeatedly a single type of furniture. Artisans in the *haut luxe* sector, varying their creation according to the wishes of the customer, were distinguished by their extreme versatility,[46] which was organized in a sophisticated and extensive division of labor. Du Maroussem clarified the French craft tradition, which associated the increased division of labor with an increase in the quality of the product. This direct proportion which inverts Ruskin's, Morris's, and Van de Velde's pejorative conception of the division of labor in craft production, may be seen in Diderot's *Encyclopédie,* where each artisanal trade was presented in a series of pages unfolding the divided labor that was joined in the final product.[47] Du

Maroussem reconstructed the many intricate phases necessary for the creation of a single piece of *haut luxe* furniture. His taxonomy reads like a list of the diverse artisans participating in the manufacture of royal furniture under Charles Lebrun; the contributions of the *haut luxe* artisans in the late nineteenth century remained essentially the same as in the seventeenth and eighteenth centuries.[48] Among the many hands collaborating in progression were the *découpeurs,* who cut the wood; the *tourneurs,* who shaped the cut wood on a lathe; the *ébéniste* proper, who assembled and carved the piece of furniture; and a proliferation of finishers, varying according to the item: the *marqueteurs,* who inlaid surface designs; the *ciseleur-doreurs,* sculptors of wood and gilded embellishments; appliers of veneers; and *sculpteurs sur bois,* sculptors of wood adornments.[49]

Not only was a complex division of labor intrinsic to producing the finest furniture, but the second enemy of radical craft reformers in England and Belgium, the machine, was an integral and distinctive feature of the French *haut luxe* sector. Du Maroussem explained that mechanization, rather than signaling the death knell of the crafts, made possible the continuity of the aristocratic traditions of luxury cabinetmaking. As early as the 1860s the *haut luxe* workshops incorporated new technology as labor-saving devices for the most rudimentary, repetitive, and time-consuming part of the production process—the initial cutting of large frames of wood into smaller blocks. Steam-powered mechanical saws were indeed able to cut the wood more precisely than human hands, in half the time. This use of mechanization, rather than undermine traditional skills, strengthened the *haut luxe* corps of producers.[50] Technological advancement and artisanal creation not only were compatible but were the distinguishing features of the only purely French and most refined aristocratic core of the Parisian furniture trade. The misery of the "human machines" in the *petit patron* "sweatshops" was due to the *patrons'* inability to afford mechanized labor-saving tools.[51] Pressed by the supply orders for the department stores, the *petit patron* was forced to ceaselessly repeat arduous tasks, some of which did not require the superior skill or attentiveness of a trained craftsman. It was the luxury sector which successfully assimilated modern forms of technology to the craft process, domesticating new machines and pressing them into the service of sustaining aristocratic traditions of artisanal refinement.

The *haut luxe* sector, despite its continued vitality in the late nineteenth century, felt beleaguered, surrounded as it was by the other sectors. The perceived threat led to two forms of self-protection: first, the reconstitution of corporate solidarity, pursued by patronal syndical chambers and, second, the direct appeal to the state to help renew the aristocratic tradition of the unity of art and craft.[52] The state was asked to provide the impetus and opportunity for this efflorescence. If the Republic had replaced the Old Regime in political structure, it should affirm and reassert its continuing cultural role as the Maecenas in whose service all the arts would again converge. Directors of luxury furniture houses, growing fearful, wanted help from above. They appealed to the republican state in the image of the Old Regime: they sought the restoration of the Colbert corporation. And with this restorative image, they dream of a state that guides public taste, a state that commissions art works, a state that would evoke again the splendors of Louis XIV in the innumerable palaces that have been bequeathed to us by the old French monarchy and would restore to our mansions and palaces the luxury of the court. A difficult task, especially in a society that rarely translates the instinct for equality into the pursuit of such memories.[53]

The luxury furniture *patrons'* demand for an official mobilization of the applied arts and the *progressiste* elite's quest for a republican modern style would converge in the special circumstances of the 1890s. The economic performance of European rivals, in both the industrial and craft sectors, motivated republican politicians to link the French modern style with the production of luxury crafts. The government coalition would focus its efforts on the institutional elevation of the applied arts, on restoring furniture making and other crafts to their Old Regime noble positions alongside the other beaux-arts. Du Maroussem's analysis of the furniture trade as a three-tiered hierarchy exposed the exclusivity of the official craft movement, whose nationalist and aristocratic celebration was appropriate only to the highest of the three strata of craftsmen in the Faubourg Saint-Antoine. By 1890 the *haut luxe* sector of *ébénisterie* was a small bastion of traditional skills in a trade teeming with foreign craftsmen and reeling under the stress of market specialization. The concentration on securing a place for fine crafts in the museum and the Salon was, in the case of furniture, an urgent operation, which rescued a French artisanal elite from the pressures of foreign invasion and commercial *déclassement*.

Du Maroussem's detailed description of the division of labor intrinsic to *haut luxe* production also offers a guide crucial to understanding the specific meaning of the division of labor in the French arts and craft movement and isolates a fundamental set of differences between it and its counterparts in England and Belgium. If we approach the French arts and crafts movement with the conceptual categories elaborated by Ruskin and Morris, we find it peculiarly lacking in a critique of the division of labor. For Ruskin and Morris, the division of labor meant the division of man, and their ideal artisan was a creator of the whole product. Du Maroussem's evidence partly helps to explain why the division of labor was not the enemy of craft reformers in France. As he indicated, in the luxury trades that flourished in eighteenth-century Paris, the division of labor was extended, and the value and refinement of individual objects was increased by the complex adornment and finishing procedures. Indeed, the division of labor was the determining feature of luxury production, and the nineteenth century continued to correlate the sumptuousness of the item with the number of both steps and artisans required to produce it. This French tradition shaped the assumptions of the elite sponsors of craft regeneration and suggests why the English and Belgian social vision of "one man–one product" had so little resonance in the French context. Not the division of labor per se but commercial pressures were the target of official reformers, who criticized these pressures precisely because they simplified the elaborate division of labor required for precious objects, lowering public taste through the rapid execution and homogeneity of consumer items. Falsity, the great moral violation that Ruskin and Morris exposed in the opulent syncretisms of bourgeois style, would be treated in France as an issue of bad taste; the *faux luxe* would be replaced by the *haut luxe* and would effect, one modernist bureaucrat predicted, "the elevation of public taste for the good of all."[54]

Elevating taste by presenting objects of superior craftsmanship in the institutions of high art—this was to be the goal of the officially sponsored movement for the unity of the arts. In the temple of art in the 1890s, furniture, jewelry, ceramics, and glasswork would recover the position beside painting and sculpture that they had enjoyed in the Old Regime, embodying a new patrimony in an era of urgently needed national solidarity.

CHAPTER FOUR

Amazone, Femme Nouvelle, and the Threat to the Bourgeois Family

Women have become men's equals. . . .
They have relinquished all their coquettishness . . . and will no longer be
women, but "*hommesses*," too masculine.
Georges Valbert, 1889[1]

CHAPTERS 2 AND 3 examined the political and economic factors that helped to formulate a French craft modernism by an official elite. Chapters 4 and 5 will explore two cultural components of fin-de-siècle France that shaped the meaning and function of an organic, interiorizing, and feminine art nouveau: the problem of the "New Woman" and the discovery of the interior world as a sensitive nervous mechanism (Fig. 17).

In the 1890s the legal and professional possibilities for middle-class women in France changed significantly. These changes bolstered the French feminist movement, adding another layer of challenges to liberal republicanism in the fin de siècle: as women called for solidarity, the working class was demanding liberation. Although the actual number of French women affected by the changes was small, the visible and unfamiliar character of the new bourgeois woman generated a powerful symbol of the *femme nouvelle,* the "New Woman."

The menace of the *femme nouvelle,* who left home and family for a career, pervaded contemporary journals between 1889 and 1898. Ranging from the sober academicism of the *Revue des deux mondes* to the ribald caricatures of *L'Illustration,* the periodicals presented the *femme nouvelle* as rejecting woman's position as the anchor of bourgeois domesticity. Alternatively envisioned as a gargantuan *amazone* or an emaciated, frock-coated *hommesse,* the *femme nouvelle* inverted traditional sexual roles and threatened the essential divisions ordering bourgeois life: public from private, work from family, production from reproduction.

Three factors contributed to the public preoccupation with the menace of the *femme nouvelle.* The first was the social question. At the 1889 Paris Exposition, the first International Congresses on Women's Rights and Feminine Institutions were held as the Socialist Workers' International convened on the fairgrounds. The 1889

Fig. 17. "Female Emancipation," *Gil Blas illustré,* 1893. Courtesy of the Department of Special Collections, University Research Library, University of California, Los Angeles.

women's congresses marked what historians have called the coming of age of the French feminist movement, stimulating "a new wave of its organizational efforts."[2] Between 1889 and 1900, twenty-one feminist periodicals began publication in France, and international feminist congresses convened in Paris in 1892, 1896, and 1900.[3]

By their own description, elaborated in a special issue of *La Revue encyclopédique* devoted to the *femme nouvelle* in 1896, the French feminists, few in number, were nonprofessional upper-middle-class mothers or matrons.[4] Among their ranks were such well-known society women and philanthropists as the duchesse d'Uzès and Madame de Witt-Schlumberger and well-placed wives or relatives of prominent republican statesmen and educators, including Madame Jules Siegfried and Madame Brunschwig.[5] These women and their cohorts shared what Karen Offen has aptly called the ideology of "familial feminism," accepting the sexual division of labor in society and the family while using the concept of "equality in difference" to enhance women's designated role in the home.[6] "Motherhood," "*patrie,*" and "pot-au-feu" were the surprising banners rallying French feminists in their campaign for limited reform during the 1890s.[7]

French feminists declared that their claims transcended politics, with its divisiveness; they emphasized their distance from socialism and other forms of radicalism.[8] Their major goals were twofold: first, they sought a broadly based solidarity among women of different social classes, which entailed, to a large extent, a moralizing crusade by wealthy women to teach infant care to poor women and to aid widows, orphans, and prostitutes; second, they wanted to reform the Civil Code to give married women some control over family finance. The existing code relegated a married woman to the status of dependent minor, requiring that she give over to her husband all her financial resources.[9]

Despite the explicit antisocialism of French feminism and the republican respectability of many of its affiliates, the movement was rapidly associated with the collectivist menace and triggered an overreaction similar to that against the socialists. For if the socialists provoked bourgeois fury by tapping the raw nerve of property, the feminists touched another—the family. Protection of the family, a highly charged political issue in the 1890s, was incorporated as a central element of the *progressiste* republican program. In 1894 Paul Deschanel, the prominent *progressiste* deputy of the new generation of republicans, published *La République nouvelle,* the manifesto of the consolidation and antisocialism that characterized the politics of the 1890s. In his book Deschanel attacked the socialists as enemies of individual autonomy, levelers of property, and amoral destroyers of family unity.[10] In a period when politicians actively defended the family from perceived socialist marauders, the challenge of the *femme nouvelle* was particularly irksome. For if the family was already beleaguered by external socialist invasion, it was now also vulnerable to internal bourgeois defection.

A second factor contributing to the perception of the *femme nouvelle* was the new access of some French women to higher education and professional careers. Bourgeois women benefited in the 1890s from the first decade of secondary and higher education funded by the state. In 1880 the republicans had implemented the Camille Sée Law, which established state-sponsored secondary education for women. With the support of Jules Ferry, Deputy Sée had proposed the new education facilities as a direct extension of anticlericalism. The only way to ensure the progressive rationality of the Third Republic was to wrest French women away from the church: "Women must belong to science and democracy, or they will remain in the hands of the church."[11] Sée stipulated strict limits to female education, which was to prepare women to pursue their roles as wives and mothers under republican, rather than ecclesiastical, tutelage. The new educational curricula were designed to dissociate female education from the professional and career orientations of its male equivalents: "I do not want women lawyers, and I worry about the possibility of having women doctors. The education of young women will certainly be set apart from all that in educating young men is geared toward preparing them for a career."[12]

Like other parts of the republican program in the 1880s, however, the Camille Sée Law had unanticipated consequences. Although it wrested female education away from the church, it also led many women to choose the very professional careers it was supposed to discourage. Between 1885 and 1900, for example, the number of lycée degrees tripled, from 4,300 to 13,000.[13] By 1896, 46,000 women worked as primary school teachers, the result of training institutes founded only in 1880.[14] In the 1890s the first women entered the prestigious world of male academe as well as male careers: in 1895 there were 842 women inscribed at the *facultés;* in the decade twenty female doctors and ten lawyers completed their studies.[15] That even a few women gained entry to the centers of respected male vocations for the first time fueled the symbolic power of the *femme nouvelle.* New divorce laws passed in 1884, giving French women the right to initiate divorce proceedings against their husbands, compounded the perceived challenge of the New Woman.[16]

A third factor contributing to the overreaction to the *femme nouvelle* was linked to another area of public concern after 1889: the decline in the birthrate and the relative stagnation of the French population. Germany in particular became a formidable demographic menace in the 1890s, matching its industrial expansion with a momentous growth in population. The birthrate in France declined gradually and continually after 1870, so that by 1891 the German birthrate was about double the French.[17]

French officials' alarm over the quadrupling of Germany's industrial capacity was accompanied by their recognition and public discussion of the decline of births in France and its implications "in terms of the manpower available for military service."[18] One of the most vociferous prophets of the German baby boom cum incipient war machine was Doctor Jacques Bertillon, who in 1896 founded the Alliance nationale pour l'accroissement de la population française. In an article in the *Revue politique et parlementaire,* Bertillon sounded the alarm against Germany, hoping to persuade the French to begin replenishing the ranks of youth as an urgent military necessity: "It is fatal that Germany will have twice as many conscripts as France in fourteen years. Then, this people filled with hatred for us will devour us. The Germans say it, print it, and they will do it."[19]

The *femme nouvelle,* a middle-class woman seeking independence and education rather than marriage and life at home, thus made her claims in a context where maternity and family were issues fraught with special political and national significance. The national apprehension over depopulation, which one journalist in 1896 described as "the problem that torments all Frenchmen,"[20] brought about an urgent response to these issues. The decline in the birthrate rigidified the response to infractions of the sexual division of labor, however moderate, and transformed the protection of the traditional family into an imperative of national security and military strength. In this highly charged context even slight tampering with female identity and female activity was experienced as a threat to the entire structure; the menace of the *femme nouvelle* was therefore met with an active campaign to relegitimate women's procreative and moral role. Doctors, politicians, and scholars after 1889 rallied to defend the traditional female role and sought medical and philosophical rationales to consign women to the home.[21]

The controversy over the *femme nouvelle* pervaded the Parisian press between 1889 and 1896. The tremors unleashed by the New Woman were registered in the *Journal des débats,* the *Revue des deux mondes,* and a major journal for avant-garde literary and artistic innovation, *La Plume.*[22] Middle-brow magazines such as *La Revue, La Nouvelle Revue,* and *La Revue encyclopédique* were also filled with discussions of the *femme nouvelle*'s challenge to traditional femininity.[23] Popular caricatures patterned after Daumier's *Les Bas bleus* (The bluestockings) appeared in the pages of *L'Illustration* and *Le Grelot* and in the best-selling book by the cartoonist Alfred Robida, entitled *Le XXe Siècle: La Vie éléctrique.* In 1896 a caricature in *Le Grelot,* for example, showed a female virago berating her husband (Fig. 18). Smoking a cigarette, dressed in bloomers and a straw hat, she announced that she was on her way to a "Congrès féministe" and blasted instructions to her housecleaning husband as she left. She would ride off on her bicycle, often depicted as the technological partner of the *femme nouvelle.*[24] The association of new technology and inverted sexual roles was repeated in popular and elite literary accounts of the *femme nouvelle.* In Robida's vision of the twentieth century, superwomen in men's clothing use machines to dominate the earth and skies, dividing their time between mechanical wizardry and teaching at the universities.[25] More solemn and more apprehensive in tone was an article in 1889 by Georges Valbert in the *Revue des deux mondes,* an academic counterpart to Robida's lively science fiction. Valbert's "L'Age des machines," written one month after the opening of the 1889 exhibition, cautioned against two distracting modern forces prefigured in the monumental exhibition. One was the leveling depersonalization of the new technology, whose standardized and prefabricated iron forms threatened individual creativity and autonomy. The other was the social effects of this new technology, which would be expressed in the elimination of differences between the sexes. Women would extend their already growing access to higher education and the professions and would become the equals of men not only in social station but in physical presence. Women leaving their traditional domestic and familial havens would be transformed into "*hommesses,*" desiccated and rigid characters divested of

26e ANNÉE — Nº 1,306   FRANCE **15** CENTIMES   19 Avril 1896

BUREAUX
5, Cité Bergère, 5
PARIS
—
ABONNEMENTS
FRANCE
UN AN........ 8 fr.»
SIX MOIS...... 4 fr.»
TROIS MOIS... 2 fr.»
15 c. le numéro

PARAIT LE DIMANCHE

—
ADRESSER
Lettres et Mandats à M. J. MADRE
Administrateur

BUREAUX
5, Cité Bergère, 5
PARIS
—
ABONNEMENTS
ÉTRANGER
UN AN........ 10 fr.»
SIX MOIS...... 5 fr.»
TROIS MOIS... 2 fr. 5
20 c. le numéro

PARAIT LE DIMANCHE

—
PUBLICITÉ
*Les Annonces sont reçues
aux Bureaux du Journal*

Voir en tête de la deuxième page les conditions auxquelles on peut recevoir gratuitement le GRELOT

REVENDICATIONS FÉMININES

-- Je vais au **Congrès féministe !** tu prépareras le dîner pour huit heures précises,
tu m'entends ? et surtout, que rien ne cloche !...

Fig. 18. "To the Feminist Congress!" *Le Grelot,* 1896.

all feminine "coquettishness." Technology and gender equality would contribute to a new world of sensual impoverishment and uniform ambitions. The model of woman as the embodiment of aesthetic spectacle and as the manipulator of a complicated weaponry of seduction would be replaced, Valbert feared, by the female-man, rigid, austere, and riddled with the appetitive combativeness of professional mobility.[26]

Although many intellectuals and politicians expressed concern with the emergence of the new woman, their responses to the potential danger varied. The art critics Camille Mauclair and Marius-Ary Leblond, for example, characterized the *femme nouvelle*'s impact on painting and the decorative arts but were not explicitly against her. In a survey of Salon painting in the 1890s, Mauclair identified a new type of female iconography executed by what he called the "painters of the 'New Woman.'" He explained that the possibility of a *femme nouvelle*—independent, critical, and mobile—was redefining the artistic theory of portraiture.[27] Throughout the nineteenth century the pictorial goals of male and female portraiture had been rigorously separated in academic doctrine. Depictions of women were tests of technical expertise and the elaborate crafting of surfaces, whereas portraits of men were occasions for exploring character and expressing inner life. Women in their fine clothes offered the painter an exercise in decorative mastery, in rendering the multicolored and multilayered envelopment of the subject, and in portraying them as objets d'art as luxuriant as the decor surrounding them. This equivalence between woman and the life of the surface was now changing, according to Mauclair, because of the emergence of the *femme nouvelle:*

> A man's portrait was a psychological document subject to analysis and moral evaluation . . . but a beautiful woman's face was an unknown terrain where there were no traces and byways. . . . She was purely physical. . . . A feminine portrait was hence always a decorative work . . . a stylized landscape of which the woman's body, invisible and central, was the driving force and the prisoner of the whole ensemble.
>
> Yet a new concept of women's portraits has begun to emerge. Her decorative and nonconscious aspects will probably fade. A new woman is being elaborated, a pensive and active being to which a new form of painting will have to correspond. . . . A woman's portrait will cease to be a *tableau,* and will become an intimate, analytical, and ideational document.[28]

Marius-Ary Leblond also commented on the challenge of the *femme nouvelle* to both the pictorial traditions of female representation and the equivalence between women and objets d'art. In "Les Peintres de la femme nouvelle," Leblond identified two essential characteristics of the new woman as she migrated into pictorial form, each of which undermined the conventional divisions between male and female portraiture. The first was the active, public, mobile, and agitated character of the *femme nouvelle,* which Leblond associated with the tension and new electric energy of the city streets and the "brand new sparks" of the century of technological inventions and "eternal motion";[29] the second was the *femme nouvelle*'s repudiation of female physical display. The new woman rejected decorative opulence in appearance, and challenged the role of woman as an orchestrated objet d'art:

> The new woman is not beautiful. She looks rather like a boy, and illustrates more than anything the expression of a firm character, a serene soul, a robustly harmonious body. . . . They are no longer women of pleasure and leisure but women who study, of very sober comportment. And nothing suits them better than heavy and somber colors . . . that express firmness, . . . roughness, and decisiveness.[30]

The most striking inversion Leblond noted was the redirection of female energy from external artificing to internal cultivation. Rather than create decorative ensembles of her dress and accessories, the new woman analyzed ideas:

> They have learned to understand, . . . have made their lives complex, educated their minds. . . . They appreciate the silhouette of ideas, the fine laces of psychology, bejeweled words, and the beauty of simplicity. So they form a new society . . . in which every woman . . . can be exquisitely cerebral. Indeed, what distinguishes the new woman most clearly is simplicity of appearance, which banishes luxury in the quest for an egalitarian modesty. . . . She looks like the worker's sister, with her elegant but weary body, . . . her simple but courageous gestures completely devoid of the useless illusions that can be found in the falseness of high luxury.[31]

The aesthete collector and writer Octave Uzanne denounced such simplicity in the 1890s. He asserted that both the distinctive female form and female adornment were essential to the vitality of the French decorative arts. Uzanne was a primary literary spokesman for reintegrating the arts and crafts in his generation; his ideas flourished in the 1890s in the interstices between avant-garde Symbolist aestheticism and erudite aristocratic revivalism.[32] At the center of Uzanne's extensive literary, historical, and critical works was the alliance between feminine grace, interior space, and artisanal refinement in the eighteenth century, bequeathed to the aristocracy of the spirit in the nineteenth century. Looking through the prisms of the intimate, feminine culture of the eighteenth-century rococo in which he was deeply immersed, Uzanne criticized the sartorial severity of the *femme nouvelle*.

His remarkable work *La Femme à Paris, nos contemporaines,* of 1894, registered the problematic implications of the *femme nouvelle*. This long volume was one of a series of Uzanne's studies of Parisian women of the past and present, the "queens of elegance" who transformed the tawdry urban metropolis into an earthly "garden of delights."[33] The physical and intellectual sobriety of the *femme nouvelle* undermined Uzanne's ideal type of decorative, organic Parisian woman. He devoted parts of *La Femme à Paris* to discussing the implications of the new woman for the urban and domestic orders. Uzanne equated feminism with a dangerous unleashing of social and sexual inversion, invoking medical and philosophical sources to demonstrate the unsuitability of the female temperament to public and professional activity.[34] He celebrated woman's ability to adorn both her own body and the interior spaces in which she naturally belonged. He urged young men to avoid educated, "ambitious females" who could "solve mathematical problems" and advised bachelors to "choose a young lady who does not despise crocheting, whom tapestry interests, and who loves embroidery."[35]

Uzanne modeled his vision of decorative females and female decorators on the aristocratic tradition of female crafts. Like the Goncourts, he was an avid archaeologist of aristocratic material culture. Preceding his series of books on Parisian feminine typologies was an extensive scholarly oeuvre chronicling the intricacies of female adornment in pre-Revolutionary France. Concurring with the Goncourts that history and mentality were expressed in the form and contents of such minutiae as dinner menus and belt buckles, Uzanne compiled such monographs on the accoutrements of aristocratic comportment as *L'Eventail; L'Ombrelle, le manchon, le gant;* and *Documents sur les moeurs du XVIIIe siècle*. His stated purpose in these works was to reveal "the gallant spirit animating the customs of yesteryear," to "evoke the elegant life, frivolity, and nuances of female attire, ruled by the scepter of fashion."[36]

Through the recovery of the intricate arts of adornment, Uzanne hoped to facilitate what he called the renewal of female interior arts, "intimate and decorative."[37] He invoked Madame de Pompadour and Marie Antoinette for their exemplary delicacy in rendering the surfaces of diminutive screens and promoted them as the common ancestors of all women of aesthetic sensibility, referring to them familiarly as "Mesdames our ancestors," and "our resourceful grandmothers."[38] Uzanne offered the aristocratic female artisan as a model and inspiration for the fin-de-siècle bourgeois woman, who would activate the surfaces of her home with the unprecedented flourishes of her own distinctive sensibility, offering a "truly new style" in female arts and interior design.[39]

According to Uzanne, bourgeois wives should not only decorate the walls of their homes but also cultivate luxury and artistry in an adornment ignored by their aristocratic predecessors: their undergarments. Department store democratization made impossible the uniqueness of fashion practiced in the eighteenth century. The nuances of individual personality that could no longer be expressed in outer garments could be expressed in what women wore beneath them. Madame de Pompadour's exquisite costume represented her singularity; her bourgeois descendants could achieve an equivalent form of decorative distinction in their subtle and diaphanous undergarments. Uzanne envisioned the *femme nouvelle* replaced by the contemporary woman who crafted an exquisite "vision of a beneath," where her "delicate husband" could "lose himself in soft and evanescent delicacies of colors, groping for supremely sheer and subtle textures."[40]

Uzanne's critique of the *femme nouvelle* echoed in one of the primary centers of literary and artistic innovation—the journal called *La Plume*. Originating in the 1880s as the purveyor of avant-garde rebellion, it played a major role in introducing the Symbolist rejection of material reality and celebrated the poetic liberation from Parnassian conventions in the irregular rhythms of free verse. This sponsorship of artistic innovation entailed an explicit identification with social radicalism. *La Plume* in the late 1880s found the political analogue to free verse in the newly emerging doctrine of anarcho-communism.[41] By the mid-1890s *La Plume* had become artistically multifaceted and tempered its literary and social radicalism. In 1894, in an issue of *La Plume* devoted entirely to *l'aristocratie intellectuelle,* aesthete followers of the Goncourts such as Rémy de Gourmont advocated an elite, noncommunitarian ideal of social order to be realized in the rule of an intellectual clerisy.[42]

In this deradicalized and aristocratizing context of *La Plume,* the reaction against the *femme nouvelle* appeared. The opening article in the September 15, 1895, issue was entitled "Le Féminisme et le bon sens," by Victor Jozé, a well-known writer and literatus who specialized in the psychologically realistic novella. A series of his works, under the rubric "Ménageries sociales," was devoted to "man and woman—Parisian morals"; it went through eight editions between 1888 and 1897. Jozé was also known for his relations to the Neo-Impressionist painters; one of his works was published in 1891 with a frontispiece by Georges Seurat.

According to Jozé, men's and women's fundamental differences were necessarily translated into their separate life spheres, the public world of action and the private world of emotion and maternity, respectively. Jozé assumed that any movement of the female away from the private world would violate the natural order and yield an unstable and dangerous state of social inversion.

Jozé, like others who commented on the new woman, linked her to new technology. The stable divisions between public and private space threatened by technological invasion were also subverted by collusion between the woman and a new machine, the bicycle:

> The bicycle's triumph . . . necessitates an androgynous outfit . . . worn by its adepts of the weaker sex. . . . Will we never make our skirted publishers and sociologists in dresses understand that a woman is neither equal nor inferior nor superior to a man, that she is a being apart, another thing, endowed with other functions by nature than the man with whom she has no business competing in public life. A woman exists only through her ovaries.[43]

Jozé ended his manifesto against the *femme nouvelle* by proclaiming woman as the queen of the interior, her place in the home dictated by nature's laws:

> Feminists are wrong when they turn women away from the duties of their sex and when they turn their heads with illusory emancipatory ideas, which are unrealizable and absurd. Let woman remain what Nature has made her: an ideal woman, the companion and lover of a man, the mistress of the home. . . . Let her not pose as a virago: it does not suit her. . . . Let there be no . . . androgynes![44]

Republican politicians were as preoccupied as other Frenchmen with the "woman question" in the 1890s and registered a range of reactions to the menace of the *femme nouvelle.* Although they avoided the ferocious antifeminism of conservatives like

Gabriel Tarde and Gustave Le Bon, most republicans assumed that the social order was based on biological difference and the strict operation of "separate spheres." Republican statesmen accordingly developed various strategies to contain and interiorize women, to resolidify the boundaries between public and private, home and work, that the new woman had transgressed.[45]

Official responses to the new woman conformed to the dual program of republican response to the social question in the 1890s. As we have seen, the Third Republic developed a conservative and progressive stance to confront the challenge of socialism, shifting from the aristocratic and clerical rapprochement of the *ralliement* to the social revision of its liberal legacy in the modern doctrine of solidarism. Republicans formulated similarly defensive and resilient strategies toward the new woman, including the affirmation of an antifeminist aristocratic tradition and a subtle endorsement of those feminist goals that could be used to strengthen woman's designated role in the home.

Senator Jules Simon represented the antifeminist tendency among French republicans in the 1890s and lobbied both in the Senate and in print against changes in the legal status of women from 1888 to 1896. Simon identified the moral and national dangers inherent in the aspirations of the *femme nouvelle* and vigorously defended patriarchy, maternity, and female inferiority.[46]

A philosophical liberal, Simon did not accept Tarde and Le Bon's denigration of women and promoted limited extensions of women's education. Yet he was distressed by the intellectual and professional aspirations of women that had been brought about by compulsory schooling. In an 1896 article Simon argued that education had to be carefully monitored, with separate tutelage for men and women, appropriate to their distinct capacities and destinies. Women had to be trained for nurturing, tenderness, and maternity, according to their unique biological imperative and unalterable social function: "Everything in a woman, her body, her mind, and her character, has been planned by nature's creator as a preparation for childbearing."[47]

Simon's advocacy of strictly separate education for women expressed the republican proximity to clerical traditions, confirming the *ralliement* tendencies of fin-de-siècle political history. As Karen Offen has demonstrated, republican justification for gender-specific education in the 1890s relied on clerical, monarchist, and aristocratic authorities. Despite their secular goals, republican administrators drew on the writings of the bishop of Orléans, Monseigneur Dupanloup, who expounded the church doctrine of female education as a preparation for maternal and domestic duties. And the cultivated noblewoman Madame de Maintenon, companion of King Louis XIV, was also frequently invoked in republican education literature as a model to be adapted for young bourgeoises.[48]

Political reaction to the *femme nouvelle* included a second, more flexible, attitude than Jules Simon's. Proponents of the new republican doctrine of solidarism endorsed some changes advocated by French feminists. Solidarist republicans were as determined as antifeminists to preserve the structure of the separate spheres and keep women in the home. Yet their methods were cooptive rather than defensive, as they pressed some feminist reforms into the service of enhancing women's prescribed function in the family. Solidarists met the feminists' challenge as they handled the socialist claims: by stealing their opponents' thunder. As solidarists had inserted a social concept into their individualist legacy, they also absorbed feminist reforms into the existing structure of role division. They directed the powers of the new woman back into the home, channeling them to extend the range of woman's activities and responsibilities within her assigned domestic sphere.

Solidarists promoted limited reform for women through an alliance with the French "familial feminists." Solidarists such as Léon Bourgeois and Alfred Fouillée and republican feminists shared fundamental assumptions as well as social backgrounds. The two groups emphasized cross-class national solidarity, and in the 1890s both supported changes in the laws pertaining to married women's earnings and the extension of hygiene and child-rearing education to lower class women. These efforts conformed to the vision of "equality in difference," and both solidarists and republican feminists meant their reforms to animate women's distinctively domestic functions and maternal obligations.[49]

*

The attitudes expressed by Mauclair, Simon, Uzanne, Jozé, Bourgeois, and Fouillée, spanning the realms of republican politics and elite culture, would resonate in the official craft movement of the 1890s. During the decade of controversy over the new woman, the members of an official craft coalition defined and promoted women as the natural allies of luxury artisans and as the artificers of a unitary interior design. The specter of the *femme nouvelle* contributed to their efforts to invest women with a central role in aesthetically renovating domestic space.

The range of responses toward women and feminism among republican politicians would be replicated in the craft movement, whose members expressed both the defensive antifeminism and the cooptive "familial feminism" of republican figures. Yet the craft officials united in forging a specifically cultural route to contain and interiorize women. By celebrating women as queens and artists of the interior, they developed a powerful antidote to the *femme nouvelle,* who threatened to relinquish her role as decorative object and decorative artist.

CHAPTER FIVE

Psychologie Nouvelle

We wander all over the Champ-de-Mars and the Gallery of Machines . . . we stroll among these tamed monsters that, roaring, howling, hissing, and spitting, perform the most exact and precise tasks with methodical violence. It will hence surprise you that the age of machines has been inclined, above all others, to exalt the human personality, while it appeared to be diminishing it. Egotism has developed to unprecedented proportions in this century of the machine. . . . *In no other time has the self had so many pretensions, held so high a status, been so widespread, and yet everything blocks the free development of the individual, reduces that part of himself he puts into work, disappoints the yearnings he may have to shape himself according to his own way. The society in which we live aligns us in conformity, and it has never been more difficult to be somebody.*

Yet we love to make ourselves complex, to contort ourselves, to twist and straighten ourselves, to torment our language as well as our thoughts. . . . We are not solely complicated beings but agitated ones as well. All invites us to add to our being, to multiply ourselves, to vary our sensations ceaselessly. . . . We are like . . . neuropaths who cannot believe in the impossible but attempt adventures. . . . We are [like] birds so light that the branch on which we land does not even flinch, and we leave quickly on a quest for something we cannot name and that we never find.

Georges Valbert, 1889[1]

The unconscious activity of the mind is a scientific truth established beyond any doubt. . . . Even in daily life, our conscious mind remains under the direction of the unconscious.

Jules Héricourt, 1889[2]

EIGHTEENTH-CENTURY traditions and late nineteenth-century problems helped to redefine the distinctively French modern style from one of geometric expansiveness to one of serpentine involution. This chapter turns to psychology, the fourth and final contextual component that facilitated the artisanal movement of the 1890s, providing the indispensable intellectual tools to redirect modernity to the interior. A psychology specific to France in the 1890s invested the enterprise of interior decoration with new meanings and transposed the eighteenth-century associations of modernity, intimacy, and interiority into the new key of nervous vibration, spatial self-fashioning, and unconscious projection. By 1889 a decade of clinical exploration of new dimensions of the self had already gained public attention. Georges Valbert, writing for the *Revue des deux mondes,* noted that a cult of the self had emerged to compensate for the challenges to individuality wrought by machine production and colossal technology. Valbert commented that at the very moment that spatial forms and social life threatened the individual with anonymity and insignificance, self-cultivation and self-analysis had been given new life and power. If "society aligns us to conformity" and machines rule us "by the spirit of symmetry, exactitude, and precision," psychological man liberates himself by relentless self-expansion and convolutions of thought and speech. The continual search for new and varied sensations, however, denied to the ego both contentment and stable boundaries. If self-reflexiveness countered regimentation and social leveling, it also transformed modern man into an "agitated" and weary "neuropath."

Restless neuropaths and contorted interior meanderings were themselves the objects of clinical discussion at scientific congresses held during the 1889 Paris Exhibition. The International Congress on Physiological Psychology addressed the conventional topic of psychological heredity but also explored the controversial and less definitively physiological issues of hypnotism and hallucinations in nonpsychotic individuals. The exhibition also provided the occasion for the First International Congress on Experimental and Therapeutic Hypnotism, whose three hundred participants included "philosophers, neurologists, psychiatrists, and practitioners of hypnotism."[3] Although delegates vigorously debated the extent of receptivity to hypnosis and its use as a curative tool, a consensus was evident in the scientific community by 1889 that hypnosis had revealed that the mind was subject to divided consciousness, incorporating a double ego: a conscious ego and an unconscious one that, unknown to the conscious one, acted autonomously.[4] Jules Héricourt's survey on the nature of the unconscious, based on a wide range of sources, concluded in 1889 that "even in our daily life, our conscious mind remains under the direction of the unconscious."[5] The expansion of the discoveries, debates, and personnel of French mental medicine between 1889 and 1900 deepened public awareness of and preoccupation with unconscious domination, calling into question the Enlightenment legacy of self and social mastery.

In charting the emergence of a new cult of the self and the primacy of the irrational in fin-de-siècle France, historians usually invoke the ideology of Symbolism. French Symbolism originated as a literary movement but emerged in the 1880s as a broad theory of life and an attitude toward the material world that inverted outer and inner reality. Conceived as an attack on Parnassian naturalism, Symbolism was officially launched by two poets, Jean Moréas and Gustave Kahn, in 1886. Their published statements of that year articulated four goals that were to galvanize a varied segment of the artistic community in a "reaction against positivism."[6] The first was idealism, a commitment to disengage an essential order of reality beneath the surface of appearances. Kahn asserted that "the aim of art is to objectify the subjective," the "externalization of the Idea." The second was subjectivism, the redirection of artistic activity to an inner psychic world, with particular emphasis on the dream state.

Kahn stated that "we carry the analysis of the self to the extreme," where "the dream is indistinguishable from life." Third, Symbolists redefined artistic language, aiming to communicate through suggestion, allusion, and association rather than by direct statement, description, or depiction. The purpose of Symbolist art was to express the inexpressible, to convey and evoke emotional states in the reader or viewer similar to those experienced by the artists. Fourth, the Symbolists sought to appeal directly to the inner world of the audience through the suggestive power of sound and the dynamic formal elements of the visual arts—line, color, and shape.[7]

The extension of Symbolist ideals to the applied arts was one source for the redefinition of the interior from an accretion of material objects to an arena of self-discovery. For the setting for the Symbolists' exploratory subjectivism was in private ensembles coordinated for the purpose of continually extending the boundaries of sensibility; the decor functioned not to locate the inhabitant historically but to stimulate him visually. The brothers de Goncourt had established this link between interior decoration and psychological interiority. Their vision of the interior as activator of both nervous vibration and visual suggestion became a central feature of the Symbolist enterprise. Where the Goncourts were delicately poised between historicism and psychology, between realism and subjectivism, the Symbolists embraced the cult of artifice, of life from the inside out. The interior was no longer a refuge from but a replacement for the external world.

The Goncourts were directly connected with the literary Symbolists of the 1880s who redefined the interior as a field of visual evocation and nervous palpitation. Joris-Karl Huysmans, a friend and admirer of the Goncourts', stated that his manifesto of Symbolism, the 1883 novel *A rebours,* was inspired in form and in substance by Edmond's *Maison d'un artiste.*[8] Like Edmond's book, Huysmans's work repudiated conventional narrative coherence and descriptive action. It recorded the inner world of one major character, Des Esseintes, through the unfolding of his experience in a succession of elaborate interiors he himself had crafted. The objects in those interiors were the vehicles for his synaesthesia and visual fantasies; his dependence on this continuous aesthetic stimulation consigned him to physical lassitude and nervous hypersensitivity. One of the models for Huysmans's protagonist was Count Robert de Montesquiou-Fezensac, a Symbolist poet and visual artist who also engaged in a form of interior decoration in direct emulation of the Goncourts' aesthetic and psychological model.[9] De Montesquiou organized his apartment on the rue Franklin as an evocative scene in which individual objects dissolved into a field of suggestive visual energy.[10]

We can thus trace affiliations in the artistic avant-garde that explain the new link between psychological self-exploration and interior space as a domain of suprahistorical self-projection. This diachronic line extends from the Goncourts, via Huysmans and de Montesquiou, to Marcel Proust Proust amplified the Symbolists' ideal of the expressive and visual capacities of language to evoke the fluid, suggestive power of the interior realm. He chronicled a flowing give-and-take between the insulated narrator and his furnished decor, correlating the materials of the inner space with the nervous vibrations they stimulated, even as the concrete rooms dissolved in the transfiguring fevers of inner vision.[11] The Goncourts' projection of visual animation onto the walls of the bedroom in the *Maison d'un artiste* led finally to the whirling room envisioned by the narrator in the opening section of Proust's *Swann's Way*. Edmond de Goncourt had relished lying in bed at night, half-asleep, thinking of the bed's former inhabitant, the princesse de Lamballe, and gliding his eyes about the room. His inner vision assumed visual and dynamic shape as he imagined the figures woven into the eighteenth-century Aubusson-tapestried walls coming to life, dancing, cavorting, and encircling him.[12] In Proust's version, the narrator no longer needed historical cues to provide an anecdotal frame for visual projection; the tumult of mental energy set the room spinning around, trapping all the furnishings in the centrifuge of the psyche.[13]

Significantly, the transformation of the interior to a subjectivist dream room was not confined to the artistic avant-garde. Indeed, the association between psychological knowledge and interior decoration had wider cultural resonance and broader historical meaning. At the same time the Symbolists were inventing the interior as the emblem of self-fashioning, a new body of medical knowledge was being consolidated and generalized, called the *psychologie nouvelle*.[14] The medical clinicians concentrated their efforts in two areas: first, the exploration of the interior of the human organism as a febrile, mechanistic system of nerves and, second, the examination of visual dimensions of the thought process, with particular emphasis on the role of images in the mental operations underlying states of hypnotism, suggestion, and dreams. Originating in studies restricted to individual pathologies, the conceptions of nervous excitation and degeneration and of the dynamic visual properties of thought extended well beyond the boundaries of medical science. By the 1890s the diffusion of the *psychologie nouvelle* had indelibly stamped elite and popular culture.

Although the Symbolists are usually credited with redefining rational consciousness and with championing a new subjectivist relation to the world, the diffusion of medical psychology facilitated a broader reevaluation of space and self in the French fin de siècle. Some evidence, indeed, indicates that the Symbolists themselves drew directly on medical sources for their conception of the psychological interior. To Des Esseintes, for example, Huysmans attributed clinical states of nervous excitation and exhaustion that he had absorbed from a careful reading of Doctor Alexander Axenfeld's 1883 text *Traité de névroses*.[15] More broadly, the four goals of Symbolist artistic philosophy—subjectivism, idealism, the dream world, and the power of visual and aural suggestion—were the very objects of medical research on the mind. They appeared at the center of medical debates on contending models of the unconscious, the results of which were widely publicized in late nineteenth-century France. Most important, the widespread dissemination of medical ideas about the workings of the nerves and the visual dynamism of cognition were assimilated by artists and sponsors of the decorative arts movement, shaping their understanding of the modern style as one of psychological interiority.[16]

The *psychologie nouvelle* in the 1890s originated with the discoveries of the two medical pioneers, Doctor Jean-Martin Charcot of Paris and Doctor Hippolyte Bernheim of Nancy. In three ways the generalization of this *psychologie nouvelle* had direct relevance for the redefinition of interior decoration. First, in the wide-ranging political discussion of the pathological degeneration of the national body, attributed to the sensory overstimulation of the urban metropolis, the city was identified as an agent of "neurasthenia"; the interior took on a new role as a soothing anaesthetizer of the citizen's overwrought nerves. Second, the meaning of interior space was transformed by its new association with the visually charged fluidity of the "*chambre mentale.*"[17] If the overstimulated citizen could find refuge in the interior from the sensory barrage of the metropolis, he nonetheless transported with him the propensity for animating the interior by that very same mechanism of the nerves. No longer could the interior be construed as a stable and static historical setting. Rather, by the 1890s it had emerged as an arena of dynamic and reciprocal interaction between subject and object. Finally, the convergence of interior design and the new psychology was sealed by the engagement of a medical psychologist in the decorative arts. The new space and the new self were bound together by Doctor Charcot's practice as an artist and interior decorator.

From Decadence to Degeneration: Aesthete Debility to National Pathology

In 1862 Jean-Martin Charcot, the son of a Parisian carriage builder, was appointed resident physician to the Salpêtrière Hospital. Charcot had studied medicine at the University of Paris and was awarded his medical degree in 1853, upon presenting a doctoral thesis on gout and chronic rheumatism. Beginning in 1862, Charcot devoted his research exclusively to neurological disorders, and within the next eight years he founded the field of modern neurology. His publication of a series of studies and his innovative teaching techniques gained him widespread recognition. In 1872 he was appointed professor of pathologic anatomy in the faculty of medicine, and in 1892 he accepted the chair for the study of nervous disorders at the Salpêtrière. This appointment represented the first official acknowledgment of neurology as a specialty in its own right.[18]

Charcot's work unfolded in two directions that were destined to have significant public impact by the late 1880s. First, he defined and characterized a series of diseases of the nervous system, called *maladies nerveuses,* each of which was associated with a set of interior lesions on the spinal cord. Second, Charcot developed a variety of new therapies to treat the different pathologies of the nervous system. These included "galvanization," or electric shock therapy; "ferronization," or the ingestion of iron; and the suspension of the patient from the ceiling in a contraption resembling an iron harness.[19] Underlying these treatments was a belief in the physical and organic origins of nervous disorders, whose causes were attributed to the atrophy, or degeneration, of the nervous system.

By 1885, French creative artists had assimilated Charcot's elaboration of nervous pathologies, with particular emphasis on a condition called neurasthenia. This was a clinical state of mental hypersensitivity and physical debility, resulting from continuous mental exertion unrelieved by physical action. Following the mechanistic model of the nervous system formulated by Charcot, neurasthenia was diagnosed medically as a condition of nervous exhaustion, in which excessive stimulation atrophied the nerves to a point of extreme irritability and physical lassitude.

The clinical states of neurasthenia and degeneration were transposed into literary form by such writers as Edmond de Goncourt, Paul Bourget, Joris-Karl Huysmans, and Emile Zola, who attributed the qualities of individual degeneration to the nation as a whole. In 1880, for example, Edmond de Goncourt characterized the nineteenth century as a "feverish, tormented" century, one of "anxiety and nervous corrosion."[20] In 1896 Emile Zola traced infirmity to the nervous tension of modern life:

> Ours is a society racked ceaselessly by a nervous erethism. We are sickened by our industrial progress, by science; we live in a fever, and we like to dig deeper into our sores. . . . Everything suffers and complains in the works of our time. Nature herself is linked to our suffering, and being tears itself apart, exposes itself in its nudity.[21]

The extension of the pathological findings from the individual to the national body went far beyond the confines of aesthetic culture after 1880 because of the widespread diffusion and generalization of the Salpêtrière discoveries. As the typologies of the *maladies nerveuses* left the halls of the Salpêtrière and permeated the public domain, the arena of susceptibility expanded; politicians, journalists, literary critics, and social theorists were faced, in the late 1880s, with the startling revelation that nervous debility was not restricted to the hothouses of literary decadence but was incubating as a collective condition of national degeneration. The urban metropolis, whose inhabitants faced a relentless barrage of sensory excitation and lived at an accelerated pace, threatened to transform France into a nation of physically exhausted and mentally hypersensitive Des Esseintes.[22]

Charcot and his followers had systematized the link between disorders of the nervous system and the urban metropolis. When the American physician George Miller Beard first defined neurasthenia in 1880, he attributed Americans' nervous exhaustion to their excessive zeal for the Protestant ethic. Restricting neurasthenia to the middle and upper-middle classes, Beard attributed the condition to overwork. He believed neurasthenia could be eliminated through a combination of rest cures and electrotherapies. As neurasthenia traveled to the European continent, however, it assumed a more menacing and intractable form. French clinicians did not share the American's belief in ready cures or his restriction of nervous exhaustion to particular classes. Indeed, they suggested that the wear and tear of life in the city promoted neurasthenia as a general condition of modernity.[23]

Between 1885 and 1893, French medical researchers explored the relation between urban existence and nervous tension in a number of publications. For example, in a series of articles in the *Revue scientifique* Charles Richet, a noted physiologist and a colleague of Charcot's, affirmed the potential of international communication networks, travel, journalism, and such technology as electricity and telegraphs to promote a new unity among nations. Yet he also indicated the psychological cost for the citizen of the urban center where these innovations converged. The expansion of information to be assimilated and the speed of city life developed the urban dweller's mental sensitivities at the expense of his physical vitality.[24] Richet returned to these themes in 1890 in *Le Surmenage mental dans la civilization moderne*.[25] *Surmenage*, the overtaxing or overexertion of the nervous system, emerged as a central criterion with which to evaluate urban existence in the fin de siècle.

A second medical figure who identified the city as an agent of nervous pathology, Doctor Fernand Levillain, published the relatively inexpensive, small-format book entitled *La Neurasthénie* in 1891, with an introduction by Charcot.[26] Part of Levillain's intention was to introduce the public to the etiology and varieties of the neurasthenic condition and to provide a typology of the medical therapies to remedy it. Levillain explained that neurasthenia had a natural breeding ground in the urban metropolis. He emphasized that women and men contracted it; the decisive factor was not gender but the agitated pace of urban life. The city generated neurasthenia across class lines, in unskilled workers as well as in intellectuals. The modern metropolis, demanding continuous nervous exertion, could lead all of its inhabitants into a state of *surmenagement*, "overtaxing neurosis."[27]

Concern over collective devitalization and degeneration resonated throughout high and low culture in fin-de-siècle France. Popular journals such as *L'Illustration* devoted explanatory articles and bold images to the discoveries and therapies of the Salpêtrière.[28] Women's magazines such as *La Grande Dame* provided space in their columns for medical experts, who advised their readers to adjust the color schemes of their clothing to the tonalities psychophysical experimentation had found to be least corrosive to the nervous tissue of the spectator.[29] Octave Uzanne presented his menagerie of *La Femme à Paris* against the backdrop of the debilitating "*fin-de-siècle névrosée*."[30] Art criticism in the pages of *La Plume* recommended the complexities of Symbolist painting to an audience rendered highly sensitive by an "overtaxation of the nervous system" and affirmed that as civilization evolved, physical agility was generally superseded by the cultivation of the higher faculties, "the refinement of cerebral capacities."[31] The middle-brow journal *La Revue* was filled, after 1890, with articles devoted to the new *psychologie*, which suggested such panaceas for "our exhausted generation" as the "massage of your muscles' nerves."[32] And even in that sober academic bastion the *Revue des deux mondes*, writers debated the implications of urban nervous degeneration for social policy.[33]

The broadly based tendency to apply the discoveries of nervous pathologies to the national body culminated in 1895 with the publication of the controversial and widely debated book *Degeneration*. The author of this work, Max Nordau, was a practicing physician from Germany, who had studied in Paris under Doctor Charcot. Nordau drew on his clinical knowledge of medical pathologies in his effort to become an amateur sociologist and cultural critic. Living in Paris throughout the 1880s, Nordau was appalled by what he considered to be the corruption and immorality of the Symbolist poets and painters. After haunting the cafés of the Latin Quarter, visiting the art exhibitions at the offices of *La Plume* and the *Revue indépendante,* and attending performances at the Théâtre Libre, Nordau unleashed an indiscriminate attack on all forms of modernism in the arts.[34]

Nordau's work, which soon became "a sensational best-seller,"[35] had two significant dimensions, which provoked responses from renowned political theorists in France. The first was his scientifically based redefinition of artistic decadence as a condition caused by nervous disorder. Equipped with Charcot's list of the physical signs of nervous debility, Nordau diagnosed the literary aesthete as the victim of neuropathology:

> The physician, especially if he has devoted himself to the special study of nervous and mental maladies, recognizes at a glance, in the . . . tendencies of contemporary art and poetry . . . the confluence of two well-defined conditions of disease, with which he is quite familiar, viz., degeneration (degeneracy) and hysteria, of which the minor stages are designated as neurasthenia.[36]

Nordau extended his characterization of the individual aesthete-degenerate to the nation. A second feature of his book was to illuminate a general "fin-de-siècle disposition" or "frame of mind."[37] Artistic decadence was symptomatic of national degeneration and decline. Nordau identified nervous pathology as a collective pathology, not a condition limited to a small coterie of debilitated aesthetes. The physically exhausted and overstimulated artist was merely the forerunner of all the citizens of urban centers in France. The city, condenser of anxiety, concentrator of speed and sensory bombardment, and spatially de-natured, depleted national energy and eroded national nerve fiber to the point of collective neurasthenia.[38]

Though Nordau's book aimed to characterize the degeneration of all contemporary European nations, he located in France the most extensive collective pathology. Historical events such as the Napoleonic wars had already exposed France to "nervous strain" and "derangement," according to Nordau; the Franco-Prussian War and the Commune of 1870–1871 intensified the Gallic predisposition to national "neurasthenia."[39]

Despite the shrill tone of his book, Nordau identified sources of French degeneration that contemporaries found were too powerful to dismiss. One of the most telling responses to Nordau was articulated by a central spokesman for the Third Republic in the 1890s, Alfred Fouillée, an intellectual originator of solidarism, who sought to revitalize the republican tradition by replacing its desiccated atomism with cooperation. Although Fouillée rejected the fatalism of Nordau's indictment, he provided a telling summary of Nordau's findings in an article in the *Revue des deux mondes.* Fouillée was particularly struck by the evidence connecting degeneration and urban life. The full-fledged immersion of Fouillée's discussion in the categories of neuropathology demonstrates that the Salpêtrière taxonomies had permeated the political elite:

> Neurosis is a danger to the individual, but it is much more a danger to the nation. . . . We fear a certain rupture in the equilibrium of a people's constitution. . . . We fear a weakening of moral vigor, of courage, consistency, firmness, of all the qualities that create the life force. Intelligence is refined along with the nerves, but willpower is weakened along with the muscles. . . . From this we must conclude that France needs . . . better physical hygiene, capable of counterbalancing the effects of our intellectual overexertion . . . and a vigorous reaction against our abandonment of the countryside for the city.[40]

In this context of widespread application of the medical studies of nervous pathologies to national life and of worry over collective degeneration, the official craft sponsors promulgated a modern interior style based on vitalizing organic forms. Their retreat to a healthy chamber of naturist physicality was posed against the nervous erosion wrought by the overloaded metropolis. But a second feature of the *psychologie nouvelle* undermined the possibility for a stable and concrete interior anchorage. By 1890 the psychological phenomena of suggestion, hypnosis, and dreaming had left the Salpêtrière and had shaped a new theory of mind and attitude toward reality, inextricably joining the practice of interior decoration to the unstable fluidity of the *chambre mentale*.

Hypnotism, Suggestion, Visual Thinking, and the New French Concept of the Irrational: Psychopathology or Model of Mind?

After 1875 Charcot shifted the focus of his work from the systematic characterization of nervous disorders and their clinical remedies to the particular study of hysteria. This pathology posed a special challenge to the medical pioneer, for unlike the other diseases of the nervous system classified by Charcot, it had no discernible and consistent anatomical base. Moreover, hysterical patients demonstrated a host of bewildering symptoms: amnesia, paralysis, anesthesia, contractions, and spasms. Charcot observed these patients intensively, using hypnosis as one method of investigation.[41] By the 1880s the results of these studies, together with Charcot's volatile debates with another clinician of hypnosis, Dr. Hippolyte Bernheim of Nancy, yielded a reevaluation of rational consciousness. The Charcot-Bernheim conflict over hypnosis and mental suggestion is usually noted for its impact outside France: Sigmund Freud went to Paris and Nancy between 1884 and 1886 to absorb the lessons of both Charcot and Bernheim, transposing their conclusions into a radically new theory of sexuality and the unconscious. But the clinical explorations of hypnosis and suggestion had an equally powerful effect in France in the fin de siècle. To

French psychologists, hypnosis unveiled a nondiscursive, dynamic ideational flow. Images were discovered as an irresistible force in the thought process, permeating the brain directly from the outer world, and projected outward as if to shape the world in accord with inner visions, unmediated by rational discretion. Although less shattering to the rationalist legacy than the Freudian formulation of the connection between the unconscious and the unbridled aggressiveness of the id, French explorations of hypnosis, suggestion, and the peculiar propensity of the mind to receive and project images posed a striking challenge to the positivist understanding of the relationship between the mind and the external world.

Hypnotism had been discredited in medical circles in the nineteenth century by its relation to the eighteenth-century practices of Mesmer and his animal magnetism. Charcot dismissed the Mesmer legacy as metaphysical quackery but defended the utility of hypnotism and suggestion under carefully controlled conditions. The enlightening forces of modern medicine revealed that hypnotism and suggestion had nothing to do with the supposed magical power of the inducer but were attributable to physiological causes in the subject to whom they were applied. The highly sensitive and pathological state of the nervous systems of hysterical patients rendered them receptive to hypnosis, a tool whose therapeutic use Charcot intended for only this type of nervous disorder. His presentation on hypnosis and hysteria to the Académie des Sciences in 1882 marked the official recognition of hypnotism as a respectable subject of scientific investigation.[42]

After repeated experimentation, Charcot divided the phenomenon of hysterical hypnosis into three phases. The first was lethargy or drowsiness, which the doctor induced by having the patient concentrate intensely on a moving object. The second stage, called catalepsy, referred to a state in which the patient was irresistibly receptive to suggestion from the doctor, due to the contraction of consciousness to a single idea or impression, unimpeded by other ideas or impressions. During the third and final phase, somnambulism, Charcot observed what he described as the dissociation of personality—the hypnotized patient was able to act out suggested commands with no recollection afterward. Charcot considered this acting out of gestures, signs, or other behavior suggested by the doctor a splitting and externalization of states of consciousness normally coordinated and controlled. Suggested ideas, implanted in the mind of the patient, settled in "isolation from the Ego," revealing an autonomous inner development and a direct outer materialization.[43]

During the three phases of the hypnotic process Charcot discovered the particular potency of images to affect the minds of hysterics. The hypnotic trance was induced when the patient concentrated intensely on a moving object. Of the many types of suggestion that provoked automatic behavior among hypnotized patients, Charcot found that visual materials—colored discs and signs—were often more effective than verbal commands. Charcot explored this special receptivity of hysterical patients to visual material in a series of experiments during the 1880s. In one session, two of Charcot's colleagues tested the effects of various colors on the hypnotized patients. Not only did they find that visual stimuli provoked an immediate and

visible set of gestures among the patients, but the clinicians were also able to correlate specific colors with emotional states.[44] This correlation paralleled in the medical
sphere the Symbolist artists' attempts to discover the emotional equivalents of visual
language. During the 1880s Seurat and Gauguin, among others, proposed the evocative power of colors, believing that painters could formally convey and evoke in
the viewer emotional responses independent of the subjects they represented. In the
Salpêtrière experiments, doctors exploring the visual effects of suggestion confirmed
the propensity of color to assume evocative, emotional form. Red colored discs provoked gestures of joy and pleasure among the patients; blue triggered a sad, dejected
look; yellow produced signs of panic and fear. The visual artists of the 1880s had
similarly construed the emotional valences of these colors.[45]

Besides the particular susceptibility of hypnotized patients to visual material,
Charcot and his co-workers discovered the tendency of these same patients to externalize their inner visions. The acting out of what Charcot called sensory hallucinations[46] during the last stage of hypnosis was considered the projection outward of
"the true nature of the painting that is drawn in the brain of the sick."[47] Those who
observed this imagistic projection by hysterical patients described it as dreaming,
which had been discussed earlier in the century but which Doctor Charcot isolated
with clinical accuracy. One systematic account of the dreaming of hysterical patients
was discussed by Charcot in 1889:

> Visual hallucinations are frequent. . . . They preside especially in the third
> stage: The patient becomes a character in a scene and it is easy to follow all the
> sudden changes of the drama he believes to be unfolding and in which he plays
> the principal role by the expressive and animated mimicry to which he has
> given himself over. When the patient is a woman, two very different orders of
> ideas share in the hallucinations. That painting has two aspects, one happy, the
> other sad. In the happy phase, the patient believes herself to be transported to a
> magnificent garden, a kind of Eden, where flowers are often red and inhabit-
> ants are dressed in red. Music is playing. The patient meets there the object of
> her dreams and her previous affections, and scenes of love-making sometimes
> ensue. But this erotic part is often lacking and plays a secondary role in the
> numerous and varied manifestations that constitute the great hysterical attack.
> The sad paintings are fires, war, revolutions, assassinations, etc. Almost al-
> ways blood flows. Among men, these dismal and terrifying visions alone oc-
> cupy almost the entire third period.[48]

Charcot consistently emphasized that the special visual receptivity and imagistic
exteriorization that he observed among hypnotized patients were abnormal, pathological phenomena, attributable to the irregularities in the nervous systems of hysterical subjects. The confinement of hypnosis, suggestion, and visual projection to
individuals afflicted with nervous disorders, however, was vociferously contested in
the 1880s. A respected medical center outside of Paris, which followed a system of
clinical experimentation equal to that of the Salpétrière, arrived at conclusions very

different from those of Charcot. The Ecole de Nancy, officially established in 1882 under the direction of Doctor Hippolyte Bernheim, entered into protracted debates with the Salpêtrière during the 1880s. These debates undermined the primacy of rationalist regularity in the thought process.

Doctor Hippolyte Bernheim was forty-two in 1882 and had worked for ten years as an assistant to Doctor Ambroise-Auguste Liébault at the Faculté de Médecine in Nancy. Liébault was the first medical practitioner to embrace hypnosis as a serious clinical tool. Beginning in the 1850s, he conducted numerous experiments with hypnosis, inducing artificial sleep in patients suffering from functional handicaps as well as nervous disorders. It was his intention to discredit definitively the mesmeric theories of magical fluid transmission and faith healing that stigmatized hypnosis and to examine its physical and psychological underpinnings. Until he began to collaborate with Bernheim, however, Liébault had little success in convincing his medical colleagues that hypnosis was a useful therapeutic tool. The lengthy treatise he compiled in 1866 was largely ignored; indeed, it was read by only five readers in seven years.[49]

Hippolyte Bernheim was one of them. After adopting Liébault's position, Bernheim worked with his mentor in the hopes of expanding the purely medical and therapeutic uses of hypnosis and suggestion. By the late 1870s, however, Bernheim's experiments yielded unanticipated results, which led him beyond Liébault's theories and into a collision with Charcot and the Salpêtrière school.

Bernheim discovered four startling phenomena. First, he was able to alter patients' behavior by visual and verbal suggestion *without* initially hypnotizing them, thereby reversing the order stipulated by Charcot. The linchpin of Charcot's theories and methods was the assumption that suggestion was a function of hypnosis, which produced a state of mental passivity in the subject; only *after* this artificial sleep state was induced could a patient be receptive to suggestion. Bernheim found, on the contrary, that hypnotism was itself a function of suggestion, to which the subject was susceptible in a waking state—"*la suggestion à l'état de veille.*"[50] Related to this reversal was Bernheim's observation that the impact of suggestion lasted longer than the duration of the hypnotic state. When he instructed hypnotized patients to perform certain tasks in a month's time, they did as they were told at the appointed date but recollected neither the instructions nor the performance of the tasks. Bernheim attributed this gap between memory and action to the splitting or dissociation of personality, which Charcot had also defined as the mechanism underlying the actions performed upon suggestion. But Bernheim argued that this mechanism could carry over from the immediate situation of suggestion into future actions by what he called the "transmission" or "extension" of thought.[51]

Bernheim's most important challenges to Charcot related to two of his conclusions regarding the mechanisms of suggestion and hypnosis in healthy individuals. Charcot insisted that hypnosis was a clinical tool for examining one type of nervous pathology: only hysterical patients were hypnotizable, and hypnosis itself was a manifestation of hysteria. Yet Bernheim executed repeated experiments with normal individuals, who revealed a striking susceptibility to suggestion and hypnosis, equal

to that of abnormal patients. Finally, he found that the particular potency of imagistic suggestion and the tendency to externalize visual material, identified by
Charcot as the exceptional features of nervous pathology, were in fact characteristic
of normal subjects. Bernheim's findings led him to elaborate a fundamental redefinition of consciousness.

In his 1884 treatise *De la suggestion dans l'état hypnotique et dans l'état de veille,*
Bernheim explained that "visual images" penetrated the mind directly from the external world. The thought process transformed ideas into images: "One should not
consider the transformation of an idea into an image as a morbid operation but
rather a normal property of the brain."[52] Bernheim argued that the mind was an
acutely sensitive chamber, receptive to the dynamic flow of images and ideas and to
the subtle influences of social interaction, independent of rational control. Energy,
visual impressions, and intangible forces emanating from the external environment
were elements as powerful as conscious decision making or assimilation of information about the world. Rather than a concrete surround from which the individual
selected and processed information, the external world was a torrential flow of stimuli, to which the individual was unpredictably and imagistically impressionable:

> Suggestion, that is, the penetration of the subject's brain by the idea of the phe-
> nomenon through a word, a gesture, a view, or an imitation, seems to me the
> key to all the hypnotic phenomena that I have observed. Supposedly physio-
> logical phenomena seem to be, in their greater part if not in their entirety, psy-
> chic phenomena. . . . Suggestibility is such that, in the waking state, an idea
> accepted by the brain becomes . . . an image. . . .
>
> Suggestive phenomena do have their analogies in everyday life . . . ; nature
> produces them spontaneously. . . . Sensorial illusions, hallucinations, realize
> themselves in all of us. . . . We are all suggestible and can experience hallucina-
> tions by our own or other peoples' impressions. . . . No one can escape the
> suggestive influence of others.[53]

Accompanying Bernheim's discovery of the mind as a febrile, permeable chamber
was the notion that the individual projected this animated imagistic material back
out, shaping the external environment in accord with his inner vision. Although
Charcot insisted that externalized visualization, or dreams, were the identifying features of hysterical abnormality, Bernheim retorted that "sensorial hallucinations"
formed part of the daily existence of all individuals:

> The truth is that we are all subject to hallucinations for a great part of our
> lives. . . .[54]

> Poor human reason has taken flight. The most ambitious spirit yields to halluci-
> nations and becomes . . . the plaything of dreams evoked by the imagination.[55]

Bernheim initially considered the primacy of "sensorial hallucinations" a short-
term condition of normal sleep, when the relaxation of what he called the higher

centers of judgment and verification tumultuously released unconscious images. But his study of suggestibility in the waking state led him to conclude that the mind yielded to the "flight of reason" and to the domination of hallucinations "for a great part of our lives." He observed in normal subjects what Charcot had identified in hysterics: the implantation of suggested ideas, their isolation from "the ego proper," and their direct and unmediated materialization into acts. Bernheim called this irresistible influence of suggested "ideas over acts" "cerebral automatism," or "ideodynamism."[56] Bernheim was particularly interested in the visual dimensions of ideodynamism, and he devised experiments to test visual perception and suggestion. He noted that "suggested images" were "fictitious," "subjective images" "evoked by the subject's imagination."[57] Yet these subjective images were projected outward onto physical reality, even in ways contrary to the laws of optics:

> The hallucinatory image may be as distinct, as bright and as active to the subject as reality itself. . . . He sees it as he conceives it, as he interprets it. . . . It is a psychical cerebral image and not a physical one. It does not pass through the apparatus of vision, has no objective reality, follows no optical laws, but solely obeys the caprices of the imagination.[58]

Bernheim stated in these writings that "imagination rules supreme,"[59] and his experiments demonstrated clinically the Symbolist ideal of the "objectification of the subjective," the referring of interior images to the outer world as if they were true.[60] Charcot associated the "*rêve vécu*" ("living out the dream") with hysterical ideodynamism.[61] Bernheim, in contrast, found that "hallucinations" were "universal" and that "supposedly physiological phenomena seem to be in their greater part, if not in their entirety, psychic phenomena."[62] Two years before the Symbolist assault on positivist materialism and rational discourse in the manifesto of 1886, Doctor Bernheim proclaimed, with scientific authority, the dissolution of the stable boundaries between inner and outer, subjective and objective, reality.

The epistemological and social challenges inherent in this model of a mind prone to suggestion and imagistic externalization were widely recognized and debated in fin-de-siècle France. As early as 1885 the Chamber of Deputies heard an official statement of the problematic implications of suggestion for the law: M. Liégeois's *De la suggestion hypnotique dans ses rapports avec le droit civil et criminel*. A number of well-publicized trials began to rely on the theory of actions induced by hypnosis as the basis for a criminal defense. The most sensational of these was the trial in 1888 of Henri Chambige, who claimed he murdered a married woman under the influence of hypnosis.[63]

Hypnotism and suggestion also inspired numerous novels, some of which were the result of writers' direct contact with Doctor Charcot. Charcot's weekly public demonstrations of hysterical hypnosis drew a surprising range of "tout Paris" to the Salpêtrière. Artists in the audience found it difficult to confine Charcot's lessons to the afflicted inhabitants of the hospital wards, and they explored what one Symbolist writer called Charcot's revelation of the "unsuspected realms of the mind."[64] The protagonist of Guy de Maupassant's novella *Le Horla* suffered from strange visions and unaccountable actions, only to realize that he was a victim of his own unconscious cerebral automatism: "Someone possesses my soul and governs it. Someone directs all my actions, all my movements, all my thoughts. I myself am nothing but a terrified, enslaved spectator of the things I am accomplishing."[65] Jules Clarétie, who attended the Salpêtrière lectures regularly, wrote a novel, *L'Obsession, moi et l'autre,* describing a painter's preoccupation with the involuntary actions that might be performed by a hidden second personality lurking within his own psyche.[66] Even Charcot's medical colleagues adopted fictional form to examine some of the perplexing implications of the new discoveries of the mind. Charles Richet, under the pseudonym Charles Epheyre, published a novella in the *Revue des deux mondes* that told the story of a split personality.[67] Alfred Binet, a respected clinician who experimented widely with suggestion and visual thinking collaborated with a playwright, André de Lorde, in dramatizing Charcot's lessons at the Salpêtrière, hypnotic somnambulism, and states of hallucination. Three of these plays were performed at important Paris theaters after 1901, and two became puppet shows at the Grand Guignol.[68]

A range of popular sources registered the intellectual tremors of suggestion and hypnotism during the 1890s. Alfred Robida, the writer and illustrator of best-selling anthologies, devoted a section of his volume *Le XIXe Siècle* to a humorous tale of hypnosis used to extract a confession and description of a lurid amorous past.[69] The columns of *L'Illustration* contained a fictional account of the hypnosis of an idle bourgeois matron in her home.[70] Caricatures in this same popular journal recorded the use of hypnotism and suggestion to implant ideas in the minds of powerful friends: in 1892 a cartoon presented Edmond de Goncourt hypnotizing Emile Zola to induce, by suggestion, the idea that Zola approach the ministry and recommend that Edmond be awarded the Legion of Honor.[71] An entry in the popular press indicated that the implications of hypnosis for a fundamental redefinition of the ego were widely understood: Hypnotic experiments "demonstrate that the personality is neither really defined, nor permanent, nor stationary; that the sense of free will is essentially floating and illusive, memory multiple and intermittent; and that character is a function of these variable qualities and can be modified."[72]

The discovery of the febrile, suggestive power of the external world and the dynamic extension of inner vision outward also transformed assumptions held by the elite in culture and politics. Henri Bergson, whose writings mark the intellectual center of fin-de-siècle French redefinitions of reason, was deeply involved in neuropsychiatric research on hypnosis, suggestion, and ideodynamism. His conceptions of the fluidity and indeterminacy of the mind, first expounded in his 1889 *Essai sur les données immédiates de la conscience,* depended in part on his incorporation of the findings of medical clinicians. As professor in Clermont-Ferrand between 1883 and 1888, Bergson observed hypnotic sessions organized by a Doctor Moutin. In 1886, Bergson himself experimented with the effects of hypnosis and suggestion on the perception and mental processes of a number of subjects.[73] He witnessed in particular the unmediated penetration of images from the outer world, the tendency, as Bernheim had indicated, to "transform ideas into images," and the deep unconscious "imprinting" established between the hypnotizer and the subject.[74] In the *Données,* Bergson pressed his clinical understanding of imagistic suggestibility into the service of a new theory of the mind, ascribing a fundamental position to the artist. The book opened with a discussion of the way that the artist replaced the hypnotist as the agent of a direct, unmediated access to the unconscious. The artist, like the hypnotist, functioned to "put reason to sleep" and "to trigger emotional states by suggestion."[75] The artist's visual material "fixes our attention," "suspending the barriers" blocking the release of the unconscious. Caught in the "contagion" of the artist's vision, the boundaries of individual consciousness dissolve, and we are automatically transported to a dream state, where we experience irresistibly the same emotional state provoked in the artist.[76] In a subsequent passage, Bergson indicated that the intensity of the artist's "imprinting" on us corresponds to the stages of hypnosis. At its most intense, we experience what Bergson described as a total loss of self; even our physical being becomes inhabited by another, whose movements our bodies mechanically imitate, while our consciousness is completely given over to "the indefinable psychological state experienced in the other."[77] Bergson construed the artist's compact with the unconscious only as the most concentrated form of suggestibility present in all interactions. The *Données* developed the idea that all of nature is dynamically charged and affects us, like art, by suggestion. We are irrevocably "oscillating," Bergson noted, between consciousness of self and the dissolution of the ego. Even a hint of an idea, suggested without our being cognizant of it, suffices to "absorb" our entire psyche in unconscious simulation.[78]

Like Bergson, important republican thinkers also used the discoveries of the new psychology to redefine reality and individual consciousness. In the 1880s Alfred Fouillée began to chronicle the experiments with hypnotism and suggestion at the Salpêtrière and in Nancy for the *Revue des deux mondes.*[79] By 1891 Fouillée had written a series of articles for the same journal, summarizing the medical debates and transposing the psychiatric discoveries into a radical inversion of outer and inner reality.[80] Fouillée's articles reveal the elements of clinical material that interested him. First, the medical experiments with suggestibility contributed to Fouillée's antimaterialism; he came to construe the external world not as a clear, legible structure but as "a tumultuous ocean,"[81] "a continuum" of unstable energy.[82] "The material world that surrounds us is animated by an atmosphere of psychic life. . . . We are not plunged into a material world, we bathe in mental atmosphere. . . . All is sympathetically and telepathically related."[83]

Second, the new psychology revealed to Fouillée what he called the subterranean disaggregated parts of the self that were released during induced hypnosis or, as in Bernheim's view, during normal sleep or in a relaxed waking state.[84] For Fouillée this finding disclosed the mind as a psychic "theater," where a "troupe of different, multiple actors enacted an interior drama."[85] Third, Fouillée was fascinated by the neuropsychiatric research on ideodynamism. Concurring with the Bernheim school of "universal hallucinations," Fouillée was struck by the dynamic extension of inner vision to the outer world. He explained that hypnotism had revealed the "astonishing influence of the mental over the physical" and cited Bernheim's experiments with sensorial suggestion in which blank white pieces of paper were perceived distinctly as red.[86] Fouillée concluded that "hypnotic phenomena demonstrate precisely that completely psychic images can be projected outward in the form of real objects."[87]

Fouillée assimilated these psychiatric discoveries into three striking revisions of liberal rationalism. First, he transposed ideodynamism into a philosophical doctrine of "*idées-forces,*" the power of ideas over action. This was a new idealism, anchored in nonrational sources.[88] Fouillée extended the principle of *idées-forces* to the national body, arguing that France's preoccupation with decline and degeneration operated as a powerful form of autosuggestion that could be countered by promoting ideas of national strength and vitality.[89] Second, he used suggestibility to resolve the major problem of liberal political theory of the 1890s—how to move beyond atomism to community. Fouillée asserted that the "new psychology has wrested from us the illusion of a bounded, impenetrable, and autonomous ego."[90] Our pride in our discrete individuality, he explained, is utterly compromised by the irresistibility and omnipresence of suggestion. The permeable, shifting centers of personality rendered the mind itself a vessel of the social, injected, by "mutual penetration," with "a vast society of beings."[91] Fouillée thus celebrated suggestibility as a new, unconscious imperative for the "law of solidarity and universal fraternity." "Rien de si un qui ne soit multiple, rien de si mien qui ne soit aussi collectif":[92] this was the lesson he drew for republicans from the revelations of antirationalism. Finally, the new psychology compelled Fouillée, like Bergson, to redefine the self as an artist, involved in a continuous process of ego creation. The clinicians of the psyche exposed to Fouillée the fragility of the notions of the unity of being, of reality as a given, and of free and conscious will. He responded with a call to liberation: the self is not a discrete substance but an idea, and we are each therefore responsible for constructing and reconstructing our own self-image.[93] Identity, like the rest of external reality, is a representation, and we must extend the idea of our ego outward. "Like an artist who invests the idea with material and real form," we must select and project the form of our self, materializing our shifting inner vision of an identity.[94] Without interior construction and representation, Fouillée concluded, we risk being "swallowed up in the vast, disordered, tumultuous ocean that envelops us."[95]

"Charcot-Artiste":
Visual Medicine and Interior Decoration

While philosophers, novelists, and journalists interpreted Charcot's theories as catalysts for new models of mind and society, the doctor himself maintained a stringent positivism, insisting that the powers of suggestibility and imagistic externalization were restricted to patients suffering from nervous disorders. Yet evidence indicates that Charcot understood some of the radical implications of his own clinical discoveries for a redefinition of consciousness. Contemporary accounts and Charcot's own

Fig. 19. Dr. Charcot and suggestion, from *Les Hommes d'aujourd'hui,* 1889. Courtesy of the Bibliothèque Nationale, Paris.

behavior suggest that he was drawn to the underside of rationality and acknowledged the power of dreams, suggestion, and visual thinking not only in hysterics but in all normal minds, including his own (Fig. 19).

Charcot was particularly fascinated by artistic creativity, and although officially he linked artists to hysteria and neurosis, both his scientific work and his personal history were marked by the primacy of the visual. Charcot's own unprecedented clinical methods and innovative educational techniques were based precisely on a model of imagistic thought, on "raising the image," as one of his students noted, "to the rank of the first order."[96] Indeed, Charcot was celebrated by his contemporaries, Sigmund Freud among them, specifically for transporting artistic categories to medicine and for creating a new visual language of diagnosis. Charcot's organization of a visual medicine at the Salpêtrière was complemented by his lifelong practice of drawing, design, and interior decoration at home. In this concluding section, I will examine the ubiquity of the visual in Charcot's professional and vocational endeavors. The significance of Charcot's artistic practice for this analysis is twofold. First, his involvement in interior design brought him, and members of his family, into direct contact with the institution of decorative arts renovation after 1889. Second,

Charcot's preoccupation with art exposed a split in his own identity, and provided him with an avenue to explore the role of fantasy, unconscious visualization, and ideodynamism in his own psyche. Charcot expressed this tension in his interior design, where he combined the forms of historical eclecticism with suggestions of personal memory and private, subjective fantasy.[97]

Both the elaboration of a visual medicine and the practice of interior decoration originated in personal history—Charcot was an artist. The son of a carriage maker, Charcot began as a child to draw the decorative motifs on the ornaments that his father applied to the carriage surfaces.[98] Throughout his adolescence, Charcot devoted all his free time to drawing and sketching from nature. His early drawings refined his visual acuity, and developed his skill at seizing essential configurations by observation:

> At the age of seventeen, Charcot was drawing. [From his drawings] we can deduce . . . a quick and good grasp of an ensemble, of its main lines. . . . Charcot's drawings are always synthetic. They are, most often, a true schema. But that schema has nothing artificial to it, and every line in it sums up a whole set of natural lines. From this comes our impression of truth, often even of life. The faculty to discern the essential traits . . . of a landscape, to instantly perceive an ensemble, to isolate in this ensemble the traits needed for its expression . . . this faculty Charcot possessed to the highest degree.[99]

Whereas his three brothers chose the army, the sea, and the carriage shop, respectively, Jean-Martin was offered a choice: as he had shown his talents for both art and book learning, his father would sponsor his higher education, either as a painter or as a doctor.[100] At eighteen, Jean-Martin Charcot chose medicine. Yet he still retained yearnings for an artistic vocation, which deeply affected his relation to his chosen medical career. Charcot pressed his acute visual thinking into the service of his medical practice by advocating in his clinical methods and educational techniques the power of images above all other forms of communication and diagnosis. The fusion of art into medicine provided a means of personal integration while it revolutionized the practice of nineteenth-century psychopathology: "That he knew how to put the artist's temperament with which he was naturally gifted to the service of his medical studies is not the least of the reasons for his scientific success. . . . For Charcot, the artist went hand in hand with the physician."[101]

Charcot applied his emphasis on the visual at the Salpêtrière in his method of clinical education. Freud, who came to study under Charcot in 1885, was fascinated by this emphasis, by Charcot's attentiveness to observation.[102] Another of Charcot's students, the Frenchman Henri Meige, who described Charcot's pedagogical tactics in vivid detail, noted that Charcot's teaching relied on the capacity of images to penetrate the mind directly. Charcot conveyed to students mental pictures, transforming complex ideas into the linear clarity of an imagistic "schema." Meige identified Charcot as an "incomparably visual teacher," who used drawing and gesture to "penetrate the mind through the eyes." Restrained in "oration," Charcot would always describe a symptom by illustrating it, by drawing its "schema" with "colored chalks." "With a few strokes, a few hatchings," he would "objectify the idea," translating ideas into images. In anatomical discussions, Charcot provided "panoramic" descriptions, again drawing synoptical models on the board in vivid colors. "Teaching to the eyes," Meige claimed, was Charcot's special innovation. Under his spell, the Salpêtrière "glowed with an artistic efflorescence that cast a hitherto unknown luster onto clinical education." [103]

Charcot's own practice of thinking in images made possible the invention of a new visual language for diagnosis, which was his greatest contribution as a clinician. Until Charcot, the identification of nervous diseases rested solely on postmortem examinations, which located particular organic lesions or deterioration related to a specific nervous pathology. Charcot systematized an unprecedented method of diagnosing the diseases of living subjects. By acute observation, he correlated external signs and symptoms to an internal state of deformation and degeneration. Charcot's "clinical-anatomical method" celebrated the correspondences between external physical form and internal organic essence:

> The anatomy of the human body's exterior forms does not concern only artists. It is of primary use to doctors. . . . It is not on an inert corpse that one can chart the incessant movements that life, with its infinite variations of movements, impresses on all parts of the human body. It is hence on the living that the anatomy of forms should be studied. . . . Its procedure is the synthesis. Its means are the observation of nudes, its aim to find the multiple causes of the living form and to fix it into a description. . . . Exterior forms show, through their relations with interior ones, . . . what is hidden in the depths of the body through what is visible on the surface. [104]

Sigmund Freud watched Charcot at work and noted how the French clinician scrutinized a procession of patients, seizing an essential image of their inner disorder by penetrating observation. Freud called Charcot not a "thinker" but an "artist" and quoted Charcot telling him, "Je suis un visuel." Freud characterized Charcot as an "impressionist," registering visual material directly and able to distill an essential pattern immediately. [105]

Visual morphologies and design patterns formed the grammar of Charcot's language of clinical identification. Manifest physical curvatures, contours, contortions, and distended facial gestures provided the correlation between external appearance and internal disorder. The essential visual "trope" in Charcot's system of correspondences between outer physicality and inner pathology was the curve. Nervous diseases, Charcot believed, were caused by lesions or "trophisms" along the spinal cord, which found their physical equivalents in the irregularity, asymmetry, contortion, and curvature in the patient's comportment (Figs. 20, 21).

Charcot documented various outward signs of internal disorder not only during clinical lessons at the Salpêtrière blackboard with colored chalks but also in a series of works he conceived as clinical picture books. One of these was the remarkable project called the *Nouvelle Iconographie de la Salpêtrière: Clinique des maladies du sys-*

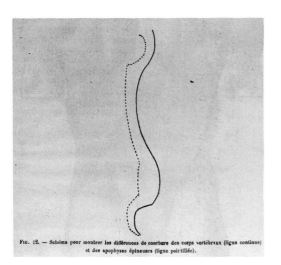

FIG. 12. — Schéma pour montrer les différences de courbure des corps vertébraux (ligne continue) et des apophyses épineuses (ligne pointillée).

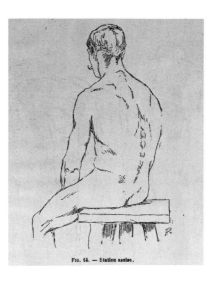

FIG. 14. — Station assise.

Fig. 20. Pathological curvature, by Paul Richer. From *Nouvelle Iconographie de la Salpêtrière* 4. Courtesy of the Bibliothèque Nationale, Paris.

Fig. 21. Pathological curve, by Paul Richer. From *Nouvelle Iconographie de la Salpêtrière* 4. Courtesy of the Bibliothèque Nationale, Paris.

FIG. 81. — Attitude de la paralysie agitante dans la station debout et pendant la marche. Type de flexion.

Fig. 22. Pathological movement, by Paul Richer. From *Nouvelle Iconographie de la Salpêtrière* 4. Courtesy of the Bibliothèque Nationale, Paris.

tème nerveux. Published every year after 1888, the *Iconographie* collected and presented case histories of patients at the Salpêtrière. The volumes were committed to the new "method of analysis that completes written observations with images."[106] Each case was described through a combination of text and image, identifying the physical features of the disease and illustrating the gestures and movements of patients under different therapeutic conditions (Fig. 22). Different media were used to give a detailed and comprehensive visual rendering of the subjects. Gestures, contortions, and physical curves were depicted in extensive photographs, engravings, and drawings. Charcot himself and his assistant Paul Richer, a former artist and sculptor, supplied the drawings and prints in the volumes.

Charcot and Richer did not invent a new scientific language of curve and distention, but their analyses derived formal coherence from their explicit reference to artistic monuments from the past. Indeed, only half of the material recorded in the volumes consisted of case histories from the Salpêtrière; the other half consisted of descriptions and reproductions of many images by the Great Masters, including Rubens, Dürer, Goya, Raphael, Michelangelo, and Leonardo. Deeply immersed in the artistic tradition, Charcot was familiar with painting, sculpture, and prints from the twelfth to the eighteenth century. He was especially attentive to the artistic renderings of abnormal states—satanic possessions and exorcisms, religious ecstasy, and healing of the sick. Henri Meige recounted how Charcot came to realize the striking affinity between the artists of the past and the clinicians of neuropathology:

> One day, Charcot studied a painting by Rubens, representing the *Healing of a Possessed Man*. A striking resemblance occurred to him: was not the grimacing, contorted, and convulsed man a realistic portrait of one of his patients at the Salpêtrière? And it seemed to him that Rubens had painted one of the three phases of the great hysterical attack. And this painting by Rubens was not the only one of its genre. Were there not many lessons to be drawn from the study of great artistic works of the past? What a fascinating collection of clinical documents could be made with these images![107]

After 1880 Charcot, in collaboration with Paul Richer, began an exhaustive inventory of artistic images of pathology. He examined statues by Leonardo and Michelangelo, architectural sculptures on French cathedrals and Italian chapels, paintings by Goya and Rubens, and innumerable prints and performed on them what he called retrospective diagnosis. He filled the pages of the *Nouvelle Iconographie de la Salpêtrière* with discussions of these artifacts and offered them as the documents of disease. Rather than expressions of artistic creativity, Charcot argued that the writhing contortions of Michelangelo's statues, the facial grimaces of gargoyles on Notre-Dame, and the tortuous asymmetries of Rubens's possessed man were objective records of clinical pathologies. Writing about the architectural sculpture on the Venetian church Santa Maria Formosa, for example, Charcot analyzed its clinical value (Figs. 23, 24):

> The deformed traits that give the mask such a grotesque and hideous air are not the result of a simple artistic fancy. . . . The artist of Santa Maria Formosa . . . reproduced the marks of a pathological deformation with great fidelity, the marks of a clearly defined nervous affliction of which we have at this time some interesting examples in the Salpêtrière. . . . We note . . . the very special manner of sticking out the tongue, the face being turned aside, as if convulsed. . . . This illustration of special symptoms makes the mascaron of Santa Maria

Fig. 23. Grotesque mask, Santa Maria Formosa, Venice, by Paul Richer. From *Nouvelle Iconographie de la Salpêtrière* 4. Courtesy of the Bibliothèque Nationale, Paris.

HÉMISPASME GLOSSO-LABIÉ HYSTÉRIQUE

Fig. 24. Hysterical glosso-labial hemispasm, by Paul Richer. From *Nouvelle Iconographie de la Salpêtrière* 4. Courtesy of the Bibliothèque Nationale, Paris.

Formosa a naturalistic work of the first degree. . . . It gives us an image of
nervous deformation, reproduced by the artist with rare acuity.[108]

In practicing this extraordinary retrospective diagnosis on the art of the past, Charcot
embraced artists as the predecessors of clinicians in the nineteenth century. Long before scientists discovered a language to articulate the curvilinear irregularities sig-
nifying disease, artists described pathology with clinical accuracy:

> Is it not interesting to see art preceding science, to show how Albrecht Dürer,
> copying a leper, not only gave an exact image of leprosy but formulated in an
> absolutely accurate manner in 1515 the morphological characteristics of a mus-
> cular alteration that a scientist has to describe routinely more than three cen-
> turies later? . . . From the hand's deformation to the limited movement of the
> patient's limb, . . . everything conforms perfectly to the most precise scientific
> findings. . . . We know that the muscular atrophy that afflicts certain lepers is
> exactly similar, at least in its exterior manifestations, to the ones constituting
> the exclusive sign of another affliction of solely nervous origin, an affliction by
> the name of progressive muscular atrophy discovered by an eminent clinician
> of our era, Duchenne.[109]

The affirmation of a continuum between artistic tradition and medical invention
did not end with the *Nouvelle Iconographie de la Salpêtrière.* Charcot and Richer published two separate volumes devoted to the "documents" of pathology by artists
in the past and the continuation of their work by the medical practitioners at the
Salpêtrière. The first of these, *Les Démoniaques dans l'art,* appeared in 1887. In it
Charcot assembled and examined images of supernatural possession and satanic convulsions, beginning in fifth-century Ravenna and ending with mesmeric trances. He
explained how these depictions accurately rendered what medical clinicians later defined as the signs of nervous degeneration and the phases of attacks of hysteria. Indeed the last part of the book was devoted to Charcot's own discovery—hysteria,
"the great convulsions of today."[110] Charcot's account, replete with extensive illustrations, unfolded the various phases of the hysterical attack through the visible contortions of the patient, his "plastic poses."[111] Charcot demonstrated the direct visual
resemblance between the physical forms and gestures of hysterical patients—kneeling, screaming, and twisting their bodies into a "rainbow" shape, an *"arc-en-ciel"*—
and the repertoire of images of "possessed" religious states from the annals of the art
historical past (Figs. 25, 26). The long train of artistic expression culminated in the
visual clinicians at the Salpêtrière.

As Jan Goldstein has demonstrated, Charcot's presentation of the iconography of
religious ecstasy as documents of psychopathology was charged with the politics of
anticlericalism.[112] Yet Charcot's engagement with images was not restricted to a repertoire of religious art and transcended a conscious political function. His visual
medicine was driven by a larger emotional project of equivalence: to demonstrate
the identity between artistic creations and his own clinical enterprise. Charcot satu-

Fig. 25. Religious Ecstatic State: Saint Catherine of Sienna, by Paul Richer. From *Les Démoniaques dans l' art,* by J.-M. Charcot and Paul Richer.

Fig. 26. Hysterical Ecstasy: Salpêtrière Patient, by Paul Richer. From *Les Démoniaques dans l' art,* by J.-M. Charcot and Paul Richer.

rated the Salpêtrière with art of all types. He organized a museum and a photographic laboratory at the hospital, and he created a sculpture studio for Paul Richer. Charcot's office, a sterile cabinet before his arrival, was enlivened by what Meige describes as a "startling profusion" of images, tacked to the walls.[113]

As Charcot packed the Salpêtrière with art, he was driven to deny that it related to those qualities with which it was so readily associated in the late nineteenth century: fantasy and the release of figurative boundaries. In the preface to *Les Difformes et les malades dans l'art* (1889), Charcot explained that the value of visual art derived from its "scrupulous recording of nature."[114] He affirmed that artists were the natural allies of the scientist when they devoted themselves to a dispassionate realism; in this way they provided the clinician an indispensable tool for systematizing the visible signs of psychopathologies. He went on to discuss how science gave the artist something in its turn, offering an important and necessary check on his imagination, securing the limits of his fantasy. Charcot cited Leonardo da Vinci as an authority for this view: "Science distinguishes what is impossible from what is possible. Left to itself, imagination will yield to implausible dreams; science contains it by teaching us what cannot be."[115] Charcot concluded that "art has nothing to fear from that control which, when it is imposed by the artist himself on his own works, will become a new force."[116]

Charcot's indictment of artistic fantasy recurred in other settings. His students noted his "horror of inexactitude" and his detestation of "movement that displaced the line."[117] He was predisposed against what he called the vague and imprecise qualities of Impressionism and Symbolism.[118] Indeed, in his medical demonstrations Charcot compared the unchecked imaginations of his hysterics to the visual abstractions of the proponents of "art for art's sake," the term usually associated with Symbolism. Artists unanchored in figurative reality were as deluded and deceitful as his patients, who projected their own illusory alternative world:

> There is a point to bring to your attention which . . . has to do with simulation; not the sort of imitation of one disease by another . . . but rather intentional malingering, in which the patient voluntarily exaggerates real symptoms or even creates in every detail an imaginary symptomatology. Indeed, everyone is aware that the human [*sic*] need to tell lies, whether for no reason at all other than the practice of a sort of cult like art for art's sake or in order to create an impression, . . . is a common event, and this is particularly true in hysteria.[119]

Charcot's preoccupation with uniting visual and medical naturalism belied a deep attraction to the forbidden world of fantasy and imagination. His invocation of Leonardo as the apotheosis of artistic science resonated with this tension; for da Vinci was both the rigorous anatomist and the excavator of the full torrent of his own inner visions.[120] Charcot emphasized that he relied on images as purely illustrative documents, as scrupulous confirmations of his own pathologic diagnoses. Yet Charcot's definition of art as flat *reportage* was accompanied by his interest in art as complex interior *voyage;* in secret, separate regions of his identity and in his own practice of the arts we can glimpse his uneasy movement from Realism to Symbolism and back again.

Students and colleagues of Charcot's noted that an intense "taste for the fantastic"[121] and a surrender to flights from reality operated beneath the impassive mask of the "Napoléon of the neuroses."[122] Both Léon Daudet and Pierre Marie identified Charcot's inclination for private absorption. Marie noted that Charcot locked himself away for three weeks as he prepared a clinical article, relinquishing all daily routine and social contact for the world of his ideas.[123] Daudet observed Charcot, who was unaware of his presence, in a state of fixity and contemplation in his library and described the doctor as riveted, immobile, staring rigidly ahead, embodying all the features of a hypnotic trance that proceeded undisturbed for almost an hour.[124] Henri Meige offered another instance of Charcot's intense capacity for withdrawal. During a period when he was completing research on aphasia, Charcot worked successively through the nights. One night, completely absorbed by the figures he was drawing to illustrate various forms of aphasia, he mechanically wrapped some of his hair around his forefinger, turning it in tighter and tighter circles. Later, when he realized what he was doing, Charcot had to cut off the hair to release his finger.[125] This automatic behavior, carried on during a state of artistic concentration, contained all the features of the involuntary actions carried out during the hypnotic state, what Charcot identified in his patients as "cerebral automatism."

If Charcot openly rejected nineteenth-century artistic fantasy, he experimented himself with its forms. As a medical student in the 1850s, Charcot drew prototypes of artistic marginality, the dandy and the bohemian.[126] He also tried to become one of them. After smoking hashish in 1853, Charcot executed a drawing marked by the very features he would later assign to hysterical crises: zigzag contorted forms and jumbled hallucinations (Fig. 27). Henri Meige described the experience and the drawing:

Fig. 27. Hallucinatory drawing, by J.-M. Charcot. Bibliothèque Charcot, Paris.

One evening . . . Charcot decided to try himself the effects of smoking hashish and to record his impressions. As soon as he was under the influence of the narcotic, a tumult of phantasmagoric visions flashed across his mind. He began to write in characters that became more and more strange and more difficult to decipher: "What a disorder of ideas, and yet what a pleasant carousel. . . . Fantastic unbridled impulses which, however, are not entirely free from voluntary control. . . . Everything I touch has an electric quality . . . and yet . . . yet." Then the words became illegible, the script of the letters became measurably longer, became distorted into zigzags, spirals, interlacing patterns, and transformed themselves into the forms of leaves, floral petals, and architectural motifs . . . and no more writing. The entire page is covered with drawings: prodigious dragons, grimacing monsters, incoherent personages who were superimposed on each other, and who were intertwined and twisted in a fabulous whirlpool, bringing to mind the apocalyptic conceptions of Van Bosch and Jacques Callot.[127]

As the despotic, positivist psychopathologist, Charcot exercised on himself the imperative he later invoked from Leonardo: to contain and limit the surrender to unrealizable dreams. He displaced to hysterics and abstract artists the experience of externalizing a fluid, mobile, and dynamic interior vision. In later research on visual fields, Charcot returned to the zigzag forms of his early drawing, this time attributing them to the condition of a migraine pressure; when the pressure subsided, he noted, the zigzag was replaced by a regularized grid: "Tout revient à l'ordre."[128] Pressing art into the service of his medicine, Charcot may have discovered his own psychological integration by inventing the visual identification of pathology in others. In so doing, he unwittingly strengthened Bernheim's redefinition of reason in the fin de siècle.

The tension between reason and fantasy, order and disorder that shaped Charcot's artistic-medical persona was expressed in his personal practice of interior design. Charcot collaborated with his family to create a unified personal environment where historical materials were animated by private memories and "exteriorized dreams."[129]

The Charcot family's first residence was in a wing of the Hôtel de Chimay on the quai Malaquais, adjacent to the Ecole des Beaux-Arts. The other wing was inhabited by the family of the writer Edouard Pailleron, who introduced Charcot to many other artists. In 1884 Charcot, at the height of his medical preeminence, moved the family to a mansion on the boulevard Saint-Germain. The splendid residence and gardens had originally been built as a rococo palace, the Hôtel de Varengeville.[130] Charcot transformed the interior into a showcase for his art collection and his own artistic designs. There, at his weekly evening salons, which became as well known as the doctor's weekly hysteria demonstrations at the Salpêtrière,[131] sculptors, painters, writers, and art connoisseurs mingled with politicians and medical colleagues.

An avid traveler, Charcot sketched incessantly throughout his frequent trips to Italy, Holland, and England, trying out models for his own interior decor by copying the "decorative relics of the past" in European museums.[132] Aided by his marriage to an extremely wealthy widow, the carriage maker's son supplied himself with rich, fine woods and precious stones, which he used for the armoires of his own creation. When Sigmund Freud was invited to Charcot's home, he was dazzled by the "magic castle in which he lives." He noticed "cases containing Indian and Chinese antiques," "walls covered with Gobelins and pictures," and "the walls themselves painted terra cotta."[133] Freud did not note that the painted walls and the wood cases were Charcot's own work or that Charcot had carefully coordinated the space and contents:

> Charcot participated directly in ornamenting the interiors. Certain ceramic panels in the hearth . . . were designed by his own hand. . . . His choices of those art works with which he surrounded himself, his care to direct the ornamentation of his interior space personally, the active part he took in this decoration make Charcot appear not only like an informed connoisseur but like a fervent devotee of beauty's purest manifestations. One has . . . praised the arrangement of his apartment on the boulevard Saint-Germain. . . . No frame could have better harmonized with Charcot's personality. This frame was also his masterpiece. Vast rooms, . . . furniture of dark luxury, of faded golds, of faultless designs, paintings, sculptures: all were set up to form the most perfect harmony of an ensemble and to be the most satisfactory to the eyes. The walls covered with tapestry . . . the wooden panels' alternating columns with elegantly interlaced leaves, . . . arabesques of ironwork highlighted with gold. . . . In this interior, a total synthesis, Charcot liked to rest.[134]

Charcot did not design and coordinate the ensemble of his interiors single-handedly. Indeed, he was the *chef* of an artisanal "atelier," whose members were all female and familial—his wife and two daughters. As in any other atelier *de haut luxe,* the production of any one object necessitated an extensive division of labor. Together the family workshop made furniture designed by Charcot, hammered leather bindings for books, embellished lamps, sculpted bas-reliefs, and carved terra-cotta figures (Figs. 28, 29):

> Charcot found in his family entourage affectionate and skilled helpers who knew how to fashion the beautiful things to which he was accustomed. . . . Under his inspiration, everyone fulfilled her task and did her part for the decorative project. . . . Charcot provided the idea, the initial design—its execution would follow. Once the work had started, he would supervise its progress, making a comment and correcting an error here and there and would be happy only if the smallest details conformed to his aesthetic desires. Thus he was the master of a studio of the decorative arts, instituted through his care in his house, with his family as practitioners and students. All raw material was used: earth, metal, glass, wood, leather, and tissue. From them would come sculptures of round shapes or bas-reliefs, chiseled or compressed ornaments, gilded

Fig. 28. Faience and painted lamp, by Madame Charcot. From *Revue des arts décoratifs,* 1900.

or painted table settings, stained-glass windows, enameled works, furniture with sculptures, engraved, and colored panels . . . small coffers, tables, and a flood of statuettes.[135]

The component parts of the Charcot home, objects with clear historical reference, were unified by personal expression and the themes of personal memory and family intimacy. Meige noted that the furniture and decorations Charcot re-created from

Fig. 29. Mantle and fireplace, by J.-M. Charcot, with Madame Charcot. From *Revue des arts décoratifs,* 1900.

his sketches of historical styles were marked by an infusion of his own "artistic fantasies" into both the drawing and design processes. In interior decor he could "exteriorize his dreams."[136] Not historical accuracy but subjective transformation characterized Charcot's replication of fifteenth- and sixteenth-century furniture and objets d'art. In re-creating objects, Charcot stamped them with personal memory, suggesting and evoking the places he and his family had visited on their many travels.[137] The Charcot interior ensemble thus became an envelope of *personnalité:*

> No frame could have harmonized better with Charcot's personality. . . . How many platters, how many plates were transformed by his hand into little commemorative paintings! . . . They are composed of unconsciously evoked memories that . . . would materialize and take shape.[138]

The interjection of personal memory and fantasy into the interior was complemented by a second level of personal feelings: family insulation. A second commentator on Charcot's art and design joined Henri Meige in emphasizing the unity of the doctor's interior ensemble in the theme of "familial intimacy." Surrounded by their own creations, the family bonds were encrusted in the very walls and material objects of daily use. The interior was charged with powerfully personal meanings. "This artistic project," "this ensemble," is "a *chez soi* of the dream wherein everything is precious, where every object calls out. . . . This splendid residence . . . is charged with such beautiful artistic dreams."[139]

The personal meanings and evocative memories animating Charcot's interiors may not have been confined to pleasant remembrances of travels and family occasions. Some of the objects Charcot created may have stimulated darker fantasies. What is one to make of Albrecht Dürer's *Dance of Fools,* whose images of madness and the macabre Charcot reconstituted as a set of porcelain slabs attached to the facade of his house?[140] Charcot probably selected this set consciously as an example of a retrospective diagnosis, an artistic anticipation of his own discovery of the forms of hysteria. But the writhing dance may have functioned more ambiguously as an announcement of the dark insulated chambers where "he liked to rest." Dürer's contorted shapes prefigured the visual themes of Charcot's work on the interior, the wood columns Meige described as having "interlaced leaves" and "arabesques of ironwork."[141] All of these elements of spatial design suggested a hidden "total synthesis" vitalizing the historicist frame. Together they composed an evocative image of irregularity, a dynamic cue to the memory of the phantasmagoric "interlacing leaves" and "zigzags" unleashed by the younger Charcot's artistic intoxication. These traces of a hallucinatory organic interior as well may have been more than a reinvoked memory of youthful abandon: Edmond de Goncourt stated that the mature Doctor Charcot relied on a powerful narcotic potion of bromide, morphine, and codeine to "procure" such "exhilarating dreams on a daily basis."[142]

*

The discovery that the interior of the human organism was a sensitive nervous mechanism, prone to suggestion, visual thinking, and imagistic projection in dreams—these elements of a new psychological knowledge would alter the meaning of interior decoration in the fin de siècle. This specifically French version of psychological interiority provided the intellectual vehicle for the transformation of the domestic interior from a place to display a historical anchorage to one that expressed personal feeling. Aware of the first level of psychological exploration from the Salpêtrière—nervous vibration—the brothers de Goncourt had realized in the 1860s a personally designed environment that lay poised between historical reference and subjectivity: they fused a *Gesamtkunstwerk* of rococo nature and literary nerves. Jean-Martin Charcot, the clinician who had penetrated that inner world of the nerves, offered a second example of the interior ensemble between history and the psyche. Although he consciously rejected the antirational implications of his own discoveries, Charcot's practice of interior design translated into spatial form the principles of subjective self-projection and imagistic suggestibility. The artist, never purged from the interior of Doctor Charcot, unwittingly brought fantasy, memory, and dreams into the concretion of private space.

PART THREE

Rococo Revival and Craft Modernism: Third Republic Art Nouveau

CHAPTER SIX

The Central Union
of the Decorative Arts

DURING THE LAST two decades of the nineteenth century an interlocking elite, drawn from the varying arenas of politics and official culture, joined together in a single organization to revitalize the arts and crafts: the Central Union of the Decorative Arts. This chapter analyzes the internal history and development of this union. The commingling of political and cultural officials with collectors, art historians, and luxury craftsmen in the Central Union of the Decorative Arts, with their common program of institutional craft elevation in the 1890s, represented only the final phase of the union's evolution. The internal development of the Central Union reveals two significant features: first, a trajectory from a private association to a public consortium and, second, the shift in its focus from the producer and the commercial potential of the *industrial arts* to the collector and the cultivated refinement of the *decorative arts*.

The Central Union of the Decorative Arts was founded in 1864 as the Central Union of Fine Arts Applied to Industry.[1] After the British sponsorship of the industrial arts was revealed at the 1851 World Exhibition, a group of French artists and manufacturers united in a producers' association, designed to keep pace with British rivalry and ensure the French position in the world export market. This Society for the Progress of Industrial Arts was composed of commercial artisans, such as the architect–decorator E. Guichard; Philippe Mourey, a metalworker specializing in the application of silver and gold finishings; Clerget, an industrial designer and ornament engraver; and Klagmann, an ornamental sculptor.[2] In 1852 Clerget and Klagmann each sent treatises to Napoléon III advocating the creation of an industrial arts museum, a central school of the industrial arts, and a yearly Salon for the display of commercial and industrial designs.[3] The first separate gallery for the designs and products of the industrial arts was established at the 1855 Paris Exhibition. The structure built to house this display, the Palace of Industry, embodied a lasting record of Second Empire attention to the industrial arts. The participants in the 1855 industrial gallery aspired to more permanent, yearly, exhibitions of their labor, and in 1861 they discovered an enthusiastic state sponsor, Baron Taylor. In 1861 and 1863, displays of industrial arts were mounted for public view at the Palace of Industry.[4] By 1864, the producers active in the exhibits had established a new organization, legally recognized under the name Central Union of Fine Arts Applied to Industry. One hundred and thirty-six founding members agreed to pay thirty-six francs per year and to rent the second floor of a house in the place Royale as the union headquarters.[5] The location in the place Royale (now the place des Vosges) situated the organization squarely in the center of the artisanal quarter of the Marais. Guichard was elected president, and the eleven-member steering committee of the union included manufacturers of lace, wallpaper, rugs, and pianos as well as a tapestry designer, silversmith, and upholsterer.[6]

The ideology of the union during the 1860s was carried in its title: Fine Arts Applied to Industry. "The unity of the arts" was its major goal, conceived as the commercializing and democratizing process of integrating "beauty and utility." The founding members accepted the exigencies of a new consumer structure and wanted both to industrialize art and to make industry more artistic:

> Our goal is to honor, encourage, and stimulate in industrial works everything that contains art . . . to propagate in France . . . the realization of beauty in utility; to aid men in the elite in their efforts to raise the standards of work, from apprenticeship to mastery; to encourage the emulation of those artists whose works, while vulgarizing the sense of beauty, also maintain the just preeminence attributed to our industrial arts by the world.[7]

At its inception, the Central Union considered itself a private association, "relying on private initiative" and the distant but benevolent sanction of the government.[8] It set out several strategies to revitalize the industrial arts and to wed beauty to utility. First, soon after its organization, the Central Union accepted donations for a museum of industrial art, to be divided into retrospective and modern sections. Second, it inaugurated a working library at its headquarters. The library, with designs of both "historical and contemporary" character, was conceived as a center for artisans of the *quartier,* an archival storehouse to facilitate production. Third, the new Central Union sponsored a series of free public lectures devoted to historical and technical aspects of different applied arts. Finally, it initiated design competitions and exhibitions, which were nationally publicized. Parisian and provincial artisans were invited to submit projects for various adaptations of art to industry.[9]

By 1889, the Central Union of Fine Arts Applied to Industry had undergone a profound transformation, which unfolded in two phases. The organization established in the 1860s as a producers' association aiming to industrialize art for a broad public had become the institutional base for a coalition of government ministers, aristocratic collectors, museum curators, and a small circle of producers in the luxury sector. The union had been assigned a new name that eliminated the term *industry* and inflated the domain of art: the Central Union of the Decorative Arts. Underlying this titular alteration and the change in social composition were profound transformations in ideology, goals, and programs. By 1889 the aims of the 1860s were reversed: rather than to "vulgarize the sense of beauty" and democratize art, the Central Union sought to purify the sentiment of beauty and aristocratize the crafts. Whereas earlier artists were called upon to reject the lofty, separate realm of beauty and join the industrial creators of "useful arts," in the 1890s the artisan was invited to "elevate himself to the rank of artist" by the power of his creative imagination.[10]

The Central Union during the 1870s: Philippe de Chennevières and the Rococo as "Patrimony"

The Paris Commune of 1870–1871 initiated the internal transformation of the Central Union. The civil war in Paris had left the Hôtel de Ville and the Tuileries Palace in ruins, and a fire had destroyed parts of the château at Saint-Cloud, the favorite suburban retreat of Napoléon III. In each of these monuments, furniture, sculptures, paintings, ceramics, and woodworks of the Old Regime were damaged or destroyed.

Alarmed by this desecration of cultural artifacts, a group of Parisian collectors, both aristocrats and bourgeois, joined the Central Union to promote the reappraisal and reconsolidation of the applied arts of the French aristocratic past. Until the 1870s these collectors, called *amateurs,* had, like Edmond de Goncourt, maintained the splendors of the applied arts in their homes, in jealously guarded isolation. After the Commune, they allied with the Central Union to present the first public exhibitions of the drawings, engravings, tapestries, ceramics, and woodworks of the seventeenth and eighteenth centuries. Their purpose was to disprove the Davidian idea of a hierarchy of the three beaux-arts by documenting the illustrious royal and aristocratic history of the craft arts. They appealed to the public to accept these artifacts as expressions of "French genius" and called attention to the exile of many parts of this "patrimony" to foreign collections, such as the rococo decorative arts in the Wallace Collection and at Baron Alfred de Rothschild's Waddington Manor.[11]

The collector-*amateur* had a special significance in the Central Union after 1870. He was the antithesis of the nouveau-riche collector of the Second Empire, who amassed precious stuffs as the signs of financial success. The *amateur* in the Central Union was the counterpart of the Goncourts—specialists in a particular period or medium, connoisseurs and scholars of the objects in their collections, recognized for their superior sensitivity and taste as much as for their often illustrious social positions. Money, the marquis Philippe de Chennevières explained, was only the prerequisite for a collector, but "taste and erudition" rendered him a true *amateur,* worthy of his renowned colleagues in the Old Regime from Mazarin to the comte de Caylus.[12] The *amateur* was not a passive consumer but an active re-creator of the past, and his efforts at reassemblage were like the creative work of an architect or poet. This definition of the *amateur* was expressed by an admirer of Gustave Dreyfus, a founding member of the Central Union and a specialist collector of medals, coins, and terra-cotta sculptures: "One built a collection as one built a monument. Day after day, . . . one added to the ensemble, . . . a testament to taste, erudition, and sensibility. . . . The *amateur* needs money in order to buy, but it is his intuition, his exquisite sensibility, and his sophisticated competence that enable him to discover rare objects for sale." [13]

The first official infusion of *amateurs* into the Central Union came in 1874, when the steering committee was reconstituted "on new bases." [14] President Guichard, the architect-decorator, was replaced by Edouard André, a wealthy collector who would later donate his rococo ensembles to the state as the Musée Jacquemart-André. Henri Bouilhet, one of the directors of Christofle, the luxury silversmith manufacture; Paul Christofle himself; and the publisher-collector Alfred Firmin-Didot all joined the administrative council. [15] In the 1870s the Central Union extended its educational efforts of the 1860s. The library continued to grow through donations and acquisitions, and exhibitions were mounted in the Palace of Industry: in 1874 a display on the "history of costume," including rare "ancient robes," and in 1876 an exhibit on "the history of tapestry." In 1880 the Central Union initiated exhibitions organized according to the raw material used by the "great luxury industries." [16] Called Technological Exhibitions of the Industrial Arts, these exhibits were inaugurated with a display of the "arts of metal." Metal arts were subdivided and displayed in thirteen categories, including "jewelry, precious stones, gold and silver work, decorative clocks and watchmaking, artistic bronzes, luxury arms, and artistic locksmithery"— the artifacts of aristocratic *arts somptuaires*. Master craftsmen produced these objects, with their diminutive and intricate shapes. [17]

If the new steering committee of the Central Union reflected the arrival of the *amateur,* the elite, erudite collector assumed the dominant role in organizing a permanent museum for the applied arts. In 1874, the magazine *L'Art* opened a subscription to create a "French South Kensington Museum." [18] This project was conceived as different from both the government-sponsored industrial arts center in England and the producers' archive envisioned in the 1860s as a French museum of the industrial arts. As a result of it aristocrats and wealthy *amateurs* in 1877 formed an association, the Society for a Decorative Arts Museum. [19] The society, established in cooperation with the Central Union of Fine Arts Applied to Industry, took over the union's attempts to find the capital and space necessary to convert its collections into a museum. [20] Capital and distinction: with both of these the new society was well endowed. Its honorary president was the duc d'Audiffert-Pasquier, president of the Senate; its president was the marquis Philippe de Chennevières, director of the beaux-arts. The steering committee of the Society for a Decorative Arts Museum was composed of the duc de Chaulnes, a renowned scholar and *amateur;* the collector vicomte de Ganay; and Alfred de Champeaux, de Chennevières's deputy. [21]

Between 1878 and 1882, the society established a journal—the *Revue des arts décoratifs,* jointly sponsored by the Central Union of Fine Arts Applied to Industry—and mounted exhibitions, primarily of artifacts in the collections of its illustrious members. The most important of these was the Exhibition of Old Master Drawings of Decoration and Ornament. Organized by the two Central Union members, Gustave

Dreyfus and Charles Ephrussi, this exhibition displayed the decorative designs of artists under royal and aristocratic patronage. The engravings, watercolors, and etchings of furniture designs, picture frames, and coats of arms came primarily from the collections of the marquis de Chennevières, the duc d'Aumale, and Edmond de Goncourt. Mounted initially under Central Union sponsorship at the Ecole des Beaux-Arts in 1879, the show traveled to the Palace of Industry in 1880 and ended as one of the first major shows devoted to drawing and the decorative arts at the Louvre in 1882.[22]

Despite Edmond de Goncourt's stated aversion to the institution of the museum, he cooperated with the supporters of the Decorative Arts Museum. The Exhibition of Old Master Drawings of Decoration and Ornament marked the first loan of the extensive eighteenth-century print collection from the Goncourts' living room to a public gallery. The marquis de Chennevières, a friend of Edmond's, perceived in the opening of the 1879 exhibit the inauguration of "a great movement of national renovation," which restored the eighteenth century to its rightful place.[23] De Chennevières welcomed the recovery of all the eighteenth-century arts, which "manifest the genius of our country." The exhibit made clear that the "poetry of Watteau was as great as the works of the great poets, political writers, and moralists of his time. . . . Never before had anyone seen such a magnificent array of Watteau, Gillot, Pater, Lancret, Boucher, Vanloo, Oudry, La Tour, Moreau le Jeune, the Saint-Aubins, and the great illustrators and decorators of the period of the *fêtes galantes*." The exhibit ended with a drawing by Jacques-Louis David, who, according to de Chennevières, had "strangled the adored epoch in his terrible revolutionary hands."[24]

The marquis Philippe de Chennevières's leadership of the Society for a Decorative Arts Museum marked the first phase of interlock between the institutions sponsoring the rehabilitation of the applied arts and the official centers of cultural administration. De Chennevières was a pivotal link between the Central Union and the beaux-arts ministry. To each he carried his personal commitment to the cultural riches of the Old Regime, where his lifelong ideal, "the unity of the arts," had found its most glorious realization.[25]

De Chennevières's service in a number of positions in the Second Empire beaux-arts administration had brought him into contact with painters, art critics, and a circle of collectors and writers that included the brothers de Goncourt and the princesse Mathilde.[26] He shared with them "the love of the fine and elegant art of the eighteenth century."[27] During the late 1850s, de Chennevières began, under the influence of the Goncourts, to collect eighteenth-century prints, drawings, and *paperasseries,* "printed ephemera," which he added to his already extensive collection of rare books and the creations of little-known Norman painters and craftsmen. Among the items in de Chennevières's holdings were the painted ivory shoe buckles of Louis XV and a metal lock fashioned by Louis XVI, the king who liked to "dip his hands into metal molds" during his leisure hours.[28] De Chennevières transformed his native home in Normandy into a living museum. He published an elaborate description of the rooms in his house and their art historical contents from the Old Regime in a series of articles in *L'Artiste* modeled explicitly on the inventory method in the Goncourts' *Maison d'un artiste*.[29]

As director of the beaux-arts from 1873 to 1880, the marquis de Chennevières used the administrative bureaucracy to establish a national network for the reconstitution of the decorative arts. Together with the minister of public instruction, de Chennevières devised a plan in 1874 for a comprehensive inventory, classification, and attribution of the cultural riches of France. Entitled *Inventaire générale des richesses d'art de la France,* the work was conceived to describe the external architectural forms and the internal decorative ensembles of all edifices in the national domain, both civil and religious. The project would eventually yield a written record enumerating all the material art forms, their artistic creators, original patrons, provenance, and present condition and location. The organizing committee of the *Inventaire* included Edmond de Goncourt and members of the curatorial and administrative staffs at the Louvre and the beaux-arts, such as Paul Mantz and Jules Guiffrey. The first two volumes of the *Inventaire* were published in 1876 and 1878.[30] The tome devoted to secular buildings began with detailed inventories of two monuments of the seventeenth and eighteenth centuries—Versailles and the Hôtel de Rohan-Soubise. The massive entry on Versailles presented all the stages of the palace's construction and transformations, with elaborate accounts of the insertion of intimate rococo "small apartments" by Louis XV, including the measurements, dates of origin, and craftsmen of everything from Louis's private gallery of pictures of his five daughters to the minutiae of serpentine stucco cornices on the gilded, woodworked ceilings.[31] The subsequent volumes of the *Inventaire,* which appeared at intervals from 1879 until 1914, were prepared by regional *amateurs* and antiquarians. De Chennevières appealed to local scholars to join the task of national cultural classification and envisioned a national "fraternity" devoted to the patrimony.[32] The *Inventaire* was the first comprehensive compendium that applied the tools of erudite art history and connoisseurship to all the arts. De Chennevières considered this work of classification an act of national rehabilitation as important as military and educational reform in the post-Commune period. In the introduction to the first volumes, he explained that taking stock of national greatness in all the arts would regenerate those "virile forces" that had languished on the battlefields against the Prussians.[33] And the massive inventory would also provide cultural insurance against internal social crisis: future acts of artistic destruction would be countered by intricate written records of description and location.

The marquis de Chennevières continued his project of the erudite reconstitution of all the arts as director of the Society for a Decorative Arts Museum. In the society and its partner, the Central Union of Fine Arts Applied to Industry, he found what he called "a confraternity of dedicated collectors,"[34] who joined him in bringing to public view the artifacts of artisanal grace from pre-Revolutionary France. In his speeches, writings, and notes to exhibitions, de Chennevières clarified two assumptions that were to underly the efforts of the union during the 1870s and which had a lasting impact on its subsequent development: the unity of art and craft as an aristocratic legacy and the role of the nineteenth-century *amateur* as the inheritor of that legacy.

De Chennevières brought to the society and the Central Union his talents not only as a collector but as a "connoisseur of delicate tastes" and "erudite historian."[35] He spent years of researching and reconstructing the world of art patronage and practice during the seventeenth and eighteenth centuries. In works like the long scholarly foreword to the first monograph on the eighteenth-century draftsman Aignan-Thomas Désfriches (1715–1800),[36] de Chennevières brought to light an important tradition, the aristocratic practice of the art of drawing. Désfriches was not only a painter and designer but an *amateur* and collector. His home at Orléans was a center for cultivated nobility, men and women, who were themselves members of amateur drawing societies, the first "free drawing schools."[37] De Chennevières emphasized that this noble "confraternity of sketchers" common in the eighteenth century celebrated the sense of sight, "things seen."[38] For them, the media of drawing and printmaking, later devalued, were equal in value to "excellent paintings"; even a "rough sketch" could be rendered with a distinctive "fantasy," "fluid poetry," and "vaporous suppleness."[39]

The 1879–1882 Exhibition of Old Master Drawings of Decoration and Ornament organized by the Society for a Decorative Arts Museum gave de Chennevières a chance not only to display his own print collection but to "initiate" the public into the noble traditions of unity among the arts.[40] He hoped that the public seeing the exhibit would be forced to reevaluate their assumptions about aristocratic *dérogation*. Invoking the metaphor of illumination, he glorified the rediscovery of the French traditions of the integration of art and craft, artist and artisan:

> For the first time we have brought to light . . . drawings of ornaments, which have never been the object of scholarly study. . . . Only fools and pedants construe these as products of inferior creativity; they are the works of great painters, great sculptors, and great architects, who considered them the elegant ornaments for royal palaces and the luxurious exteriors of aristocratic residences. . . . Our exhibit helps us prove that the nation of Boules and Gouthières knew how to value the ingenious and skillful combination of forms, lines, and figures in vases, furniture, and rugs as equal to the severe compositions of painted historical subjects. . . . The former group are exquisite monuments in their own right; they charm the eyes, lift the spirit, and formed the pride and riches of families who knew how to preserve them with respect.[41]

Like his friend Edmond de Goncourt, de Chennevières did not propose an archaistic revival of aristocratic culture. Rather, he affirmed that the delicacies of rococo ornamentalism could bring about a new understanding of the riches of the "French School"—"the genius of our country."[42] He hoped that artisans would absorb the lessons of craft integrity and that the exhibitions of decoration and design would thus catalyze improvements in their work: "The Decorative Arts Museum has as its goal to develop the taste of artists and artisans, who carry with them the traditions of our national applied arts."[43] Such improvement was a matter of elevating and "perfecting" taste.[44] Its agents were the *amateurs,* who replaced the old legal aristocracy as the carriers of culture and cultivation. These *amateurs,* including de Chennevières himself, joined the descendants of noble families with bourgeois men of cultivation and expanded sensibilities. In his introduction to the catalogue of the 1880 exhibit, de Chennevières gave special mention to this group of "initiates" who lent their collections for public view—the duc d'Aumale, the baron Pichon, the marquis de Valori, the comte de la Baudrière, and the Goncourts, Alexander Dumas, Jean Dolent, and Beurdeley.[45]

De Chennevières's conception of the *amateur* wavered between an attribution of public responsibility and an affirmation of private cultivation. The *amateur* was to "educate taste," a work of "truth and sincerity" that would raise the level of artistic facility among artisans.[46] The Decorative Arts Museum and its patrons would bring about a multiple transformation—among "those who create, those who direct, commission, and acquire."[47] In this way the *amateur* was invested with a role of public leadership that had hitherto been exercised by a noble elite in politics. Indeed, de Chennevières wrote that he considered his task of art administration and exhibition as the cultural analogue to the judicial practice of his ancestors in the local *parlements.* Before visiting an art dealer or an auction house, de Chennevières marshaled his powers of analysis and discretion just as his forebears had done before hearing a legal argument—he would eat and drink nothing and would carry out the transaction in the morning, the time the courts had met during the Old Regime.[48]

If de Chennevières's reverence for the aristocracy shaped his conception of the elite *amateurs'* responsibility to elevate national taste, his immersion in the mid-nineteenth-century art world fostered a second, alternative, tendency—an appreciation of the private, isolated, and inaccessible pleasures of collecting and erudition. His friendship with the Goncourts, Théophile Gautier, and Baudelaire nourished his aestheticism and withdrawal and led him to glorify the personally designed environment.[49] De Chennevières understood the relation between overwrought sensibilities and the creation of a self-reflexive individual space, and he recognized in the Goncourts the coupling of the hyperaesthetic needs of neurasthenics, relentless collecting, and interior design.[50] Of his own insatiable acquisitiveness he said that he was driven by a virtual "mania for prints,"[51] a compulsion shared by all *amateurs.* Those driven by this mania reveled in the smallest detail related to prints, communicable only to a restricted circle of specialists equally impassioned and informed. And these same prints provoked hours of reverie and self-absorption, sending the hermetic imagination on inward flights to what de Chennevières called the world of "dreams, visions, and hallucinations."[52]

The tension de Chennevières expressed between producer improvement and elite cultivation also characterized the *Revue des arts décoratifs.* First published in 1880, this journal was established as the joint voice of the Central Union of Fine Arts Applied to Industry and the Society for a Decorative Arts Museum. During the first year the editor was the marquis de Chennevières. Complementing the diffusion of knowledge of art-craft excellence provided by the exhibitions of 1879–1882, the *Revue des arts décoratifs* would introduce the public to the varieties of the *arts somptuaires*. Examples from the private collections of the Central Union *amateurs* were illustrated or photographed for the journal. De Chennevières hoped that the *Revue* would thus yield "the initiation of the masses to the intimate history of the design arts of great historical periods."[53]

Despite his prescriptions, the *Revue des arts décoratifs* was better suited to elite *amateurs* than to artisans, broadly defined, or the mass public. The journal, with its large folio-size pages and abundant illustrations, was expensive. Each monthly issue included a detachable portfolio of photographs and engravings of craft items for collectors. The intellectual standard was also high, and many of the articles were inaccessible to all but a small circle of connoisseur-specialists. During the first year of publication, the typical article in the *Revue* was an exercise in art-historical erudition, focusing on the scholarly reconstitution of the decorative arts commissioned and owned by royalty and the aristocracy, particularly those of the eighteenth century. Indeed, from its first year of publication, the *Revue des arts décoratifs* provided a journalistic forum for authors of scholarly monographs on the rococo applied arts. A major contributor to the inaugural volume in 1880 was the comte Henri de Chennevières, son of the marquis Philippe de Chennevières and adjunct curator of prints in the Louvre. Henri de Chennevières devoted a series of articles to Jean-Nicolas Servandoni, who under Louis XIV and Louis XV practiced the arts of the "painter, architect, decorator, set designer, and organizer of public spectacles."[54] Servandoni, an Italian court artist who moved to France, was the most renowned and imaginative of *animateurs* at the service of the eighteenth-century French kings. In his decorative ensembles he combined sophisticated technical inventiveness with spectacular ornamental effects. Lavishly illustrated and painstakingly researched from primary sources, Henri de Chennevières's articles typified the erudite efforts to reconstitute the aristocratic unity of the arts that characterized the *Revue des arts décoratifs* from its inception.

Other contributors to the *Revue des arts décoratifs* during its first year of publication deepened the connection between art administration, connoisseurship, and the Central Union embodied in the marquis de Chennevières and his son the comte Henri. Paul Mantz, for example, wrote a long commentary for the *Revue* in 1880 delineating the historical development of the fine silversmiths' and goldsmiths' work on exhibit at the union's Exhibition of the Arts of Metal.[55] Mantz was a specialist in the history of silver and gold crafts. A friend of Edmond de Goncourt's, he completed in 1880 one of the first scholarly treatments of three rococo artists, a work entitled *Boucher, Lemoine, et Natoire*. Mantz was also a colleague of the marquis de Chennevières's at the Ministry of Public Instruction and Beaux-Arts, serving as a pivotal figure on the committee overseeing the massive *Inventaire des richesses d'art de la France*.[56] Jules Guiffrey also wrote for the *Revue des arts décoratifs* in 1880. With Mantz, Guiffrey was one of a handful of specialists on reconstructing the arts of the seventeenth and eighteenth centuries. Building on archival materials exhumed by the Goncourts, Guiffrey became an expert on silvercrafts and crockery, particularly the tableware of the French kings and of their wives and mistresses. Trained at the School of Chartres and a member of the permanent staff of the National Archives, Guiffrey also worked closely with de Chennevières, Edmond de Goncourt, and Mantz on the committee for the *Inventaire* after 1879.[57] Guiffrey's 1880 article "Notes on French Silverware: Nollin, Ballin, and Lebrun, 1740–1753" provided descriptions and inventories of the silver dinnerware of such aristocrats as Madame d'Angervilliers, created with rococo flourishes by master craftsmen such as Ballin.[58] Guiffrey enlivened his lists of crockery with anecdotes of the nobles' luxurious lives, a mixing of narrative and inventory that Edmond de Goncourt had employed in recounting the varieties of porcelain dinnerware and their suitability to the multiple courses served at aristocratic gatherings.[59]

Politicians and *Amateurs*: Antonin Proust and the Central Union of the Decorative Arts, 1882–1889

In 1882, the Central Union of Fine Arts Applied to Industry and the Society for a Decorative Arts Museum joined to become the Central Union of the Decorative Arts.[60] The selection of *arts décoratifs* as a title, and the exclusion of the word *industrie*, expressed the domination of the *amateurs,* art-historical scholars, archivists, and administrators who had allied with the union and the society in the 1870s. The new organization, whose statutes were approved by the state in 1882, institutionalized the contraction of the ranks of craft producers who had flourished in the Central Union in the decade after its founding in the 1860s. Public "initiation" into the exquisite refinements of the applied arts of the past replaced the initial campaign for public consumption of useful industrial art products of the present.

The first official acts of the union were to form a new governing committee and appoint new officers. The major figures from the 1870s remained on the administrative council, with new members largely drawn from circles of collecting and erudition. Among them were Germain Bapst, a bibliophile, jeweler, and eighteenth-century decorative arts scholar; Lucien Falize, the jeweler and director of a *haut luxe* jewel and silver house; the baron Gérard; the art dealer and luxury art book publisher A. Goupil; Paul Mantz; the baron Gustave de Rothschild; the duc de Sabran; G. Schlumberger; and the director of the Ecole des Arts Décoratifs, Louvrier de Lajolais. The union's officers remained primarily the same, with Henri Bouilhet and the comte de Ganay as vice presidents. The reigning president, Edouard André, retired but remained honorary president; André ceded his place not to the marquis de Chennevières, who became a member of the administrative council, but to a new figure, the political deputy and former minister Antonin Proust.[61]

Proust's appointment widened the union's network of influence to include political as well as cultural officials. Proust carried the message and program of craft regeneration from the meeting rooms of the Central Union to the chambers of the National Assembly.

Antonin Proust was an interesting and ambiguous figure, who experienced a tension between his republican political ideals and his cultural elitism. Committed to the ideals of 1789, he desired a republic based on progress through enlightenment and education. He had been called to administrative service by his friend Gambetta, who in 1880 appointed Proust the first minister of arts. Gambetta wanted this new ministry to democratize and reclassify the arts. Noting the recognizable gains in European industrial arts production outside France, Gambetta proposed to reorganize art education and administration by eliminating the old hierarchy that placed the Institut de France and the Ecole des Beaux-Arts at its pinnacle. The Arts Ministry was founded to reunite the fine arts and the applied arts through a new uniform system of education. Strident resistance, however, prevented the consolidation of the new Arts Ministry, which under Proust's direction lasted less than a year.[62]

Proust's selection as president of the Central Union in 1882 signaled the defeat of a comprehensive governmental project to improve the education of artisans; the focus of the craft cause shifted from the state to a private association. Proust's position in the union confirmed his long-standing commitment to the conservation and restoration of French treasures in the arts and crafts and reflected his social connections to collectors and art scholars. Antonin Proust had always combined his political career with art patronage and criticism. A boyhood friend of Manet's, Proust was an early champion of Impressionism and wrote accounts of the painting Salons during the 1880s.[63] He was also a friend and patron of Rodin's; during Proust's tenure as president of the Central Union, Rodin executed an important bust of him.[64]

Some of Antonin Proust's connections with the *amateur*-collector milieu of the Central Union resulted from his participation in the post-Commune inventory project directed by the marquis de Chennevières. Proust served as vice president of the Commission of Historical Monuments, the architectural division of the comprehensive classification program begun by the Commune.[65] Proust also attended the salons where artists, politicians, and collectors met for evening entertainment. One of these was the weekly event at the home of Doctor Charcot. There Proust met other regulars like Gambetta and Waldeck-Rousseau and members of the Central Union, such *amateurs* as Gustave Dreyfus and Philippe Burty.[66]

With the transfer of power from the marquis de Chennevières to Antonin Proust, the leadership of the Central Union shifted from the hereditary aristocracy to the aristocracy of the spirit. Although Proust was committed to political democratization, he was also a social and cultural elitist. His writings and speeches as president of the union identified for the *amateur* a new role in shaping national taste and improving artisanal production. These *amateurs,* "elite spirits," understood the aesthetic power that both Edmond de Goncourt and the marquis de Chennevières had also attributed to the decorative arts: *séduction.*[67] Proust affirmed the Central Union as a fraternity of art and cultivation, an artistic elite that transcended the divisiveness of politics, uniting its members in a common brotherhood of refinement. Proust contrasted the pettiness of politics with the superior and binding powers of art—a curious position, perhaps, for a major politician to articulate yet one that republican politicians attached to the Central Union in the 1890s would clarify and strengthen. Proust isolated a resonant theme among the governing classes of late nineteenth-century France: the division of contingent political realities from the transcendent cultural patrimony:

> The Central Union is a French society founded for the purification of French taste, for the restoration of French methods. . . . In the course of this century French art has maintained its profound unity, despite the diversity of genres and temperaments. . . . French collectors . . . are devoted to everything that relates to the glory of the nation. . . . One must celebrate these eminent and illustrious persons. . . . As diverse and disparate as the branches of government may be, there exists a republic of intelligence where the petty concerns of politics cannot penetrate.[68]

Antonin Proust's major responsibility as head of the Central Union was to act as liaison between it and the government; the administrative council of the union perceived him as "an eloquent spokesman in the very center of parliament."[69] Proust advocated the union's major proposal of the 1880s: the establishment of a permanent decorative arts museum. The union needed government funds and space, and Antonin Proust became its primary political publicist. The negotiations for the museum were complicated and protracted; a site was not agreed on until 1895. During the 1880s, Proust lobbied for the government to cede a site along the Seine across from the Tuileries: the former Palais de la Cour des Comptes, the accounting offices of Napoléon III. With the vast terrain surrounding the palace, the site resembled a Piranesian ruin. Burned by the Communards, it formed with the Tuileries Palace, also a ruin, a gaping hole in the center of Paris.[70] Antonin Proust and the union wanted their museum to be centrally located, splendid, and massive. They wanted to transfer the museum and the union presence from the artisanal quarter where the union had its origins and its headquarters to the fashionable area of the city near the other cultural institutions of Paris, particularly the Louvre. The land and foundations of the Palais de la Cour des Comptes were thus desirable, and reconstruction would rid the Republic of the physical evidence of its tragic origins.[71]

In 1882, Antonin Proust entered into negotiations on behalf of the Central Union with the ministers of finance and of public instruction and beaux-arts. They agreed to the idea of the decorative arts museum, under joint government and union auspices. State underwriting would be acceptable if the union ceded the museum to the state after ten years. The union was to pay the initial costs of construction. Proust organized a national lottery to collect funds, but it was less successful than the union had hoped: between 1882 and 1886, ticket sales resulted in only six of the necessary twelve million francs. Internal feuding in the union administration and the failure to meet expenses forced the planners to postpone the establishment of the museum and to reevaluate the feasibility of the Palais de la Cour des Comptes as the site.[72]

In addition to negotiating for a permanent location of the decorative arts museum, the Central Union continued to use its journal as a forum for scholarship and connoisseurship in the applied arts. Between 1882 and 1887, the *Revue des arts décoratifs* devoted attention to the erudite classification of the arts and to reconstituting their pre-Revolutionary unity. The rococo arts of the mid-eighteenth century, unveiled in the collector exhibitions of 1879–1882, maintained their priority in the published articles in the *Revue*. The generation of scholar-*amateurs* who built on the archival and descriptive information exhumed by the brothers de Goncourt discovered in the *Revue des arts décoratifs* an enthusiastic sponsor.

The rococo and its organic ensembles of art and craft were celebrated by a new cover that appeared on the *Revue des arts décoratifs* in 1882 (Fig. 30). The title of the journal was framed by a cartouche in the pure rococo style—a composite of shells, vines, ribbons, and trellises. These "picturesque" motifs were repeated throughout the *Revue*, usually at the beginning or end of articles. Illustrations of fragments of sculpted woodworks, chinoiseries, and delicate vines from the eighteenth-century *style moderne* were abundantly reprinted for the first time in the *Revue des arts décoratifs* during the 1880s (Figs. 31, 32).[73]

The *Revue des arts décoratifs* gave special priority to the scholarly recounting of the organic, exotic, and erotic character of the mid-eighteenth-century decorative ensembles. In 1884, for example, it published Henri Thirion's account of the life, work, and destiny of the rococo sculptor Clodion.[74] Thirion's article, like others in the *Revue*, summarized a major monograph in progress; his book on Clodion, a lavish, illustrated folio with "extracts of unpublished documents," was soon to be published by Quantin.[75] In his article Thirion celebrated the recently recovered appreciation of mid-eighteenth-century arts:

> Clodion, a greatly gifted artist, . . . has suffered from the caprices of public opinion; he was indicted for adapting too well to the tastes of his time. . . . This dismissal of his work held sway until very recently, when Clodion was rescued by the enthusiastic return to the graces of the eighteenth century. . . . It is time to restore to this charming master his true character.[76]

Thirion emphasized that Clodion's polished marble nymphs, delicate terra-cotta fauns and satyrs, and "amorous shepherdesses" were efforts of skill and technical expertise equal to those demonstrated by sculptors of grandiose historical works. He included detailed information on the way that the "seductive grace" of Clodion's sculptures harmonized with spatial ensembles celebrating "coquettishness, gallantry, and preciosity."[77] Relating Clodion's style and subject to an underlying social and cultural transformation following the reign of Louis XIV, Thirion explained that Clodion was not so much a "creator or inventor" as a skillful and stylish "interpreter of the artistic sensibility that reigned during his time," a time when France became "the most delicate and playful nation in Europe."[78]

The delineation of the eighteenth-century shift from the *grand goût* of Louis XIV to the *grâce* of Louis XV was further explored in articles by Victor Champier.

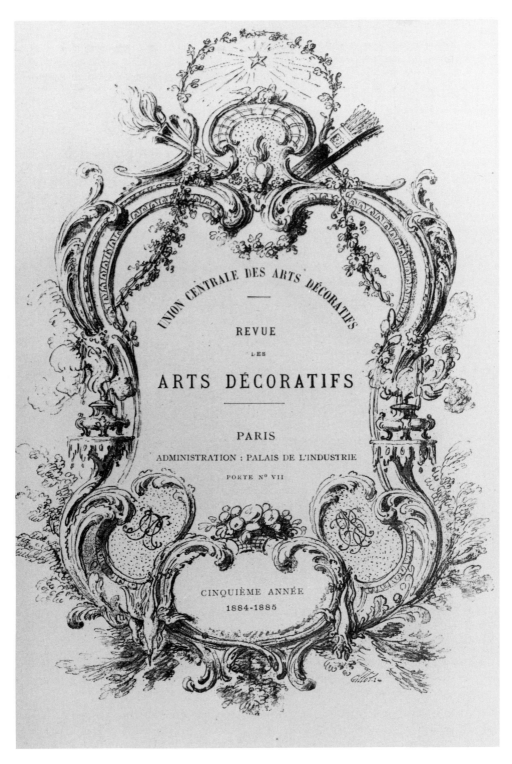

Fig. 30. Cover, *Revue des arts décoratifs,* 1884.

LES

MEUBLES DU XVIII° SIÈCLE

Fig. 31. Rococo illustration. From *Revue des arts décoratifs*, 1883.

Fig. 32. Rococo framing. From *Revue des arts décoratifs*, 1885.

Champier, an art critic and scholar, was the editor of the *Revue* after 1882, and his contributions to the journal reflected his erudite immersion in the art and culture of the rococo period. He was careful to indicate the change from "solemnity" to "coquetry" after 1724: "Apartments were used for receptions; furniture, transformed under the influence of intelligent and refined women, became smaller, more intimate, and more coquettish in order to conform to new needs. In living rooms, heavy draperies were replaced with pastel-painted wood panels, radiating gaiety and light."[79]

Champier expanded his treatment of the "seductive grace" of the rococo applied arts in one of his articles of 1884, "The Silverware Collection of M. Paul Eudel,"[80] which detailed the history and provenance of Eudel's collection, illustrated with acutely rendered engravings of the prize attractions, such as the silver soup tureen executed by Antoine Jean de Villeclair for Louis XV himself, a candelabrum with flowing molded *rocailles* for Madame de Pompadour, and an exquisite engraved silver pitcher, originally designed for the queen in 1765. Accompanying the captions below each illustration were the insignias of the noble craftsmen who had helped to create the object and the coats of arms of the owner. One of Champier's more interesting archival sources was an account book that recorded the names of the Parisian noblewomen who were forced to bring their precious silverware to the treasury office to be melted down into money for the new Republic in 1790. Champier mourned this destruction of what he considered as some of the finest objets d'art ever created in France.[81]

The intimate, organic character of the eighteenth-century *style moderne* also received exhaustive discussion in a series of articles in the *Revue des arts décoratifs* by Paul Mantz. Mantz's "Eighteenth Century Furniture" chronicled the evolution of the rococo style in furniture, and identified the distinctive technical and ornamental contributions of the major cabinetmakers. Beginning with the transitional works by the master Boulle under Louis XIV, Mantz described the rococo furniture by Oppenordt, Pineau, Meissonnier, Oeben, and Migeon, delineating the multiple stages in which the objects were made and noting the collaborators who embellished the flowing wood surfaces with matching bronze, gilded, and ivory rococo carvings. Mantz's account was full of hitherto unpublished material, which he called the evidence of "our new erudition."[82] He mined hundreds of memoirs, inventories, and account books of both the cabinetmakers and their aristocratic patrons for information on the cost and installation of the furnishings.

Like his mentors the Goncourts, Paul Mantz used his erudition in the service of cultural history. He related eighteenth-century applied arts to the ethos and values of the society for which they were produced. The "new furniture" articulated a "new worldview," the external sign of the shift from the "solemnity of the *grand goût*" to the *grâce* of private pleasure:

> Furniture . . . expresses the spirit of its time; it contains memories, and it tells us about the values and tone of a period that history books scarcely sug-

gest. . . . Indeed, we learn less of the eighteenth century in a grandiose canvas of official painting than we do from a console or a small dressing table. From 1715 to the Revolution, furniture makers articulate the changing phases of taste with the same exactitude as Vanloo and Lemoine. . . . One senses that from the death of Louis XIV we enter a new world, and furniture expresses it, becoming less severe and solemn and more elegant, intimate, and playful. . . . Under Louis XV, furniture . . . assumes the frivolousness of aristocratic and royal manners. The heavy table of sober court feasts would not do for a period of intimate dinner parties.[33]

Mantz went on to emphasize the specifically feminine and anthropomorphic qualities of the rococo ensembles, and he enumerated the new repertoire of fragile pastel-painted objects, designed for intimate space, which suggested erotic dalliance: "Furniture spoke in the eighteenth century. . . . Hearts were imprisoned as captives in the amorous curves of sofas the color of rose. . . . Eroticism in ornament reigned . . . in all the luxury arts; the ideal had become feminized."[84]

Besides chronicling female form in the rococo applied arts, Mantz detailed the participation of aristocratic women in the design arts. A long section in the first of his three articles revealed the fad that arose suddenly in the late 1720s and continued through the 1740s for cutting apart images and pasting them, in collagelike form, on the surfaces of furniture, carriage walls, and utensils. A kind of "delirium" overtook the women of "elegant society," who "scissored out engravings, arabesques, and ornaments and affixed them to chairs, tables, and the interior of carriages. Even the most serious noblewomen were transformed into mischievous children by this mania for cutting and pasting."[85]

The end of Mantz's dispassionate and exhaustive history, a commentary on the destructive divisions imposed by the rebel David, intimated the author's attitude toward his subject. The marquis de Chennevières, like the Goncourts before him, had lamented the French Revolution for both social and aesthetic reasons; 1789 not only exploded social structures but eliminated artistic unities. Mantz indicted the Revolution on similar grounds. De Chennevières had accused David of "strangling" the effusive life of the eighteenth century, the "adored era";[86] Mantz, more soberly, warned the historian examining the arts of the post-Revolutionary period to prepare himself for a chilling experience:

The cult of the straight line, the pseudoantique tendencies: this was the beginning of the end, the transition that prepared the cruel triumph of the empire and of boredom. Already the painter of Horaces introduced menacing furnishings in his canvases, and already an arbitrary and simulated Egypt set facile sphinxes in every angle. Gone was the smile set in form, and gone was the warmth! By the fatal door opened by David, one felt the arrival of an icy wind. The time had come when, in the face of the frozen ideal, the chilled historian must request his coat.[87]

*

If the aristocratic and feminine legacy of eighteenth-century art and craft was central to the journal published by the Central Union, the organic forms and applied arts of Japan also received considerable attention. The interest in Japanese decorative arts derived partly from the union's rediscovery of the French rococo, which had incorporated Oriental motifs and objects. The Goncourts, who reveled in Japan as the "country of truth and dreams," had classified the Japanese presence in the eighteenth-century French *style moderne*. During the 1880s, scholars and *amateurs* attached to the Central Union of the Decorative Arts reconstructed, as precisely as they did the rococo applied arts, the origins and provenance of Japanese objects collected by eighteenth-century French elites.[88]

The scholarly interest in Japanese arts coincided with the unprecedented export of Japanese applied arts to the Parisian market after 1870. These applied arts of traditional Japan had been jealously guarded from Western plunder. With the Mejii restoration of 1867 and the new constitutional Japanese state, the cultural artifacts of the traditional warrior caste began to be sold to the West.[89] The new Japanese government encouraged visits from foreign travelers and traders, among whom were such enterprising merchants as Siegfried Bing and Philippe and August Sichel from Paris, Louis Comfort Tiffany from New York, and Liberty of London.[90] The French contingent, led by Bing, concentrated on the accoutrements of the Japanese feudal elite—samurai swords, spears, and daggers with jeweled and sculpted cases; silk embroidered *fukasas*, which had been used to wrap gifts exchanged between princes; tiny ornamented boxes for medicine, which were always hung from the waist between the two swords of the warrior; and the gilded, jade, and onyx bodies of slender writing quills and their cases.[91] Bing indicated that the Franco-Prussian War and the Commune of 1870–1871 made the arts of Japan especially attractive to his French public. Part of the appeal was relief and diversion from internal devastation: "In 1871, at the moment when our spirits, crushed by recent catastrophes, had begun to breathe again, we could surrender ourselves to such fruitful studies."[92]

Siegfried Bing is usually credited with supplying Japanese decorative arts to a small circle of aesthetes and collectors. His Paris Oriental arts boutique on the rue Chauchat, opened in 1875, became a favorite haunt of such collectors as Edmond de Goncourt, Cernuschi, and Philippe Burty, who admired Bing's expertise in the history, techniques, and traditions of Japanese applied arts.[93] Yet the Japonist applied arts, like the French movement to reunite art and craft, had an important institutional nexus during the 1880s, which brought together the merchant Bing, his aesthete-collector clients, and official administrators. As early as 1878, Bing lent part of his own collection of Japanese artifacts to the Society for a Decorative Arts Museum for an exhibition.[94] In 1883 and 1884 Bing was put in charge of a series of Central Union special exhibitions, held at the union's temporary quarters at the Palace of Industry. The exhibits featured Japanese painted screens, scrolls, fans, and silks.[95]

The Central Union's fascination with Japanese applied arts in the 1880s was translated into projects of erudite classification and attribution. In exhibitions like the Glass, Wood, Stone, and Earth, in 1884, Japanese pottery and glass were given ample display space. Victor Champier's scholarly catalogue for the show celebrated Japan as the "nation of decorative art par excellence."[96] Catalogue entries gave a wealth of technical and historical information on each artifact, comparing and contrasting it with the eighteenth-century French porcelains and ceramic miniatures also featured at the show.[97]

The scholarly treatment of the arts of Japan extended to one area for which there was no equivalent analysis of the eighteenth-century rococo: ethnography and anthropology. The scholar-collectors writing for the *Revue des arts décoratifs* during the 1880s indicated that the French integral craft style of the 1720s expressed the ethos and attitudes of the elite for whom it was produced. But the lecturers and writers on Japan for the Central Union went further, relating the arts to the customs, traditions, and rituals of an ancient and unfamiliar foreign culture. Evidence suggests that the scholarly writers on the arts and crafts of Japan were particularly attracted, in the post-Commune period, to a society bound by ties of deference, status, and a sacred union of the human and natural orders. When Victor Champier, Philippe Burty, and Lucien Falize investigated the applied arts of Japan, for example, they emphasized the plethora of forms in the outer world that resonated with inherent order, a shared system of values, and a universe charged with meaning.[98]

The scholarly and ethnographic analysis of Japanese crafts had two overlapping centers, demonstrating the indivisibility of institutional and aesthetic circles during the 1880s. One was the *Revue des arts décoratifs,* which reviewed recent books on Japan and published articles on the forms and functions of Japanese crafts. The other was *Le Japon artistique,* the journal founded by Siegfried Bing in 1888. Bing's stated purpose for publishing *Le Japon artistique* was to replace stereotyped visions of the exotic East with an empirical project. He modeled it on a "graphic encyclopedia," a blend of scholarly articles and extensive, large-scale multicolored plates. Bing stressed the difference between the Far East as an exotic curiosity and the Far East as revealed in his own project of painstaking scholarship.[99] The journal fastidiously delineated the technical and cultural history of each art object. The same group of people wrote on Japanese art and culture in Bing's journal and in the *Revue des arts décoratifs:* Paul Mantz, the scholar of rococo furniture; Edmond de Goncourt; and Philippe Burty, the collector-scholar who delivered a series of lectures on Japanese pottery and porcelain at the Central Union in the fall of 1884.[100]

The lectures and articles of Philippe Burty exemplified the incorporation of Japonism into the elite art and craft program of the 1880s. Like his close friends the brothers de Goncourt, Burty (1830–1890) came to the applied arts through active participation: he had spent his early adulthood executing drawings and engravings.[101] For him, as for the Goncourts, art criticism, collecting, and art practice flowed in a continuum and were mutually reinforcing. Beginning in the 1860s, Burty assembled a collection of watercolors by French artists, including Delacroix, Manet, Whistler, Puvis de Chavannes, and Paul Huet. Alongside these he hung prints by eighteenth-century draftsmen such as Fragonard, Watteau, and Moreau le Jeune. In journals such as the *Gazette des beaux-arts* and the *Chronique des arts et de la curiosité,* Burty publicized the aesthetic qualities inherent in the print media and sketches. In addition, he was called on to edit and publish exhibition catalogues and sale catalogues, both primary vehicles for disseminating new ideas on the value of arts outside the Great Tradition.[102] Burty's elevation of the print media, like the Goncourts', derived from both his eighteenth-century erudition and his nineteenth-century aestheticism. Burty celebrated the craft patronage and practice of eighteenth-century aristocrats, relying on an awareness of the same *amateur*-noble drawing societies that the marquis de Chennevières had recuperated to demonstrate the French tradition of the unity of the arts. To this tradition Burty attached a new criterion of artistic individualism, glorifying the media of watercolor and pencil sketching as condensers of visionary imagination. It was Burty who collected and published the watercolors, engravings, and etchings of the brothers de Goncourt in 1876. He brought to light for the first time the intricate connection between the technical artistic practice of the Goncourts, their identification with the eighteenth century, and the visual character of their writing style.[103]

Philippe Burty was most widely known during the 1880s for his collection of Japanese prints and objets d'art. He had been an early enthusiast of the rediscovery of Japan and joined Edmond de Goncourt and Théodore Duret in starting the vogue for Japanese prints during the 1860s.[104] Burty was equally central to the second wave of Japonism unleashed by the new availability of applied arts after 1870. He concentrated his collection and erudition on Japanese ceramics and samurai weaponry. By the time of his 1884 lectures for the Central Union and articles in the *Revue des arts décoratifs* and *Le Japon artistique,* Burty was recognized as the reigning collector *érudit* in Japonism.[105] Burty was more publicly oriented than his only rival, Edmond de Goncourt; Burty's critical writings mediated between the splendid stuff arriving from Japan and the French public. Among those to whom Burty offered expert advice on collecting Japanese objects was Doctor Charcot, whose weekly salon Burty visited along with Antonin Proust, Gambetta, and Waldeck-Rousseau.[106] Burty's critical and aesthetic credentials were complemented by official recognition—in 1881 he was appointed inspector of beaux-arts, a post held until his death in 1890.[107]

Burty's lecture series "The Pottery and Porcelains of Japan" introduced members of the Central Union to the illustrious history of ceramic production. The lectures typified the careful empirical and contextual analysis of late nineteenth-century Japonists eager to dissociate themselves from the caricatured Orientalism of eighteenth-century consumers. The first part of the lectures examined the climatic and geological conditions that made the Japanese production of pottery possible and described the patronage system emerging from a feudal hierarchy. Burty emphasized the affinity between the Japanese nobility and the objects created for them, positing, like the Goncourts, a direct correspondence between the delicate serpentine shapes of the applied arts and the refinement and elegance of those for whom they were made. Japanese noblewomen were themselves agile practitioners of the arts of drawing and decorative painting, Burty noted, echoing the Goncourts' association of Madame de Pompadour's fluid work with that of Japanese women.[108]

The lecture series on Japanese stoneware concluded by celebrating the visual grammar of all Japanese crafts: nature. Burty was fascinated by the limitless capacities of the Japanese to record the elements of the natural world. Every part of the vegetable, mineral, and animal kingdoms was regarded with equal attentiveness and rendered with scrupulous accuracy. Burty construed this style of feudal Japan as an expression of a tradition that infused even the smallest object with "moral, symbolic," and ritualistic power.[109]

Burty's glorification of Japanese organicism was not, however, limited to a mournful idealization of the feudal and religious traditions that had inspired it. Nor did he recommend that French *amateurs* restrict themselves to collecting Japanese artifacts, whose symbolic meaning and social functions would be lost in a foreign context. To his French audience of *amateurs,* cultural administrators, and luxury artisans in the Central Union, Burty offered Japan as a living example of craft integrity. For him the organicism of Japanese art and craft, like that of the French rococo, was a standard against which to measure the sterility of nineteenth-century historicism and a model that suggested the forms of a new decorative ensemble. He called for the creation of a professor's chair at the Louvre or the Collège de France to disseminate the techniques of Oriental arts. French potters and porcelain producers could profit from the tutelage of their Japanese counterparts, whose works "were full of instructive motifs."[110]

Burty emphasized that the lessons of the Japanese were to be screened through a fine filter of national character. He was not proposing that French craftsmen imitate their illustrious Japanese counterparts but that they adapt the Japanese example to express French realities. From Japan the French should learn a scrupulous attentiveness to nature. Burty glorified the long hours Japanese designers spent in their gardens or fields, studying the structure and surface of the leaf, rock, or shell they would later transfer to the face of a bowl or to a screen. This example of an art based on a direct engagement with nature prompted Burty to exhort the French to cultivate their own garden, to rekindle "the sacred fire of the love of nature," out of a "jealous regard for national beauty."[111] Japan had revealed the principle of decoration based on naturalistic observation; France would realize that principle in representations of its own distinctive soil, flowers, and rocks.

Burty's presentation of Japan crystallized a central paradox that would characterize the efforts of Siegfried Bing and the Central Union. On the one hand, Burty was steeped in the customs and hierarchies of feudal Japan, celebrating the craft arts as the physical embodiments of a particular class and a traditional social order. On the other hand, the artifacts of this highly stratified traditional culture were to liberate the French from tradition; Japanese tradition was to be the agent of French modernity. "The ornamentation in Far Eastern art," noted Burty, "is symbolic." It is different in Europe, where historical patterns ceaselessly copied and transcribed have lost their meaning, which may be found again only in nature. Burty insisted that "our flora and fauna have all the elements of an absolutely inventive and absolutely French decorative style."[112] He concluded by urging the French to follow the model of the Japanese—to discover the forms of "national beauty" in nature:

> I believe the academic education that we receive is absolutely contrary to human truths. . . . It is clear that each race follows its own laws. I believe that the conditions of our climate, the earth on which we stand, . . . the air that we breathe, and the physical beauty that surrounds us are the matrix of a race. Therefore, those peoples that fashion an ideal based only on copying things already made in the past are profoundly wrong.[113]

Siegfried Bing, whose expertise and artifacts Burty praised in his lectures, also noted the paradox inherent in using the arts of feudal Japan to promote a new French anti-academicism: "The glimmerings of a new aesthetic that suddenly appeared on our horizon as a new dawn were, in the Oriental skies, the last rays of a dying antique culture."[114] The two exhibitions Bing organized for the Central Union in 1883 and 1884 aimed precisely to undermine French eclecticism with a vision of unified organic arts. Bing arranged these shows in collaboration with a Japanese institution for craft arts strikingly similar to the French Central Union of the Decorative Arts. Called the Ruitshikuai, the Japanese organization included the minister of the beaux-arts and "senators from the empire."[115] The Ruitshikuai affirmed, as "a patriotic cause," the task of conserving the traditional Japanese arts disinherited by the new constitutional and bureaucratic order.[116] The site of this national preservation was in France. In their turn the French, represented by Bing, welcomed the objects as an exhilarating deliverance from history and tradition:

> The appeal of Japanese artists has begun to be extensive. In artistic matters, there is no country more hospitable than ours, and there is no European country to whom our doors are not open. But however open these borders may be, they still exist; perhaps now that our attention is drawn beyond our own continent, we will recognize that it is time to overturn the last barriers. . . . It is important to recognize that as the evolution of our old art began to show significant symptoms, we were open to mysterious influences; the subtle art of the Far East . . . is hardly foreign. There are benefits to be gained from this, for as our movement of transformation, our new genesis, approaches, there are lessons to be learned from an art whose origins are so completely independent of the sources of our old aesthetic.[117]

Bing's enthusiastic embrace of Japanese applied arts was tempered, however, by the same nationalism that Burty had articulated. Although he affirmed the openness of France and its willingness to absorb artistic innovation from other countries, Bing shared the nationalist ethos underlying the Central Union's craft sponsorship. But elements of Bing's own background and experience shaped his desire to reject the constraints of national borders in matters of art and taste. Born and raised in Hamburg, he had migrated to France to work in his family's lucrative business importing and manufacturing art ceramics. He became a naturalized French citizen in 1876.[118] His subsequent work as a merchant-middleman made him a continual traveler, an avid promoter of international influences in the arts.[119] Bing's background developed his enthusiasm for the Japanese as an example to the French members of the union and led to his affirmation of an international "kinship of sentiment" that necessitated French openness to external models.[120] Yet Bing was also at pains to show that Japan "is hardly foreign,"[121] that Japonism was already an important part of the French tradition in the eighteenth century, and that the French cultural identity would not be undermined by an influx of art from the Orient. As a new citizen, a German, and a Jew, Bing was, and would remain, acutely aware of a need to prove his membership in the French national community. His statements expressed a continual identification with France as "our race,"[122] and his assertions of the particular strengths of the "French taste and traditions" increased as the new nationalism of the 1890s was consolidated.

During the 1880s Bing's participation in the Central Union of the Decorative Arts exposed his lifelong delicate ideological balance between an expansive "kinship of sentiment" that united all countries and a protectionist fortification of "national beauty." In the statements about Japan, he tempered his euphoric calls for emulation of the Japanese with demonstrations of French resiliency. He reassured the union members and his magazine readers that receptivity to external influences could strengthen French vitality. The capacity for assimilation had long precedents in the French cultural past and had facilitated such quintessentially French styles as the rococo, melded from European baroque sources, and Louis XIV classicism, a French response to Italianate artistic domination.[123] Thus Bing explained that the celebration of Japanese art would pose no threat to national cultural solidarity. Rather than erode the foundations of national integrity, a transfigured Japan would help to regenerate the "French genius":

> In the novel artistic models that have come to us from the Far East . . . we will find examples that deserve to be followed, not, certainly, to dislodge the foundations of our old aesthetic edifice, but to add one more force to all those that during centuries past we have appropriated to revitalize our national genius. How can we maintain our vitality without continual infusions from new sources? What civilized country, ancient or modern, near or far, have we not borrowed from? . . . We have made a law of the need for eternal evolution; . . . is it any wonder, then, that our artists . . . have so passionately embraced the new arrivals?[124]

The exhibition and explication of Japanese applied arts in the Central Union served to catalyze new ideas about craft revitalization in the 1880s. The Japanese embellishment of objects with delicate organic forms stimulated members of the union to envision a regenerated French craft style based on natural, rather than historical, models. The reconstitution of the rococo central to the union's efforts during the 1880s provided an indigenously French precedent for a *style nature;* the Japanese influx, transposed by nationalist standards, prompted Frenchmen to look anew at their own flora and fauna. Burty's and Bing's celebration of Japanese decorative naturalism contributed to a slow redirection of the union from craft restoration to craft renovation. Nature, the source of both eternal national character and continually changing forms, offered a bridge between the glories of the French tradition and the possibilities of French rejuvenation.

Although the explicit links between nature style, craft integration, and modern style were not articulated until after 1889, in the mid-1880s the Central Union grappled with the issue of craft innovation. Victor Champier, who glorified Japanese artifacts but warned that "one is guided to create only by one's own genius and that of his race,"[125] argued in 1884 that French artisans should emulate their own ancestors not by servile imitation but by producing new forms in the spirit of the immutable "French taste"; "to create not *what* our ancestors did, but in their spirit."[126] Articles in the *Revue des arts décoratifs* after 1884 focused on the renovation of traditional national craft institutions, such as the Sèvres national manufacture. One writer of 1885 examined the history of ceramic production in France since the seventeenth century and then proposed a new formula for national preeminence: reverence for tradition, and revision through nature.

> We have not honored our forefathers enough. They were accomplished even in the minutest objects they bequeathed to us. . . . The true carriers of progress are those for whom the point of departure is respect for the past and for our ancestors. Let the Germans keep their oversized goblets, with their dull ornamentation; leave the English their heavy and ugly forms. . . . We are French; let us remain French . . . ! blue, white, and red! The blue of Nevers, the white of Sèvres, the red of Rouen! Long live the flower! Let us study more and more our own. . . . Let us recover the fecund sources of our sovereign mother, *la patrie;* then we will march firmly toward what is best.[127]

By the mid-1880s, Central Union publicists Philippe Burty and Louis de Fourcaud had asserted in the pages of the *Revue* that union efforts should be bolstered and extended by active state intervention if France was to maintain its traditions of artisanal excellence. In 1884, Burty charged that "the Republic must follow the example of the monarchy and refined aristocracy and lend aid to the national manufactures."[128] De Fourcaud chastised the Republic for failing to regenerate the applied arts, in contrast to the steady succession of innovative unitary decorative styles under the French monarchy; the republicans, zealous devotees of political liberation, were culturally enslaved to the styles of their privileged forebears. Rather than seek out the forms of the Republic's own distinctive image, republicans affirmed "false luxury" and the "taste for archaism." De Fourcaud called on the government to support the Central Union's developing program to revitalize the crafts through nationalism, renewal, and direct engagement with nature: "Restore our French genius," he urged; "help our French art works to triumph."[129]

*

The demands of de Fourcaud and Burty were to be met in the 1890s. The immediate post-Commune decades had prepared an important institutional base: a decorative arts organization with a dual program of craft restoration and artisanal innovation. Responding to the cultural desecrations wrought by the events of 1870–1871, a group of aristocrats and collectors had emerged in the dominant position in the Central Union of the Decorative Arts, altering its character and goals. During the 1880s, the union forged its first links with political figures, with Antonin Proust as its president. Through the influx of Japanese arts and the scholarly resurrection of the rococo nature ensemble, new ideas about the creation of a natural, and national, artisanal style began to percolate. Yet it was not until after 1889 that the full institutional bonding between the Central Union of the Decorative Arts and the Third Republic was sealed. During the 1890s the principal members of the political elite actively embraced a craft program and defined a distinctively French modern style as a style of craft luxury. The Paris Exhibition of 1889 revealed the realities of French beleaguerment by other producers of luxury goods, including Germany, Denmark, America, and Austria. The economic emergence of protectionism and industrial competition dimmed the hopes of the republican elite for technological triumph of the type prefigured in the Eiffel Tower. The political reshuffling of the republican elite resulted in new men at the top, who were sympathetic to a government alliance with an institution of craft regeneration. *Ralliement* and *solidarité* found their cultural analogues in state-sponsored restorations of landmarks of aristocratic crafts and in official support for artisans who heralded an organic and interiorizing *style moderne*.

CHAPTER SEVEN

Esprit Nouveau:
Politicians, *Amateurs,* and Artisans

The social unity shaped by morality, education, and metaphysics is incomplete; this is only a community of ideas . . . the community of sensations and feelings remains to be established. . . . It is sensations and feelings that divide men the most; . . . yet there is a way to *socialize* them, to make them identical for each individual: through art. From the inchoate discordance of individual sensations and feelings, art can shape an ensemble of sensations and feelings to be shared by all; it can create an *association* of pleasures. These pleasures . . . become an essential "solidarity." Like metaphysics, like morality, art lifts the individual into the realm of the universal, not simply by the communion of ideas and beliefs . . . but by the communion of sensations and feelings. . . . Art is therefore a tool of social concord more profound than others; for thinking alike is a lot to achieve, but it is not enough to make us *will* in the same ways. The great secret is how to make us *feel* in the same way, and this is the wonder that art accomplishes.

Alfred Fouillée, 1892[1]

AMID THE FRACTURES of political challenges, the pressures of economic nationalism, the claims of feminist reform, and the discovery of divided consciousness, French republicans turned to art as a source of unity. Despite the articulation of the reconciling powers of an *esprit nouveau* and the projection of a harmonic, functional organicism of *solidarité,* political integration remained incomplete in the 1890s. Fiscal policy, education, foreign affairs, and social reform continued to divide political leaders.

Alfred Fouillée, one of the primary philosophers of republican solidarism, suggested in 1892 the potential of art to transcend dissension and discordance. He argued that a social system operated on the basis not only of common ideas but also of common feeling, collective "sentiments and sensations." Thinking alike was not enough; the will that led to action derived from emotion. One way to tap this means to social "solidarity" was through art, the plastic power for focusing attention and mobilizing a "communion of emotions." Art was the "great secret" for molding "social concord"; it lifted the individual from the confines of egoism to the life universal.

The republican elite of the 1890s actively pursued the goal of solidarity through art, extending the political initiatives of *ralliement* and *solidarité* into culture. All of the primary political spokesmen for both of these initiatives embraced the cause of "solidarity among all the arts."[2] As a result of the new official devotion to art as a source of spiritual renewal and social cohesion, the Central Union of the Decorative Arts was reshaped. The program pursued by the official elite in conjunction with the Central Union, like the two phases of republican political transformation, balanced respect for tradition with the goal of renewal.

This chapter describes the new social composition of the Central Union of the Decorative Arts after 1889 and the convergence of politicians, cultural administrators, and official educators with the union's core of aristocratic collectors and luxury craft producers. It goes on to suggest the general contours of the dual program of aristocratic craft revival and organicist craft modernism pursued by a network of individuals who were affiliated with the Central Union and played official roles in cultural and political administration.

*

Three statements exemplify the individuals attached to the Central Union of the Decorative Arts in the 1890s and the ideas they shared as official spokesmen for a craft *art nouveau.* Here is Raymond Poincaré, minister of public instruction and beaux-arts from 1894 to 1895:

> The century in which we live is infatuated with the reproduction of old styles . . . a nation that dawdles in this retrospective contemplation will soon become sterile and impotent. While there is surely a place for curiosity about the talents of our ancestors, it must not be our primary preoccupation. We must not look behind us, but around and ahead of us. . . . Let us not be hypnotized by the corpses of dead centuries. Let us rather extend, expand, enrich, and augment the heritage that we have been bequeathed.[3]

Gustave Larroumet, professor of modern literature at the Sorbonne, echoes Poincaré:

> Our decorative art is being crushed under the weight of the past, all its forces of invention have been paralyzed. . . . Dominated by archaism, . . . decorative art has been relegated to mere pastiches and sterile copies. . . . Our interiors, a prodigious mélange of form and color, lack all unity and harmony. . . . We love decorative art, and though we must learn from the past, we must reshape it in our own image. Artists are now at work, and they will discover the elements necessary for an art nouveau. It is time to create for the present, that is to say, according to our taste, our needs, and our mores.[4]

Roger Marx, inspector-general of provincial museums, sounds a similar theme:

> The fanatical cult of the past has stifled inspiration, crushed all initiative, and shackled us to relentless copying and imitation. . . . Yet the adornment of the home can only respond to the needs and aspirations of a society in continual transformation by varying with it, . . . by keeping pace with the modern

spirit. . . . This does not mean, however, that we should celebrate those creations that have no attachment to or evocation of a style from the past. . . . Indeed, modern decorative masters will command more of our admiration when they project among us the reminders of our gifts of elegance, grace, and verve, which have always signified the particularism of our national temperament. . . . We recognize and admire in them . . . the power to incarnate in matter the characterizing features of French genius. . . . We value comfort only when adorned with elegance and seduction.[5]

The three men exemplified the interpenetration of government and cultural administration in the Central Union of the Decorative Arts. After 1889 the president of the Central Union was Georges Berger, an important deputy in the Chamber and member of the parliamentary budget committee for the beaux-arts.[6] From this strategic position, Berger was able to promote the interests of the Central Union and to direct attention to the luxury artisan, whom he lionized as the agent of French commercial salvation in a period of international protectionism. Raymond Poincaré, who spoke to the union in 1894, was a leading politician of the *ralliement* and solidarist Republic affiliated with the Central Union. He was a pivotal spokesman for the renovation of the decorative arts throughout the 1890s.

Poincaré himself sealed the government's association with the Central Union when he finalized the agreements for a decorative arts museum to be housed in the Pavillon de Marsan at the Louvre complex.[7] His 1894 speech emphatically demanded a modern style, freed from the sterile repetition of historicist formulas. The quest for a new style did not imply the rejection of tradition but its revitalization, the "extension" and "enrichment" of the national heritage. Poincaré celebrated Edmond de Goncourt as a model of this affirmation of tradition, and its transformation, in a speech awarding Edmond the Legion of Honor in 1895. Poincaré praised Edmond's historical work of rehabilitating the applied arts of the eighteenth century; he also appreciated the essence of Edmond's literary modernism: the infusion of language with visual categories and the movement away from a realistic description of the world toward a subjective expression of the effects of stimulation on sensibility. Edmond, in turn, admired Poincaré as "a true literatus."[8] And in fact Poincaré's tribute to Edmond was more like that of a literary critic than a political official:

> Your greatest pleasures have been those of ideas, lines, and colors; and the sensations that you have felt, you have tried to render with the aid of new forms and the tremblings of personal notations. You have made your language supple to capture the complex painting of observed reality, the continually changing shifts of mood, the caprice of fugitive impressions. You have infused your style with light, coloring, and palpitations from the outer world; you have also infused it with subtle emotions, with the shudderings of the inner world. Anxious to evoke in your phrases all that vibrates and quivers, . . . you have called on the richness and diversity of artistic forms to express the infinite multiplicity of experience.[9]

Poincaré's speech to the Central Union in 1894 was characteristic of an individual with a commitment to a nationally distinct form of artistic innovation. It was no accident that Poincaré cast his critique of imitative historicism in the language of hypnotism. Just as he recognized Edmond de Goncourt as a writer of "interior shudderings," so the republican minister could draw on the psychology of hypnotic states in his Central Union speech.[10]

Other prominent republican leaders of the 1890s joined Poincaré in working with the Central Union for craft renovation. Eugène Spuller, former Gambettist and architect of the *ralliement,* had approved, as early as 1889, a program to restore Versailles and make it a national gallery of art and a cultural center.[11] In 1894, soon after the goals of the political *esprit nouveau* had been articulated, Spuller helped organize what he called the *esprit nouveau* in culture: an officially sponsored Congress of the Decorative Arts, run by the Central Union. The congress assembled government leaders, museum and beaux-arts administrators, art critics, and luxury artisans to discuss a new program for the applied arts. Among the topics discussed were education; the rights of artisans to sign the final product of collaborative labor; the role of women in the crafts; and international competition. Among the speakers at the opening and closing of the congress were the new president of the Central Union, Georges Berger, and Emile Guillaume, the head of the Ecole des Beaux-Arts.[12] Eugène Spuller also spoke, celebrating the congress as the alliance of the government and the craft association, embodied in the union, and describing the partnership as the "disinterested league of pure beauty." He characterized the congress as a meeting place where, above other "orthodoxies," "the great religion of one art" could flourish. The theme of elites joined through art despite the fractures of politics emerged again at the end of Spuller's speech: "It gives me great satisfaction to see that despite all sorts of changes, disruptions, revolution, worries of all types, and even the shock waves of violent acts, those men who love great and beautiful things still come together in association."[13] In a speech resonating with the political problems of socialism and anarchism, Spuller offered national art as a bond above the vicissitudes of politics. The unifying goals of the *esprit nouveau,* originally defined as a political realignment with old elites, were thus transferred to the realm of culture.

Other political leaders of the 1890s were affiliated with the Central Union of the Decorative Arts. Léon Bourgeois was minister of public instruction and beaux-arts from 1891–1892 and during that year made important decisions about the national manufactures—Sèvres, Gobelins, and Aubusson. His policies were reprinted and discussed in the *Revue des arts décoratifs.*[14] In 1891, for example, he ensured the continuity of the manufacture at Sèvres while changing its orientation to meet international competition. Rather than strive for technical efficiency, increased production, and the implementation of mechanical innovations, Bourgeois stated that the French crafts should strive for quality. Art, not science, was to be the strength of French fine porcelain production. To this end, Bourgeois appointed an artist as head of the Sèvres manufacture, demoting its former head, an expert chemist, to second-in-command. Bourgeois argued that France would remain the international "school of taste" not by flooding the market with predictable patterns but by continually inventing delicate, inimitable designs.[15] Following this new directive, the Sèvres manufacture in the 1890s varied the models produced and promoted a new version of the celebrated porcelain type of the eighteenth century, *pâte tendre,* "soft-paste." Originating under the auspices of the Sèvres manufacture's founding patron, Madame de Pompadour, soft-paste porcelain was renowned for its fragile texture and pastel palette. The Sèvres manufacture rediscovered this porcelain in the 1890s, shifting from the hard-paste porcelain dominant since the beginning of the nineteenth century.[16]

Léon Bourgeois's interaction with the Central Union and his special efforts for the decorative arts were also evident in his attempt to reorganize the administration of the beaux-arts in 1891–1892. As part of a campaign to widen the government's interest and involvement in the decorative arts, he solicited a special report from Victor Champier, editor of the *Revue des arts décoratifs* in 1892. Bourgeois's arts initiative was left unrealized when changes in the cabinet led to his removal from the ministerial post.[17]

Léon Bourgeois's commitment to the crafts extended to the years of his solidarist ministry, 1895–1896. In 1896 the *Revue des arts décoratifs* noted Bourgeois's presence at a banquet whose theme was the dissemination of art to the people.[18] Bourgeois's keynote address suggested adapting the message of William Morris to France. Morris's writings had entered France beginning in 1892, when translations of his work appeared in the anarchist journal *Les Temps nouveaux.*[19] The syndicalist radical Fernand Pelloutier publicized Morris's revolutionary message in his articles on labor in the 1894 *Société nouvelle.*[20] Official circles also invoked Morris in the 1890s, though with emphases different from those of their left-wing counterparts. In 1896, for example, the Chamber of Deputies debated the adoption of Morris's craft principles to foster local associations of artisans devoted to the preservation of indigenous traditions.[21] Léon Bourgeois's interpretation of Morris, like that of his official colleagues, was highly selective; it omitted the critical and radical meaning. Morris's theory was based on the indictment of the market system and the return of art to the people when capitalism was overthrown. Léon Bourgeois refracted Morris through the prism of antisocialist solidarism, using Morris's writings to bolster the solidarist ideals of duty, cooperation, and community interdependence under capitalism:

> M. Léon Bourgeois commented in a very felicitous manner on the slogan of William Morris: "Art by and for the people": "The artist who works only for himself will not go very far. He must draw continually on the underlying sources that nourish the soul of an entire people. And, just as the artist will soon lose his creative spark if he does not renew himself in the communal fount, so too he will be remiss in his duty if he does not offer his share to the whole community."[22]

Morris had concentrated his analysis on workers and the work process, exposing the separation of artists from society as an unnatural phenomenon, a particular manifestation of the general problem of the division of labor under industrial and com-

mercial capitalism. Revolutionary change would transform work into an act of pleasure and all workers into artists. Léon Bourgeois's transmutation of Morris stressed
the correct role of the artist—by definition different from other people—in the
existing system. The artist could heal the split between self and others by internaliz-
ing the ideology of debt, duty, and solidarity. Continual contact with "communal
sources" would discharge the debt to society while this duty to the whole would
enliven the artist's creative spirit.

Other political leaders affiliated with the Central Union of the Decorative Arts
were Paul Doumer and Réné Waldeck-Rousseau. Doumer, minister of finance in the
1895 solidarist cabinet of Léon Bourgeois, drew public attention to the metal-art
crafts by proposing a new coinage, which I will analyze in detail in a later chapter.
Waldeck-Rousseau, who returned to the Chamber in 1895 after a six-year absence,
began serving in 1894 as a lawyer on the Central Union's judicial council.[23] Waldeck-
Rousseau's services were enlisted for the Central Union of the Decorative Arts by his
wife, the stepdaughter of Doctor Jean-Martin Charcot, who was an active member
of the Central Union's women's committee. The luxury crafts promoted by the Central Union were compatible with Réné Waldeck-Rousseau's own political inclination
toward associations of small producers; Waldeck-Rousseau himself forged new links
with the artisan sector.[24]

The official coalition for the arts and crafts encompassed not only the political
elite of the 1890s but also important figures in museum administration, the beaux-
arts bureaucracy, and art criticism and education. The continuum between the institutions of official culture, the Central Union of the Decorative Arts, and the ideology of eighteenth-century grace and nineteenth-century craft renewal was evident
in a single figure, Roger Marx. He played a pivotal role in the official movement to
revitalize the arts and crafts in the 1890s, becoming affiliated with the Central Union
while holding influential positions in cultural administration. As secretary to the director of the beaux-arts between 1883 and 1888 and then as inspector general of provincial museums after 1889, Roger Marx was a well-placed and effective promoter of
the decorative arts.[25] A devoted follower of the Goncourts, he was immersed in the
newly recovered tradition of the eighteenth-century unity of the arts. He lamented
the erosion of an enlightened aristocratic patronage that had yielded what he called
the "intimate dwellings" and "pleasure houses" of the rococo period.[26] As a bureaucrat and art critic, Roger Marx urged the state to sponsor the regeneration of the arts
and crafts. His conception of modernism was based on the same interplay of change
and continuity articulated by Raymond Poincaré. Repudiating ostentatious "false
luxury" and inchoate eclecticism, he lobbied in the 1890s within the administration
of the beaux-arts for Daumier's position of the 1840s—"Il faut être de son temps"
("Let us be of our own time").[27] Yet Roger Marx's progressive aestheticism denied
any bold rupture with the past and rested on a vitalist affirmation of French "genius"
and "temperament." The forms of a style in accord with contemporaneity were to
be national and particularistic, embodying new variations on the distinctively French
theme of "elegance" and "seduction."[28]

Roger Marx was joined in the Central Union by Gustave Larroumet, who also carried the ideals of integrating art and craft into an official cultural center: the Sorbonne. Larroumet played a central role in rehabilitating the arts of the mid-eighteenth century, offering the first literature course at the Sorbonne devoted entirely to the eighteenth century and publishing the first book on the literary "modernist" of the rococo period, Marivaux.[29] From the podium at the Sorbonne, Larroumet celebrated the special character of rococo intimacy and identified the shift from the solemn grandeur of Louis XIV to the supple grace of Louis XV. In this shift he found reason to hope for "the emergence of elegance as a French quality par excellence."[30]

Larroumet combined teaching at the Sorbonne with lecturing and writing for the Central Union of the Decorative Arts, where his activities included reconstituting the eighteenth-century *style moderne* and defining a nineteenth-century art nouveau. At evening lectures, Larroumet introduced members of the union's women's committee to the stylistic and cultural characteristics of the music, literature, and decorative arts of the mid-eighteenth century.[31] At the same time, he publicized the demand for a new style, liberated from moribund historicism and in accord with the needs of a new era. To reject routinized eclecticism did not mean to repudiate French history and tradition. What Larroumet called the "solidarity between generations" lay at the center of the craft regeneration sponsored by the Central Union.[32] The late nineteenth century would discover new forms for expressing elemental French elegance, forms that balanced invigorating change and national continuity. Larroumet gave particular emphasis to the bonds between the eighteenth and nineteenth centuries:

> If the nineteenth century is great, it is because all of the elements of its greatness were prepared in the eighteenth century. . . . To wish to break suddenly from the past is not only the most dangerous but also the most vain of chimeras. . . . National tradition forms the conscience of a people and its collective personality across the ages. . . . To be sure, every generation has the right to define itself and to reject a servile tutelage that would sacrifice the rights of the present to those of the past. But its own identity would be compromised . . . if each generation did not press the past into the service of the present.[33]

*

Thus in the 1890s a network of important individuals coalesced, affiliated with both the Central Union and the official centers of cultural and political administration. This amalgamated official coalition was described by its members as "the elite of intellectual and patriotic France" and "at the same time official and lovers of the arts."[34] Among them were the art critic, collector, and educator Louis de Boussès de Fourcaud, who was Taine's successor as professor of the history and philosophy of art at the Ecole des Beaux-Arts; the Louvre curators and art history scholars Gaston Migeon, Emile Molinier, André Michel, and Louis Curajod; the curator of the Garde-Meuble National, E. Williamson; scholars of the history of art and connoisseurship Paul Mantz, Charles Ephrussi, the baron Roger Portalis, Léon Deshairs, and Alfred de Champeaux, also an undersecretary in the beaux-arts; inspector of beaux-arts and writer Henry Havard; and director of the Ecole des Beaux-Arts, Eugène Guillaume.

All of these figures participated in the Central Union, appeared in its journal, the *Revue des arts décoratifs,* were consulting members of union committees for exhibitions and craft programs, and played central roles at the 1894 Congress of the Decorative Arts.[35] At the same time, each one had a particular association with the institutionalization of the rococo revival. The Louvre curators Migeon, Molinier, and Michel were scholars of eighteenth-century decorative arts, and together they were responsible for the first museum assemblage of rococo objets d'art and furniture. Migeon was himself a direct descendant of the personal cabinetmaker to Madame de Pompadour, Pierre Migeon.[36] André Michel wrote one of the first scholarly monographs on François Boucher, whom he celebrated as an "artist of the race," who encapsulated the elegance and grace of the epoch of Louis XV.[37] Michel also initiated a lavish journal, *Les Arts: Revue mensuelle des musées, collections, expositions.* The unity of all the arts—conceived as the luxurious accoutrements of pre-Revolutionary France—assumed pride of place in the magazine, which also celebrated the central role of the *amateur* as the guardian of the French patrimony.[38] Finally, Henry Havard, scholar and inspector of beaux-arts, was a publicist of the long French tradition of craft unity and the special role played by the eighteenth-century nobility in the golden age of interior design and applied arts. Among Havard's many books was *L'Art dans la maison,* first published in 1884. In 1891, the government adopted this book, a cross between a manual for interior decoration and a history of French aristocratic ensembles, as the official decorative handbook for the Third Republic: it was chosen as the one book on the decorative arts to be included in all teacher-training centers, the normal schools.[39]

The well-placed political and cultural officials of the Third Republic in the 1890s attached themselves to the existing core of *amateurs*-collectors and luxury artisans already assembled in the Central Union of the Decorative Arts. The union's administrative council in the 1890s included Gustave Dreyfus, Jules Maciet, Charles Ephrussi, Paul Mantz, the comte de Ganay, Henri Béraldi, the marquis de Biancourt, the baron Gustave de Rothschild, and T. Schlumberger.[40] The luxury artisans who regularly wrote for the journal included Lucien Falize, who crafted works in gold and silver, and Emile Gallé, who produced work in glass and ceramics.

In the 1890s the craft coalition formulated a program that was both restorative and modernist. Its dual aim was to reassemble and publicly display rococo ensembles and to find a craft modern style that would temper formal change with national continuity, uniting naturism and nationalism.

The chapters that follow discuss the official rehabilitation of rococo monuments pursued by the Third Republic in collaboration with the Central Union and then turn to the programs of craft modernism pursued simultaneously by the state and the Central Union of the Decorative Arts, efforts that converged in the reform of the Salon in 1891.

CHAPTER EIGHT

The Third Republic
and the Rococo as National Patrimony

THE THIRD REPUBLIC undertook an important series of eighteenth-century restoration projects after 1889, including renovations of the châteaux at Versailles and Chantilly, the reconstruction of the original rococo core of the National Library in Paris, and the establishment of permanent displays of eighteenth-century furniture and applied arts in the Louvre. These projects marked the first official celebration of pre-Revolutionary aristocratic culture by a Republican government. Taken together, this series of institutional restorations represented the entry of the rococo unified arts into the national heritage, the French *patrimoine*.

Unlike their official predecessors of the Second Empire, for whom the eighteenth century provided a glittering backdrop for an exclusive court coterie, the Third Republic institutionalized the rococo, making it a legitimate part of the national cultural trust. In the 1890s the elite recovered the arts of the mid-eighteenth century from the arriviste pleasure-seekers surrounding Napoléon III and installed these arts in national museums and monuments. The rococo reconstitutions of the 1890s were made possible by the scholarly archaeology of the eighteenth-century applied arts, initiated by the Goncourts and extended during the late 1870s and 1880s by the erudite members of the Central Union of the Decorative Arts.

Although it is difficult to account fully for the voluminous literature on the mid-eighteenth century, it is clear that the number of books increased dramatically during the last two decades of the nineteenth century. The registry of books deposited at the National Library between 1865 and 1882, for example, includes thirty books on the Louis of the Old Regime. Between 1882 and 1894, the number of books under the broad rubrics Louis XIV, Louis XV, and Louis XVI increased to 112. Between 1894 and 1925, the number jumped to 245, of which 207 were published between 1894 and 1909.[1]

More important than a rough count of book titles, however, is the profusion of scholarly writing on the arts of the eighteenth century after 1880. The writers of the articles and books on the painting, applied arts, and sculpture of the eighteenth century belonged to a tightly knit group, many of whose members were attached simultaneously to the Central Union and to the state arts administration or a museum

staff. Among this group was the beaux-arts administrator and Central Union affiliate Paul Mantz. Another scholar contributing to the erudite and technical knowledge
of eighteenth-century arts was Samuel Rocheblave, friend and colleague of the Sorbonne professor Louis de Fourcaud, who published books on the eighteenth-century
amateur-collector-engraver the comte de Caylus (1889) and on the brothers Cochin
(1893).[2] In 1880 the baron Roger Portalis, a wealthy collector and art historian, began a series of books entitled *Les Graveurs du XVIIIe siècle*. Eventually filling five
volumes, Portalis's work constituted the first *catalogues raisonnés* of eighteenth-
century engravers. A member of the Central Union, Portalis defined his scholarly
efforts as the attempt of a new generation to render homage to the eighteenth century, whose multiple arts were worthy contributors to "the glory of French art."[3]

Indispensable to the reconstruction of rococo monuments executed during the
1890s were a series of newly available folio volumes reproducing the drawings,
plans, and tools of the eighteenth-century rococo decorators. In 1881–1882, for example, Désiré Guilmard, an *haut luxe* designer, compiled a two-volume work, *Les
Maîtres ornemanistes,* an extensively illustrated visual history of the interior ensembles
fashioned under Louis XIV, Louis XV, and Louis XVI.[4] The rococo masters Pineau,
Oppenordt, and Meissonnier were heavily represented, and archival documents explaining their working methods and patrons were recorded with Guilmard's commentaries. Guilmard's lavish craft manuals were followed by two other folio collections of rococo masters. Nicolas Pineau, the designer of ornamentation credited,
along with Meissonnier, with originating the eighteenth-century organic *style moderne,* was the subject of scholarly study; his collected drawings were published in
1889 in a Rouvèyre art folio in the series Library of Fine Arts Applied to Industry.[5]
This volume included reproductions of Pineau's own sketches for the tables, vases,
consoles, medals, and wood engravings executed while Pineau was "sculptor and
engraver of the Regent." Also represented were Pineau's extensive commissions for
the Russian monarch Peter the Great. The 1889 volume was soon complemented by
a voluminous scholarly work on Pineau by Th. Biais, a member of the Central
Union of the Decorative Arts. Biais's book, published in 1892, enumerated many of
Pineau's works in private collections in France and Russia that had hitherto been considered lost.[6] In 1898, Léon Deshairs, the curator of the Library of the Decorative
Arts, began compiling another folio collection of Pineau's oeuvre, for which he relied heavily upon Biais's scholarship, classification, and research into provenance.[7]
Deshairs's work extended the eighteenth-century collection of the union's library,
whose acquisitions, donations, and holdings favored the eighteenth-century artists
and designers of ornaments above all others.[8]

One of the scholarly propagators of the arts of the eighteenth century, Pierre de
Nolhac, received official recognition in 1892. Born in 1859, de Nolhac had been
trained as a historian and classical philologist, and he was appointed to the archival
staff at the National Library in 1886. His early writings had dealt with the Renaissance humanists, including Joachim du Bellay, whose letters he published in 1886,
and Fulvio Orsini, whose library he catalogued, with commentary, in 1887. By

1890, however, the subject of de Nolhac's erudition had changed; he devoted himself to the arts and the royal women of the reigns of Louis XV and Louis XVI. In 1890 he published a lavishly illustrated monograph *La Reine Marie-Antoinette*.[9] Not only was the book one of the first scholarly biographies of the queen, but it also contained a series of portraits and engravings of her, reproduced for the first time. Photoengravings at the back of de Nolhac's work also depicted the furniture and woodwork in the queen's private apartments. The publisher's announcement praised de Nolhac's work for skillfully evoking the tone of a society of pleasure and sophistication; the book was "amusing, feminine, and true history":

> The book we are editing, composed by a historian, is written by an artist. M. de Nolhac . . . evokes the phantoms of vanished queens. His book is neither pamphlet nor apologia, but it is tender, crying for royal miseries, relishing its pleasures, glorying in its parties, laughing at its anecdotes. . . . Nothing has been neglected to turn this book into a true monument to honor Marie-Antoinette.[10]

In 1892 Pierre de Nolhac was appointed chief curator at the new National Museum of Versailles. The palace at Versailles had only recently attained the status of cultural monument. Between 1871 and 1879, Versailles was the political seat of the new French Republic, which protected itself from the aftershock of the Commune by governing away from Paris. Eugène Spuller, the spokesman for the *ralliement,* had lobbied since 1887 for the preservation of the palace and for public access to Versailles as a state museum. This plan was finally realized with the assignment of de Nolhac as official curator.[11]

De Nolhac used his new position to continue his research and writing on the artistic and cultural dimensions of the last half of the eighteenth century. Between 1895 and 1898 he published inventories and histories of the private apartments inserted into the Versailles palace after 1720, the "intimate chambers" of Louis XV and his mistresses, the apartments of Madame Du Barry and of the Dauphin. Initially written as a series for the *Gazette des beaux-arts,* these articles were expanded into a multi-volume work, *Le Château de Versailles sous Louis XV* and the *Histoire du Château de Versailles* (1898–1899). These works contained exhaustive object-by-object discussion, with information on the artisans responsible for coordinating the private royal apartments.

Remaining devoted to the women of the mid-eighteenth century as official curator, de Nolhac compiled an extravagant limited edition called *Les Femmes de Versailles* (1901). The folio volume, which sold for one thousand francs, comprised a running portrait gallery of the women who had graced the palace during the eighteenth century. Most of the portraits were reproductions of those in the vast collections of Versailles, never before seen by the public. They testified to the grace and refinement with which France had been endowed when she had "ruled all Europe." Following the suggestive visual history propounded by the Goncourts, de Nolhac's scholarship relied on pictorial representation to evoke "the quality of life" printed sources could not evoke:

> For those who do not look at history as a chronological manual where dates
> follow names of kings one by one; for those who do not concern themselves
> solely with political matters and with war; . . . for those who research above
> all . . . the stages of civilization, the forms of society, the power of women—
> . . . for all of you this study is intended, a charming study visualizing each
> period. Through this study of painted or sculpted works a history that has thus
> far been confused and intangible will emerge from the mist, define itself into
> human beings, assume the contours of the visible signs of the passions, virtues,
> habits, and customs of an age. The women of Versailles—therein lies the soul
> of France during the times of our true sovereignty over the world. Over this
> society ruled, not the Christian kings, but women. . . . They are all beauty
> and grace.[12]

Organizing Versailles into a national monument presided over by a scholarly ele-gist of eighteenth-century women was only one of several ways in which the Third Republic institutionalized its celebration of the eighteenth century. In 1890 the two chambers of government passed a new budget for the beaux-arts, tripling the amount of money allocated twenty years earlier.[13] Among the beneficiaries of the funds was the château at Chantilly, which became a public museum in 1897. The financial and restorative measures necessary for the château's entry into the national patrimony were jointly executed by the Institut de France and the château's owner, the duc d'Aumale.[14]

During the eighteenth century Chantilly had been a nucleus of rococo architecture and interior design. Louis-Henri, prince de Condé (1692–1740), had reconstructed the domain around four masterworks of the rococo *goût nouveau*. He installed a series of elegant private apartments in the *petit château*, featuring wall-painted pas-torales and matching furnishings by Huet and Leprince; he established a porcelain manufacture at Chantilly whose delicate *pâte tendre* objects were soon emulated by Madame de Pompadour at her new Sèvres manufacture; he commissioned the archi-tect Jean Aubert to build the *grandes écuries*, completed in 1753. The stables' interior grotto-works and animated exterior stonework epitomized the tumultuous asym-metry of the *style pittoresque*. Finally, the prince constructed at Chantilly the *cabinet des singeries*. The tiny room's walls, ceilings, and doors were covered with twisting gilded vines and plants, and delicately painted panels depicted monkeys, maidens, and children frolicking in an imaginary Chinese *fête galante*. These efforts by the prince helped to make Chantilly a central monument of the eighteenth-century *style nature*, rivaled in its time only by the Hôtel de Soubise-Rohan and by the additions to Versailles under Louis XV.[15]

After being partially destroyed during the French Revolution, the château at Chantilly languished until it was returned to its original owners, the Bourbons-

Condé, after 1815. The property was transferred by the second duc de Bourbon to his godson, Henri d'Orléans, the duc d'Aumale (1822–1897), fourth son of Louis-Philippe.[16] A former governor-general of French colonial Africa, Henri d'Orléans engaged in an extensive refurbishing of Chantilly between 1872 and 1884. His deep involvement in artistic and architectural projects won him election to the French Academy in 1873 and to the Academy of Beaux-Arts in 1880.[17] Despite such acclaim, the duc d'Aumale was dissatisfied with a republican France and in 1884 joined a plot by royalist princes to overthrow the Ferry government. He was subsequently stripped of his generalship and banished in 1886. In 1889 he was allowed to return to France, his political exile revoked by his payment of a cultural ransom: he donated the domain of Chantilly to the Institut de France.[18] Pledging himself to cultural preservation rather than political subversion, the duc was welcomed back by a government in the process of fashioning a new program of artistic consolidation. In his written statement to the Institut de France, still inscribed today on the doors of the main hall of the *grand château,* the duc proclaimed the durability of aristocratic cultural contributions over the vicissitudes of politics:

> I want to conserve for France the domain of Chantilly integrally, with its woodworks, its lawns, its waters, its edifices and all that is in them, that is, trophies, paintings, books, art objects, the entire ensemble that constitutes a varied and complete monument to French art in all its forms and to the history of my country's glorious epochs. I resolved to entrust the estate to an illustrious body of people who have honored me with the call to join their ranks. Though they cannot escape the inevitable transformations of society, they are free of the spirit of factionalism and of sudden upheavals and preserve their independence in the midst of political fluctuations.[19]

The duc d'Aumale's celebration of the binding power of art above political upheaval extended to his own sponsorship of a variety of contemporary artists at Chantilly. Between 1872 and 1884, and then after his return to France in 1889, the duc d'Aumale played a pivotal role in revitalizing the arts and crafts. Chantilly was not only a center of the newly recovered rococo decorative style but also a focus for late nineteenth-century luxury craftsmen, from metal workers to wood sculptors. In 1884 the brothers Moreau completed a magnificent iron ramp for a new circular stairway inserted into the hall of the *grand château.* At the Paris Exhibition of 1889, Roger Marx cited this ramp as an example of the excellence French artisans could achieve if they were given proper commissions and support.[20]

The duc d'Aumale not only commissioned *haut luxe* craft teams but presided over a salon where many of the active participants in the movement for an artistic artisanate appeared. The duc held his literary and artistic gatherings in one of the chambers in the *petit château,* the Hunt Gallery. Here he welcomed such artists as the glassmaker Emile Gallé and the sculptor Auguste Rodin. The comte Robert de Montesquiou-Fezensac, a friend and admirer of the duc's, was responsible for inviting both Gallé and Rodin.[21] These artists and others toured the château with their host and were

able to see paintings by the newly rediscovered "lesser masters" of the period of
Louis XV: Lancret, Drouais, Van Loo, Watteau, Gillot, and Saint-Aubain. Among
the portraits in the collection were Drouais's 1764 representation of a smiling Madame
de Pompadour at her glistening ebony and onyx embroidery frame and Rigaud's
official portrait of Louis XV.[22] Beneath these paintings in the painting gallery at
Chantilly were low rows of bookcases. Here the duc d'Aumale displayed both his
erudition and his association with the craft movement launched by the Central
Union of the Decorative Arts and the Third Republic. The duc served on Central
Union consulting committees for decorative art exhibitions. The books in his library featured all of the primary scholarly representatives of the rococo revival,
many of them affiliates of both the Central Union and the institutions of cultural
administration.[23] Thus the Chantilly château joined the masterworks of the rococo
arts to the intellectual celebrators of luxury art-craft integration of the late nineteenth
century.

That the Third Republic embraced Chantilly and its former master typified the
political and cultural reorientations of the decade of *ralliement*. If the Ferry republicans banished the Orléanist heir and removed him from the army and the country as
a monarchist conspirator, the "new generation" of *progressiste* republicans glorified the duc as a cultural leader. Befitting a political program of reconciliation with
the Republic's former royalist and religious enemies, the reinstatement of the duc
d'Aumale extended the *ralliement* to culture. The *progressiste* republicans launched the
1890s with a political program composed of essentially unpolitical ingredients—
the effort to end divisiveness by propagating a solidifying *esprit nouveau*. The duc
d'Aumale had expressed the same ideals in a different context: he offered Chantilly as
an exemplar of the power of art to transcend political dissension by its binding, unifying character. The goals of the new republicanism and the Orléanist heir converged after 1889.

In addition to government subsidies for the refurbishing and public display of two
Old Regime châteaux, two Parisian projects received official sponsorship: the restoration of the eighteenth-century interiors and facades of the National Library and the
preparation of a separate wing of the Louvre for the furniture and decorative arts
from the era of the three Louis.

The National Library had become famous for the vast iron and glass reading
room designed by the architect Henri Labrouste and executed in the 1860s. Labrouste
inserted his huge sunlit structure into an existing core of buildings that had comprised the library since the seventeenth century, when it was known as the Library of
the King. Labrouste built his massive reading room as an extension of one wing of
an existing structure, providing seating space for eight hundred readers and shelf
space for thousands of books.[24]

The use of wrought iron made possible both the scale and lighting of Labrouste's
hall. Iron not only provided the skeletal structure of the building but also visibly
supported the body of the hall in its center by multiple piers. Although both the cupo-
lated skylights and the painted embellishment of the wrought-iron poles adapted the

new materials to traditional idioms, Labrouste's reading room was perceived as a major technical breakthrough and a cultural revolution. For the first time a cultural monument of Paris was constructed of iron and glass, which were exploited to span vast open spaces while ensuring light and safety.[25]

Beginning in 1890 the National Library again became a site of major reconstruction. This time the building program called not for adding new public spaces but for restoring existing apartments. Labrouste's project had left the adjoining buildings— a cluster of interlinked *hôtels* from the seventeenth and eighteenth centuries—in disarray. These various *hôtels* had originally been unified into a single suite of interior ensembles and exterior facades by the architect Robert de Cotte, commissioned by King Louis XV in the 1730s. In the 1860s Labrouste dismantled the gilded woodwork and removed the delicate painted panels from the walls of the eighteenth-century chambers. In the 1890s the Third Republic commissioned the architect A. Pascal to reconstitute these rococo ensembles.

Leaving Labrouste's reading room intact, Pascal focused on four suites originally of rococo design and their accompanying courtyard facades—the Manuscript Room, the Vestibule of Honor, the Office of the Administrator-General, and the Medals Chamber. Emulating Robert de Cotte before him, Pascal considered all elements of the decor as integral parts of the ensemble and spent long hours studying the woodwork, cornices, iron grills, and furniture that had harmonized the eighteenth-century chambers. His researches were facilitated by new documents on the eighteenth-century *goût moderne* rediscovered by the Goncourts and consolidated by the scholars and publicists associated with the Central Union of the Decorative Arts. In the 1880s, for example, Alfred de Champeaux assembled archival sources describing the consoles and vases installed by de Cotte in the Medals Chamber.[26] A second union figure, Germain Bapst, assembled manuscripts delineating the daily work schedules and design processes of the royal carpenters who originally constructed the rococo furniture for the Library of the King, recovering intricate descriptions of the sculpted wood cases for medals.[27]

Pascal was thus able to reconstitute with painstaking accuracy the eighteenth-century splendor of the library chambers. Teams of artisans were hired to regild the exfoliating table legs, door handles, and picture frames. Wood sculptors cleaned and retouched the serpentine woodwork on the wall and door panels of the four rooms. Bands along the ceilings were repainted and the flamelike pattern of trellises and vines exposed. The artisans in all the different media worked arduously to bring to view at every turn—in cornices, door panels, table supports, and iron ramps—a glistening emblem; the serpentine interlacing L's of the royal insignia. Erudite restoration by the Third Republic architect concretized the aristocratic imprint on cultural style.

After 1890 a visitor to the Medals Chamber would find an elegant room whose walls, painted green, were ornamented with gilded woodwork (Pl. 2). Around the room ran a stucco band, with vines that formed interlocking L's at the ceiling cornices. Pascal reinstalled the two royal portraits that had originally hung at either end of the room: Louis XIV at the east end, and Louis XV at the west. Each painting was

framed in gilded wood representing vines, roses, and rockwork. A winged cartouche above each painting contained a lacy crown and a shell emblazoned with
three fleurs-de-lis. Pascal reattached the Boucher and Natoire panels above the doors
and along the walls; their painted shells, ribbons, and vines echoed the shapes en-
livening other parts of the room. The eighteenth-century leather-embossed cabinets
for medals were freshly sewn and polished, their legs elaborately sculpted with fanning shells, interlacing L's, and roses (Pl. 3).

The Manuscript Room adjacent to the Medals Chamber also reemerged in the
1890s as a masterpiece of the rococo ensemble. All the elements of the Manuscript
Room—furniture, bookcases, overdoors, ceilings, and panels—composed a single
fluid line and drew upon a single repertoire of organic forms. The ensemble character of the room derived largely from the floor-to-ceiling bookcases: books were set
into rich mahogany shelves running the length of the room, forming a wall of brightly
colored leather bindings. An iron ladder rolled along the bookcases, each of its ends
molded into delicately curving scrolls. The room was further unified by the special
stairwells for entry and exit, each one encased in a swooping curve of wood that
followed the curve of the stairs (Fig. 33). The elegant casings resembled conches,
thus matching the shell forms incised into the wood itself. The furniture was graceful, its shapes echoing the sinuous architectural elements of the Manuscript Room as
a whole. Elongated mahogany consoles, embossed with leather, filled the room.
The legs of both consoles and chairs tapered to a delicate flourish of roses and shells.
Even the bookrests for the folios replicated the gracious curving lines. A diminutive
shell on each end offered a miniature variant on the chamber's rococo theme.

Pascal renovated other rococo chambers of the National Library as well. A visitor
entering the main halls of the library who turned left instead of right into the iron
and glass reading room of Labrouste would be guided through a succession of wood-
paneled corridors to two majestic locked doors. Behind these were two suites reserved for private meetings. Visitors admitted into the first chamber beheld the Vestibule of Honor of Louis XV, designed by de Cotte for the reception of privileged
guests and glowingly restored by Pascal. In the vestibule Pascal reassembled and reattached the Boucher and Natoire overdoors, the ceiling cartouches with the royal
L's clearly marked, and the elegant furnishings of the rococo ensemble (Pl. 4). The
doors of the Vestibule of Honor opened into a small splendid chamber reserved as
the private office of the director of the library, the administrator-general. Pascal
reconstituted the diminutive room, originally created by de Cotte for the king's
archivist, the abbé Brignon, for the Third Republic officer, using spatial devices
similar to those unifying the Manuscript Room immediately above it. Like the
Manuscript Room, the office had floor-to-ceiling bookcases, with wooden sculpted
cartouches of shells, fleurs-de-lis, and interlocking L's on the panels between them.
The cornices repeated in stucco the same interlacing L's and flamelike winding leaves.
A sumptuous armoire with an inlaid marble top was set into one wall of the room. A
clock hung above the mantle, its porcelain and gold case twisted into asymmetrical
vine and shell forms. In the small sumptuous room was a set of matching chairs and

Fig. 33. Manuscript Room, restored stairwell, Bibliothèque Nationale, Paris. From *Revue des arts décoratifs,* 1892.

tables with curving slender legs. On the back of each chair were a shell and a rose like those on the chairs in the Manuscript Room. A desk was modeled on the one originally created for the abbé Brignon. A replica of the elegant desk once used by the royal servant was thus provided for his republican descendant.[28]

The official restorers of the National Library in the 1890s celebrated the eighteenth-century heritage of the building and criticized Labrouste's reading room. Its "destructive" "pseudo-Greek orderliness" reminded them of the ruthless David; in dismantling the library's rococo elements, Labrouste engaged in "acts of vandalism."[29] Members of the Central Union welcomed the reappearance of the eighteenth-century library as the triumph of the "palace" over "a railroad shed."[30] Henri Bouchot, an eighteenth-century scholar writing in the *Revue des arts décoratifs*, contrasted the social and historical worlds represented by the Labrouste and Pascal parts of the library: "These eighteenth-century works . . . saved from disaster . . . are linked to the heavy and harsh building on the rue Richelieu. . . . They are to Labrouste's art what a powdered marquise of Moreau le Jeune looks like to a parvenue bourgeoise."[31]

The difference between the architecture of palace and shed was the difference between anonymity and individuation. The Labrouste addition of the 1860s, Bouchot argued, typified the technological process of building and design: prefabrication, rationalized planning, and the on-site assemblage of a structure whose details had been orchestrated at the office of the technical designer. In constructing the palatial eighteenth-century chambers, the contribution of every artisan at the site was essential; the division between designer and executant was less visible. Restoration reinstated both the eighteenth-century lineaments and the status of the artisan who did the work. In contrast to the reliance on a single mind, capable of rationalized planning and technical wizardry, the eighteenth-century chambers relied on the collaborative effort of many skilled and creative craftsmen. Labrouste made his monumental shed according to fastidious calculations of the stresses of iron and glass; de Cotte's palatial wings were restored through painstaking attentiveness to the decorative malleability of woods, stuccos, and iron ramps. On-the-spot handiwork by teams of artisans consolidated a single organic whole; prefabrication divested workers of both individual and collaborative creativity. Bouchot concluded that "the work of rebuilding done by M. Pascal constitutes a more serious expenditure of means and of wills than the construction of a monument completed in the silence of an office and built according to a calculated plan."[32]

Although Labrouste's reading room represented a bold technical innovation, it was in fact decorated by artisans working, though in a larger setting, like the craft teams hired by Pascal for the eighteenth-century renovations. Bouchot's misrepresentation of Labrouste was significant and derived from his retrospective evaluation of the iron and glass reading room in relation to the Eiffel Tower. The characteristics of the wrought-iron monument of 1889 resonated in Bouchot's contrast of the two parts of the library in 1891. Intricately planned by an engineer "in the silence of an office" and riveted at the site, the iron colossus was the absent presence in Bouchot's analysis. The antinomies Bouchot used to distinguish the architecture of Labrouste from that of de Cotte—railroad shed and palace, "powdered marquise" and "parvenue bourgeoise"—replicated in the library context the larger debate on the encroachment of iron technology on the heart of Paris in 1889. To Bouchot, the reconstitution of de Cotte's intimate rooms signaled the victory of gracious handiwork and aristocratic history over the prefabricated technics and unanchored industrial world prefigured in Labrouste's iron and glass shed.[33]

The official rococo restoration in the National Library was one of a series of symbolic dismantlings in the 1890s of the world represented by the Eiffel Tower. Pascal's reconstructions juxtaposed strikingly with the Labrouste sections. The two kinds of architecture, cemented uneasily together without mediation, concretized two social worlds, one of which the republicans of the 1890s promoted over the other. The outer courtyard of the library displayed the spatial and social division repeated within. The facade of the left side of the courtyard, behind which lay the Vestibule of Honor and the Office of the Administrator-General, comprised a decorative program typifying the eighteenth-century picturesque—masks of smiling female faces; cartouches cascading with ribbon, roses, and rockwork; and banners of wheat and pastoral elements. The facade on the right side of the courtyard, with the main entrance to Labrouste's reading room, was a somber unarticulated facade, marked by masks of expressionless men atop stringently classical columns. The contrast outside only intensified inside. The Labrouste reading room of iron and glass formed the public arena of the library. The eighteenth-century chambers reassembled by Pascal encompassed the private areas of the library, the spaces reserved for special guests, administrative power, and precious collections of medals and manuscripts. The Labrouste wing revealed the new materials and new structures of nascent technological strength; the Pascal wing celebrated the glorious traditions of cultural refinement.

By reasserting the architecture of de Cotte in the context of Labrouste, the Third Republic testified to the dual strands of both the French economy and French society. The Labrouste wing was left standing, a monumental reminder of new industrial growth. The Pascal wings signaled a redirection of the French Republic to the crafts, a repudiation of the promises of technology initiated by Labrouste and culminating in the Eiffel Tower. The rococo reassemblage of the 1890s solidified in stone the politics of *ralliement;* the realignment of old noble elites and republicans in the Chambers shifted to the domain of culture. The enlightenment liberals of the 1880s had projected in engineered iron an "arch of triumph to science and industry."[34] The *progressiste* republicans of the 1890s subsidized in crafted woodwork the evocations of pergola *folies* in royal cabinets. The artisanship of pre-Revolutionary aristocratic dalliance triumphantly entered the Parisian architectural patrimony.

*

Not far from the Opéra *quartier* where the eighteenth century reappeared in the National Library, the Louvre museum complex was also undergoing a rococo renovation. Long a treasure house for painting and sculpture, the Louvre was reformed by official decree to house the abundant riches of arts and crafts as objects for public veneration. Harking back to the continuum of fine and applied arts under the French kings, the Third Republic reassembled the furniture, overdoors, woodwork, porcelains, silverware, jewelry, and tapestries that once constituted the royal collections, adding these elements to new galleries of the Louvre: precious gems, silverware, and some faience were displayed in the galleries of the new Department of Art Objects, founded in 1894;[35] furniture, ceramics, tapestries, and painted wall panels from the eighteenth century were reassembled as a succession of rooms, christened in 1901 the Museum of French Furniture.[36]

The reentry of the applied arts into the Louvre resulted from a new budget program of the Third Republic after 1889. Beginning in 1890, the monies allotted to the Louvre almost tripled, increasing from 160,000 francs to 400,000 francs.[37] A new institutional arrangement governed the flow of these funds: in 1890 the Louvre was recognized as a separate "civil personality," a separate national trust, with its own museum treasury. Before, the Louvre had shared with the many other national museums a single allocation. With this new financial organization, the Louvre expanded, and most of the new funds were funneled directly into the decorative arts—acquisitions for the Department of Art Objects and the reconstitution of ensembles for the Museum of French Furniture.[38]

This glorification of rococo arts in the Louvre was not completely unprecedented. The revival of the art of the *fêtes galantes* had proceeded in successive waves in nineteenth-century France, fostered by both official and literary circles. These various groups adapted the eighteenth century to distinctive needs and goals, ranging from the anti-imperial restoration of Louis XVIII to the antibourgeois aestheticism of Théophile Gautier. The enthusiasm of Napoléon III and Empress Eugénie for the rococo left its mark on the Louvre. During the 1860s the first donations of eighteenth-century paintings were accepted and given ample space in galleries hitherto reserved for monumental classical and historical works. The donations of La Caze and Walferdin, together the greatest nineteenth-century collectors of the eighteenth century, enabled the Louvre to install a separate gallery for the painters of the *fêtes galantes*. Fragonard, Boucher, Watteau, Lancret, and Van Loo were particularly well represented.[39]

Nevertheless, institutionalization of the rococo arts by the Third Republic differed from the arrival of rococo painting at the Louvre during the Second Empire. The Second Empire continued to separate painting from the other arts, accepting the decorative panels of Boucher and Fragonard as entries in the galleries of the beaux-arts of painting.[40] The program of the Third Republic restored the images of Fragonard and Boucher to their position as decorative panels in ensembles of interior design. The Museum of French Furniture reunified the fine and applied arts of the eighteenth century in intimate rooms whose furniture and picture frames echoed the shapes and scenes depicted in painted panels. The Third Republic glorified, in an official setting, the decorative arts of the *fêtes galantes* and integrated them into ensembles of private interiors. The "lesser arts" were elevated to center stage in the national trust, identified for the first time as elements of the French patrimony.[41]

The Central Union of the Decorative Arts was a catalyst in the organization of the Museum of French Furniture as a wing of the Louvre. Indeed, the reassemblage of eighteenth-century interiors in the Louvre, exemplifying the unity of art and craft, realized one of the main goals of Central Union affiliates in the 1890s. Before the creation of the museum, furniture and applied arts from the eighteenth century were housed in the dilapidated Garde-Meuble National. During the 1880s scholar-bureaucrats like Alfred de Champeaux, the first librarian of the union, had demanded that the contents of the Garde-Meuble National be transferred to a special museum within the Louvre.[42]

The Garde-Meuble National had originally been constructed by Jacques Gabriel, the architect of Louis XV, under the name Garde-Meuble de la Couronne. From the 1740s until the French Revolution, the Garde-Meuble de la Couronne functioned as a royal storehouse for furnishings and objets d'art. The revolutionary government converted the Garde-Meuble into a national trust, renaming it the Garde-Meuble National. The political radicals of the 1790s were conservative in cultural matters; rather than destroy the royal furniture, they left intact many of the applied arts from the Old Regime. The Garde-Meuble provided a remarkable reservoir of cultural continuity throughout the political vicissitudes of the nineteenth century. Every government, from that of Napoléon I through the bourgeois monarchy and Second Empire, utilized the objects housed in the Garde-Meuble for official furnishings and ceremonial display. Louis Philippe decorated his château with components from the Garde-Meuble, while the Empress Eugénie depleted the sources with her decorations at Malmaison, Saint-Cloud, and the Tuileries palace.[43]

Before the 1890s, the Third Republic, like governments before it, used the Garde-Meuble National as a storehouse for state furnishings and for ceremonies welcoming foreign dignitaries. Beginning in the 1890s, however, pressure mounted within the Central Union to create a permanent home for the furniture of the Old Regime. Scholars and critics like Edmond Bonaffé and Edmond Williamson urged the government to end the ebb and flow of objects, to freeze the contents of the Garde-Meuble and make it a national museum.[44] Some response to this demand was given in the 1882 decree that the Garde-Meuble display part of its holdings in its own museum, though critics noted that the result was poorly publicized, badly lit, and rarely visited by the public.[45] Significantly, before 1890 the Garde-Meuble museum was used most profitably by the Central Union of the Decorative Arts. Williamson, appointed curator of the Garde-Meuble in 1882, worked closely with union members and lent objects from the museum collection for union exhibitions in 1882 and 1884.[46]

Plans to establish a museum of French furniture gained new momentum when the budget of the Louvre was tripled and the Department of Art Objects was created in 1894. The curators of the new department, Gaston Migeon, Emile Molinier, and Carle Dreyfus, were particularly eager to transfer the Garde-Meuble to the Louvre and to reassemble there authentic interior ensembles for the new museum. Each curator had close ties to the Central Union; each was a scholar specializing in pre-Revolutionary arts and crafts.[47] The campaign they undertook together, inextricable from official politics, illuminates the overlap of political and cultural elites in the 1890s. Furthermore, the enlistment of politicians in institutionalizing the Museum of French Furniture exemplifies the power of the cultural patrimony to unify different factions in the governing classes.

The involvement of politicians in creating the Museum of French Furniture grew out of the dispersal of eighteenth-century furniture and applied arts throughout various ministries. The curators Molinier and Migeon conceived of the museum not only as the transfer of the Garde-Meuble to new quarters but as the recuperation of royal treasures housed in other government offices. The Third Republic had inherited and retained decorative objects from the eighteenth century, most of which remained in their original dwellings in the seventh arrondissement. In the nineteenth century, these same *hôtels* were converted into state ministries: the Ministry of Justice, the Ministry of War, the Ministry of the Navy, and parts of the Interior Ministry. Another official institution, the National Archives, was housed in former quarters of aristocratic dalliance in the Marais: the Hôtel de Rohan-Soubise, a paragon of rococo interior design.[48]

Molinier and Migeon were especially determined to rescue elegant eighteenth-century furnishings from the clutches of republican bureaucrats. Their goal was to lift the furnishings of these eighteenth-century *hôtels* out of the realm of utility and into the realm of cultural display. Rather than serve as the desks, wall clocks, and ashtrays of irreverent officials, these applied arts would testify, unsullied, to what Migeon called the exquisite distinction and good taste of pre-Revolutionary craftsmen.[49] Migeon was also perturbed by the carelessness with which these splendid objects had been treated. The Museum of French Furniture would protect precious eighteenth-century furniture from the "negligent" broomsticks of the ministries' janitorial staffs: "Oeben, the great cabinetmaker of Louis XV, made a splendid chest . . . an exquisite model of good taste and distinction. . . . Fortunately, it can be saved from the negligence of the War Ministry's cleaning boys. Their daily sweeping has hardly spared the inlaid work of its feet."[50]

Molinier and Migeon successfully mobilized the political staffs of the ministries to aid them in transferring the remnants of aristocratic habitations to the Louvre. Their main contact and supporter was Henri Roujon (1853–1914), director of the beaux-arts from 1891 and a scholar of seventeenth- and eighteenth-century arts.[51] Molinier worked closely with Roujon to ensure that the ministerial staffs would comply in the donation of furnishings and art objects to the Louvre. One politician who proved especially helpful was Georges Clemenceau, whom Migeon singled out in his celebratory essay:

M. Clemenceau has never ceased to be interested in the salvaging of precious furniture in the ministries. . . . His energetic authority has often contributed

to their quick entry into the Louvre, and now . . . he has had delivered . . . a
beautiful bronze . . . on which is engraved the inventory number of the royal
furniture collection and a charming Louis XVI clock, in white marble and
gilded bronze.[52]

Though Clemenceau is often associated with such avant-garde artists as Monet and
Rodin, he was also devoted to the conservation and display of the cultural riches of
France's aristocratic heritage.[53]

The collaboration of republican officials facilitated Molinier's treasure hunt. Between 1895 and 1900, the following artifacts of pre-Revolutionary craft arts were
recuperated: the personal desk of Louis XV, Clodion statuettes of nymphs and satyrs;
women's dressing tables by the royal cabinetmaker Oeben; consoles and end tables
originally in the possession of Madame de Pompadour; Beauvais tapestries with
Boucher cartoons; and embroidered firescreens once belonging to Marie Antoinette.[54]
Molinier and his staff worked to coordinate these recaptured pieces into ensembles,
replicating at the highest level of official national culture the reconstitutive work of
the brothers de Goncourt thirty years earlier.

The re-creation of intimate eighteenth-century rooms by museum curators in
the 1890s lacked the extreme aestheticism and subjectivism that had transposed the
Goncourts' project from archaeology to psychology. Yet the Louvre curators gave
certain indications that theirs was not simply a project of archaistic restoration. First,
they construed the Museum of French Furniture as a catalyst for revitalized artisanal
invention. Molinier and Migeon adhered to the incipient formula for craft modernism defined by union members Proust and Champier in the 1880s: to renew style by
affirming national endowments. Champier's distinction between "what was made"—
the imitation of patterns inherited from the past—and "the spirit in which it was
made"—the articulation of new forms flowing from the same national substance—
shaped the understanding of the Louvre curators. The museum was not to house
static objects of reverence but to stimulate artisans to match the glories of their ancestors. Migeon anticipated that the "modern artisan" would visit the Museum to
sketch and design: "The artisan can come and comfortably make a quick sketch or
decorative motif far more suggestive than a drawing he could execute by copying
from an album of old prints that he got out of the library."[55] Migeon hoped that this
direct contact with the artifacts of the illustrious past would generate artisanal renewal: "From the ensembles thus assembled will spring the seeds of a style."[56]

This vision of artisans sketching in the halls of the Louvre was necessarily selective; Migeon's idea resonated with the artisan of the luxury sector, who would have
the time, energy, and initiative to stroll over to the solemn national museum from
the Faubourg Saint-Antoine. The celebration of the Louvre Museum of French Furniture as both the historical reconstitution of the national patrimony and a workshop
for luxury craftsmen typified the French arts and crafts movement as a whole. The
original impetus during the 1860s had been to create in Paris a museum-atelier of the
industrial arts à la South Kensington. It was to be in the heart of the faubourg, an

extension of the workshop, directly linking design, execution, and production with
the aid of models from both contemporary and past generations of artisans. The
Museum of French Furniture represented the final phase of the transformation and
aristocratization of the 1860s project. Rather than a museum-atelier in the heart of
the Faubourg Saint-Antoine, the curators of the Louvre established a museum within
a museum, available to those artisans able to approach the national temple of art.

Migeon's other comments on both the public he anticipated would visit the museum and the impact of the museum on that public clarified the theme of the elevation of the crafts. In an article recalling the opening of the museum, Migeon glorified the ensembles in the Louvre as having a "great appeal," "for they speak to the
instincts of the greatest number."[57] Unity of all the arts, and the "appeal to the greatest number": Migeon's ideals corresponded to those of other European advocates of
integrating the crafts and of art for the people. Yet how telling that in France the
spokesman for these ideals was a curator of the applied arts of eighteenth-century
elegance at the Louvre and that the meaning of the ideals derived from the impulse to
elevate the crafts to the museum, the artisan to artist, rather than to send art down to
the street and reclaim the artist as a humble worker. Migeon went on to characterize
the public to whom the glistening interior decors would appeal: first, the "refined
amateur, the possessor of old family collections," who "will find useful comparisons
with the furniture he owns"; second, the artisan, who would use the objects for
sketching, generating new designs by their emulation; third, the foreigner.[58] The
foreigner continually appeared in both Migeon's and Molinier's writings on the
eighteenth-century decorative arts, most often in a lament. Many of the prize pieces
of French furniture and applied arts had been bought by foreigners and taken out of
the French domain.[59] Both Molinier and Migeon castigated the French for neglecting
the "finest fruits of the national patrimony" and for letting objects fall into foreign
collections.[60] The new Louvre museum would demonstrate French cultural power to
foreigners. The restored ensembles would remind them that the French had dominated European sensibility for two centuries: "The foreigner will be thrilled with
these works of a taste so pure and chaste. In his country he saw their reflections.
Now he will see them radiating from the center that had ruled Europe for two
centuries."[61]

The final element of the public Migeon envisioned for the new furniture museum
in the Louvre was "the people," an undifferentiated mass for whom the splendid
objects of intimate aristocratic life would have an intangible but indelible "general
educating interest."[62] "Ignorant" but "instinctive" and malleable, the people had a
"natural taste" for richly rendered surfaces and objects with strong "effects": they
sensed "in a confused way that these harmonious forms, these decorative fantasies,
this wealth of effects correspond best to [their] natural taste, one stimulated above all
by glitter and fantasy."[63]

Thus the interior ensembles in the Louvre, which, according to Migeon, would
"envelop the spectator in the authentic atmosphere of the epoch,"[64] would have an
uplifting function for "the greatest number." In other countries, reintegrating the

fine and applied arts was also conceived as a way to provide art for the greatest number, "the people." In England and Belgium, William Morris and Henry Van de
Velde proclaimed a similar aim. For them, however, art for the people necessarily
implied "art *by* the people"; healing the split between artist and artisan meant focusing on the process of work in which each artisan could express "pleasure." In France,
by contrast, art-craft for the greatest number signified the diffusion of taste and traditions of national refinement from above, from an official institution of the cultural
elite. A catalyst for at most a small number of luxury artisans, the objects in the
Louvre furniture museum would confirm the "people's" inclination to be dazzled
and overawed by richness and splendid effects unavailable to their class and distant
from their experience. For Morris and Van de Velde, integrating art and craft meant
infusing art into life, into the street; it meant the end of art as a separate and autonomous sphere. In France, the reuniting of art and craft solidified exclusiveness; applied arts were elevated to the status of painting and sculpture and incorporated into
the elite temple of national art. Furniture and objets d'art hitherto used by government officials in ministerial offices were indeed divested of their function and removed from practical life; Molinier's curatorial teams lifted them out of their offices
and into the Museum of French Furniture.

Molinier and Migeon's Louvre project realized a Central Union ideal articulated
by Louis de Fourcaud. In one emphatic statement of the need to reunite art and craft,
painting and decoration, de Fourcaud castigated David for banishing artisans from
the Academy and repeatedly invoked the illustrious aristocratic traditions of art as
craft. Significantly, de Fourcaud assured his elite audience that the reintegration of
art and craft, artist and artisan, would *not* mean the descent of art to the street or the
subversion of the meaning of art as a separate and special realm of experience.
"Troublesome democratization of the ideal?" he asked. No—the unity of art and
craft meant, by contrast, "the aristocratization of the producers."[65] The reentry of
elegant rococo furnishings and art objects into the Louvre in luxurious ensembles for
emulation by artisans provided a striking and prestigious realization of de Fourcaud's
ideas by his curatorial colleagues.

Plates

Plate 1. Lounge chair, called *la marquise brisée.* Musée Carnavalet, Paris.

Plate 2. Medals Chamber with portrait of Louis XV. Bibliothèque Nationale, Paris. Restoration by A. Pascal.

Plate 3. Medals Chamber, refurbished cabinetry, Bibliothèque Nationale, Paris.

Plate 4. Restored ceiling design with insignia of Louis XV, Vestibule of Honor, Bibliothèque Nationale, Paris.

Plate 5. Place Stanislas, Nancy, France, gates by Jean Lamour.

Plate 6. Place Stanislas, Nancy, France, Guibal sculptures.

Plate 7. Pont Alexandre III with rococo lamps, Paris.

Plate 8. Talking Fluted Bowl, 1892, by Emile Gallé, with poem by Maurice Rollinat. The Chrysler Museum Institute of Glass, Norfolk, Va., the Jean Outland Chrysler Collection. Photograph Courtesy of the Corning Museum of Glass.

Plate 9. Portrait of Emile Gallé, by Victor Prouvé. Courtesy of the Musée de l'Ecole de Nancy. Photograph by Cliché Studio Image, Nancy.

Plate 10. Crown and cartouche at the back of the bronze model for the *Monument to Claude Lorrain,* by Auguste Rodin, 1889. Rodin Museum, Philadelphia.

Plate 11. *The Gates of Hell,* by Auguste Rodin, 1880–1917. View of doors and Thinker. Musée Rodin, Paris.

Plate 12. Entry gate, Petit Palais. Gilded iron. 1900.

Plate 13. Ceiling painting, by Albert Besnard. Grand Palais, 1900.

Plate 14. Paix au foyer, by Jean Dampt, 1900. Ivory, wood, and bronze statuette. Courtesy of the Musée des Arts Décoratifs, Paris.

Plate 15. Glass hand, by Emile Gallé, 1900. Exposed nerves and ocean forms on a blown-glass hand.

CHAPTER NINE

Rococo Revival and the Franco-Russian Alliance

THE RENOVATIONS OF the National Library, the château at Versailles, and the château at Chantilly, and the reassemblage of the applied arts that reentered the Louvre, testified to the promotion of the rococo patrimony by the republican administration. If *ralliement* politicians found in craft culture the extension of their internal program of rapprochement, so in the international arena the rococo applied arts provided the necessary basis for a delicate diplomatic maneuver. Such diverse individuals as the duc d'Aumale, Pierre de Nolhac, Eugène Spuller, Georges Clemenceau, and Gaston Migeon had joined in the official rococo revival; an international event, the Franco-Russian alliance, united a secular, liberal republic and a theocratic, absolutist autocracy. One bridge between the two politically distinct nations was thrown by the delicate handiwork of the luxury artisans. The official affirmation of the rococo as a French *patrimoine* received a powerful impetus from the Franco-Russian alliance. The ceremonial aspects of the alliance were multiple and elaborate and pressed the decorative arts into important service to the state.

Until 1889 French republicans refused to consider a solution to post-Commune international isolation through a union with czarist power. At the same time, Russia's czar, Alexander III, distrusted the Gallic nation, spawned from regicide and revolution. But as the zealous anticlerical campaign of the Ferry Republic diminished, an alliance with Russia became more palatable, particularly to the republican politicians of the "new generation." Several factors after 1890 facilitated new attitudes on both sides. First, Russia had become isolated internationally after the fall of Bismarck resulted in the nonrenewal of the reinsurance policy. Second, France and Russia were exposed to the menace of the Triple Alliance, from which both were excluded. Third, the French hoped to invest in Russian industrial development.[1]

By 1892 General Boisdeffre, army chief of staff, began negotiating a military agreement. The two nations accepted it in December 1893, and the politicians of the Third Republic ratified the alliance in January 1894, in exact synchrony with the internal program of *ralliement*.[2]

The Franco-Russian alliance had significant cultural consequences that directly affected the officially sponsored arts and crafts movement. Before and after the treaty was ratified, from 1891 to 1897, France and Russia engaged in a series of cultural exchanges and state ceremonials. These included the mounting of art exhibits, the presentation of precious gifts, monument building, and mutual visits by heads of state. Czar Nicholas II and Czarina Feodorovna traveled to France in October 1896; President Félix Faure visited Russia in August 1897. Each official event necessitated the orchestration of craft ensembles and the commissioning of precious objects to be made by artisans. Urban festivals were staged to greet the czar and czarina on their visits to French cities, and teams of craftsmen were mobilized to embellish urban facades with the magnificence appropriate to a royal entry. In Paris the visit of the Russian family in 1896 culminated in the inauguration of the Pont Alexandre III, honoring the recently deceased father of Nicholas II.

If cultural events in general provided important opportunities for the rapprochement of French and Russian ruling elites, the French crafts—particularly the rococo crafts—derived special benefits from the Franco-Russian alliance. For the unlikely kinship of French republicans and Russian czarists was consecrated in a shared cultural heritage. France and Russia celebrated their late nineteenth-century union by invoking their common cultural history of the mid-eighteenth century, when the first Franco-Russian alliance had occurred, the union of the Sun King and Russia's great Westernizer, Peter. This alliance had stimulated a rich cultural exchange, particularly of the splendid applied arts. The flow proceeded mainly from France to Russia, largely because of Peter's aspirations to Europeanize Russian culture. After the death of Louis XIV, the outpouring continued, culminating during the height of the fashion for the rococo *goût nouveau*. Russian courtiers and aristocrats avidly patronized the French artisans of the new organic style in the mid-eighteenth century. Indeed, many rococo architects, sculptors, and decorative artists left France to work for the elite in Russia. In 1720, for example, Peter initiated the transformation of St. Petersburg, commissioning the French architect Leblond to design Peterhof Palace. The interior of the massive royal residence was executed by teams of rococo craftsmen, including Nicolas Pineau, the wood sculptor, and Falconet, the favored marble sculptor of Madame de Pompadour.[3] François Boucher, Falconet's colleague at the manufacture at Sèvres, also had important Russian clients; Clodion, the fashionable terra-cotta sculptor of the lubricious adolescent nymphs favored by the rococo, exported his work to St. Petersburg courtiers.[4]

This eighteenth-century legacy of rococo arts in Russia was rediscovered by French scholars and *amateurs* in the 1880s. Many of the art historians responsible for this rediscovery were affiliated with the Central Union of the Decorative Arts, whose Exhibition of Old Master Drawings of Decoration and Ornament in 1880 identified and exhibited those works of Boucher, Falconet, Pineau, Clodion, and Wailly originally collected by eighteenth-century Russian clients.[5] The catalogue for the exhibition contained scholarly information on the commissioning and disposition of the art objects in Russia.[6] The article on Clodion in the *Revue des arts décoratifs* of 1884–1885 discussed the Russian patrons of the French rococo sculptor.[7] The 1889 monograph on François Boucher by André Michel of the Louvre detailed the painter's Russian clientele.[8] The most extensive scholarly treatment of the rococo-Russian connection emerged in the scholarship on Nicolas Pineau, who had designed grottoes and fountains surrounding the Peterhof Palace. An 1889 folio collection of Pineau's applied arts designs replicated numerous drawings, hitherto unpublished, of objects originally executed for Russian patrons. The plates were accompanied by texts giving the dates and locations of the Russian artifacts.[9] In 1892, Th. Biais, a Central Union member, collector, and scholar, published the first monographic biography of Pineau, a detailed account of the artist and his Russian period.[10] In preparing the book, Biais consulted Russian experts to ferret out information on the whereabouts and condition of Pineau's work in Russian museums and private collections. Part of Biais's personal collection of Pineau drawings was purchased by the Stïeglitz Museum in Russia, though after 1896 the Central Union administration campaigned to buy them back for the union's decorative arts library.[11]

The scholarly reconstitution and classification of French rococo arts in Russia during the 1880s provided the intellectual groundwork for reinvoking eighteenth-century culture associated with the crafts during the decade of the Franco-Russian alliance. Artistic solidarity between the two nations began in the apolitical milieu of collecting and erudition, for example, in the baron Pichon's collaboration with Russian art scholars and *amateurs* for his work on Nicolas Pineau. Russians and French mingled during the 1880s in Parisian salons, such as that of Doctor Charcot, who every Tuesday received a regular group of guests in his mansion on the boulevard Saint-Germain. Visitors to Charcot's salon included the emperor of Brazil, the grand dukes of Russia, Cardinal Lavigerie, Antonin Proust, Réné Waldeck-Rousseau, the painters Jean-Léon Gérôme and Georges Rochegrosse, the sculptors Jules Dalou and Jean Falguière, the architect Charles Garnier, the writers Alphonse Daudet and Théodore de Banville, and the applied arts collectors Enrico Cernuschi and Philippe Burty.[12] Charcot's devotees emphasized that neither the doctor himself nor the Tuesday salons meddled in the pettiness of politics.[13] There was one exception to Charcot's nonpolitical amalgamation of officials and artists in his salon. In 1881 he provided the occasion for a prologue to the Franco-Russian alliance by arranging an early formal meeting between his friends Prime Minister Gambetta and Grand Duke Nicholas of Russia as representatives of their respective governments.[14] Thus on a cultural ground, in a meeting promoted by the neurologist-aesthete, the two powers joined in an informal entente. Ten years later, culture would again provide a binding power for the official international alliance.

The first official cultural program for Franco-Russian rapprochement preceded the political alliance of 1894 by four years. In the spring of 1890, the French government transported an elaborate exhibit to Russia, the French Exhibition in Moscow. It featured the luxury sector of the applied arts and was dedicated to the Russian emperor, Alexander III, as an expression "of our country's sympathy and of our industrial artists' skills."[15] French artisans and manufacturers accompanied the exhibition to its mountings in both Moscow and St. Petersburg. At the closing of the exhibition, the French artisans offered the emperor two magnificent gifts as testimony to the new rapport established between the two nations.

The first gift was a splendid ceramic tableau, set into a silver and gold frame, inlaid with precious stones and decorated with enamel overwork. The tableau represented the genealogical line descended from Czar Nicholas I. The plaque and its frame typified the collaborative, divided labor that marked the crafts of the luxury sector: the silver and gold frame was executed by a team of jewelers; the genealogical tableau combined the work of enamelers, ceramicists, and jewelers. The second gift united the labor of even more artisans in a single item. All the participants in the show contributed to the creation of a large folio volume, printed in one copy only, containing the name and works of each exhibitor. On the book's cover was a hammered plaque of gold, silver, and enamel. The leather binding was executed by the artisans Gruel and Engelmann, and the elaborate ornamental cover was designed by the silversmith Paul Christofle and six associates (Fig. 34). The Christofle plaque comprised a silver band around an allegorical frieze. In the band on either side of the frieze were twelve incised panels, each naming a product from four categories: science, art, industry, and agriculture. Among the products inscribed on the panels were bronze, furniture, jewelry, and silversmithing. Flowing wreaths and ribbon work surrounded the panels, reminiscent of the bouquets gracing rococo cartouches. At each corner of the leather volume was a raised enamel escutcheon representing the arms of Russia held by the double eagle. This escutcheon also had a rococo precedent: one of the designs favored by Nicolas Pineau in eighteenth-century St. Petersburg was a cascading escutcheon heralding the double eagle and flowing leaves, both of which reappeared on the 1890 commemorative volume.[16] At the center top of the band was a carved shield bearing the insignia of the French nation, the intertwined R and F. The shield was framed in silver, replete with fanning shell forms and a bouquet of leafy branches.

The allegorical frieze in the center of the Christofle plaque was designed by the sculptor Jules Coutan and executed by an artisan who worked in leather and ceramic. The allegory was set against a long silver olive branch, bound at the bottom by a banderole with the inscription *Pax et labor*. The allegorical panel revealed France as a woman in flowing robes, seated beneath a leafy tree, with a cornucopia to her right. At her feet two putti embraced. Arms outstretched, La Belle France held a sign in one hand, Paris, while the other pointed toward a distant city, Moscow, visible through the trees, which displayed "symbols of abundance and peace."[17] To the woman's left were two figures. One was a seated, bearded man in robes, pensive and absorbed. Poised near an anvil, he represented Industry. He sat, head in hand, contemplating the scroll on his lap. Behind him appeared the attributes of the beaux-arts—a palette and brushes. The second figure beside him, a young Mercury, was turned, his eyes riveted on La Belle France. He stood "ready to propel the objects born of his genius" in the direction of Moscow.[18]

The Christofle plaque for the Russian czar symbolized the cultural *ralliement* of

Imp. phot. ARON Frères, à Paris.

PLAQUE DE RELIURE EN ORFÈVRERIE (Argent, or et émail)

COMPOSÉE ET EXÉCUTÉE PAR MM. CHRISTOFLE

POUR L'EXEMPLAIRE COMMÉMORATIF DE L'EXPOSITION DE MOSCOU, OFFERT A L'EMPEREUR ALEXANDRE III
PAR LE COMITÉ D'ORGANISATION ET LES EXPOSANTS FRANÇAIS

Fig. 34. Gold, silver, and enamel book cover, by Paul Christofle. From *Revue des arts décoratifs,* 1892.

two nations, forged on the common ground of their eighteenth-century heritage. It embodied on its surface of silver, enamel, gold, and embossed leather the potential binding power of culture above the vicissitudes of politics. Along the four corners of the silver frame, for example, the Pineau-inspired Russian double eagle appeared, bearing, as it had in the eighteenth century, the insignia of czarist sovereignty. France, on the other hand, retained a rococo cartouche with new republican content. Not the interlacing L's of the Louis but the linked R and F emblazoned its shield. Yet the grottolike frame around the R and F and the leafy branch that supported it resonated with those eighteenth-century cultural forms that had expressed a previous bond with France's Russian ally. The creators of the leather volume for the czar, artisans like Christofle, Coutan, and Oscar Roty, all retained their ties to the traditions of their eighteenth-century colleagues. The products exhibited in Russia, evoking the flowing graces of eighteenth-century organicism, constituted a living memory for both republican France and czarist Russia.

The French Exhibition in Moscow of 1890 and the masterpieces of artisans commemorating it were only the beginning of a series of cultural exchanges between France and Russia. In the year 1893, when negotiations for a formal political alliance intensified, the Russians sent a military squadron to visit French cities to promote friendship and goodwill between the two nations. One stop on the Russian squadron's tour was the city of Nancy, in Lorraine. The city's official reception brought in its train a significant production by artisans in the luxury sector in a setting where the splendors of rococo elegance were still very much alive.

Nancy was a paradigmatic rococo city. The duke of Lorraine, Stanislas Lesczinski, the father-in-law of Louis XV, had transformed his fief into a monument of elegant *goût nouveau* design. A graceful central square, the place Stanislas, was the center of the city's eighteenth-century reconstruction (Pls. 5, 6). Dazzling gilded iron gates surrounded the square, designed by the royal locksmith Jean Lamour, who laced together the slender iron posts with gold-covered iron foliage that twisted through them like multiple vines. Sculptured fountains of Neptune and female sea goddesses were framed by the gates at one end of the square.[19]

In 1893 Russian sailors marched in Nancy through these shimmering gates, still fully intact and still crowned with their original gilded shields of Louis XV, visible with the interlacing L's. After the city fathers had welcomed the foreign emissaries, artisans from Nancy presented precious gifts to the sailors. These offerings were inspired by vital traditions of eighteenth-century artisanship, such as those represented by the illustrious Nancéen Jean Lamour. One of them was a commemorative volume, a *livre d'or,* containing a message to the czar from the municipal councils of all the cities of Lorraine. Similar to the volume presented to the czar after the 1890 French Exhibition in Moscow, the *livre d'or* was an opulent masterpiece of the applied arts, produced collaboratively by workers in leather, silver, gold, and ceramic. So weighty with ornament and thick with heavy folio pages was the precious volume that a table was needed to support it. Emile Gallé of Nancy, commissioned to design this special table, created a furnishing as elaborate and unique as the volume itself.[20]

Emile Gallé, soon to be known as one of the central founders of a French art nouveau, participated in 1893 as an official cultural spokesman for the impending Franco-Russian alliance. As an exhibiting member of the Central Union of the Decorative Arts in the 1880s, Gallé had participated in rediscovering the splendors of the eighteenth-century craft traditions; in Paris he had evoked the shapes and forms of Jean Lamour's gates.[21] Now, in his native town Gallé again revitalized eighteenth-century traditions, this time for a cultural consecration of an international alliance.

Gallé's exquisite table fused eighteenth-century forms and nineteenth-century meanings. Over twenty craftsmen of varying levels of skill had participated in creating it—a division of labor typical of an *haut luxe* workshop. Each artisan carved his signature at the base of the finished table, testifying to the collaborative venture and to the long and specialized process of production. In addition, each participant described his hopes and feelings on a parchment that was inserted and sealed inside the table.[22]

The shape of the table evoked the slender curves of a rococo furnishing, while the marquetried tabletop continued the eighteenth-century fashion for inlaid designs. Yet if rococo marquetry would ordinarily have been used to represent a playful landscape of fantasy, Gallé's inlaid wood design symbolized a solemn truth of embattled nature: the contested soil of Lorraine. Gallé used the Russian occasion to visualize Franco-Russian union and anti-German sentiment. He created an intricate tabletop design to depict a particular, politically charged landscape scene. Even the legs supporting the tabletop were symbolic. Carved into flowering colonnettes, they were attached to the table by copper and bronze plates, hammered out to represent the interlacing of a Russian pine and a Gallic oak and inscribed "I unite and I attach." This metaphor for the union of the two nations was reiterated in the interlocking trees that took shape as the table legs ascended. The wood design inlaid in the tabletop infused the anti-German nationalism of Lorraine into the message of Franco-Russian solidarity. To proclaim his "pious attachment to the mother country," Gallé included in his design a multiplicity of flowers specific to the hamlets of Lorraine: "The big gentian symbolizes antique Donan and Dabo, . . . the wood lily Domremy, . . . the snapdragon Belfont . . . all these names twist around the bough like vines. Nancy's signature is a nervous and coquettish thistle."[23] Gallé's language of flowers culminated in the botanical symbols of loss and mourning. The centerpiece of the inlaid design was a large cross of Lorraine, wrapped in a flowering diclytra wreath. Along the cross of Lorraine were the flowers of grief. Behind the cross and through a mist, Gallé represented the aureole and rays of a distant rising sun. Other flowers peeked through in the distant sun on the horizon—the flowers of that part of Lorraine annexed by the Germans. Gallé, a botanist, noted these flowers were "catalogued scientifically in the *Flore de Lorraine*" but were "now cut off from the *flore française*."[24] In Gallé's design, these flowers reached, tropistically, toward their native soil.

Following the reception of the Russian squadron at Nancy in 1893, one occasion in particular strengthened the solidarity between France and Russia while expanding the official impetus given to reinvoking the rococo crafts: the visit of the czar and czarina to France in October 1896. To celebrate the reception of the royal guests and to welcome them in appropriate manner, the government commissioned teams of artisans to embellish the city of Paris, mount festivals, and create decorative arcades along the routes of the royal entry. The luminous ornamentation for the Franco-Russian festivals transformed sections of the first, seventh, and sixteenth arrondissements in Paris for well over two weeks.

Promoters of the unity of the arts in the Ministry of Beaux-Arts and in the Central Union pondered a common question: "Does French democracy possess the necessary elegance to receive the czar Nicholas?"[25] Victor Champier, editor of the union's *Revue des arts décoratifs,* commented that the city of Paris could receive its royal visitors in appropriate style if it were armed with all the aesthetic weaponry of female seduction: "Like a woman who freshens up and changes her dress to please those she loves, the city of Paris is beautiful. . . . She will create a dreamy atmosphere, . . . a loving halo . . . a smile's seduction, . . . the winning charm of the smiling person."[26]

The model for the artful transfiguration of urban reality into fantasy was the French royal festival, particularly that of the era of the three Louis. The museum administrator Roger Marx spoke repeatedly of the genius of Charles Lebrun as the organizer of royal festivals, identifying the eighteenth-century tradition of spectacle as an enduring feature of the French national temperament:

> The French, especially the Parisian, preference for public festivals is characteristic of our national temper, a sign . . . of the expansiveness of our national temperament. Our monarchs were wary of neglecting this inclination of the popular soul. I know of no event in the eighteenth century—new king, royal birth, or royal wedding—that did not give rise to some public celebration. These events were infused with art to the last detail.[27]

Victor Champier echoed Roger Marx's invocation of eighteenth-century royal festivals in his articles entitled "Reception of the Russian Monarchs."[28] Champier singled out royal artist-artisans such as Jehand Perréal and Charles Lebrun for their ingenuity in staging court spectacles and "ceremonies of royal entries." Champier was particularly enthusiastic about Jean-Nicolas Servandoni, the director of royal festivals under Louis XV, whose works had been explored in the *Revue* in 1881 by Henri de Chennevières. In 1896, Champier could appeal to this recently recovered illustrious tradition as a point of emulation and inspiration for a contemporary royal entry.

With their eighteenth-century royal predecessors in mind, teams of artisans embarked on the decoration of Paris for the benefit of the Russian autocracy. The train station at Ranelagh in the sixteenth arrondissement, the site of the czar and czarina's arrival in Paris, was bedecked with multicolored banners and flowers (Fig. 35). Ceramic and silver artisans worked a huge escutcheon into a medley of rococo form

Fig. 35. Reception Station at Ranelagh.

and republican insignia. The R and F interlocked in a silver shield, whose edges curled like fanning shells. A garland of flowers and ribbon, similar to rococo garlands, festooned the shield, its flowers spilling over the pilasters of the train station's small waiting room.[29]

Plaster and papier-mâché pylons, miniature triumphal arches, ceramic and silver emblems, multicolored and painted banners—all these appeared in the Parisian center for the Russian visitation. Besides such ephemeral decorations for the royal entry, luxurious gifts also played an important role in welcoming the czar and czarina in 1896. The members of the Central Union of the Decorative Arts appeared with splendid offerings in the Parisian ceremonies for the royal family. Emile Gallé collaborated with the famous goldsmith Lucien Falize to create a vase for Czarina Feodorovna. Gallé fashioned a crystal vase, layered with carved cameo in the shape of long-stemmed irises (Fig. 36). Falize provided for the vase a splendid stand of carved gold finished with precious stones. Another member of the union, Jules Chaplain, gave the czar a special commemorative medal, on whose surface appeared the faces of two women—the crowned head of the czarina, her neck ringed with strands of pearls, and the stalwart Greek profile of Marianne (Fig. 37).[30]

Appropriate to the theme, the continuity of the eighteenth-century crafts that united the two countries, the czar and czarina paid a special visit to the manufacture at Sèvres, whose eighteenth-century directors, Boucher and Falconet, had had im-

Fig. 36. Crystal and cameo vase, by Emile Gallé. Presented to the Czarina Feodorovna, 1896. From *Revue des arts décoratifs,* 1896.

Fig. 37. Commemorative medal, by Jules Chaplain. Presented to the Czarina Feodorovna, 1896. From *Revue des arts décoratifs,* 1896.

For the groundbreaking ceremony, artisans created special tools for each head of state, each one ornamented. Lucien Falize, the goldsmith who collaborated with Emile Gallé in making the mounted vase for the czarina, created three gold hand tools. The first two were matched gold hammers, one for Félix Faure, one for Czar Nicholas II. One hammer had the insignia of the superimposed R and F on one side of its ivory handle, the initial N for Nicholas on the other. The second hammer matched but had the initial F on its ivory handle.[34] Falize prepared a third tool for presentation to Nicholas II. This was a solid gold trowel for turning the dirt near the stone placed by the bridge pier (Fig. 38). The handle of the trowel had a carved image and sign: the ship of the city of Paris and its motto, *Fluctuat nec mergitur.* Around the ship were fleurs-de-lis. Where the handle of the trowel joined the base, gold plaits were molded in the shape of waves, symbolizing the river Seine.[35]

The fleurs-de-lis and the ship of state, cleaving through the waves but not capsizing—this iconography on a miniature golden trowel offered a thematic summary of the interaction of politics and culture in the Franco-Russian alliance. The fleur-de-lis was the symbol of the French kings, the legacy of the two Louis with whom Russia had cooperated in the seventeenth and eighteenth centuries. The sailing ship and its emblem, originally a royal symbol repudiated during the French Revolution, were restored to service by Napoléon III; in the 1890s, the motto *Fluctuat nec mergitur* was added below the ship and the emblem became an official stamp of the Third Republic. In the context of the Franco-Russian alliance, it resonated with particular meanings. As the Republic tried to chart a smooth and continuous course between socialism and right-wing nationalism, so too it attempted to assimilate cultural elements from France's aristocratic and pre-Revolutionary past into a binding national patrimony. The Franco-Russian alliance, moored in the history of eighteenth-century diplomacy and eighteenth-century culture, intensified the impetus toward rococo reaffirmation.

CHAPTER TEN

Art Nouveau:
Craft Modernism in the State

THE TWO PRECEDING chapters examined the revivalist dimensions of the 1890s craft program, which centered on the excavation, reassemblage, and public display of eighteenth-century ensembles of the rococo *style moderne*. This chapter identifies the comprehensive program of innovation in the crafts pursued simultaneously with these revivalist efforts.

The official program for craft innovation had two institutional centers. The state provided one, which was guided by government officials affiliated with the Central Union: Roger Marx, Louis de Fourcaud, and Georges Berger; the Central Union of the Decorative Arts provided the other.

The state's direct action on behalf of craft modernism was manifold. Among its initiatives during the 1890s were the patronage of innovative artists such as Emile Gallé, Auguste Rodin, Albert Besnard, Eugène Carrière, and Louis Falize; the opening of a renovated museum, the Musée de Luxembourg, designed specifically to house new works of art in all media; participation in a national Congress of the Decorative Arts held in Paris in 1894; the issuing of new coinage; cooperation with the Japanese government in promoting Japanese applied arts in France; and commissioning official advisors to study non-French attempts at craft renovation. One such advisor was Siegfried Bing, the scholar and art dealer of Japonism, who was an affiliate of the Central Union during the 1880s. During the 1890s Bing assumed an official role, drafting recommendations for the director of beaux-arts on the basis of his study of the applied arts of Japan and the United States.

Rather than examine all these state initiatives, I will concentrate on the last three, which most clearly reveal the meanings attributed to French craft modernism by both official administrators and advisors. This chapter, then, analyzes the issuing of new coinage, the Japanese arts in France, and the reports of Siegfried Bing and situates them in the context of solidarist political culture. It identifies the emerging common assumptions articulated by both state officials and advisors like Bing with respect to the organic and national character of a French *style moderne* and suggests the special resonance of an artistic style patterned after the forms of nature in the decade of republican solidarity.

Republican Solidarity:
The Aestheticization of Money, 1892–1895

As the call to reintegrate all the arts, to reunite artist and artisan, spread from England to the Continent, artists in many countries embraced a common ideal: to infuse the products of daily use with beauty in a quintessentially modern spirit. Efforts to realize this common ideal assumed divergent forms, one born of political and social radicalism, the other derived from the acceptance of the role of the state as it existed.

In England and Belgium the fusion of beauty and utility was inseparable from an indictment of the capitalist system and a demand for social reform. For William Morris and his Belgian disciple Henry Van de Velde, artist and artisan could be reunited only when the market was obliterated; only then would art no longer serve an elite but flow from all men, expressing their new and equal pleasure in work.

William Morris's vision of the postrevolutionary infusion of all of life with art was limited. He projected an archaistic paradise of simplicity and contracted needs. The utopian world sketched out in his *News from Nowhere* was a spartan terrestrial heaven; the permeation of sensual adornments was restricted by the hold of Protestantism on Morris's medievalizing imagination.[1]

In Catholic Belgium, where carnivals, masks, and Corpus Christi processions were part of the lived experience of social radicals preaching Morris's gospel, the role attributed to art in daily life was prodigious. Less archaistic than Morris and more accepting of the pleasures afforded by plastic form, the Belgian radicals projected a postrevolutionary society where all aspects of daily existence were transfigured by art. Henry Van de Velde's friend and fellow socialist Jules Destrée, a poet and art critic, described the pervasive role of art in a platform paper he wrote for the Parti Ouvrier Belge in 1894. According to Destrée, art nourished the senses and embodied the collective pleasures of the new society. His vision, in contrast to Morris's, detailed the extensive infusion of art in noncapitalist life. Destrée projected colorful secular festivals, the adornment of vast public buildings such as railroad stations, and the creation of beautiful necessities, such as pictorial postage stamps.[2]

In Austria and France, the marriage of beauty and utility did not await a socialist future but was consummated by official decree in the capitalist present. In Austria, the Arts Council of 1899 and the Koerber Ministry of 1900 sponsored innovative artists seeking a uniquely modern design in the applied arts. Leading Secessionist artists such as Otto Wagner, Karl Moll, Koleman Moser, and Alfred Roller helped to formulate state cultural policy by serving on the Arts Council, where they operated as a "pressure group for the modern movement within the state apparatus."[3] As a result, "not only some of Austria's major public buildings, but even their postage stamps and currency were designed by Secessionists."[4]

According to the historian Carl Schorske, the motive behind state sponsorship of art and craft modernism in Austria was the divisive problem of nationality, "which

had virtually paralyzed the government with its conflicts over language rights in administration and schooling."[5] Modernism, implemented by bureaucratic rule, was
to provide the riven empire with a unitary language, transcending national differences. Universalist, nonhistorical, supranational modern design offered, according
to a Secessionist spokesperson, "a form of art that would weld together all the characteristics of our multitude of constituent peoples into a new and proud unity."[6]

France shared with Austria the capacity to promote, by official policy, the modernist creators of unified arts and crafts. Like the Austrians, French liberals sought
unity above division during the 1890s, and art provided an important source of that
unity. Yet the French legislated out of strength whereas their Austrian counterparts
decreed out of weakness. Austrian modernism was sponsored by disheartened liberals who "reverted to an 18th century tradition of enlightened absolutism and bureaucratic rule" after the nationality question had paralyzed the normal channels of
parliamentary rule.[7] The French brand of modern design was implemented by republican solidarists, who practiced a version of liberalism successfully modified to
meet the challenges posed by Right and Left. In Austria, modernist art offered a last
resort, a compensatory binding power in an empire split into competing ethnic elements. In France, the policy of "solidarité entre tous les arts" flowed from a single
national heritage, the cultural *patrimoine*.[8] If the Austrians embraced modern design
in order to transcend the national question, the French adopted the cause of art
nouveau in order to affirm it. As political unity was asserted by the solidarist minister Léon Bourgeois through state social programs and an organicist political theory,
so cultural unity was forged by the official promotion of an organic, specifically
French *style moderne*.

Beginning in 1892, government representatives campaigned for a goal that echoed
throughout the European arts and crafts movements: "the diffusion of beauty," "to
infuse the multiple objects used in daily life with beauty and spirit."[9] English and
Belgian radicals had called, similarly, for the embellishment of utensils, clothes, and
work tools by art. In France, however, the union of beauty and utility was realized in
1895 in a way that would have been distasteful to William Morris and Jules Destrée:
the execution of beautiful images on the surfaces of coin money.

Two government officials were responsible for creating the new coinage, Roger
Marx and Paul Doumer. Beginning in 1892, Roger Marx, then an inspector of provincial museums, advocated an administrative initiative to redesign French coins. He
regarded this initiative as a means to revitalize the French craft of medal making, a
source of pride in French cultural history unjustly overlooked by the Third Republic. In addition, as a liberal republican from Nancy, Marx perceived the new coinage
as a way for the Third Republic to claim its own distinctive style, to free itself from
images and allegories used by other regimes.

He outlined his platform for the beautification of coins in articles in the journal *Le
Voltaire*.[10] "We must aspire to insert in even the smallest of vessels so much poetry
and so many dreams."[11] In presenting his program for coin reform, Marx invoked
the special French talent for continuing the ancient art of medal engraving, claiming

that in this field only the French were able to rival the works of Evainelos and Pisanello.[12] Following his observation on French tradition, he argued that all periods in French cultural history had redesigned the coinage; every regime in its own style had inscribed its face on the coins it minted. A regime that did not do so "risked being ignored by posterity."[13] Here Roger Marx reiterated, in the case of coins, the logic of an argument about the imperative in the French tradition for continuous innovation and the evolution of style, calling this special progressive force the law of innovate or perish.[14] His official colleagues in the administration of the Garde-Meuble and the Museum of French Furniture—Williamson, Migeon, and Molinier—had used similar arguments for the development of a new style in decoration. Rather than reject history, the new style would affirm the best part of French tradition: stylistic change marked by the enduring substance of *le goût français*.[15]

Roger Marx was particularly critical of the Third Republic for relying on allegorical images from previous regimes for its coins. Rather than proclaim its affinity with the First and Second Republics by imitating their classical symbols and figures, the Third Republic should find new emblems. The new images would capture, on the surface of the coin, the idea of France under the Third Republic; it would crystallize a "specific time, nation, and state." "We cannot live with the borrowed allegories of other republics." The Third Republic must choose an original image, "in accord with the modern spirit and resonant with its distinctive republican ideal."[16]

In 1892 Roger Marx did not propose a specific image or allegory that would capture the modern spirit and express the ideal of the Republic. He merely urged the government to commission three medal engravers to execute new coinage. For bronze pieces he recommended Chaplain, for silver Roty, for gold Dupuis. The first two were members of the Institut de France. Marx was confident that all three could embody both the modern spirit and the "distinguishing features of the French genius."[17] He characterized their work as full of "elegance," "charm," and "grace," that "decorative verve"[18] that he construed as the "particularism of our temperament."[19]

The Central Union of the Decorative Arts avidly supported Roger Marx's coin reform plan. In 1892 the *Revue des arts décoratifs* reprinted the articles from *Le Voltaire* and added its own editorial comments. The creation of beautiful money could be the most effective and direct means of diffusing art to all levels of society. The new coins would function as the most powerful agent of the elevation of taste: "Coins are the most precious agents for the diffusion of beauty. The modest and simple French sou, recast with a noble engraving, embellished with a pretty symbolic image, may become an educator of taste."[20] As the simplest and most modest of coins, the French sou, could be transfigured and ennobled by a "pretty image," so the lowliest of men could fondle a masterpiece: "Soon even the most humble among us will be able to have a masterpiece in his pocket."[21]

In 1895 Roger Marx's program for the reform of monetary images was realized, largely because of the intricate network linking culture and politics in the 1890s. A new prime minister, Léon Bourgeois, came to power in 1895, a republican carrying the new banner of solidarity. Bourgeois's political career, as I have noted, had brought

him in direct contact with the Central Union and craft renovation in the years prior
to his prime ministership. Bourgeois appointed to his new cabinet Paul Doumer as
his minister of finance, with direct consequences for the cause of craft modernism in
France. Doumer was apprenticed as a youth to a medal shop, where he learned the
art of engraving on precious metals. Rather than a career as a craftsman, Doumer
chose political journalism. He spent several years as a writer for the magazine *Le
Voltaire,* where he met and collaborated with Roger Marx.[22]

One of Doumer's first acts on entering into ministerial affairs was to implement
Roger Marx's plan for the artistic reform of coinage. Following the plan of 1892,
Doumer offered government commissions to three medal engravers: Chaplain for
bronze, Roty for silver, and Dupuis for copper. Roty, jubilant over the commission,
exclaimed, "French money has for too long remained mute; it is time that it said
something!"[23]

What did the new French coins say? How did they signify the "modern spirit"
and express the "distinctively Third Republic ideal," as Roger Marx had demanded?
The image cast by Roty, which was stamped on the one-franc silver coin, visibly
broke from the sober classicism and solemn abstractions of the First and Second Republics. His emblem of the Third Republic assumed the form of an active, full-length
female figure: Marianne as a sower (Fig. 39). Roty's sower was a young, agile woman
in long flowing robes, with hair that cascaded from under her small bonnet. Barefoot, legs astride in motion, she held a sack of seeds, which she scattered about her.

The association between the Republic and a woman had a long history in France.
Maurice Agulhon has demonstrated the correspondence between the changing political spectrum of the French republics and their varying symbolic representations of
the Liberty figure, Marianne. Until 1880 there were two distinct Mariannes, inherited from the liberal and social republicans, who split in 1848. One was the Marianne
of popular revolt, an active, youthful figure wearing the red Phrygian cap associated
with the Revolution; the second was the Marianne of legalistic moderation, an immobile, mature woman crowned by a star or by ears of wheat or corn. In the early
years of the Third French Republic, officials such as Jules Grévy avoided the active
Marianne, and the Phrygian cap was excluded as a "seditious emblem." The allegory
of the republic was highly didactic: in both the sculptures for the entrance to the 1878
Paris Exposition and the medals struck in 1879 for the government, for example, the
Republic was personified as a sedate Athenian matron, draped in heavy classical
robes, crowned with laurel leaves, and holding the tables of the constitution.

After 1880 the sharp division in the language of allegory subsided. The official
Marianne incorporated features hitherto associated with the problematic radical variant; the "victorious Republic" became a young, serious female, who wore on her
head either traditional signs of "rustic well-being"—foliage, wheat, ears of corn—
or the Phrygian cap.[24]

Roty's 1895 image of the Republic as a young, active female extended the process
of redefinition by continuing the recuperation of the radical Marianne: this figure
wore a Phrygian cap; she was barefoot, stood in a mobile posture, and had free-

Fig. 39. Marianne figure for the French one-franc piece, by Oscar Roty.

floating hair; and she lacked the surround of didactic banners—all elements that had typified the populist Marianne before 1880. In the context of 1895, Roty's was an appropriate incarnation of the Third Republic. As the aggressive anticlerical liberalism of the 1880s was modified, the republicans tempered their visual stridency and no longer used didactic allegories of Reason, Law, and the Constitution as Marianne's symbolic shields against the Right. As the Republic consolidated, its personification became generalized and simplified. Evolving in the late 1880s from a symbol of one party or regime to a symbol of France, the republican Marianne relinquished the specific and legible reminders of what she represented and emerged as an allegorical compromise, fusing the qualities of both the populist Marianne and the nation "pure and simple." [25]

Although Roty's Republic exemplified the general tendencies Agulhon proposed, it also contained strikingly new features. Marianne as a bounding, graceful sower was new and departed from the usual representations of Marianne in an inactive stance. The sedate Marianne had been crowned by vegetation—foliage, or ears of wheat or corn. Roty shifted the Marianne from passivity in relation to nature's bounty to active production of it. The elegant, vigorous female sower also differed markedly from male sowers depicted in works of art. Between 1848 and 1852 Jean-François Millet's lumbering massive peasant sower carried radical content to audiences menaced by rural laborers' uprisings.[26] Millet's raggedy giant was replaced by Roty's miniature image of a sprightly female, light of foot.

The union of a woman and an agrarian setting fulfilled Roger Marx's call for an image cast in the "modern spirit," and in "accord with our distinctive republican ideal." The sower represented the world of natural rhythms and seasonal renewal, above the specificity of historical moments. Solidarist politics looked precisely to this organic realm, where cyclical renewal and unity in diversity ruled. Earlier Marianne figures had bound nature to codes of law, whose imperatives were inscribed on shields or tablets surrounding them. Roty's figure abandoned the invocation of the law for organic power; rather than display society's rules, she activated nature's force, a solidarist working as nature's partner to affirm the fundamental harmony beneath the surface of words and appearances. Roger Marx expressed this inherent organic order, which moved from the natural to the social:

> The structure may vary infinitely while the working relation among its parts remains constant. Each organism contains nothing superfluous; as a tightly co-ordinated ensemble, each part has its role and its function. . . . As the sun on the horizon slowly and surely rises, so the general order of things is revealed to us. The interdependence of nature may not be apparent to the observer; the lake, the valley, the hillock may seem isolated; yet in the distance, one discovers how each part is intricately linked to the next, expressing the unity of the whole. Man's predicament is subject to these same remarks concerning the totality of nature. Despite apparent dispersion, a moment comes when one perceives the common goal that binds all men together.[27]

The Roty sower expressed solidarist organicist hopes and typified the work of modernist craft artists who looked to nature as the source of revitalization. Nature and national roots as symbols appealed to both artists and the politicians who supported them. Like their official sponsors Roger Marx and Léon Bourgeois, the artists looked on nature as the crucible of change in continuity, of cyclical renewal, and of unity in diversity. They translated these shared assumptions into a guiding formula in a metaphor related to that of the sower: the tree bearing fruit each season. Stylistic progress divested of violent breaks and radical departures was symbolized by a French tree, which bore new fruit each season but continued to be nourished by the same trunk and roots. Organicist craft art such as Roty's would similarly discover a new repertoire of forms while expressing the permanent, essential core of the "French temperament."[28]

Art Nouveau by Example:
Japanese and American Crafts, 1890–1895

The goal of "solidarity among the most varied arts" in accord with "our modern visions" was championed in official culture not only by Roger Marx but by a second government advisor, Siegfried Bing.[29] Between 1890 and 1896 the Third Republic supported Bing in two major projects related to craft innovation: the Exhibition of Japanese Engraving at the Ecole des Beaux-Arts and a visit to America as official emissary to review the progress of the arts and suggest recommendations for French policy. In carrying out these two projects, Bing expressed ideas and values that revealed striking affinities with those of other official advocates of the crafts. Indeed, Bing shared an attitude that characterized the French craft movement as a whole and rendered it particularly French.

Bing had collaborated with the Central Union of the Decorative Arts in their exhibitions of Japanese painting of 1883 and 1884. These exhibitions, sponsored by the Japanese government association, the Riutshikuai, pursued the paradoxical program of saving ancient treasures of Japanese art by displaying and selling them abroad. The magnificent variety of Japanese artifacts was welcomed by French collectors, who were particularly receptive to the cultural vestiges of a foreign traditional feudal caste after the bloody class warfare of the Commune.

During the 1880s, the interest of the Central Union in Japanese organic arts was encouraged by the French rococo revival promoted in the union journal and shows. But the revivalist impetus had already been transformed, on the eve of the 1884 exhibition, into the stirrings of craft modernism. The union associates Burty and Bing, along with the editor Victor Champier, had seen in Japanese organicism the elements needed for craft revitalization in France. In 1883 and 1884 these men shared the idea that the forms of nature in Japanese art should be emulated and could be liberating, but they would have to be reinterpreted and adapted by French artists in accord with their own national temperament.[30] In the Exhibition of Japanese Engraving in 1890 this idea returned, and was expanded, with official government support.

The Exhibition of Japanese Engraving took place at the Ecole Nationale des Beaux-Arts in Paris. The organizing committee, made up of important figures in politics and culture, included Georges Clemenceau, Roger Marx, and Antonin Proust. Clemenceau participated largely because of his collection of Japanese prints and illustrated books, many of which were included in the exhibition. A Japanese minister, Tanaka, was also represented on the organizing board. Participants from the art world included Edmond de Goncourt and Philippe Burty, each of whom contributed works from his collection of Japanese art for the show.[31]

As in earlier exhibitions of Japanese visual art, an effort was made to reveal the multiple functions and applications of the medium on display. For the 1890 print show, engravings, lithographs, wall hangings, wallpaper, illustrated books, designs for screens, and bronze, ceramic, and wood engravings were all exhibited as "*gra-*

vure."[32] The exhibition was organized chronologically from the creation of the *es-tampe* under Monorobu (1675–1720) to the illustrated books from the years 1720–1760 to the "apogee of the chromoxylograph" under Outamaro (1760–1800) to the era of Hiroshighe and Hokusai (1800–1860).[33] All the varied artifacts from the different eras depicted nature—floral, faunal, and feminine. Typical of this organicism was a colored print of two women in a boat, rocked by waves; a wood engraving of noblewomen covered with cherry blossoms; a lithograph of a mandarin duck among irises; and a scene of flying cranes near Mount Fuji.[34] One print on display had particular resonance in the French context in which it was exhibited. A work of 1790 by the artist Toyokouni, entitled *The Storm,* depicted a series of individuals from different social classes thrown together by a sudden downpour. Bing's catalogue entry described it:

> A gigantic tree in the center of the composition forms the shelter where all those surprised by the sudden downpour find refuge. It is a motley crowd, confounding all the classes of society, from the young nobleman out with his falcon to the washerwoman, the monkey man, the woodcutter, and several blind men who tumble and fall in their haste.[35]

In a decade marked by the search for political unity, for a new power to bind the nation, here was a resonant image for the French state sponsors, one in which nature eliminated social differences, confounding members of all stations of society in a common predicament, a storm. The rain leveled, and the tree united; no one was protected from the storm except in the collective shelter of the massive tree.

Siegfried Bing wrote not only the catalogue entries for the Japanese exhibit but also its thematic introduction, in which he expressed the assumptions he shared with other members of the official craft movement. The conceptual core of Bing's essay was stylistic evolution, regulated by tradition. With his colleagues in the Central Union and the cultural administration, Bing believed that the Japanese had a special national gift, an endowment bestowed by nature upon the people of the "Country of the Rising Sun." Bing characterized Japanese artists as the exponents of this national temperament, in their "exquisite expression of taste," "their extreme suavity," their "extreme delicacy," and their "refined and tender taste, often caressing." These qualities constituted the enduring essence of the Japanese "national art," providing continuity in Japan's visual arts, despite changes in both technique and subject matter.[36]

Bing described the important transformations in the medium of the Japanese print from its inception in the seventeenth century. He complemented his analysis of the Japanese "national art" with a discussion of what he called the art nouveau of Japan: the work of the realist printmakers and illustrators Hiroshighe and Hokusai.[37] This nineteenth-century "youthful school" was noted for expanding its subject matter to include elements of the daily life of the popular classes, especially the theater, and for its attentiveness to organic forms.[38] But even while applauding its innovations, Bing emphasized the central core of continuity embodied in this art nouveau, which linked it to an essentially Japanese spirit. Particularly revealing was Bing's comment that even in depicting subjects geared to a popular audience, Japanese printmakers retained the refined, delicate, and exquisite sensibility of their aristocratic ancestors:

> These impressions in color . . . these suave impressions full of seductiveness. What a fine idea it is to create with taste and artistic sentiment, qualities required by a people who demand works of sufficiently exquisite distinction. How different from the crude imagery, aimed at brutal effects, which, ordinarily, has the sole privilege of captivating the masses! Today, in this aspect of Japanese art as in all others, tradition again survives.[39]

In the 1890 essay, Bing identified the pattern of artistic innovation and national affirmation in Japanese prints without drawing explicit lessons for the evolution of art and design in France; in 1895, however, he consolidated these ideas and developed a general law of stylistic evolution that he wanted the French to obey. Bing adapted lessons he had learned from the Japanese, which had been confirmed and extended by his observation of a similar pattern of continuity and change in the arts in a second national context: the United States.

Bing explored his conception of stylistic evolution in 1895 in an official report to the director of beaux-arts in France, Henri Roujon, who asked Bing to comment on "the development of art in America."[40] This report interpreted "the artistic culture in America" in the light of three concepts: artistic innovation within the framework of the national temperament, solidarity based on unity in diversity, and organic forms as the basis for a regenerated decor. Each of these concepts revealed Bing's affinities with the other official sponsors of renovation in the French crafts. Indeed, this report stands as central expression of the values and attitudes of the variegated official elite promoting a French modern style in the 1890s.

Bing examined American painting, sculpture, architecture, and the industrial arts. His assessment of American production in the beaux-arts was largely negative; without a deeply rooted cultural heritage of their own, Americans sought compensatory historical legitimation by importing the styles of European masters. Only in the applied arts, "the luxury arts" applied to the "interior of the home," did Bing find important lessons for European artisans.[41] Glassmakers like Louis C. Tiffany had first riveted the attention of French spectators at the World Exhibition of 1878. By 1889 Tiffany and Company had dazzled the public, and the success of its display was one of the motives behind Roujon's request that Bing investigate the development of the arts in the United States. Bing's observations confirmed the special qualities of modern American glass design. He also singled out other fine crafts for special mention, including the work of goldsmiths and silversmiths like Gorham and Company, of pottery makers like Rookwood, and of furniture makers. In the crafts produced by these varied artisans Bing discerned "a new movement," fueled by an uncommon spirit, "a singular spirit of initiative, a youthful vigor."[42]

Though a German and a Jew, Bing identified deeply with France and French culture.[43] He repeated this propensity in the 1895 report. Although Bing's official mission was to observe American techniques and to compare them with French ones, his discovery of a vigorous American craft movement wounded his pride in his adopted nation, France. As he reported American ingenuity and advised emulating the American example, Bing commented on the ironic reversal of cultural fate: France, which for centuries had led the world in taste and style, now was forced to look to the New World, to a country without a long history, for help in revitalizing its arts. The special French gifts had been overshadowed:

> Suddenly, America, which only shortly before had experienced its first artistic stirrings, was to bear proof of singular powers of initiative and youthful vigor, in sharp contrast with the thinning blood that has progressively weakened our industrial arts and made impotent our most precious artistic heritage. By what surprising phenomenon were the roles reversed? We French, tireless educators of all nations, who for centuries have sowed the seed of our artistic knowledge, should be especially awed by this sudden flowering in a barren, far-off land. And it would be still more appropriate to translate our wonder into discovery of how America can enlighten us in our present weakness.[44]

Significantly, Bing learned from the new American craft movement not to seek a release from history and tradition but to discover, selectively, how to affirm and be inspired by them. The genius of the Americans was their capacity to look back and to reshape. Bing celebrated the ingenuity of craftsmen like Tiffany who emulated the art of ancient civilizations, transposing it into an American idiom. Lacking a long history of artistic development of their own, American artisans drew on designs from the decorative arts of Byzantium, China, Japan, and the Middle East. From this mélange a distinctively American style emerged. Bing noted that the artists of the New World "select judiciously from the past, combining their study of ancient creations with an immersion in nature's forms." The Americans were able "to adapt artistic forms from the past to new needs, to modern conceptions, rather than engaging in the tricks of sterile archaeology." These combinations of past and present, Bing concluded, "have become the point of departure for a new ideal, a new aesthetic."[45]

In this assessment of American craft modernism, Bing restated the primary assumption of the official sponsors of innovation in the French arts and crafts: that the past was a source of creative inspiration. Beginning with Victor Champier's distinction between the renovation of style based on "not *what* was made," but "*how* it was made," the French craft movement had developed a healthy tolerance for history and tradition. Those who wanted to unify the arts and crafts urged French artisans to continue the *spirit* of their ancestors: a new style would discover an innovative repertoire of plastic forms while expressing the permanent, essential core of the "French temperament." In characterizing the Americans, Bing restated this concept of the interplay between past inspiration and contemporary renewal. Like Champier, he distinguished between an adaptation to modern "conceptions" and needs and a servile repetition of past styles.

From his analysis of the interplay of history and contemporaneity in the American applied arts Bing developed a general law of stylistic evolution for his French official sponsors. The linchpin of modernism in the arts for France lay not in the repudiation, but in the renewal and revitalization of the exceptional French talents for adornment and tasteful fashioning. The "youthful vigor" of America had exposed, by contrast, an "anemic" debility in the production of French crafts. Yet Bing was certain that "parvenu" America would be no match for a regenerated France, whose national artistic faculties had been finely honed through centuries of stylistic successions: "We bear as our heritage an ancient patrimony, . . . we are fortified by long experience nurtured by all the phases of a long development; we possess faculties of sensation rendered more acute each day—a vital bloodstream that, in spite of periods of sluggishness, is capable of being at any moment quickened by new infusions of creativity."[46] "An infusion in the national bloodstream" would bring about a modern style. French craftsmen should revere their illustrious ancestors and be inspired by them while evolving their own distinctive vocabulary, suited to the new needs of the present:

> We do not suggest the renunciation of our glorious heritage. Quite the contrary. . . . If we think about it, we do an injustice to . . . these works of art, . . . if we use them as instruments of imitation, in the sole aim of absolving ourselves from the exhausting labor of creation. Why, instead of continuing to reproduce the forms of earlier art, do we not try to equal the creative genius that gave them birth?[47]

The best way to affirm the essence of the French tradition was to promote stylistic change inspired by the "creative genius" embodied in the artifacts of the past. Repetition of the forms of other eras violated "our most precious hereditary gifts,"[48] gifts which Bing described elsewhere as "grace and elegance—which are the tradition of our race."[49]

In emphasizing the interplay between past and present, the exceptional French talent for embellishment, and the imperative of continuous stylistic evolution based on the inspiration from, rather than the imitation of, splendors from the French past, Bing echoed the central concepts not only of Victor Champier but of Roger Marx. The law of French tradition for Roger Marx was "innovate or perish."[50] In 1895 Bing stated similarly that it was "a fundamental law to be ever and always equal to the perpetual metamorphoses of the times, the day, and the present hour."[51] Roger Marx had qualified his declaration by emphasizing that if "interior decoration" had to "vibrate in unison with the modern soul," it was also bound to extend and affirm the essential core of the national temperament:

> The masters of modern decoration . . . project among us the signs of our national gifts of elegance, grace, and verve, those gifts that have always expressed the particularism of our temperament. We recognize and admire in them . . . the power to cast in matter the distinguishing features of French genius. We value comfort only when it is sheathed in elegance and seduction.[52]

Bing similarly extolled a modernism governed by "our most precious hereditary gifts," gifts of "elegance and grace that are the tradition of our race." A French modern style must rest on the renewed expression of those immutable "distinguishing features of French genius," just as the "new aesthetic" in America was "framed by local conditions, a particular time, and the spirit of a race."[53]

Bing's essay of 1895 revealed his ideological affinities with other members of the official craft coalition not only in affirming artistic innovation within the framework of the national temperament but also in glorifying a particular type of solidarity. His report propounded a collaborative model of artistic production, based on an appeal to organic logic. Collective solidarity celebrating unity in diversity: this was Bing's vision of the social formation binding the creators of an art nouveau.

Written during the very year that the republican solidarists came to power, Bing's official report resonated with the underlying intellectual assumptions that guided the organicist politicians. Léon Bourgeois posited a vision of community through an appeal to an organic logic of union in diversity: harmony and solidarity in social relations mirrored the interdependence and individuation in nature. Each cell in the body was essential yet functioned only in relation to the whole organism; similarly, society valued each individual but demanded its contribution to the whole. Roger Marx had expressed his attachment to organic logic in his statements transporting the model of natural order to the social order, as when he compared the differentiation and interdependence in nature to the working totality of society. Siegfried Bing replicated the form of this organic logic; he applied it not to the whole society of the macrocosm but to the artistic community in the microcosm.

Bing's affirmation of unity in diversity in a modern craft community derived from his observation of Louis Tiffany in the American scene. Tiffany had just expanded his operations to include not only glassmaking but all parts of the design, execution, and installation of interior ensembles, thus necessitating the coordination of artisans from many different branches of the applied arts, who worked together in a common plan and stylistic pattern. Bing celebrated Tiffany's organization of a "vast central workshop" where metalworkers, jewelers, cabinetmakers, ceramicists, and glassblowers collaborated under one roof, guided by a "common current of ideas."[54] Bing claimed not only to have witnessed Tiffany's coordination of diverse artisans but to have perceived a "moral bond" uniting all the dispersed individual craftsmen in America: "It is primarily the moral ties that draw them together and the close communion of their various characteristics that today distinguish the industrial arts in America."[55]

Moral bonds and "communion"—individual efforts and powerful unitary goals— what Bing observed in the American arts scene mirrored what the republican solidarists sought in the French political scene. Bing's own recommendations in the 1895 report corresponded to the intellectual outlook of the political elite to whom he submitted his findings. He focused on the need to facilitate the unity of the arts as well as the moral solidarity of artisans. The republican solidarists had used the language of "communion" and "moral bonds" in their attempt, after a decade of anticlericalism, to discover new spiritual bonds to unify a secularist community. Bing offered a model of such collectivity and diversity in his vision of a modern craft initiative:

> A moral bond and tacit collaboration uniting scattered efforts; over a multitude of external forms, identical tendencies, . . . adapted to the particular conditions of time and place. . . . Establishing close ties and a real sense of solidarity among the most diverse art forms, major or minor, summoning the most humble individual skills to the most lofty plans for an ensemble. And harmony emanates from all these diverse contributions, riveted on a common goal: unity within complexity.[56]

Bing thus expressed a solidarist political goal in the context of artistic revitalization. If harmony based on both unity and the division of labor was difficult to forge for society as a whole, Bing's report offered republicans the comforting compensatory possibility of facilitating harmony in diversity within the craft community.

Bing's organic logic coincided not only with solidarist republican social theory but with the solidarist conception of historical time. Cyclical renewal, bound by the irrevocable rhythm of the unfolding of the seasons, was the essence of organicist time; the particular problems of the moment were tempered by the assurance that nature would continue on its immutable course. The image of the sower on the coins of the Third Republic gave striking visual expression to the solidarist quest for a unifying, eternal national time, as it appealed to the primal and predictable rhythms of planting, sowing, and reaping.

For Siegfried Bing the historical process responded to two forces: national temperament and the coercive power of nature. Bing's conception of national temperament not only led him to project different modern styles for different nations but also affected his understanding of historical time as governed by the eternal and essential forces of nature. Throughout his 1895 report Bing discussed the development of artistic style in organic metaphors. The motive force behind artistic creation, for example, was a vital bloodstream, an organic national "*sève vivace.*"[57] And verbs associated with planting and growth, "*germer,*" "*semer,*" and "*surgir,*" appeared repeatedly in his report of 1895.[58] The modern style would take root in "a fertile field."[59] And the French were the sowers of taste and art, the "tireless educators of all nations, who for centuries have sowed the seed of our artistic knowledge."[60] Bing's final practical recommendation was to support artistic regeneration based on the design of organic forms. His observation of craftsmen like Tiffany in America bolstered the vision Bing had already adopted from Japanese arts and crafts. The "art nouveau" of Japanese prints and screens and the "youthful vigor" of American design were joined by a common appeal to nature as the source of integrated artistic ensembles. As nature provided the model for social unity in diversity and the basis for an appeal to a suprapolitical cycle of time, so it was the crucible of a modern style, adapted to each nation's temperament and needs. "The return to Nature is the point of departure of a new aesthetic, framed by local conditions, a particular time, and the spirit of a race."[61]

CHAPTER ELEVEN

Art Nouveau: Organicizing and Feminizing the Crafts in the Central Union of the Decorative Arts

WHILE THE GOVERNMENT embarked on a program of craft revitalization based on national roots and natural forms, the Central Union pursued its own program of craft modernism during the 1890s. Shifting its efforts from rococo revivalism after 1889, the Central Union launched its "new program,"[1] whose character and ideology were closely aligned with those of state initiatives for the crafts. Union leaders promoted three central ideals during the 1890s: the imperative of stylistic evolution, guided by the special and immutable qualities of the "national genius"; the reunification of all the arts; and the derivation of an art nouveau from the ever-flowing source of nature.

Although the goals of the Central Union during the 1890s thus echoed those being promoted in official circles, the union injected a new element into its program: the special role and responsibility of French women in regenerating the national applied arts. During the 1880s, scholars affiliated with the union had examined the tradition of the aristocratic woman as both a producer of decorative arts and the inspiration for artisans of rococo organic ensembles. The special link between aristocratic women and the applied arts had been celebrated by the Goncourts and researched by union scholars such as Henry Havard, Paul Mantz, and Henri Bouchot. During the 1890s the Central Union modernized this tradition, launching a series of initiatives to create a contemporary equivalent of the aristocratic female contribution to the crafts. The union campaigned for the reentry of women into the leadership of luxury craft production and consumption. The creativity and refinement of aristocratic female ancestors provided a model of inspiration for contemporary participation. The new women of the late nineteenth century could aspire, under union auspices, to be the queens of the decorative arts, joining together as a female aristocracy of the spirit rather than of lineage. The "elegance and grace" that were so consistently touted as the "distinguishing features of the French race," were thus to be returned to the vessels that inspired them: the bodily forms and the "magical, deft" hands of French women.[2]

The Exhibition of the Plant
and the Exhibition of the Arts of Woman,
1889–1892

On the eve of the closing of the Paris World Exhibition of 1889, the Central Union of the Decorative Arts embarked on its first major initiative to promote a craft modern style. The union organized its own exhibition, designed to explore and display a new source for craft invention, based on nature; the Exhibition of the Plant was to combine a massive botanical display with a display of the applied arts, interior ensembles, and furniture inspired by living organic forms. Scheduled to open in 1892, the Exhibition of the Plant enlisted the efforts of all the major artisans belonging to the Central Union: Gallé, Falize, Couty, Galland, Christofle, and Delaherche (Fig. 40).[3]

For the display of plants and the decorative arts derived from them, the union planning committee chose the Gallery of Machines on the Champ-de-Mars. Until 1889, the union had installed its craft exhibits—the Exhibition of Metal, that of Glass, Earth, Stone, and Wood—in galleries rented from the Palace of Industry. Indeed, the Palace of Industry functioned as the temporary headquarters of the Decorative Arts Museum while protracted negotiations continued for a permanent structure. The choice of the massive Gallery of Machines as the site for the Exhibition of the Plant signified a particular and striking decision about the character of a French modern style. In the 1889 exhibition, the Gallery of Machines and its pendant structure, the Eiffel Tower, had boldly proclaimed the birth of a French technological aesthetic. The Gallery's vast iron and glass architecture and the whirring machinery it housed overwhelmed the public and transported it into a collective mechanical future.[4] In planning the Exhibition of the Plant, the Central Union of the Decorative Arts aimed to replace the working machinery of 1889 with diminutive organic crafts and endless rows of plant and flower beds. In the very belly of the structure that embodied the potential of a new technological world of the future, the Central Union would plant a garden, thereby associating the iron and glass edifice with the greenhouse and its traditional and familiar purpose.[5]

The silversmith Lucien Falize welcomed the Exhibition of the Plant as a way to reconquer for nature the denuded Gallery of Machines, which was a vast lifeless "desert." Like many others in 1889, Falize was terrified of the immensity of the gallery's span, feeling that there he was "diminished almost to nothing."[6] Initially the idea of the union exhibition in the gallery frightened Falize equally; the structure was so vast that it would overwhelm anything in it. But after visiting the gallery, he became an enthusiastic supporter of the exhibition. He welcomed the transformation of the Gallery of Machines into a gigantic greenhouse, and envisioned the sprouting of gardens where machines had once whirred as "the realization of Paradise, a second Eden." The transformed gallery, bursting with innumerable varieties of organic life, would provide lush terrain for promenades protected from sun, rain, and dust.

Fig. 40. Model drawing for the use of plant forms in goldsmithing and silver-smithing, by Paul Christofle. From *Revue des arts décoratifs,* 1891.

The cathedral raised to the gods of science, technology, and engineering would be replaced by a "cathedral raised as a temple to Nature."[7]

Falize and his co-workers, however, were never to enter the new promised land. In 1891, as the committees for the Exhibition of the Plant were meeting, another major enterprise undertaken by the Central Union was coming to fruition. For over three years the union had lobbied in the Chamber of Deputies for the creation of a permanent decorative arts museum to be housed on the grounds of the former accounting offices of Napoléon III along the quai d'Orsay and the Seine. In 1891, the project proposal was evaluated by a state budget committee and presented to the Chamber of Deputies, which voted to accept it, provided that both the Chamber and the Senate approve the architectural plans and that the Central Union, though aided by state subsidies, bear the major financial responsibility for the project's construction.[8]

Although the Central Union's administrative council members were pleased with the approval, the union decided that it could not cover both the initial costs of reconstructing the quai d'Orsay and the cost of mounting the exhibition in the Gallery of Machines. The plan for the exhibition was canceled; in its place the Central Union proposed a smaller but related exhibit for 1892, to be mounted in the galleries the union usually rented in the Palace of Industry—an Exhibition of the Arts of Woman.[9]

The movement from plants to women was fitting. If a French art nouveau conceived as artisanal luxury could not be implanted in the belly of the machine, it would flourish in another site under the charming guidance and fecundity of women. Financial constraints did not eradicate the union's interest in exhibiting the shape and scope of a new organic artisanal modern style in 1892; the union merely shifted the focus of the show from one form of organicism to another. What "more ingenious way to replace the flower" than with the woman? The new exhibition, a union committee member suggested, would "charm us with its 'Parisianisms' and its studied flirtations."[10] Another union writer affirmed that nature, ceaselessly revitalizing itself, had its social analogue in women, who devoted themselves, in self-presentation, to the art of continual renewal. And it was "woman's role and mission in society" to embody "nature's freshness" in her seasonally changing physical adornments and interior surroundings.[11]

The Central Union president, Georges Berger, welcomed the alternative to the plant show as a reaffirmation of "old French gallantry."[12] He invoked women and the aristocratic French past as rich resources for a French modernism construed as crafted luxuries patterned after the forms of nature. Modernity, once prefigured in the colossal power of iron and glass technology, would now be embodied in the French "national genius" for "elegance, grace, and luxury objects":

> Represented will be women from all the enlightened classes of society, . . . who charm their leisure hours with the artistry of delicate needlework, wrought by enchanted fingers. . . . In the name of old French gallantry, let us give the patronesses of the decorative arts a meeting place worthy of their talents and devotion.[13]

In the eighteenth century, as the Goncourts and union scholars had demonstrated, noblewomen had amused themselves by engaging in delicate, deft handiwork, such as the "lace" and "knotting" activities pursued by the daughters of Louis XV. On their dresses, in their hair, and on chairs and pillows women had applied their craft of adornment and fantasy. Berger reinvoked this tradition by describing the "enchanted fingers" of "enlightened women" who "charmed their leisure" with artistic diversion. Yet Berger called such women in the 1890s not to a diversionary fantasy but to a duty of national salvation. Declaring that the "women belonging to all the enlightened classes of society" were the directors and protectors of the decorative arts, Berger assigned them the task of ensuring French economic and artistic ascendancy.[14]

The First Exhibition of the Arts of Woman, 1892

The first Exhibition of the Arts of Woman was organized in two major parts, "modern and retrospective," following the format of previous Central Union shows. Both parts of the show were subdivided into sections. The three retrospective sections of the exhibition illustrated the decorative arts practiced by women and the work of artisans who had adorned women both in "the art of dress," and in the "art of decorating the home."[15] One group in the retrospective section encompassed "works of the female arts," such as tapestries, embroideries, painting, engraving, and lace fashioned by women beginning in the sixteenth century. A major attraction of this group was the decorated harpsichord of Marie Antoinette.[16] The committee charged with executing this historical exhibit had many illustrious members, among them the union council members Heron de Villefosse, the comte de Ganay, the marquis de Biancourt, and the baron G. de Rothschild; the rococo scholars Germain Bapst, Henri Béraldi, Alfred de Champeaux, Henri Bouchot, and Edmond Bonaffé; and specialists on the decorative arts of the Far East: Siegfried Bing, Louis Gonse, and Charles Ephrussi.[17]

In addition to the works of female arts, the retrospective section included displays on the history of woman's costume, and the history of the art of hairdressing. Each of these was directed by a committee with scholarly expertise. Marius Vachon, author of the massive *La Femme dans l'art, les protectrices des arts, les femmes artistes,* was responsible for the display on hairdressing. Vachon's helpers were members of "a guild of Parisian hairdressers," who created a series of elaborate wax busts of women of previous eras to show the variety and complexity of "the art of coiffure."[18]

The catalogue for this section of the exhibit suggests the type of women identified with the art of adornment. The cover depicted a delicately ornamented woman of the eighteenth century, her dress billowing as she emerged from a portable *chaise* (Fig. 41). The *chaise,* resembling at once a throne and a chariot, was decorated with tassels and sparkling jewels much like those the woman herself wore. A man to her left held open the door of the carriage to watch her emerge. He was the artist-coiffeur, who had fashioned the woman's hairdo to enhance and harmonize with her magnificent costume. A servant bowed, one arm on a pole of the *chaise;* it is clear that this servant also carried the woman in her elegant box.

The wax figures for the hairdressing exhibit continued the theme of aristocratic feminine decoration. All periods of female coiffure were represented, from antiquity to the Second Empire, but the display favored the eighteenth-century woman. Multiple examples of coiffure in the time of Louis XV and Louis XVI related the adornment of women's hair to their other adornments. The ornaments in the hair of the three wax women from the time of Louis XV, for example, matched exactly those affixed to the women's bodices—feathers, bows, and floral wreaths. Thus the noble tradition of the woman as an elaborately orchestrated objet d'art served by artist-craftsmen was given a prominent place in the exhibition.

The eighteenth-century woman in the retrospective sections of the Exhibition of the Arts of Woman, however, was overshadowed by her modern equivalent, the woman of leisure, an applied artist whose needs were served by male artisans. The union emphasized what the program called the "modern woman, with her elegances and the arts she practices, moving in the framework of the residence she artfully adorns."[19] The union president Georges Berger urged the participants in the show to

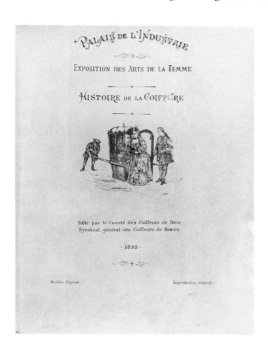

Fig. 41. Exhibition of the Arts of
Woman catalogue cover, 1892. Courtesy
of the Bibliothèque Nationale, Paris.

endorse originality and stylistic integrity and to aspire to a "vital innovative spirit in
expressive form, . . . an absolutely new environment."[20] To this end, the modern
section of the exhibition included a display entitled Manufacture, Objects of Female
Usage, whose ten subclasses spanned the range of applied arts by or for women,
including furniture, leather work, basket weaving, cutlery, jewelry, feathers, artificial flowers, lace, embroidery, clothing, and apparel accessories. On the committee responsible for mounting this section of the show were representatives from syndical chambers, Central Union council members, and arts administrators: Henri
Bouilhet, vice president of the union and manager of the Christofle silverworks;
Fould, Christofle, and Falize; and Edmond Williamson, director of the Garde-
Meuble National.[21]

Some of the decorative objects produced by women themselves were donated by
professional schools that trained young women in "the techniques of luxury goods'
manufacture: screens, feathers, flowers, lace, and embroideries."[22] Other objects had
been fashioned by "high society women," some of whom were the wives of Central
Union council members. One reporter at the show noted that though in this area
there was a mélange of styles reminiscent of Japonism, the Renaissance, and the
eighteenth century, the group as a whole favored variations on the styles of the eighteenth century.[23] The objects created for this section of the show included screens,
piano covers, and draperies by the comtesses de Greffulhe, de Pailleron, de Gramont
Aster, and de Saint Marceau and children's clothes and small bronzes by the comtesse
de Biancourt.[24] The princesse de Bibesco and Madame Jean-Martin Charcot contrib-

uted the most ambitious projects of craft design and application. The princesse de
Bibesco created a carved wooden crib, decorated with colored *pyrogravure,* a new
technical process of electrical incision on wood. If the chatelaine of old had sat, like
Madame de Pompadour, at her embroidery frame, the nineteenth-century aristocratic female artisan used new technology to create diminutive graceful objects. Like
the *haut luxe* sector of the furniture trade, which was able to incorporate the newest
technological inventions to produce goods of the highest quality, this female artisan
could afford sophisticated modern tools for luxury objects.

Madame Charcot's contribution to the exhibition added a note of cultural modernism to the princesse de Bibesco's technological advances. Madame Charcot,
along with her daughters Jeanne and Madame Waldeck-Rousseau, was a participant
in the family atelier directed by Doctor Jean-Martin Charcot. Madame Charcot's
1892 exhibition piece was a large wooden coffer, covered with colored arabesques
(Fig. 42). It had two heavy wooden doors that opened to reveal a large carved and
decorated surface: On this surface Madame Charcot had incised ten compartments
of equal size. On each compartment Madame Charcot had designed images that appeared to be a form of hieroglyphics: stylized birds, fish, and other elongated creatures. A central panel represented another unfamiliar creature: a black owl with a
humanoid face; two other birds, one white, one black, seem to be pecking at it.

COFFRET DE Mme CHARCOT.

Fig. 42. Coffer by Madame Charcot, 1892. Courtesy of the Bibliothèque Nationale, Paris.

Madame Charcot's coffer, heavy, black, and wooden on its outer layer, and color-ful, fantastic, and grotesque on its inner layer, had suggestive overtones, particularly for the wife of the doctor who explored the inner chambers of the mind and its imagistic receptivity and capacity for externalization. The coffer, with its dual struc-ture, corresponded to the divided psyche: a rational facade and an irrational interior lurking beneath the surface of appearances—the dream world where grotesque pic-tures could be unleashed when the critical faculties were relaxed. Indeed, the coffer's birdlike creatures resembled some of the hybrid animals populating the hallucina-tory drawing of the young Doctor Charcot. Madame Charcot's craft work brought to the Central Union exhibition an evocation of a psychological structure whose generalizable features were still being debated by the followers of her husband and Doctor Hippolyte Bernheim.

Modernism, the New Woman, and Central Union Ideology, 1892–1896

The Exhibition of the Arts of Woman in 1892 represented the initial efforts of the Central Union to concentrate on promoting a French modern style based on or-ganicism, the luxury crafts, and female allies and producers. Between 1892 and 1896, the momentum for this kind of modernism intensified. The campaign to link a French modern style to women as both the artists and ornaments of the home flowed from the recovered aristocratic tradition of women's central role in the decorative arts. But the "woman question" in the fin de siècle colored the motives and mean-ings of the feminization of the decorative arts between 1892 and 1896.

The celebration of women as the central inspiration for modern artisans and as creators of objets d'art was proclaimed in the new cover of the *Revue des arts décoratifs* after 1895. Until that time, the cover had had a rococo design, with the title in a typical mid-eighteenth-century frame. Rococo details—a picturesque mélange of trellises, leafy foliage, and grotto-work—were incorporated into this design, and shells, flora, putti, and trellis netting also provided a decorative motif inside the jour-nal (see Fig. 30).

The new cover did not eradicate the rococo motifs but significantly transformed them. Vestiges of the rococo organicism remained even as new forms and figures gave the cover a quintessentially fin-de-siècle composition (Fig. 43). The *Revue* title was now emblazoned above an arch of birds, resembling doves, that hovered over a central female figure: a young woman with long flowing hair and elegant billowing robes. The woman perched calmly on the branches of a tree rich in foliage, flowers, and fruits. Wide-eyed, she stared straight ahead, in her right hand a flower, appar-ently a lily. The woman blended into her organic surroundings. Her delicate feet showed under her long robes as she reclined against the branches of the tree. Her hair flowed in and around the foliage and fruits on the tree branches. Her costume inte-grated real and artificial flowers: the long dress was adorned with a band of flowers at

Fig. 43. Revue des arts décoratifs cover,
1898. Courtesy of the Bibliothèque
Nationale, Paris.

the chest and a wider band of flowers and leaves at the hem. She wore a wreath of
flowers on her head. The woman sat between two poles—not branches of the tree
but suggestions of a throne: she was the queen of organic design, enthroned in a tree,
a delicate and receptive ruler.

Even before the *Revue des arts décoratifs* adopted its new cover, its pages affirmed
women's role in craft renovation. In campaigning for women as rulers of the decorative arts, situated in the home, the union directly confronted organized French
feminism and the "new woman" after 1892. The Central Union appointed a Madame
M. Pégard to prepare a report to its National Congress for the Decorative Arts,
jointly sponsored with the Ministry of Beaux-Arts, at the Ecole des Beaux-Arts in
Paris in May 1894. Madame Pégard's task was to explore one of four key areas identified in the congress's program as guiding the future of the French decorative arts:
"the role and influence of women on the artistic development of our country."[25]
Madame Pégard was a participant in and official stenographer at French feminist
congresses,[26] and her political commitments shaped her report to the Central Union
on the role of women in the arts. The statements she read to the decorative arts congress marked her as a republican "familial feminist"; she articulated claims for wom-
en's rights within the framework of national obligation.

Madame Pégard began her presentation with a polite but forceful account of her
experiences at the 1893 Chicago World Exposition, where the first Women's Building was constructed as a showcase of arts by and for women. She explained how

deeply impressed she had been by the "independence, initiative, and authority" of the American women organizers of the Women's Building and how their efforts had inspired female solidarity, revealed to the public the diversity and quality of women's artistic works, and offered the participants a strong and needed boost in their own sense of "self-worth."[27] The American example suggested to her the untapped potential of French women, who were treated with "flagrant injustice" and "imprudent, unmerited exclusion" by French men.[28] She chastized her male audience for making women the "victims" of unequal laws, institutions, and salaries, and she articulated general claims for more equitable opportunity for females.[29]

Yet as Pégard turned to the specific question at hand—the role of women in the arts movement—her feminism was tempered by her nationalism. Her praise for the American women was muted by her belief in the "superiority" of French women and the arts they produced.[30] Pégard's *mémoire* subordinated the feminist critique to an affirmation of the special endowments shared by all French citizens: what she termed "the innate gift of our race for taste in the arts."[31] Echoing her union colleagues, Pégard indicated that this taste was no longer sufficient to retain primacy in a competitive international market. She identified the conservation of French craft preeminence as the most urgent problem besetting the decorative arts, to which women's actions and claims had to be referred. She proposed that women collaborate with men in the "national defense" of France's decorative arts.[32]

What did this effort entail specifically for French women? Pégard's recommendations centered on women's roles as homemakers, wives, and consumers. "Does not woman organize the home? Does she not preside over the arrangements of the interior? Does she not choose the furnishings, porcelains, bronzes, laces, silverware, tapestries, all those trinkets and a thousand things that give a residence its elegance and charm? And does she not select those numerous objects that add to female beauty: the textures, laces, embroideries, jewels, flowers, etc., etc.?" Pégard explained that it was thus upon women, the artificers of interior spaces and of themselves as objets d'art that the progress of the decorative arts depended.[33] Because women's choices and acquisitions were so directly responsible for the fate of the national applied arts, Pégard's main proposal was for the reeducation of French women's tastes by instructing women buyers to recognize and sponsor French products of good quality. French women's innate propensities for elegance and refinement were deflected by the sheer volume of the goods available in department stores and by women's need to economize. Pégard suggested that women be deterred from buying the "shoddy" product in the large stores and that they learn to patronize individual French artisans. Women consumers should be advised that it was preferable to spend more money on an expensive object of high quality made in a shop than to economize by purchasing a poorly made product from a department store.[34] She appealed to her male audience to enlist women for the "patriotic duty" of supporting the national crafts:

> You must instruct woman more . . . raise her spirits, . . . provide a goal for her activities, and enlist her in . . . the cause of national prosperity. . . . Gentlemen, solidarity is a great power. . . . Call on women! . . . Use her talents for

the wisdom and prosperity of all—do not forget that she is the buyer of your arts products. . . . When she knows she has been called on . . . she will not betray the trust you have placed in her. . . . Thus we will work together for a common goal, the primacy of our arts and . . . the grandeur and wealth of our *patrie.*[35]

Madame Pégard's report sounded the themes of bourgeois "familial feminism," whose adherents accepted the sexual division of labor, proclaimed their nationalism, and allied themselves politically with republican solidarists, with whom they shared social backgrounds as well as reformist tendencies.[36] Pégard assumed the continuity of women's assigned role in the home. Despite her general claims for equality and opportunity, her specific recommendations hinged on women's roles as domestic consumers and organizers of the interior world. Although Pégard's report included propositions for the improved education of women craft designers, her main focus remained bourgeois female production in and for the home. Like familial feminists, she emphasized those changes for women that enhanced their activities in their assigned sphere. And her nationalist discourse corresponded to the bourgeois feminists' affirmation that national and maternal duties took precedence over the claims of the individual. Her appeal to "solidarity as a force" extended the alliance of "familial feminists" and republican solidarists from legal reform to craft reform. In each case the collaboration of the women and politicians was predicated on maintaining the "separate spheres" while expanding women's activities within the designated domestic realm.

Madame Pégard's male colleagues at the decorative arts congress enthusiastically endorsed her proposal to grant French women a central role in revitalizing national crafts; at the same time, they firmly refused to confront the general issues of women's rights that Pégard raised in her introductory remarks.[37] In the aftermath of the 1894 congress, the Central Union moved to institutionalize Pégard's suggestions that women be involved in elevating the quality of the crafts and in educating French taste by creating a *section féminine* within the organization, directed by a Comité des dames. Madame Pégard was appointed to direct the new Women's Committee. Joining her were aristocratic and bourgeois *grandes dames,* many of them the wives of Central Union associates. The president of the Women's Committee was Madame la générale Fevrier; the four vice presidents were Mesdames la princesse de Broglie, Paul Christofle, marquise de Nadailhac, and Jules Siegfried. The full membership list of the committee is worth enumerating:

La comtesse de Baulaincourt, la comtesse Réné de Béarn, Madame Georges Berger, Princesse Bibesco, Madame Bouilhet, Madame Cavignac, Madame Charcot, Madame Délaville-Le Roux, Duchesse d'Estissac, Baronne de Gartempe, Madame de Gosselin, Comtesse Greffulhe, née la Rochefoucauld, Comtesse Greffulhe, née de Caraman-Chimay, Madame Lefébure, Madeleine Lemaire, Madame Moreau-Nélaton, Madame Pailleron, Madame Réymond, Madame Emile Rousseau, Madame Paul Sédille, Madame Schlumberger,

Duchesse d'Uzès, Madame Georges Ville, Madame la comtesse Louis de Vogüé.[38]

All of these women were practitioners of the decorative arts, and many had exhibited their artifacts in the 1892 Exhibition of the Arts of Woman. In their craft creations they expressed their continuity with the artistic practices of their illustrious female ancestors, whose drawing circles and applied arts creations reached their apogee in the eighteenth century. The bourgeois women committee members and producers were linked to the crafts through their husbands, some of whom, as artisans themselves, were leading producers of luxuries or officials of the Central Union. Among this group were Paul Christofle's wife, Henri Bouilhet's wife, and Moreau-Nélaton's wife.

The Women's Committee was granted a "certain autonomy" in the union organization while remaining under the final authority of the union's administrative council. In its charter, prepared by Madame Pégard, the new committee proclaimed that women must "involve themselves in the progress of the arts and in expressing their love of country and of solidarity."[39] The charter restated the responsibility of women to create in the home an artistic ensemble and hence their importance for the future of the decorative arts. The charter appealed to *femmes du monde,* "society women," to embrace their role as patrons and producers of fine interior objects and decors, and it also asked them to serve as instructors both in refining taste and in choosing worthy artistic models and associates for craft renovation. In addition, the charter articulated the need for a cross-class alliance between elite women directors of taste and women craft workers; the committee proposed programs whose goal would be "works of philanthropy and social fraternity." Toward this goal, the charter noted plans for future exhibitions that would combine displays of objects produced by leisured society women and by women who were employed as artisans and stated that the committee would investigate the range of artistic training available to young girls seeking employment in the design and applied arts industries.[40]

As its first official acts, the Women's Committee announced a competition for the design of an umbrella with an ornamented handle and case and scheduled meetings to discuss the creation of a national school of fine needlework, to teach a skill whose ancient traditions and women practitioners were endangered by foreign competition and mechanization.[41]

The new Central Union Women's Committee included some prominent advocates of French republican "familial feminism": Madame Jules Siegfried, the duchesse d'Uzès, and Madame Schlumberger along with Madame Pégard herself strongly represented reformist feminism.[42] Respecting existing role divisions, these elite figures aimed to widen women's opportunities while enhancing their special nature and separate functions. The association of Mesdames Siegfried, Uzès, and Schlumberger with the Central Union, like that of Madame Pégard, enabled them to act on their particular form of feminism. The Central Union's campaign for women as the directors of revitalized interior design extended the doctrine of "equality in difference" to cultural action. Familial feminists could rally to a program that invested women with a special mission concordant with their assigned domestic duties: the renovation of the decorative arts and the artistic regeneration of the interior. The appeal to philanthropy, class solidarity, and nationalist sentiment in the charter of the Women's Committee reflected ideas similar to those that led familial feminists to join forces with republican solidarist politics.

While the familial feminists found in the Central Union Women's Committee a forum for promoting and expanding women's special capacities, the male associates of the Central Union had other motives for celebrating women's unique responsibilities for interior decoration. Union officials and writers were preoccupied, after 1892, with the menace of the "new woman." Like their republican counterparts, Central Union spokesmen expressed a variety of attitudes toward the woman question, ranging from strident antifeminism to a more guarded endorsement of limited domestic reform. Whatever their attitude, however, they were made uneasy by the possible changes in sex roles and the compounding problem of the declining birthrate. They glorified women as the creators of private spaces, redirecting new energies for women's actions from the public professionalism of the "new woman" to the productive artistry of the maternal decorator. They tried to defuse the threat of the unattractive careerist *amazone* or *hommesse* by attributing to women special powers over the domestic interior and the arts called upon in furnishing it.

Louis de Fourcaud made the first explicit reference to the menace of the *femme nouvelle* in relation to the special feminine mission for the decorative arts. De Fourcaud reviewed the Union's first Exhibition of the Arts of Woman in 1892, articulating his ideas about women's peculiar propensity for the applied arts and their destiny as the objects of male delight and his assumptions about "female genius" and the "weaker sex." Regardless of her social station,

> Woman is endowed with a penetrating charm, with a persistence that makes us her slave, a tenderness that bewitches us . . . , and with so many jumbled fantasies that we ceaselessly attempt to satisfy. . . . By recognizing within her nothing but the enchanted and drunken fullness of life, we have too narrowly defined her role; she is, at all levels, the stimulant and the pivot. We lose ourselves for her and save ourselves through her. Do not decry it; that is how it is. [43]

De Fourcaud's conception of the female as the source of life, fantasy, and vitality was almost a characterization of nature itself: the "stimulant" and the "pivot" of all creation and the source of continuity and renewal.

Yet in de Fourcaud's analysis women were not only the spark for male creation. They themselves produced personal and domestic adornments and decorations. Even though De Fourcaud applauded the vast array of the "female arts" at the exhibition of 1892, he perceived in them—cribs, pillows, embroidered chairs, piano covers, and so forth—the limits of female art. Women were talented in application but had no access to creative inspiration. They could endow objects with the delicate asymmetries of fantasy but could not be trusted with the transcendent realm of painting:

What a woman suggests is worth more than what she conceives. . . . She as-
similates, she adapts, she imitates with extreme delicacy. . . . Technically a
woman excels at small tasks, no matter how minute, as long as they require
nimble hands. As regards invention, woman is superior when she derives a
modified impressionability from her constant contact with practical matters,
such as directing manners, the endless composition of attires, the expressive
organization of furnishings, and the overall harmony of interior details. She is
a born upholsterer, seamstress, refined decorator of intimate space, an inex-
haustible orchestrator of worldly elegance. For everything else, her lofty function is to be an inspiration, even when she does not know it.[44]

De Fourcaud disagreed with those who argued that women should, like men, work
in many varied areas. That could only lead women to pain and failure. "To struggle
categorically with men violated woman's nature and diminished her." "Only a fool
would give herself such trouble, only to be defeated"; woman could better win over
"the sons of Adam" by remaining her inspirational and enchanting self.[45]

The president of the Central Union, Georges Berger, defined women's roles with
a different emphasis. In 1895 he wrote "Appeal to French Women," published some
months later in the *Revue des arts décoratifs.*[46] Rather than declare categorically that
women were destined to the applied arts because they could not rise to the demands
and visionary power required for the beaux-arts of painting and sculpture, Berger
strove to elevate the domestic applied arts of women to the rank of high art. By
making a positive claim for women's artistic powers, Berger attached himself to the
ideals of familial feminism. He confronted the issues of women's rights, education,
and productivity but redefined them: women had a productive role, for example,
but it was a specifically domestic one. According to Berger, women had to be acknowledged for their contribution to the nation and were to be celebrated as artists
in their own right—artists in and of the interior.

Berger began where de Fourcaud had left off. De Fourcaud had emphasized that
woman stimulated and inspired men, especially painters: "The activity that she elic-
its is far more profitable to art than her own creative mind."[47] Berger acknowledged
at the beginning of his discussion that indeed "many a seductive page could be filled
with proofs of woman's permanent influence on artistic movements." This influence
was indirect, the effect of female eros on the male imagination: "Passion, inspired by
and felt for women, has certainly determined the great artistic vocations."[48] Intent
on distinguishing influence from aptitude, Berger cautioned lest "sentimental" and
"historical reminiscences" blind us to "certain natural aptitudes of women in the
arts, especially the decorative arts."[49] He confronted directly the issue of female
"emancipation" and role reversal represented by the *femme nouvelle,* responding that
the magical work of decoration belonged singularly to the woman and should be
celebrated and recognized accordingly:

The Central Union will try neither to discern nor to decide if women should
dream of the emancipation some wish for them, an emancipation that would
enable her to fulfill those functions that thus far have been man's. . . . What the

union knows and wants to be known is that woman has been considered, for as long as she has existed and as naturally as she is woman, mother, and lover with her heart and her soul, the marvelous fairy of manual labor. This woman's work . . . galvanizes her artistic sentiment, her innate taste for delicate and gracefully treated things. The union has never hesitated to recognize the manual labor of women in the work of the decorative arts. . . . The union appealed to society women, to women who know how to devote their leisure hours to the production of a thousand little tasks. Their seemingly fatal futility disappears beneath an incontestable appearance of elegance, of alluring originality, and of relative beauty.[50]

Berger's ideas about female productivity and artistic talents were revealing on two counts. First, though he tried to differentiate the instinctual role of women ("by her heart and soul") as mothers and lovers from their potential as producers, their activity was still defined by women's instinct and sensual charm. For Berger could not detach his notion of women's creation of decorative arts from their "innate taste" for the objects that allowed them to express their distinctive "artistic sentiment." Second, he consistently linked women's "manual labor" to the aestheticization of the work itself; women were magical artificers who could turn the "fatal futility" of repetitive and painstaking labor into objects that captured their gracious, elegant fantasy. And Berger's description of these objects' "relative beauty" suggested that women's decorative artistry lacked the quality of other inspired art.

A third spokesman for the Central Union added his voice to that of President Berger in promoting those "delicate and gracefully treated things" created by women. In 1896 Gustave Larroumet, by then a member of the Institut de France, wrote an article in the *Revue des arts décoratifs* entitled "Women and the Decorative Arts." In it he extended the campaign, already under way, to enlist women as the allies of craft innovation and as the creators of revitalized applied arts. Larroumet's article raised the discussion of women and the crafts in the Central Union to a new level. Arguing that women were the natural national resource for taste and elegance in the arts of decoration, Larroumet wanted to make them the leaders of the entire movement. Where de Fourcaud denigrated, and Berger elevated, Larroumet abdicated.

The theme of Gustave Larroumet's 1896 article was reversal: not the role reversal of men and women envisioned by proponents of the *femme nouvelle* but a reversal to reestablish the natural balance of artistic leadership in the applied arts. In Larroumet's mind the decorative arts belonged, by nature, to women, who were endowed with special talents for ornamentation and who developed refined skills through "the adornment of themselves and their homes." He introduced his theme at the beginning of the article, claiming that until the nineteenth century, "the decorative arts had always been the special domain of woman." In the nineteenth century "woman had been overthrown as the director of the decorative arts," a situation that had to be reversed for all the arts to flourish again. "A reversal of roles has to take place," according to Larroumet, for women to resume their natural position as the sovereigns of the decorative arts.[51]

For Larroumet the former splendor of the applied arts and glory of French culture were the fruits of the feminization of those arts. In the nineteenth century sovereignty over the decorative arts had been wrested from women, even though they were naturally suited for it, and they were assigned to the home, the private interior, where embellishment and artistic orchestration were necessary:

> The decorative arts exert their power in our homes and on our persons. They embellish our residential walls; they impress their mark on our everyday objects; they regulate our attire. In all these, the influence of woman rules, or ought to. While man, even the most sedentary, spends a great deal of time outside the home, the most expansive woman remains much of the time at home. In addition, the arrangement of "home" depends on her; it is what she makes of it, either agreeable or sullen, elegant or vulgar. Living room, dining room, bedroom, the most public and the most private chambers, bear her mark. An interior tells nothing of the man who inhabits it; it always reveals the character and taste of the woman who assembled it.[52]

After assigning the fate of the decorative arts to French women, Larroumet articulated a startling and important idea: Petrified archaism, servile imitation, and banal historicism began to characterize the applied arts in France when women ceased to inspire and collaborate with innovative craftsmen. French women should be allowed to resume their rightful places as the queens of the decorative arts. Applauding the many initiatives of both the state and the Central Union to renovate the crafts since 1889, he cautioned that a genuine revitalization awaited women's regaining the power to guide, inspire, and harmonize them. For the center of the applied arts was in the home, and the "quest for intimate decoration" had to begin with women, the guardians of the home.[53]

In the last section of his article, Larroumet linked nature, the role of women, and the modern style of luxury crafts. The fate of modernism, a "new taste," and an "art nouveau" rested with women because they were the agents of renewal, the carriers of youth and vitality. By instinct, women dislike history and the past; they hanker for the present and future. In supplying them with vestiges of historical culture as the raw material for interior design, men violated women's nature, which quested for life, for continuous mobility, for the new:

> For, by nature, women detest any form of archaism. Everything old shocks and shames them. They instinctually move away from what time has touched because of their taste for agreeable sensations and for laughter. Not only do they prefer the present to the past, but they also anticipate the future. They are almost always at the forefront in matters of art.[54]

Because of the proclivity to sensation and its ever-changing patterns and their natural liberation from history, women embodied and represented the organic renewal of the crafts. For women offered what nature itself offered: a stylistic source and a binding potential above the divisive particulars of history. The return of women to the leadership of the decorative arts would insure the embrace of the new, the modern, and the future:

> The time has come to press this taste for youth and novelty into the service of the decorative arts. . . . Let women take over the direction of the movement; let us ask them for their help, and since they have better and more refined taste, since their instinct for elegance is far more developed than ours, they will soon guide us to tomorrow's style. Make no mistake about it; they are tired of the past, its crude forms and dark tints. They prefer softer lines and lighter colors. . . . The time has come for the present, that is, for our customs, our tastes, and our needs to take a preeminent place among our everyday objects of use. By enlisting women in this quest, . . . we will arrive sooner; without them we will not arrive at all.[55]

Larroumet subtly and powerfully subverted the impact of the new woman; his argument, like Berger's, converged with the ethos of familial feminism by widening the realm of women's responsibilities within the framework of the *foyer*. Larroumet appropriated the new theme of women's role and rights to restabilize the traditional female purposes to orchestrate the home and to embellish themselves as objets d'art. He assigned to women the qualities of nature itself and vested them with both the power of artistic regeneration and the leadership of the renovation of the crafts.

In his article Larroumet tied an important modernist ideal to the theme of domesticating and aestheticizing women. He championed women's instinctual antihistoricism; he also identified their natural inclination to "harmony and unity" in the design of interior space. As artistic orchestrators of the interior, women put their talents for harmony, elegance, and unity in design to the service of seduction and pleasure: "Since they spend more time at home than we do, they will arrange for the most comfortable, the most agreeable, and the most flattering setting possible, the one most becoming to their beauty and one to direct, even concentrate, admiring and attentive looks on them."[56] In asking women to return to directing the applied arts, Larroumet celebrated the potential for an integrated design he hoped would result. The essence of this design was feminine, and its goal, what he called art nouveau, was to coordinate all interior surfaces to harmonize with and enhance the beauty of their female inhabitant. Here was a new version of the aristocratic ensemble that Madame de Pompadour had inspired and fashioned: the bourgeois matron, too, should establish herself as a graceful part of an interior setting.

Modernism and the Feminization of the Decorative Arts: The Second Exhibition of the Arts of Woman, 1895

The articulation of the innate talents and social mission of women for the applied arts and the identification of women as the carriers of renewal and organic form flowed directly into the organization of a second Union Exhibition of the Arts of Woman in 1895. The logic of Central Union leaders had crystallized as the perception of the menace of the *femme nouvelle* was heightened, and the 1895 Exhibition resonated with the themes of the new woman. The Second Exhibition of the Arts of Woman differed from the first partly because of feminism and the *femme nouvelle*.

The organization of the exhibition changed in several respects. First, only female artisans could participate; second, the historicist aspect of the show was eliminated and attention given solely to the "modern woman" and the objects of her creation; finally, full responsibility for planning, selecting, and mounting the exhibition was entrusted to the Women's Committee, led by Madame Pégard.

In making these changes, union officials expressed a new theme, which had already surfaced in the charter of the Women's Committee: cross-class female solidarity. Both the objects created by wealthy women in their leisure time and those created by women who were paid for their handiwork were displayed. The union bulletin announced the exhibition's goals: "to develop elegant taste in society women who create physical and household adornments" and to "draw attention to those women who executed decorative works as a financial necessity."[57] With this dual goal President Georges Berger hoped to isolate the problem of the working woman and to reassert woman's role in the home. He acknowledged that many women needed to earn income for their families; if so, they should seek work that would most closely confirm their natural aptitudes and their social duties as wives and mothers: "Woman is especially made for the kind of work that removes her the least from her domestic hearth, permitting her to meet her family obligations with as much ease as possible."[58] Thus the exhibition would encourage women's work in the home, their creation of objects in and for the domestic interior:

> The Central Union is particularly preoccupied with encouraging the production of the numerous tasteful manual arts that a woman can perform at home. The intelligent society woman makes the accomplishment of these works the delight of her interior life; we ask her to take an interest, if only morally and as an example, in the women who make their living from these activities.[59]

Berger's identification of the "intelligent society woman" as a model for the women who must work was revealing. It was consistent with his affirmation of the solidarity between women, across class lines, in their role as artificers of the home. He called on leisured society women to forge moral and artistic bonds with the female decorative arts laborer. Despite their social distance, their feminine talents for the crafts joined them in a common expression of the quintessentially French qualities of "grace" and "taste." The Central Union applauded women in the social elite for both their artistic and their moral contributions; as skillful decorative artists and as philanthropists these women have "recognized the expert and charming works of the paid female decorative artist, and her social condition," generously consenting "to include [in the exhibition] the works of all those young girls who prepare . . . the splendors of the French arts of fashion, attire, and furnishings with such opulent fantasies."[60]

Although Berger wanted to rescue the "hidden personalities" of the "female decorative arts laborer" and to affirm her solidarity with leisured "society women," he sidestepped a central problem: the arduous, even demeaning, work of women in the applied arts. In celebrating women who could work for income at home, Berger ignored the sweat-shop conditions in which some women helped to make the "splendors of French arts." The fan painters, lace makers, and artificial flower and feather makers, for example, were ill-paid; their work places permitted none of the fluid integration of "family obligation" and labor proposed by Berger.[61] The trades that employed women to produce luxury consumer items, particularly costume accessories, were marked by increased specialization, intensified division of labor, and the lowering of wages in the 1890s. Like the furniture trade, the trade in consumer goods catering to women was internally stratified; from dressmaking to screen painting, from porcelain making to artificial flower making, each craft had its upper echelon of producers and its lower tier of sweated laborers.

The selection of items for the Second Exhibition of the Arts of Woman revealed the Central Union's emphasis on artisans in the highest tiers. This was to be a display of works executed by hand, in four main groups: needlework, paintings and drawings, sculptures and engravings, and "diverse works" from basket weaving to leather work and toy making.[62] These four groups of female applied arts were displayed in three rooms: one was devoted to the objects wrought by "society women," many of whom sat on the Women's Committee;[63] a second was devoted to the designs and objects created by young women in the few French schools that existed for women artisans, called the *écoles de dessin* and the *écoles professionelles de jeunes filles;*[64] the third room was given over to works by women artists and female craft associations in both Paris and the provinces.[65]

The themes of aestheticization and feminization of the crafts, removed from the grimy realities of the workplace and centered in the home, resonated in the exhibition's poster and catalogue. The graphic artist Jean Louis Forain executed the poster, on which an elegant woman embodied the relation between women and the arts (Fig. 44). She stood very tall in a long sleeveless gown tied tightly at the waist with a dark sash, arranging a billowing drapery. In her left hand she clasped a fan; on her right arm she wore a long white glove.

Forain's poster was complemented by the exhibition's catalogue cover, which confirmed the theme of the interior, nonindustrial feminine applied arts. On the cover were two women engaged in "the arts of woman" (Fig. 45). The woman on the left was seated, embroidering, her work resting on a small rococo table, partly visible, with slender legs, delicately rounded. Behind her was another table with bottles, vases, and ceramic bowls as well as a plate suspended against the wall—all examples of the arts of women. The intrinsically female character of the applied arts was suggested in the shape of the woman's body that was echoed in the objects around her: the table legs followed the curve of her torso; the slender base and tapered neck of the bottle near her mirrored her bodice and high-necked collar. Indeed, this identity of shape between women and the bottle had been noted in the

Fig. 44. Exhibition of the Arts of Woman
poster, by J.-L. Forain, 1896. Courtesy of the
Bibliothèque Nationale, Paris.

Fig. 45. Exhibition of the Arts of
Woman catalogue cover, 1896. Courtesy
of the Bibliothèque Nationale, Paris.

eighteenth century in Sèvres porcelains called *dames jeannes* and *couper la gorge,* names designating the feminine anthropomorphic character of the objets d'art.

To the right of the seated figure was a second woman, standing, whose long black robes contrasted with the lighter dress of her embroideress neighbor. Wrapped in tenebrous shadow, the tall woman extended her right arm and sketched on the wall the title "The Arts of Woman." Over her head two forms floated mysteriously on the page: a butterfly and a flower, bent tropistically toward the butterfly. The butterfly seemed to fly from the top of an M in the word *Femme* toward the flower, and they appeared about to converge in magnetic attraction. The form and content of the catalogue reflected the various themes of women and the applied arts in the show. The intimate, domestic locus of the crafts was evident, with light and shadows suggesting its mystery and enclosure. The activity of women, with their "enchanted fingers,"[66] was illustrated in the crafts they had fashioned. The eighteenth-century tradition of the particularly female character of the applied arts was suggested visually in the repeating contours of the women's bodies and the delicate objects around them. The new theme of women's role in the late nineteenth-century renovation of the crafts appeared in the connection between the women, the interior, and organicism—suggested by the butterfly and flower. Long the symbol of metamorphosis, the butterfly was a perfect symbol for women and their assigned powers of evolution and organic transformation. As union spokesmen such as Berger and Larroumet had identified woman as the carrier of the present and the future, so the image of the butterfly on the 1895 catalogue celebrated the identity between nature's powers of regeneration and her agent, woman. The flower affirmed the union theme of the *femme-fleur:* fresh, variable, receptive, and revitalizing as nature herself.

Seven months before Siegfried Bing opened his Maison de l'Art Nouveau, Central Union officials and their Women's Committee had articulated all of the elements of the French modern style—feminine, interiorized, and organic. Fueled by the concerns of a "new woman" breaking out of the confines of domesticity, the Central Union endowed women with new powers of decorative creativity and elaborated a conception of an art nouveau propelled by women's instinctual resources for continuous renewal.

CHAPTER TWELVE

Art Nouveau in the Salon, I:
Institutional Reform and Craft Champions

WHILE THE REPUBLICAN government and the Central Union of the Decorative Arts each pursued independent initiatives to promote a French modern style, these two sponsors of craft innovation also converged in a single attempt to unite all the arts. The association between Third Republic cultural administrators, Central Union publicists, luxury artisans, and aristocratic collectors flourished in their common contribution to the reform of the yearly academic Salon. Long the exclusive bastion of the three beaux-arts, the Salon began, after 1889, to include decorative arts as the equal partners of painting, sculpture, and architecture as vessels of beauty. The re-formed Salon represented the realization in France of goals that artists in other European countries won only by defying and rejecting official institutions. While Belgian, German, and Austrian artists championed the unity of the arts and the quest for a modern style of integral design in separate secessionist organizations, many French artists found a comfortable home in their institutions of official culture.

This chapter and the one that follows examine the internal reform of the Salon and the destiny of the decorative arts that were granted entry to it. Particular attention will be paid to the meanings attributed to the applied arts by key critics and creators of French art nouveau in the Salon. This chapter analyzes the interplay of aristocratic tradition and innovative organicism articulated by the critics and creators of the new Salon works. The next chapter discusses some of the Salon artists whose clinically inspired visions of psychological discovery transformed rococo precedents.

The Salon Splits, 1889–1890

Both the academic doctrine and the canons governing exhibition of the three beaux-arts had been solidified by Jacques-Louis David during the French Revolution. After establishing the Institut National, David systematized the division between the "lofty" arts of painting, sculpture, and architecture and the "inferior" arts of decoration and application. His theory emerged from a radical moralistic attack on the opulent indulgences of pre-Revolutionary aristocratic culture. In a period when a new, national, citizenry was in the making, all forms of communication were mobilized to serve the Revolution. The elevation of the three beaux-arts, especially paint-ing, derived from their capacity to carry moral and political messages and to instruct the people in the lessons of virtue and reason.

In the aftermath of the Revolution, the Davidian canons for the Institut remained rigidly in force, divested of their original raison d'être. As the rules for artistic prac-tice petrified, some initiatives for reform were undertaken, the most notorious among them the reforms of 1863, which resulted in the temporary reorganization of both the award system and teaching at the Ecole des Beaux-Arts.[1] These reforms, how-ever, were short-lived. By 1874 the jury and prize system had been reestablished. In 1880 the organization of the yearly Salon of painting and sculpture was transferred from the Academy to the artists themselves, in the form of the Society of French Artists, whose members consisted exclusively of former exhibitors in the Salons in preceding years. They elected the Salon jury and placed at its head illustrious mem-bers of the Institut.[2]

The split within the Salon in 1889–1890 must be understood in this context of three decades of partial internal reforms. The split was precipitated by the dissatis-faction of some artists with the system of rewards to those who participated in the Paris World's Fair in 1889. This dissatisfaction soon broadened to include the issue of the applied arts, some artists arguing that decorative arts should be exhibited along-side painting in the yearly Salons, while others argued that they should not. In 1890 the Salon split into two wings: the Society of French Artists, led by Bouguereau, mounted its Salon in the galleries of the Palace of Industry along the Champs-Elysées; the dissident wing, comprising artists who wanted reform in the selection and reward processes, called themselves the National Society of the Beaux-Arts.[3] The new group mounted its own Salon in the Palace of the Beaux-Arts constructed on the Champ-de-Mars for the 1889 fair. Led by another well-known academicist, Meissonier, the National Society of the Beaux-Arts was considered one of the two wings of the official Salon. Among its members were many artists who were de-voted to the decorative arts, including Auguste Rodin, Eugène Carrière, Puvis de Chavannes, Jules Dalou, and Edouard Dubufe.[4]

The dissenting but highly respectable National Society of the Beaux-Arts held its first Salon exhibition in May 1890. One commentator described the group as "in-cluding youthful elements, but on the whole nothing revolutionary."[5] The main in-novation of this Salon was that the decorative arts were exhibited as objets d'art alongside works of sculpture and paintings. In the announcement of their Salon, the National Society of the Beaux-Arts promised "isolated producers" of fine crafts, "whose work is rarely shown in the cluttered, mercantile exhibition of the 'deco-rative arts,' [that it would] do all in its power to display those works and thereby assure these unique inventions a proper success and personal property."[6] Behind this statement were two goals: to lift the crafts out of the market and into the temple of high art and to highlight the problem of artistic "property," or copyrighting the deco-rative arts. Because the applied arts were produced in stages and because design pat-terns were easily replicable, decorative art could not easily be identified as the personal property of any one artisan. Indeed, few artisans could affix a signature to the finished product to which they had contributed.[7] In calling on artisans to display their work alongside painters, the society aligned itself with those who wished to apply to decorative art the criteria used to judge quality in painting; it defined the objet d'art as the product of a singular, personal, artistic vision. In reaching out to "isolated workers" and in assuring them of the "property" carried in their "unique, personal inventions," the members of the society appealed to that tiny core of craft artists who were involved in all stages of the creation of a single object.[8]

The decorative arts in the reformed Salon were an immediate success. One critic noted a few years after the opening of the National Society of the Beaux-Arts that it "has welcomed the decorative arts and has created a movement with a lasting impact on the artistic history of our country."[9]

As critics and journalists celebrated the reform of the Salon and the reentry of the decorative arts into the temple of high art, the name and ideals of Edmond de Goncourt surfaced again. Edmond himself applauded the inventiveness and delicacy of contributors to the new Salon and claimed in 1892 that these applied arts overshadowed the paintings in their appeal and originality: "French industrial art, under the impetus of Japanese art, with its intimate focus, is in the process of superseding great art. Baffier's tin jug, Joseph Chéret's earthen vases with their love-and-women-reliefs, Montesquiou-Fezensac's hydrangea dresser—these are the truly original works in this exhibition."[10] Frantz Jourdain, glorifying the "winds of liberalism" that had thrown open the doors of the Salon to the applied arts, noted the earlier contributions of the brothers de Goncourt and their criteria of the aristocratic traditions and aesthetic elevation of the crafts. Jourdain began an article, "Les Objets d'art au Salon," with a quotation from the Goncourts, his longtime friends: "I wonder whether Great Art is not inferior to industrial art when the latter has achieved its *summum* of perfection, if, for example, a painting is not inferior to an exceptional candelabra."[11] Like the Goncourts, Jourdain affirmed quality and perfection as the bases for a new "unity of the arts"; and he invoked the rococo works of Boulle, Fragonard, Boucher, and Meissonnier as models.[12] Jourdain applauded the entry of the decorative arts into the Salon, which restored "to the industrial artists the titles of nobility they have so unjustly and inappropriately been deprived of."[13]

Camille Mauclair, a specialist on eighteenth-century painting and applied arts and a publicist for the reform of the contemporary decorative arts, also cited the Goncourts in his writings on the new Salon. He too saw the elevation of the crafts in the 1890s Salon through the lenses of one who knew the eighteenth-century unitary arts.[14] Pleased that "the decorative arts have been cleared of discredit," he called for artisans to become "masters" by entering the Salon.[15]

The elevation of the decorative arts to the level of the beaux-arts, the invocation of the Goncourts, and the internal restructuring of the academic Salon set French efforts apart from craft initiatives pursued elsewhere during the period. Camille Mauclair equated the entry of the crafts into the reformed Salon in France to the reintegration of art and craft that had "begun in London, and then traveled to

Brussels."[16] Yet how different the Paris Salon of the Champ-de-Mars was from the Brussels organization championing the unity of the arts. The same dissatisfactions with exhibition control and interest in the applied arts that had led the French artists to add a wing to the official Salon led a group of Belgian artists to establish a new independent association, the Salon des Vingt. Vigorously antiacademic, committed to all forms of artistic innovation, the members of Les XX initiated their oppositionist exhibitions in 1884 in the spirit of the Wagnerian *Gesamtkunstwerk*—not only were paintings, sculptures, and applied arts displayed together, but musical concerts accompanied the shows.

In the context of labor activism, political crisis, and social unrest that characterized Belgium in the 1880s, the associates of Les XX quickly joined their cultural anti-traditionalism to the cause of radical social change. One of the group's founders, Edmond Picard, a lawyer, poet, and art critic whose home provided the gallery space for the Salon des XX, also served as defense counsel to striking miners after a wave of violent workers' rebellions in 1885.[17] Picard and other members of Les XX allied with the new socialist Belgian Workers' party, the Parti Ouvrier Belge (POB). Unusually receptive to artists and intellectuals, the POB, under the leadership of Emile Vandervelde, enlisted avant-garde painters, poets, dramatists, and musicians in wide-ranging projects of cultural education for workers and in developing theoretical papers on the relation between Belgian art and socialism.[18] Fernand Khnopff, Henry Van de Velde, Jules Destrée, and Willy Finch, affiliates of Les XX, lectured to Brussels workers on such topics as William Morris, Flemish medieval realism, Richard Wagner, and Symbolist free verse—all under the auspices of the POB's *section d'art* of the Maison du Peuple, later given permanent quarters in the remarkable art nouveau structure completed by Victor Horta in 1897–1898. While the artists of Les XX found no single stylistic form appropriate to the battle for social change, they strenuously connected the goal of artistic freedom and the unity of the fine and applied arts to the ideals of social liberation and of the restoration of harmony to society and the individual. In many ways Belgium in the 1890s resembled France before 1848, when artists, politicians, and intellectuals had joined together as one avant-garde in a single quest for social justice. In the 1890s, however, France was healing the split between artists and society that had taken place in 1848. Important innovative French painters of the 1890s—Pierre Bonnard, Edouard Vuillard, Ker-Xavier Roussel, and Paul Ranson (the Nabis), and even Paul Gauguin—were accommodated by the reformed Salon.[19] Significant segments of the fin-de-siècle French avant-garde were making their peace with a stable and resilient Republic and its official culture.

It was in the Belgian context of art and social radicalism that the term "art nouveau" was coined. The editors of the journalistic center of artistic innovation, *L'Art moderne,* designated themselves the "votaries of art nouveau" as of 1884.[20] In *L'Art moderne* articles, as in the exhibitions of Les XX, the ideal of "new art" was attached to that of the "new society," and William Morris was invoked as the artists' inspiration. Proclaiming that they would seek "no concessions from the public, no courting of the establishment,"[21] writers for *L'Art moderne* explored the potential of art as an agent of social change and construed the community of all the arts concentrated in Les XX as the prefiguration of Morris's goal of an art integral to all aspects of daily life, an art "made by and for the people."[22]

The artistic spokesman for the Belgian unity of art and craft was Henry Van de Velde, painter, architect, and interior designer. In 1893 and 1894, Van de Velde published a series of articles criticizing the division between the high arts and the applied arts, entitled "Déblaiement d'Art."[23] For him, as for many of his colleagues, this critique was moral and social: the division between the arts expressed the division between the classes. Following Morris, Van de Velde defined art as the expression of pleasure in work. Thus no reform of the beaux-arts was conceivable; it was necessary to eliminate completely the hierarchy between the pure plastic arts and the "inferior" decorative arts by destroying the social hierarchy and market system on which it was based. Social change had to take place before art—an art by and for the people—could flourish. Quoting Morris, Van de Velde asked, "what business have we with art at all unless we share it? . . . Real art must be made by the people and for the people, as a happiness for the maker and user. . . . The talk of inspiration is sheer nonsense, there is no such thing: it is a mere matter of craftsmanship."[24]

How differently the French worked toward the goal of unifying arts and crafts. Belgian advocates would brook "no concessions to the public, no courting of the establishment"; French advocates and producers of the crafts *were* the establishment and entered the world of the Salon precisely to reach a broad public. For Morris and Van de Velde, "the talk of inspiration is sheer nonsense, . . . it is a mere matter of craftsmanship"; for the Goncourts and their followers it was "inspiration" that counted. In the Salon of the National Society of the Beaux-Arts aesthetics, not the work process, was at issue. The critique of the division between the arts did not imply a social critique. On the contrary, the goal was not to eliminate the hierachy of the arts and with it the conception of art for an elite but to reform the hierarchy from within and thereby consolidate an elite art on a new basis. The French conceived of integrating artist and artisan in a way inverse to that envisioned by the Belgians: they wanted not to eliminate the hierarchy of the arts and recover art by the people but to extend the hierarchy of the arts to include the artisanate. In France, the Salon was able to aristocratize the decorative arts, and critical champions welcomed the "ennobling" of these arts, the admission that. like painting and sculpture, they too could express the immaterial ideal of beauty. Where the Belgians claimed that all workers were artists and that art should descend to the street, the French proclaimed that all artisans could be artists and that the crafts should ascend to the Academy.

Van de Velde himself lashed out against what he perceived as the hyperaestheticism and psychological indulgence of both the French producers of arts and crafts and the critics who defended them. In "Déblaiement d'Art," he described Emile Gallé, Joseph Chéret, and Edmond de Goncourt as elitists, misdirected in their attempts to reunite art and craft: instead of art of and for the people, theirs was an art of upper-bourgeois caprice and insulation.[25]

The French advocates of reuniting art and craft through the reform of the official Salon remained strikingly separate from a native avant-garde group that paralleled the Belgian movement binding art and social radicalism. The Belgian artists of Les XX espoused Morris's theories while practicing the applied arts. Their French counterparts—the Neo-Impressionist painters and their Symbolist literary allies—endorsed the ideal of art for the people while they explored a new abstract and non-figurative language for painting and poetry.

The Neo-Impressionists first coalesced in 1884 as founding members of the last French avant-garde separatist institution before 1905: the Society of Independent Artists. Conceived as a haven for all painters whose works were rejected by the official Salon juries, the society adopted an organizational structure with egalitarian social principles, eliminating the jury system—no group of artists was to be privileged over another—and accepting all entries on an equal basis, with each artist paying a uniform fee to cover the costs of installing the exhibition. Any proceeds from sales of paintings were to be pooled, with profits redistributed at the end of the season to all participants.[26] With the Society of Independent Artists as their institutional base, the Neo-Impressionist painters, under the leadership of Georges Seurat, formulated a coherent aesthetic program. They were committed to the scientific systematization of Impressionist luminosity, to the depiction of subjects hitherto considered unrepresentable—the industrial suburbs, or *banlieue,* around Paris—and to the revelation of an ideal harmonic order beneath surface appearances. The Neo-Impressionists were championed by some of the new Symbolist writers—Gustave Kahn, Paul Adam, and Félix Fénéon—who discovered that the painters' goals were equivalent to their own and defended them before an unreceptive and often hostile public.[27]

The Neo-Impressionists and their Symbolist colleagues related their redefinition of aesthetic form to the radical restructuring of society and during the early 1890s forged an active alliance with the French anarchist-communist movement. The anarchists' emphasis on individual freedom and anti-authoritarianism struck a responsive chord in the artists, who rejected traditional conventions and were themselves repudiated by the public. The poets and painters construed their exploration of new values in art as contributing, in the cultural domain, to the general corrosion of bourgeois values and traditions necessary for an eventual total social liberation. As Paul Signac noted, innovative artists are "revolutionaries by temperament" who, "moving far off the beaten track, paint what they see, as they feel it, and . . . give a hard blow of the pickaxe to the old social structure."[28]

The Neo-Impressionists' and Symbolists' endorsement of anarchism was, as Eugenia Herbert has shown, more than a fashionable and convenient extension of their artistic individualism. These artists developed close ties with one of the French leaders of anarcho-communism, Kropotkin's student Jean Grave. The artists subscribed to Grave's journal, *La Révolte* (later named *Les Temps nouveaux*), and they wrote articles in their own art journals advocating anarchism and social revolution. Many of the Neo-Impressionists—Signac, Maximillian Luce, Charles Angrand, and Pissarro—contributed lithographs and drawings to the art supplement that Grave appended to his anarchist journal. The artists also donated paintings for Grave to sell in lotteries to raise money for his anarchist paper and propaganda activities. The affiliation between the artists and anarchism was so well publicized that the Symbolist writer Félix Fénéon and the Neo-Impressionist painter Luce were arrested and imprisoned along with Grave in 1894, during a roundup and subsequent trial of anarchist sympathizers.[29]

Paradoxically, the Neo-Impressionists' and Symbolists' commitment to anarchist politics deepened as their aesthetic interests took them further and further away from material reality. Symbolist free verse relied on the musical associations of vowel sounds rather than the meanings of words, rendering their literary works incompatible with the didactic imperative of practical politics. The Neo-Impressionists, under the influence of psychophysicist Charles Henry, began to explore the emotional valences of the formal elements of painting—line, color, and tone—independent of the objects they represented. Through scientific experiments, Henry codified human perceptual responses to color and line, identifying the visual combinations that yielded pleasure ("dynamogeny") and those that led to pain ("inhibition"). For the Neo-Impressionists and their Symbolist friends Henry's studies demonstrated the operation of absolute, verifiable, and predictable laws of human perception that artists could exploit for the maximization of pleasure and harmony. Using Henry's findings, the painters created musical canvases, hoping that by revealing perfect harmony in the artistic domain they could stimulate perfect harmony in the social order. For Paul Signac, the potential capacities of "the people" to see beyond the subject to the painting's evocative forms justified his own visual formalism:

> Justice in sociology, harmony in art: the same thing. . . . The subject is nothing, or at least it is only one part of the work of art, no more important than the other elements—color, drawing, and composition. When the eye is educated, the people will see other things besides the subject in pictures. When the society we dream of exists, when the worker, rid of the exploiters who brutalize him, has time to think and instruct himself, he will appreciate the varied qualities of the work of art.[30]

Despite their evolving commitment to abstraction and "art for art's sake," the Neo-Impressionists and Symbolists endorsed William Morris's radical ideals. The Symbolist poet Gustave Kahn organized a weekly program—Les Samedis Populaires—to bring modern poetry to the people. He believed that the people would understand even complex works of Symbolism, for they lacked the prejudices inculcated by bourgeois values and academic training. His project of art for the people would itself be a vehicle for social change, preparing the minds of the "fourth estate" for a revolution—after which all workers would be artists, the decorative arts would flourish, and art would infuse all aspects of daily life.[31] A similar view was proposed by the Symbolist Félix Fénéon in an article in *Le Père Peinard,* an anarchist journal: "A day will come . . . when art will be part of the life of ordinary men. . . . When it does, that artist won't look down at the worker from above his celluloid collar: the two of them will be a single one. But to achieve this the Revolution must get up steam and we must build a completely anarchist civilization."[32] The painter Paul Signac developed his own plan for reuniting artist and craftsman. Signac became euphoric over one of Charles Henry's inventions, the aesthetic protractor, which replicated those combinations of lines, colors, and angles that had been found to give the maximum of pleasure to the viewer. Signac hoped to bring the protractor and Henry's text *L'Harmonie des formes* to the furniture workers of the Faubourg Saint-Antoine to enhance their work process and to guide them to create harmonic forms. Signac wrote of his plan to Vincent van Gogh, whom he tried to enlist in the project, noting the "great social importance" the protractor would have "for the industrial arts." It would "help the workers to see correctly and well" and to know "whether a form is harmonious or not."[33]

The French practitioners of the applied arts and the critics who championed them did not relate the unity of the arts to the restructuring of society. The social goals of the Belgian devotees of art nouveau and the utopian harmony sought by the anarchist Neo-Impressionists and Symbolists held little appeal for those aiming to elevate artisans to artists in the existing academic institution. Paradoxically, it was artists involved in the most abstract and immaterial of forms—Neo-Impressionists and Symbolists—who developed programs to bring art to the people and reeducate craftsmen. The French applied artists involved in the reform of the Salon were not preoccupied with social liberation or with worker education but with the dematerialization of their craft. They hoped to endow their applied arts products with the plasticity and evocative form found in pictorial abstraction and to remove their creations from the realm of function.

*

A number of individuals in the Central Union-government network devoted their energies to explicating and publicizing the new applied arts exhibited in the official Salon after 1890. Two, however, were central: Victor Champier, the editor-in-chief of the *Revue des arts décoratifs,* and Roger Marx, beaux-arts administrator, Central Union affiliate, and modernist art critic.

Victor Champier: Eighteenth-Century Organicism and Nineteenth-Century Egoism

Victor Champier was the architect of the Central Union's "new program," outlined in its journal, the *Revue des arts décoratifs,* after the entry of the applied arts into the Salon. Champier's dual attitude toward the crafts encapsulated union policies as a whole. On the one hand, he was firmly grounded in the history of the *arts somptuaires* and called for the return of the crafts to their rightful noble position: "to restore the former prestige to those arts that in our era, by singular contempt, are called 'minor arts.'"[34] By 1890, however, Champier was also fully committed to a modern style of

art and design worthy of, but not slavishly imitative of, the splendid craft forms of
the French *patrimoine:* he encouraged "the creation of original works, stamped with
a modern character," to approach "the production of modern decorative arts."[35]

In 1891, Champier wrote a celebratory article on the new reformed Salon entitled
"Les Arts fraternels au Salon du Champ-de-Mars." The word *fraternal* in the title
was significant and signaled the article's ironic theme: the destruction of artistic liberty by political democracy. Champier chronicled the liberty and equality of the arts
before the French Revolution and their suppression and division after the Revolution. Welcoming the new Salon as a "revolution in the artistic world," he construed
his "revolution" as a rightful restitution: the return of the crafts to their noble status,
equal to that of the other arts.[36]

Champier's article contained a long insert from the writings of his colleague Paul
Mantz, documenting the history of craft equality under aristocratic and royal patronage.[37] Through the eighteenth century the "fraternity of the arts was one of the
reasons for our glory." The French Revolution and its "reactionary leader, David,"
severed the bond between artistic "brothers," a split that was carried into the core of
the Academy.[38]

In reviewing the entries of decorative arts to the Salon of 1891, Champier relied
on criteria he had culled from the eighteenth century. He recalled the organic and
anthropomorphic character of rococo furnishings that were reputed to charm and to
come alive to the spectator:

> You may be sure of it: furniture knows many a story. The younger Crébillon, a
> severe and informed chronicler, heard furniture talk. He was not a victim of
> hallucination. The proof of it lies in those swelling chests of drawers, those
> pleasingly curved armchairs, those desks and their delicately wrought coppers.
> They all testify to the elegance of life under Louis XV, and they have not com-
> pleted their testimony but are still talking.[39]

Champier invoked this eighteenth-century notion of elegant suggestiveness in assessing the crafts in the 1891 Salon. One of his favorite pieces in the show was a
sculpted silver candelabrum by Bapst and Falize comprising three candle holders in
the form of three tulips sprouting from a base (Fig. 46). For Champier, this piece
"affects the sinuous movement of the Louis XV style; it has the grace of eighteenth-
century masterpieces."[40]

Champier was careful, however, not to evaluate inventiveness solely according
to eighteenth-century criteria. He celebrated the Falize candelabrum for both its
eighteenth-century evocativeness and its modern spirit, its expression of the "religion of nature." Unlike the fantasy mélanges of the rococo picturesque, Falize's
piece was "directly inspired by the flowers and plants of our gardens." This gave it
"the ever-delicate charm of novelty."[41]

The emergence of nineteenth-century modernism out of eighteenth-century fantasy was evident not only in Champier's reviews but in a series of articles he prepared
for the *Revue des arts décoratifs* as part of the union's "new program." The series, a

Bougeoir-porte-bouquet, en argent ciselé
Exécuté par MM. Bapst et Falize.

Fig. 46. Tulip candle holder, by Lucien Falize, 1892. From *Revue des arts décoratifs,* 1892.

"guide for the decoration of the modern house," [42] focused in 1891 on two model homes: the Hôtel de Madame la baronne Salomon de Rothschild, a renovated mansion from the mid-eighteenth century, and the home of the Goncourts. Champier's conception of the vitalizing influence of what he called an aristocracy of intelligence underlay the series. In the *Revue* of 1891, Champier asked, "Can a democratic society be nothing but tasteless, without love of art and lacking luxury? Are qualities like elegance and refinement the exclusive endowment of monarchies?" [43] In answer to this question, Champier distinguished aristocracies of intelligence from those of birth and of money. His own choice was an aristocracy of intelligence, which exemplified the "sensitivity of refined breeding." The articles on the *habitation moderne* offered examples of this aristocracy of intellect, those individuals vested with "true taste and spontaneity, freed from the conventional frame of old ideas." [44]

The tour, explication, and photographs of the Hôtel de Rothschild clarified the way that the lady of the house "was as delicate as she was intelligent," a true modern Maecenas. [45] Sumptuous, filled with eighteenth-century ensembles and objets d'art, the Rothschild mansion represented continuity with the first organic *style moderne,* carried on by a member of the new aristocracy of taste and intellect. The link between generations of the aristocracy of taste and money had a special meaning in the case of the Hôtel de Rothschild: the mansion on the rue Berryer had originally been built by a financier named Beaujon. He had commissioned the architect Girardin to construct a private trysting place for his amorous adventures. At the *hôtel,* called the Folie-Beaujon after the rococo fashion, the indulgent financier could devote himself to "joys of the flesh." Beaujon's epicurean imagination knew well how to "vary and refine these joys and how to draw out their refinement."[46] Champier described in detail the elaborate technology that helped to shape the Beaujon *hôtel* as "a small temple to voluptuousness." He recounted the ingenuity of eighteenth-century designers not only in integrating the rooms and ornaments into a single sensual theme but in crafting the mechanisms for surprise seductions. Among these elements were secret staircases; ceilings painted with erotic scenes visible only when a button was pushed to uncover them; and a large ceramic basket of flowers, which upon the release of a spring split in two to reveal an opening from which a bed emerged.[47]

Champier noted the difference between the original proprietor of the Folie-Beaujon and his late nineteenth-century counterparts, the Rothschilds. Yet he credited both Monsieur and Madame de Rothschild for their "true erudition" in conserving the original decor of the *hôtel* and in adding to it their fine collections of eighteenth-century furniture and applied arts. He praised in particular Madame la baronne's collection of soft-paste Sèvres porcelain, including the entire fifty-piece set originally created for Madame du Barry.[48]

After describing the decor and enumerating the objects in each of the rooms, Champier concluded on a note of criticism. Although he respected the conservational and curatorial talents of the Rothschilds and admired the completeness of their collections of eighteenth-century furniture and porcelain, he lamented their archaism. Following the "new program" of the Union in the 1890s, Champier decried an interior filled with artifacts from the past. Although it was a stellar representative of the *habitation moderne* of the eighteenth century, the Rothschilds' house could not inspire readers of the 1890s: it lacked "modernity" because it contained no art by living decorative artists. Champier concluded by formulating an imperative for modern interior design: the need "to emphasize the familiar features of our 'self,' our habits, and the distinctive character of our minds."[49]

Champier discovered a definitive *habitation moderne,* infused with such features, in the Goncourts' home. The celebration of this home in the *Revue* as the prototypically modern design brings us full circle. Originating as an acerbic and defiant critique of bourgeois design and culture, the Goncourts' personally crafted environment had become transformed by 1891 into the official symbol of a quintessentially French modern style.

Champier commissioned Gustave Geffroy, the art critic, to write the second article on the *habitation moderne.* Geffroy, along with Roger Marx, was a regular visitor to the Goncourts' home and a member of the inner circle attending Edmond's weekly *Grenier* salon. Geffroy also played his part in catapulting the Goncourts' home into the center of the official craft movement.[50]

The significance of Geffroy's account of the Goncourts' Maison d'Auteuil and its collections was his insistence on the aesthetic and psychological meaning of the interiors, which transcended their historical components. Geffroy's article answered Champier's question about the "modernity" of the Hôtel de Rothschild; the article on the Goncourts revealed that the two brothers had succeeded where Madame la

Fig. 47. The Goncourts' house in Auteuil, interior view. From *Revue des arts
décoratifs,* 1892. Courtesy of the Bibliothèque Nationale, Paris.

baronne had failed. Theirs was quintessentially an "interior decoration that emphasized the familiar features of our 'self.'"

Following the format of the first article, Geffroy described the various rooms in
the Goncourts' home and their contents. His guide to the design of the rooms was
Edmond's fastidious and psychologically charged manual *La Maison d'un artiste.* By
quoting carefully from this work, Geffroy was able to make clear to the *Revue* readers that the coherence of the home's interior derived from modern aesthetic principles (Fig. 47).

In his commentaries on the first floor rooms of the house, Geffroy described the
Goncourts' specialized collections of rococo and Japanese arts. Yet he emphasized the
way that the brothers' personal vision subordinated these historically identifiable
objects to a larger aesthetic scheme. Geffroy gave an example in recounting how
Edmond set out to invent a tonal harmony for the room that housed his collection of
eighteenth-century prints, a scheme that led him to discover the principle of color
contrast in interior design:

> To *create* a room in my house. . . . After long meditation, akin to the medita-
> tion for a chapter of a book, I was convinced that only a bright black and dull
> red would do. . . . Let us posit, in principle, that there are no harmonious
> apartments unless the objects within stand out because of the contrast and op-
> position of two largely dominant tones. Red and black is one of the best such
> combinations a decorator can use; they highlight and enhance that which fur-
> nishes a room.[51]

Geffroy concluded by assessing the modernity of the Goncourts' interior design,
which he called an "artistic arrangement, one of the most remarkable of individual

dwellings, akin to a personal creation." [52] The lessons that Geffroy derived from the house and presented to union readers were, first, the ideal of a "science of decoration," which replaced eclectic clutter with an integral, interdependent, and consistent design, and, second, interior space as distinctively personal, its design expressive of the self. Geffroy acknowledged that the Goncourts were surely exceptional, and he did not advocate that others imitate or repeat their efforts. Yet he explained to readers of the *Revue* how the Goncourts' personal design exemplified modernism. They gave their house

> a particular and signifying physiognomy, resembling their own intellectual and artistic individuality . . . There is a great lesson to be learned from this house, as long as it is not imitated directly. To proceed thus: to obey one's own taste, one's passion for the modern, to be true to oneself—there lies an imperative to be discerned by the enraptured and excited collector as he concludes his visit to this distinctly personal house in Auteuil. [53]

Roger Marx: The Aesthete-Bureaucrat as Champion of Craft Modernism in the Salon

Among advocates of the reunification of arts and crafts in the Salon and of a French modern style, Roger Marx was the most prominent. He assumed a pivotal role in articulating a theory of craft renovation and in institutionalizing craft modernism in the center of official culture. A respected art critic and collector, he supported a variety of artists and writers who sought independence and espoused modernity, and he was one of the select group who was welcomed weekly to the *Grenier* salons of the brothers de Goncourt. [54] Roger Marx also moved freely between the world of artistic innovation and the institutions of official culture, serving in the administration of the beaux-arts after 1883 and as an inspector for provincial museums after 1889. [55] Finally, he was affiliated after 1884 with the Central Union of the Decorative Arts, wrote for its journal, sat on its advisory boards, attended its congress, and worked, generally, to disseminate the goals of craft renovation. He provided a crucial bridge between all these worlds. He carried the ideals of art-craft from the Goncourts into journalism, from journalism into art administration, and from art administration into the Central Union and back to the state. This interlocking network of personnel and ideas exemplified by Roger Marx enabled France to achieve within official culture what other countries forged only through arduous efforts, resistance, and polarization. [56]

Roger Marx was born in Nancy in 1859. He began a career as a writer and art critic in his native city, contributing to the journals *Le Cocade* and *Le Voltaire.* In 1882 he moved to Paris, where he published his first book, *L'Art à Nancy,* in 1883. During his subsequent career as an arts administrator and museum official, Marx was an energetic spokesman for and representative of artistic modernism. His ac-

complishments as a mediator between avant-garde art and official culture were extraordinary.[57] For him the reunification of the arts was a central feature of modernism. Called by his contemporaries the implacable apostle of the decorative arts,[58] he
initiated and sustained the campaign to reform the official Salon to include the crafts,
lobbying in journalism and in the state bureaucracy for the admission of applied arts
into the Salon.[59] When a possible split within the Salon over this issue and that of
remuneration arose in 1889, Marx was present at the negotiations to create two separate Salon wings.[60] A friend and critical defender of many of the artists who participated in the new National Society of Beaux-Arts, including Rodin, Puvis de
Chavannes, and Carrière, he persuaded the state to buy Rodin's *The Kiss* for the
Luxembourg Museum and encouraged the acquisition of Gallé's work for the same
museum.[61] He organized some of the exhibits at the 1900 exposition, where the decorative arts were given a central role in representing the modern style of France.[62]

Because of his ceaseless efforts to reunite the arts and revitalize the artistic crafts,
Roger Marx was called the William Morris of France. The writer Anatole France, a
friend of both the Goncourts' and of Roger Marx's, called Marx "the great apostle of
a social art, like Morris in England." France celebrated Marx's belief in "the civilizing and educating role of Art in modern society."[63]

Roger Marx's campaign to elevate the crafts did indeed include the goal of a "social art," one that would infuse beauty into daily life. Yet the meaning and function
of this art in France separated him from his radical and socialist counterparts in England and Belgium. For if Morris sought to destroy art for an elite, Roger Marx
believed in the civilizing and educating role of art, conceived as a process of diffusion
from the top down. In Marx's view, the highest quality of art and craft would ema-
nate from the Salon and raise the standards of taste for all, an idea similar to his
colleague Louis de Fourcaud's notion of the "aristocratization of the producers." In
Belgium, Van de Velde defined beauty "as a weapon, . . . because its nature challenges society, wounds it with a permanent injury."[64] In France, Roger Marx perceived beauty as offering a "consolation," a breath of relief in private surroundings.[65]
If for Van de Velde, beauty challenged society by returning art to humble people and
simple things, for Marx it solidified society, creating an expanded arena of refinement, whose qualities would gradually trickle down from the elite for the pleasure
and elevation of all.

Morris's, Van de Velde's, and Roger Marx's conceptions of social art diverged
most fundamentally because Marx operated within the intellectual framework of
French assumptions. Like his colleague Victor Champier, he saw the unity of all the
arts through the lenses of the eighteenth-century aristocratic tradition rediscovered
by the Goncourts. And he transformed this tradition in his commitment to a modern
decorative art infused with aesthetic complexity, personal originality, and psychological resonance. The driving force behind Marx's campaign for the crafts was not
socialist but liberal; he was devoted, above all else, to personal independence and
originality and to the limitless capacity of artistic genius to penetrate and transfigure
raw matter. Morris and Van de Velde believed that art would flourish only in a new,

transformed, society, as the expression of communitarian pleasure in work. Marx, though he advocated a social art, remained an elitist, assuming that the function of art was to provide "charm," "reassurance," and "consolation" amid the irrevocable difficulties of modern existence.[66]

Roger Marx derived his conception of the "unity of the arts" from his immersion in the eighteenth-century French tradition of the organic applied arts. He absorbed the splendors of this tradition firsthand, from having been "raised in the school of the Goncourts."[67] Indeed, it was because of his relentless efforts that the Goncourts' version of the eighteenth-century artistic patrimony was accepted. During the 1890s Marx published extensive accounts of the Goncourts' Maison d'Auteuil, its remarkable eighteenth-century collections, and the brothers' accomplishments as interior designers. These celebratory articles appeared in journals like the *Gazette des beaux-arts,* the *Lorraine-artiste,* the *Revue encyclopédique,* and the *Grande Dame.*[68] In addition, Roger Marx contributed introductory statements to the republications of the Goncourts' articles, as in the 1893 edition of the *Etudes d'art.*[69] In these writings, he glorified the Goncourts' rediscovery of the eighteenth century as the era of "quintessential French genius,"[70] at the same time clarifying to a diverse readership the aesthetic and psychological meanings that the Goncourts attributed to their personally designed "artistic ambiance."[71]

The Goncourts' eighteenth-century collections and writings and the new scholarly material on eighteenth-century applied arts provided Marx with the intellectual tools to evaluate the decorative arts in the late nineteenth-century Salons. His journalistic efforts to promote the reunification of the arts in the Salon were rife with allusions and comparisons to the arts of the eighteenth century. In an article of 1889 demanding the reform of the Salon to include the crafts, he declared that the classification of "pure beauty" and "the lesser arts" was an "unjustifiable and damaging exclusivism that ruins our tradition,"[72] invoking the pre-Revolutionary tradition of the unity of the arts as his model. His scholarly command of the primary sources from the Old Regime was extensive. In demanding that the crafts be admitted to the Salon, he cited Lebrun and Colbert, and he invoked the royal Gobelins workshop as a model for the integration of all the arts. He discussed the original royal edict of 1688 establishing the Gobelins, describing how painters, goldsmiths, engravers, woodcarvers, and tapestry weavers all worked there together under a single roof.[73]

The eighteenth-century frame of reference also appeared in Marx's extensive critical writings on the visual arts and crafts. He isolated Deboucourt, the color engraver of the 1770s, and Watteau as the models for Chéret, the late nineteenth-century illustrator. He celebrated Lalique, the fin-de-siècle jeweler and silversmith, as a successor to the master jewelers of the eighteenth century.[74] And he invoked the noble elites of the eighteenth century as the greatest interior decorators, lamenting the nomadism and lack of taste of their nineteenth-century bourgeois counterparts. The modern passion for travel and tourism left homes empty for summer and winter seasons. The monied classes preferred to invest in their vacation spots rather than in the "tasteful decoration of their homes." What was then to happen to the "traditions of art, elegance, and intimacy . . . of France's old residences?"[75] Thus in demanding the reintegration of the arts and in evaluating such masters of the craft modern style as Chéret and Lalique, Marx invoked a national eighteenth-century model of the grace and unity of the arts.

Roger Marx transposed the eighteenth-century tradition into modernist invention on the basis of two kinds of particularism, national and personal. In embracing contemporary craftsmen in the Salon as the bearers of a modern style, he celebrated those artists who embodied the "survival of our gift for elegance," "the distinguishing features of the French race."[76] Elegance, grace, and "seductiveness" were the necessary qualities of a revitalized craft style. Marx praised those whose works both represented to him the continuity and innovation of the resilient French tradition and embodied for him the maxim of progressive evolution in national style: "One prepares for the future by linking the past to the present."[77] Two decorative artists who exhibited in the Salon typified the ideals he advocated: Jean Dampt and Albert Besnard. They were "rebels against routine," independent and free from hackneyed historicism.[78] Although emancipated from convention, they did not reject official culture but rather had been comfortably assimilated by it.

Roger Marx described the wood sculptor and goldsmith Jean Dampt as a successor to the noble artisans of the past: "No one has done more than Dampt to reestablish and honor the *arts somptuaires* of which France was once so proud." Yet Marx glorified Dampt primarily for his special transformation of these traditions of the *arts somptuaires,* infusing into craftsmanship the nuances of subjectivist fantasy and dematerializing imagination. In praising Dampt's work, Marx affirmed that this versatile artist was able to "caress," "shape," and "subject" all types of matter to his personal vision. Dampt was "a sensitive and ardent soul, haunted by dreams and dedicated to inciting dreams through the work of his hands."[79]

The effect of Dampt's work is illustrated in one of the works he exhibited in the Salon, a small statuette, *The Fairy Mélusine and the Knight Raymondin,* composed of steel, ivory, and gold and representing a kiss (Fig. 48). Roger Marx noted the contrast, in material and in pose, between the male and female figures. The knight Raymondin, standing on a platform above the fairy Mélusine, was stiff and rigid in his steel armor. Mélusine herself was "languid" and "supple,"[80] appearing to melt and bend in the arms of her helmeted lover, largely because her body had been carved in smoothest ivory. Roger Marx exalted Dampt's "virtuoso craftsmanship" in this statuette and his uncanny ability to animate matter into pulsating life: "The expression is so intense, the figures are animated by so much spiritual life. . . . Dampt extracts this radiant creation from a block where it sleeps, inertly. . . . He tames his material, all material, with imperious authority. . . . Dampt is never hindered in the embodiment of his dream."[81]

The Goncourts had celebrated artisanal creation as a process whereby "all hard and rebellious matter is made supple." Roger Marx echoed this idea in his apotheosis of Jean Dampt's *Fairy Mélusine.* Dampt had crafted his group with the "tools' caresses,"[82] a phrase that evoked the favored formulation of the Goncourts in their

La fée Mélusine et le chevalier Raymondin

Groupe acier, ivoire et or par J. Dampt.

La Grande Dame

Fig. 48. *The Fairy Mélusine and the Knight Raymondin,* by Jean Dampt, 1896. Courtesy of the Bibliothèque Nationale, Paris.

descriptions of the fluent ivory and bronze objects made by rococo craftsmen.[83] In Dampt's case, the caress of the tool merged a woman's ivory body with a steel-encased knight. This miniature group provided a striking visual symbol of the feminizing and organicizing impulses behind the modern style of the 1890s. If the wrought-iron geometry of the Eiffel Tower had projected one form of modern mastery, Dampt's *Fairy Mélusine* suggested another. Dampt had taken the most technically advanced material, steel, and had used it to shape an erotic pair. His modernity lay in both his technological feat and his decorative self-expression.

Roger Marx explicated another of Dampt's submissions to the Salon, this one expressing the themes of domestic intimacy and organicism. It was a major work, a sculpted oak bed with matching dresser. The corners of the bed were adorned with incised figures representing Prayer, Sleep, Silence, and Withdrawal. On the headboard Dampt created a frieze in which he carved a poem amid shadowy figures: "Sad as a tomb, or joyous as a love nest."[84] Roger Marx perceived in the bed and its poem an evocation of the assuring cyclical order of nature and human existence. He quoted lines from another poem that echoed Dampt's allusion to the passage from birth to death, the nest to the tomb, illustrated on the bed frame:

> It is there that man is born, rests, and makes love
> Child, Spouse, Old Man, Grandparent, Woman or Virgin.
> Be it funeral or nuptials, or to sprinkle holy water
> Beneath the black crucifix or the blessed bough,
> 'Tis there that all begins and ends
> From the first dawning year to the last candle's fire.[85]

The bed was a fitting example of what Roger Marx called Dampt's incitement, through material form, to dream. In the domestic space the wood sculptor evoked themes of continuity, timeless cycles of passages from birth to death.

In glorifying Dampt, Roger Marx proposed a message of comfort and reassurance. At the beginning of his article on Dampt, he had quoted a passage from the Goncourts' *Manette Salomon* proclaiming the nineteenth century as a century "that has suffered much, the century of scientific preoccupations and anxiety about the True." At the conclusion of the article, Marx offered the intimate, suggestive, and organic works of craftsman Dampt to quell the worry and anxiety caused by science and truth. A soothing alternative world, the world of organicized private space, would provide an oasis of peace amid the agitated present. Dampt's work "offers us absolute peace amid feverishness and agitation; to [counter] our melancholy [he gives us] a reassuring beauty."[86]

The themes of organic consolation, domestic intimacy, and personal invention also characterized Roger Marx's celebration of the decorative painter Albert Besnard, who exhibited murals and stained glass designs in the reformed Salon. Born in 1849, Besnard was the son of a famous miniaturist, Madame de Mirbel, who was the official portraitist of Louis XVIII, Charles X, and later the duc d'Orléans. Besnard had been trained in both France and England and had been awarded the Prix de

Rome. Especially interested in drawing. Besnard studied the pastels and engravings of eighteenth-century artists, particularly Fragonard and Watteau.[87] During the 1880s, Besnard rose to prominence in France as a master colorist and muralist. He was a pivotal figure in the reform of the Great Tradition from within, for he was seen as a master French painter who absorbed the innovations of colored light from Impressionism while continuing to paint figures and murals according to the canons of the Academy.[88] By the 1890s Besnard's designs could be seen in the halls of the Ecole de Pharmacie, along the ceiling of the Hôtel de Ville, and enveloping the amphitheater in the new Sorbonne. This decade of his career was crowned by the commission to paint the ceilings of the new Petit Palais of the 1900 exposition.

The central preoccupations in Besnard's work, in both public murals and private drawings, were women and nature. Roger Marx, praising Besnard's gifts as a draftsman, found in his work an "intimate poetry," which Marx related to the work of the eighteenth-century masters. And he went on to applaud Besnard's "evocations of a tender meditative softness," his "mirages of magic" that derived from his devotion to "the glory of the Eternal Feminine," the magic of "maternal suggestion."[89]

Two of Besnard's Salon entries that caught Roger Marx's attention were telling. One was a large painting entitled "*Fluctuat nec mergitur*," Besnard's attempt to give form to the device of the city of Paris. He depicted young women, "grouped together on a boat, gliding by night under an arch of a bridge on the Seine."[90] Besnard's treatment of the pictorial surface, according to Roger Marx, was marked by the flecking of colored light and by a vaporous atmosphere.[91] Marx commented that this technique represented an "accommodation," an "attenuation" of Impressionist principles. The Impressionist colorism that had been aggressively attacked and rejected during the 1870s now looked "exquisite."

Besnard's "*Fluctuat nec mergitur*" in the reformed Salon encapsulated the delicate balance between continuity and change in the official French artistic tradition. It was fitting that Roger Marx, the spokesman for modernist innovation within the cultural administration, would see in Besnard the vitality of originality, contained by the evolving strength of the French *patrimoine*. Although Marx saw Besnard as an "insurgent," an artist committed to decoration and the "lesser" media of drawing, he was hardly that. He was, instead, a primary domesticator of the Impressionist methods for the Ecole des Beaux-Arts. In painting "*Fluctuat nec mergitur*," Besnard discovered a particularly appropriate symbol of transformation and accommodation. We have encountered in an earlier chapter the way the *ralliement* Republic of the 1890s rediscovered the device of Paris—*Fluctuat nec mergitur*—and used it as a new official symbol. I have suggested that the motto and the image, that of a ship rocked by the waves but not capsizing, became a metaphor for the political history of the period from 1889 to 1898, when the Third Republic braved the storms of political crises and enacted internal transformation. I have also suggested that the emblem of *Fluctuat nec mergitur* embodied a telling metaphor of the intellectual history of fin-de-siècle France, marked by the discovery and the assimilation of challenges posed to rationalist Cartesian logic by the psychology of fluidity, suggestion, and imagistic thinking. In the same way, Besnard's painting of *Fluctuat nec mergitur* represented a striking symbol of the artistic history of the 1890s, a decade marked by the pursuit of modernism within official circles and by the internal reform of the Salon. Besnard, a domesticator of Impressionism and a resurrector of eighteenth-century intimism, was an appropriate carrier of this message of the adaptiveness of French artistic institutions and cultural traditions in the face of new realities. The strength of the French Republic, of the French rationalist tradition, and of the French artistic tradition rested in the 1890s on a common ground—the capacity for resiliency and reconciliation, for absorbing innovation and accommodating change without subverting the essential shape and foundations of the whole. In politics, intellectual life, and culture, fin-de-siècle France negotiated a course more fluid than that of Germany, Austria, or Belgium. Albert Besnard and his admirer Roger Marx testify to this achievement in culture.

Roger Marx acclaimed another entry of Besnard's to the Salon, his plan for a mural, commissioned by the Ministry of Beaux-Arts in 1895, for the new chemistry amphitheater in the renovated Sorbonne. Designed as a huge triptych, Besnard's Sorbonne mural, entitled *Life Is Born from Death,* expressed a secular version of Catholic religiosity, infused with a particular kind of organicism called transformism, a fin-de-siècle French scientific theory that assumed the continuum of being and the unity of all matter. The artistic, philosophical, and scientific roots of Besnard's *Life Is Born from Death* were explicated by Roger Marx in an article in the *Revue encyclopédique.*[92] The mural unfolded, from left to right, the passage of man from matter (Fig. 49). The left side of the triptych illustrated, in misty fusion, the fluid, dark world of matter before the emergence of man and woman. Only rocks and water were visible here, barely differentiated in a viscous flow. In the central panel of the trilogy light emanated and man erupted from nature. Beneath a "fertilizing sun,"

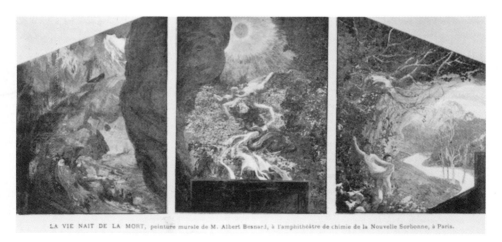

LA VIE NAIT DE LA MORT, peinture murale de M. Albert Besnard, à l'amphithéâtre de chimie de la Nouvelle Sorbonne, à Paris.

Fig. 49. Life Is Born from Death, by Albert Besnard. Mural, Sorbonne, Paris, 1896. Courtesy of the Bibliothèque Nationale, Paris.

Fig. 50. Medicine, by Gustav Klimt.
Ceiling painting, University of Vienna,
1901.

Marx noted, the body of a woman appeared, "rolling over the seeds of plants." The woman, fused with the plant, held a baby at one breast while the "river of life" flowed from the other. If the plants and the woman provided the "seeds of life" in the central panel, the third panel represented the full growth of life and its inevitable descent back into the earth. The right panel depicted a man and woman, who were destined to re-create by their union the "perpetual cycle" of "ceaseless transformation" and "the eternal becoming of all things and all beings." [93]

The transformist message of Besnard's mural—the cyclical and inevitable flow of nature—converged with Roger Marx's solidarist assumptions of the power of organic logic. Roger Marx found in Besnard's work a fitting visual form for the theoretical principles of the unity and diversity of nature and its cyclical phases.

During this same period, in Vienna, the Austrian Ministry of Culture selected Gustav Klimt to create a series of paintings for ceilings at the University of Vienna. *Medicine,* unveiled in 1901, articulated new and disturbing psychological truths, drawing Klimt directly into the battlefield of cultural politics. Klimt's *Medicine* was intended for a faculty devoted to healing (Fig. 50). His image, however, was a procession—fluid, suspended, unending—of suffering and death: on the right floated a murky fusion of bodies, tangling men and women of all ages together with a skeletal figure of Death; on the left was a nude female whose long hair swirled around her torso. Her left arm extended to join her to the mass of bodies beside her; her right

arm, behind her back, appeared to touch the outstretched arm of the nude male figure before her. At the base of Klimt's panel loomed the figure of Hygeia, suspended,
like the rest of the figures, while holding up to the viewer a snake coiled around her
right arm.

Klimt's mural hardly offered the Vienna medical faculty the allegorical vision they
wished to confront when they entered the building. Although the government,
under the new leadership of the Koerber ministry, supported the modernist art of
Klimt in an effort to transcend national divisions, forces of the old and new Right
mobilized against the artist. Though his critics failed to win an official ban on *Medicine,* the bitter conflicts over the mural drove Klimt into a period of withdrawal, isolation, and professional frustration.[94]

Albert Besnard's 1895 mural, by contrast, was welcomed at the Salon and the
Sorbonne by republican officials; his transformist vision bore a striking affinity to
the new solidarist political program. At first glance, Besnard's triptych, with women,
plants, and water rolling around in an undifferentiated mass, resembles Klimt's
Medicine, with its fusion of swirling bodies. But the subjects in *Medicine* are victims
who find no healing; Klimt's image depicts figures caught in a web of suffering, inaccessible to the curative powers of science. Besnard's mural has a succession and a
positive end; its emphasis is not on death but on the life that bursts from the continuum of matter and on the power of woman as a receptive, germinal force. Klimt's
woman offers only incitement to anguish and pain.

The commissioning and reception of these works by Klimt and Besnard suggest
striking differences between the forms and institutional settings of artistic modernism
in the painters' societies. In fin-de-siècle Austria, resources for integration eluded the
agents of politics and culture. In fin-de-siècle France, the interaction of Impressionism and academicism, Catholic tradition and secular organicism, political liberalism and social republicanism all testified to the adaptive powers of the Third Republic and linked Besnard's triptych to a revitalized program of liberal nationalism,
celebrated as an art nouveau in the 1890s reformed Salon.

CHAPTER THIRTEEN

Art Nouveau in the Salon, II:
Psychologie Nouvelle in the Works of Emile Gallé and Auguste Rodin

NOT ALL OF the art exhibited in the reformed Salon was as benign and univalent as the works of Jean Dampt, Lucien Falize, and Albert Besnard. The critical champions of the unity of art and craft in the new Salon identified the gracious, protective, and consoling intimacy of these artists' creations and their relation to rococo organicism. But the promoters of craft modernism in the Salon celebrated other artists, whose works, although also rooted in rococo traditions, were more complex and unstable than those discussed in the preceding chapter. Roger Marx, like some of his colleagues in the Central Union and the state cultural bureaucracy, not only glorified an evolving but continuous national artistic style but also committed himself to a modern art of psychological resonance. The conception of psychological complexity derived from a constellation of ideas specific to France and widely discussed there in the late nineteenth century: the psychology of nervous palpitation, hypnotic fixation, receptivity to suggestion, and the dynamic quality of images.

This chapter explores the works of two artists who expressed the new psychological ideas: Emile Gallé, a glassblower and furniture craftsman, and the sculptor Auguste Rodin. Both artists had ties to prominent figures in the official craft coalition, and both participated in the dual program of rococo revival and craft modernism pursued by the members of the Central Union of the Decorative Arts and their affiliates in the arts administration. Gallé's and Rodin's modernism was more complex and more explicitly psychological than that of the other contributors of art nouveau to the new Salon of the National Society of Beaux-Arts. Although these two artists were schooled and immersed in the French rococo precedents, they articulated unprecedented forms and meanings based on the revelations of the *psychologie nouvelle*.

The main body of this chapter closely analyzes particular works by Gallé and Rodin and the attitudes of their critical defenders to demonstrate how a specific form of psychological modernism emerged out of rococo revivalism in the 1890s. I demonstrate that both Gallé and Rodin absorbed certain ideas from neuropsychiatry and invested their artistic forms with a new knowledge of the interior of the human organism as a sensitive nervous mechanism. I indicate that, in different ways, Gallé and Rodin defined their art forms as the external manifestation of the internal world of the nerves, a world of febrile receptivity, relentless activity, and peculiar vulnerability.

Emile Gallé: Rococo Tradition, Lorraine Nationalism, and Bernheimian Suggestion

Emile Gallé began his association with the Central Union of the Decorative Arts in 1884, when his glass and ceramic works were featured at the union's Exhibition of the Arts of Glass, Earth, Stone, and Wood. Gallé's contributions to the exhibit expressed rococo, Japonist, and national themes, echoing the components of the Central Union program of the 1880s.

Gallé was born in 1846 in the Lorraine city of Nancy, a center of both eighteenth-century rococo elegance and a vital tradition of luxury crafts. The city's central place Stanislas, with its graceful iron gates, was a living testimony to the wonders of French eighteenth-century decoration.[1] Emile Gallé's father, Charles, operated a successful manufacture of luxury faience and glassware and made his name by revitalizing part of the rococo legacy. Rediscovering the ceramic molds from the eighteenth-century Lorraine faience manufacture at Saint-Clément, he reissued them from his factory in many patterns. By the 1850s he had established a solid reputation for producing fine work and had won the acclaim and patronage of the aristocracies of taste and title in many countries; he supplied glass and tableware to Napoléon III and the Empress Eugénie.[2]

The Lorraine tradition and the paternal example both influenced Emile Gallé. At the Lycée Impériale in Nancy he excelled in Latin, rhetoric, and French literature. After school hours, he learned drawing and decorative design and began at the age of fifteen to supply floral compositions to decorate the glassware and pottery executed at his father's factory. From an early age, he expressed a fascination for nature. His family spent much time together in the garden and shared a "love of flowers" and pursued a "cult of nature."[3] At the lycée, he studied under the famous botanist Professor Emile Godron, from whom he learned the variety and classifications of the many species of plant life contained in Godron's books, *La Flore française* and *La Flore lorraine*. Between 1862 and 1866, Gallé studied language, botany, and technical drawing in Weimar, Germany, and accompanied his father on business trips. In 1866 he began an on-site apprenticeship in the Saar Valley Meisenthal glassworks of Burgun, Schwerer, and Company under the direction of his father's friend and partner, Matieu Burgun.[4]

The War of 1870–1871 shattered the Franco-German bases of Gallé's youthful apprenticeship. At twenty-four he enlisted in the infantry and saw his native Lorraine partly annexed to the new German empire. Although he did not fight long, the Franco-Prussian War stimulated in him intense and enduring feelings of nationalism and anti-Germanism.[5]

Between 1872 and 1885, Gallé directed his father's glassworks with a new nation-

Fig. 51. Rococo faience, by Emile Gallé.

alist fervor. He began to choose design motifs exclusively from the repertoire of French flowers featured in Godron's writings and from those specific to the region of Nancy. Gallé discovered a stylistic source for his work by studying the elegant, twisting iron foliage on the Lamour gates as well as the colorful patterns of the reissued Saint-Clément molds (Fig. 51). Gallé transformed this rococo affiliation when he encountered Japonism. During the 1870s he became familiar with Japanese print albums, and in 1885 he met a Japanese botany student at the University of Nancy, from whom he learned firsthand the Japanese reverence for nature and the arts that expressed that reverence. Japonism supplied Gallé with new formal devices and an expanded stylistic vocabulary that included such elements as fish, insects, and sea vegetation.[6]

In 1884 Gallé sent a number of objects to the Central Union exhibition, including a magnificent goblet commemorating the splendid iron gates of Nancy, another goblet inscribed in honor of Antonin Proust, then president of the Central Union, and a shell symbolizing Lorraine, whose shape combined rococo curves with snails and sea creatures. The influence of Japan was visible in Gallé's layered glass vases, incised with dragonflies and butterflies, and in the irregular patterning of insects and flowers on ceramic bowls and bottles.[7]

Gallé's Japonism stimulated his return to the soil and roots of France as the basis for a new design legacy. In the 1880s he added a furniture manufacture to his father's glass and ceramic works and expressed an evolving commitment to the representa-

tion of living nature, divested of rococo imitation. The quotation of rococo picturesque motifs, such as the medley of ribbons, shells, fleurs-de-lis, and vines featured
in Gallé's early works, began to give way to the rendering of directly observed plant
and floral varieties. Gallé's botanical expertise aided him in developing a new decorative language, and in addition to creating organic works of art, he also published
many specialized articles in the *Bulletin of the Nancy Horticultural Society*.[8]

His botanical interest colored by anti-Germanism, Gallé often used French floral
forms to evoke themes of fierce loyalty, to mourn the French defeat, and to call for
revenge against the German invaders. The thistle of Lorraine, a favorite motif in his
glass and furniture art of the 1880s, symbolized the aggressive spirit of the Lorraine
against its German neighbor. For the Paris Exhibition of 1889, Gallé produced a
sculpted oak table whose inscription he intended as a promise of revenge for the lost
provinces: "The Rhine separates the Germans from the Gauls; I cling to the heart of
France; the more you try to wrest me away, the more I hold fast."[9]

After 1889 Gallé began to invest his works with metaphysical and psychiatric
meanings. Inspired by his immersion in the richness and multiplicity of organic life,
he conceived of nature as the "mysterious depths,"[10] where being was caught in an
irrevocable process of becoming. He construed nature not as a stable system presented to the senses but as a vitalist reservoir pulsating beneath the surface of appearances. His scientific expertise was a vehicle for other, antipositivist, ideals. He
regarded acute botanical observation as a "point of departure" for the artist as a "visionary," whose goal was to "capture the impalpable," "penetrate the depths," and
evoke the "latent spirit beneath phenomena."[11]

Gallé's metamorphic and metaphysical attitudes toward nature were shaped in
part by Romantic and Symbolist art. He read and reread the work of the early
nineteenth-century artist Jean Grandville, also from Nancy, whose *Les Fleurs animées*
offered a compelling image of the continuum of being: Grandville presented plants
invested with human characteristics, expressions, and emotions.[12] These Grand-
villian fantasies fueled Gallé's anthropomorphism. Gallé's own writings reveal how
he rejected the boundaries between animate and inanimate nature. He personified
plants and flowers, describing them as women who "smiled," "comforted," and
"seduced us" with the smoothness of their lovely skin and variety of their dress. In
evaluating a flower show in 1894, he discussed the hydrangea as a blossom of "exquisite nuance and tenderness" that has "put on her garden-party attire, her evening
gown, in order to please us."[13] In the same article, he called the rose "the eternally
adorable queen" who "caresses us" with her "velvety feel."[14] Gallé transferred this
anthropomorphic conception to the applied arts objects that he modeled on organic
forms; he considered his works "verreries et meubles parlantes" ("talking glass and
furniture") whose vitalist qualities confirmed the continuum of being that united
animate and inanimate matter.[15]

Gallé's vision combined Grandville's anthropomorphism with the ideas of nature contained in the poetry of Baudelaire and of Baudelaire's Symbolist followers
Mallarmé, Verlaine, Rimbaud, and Rollinat. To explain the meaning of his art, Gallé
cited passages from *Les Fleurs du mal* as statements of man's quest to penetrate the

mysteries of nature and, by extension, the recesses of his imagination.[16] From literary Symbolism he absorbed the use of nature in art as a means to evoke and suggest a
reality beyond the world of sensory appearances. Gallé construed nature not as a
model for description and illustration but, like Baudelaire, as a "temple," a "forest
of symbols" that by association and ambiguity aroused emotional states and created
an elusive, nonphenomenal reality.[17] As a Symbolist, Gallé aspired to convey in his
organic art a sense of the immaterial and impalpable; he compared his work to "music," with its "suggestive power," and "abstract images," whose nonrepresentational qualities effected a direct, autonomous appeal to the senses.[18] He defined his as
an art of "evocative form" and, echoing Huysmans, directed his work "au rebours
de l'imitation" ("to liberation from servile imitation"). "How much more suggestive is the image than the imitation," exclaimed Gallé.[19]

The exhibition pieces Gallé offered for the reformed Salon after 1889 expressed
his Symbolist commitment to an art of suggestion and evocative immateriality.
These "talking glass and furniture" Salon objects were featured in the *Revue des arts
décoratifs* as representatives of Victor Champier's new program for a modern craft
style. Champier often invited Gallé to submit written commentaries on the meaning
and form of his Salon contributions, thereby highlighting Gallé's vitalist and Symbolist theories for the Central Union audience. In 1892, for example, Gallé sent to
the Salon a *"vase de tristesse,"* one of a series of glass works devoted, in accordance
with Symbolist aims, to an emotional state. The color and texture of the vase elicited
the mood of sadness. Gallé used a new dark hue, hyaclite, as the ground of the glass,
whose smoky black tones ascended from the base into what he described as the in-
definite, "vaporous" edges of the vase.[20] Another of his entries to the 1892 Salon was
a crystal decanter "on a theme of Baudelaire," its body a multicolored, streaked
ground irregularly covered with raised glass shells and algae forms. Gallé inscribed
on the surface of the glass the stanza from *Les Fleurs du mal* that compares the unfathomable depths of the sea to the abyss of the human heart; he repeated the lines in
his explanatory article:

> O mer, nul ne connait tes richesses intimes,
> Homme, nul n'a sondé le fond de tes abîmes,
> Tous vous êtes jaloux de garder vos secrets.[21]

To the same 1892 exhibition Gallé submitted a glass bowl called *Blue Melancholia,*
after a poem by Maurice Rollinat (Pl. 8). The red and cream colors of the bowl fused
in places with a misty blue; the bowl was alternately smooth and rough. Above a
blue cloudy patch on the bowl, Gallé inscribed a verse from Rollinat's poem:

> How many times a languid
> Memory shows the heart
> Its blue and melancholy flower.[22]

In addition to his works in glass, Gallé sent to the reformed Salon compositions
in wood, whose Symbolist qualities were also explicated in the *Revue des arts décoratifs*. He collaborated on a number of furnishings with his friend Count Robert de

Montesquiou–Fezensac, the Symbolist poet, aesthete, and interior designer.[23] In 1892 Gallé and de Montesquiou's hydrangea dresser was included at the Salon, where it was praised by the president of the Third Republic, Sadi Carnot.[24] Newspaper commentary in April and May of that year celebrated the piece as a "laudable effort in revitalizing" the applied arts and as a "ravishing composition" that "appears to signal the discovery of a new style for modern furniture."[25] One journalist noted that the dresser suggested Symbolist interiority; it was an original work similar to one "that could have been imagined by Huysmans's Des Esseintes."[26] At the Salon of 1893 Gallé presented a large table inspired by various vegetables: its legs were sculpted artichokes; on its surface, in a marquetry mosaic of different woods, plants and vines undulated and overlapped the edges of the table top.[27] Gallé designed the mosaic to suggest the manifold and mysterious shapes inspired by even the humblest of vegetables and to evoke rather than to illustrate their "supple linearity." The table embodied his response to "chasing plants and ideas," and he proposed a Symbolist formula for transfiguring plants into visions:

> Here is a new terrain for the play of fantasy . . . for unsuspected poetry. . . . Is it not wise . . . to liberate ourselves as much as possible from realism by design and by color in order to offer semblances, more suggestive no doubt than servile imitation, of the vegetary phantoms drowning in the flat planes, the nuances in the undulating, indefinite line?[28]

For Gallé, nature as a source of "mysterious depths" included not only the outer world of organic life but also the inner world of the psyche. He formulated his conception of an art of evocative power, relying on the ambiguity of suggestion rather than the clarity of description, on the basis of an explicit clinical understanding of the mind as a sensitive nervous mechanism, prone to suggestion and peculiarly receptive to images. His own work was directly informed by the discoveries of the fin-de-siècle French medical psychologists Doctors Charcot and Bernheim.

Gallé's writings reveal his familiarity with Charcotian concepts of nervous tension. In 1896 he prepared a tribute to Edmond de Goncourt, whom he characterized in neuropsychiatric terms. Celebrating the brothers de Goncourt as modern masters of the decorative arts, he credited them with revitalizing the French tradition of unified arts and crafts. Although he acknowledged the brothers' historical attachment to the rococo, Gallé identified their use of their objets d'art to nourish their insatiable neurasthenic appetites. In discussing the Goncourts' Japonism, Gallé noted how the brothers attended to the "stealthy life of the nerves that quivered beneath the skin"[29] of their bronze miniatures. The Goncourts had taught craftsmen of his generation to "project something of their nervous tension into their molds," and he proposed that modern decorative arts should function as tremulous immaterial forces, "like secret voices that respond to our inner vibrations."[30]

Gallé defined his own works after 1889 as vessels of nervous vibration. The flowers he studied as models for his glass designs were delicate "vibrating" presences; he associated the veins visible in the leaves of plants with nerves. He had etched the

Fig. 52. *La Lorraine-artiste* cover, by
Victor Prouvé. Nature's roots and nerves.

contours of his Prouvé vase of 1896, *Olives and Pines,* to evoke the rush of wind that
made the branches "more nervous."[31] Gallé hoped that the "vibrations of my glass"
would stimulate "vibrations in the spirits" of those who saw them.[32] He construed
his sinuous organic art as exterior manifestations of the interior world of palpitating
nerves.

Other statements by Gallé after 1889 suggest his fascination with the unstable,
fluid, and visual qualities of mind that Doctor Hippolyte Bernheim claimed shaped
man's receptivity to suggestion and hypnosis. Gallé's native city, Nancy, was the
home of Bernheim's teacher, Liébault, and of Bernheim himself, Charcot's rival.
Traces of the Charcot-Bernheim debates infiltrated artistic circles in Nancy through
the journal *La Lorraine-artiste.* Gallé subscribed to it and wrote articles for it; his own
work was featured in it. The cover of *La Lorraine-artiste* in the 1890s connected nature and nerves; it depicted a large nude man vigorously pulling up from beneath
the soil roots that coiled around him and assumed the shape of pulsating nerves
(Fig. 52). In 1892 the *Lorraine-artiste* published four examples of the "new psychology." First, the magazine sent the writer Henri de Moncel to the medical faculty in
Nancy to report on lectures by Doctor Bernheim. The resulting article, "Un Discours de M. Bernheim," described the doctor's "experimental psychology" and his
discoveries of the way that suggestion, without an initial hypnosis, produced "paral-

yses, convulsions, and emotions" in ordinary people.[33] De Moncel wrote a second article in 1892, entitled "Vers l'inconscient," which presented an interior dialogue between a man's conscious self and his unconscious. The two voices explored man's actions, debating whether they stemmed from willed decisions or from the imperative of unconscious automatism.[34] Other indicators of the new psychology in the *Lorraine-artiste* appeared in the poetry it published. A poem by Jacques Turbin, "Hypnotisme," described how a man was "plunged" into a state of dreamy, automatic behavior by his lover, whose gaze and gestures acted on him as agents of hypnosis;[35] another poem, "The Divinity of the Unconscious," signed "A.G." and dedicated to Henri de Moncel, characterized the interminable struggle between "conscious acts" and the "tyranny" of the "unconscious." Replacing God, with his omnipotence and omnipresence, with the new divinity of the unconscious, the poem asserted how paltry was the force of the conscious will compared with the magnitude of unconscious animation. The full power of the unconscious emerged at night, when reason, the defender of the ego, lost its primacy:

> When conscious, you feel the strain of the Unconscious
> . . . .
> Will! Liberty! Vain works that justify
> Conscious acts! How tiny is their number!
> But the unconscious ones! In pursuing them, you are initiated
> Into the eternal law that animates the universe.
> And soon you are surprised by its beauty.
> The unconscious is constantly appearing to you. Your madness
> Is superb, and, at night, admirable power,
> You will be without your self, for the divinity,
> The perfect unconscious, sublime tyranny,
> Takes away your reason. You will be a genius.[36]

This poem registered, in literary form, two key concepts articulated by Doctor Bernheim in his psychiatric writings and experiments: the weakness of free will compared with the power of the unconscious; and the nighttime state of sleep as one in which reason's control of the self diminished, giving way to the release of the full force of the unconscious. Bernheim had asserted that "poor human reason takes flight," leaving the mind a "plaything" for the dream.[37] The poet A.G. similarly proposed the nocturnal wresting away of reason by the unconscious. In associating this nighttime state with genius, usually inseparable in this period from the artist, the poem appeared to echo the nineteenth-century idea that genius and madness were the same. But A.G. transposed this idea into a new key. His poem cast the unconscious not as a menacing madness but as a positive force, the sublime ideal, the divine energy empowering all action. Genius emerged from the capacity to surrender to the beauty and divinity of the unconscious, the "superb madness."

It is clear that Gallé knew of Bernheim's theories. In 1894 he commented in an article on a type of begonia, featured at a flower show in Nancy, that had no smell and proposed that the grower of the flower visit Doctor Liébault so that they could "put the flower to sleep" and persuade it, by suggestion, to smell like a rose.[38] Furthermore, Gallé would have known of Bernheim's work through his close friend the painter Victor Prouvé, also from Nancy. Gallé and Prouvé had collaborated in seeking new organic models for applied arts designs. And it was Prouvé who designed the cover of the *Lorraine-artiste* representing nature's roots as nerves. In 1892 Prouvé began a portrait of Gallé; in 1895 he began to paint Bernheim's portrait, which was exhibited in the Salon of 1896.[39] The portrait of Gallé represented him at work in what appears to be a state of hypnosis.

In preparing to paint Gallé's portrait, Prouvé visited Gallé's studio and observed the artist at work. The finished painting depicted Gallé caught in the midst of creating a glass vase (Pl. 9). Prouvé presented Gallé seated behind a large work table, staring intently at a vase he cradled in his left hand, while his right hand held an etching tool, poised in the moment preceding its application to the surface of the glass. The work table was strewn with papers and with the raw materials that fueled his artistic imagination—finished glass vases of different sizes and shapes and cuttings of various plants, vines, and flowers. Behind the artist was a shelf littered with sheets of paper, which appeared to be fluttering toward Gallé's left hand. A bright light shone on the wall behind Gallé, enveloping his head, which itself became a luminous orb at the center of the picture. To Gallé's right was an ambiguous space, an indistinct zone between the work table and the shelf behind it; a vase on the table seemed to meld with the shelf, dissolving the boundaries of the two surfaces. This spatial ambiguity was heightened by an oddly creeping vine that trailed upward and sideways from the largest vase in the foreground, bringing together the three parts of the picture plane; it was unclear what supported it or why it appeared to fuse with a greyish vapor in the wall.

Prouvé's visual devices animated the picture space, charging its many objects and surfaces with movement and vibration. Amid the tumult of activity, Gallé sat, rapt, completely absorbed, and insulated from the swirling matter around him by the absolute fixity of his vision on the vase before him. The hand in which he held the vase was bony and nervous; Prouvé flecked the fingers with color to suggest pulsations beneath the skin. Gallé appeared to be in a hypnotic state, engaged in a direct, intense, and unmediated exchange with his object. The vase acted on Gallé as an agent of hypnosis, stimulating the clinical condition studied by Bernheim, the "*suggestion par la vue.*" The hypnotized gaze signaled the slackening of reason's hold on Gallé's conscious mind and the release of suggested images and fantasies from his unconscious. This material was then transmitted outward, ultimately into the body of the finished glass vase. Bernheim had identified the externalization of suggested visual material as the dream, or hallucination; Prouvé represented Gallé's projection of his suggested inner vision as the basis of his art.

Gallé's own statements confirm that he understood the artistic work process as an experience of Bernheimian suggestibility. In 1889 Gallé submitted a written commentary to the jury of the Paris exposition, asserting that his work "consists above all in the execution of personal dreams"; that his goal was "to impose upon the changeable and changing material at my disposal the suitable qualities . . . in order to incarnate my dream."[40] Gallé went on to explain how his dream was elicited by the unpredictable shapes and strange effects that accidentally emerged during the glassblowing process; he would study and "play with the problems that the motley material sets before my imagination."[41] Gallé compared his transformation of this "motley material" to similar transformations brought on by visual suggestion: "In just such a way the prolonged gaze of the invalid transforms the marblings of wall-paper into thousands of strange figures, or the clouds at twilight appear to a child like immense sheep folds, while the sailor's eye sees in them rolling whitecaps and beaches."[42] The "prolonged gaze of the invalid" that unleashed dynamic figures from the static wallpaper corresponded to the visual projections experienced by Charcot's hypnotized patients; the "prolonged gaze" preceding visual creativity was also the pose in which Prouvé depicted Gallé at work. Gallé, like Bernheim, associated his visual fixity and imagistic animation with the dynamic quality of all minds. Invalids, children, sailors, and the artist were each susceptible to visual suggestion and to a subsequent externalizing of visual material. Gallé concluded by characterizing the glassmaker as yielding, during the firing stage, to visions of the depths: "I sow burning flames and then gather up with my spindle paradoxical blossoms from the depths of the dark layers where I know they lie waiting."[43]

Gallé reaffirmed his Bernheimian conception of artistic production in 1893, in commenting on a large crystal goblet presented to Louis Pasteur on the occasion of his seventieth birthday. Gallé's remarks were published in *La Revue encyclopédique* in May of that year. In explaining how he came to formulate the design of the glass, Gallé described a three-stage process of auditory suggestion, visual hallucination, and the release of images to paper, unmediated by conscious deliberation. Gallé's design for the Pasteur goblet was initiated by the incantatory power of a Victor Hugo poem. He was overwhelmed by the "abundant color" of Hugo's vision, by his "lapidary language," and noted that his own creative experience began with "images that these incantations suggested to me." The images unleashed by suggestion were "misty," "vague," and "imprecise," resembling "sooty phantoms" and a fluid, "intangible" realm.[44] Gallé recounted what happened after this initial unfolding of visual forms:

> Suddenly all sorts of shady notations took form on my paper, bizarre adaptations of beings in their vital conditions with the strange features of nocturnal animals; a cyclopean eye, the whitened stare of larva, flying foxes wrapped in coats, prosimian specters and lemurs, vampires and noctules. In order to produce these figures I would have needed not the rod of a glass-blower but the brush of a Hokusai, the demonic pencil of a Goya, the nightmares of an Odilon Redon.[45]

The rush of images transmitted to Gallé's paper closely resembled the similarly "bizarre adaptations of being" that had suddenly taken shape as the artist-clinician Jean-Martin Charcot experienced visual hallucinations induced by hashish.[46] Both Gallé's and Charcot's drawings featured swirling monsters crowding the picture surface with animated irregularity (see Fig. 27). But Gallé did not need the artificial stimulation of the drug to trigger his visual unconscious; his images were unleashed by the suggestibility of another work of art. The incantatory power of a poem acted on him as a hypnotic agent, activating visual associations that he transferred directly to paper. Here again Gallé's description corresponded to Bernheim's characterization of the febrile receptivity of all minds to suggestion and to visual projection. Gallé's artistic process conformed to Bernheim's conception of suggestion as inducing a dream state, liberated from the shackles of reason, when the "imagination ruled supreme," yielding the "objectification of the subjective."[47] Further, the last stage of Gallé's experience may be identified as a clinical form of ideodynamism, which Bernheim and Charcot defined as the way that suggested material, lodged in the unconscious, could be invoked automatically, and acted upon, without conscious control or memory. Bernheim associated ideodynamism specifically with visual fluidity, when the suggestible mind translated "ideas into images" and expressed them without conscious mediation.[48] Gallé's description of the way that "suddenly all sorts of shady notations took form" on his paper, unleashing a tangle of nightmares and monstrous animals, enacted, in artistic production, the ideodynamic qualities of all minds that the psychiatrist from Nancy had revealed to his startled contemporaries. Subscribers to the popular *Revue encyclopédique* could read how Gallé, well known for his Salon works and already an illustrious recipient of the Legion of Honor, chronicled his journey into the unconscious as the wellspring of his art.

Gallé extended his personal experience of suggestibility and visual dynamism to his conception of the function of his art. If the artist created in an altered state of consciousness induced by visual suggestion, the finished products derived from this experience would in turn create similar states of mind in their viewers. After 1889 Gallé defined his modern art objects, patterned after organic forms, as agents of suggestion, hypnotic "inducers" of the "dream state," and releasers of alternative, often hallucinatory, mental conditions, what he had once called nuanced metapsychoses.[49] In 1897 Gallé characterized decorative art as a way to put reason to sleep and allow the viewer to be transported into a dream vision:

> The painter of the walls that surround me should act as a poet, a magician; he must transfigure wood into bouquets, rugs into prairies, wallcoverings into ether, where, completely captive, I inhale. It is not enough that this music puts me to sleep for an instant . . . the decorative object must console me . . . with nuances that lead me to envision the shape of an alternative world.[50]

Gallé's theory of his art as "evocative form" derived from an immersion in new psychiatric assumptions. He considered his fluid, organic forms as artistic equivalents to his experience of the dream process that would operate in their turn as arousers of dreams in others. Gallé's "talking glass and furniture" captured the viewer for suggestion by sound or by sight, eliciting dynamic material from the unconscious. Equipped with Bernheimian concepts, Gallé created works that transformed the interior into a chamber of suggestibility.

*

The psychological qualities of Gallé's Salon works were celebrated by the critics who promoted craft modernism. Victor Champier singled out Emile Gallé for his transformation of eighteenth-century organicism. In 1891, Champier described for readers of the *Revue des arts décoratifs* two glass vases that Gallé had exhibited in the Salon. Champier welcomed them as the work of "a sensitive poet whose exquisite dreams blossom beneath the surfaces of . . . glass or wood."[51] Gallé's objects continued the rococo tradition of "talking furniture." Yet they spoke as "secret voices that respond to our inner vibrations," a language of dreams unavailable to the sybarites of the eighteenth century. In 1892 Champier called Gallé the "evoker of dreams," whose art effected a direct and immediate access to the mind of the viewer. Like nonrepresentational music, Gallé's works "have designs that open the mind to the immense space where fantasies and dreams unfold, where nothing is precise and where thought is left suspended, vaguely floating."[52] Gallé's own characterization of his work was similar to Champier's. Gallé recounted how "phantoms" and dreams unfolded in his mind, in a realm distinctive for its "vague," "imprecise," "floating," and "intangible" aspects.

Another art critic and Central Union associate, Louis de Fourcaud, also invoked psychological categories in acclaiming Gallé's art works. De Fourcaud was a regular contributor to the *Revue des arts décoratifs,* supplying a special column on the reformed Salons. A specialist on the eighteenth century, de Fourcaud published books on Watteau, Fragonard, and Chardin and was steeped in the history of the applied arts under the Old Regime.[53] Yet like his colleagues at the Central Union, de Fourcaud was committed to a modern style of decorative design that would enhance French national traditions for elegance while evolving a new, organic, language. He discovered in Emile Gallé this dynamic combination.

De Fourcaud celebrated Gallé for transfiguring humble matter into the fluid immateriality of personal vision. Gallé was a "fire magician," vitalizing lifeless form and shaping it according to his contorted and complex fantasies, "restless and impatient to express a flood of ideas."[54] De Fourcaud emphasized that no arena of matter was impenetrable to the vision of the artist. Even the toughest and least malleable of nature's elements, whether iron, enamel, magnesium, or zinc, dissolved before the voracious fire of artistic imagination. Gallé "evoked the soul through matter," de Fourcaud stated; "minerals melted into sumptuous shrouds for his visions."[55] Hard and rough metals "shudder, grow supple, and become as capricious as the inexhaustibly varied vegetable kingdom." "Dried tree bark received from art a new sap . . . that animated it for the benefit of the dream, for mysterious shifts of ideas."[56] Gallé defied the inherent differences of glass, metal, pottery, enamel, copper, and iron—all different materials with different potentialities for form and function—and shaped them according to the lineaments of his fantasy.

De Fourcaud's apotheosis of unbounded artistic will recalls the Goncourts' analysis of their rococo objects in terms of the limitless subordination of matter to the will of the artist: "How rebellious matter grows supple, how the caresses of the chisel work this mold, so it loses its rigidity and yields, taking on the slackness of its wax model."[57] Here again was the notion that no matter what their natural qualities, all substances would bend and flow according to the commands of the creator. But de Fourcaud's interpretation of Gallé also resonated with the themes of the new psychology of the 1890s, the world of fluid, febrile, and suggestive energy and of the projection of the self in images. With his boundless flow of ideas and visions, Gallé was "supremely nervous, with a tormented physiognomy."[58] In discussing the particular kind of vitalizing "new sap" that Gallé projected into all material forms, de Fourcaud consistently called it the stuff of "dreams."[59] In one example, he stated that Gallé "makes raw matter dream"; his poetry is melted glass. "It blossoms, suffused with his dreams."[50] Wrapped in the dreams of the sensitive, nervous Gallé, the inanimate objects were empowered with human feeling and became vessels of suggestion: "These mysterious inlays of the idea in hard matter, hieroglyphs of nature and feeling . . . are the essential characteristics of his art. It is a subtle, unique art, . . . an art that can come from only one man! A precious art that transforms what he touches into talking jewels!"[61]

De Fourcaud conceived of Gallé's works as Champier had conceived of eighteenth-century furniture and objets d'art—as objects endowed with speech, human confidences, and personal memories. Whereas this attribution of life to inanimate things in the eighteenth century was playfully anthropomorphic, an extension of the escapist and erotic rococo imagination, in the late nineteenth century it was profoundly psychological, a consequence of the inversion of outer and inner reality. It was no accident that de Fourcaud described Gallé's works in the language of suggestion, memory, and inner being. De Fourcaud's framework was the tremulous fluidity of "our interior source" and the suggestive palpitation of objects around the self. In Gallé's world the boundaries between self and objects dissolved into an unstable field of fluid, febrile palpitation and suggestion:

> A very special art; its every manifestation provokes dreams and enchantment! The crystal's translucence is charged with reflections where memories of flowerings and flowerings of memories palpitate. For some, this amounts to nothing more than pleasurable refinements and voluptuous eyefuls. Others will find the delights of suggestion, an abandonment to the fluid thread that springs from our interior source.[62]

"Hieroglyphs of feeling"; the interchangeability of "memories of flowerings and flowerings of memories"; the "delights of suggestion," yielding to the watery depths of the self—this was the language of the essentially French version of psychological discovery, fluid, imagistic, and metamorphic, revealing heretofore unseen layers of experience and confounding the boundaries between self and other.

In his work as an arts publicist and administrator, Roger Marx also singled out

Emile Gallé for his expression of a modern psychological language. Marx and Gallé
had become friends as young men from the same city, and when Marx moved to
Paris in 1882, he both championed Gallé's works in his reviews of Salon exhibitions
and sponsored them before government art purchase boards.

For Roger Marx, Gallé synthesized three qualities: "Frenchness, originality, and
modernity."[63] Marx perceived in Gallé's work the continuity of past and present, the
evolution of artistic innovation as a confirmation of national temperament. Gallé's
originality emerged from his formulation of an aesthetic vision of local and national
roots, derived from the Nancy traditions of "craft delicacy and grace,"[64] infused
with botanical specificity. Gallé's art, "local . . . , national . . . , a product of French
soil and the French race,"[65] affirmed for Roger Marx the solidarist ideal of nature as a
source of permanence and transformation.

Roger Marx's conception of Gallé's modernism, however, encompassed levels of
meaning that transcended the stable, scientistic categories of Marx's solidarism.
Marx isolated the Symbolist and psychiatric sources of Gallé's craft arts, linking his
work to a realm of instability and fluidity. Rather than illustrate real organic models,
Gallé molded nature into evocative glass forms, mysterious, anthropomorphic presences that held an intangible, invisible world, radiating quivering energy.[66] Marx
construed Gallé as a visionary dematerializer; he considered Gallé's science the servant of his dreams—natural roots as the point of departure for dreams and the wonders of suggestion. Like de Fourcaud, Marx depicted Gallé as an "alchemist," who
could bend rough matter to his fantasy. For Gallé, he claimed, glass and furniture
assumed the shapes of "very personal pieces," a result of the dissolving powers of
"dreams contacting realities."[67] Just as critics appreciated "the artifices of imagistic
style in literature," "they should affirm the subtleties that a glassblower or cabinetmaker can express through the language of matter." Gallé succeeded in "projecting
his creations into the pure regions of the spirit, liberated from the contingencies of
matter."[68]

Roger Marx compared Gallé as an inhabitant of that "pure region of the spirit" to
another aesthete from Lorraine, Edmond de Goncourt, who had been born and had
lived some years in Nancy.[69] Goncourt and Gallé were tied not only by their aestheticism but by their shared attribution of the new psychological categories to the applied arts in interior settings. Marx emphasized these psychological phenomena in
his writings on the Goncourts and their Maison d'Auteuil when, for example, he
described how the Goncourts' Japanese albums provided them with "cerebral excitations"[70] and with fluid emanating images, "so hallucinatory."[71] Similarly, Marx connected Gallé's evocative transformation of nature to suggestibility, citing the "intense suggestive power" and the "pensive line" of Gallé's organic forms.[72] And he
characterized Gallé's insatiable quest for artistic creation in a variety of media as a
result of the "feverish" pace of his inner life, what he called the "fever of the soul, the
quivering activity of his interior life."[73] Along with his colleagues Victor Champier
and Louis de Fourcaud, Marx noted how Gallé infused the organic sensuality of the
eighteenth century with the nervous vibration and suggestion of the nineteenth.

Auguste Rodin: Artisanal Tradition and Neurotic Tension

A second artist prominent in the Central Union and the reformed Salon expressed psychiatric ideas specific to fin-de-siècle France: Auguste Rodin. In the section that follows, I will analyze two of Rodin's works that were commissioned by members of the official craft coalition: the Nancy sculpture, *Monument to Claude Lorrain,* and the Paris project, *The Gates of Hell.* I will examine these art works in light of three issues that bind Rodin to the broader institutional and intellectual histories I am reconstructing: (1) Rodin's craft background and his immersion in the rococo precedent; (2) his association with the program of craft modernism pursued by members of the Central Union and the arts administration; and (3) his infusion of sculptural form with a radically new system of meaning, derived from the *psychologie nouvelle.* The first two of these issues have been mentioned in passing by other scholars. The third has never been explored, and provides a new key to understanding the development and reception of Rodin's unusual visual style. Rather than treating Rodin as a marginal, intractable rebel, my analysis restores his links to institutional centers and the nationalist tendencies that fueled them. And Rodin's absorption of psychiatric categories exemplified how he, like Emile Gallé, transformed rococo organicism into fin-de-siècle modernism in the reformed Salon.

In 1884 Auguste Rodin was a visible member of the Central Union of the Decorative Arts. Not only were his statuettes featured at the union's Exhibition of the Arts of Glass, Earth, Stone, and Wood, but by 1884 he was already at work at his first major commissioned monument: the massive doorway for the Central Union's planned Museum of the Decorative Arts, to be located where the accounting offices of Napoléon III had once stood. Through his contacts with Antonin Proust, then president of the Central Union, and Edmond Turquet, the under secretary for the beaux-arts, Rodin had been selected to produce the portal to the new museum, which he entitled *The Gates of Hell.*[74]

Rodin's contributions to the Central Union's exhibition and his commission for the Central Union museum confirmed his commitment to the crafts and his lifelong affirmation "I am an artisan."[75] Indeed, his personal history summarized the primary goals of the Central Union as they evolved in the 1880s: the unity of the fine and applied arts and the revitalization of national craft traditions through an immersion in nature.

Until the 1880s Rodin had made his way like any other commercial ornamental sculptor dependent on the market. Born to a marginally petit bourgeois family in 1840, Rodin trained at the Petite Ecole de Dessin, later the Ecole des Arts Décoratifs, where he learned drawing and modeling and practiced his technique by copying eighteenth-century prints, particularly the "sanguines of Boucher."[76] At night Rodin attended drawing classes at the Gobelins manufacture, where "they kept to the traditions of the eighteenth century."[77] During his apprenticeship as a sculptor-decorator, Rodin learned to create designs for a multitude of media, among them furniture, goldsmithery, jewelry, and ceramics. Two of his early mentors were founding members of the Central Union, the decorator Cruchet and the sculptor Klagmann.[78]

Fig. 53. Bacchante Statuette, by
Auguste Rodin. Design for the Sèvres
manufacture. From *Revue des arts
décoratifs,* 1891.

Rodin's attachment to the rococo tradition deepened in 1879 when he began a
three-year period of full-time work as a designer for the Sèvres manufacture. There
he copied the terra-cotta statuettes of nymphs, satyrs, and fauns favored by Clodion,
the master of rococo figurines, adapting them in Sèvres porcelains and enamels
(Fig. 53).[79] Rodin's early education and professional life thus shaped his devotion to a
"variety of handicrafts" and his particular reverence for the eighteenth century: "The
eighteenth century was a century which designed; in this lay its genius. . . . The
quality of my drawing I owe in large measure to the eighteenth century. I am nothing but a link in the great chain of artists, but I maintain the connection with those of
the past."[80]

To his training in the crafts and his familiarity with rococo forms Rodin added a
passionate love of rendering nature. By the 1880s, his artistic path, like Gallé's, corresponded exactly to that of the Central Union with which he was associated. Rodin
evolved a commitment to creation based on a direct engagement with nature, celebrated as a dynamic, erotic force comprising specifically French elements. In his
notebooks, Rodin registered his conceptions of the unity of being and characterized
organic forms as vitalist female presences. Echoing Gallé's anthropomorphic *femmes-
fleurs,* he glorified flowers as "seductive," "caressing marvels" whose profiles "together are like women with heads bowed down."[81] He also celebrated nature as a
reservoir of irregularity and of unity in diversity. Invoking the study of botany and
the Japanese respect for the minute details of organic life, Rodin directed the artist to

attend to the wondrous inexhaustibility of nature's forms. The uniqueness of each twig and leaf offered the artist a continuous reminder of the dynamic mobility of his own imagination.[82]

Rodin's probing of what he called nature's mystery extended to the interior world of the human organism as a sensitive nervous mechanism. Rodin's consciousness, like Emile Gallé's, was inscribed with psychiatric categories, transforming a legacy of rococo sensuality into a vision of nervous complication. Whereas Gallé's location and experience drew him directly into the orbit of the Bernheim school, Rodin derived his clinical understanding of the psyche from the teachings of Charcot. Gallé brought to the Central Union and the Salon an art nouveau conceived as vessels of suggestibility, the products of an artistic process of yielding to the flight of reason and the release of unconscious forces. Rodin's art nouveau for the Central Union and the Salon comprised images of neurotic tension, the emanations of an artistic process that retained the struggle between form-giving reason and abandonment to the dissolving powers of the dream. Rodin's agonistic visions represented the restraint necessary for transposing the hallucinatory dream into art.

The specific neuropsychiatric qualities of Rodin's art works for the official craft circles of the 1890s can be traced in three sources: his training and social milieu, which indicate his personal affiliation with Charcot and medical neurology; the writings of his close friend the Symbolist poet Maurice Rollinat; and the defense of his works by critics who characterized his innovations in psychiatric terms. These three sources will guide my discussion of Rodin's *Monument to Claude Lorrain* and his masterwork, *The Gates of Hell*.

In June 1892, in the Pépinière garden of Nancy, French government officials and visiting Russian dignitaries witnessed the unveiling of Rodin's large sculpture the *Monument to Claude Lorrain*.[83] A committee in Nancy had initiated the idea that the state commission a statue honoring the seventeenth-century Lorraine landscape painter. As early as 1883, this committee had selected Rodin's project, largely because of the enthusiasm of committee members Roger Marx and Emile Gallé, each of whom was a friend and admirer of the sculptor. A Parisian counterpart to the committee also chose the Rodin design, which was exhibited with twelve other projects submitted for the competition in April 1889.[84] Rodin's project contained two parts: a standing figure of the painter above, to be cast in bronze, and a pedestal below, to be carved in stone (Fig. 54).

At the time the *Claude Lorrain* was unveiled in 1892, Rodin was a prominent figure in both wings of the Third Republic movement to renovate the crafts and link them to an institutional modernism. He was still at work on the Central Union portal for the proposed Museum of the Decorative Arts, which evolved in a studio granted him by the government in the Dépôt des Marbres. In 1887 Roger Marx had secured a commission for a marble version of Rodin's *The Kiss* for the Luxembourg Museum. Rodin was appointed a Chevalier of the Legion of Honor in 1888.[85] In 1889–1890 Rodin was a key figure in dividing the official Salon and along with Emile Gallé helped to establish the new National Society for the Beaux-Arts, where

Fig. 54. Bronze model for the *Monument to Claude Lorrain,* by Auguste Rodin, 1889. The Rodin Museum, Philadelphia. Photograph by Murray White.

Fig. 55. Side view of the base, bronze model for the *Monument to Claude Lorrain,* by Auguste Rodin, 1889. The Rodin Museum, Philadelphia.

decorative arts, sculpture, and paintings were exhibited together.[86] Rodin's statue in Nancy exemplified how official circles, promoting the modernization of the rococo legacy, nurtured the birth of a new psychiatric consciousness.

Rodin chose to represent Claude Lorrain as deeply absorbed in the process of creation, paintbrush and palette in hand, poised in the moment immediately preceding the application of brush to canvas. His head raised and tilted away from the spectator, Claude studied the sunlight and scene in the distance. The moment of the painter's total immersion in the radiant spectacle before him was rendered by Rodin as physically awkward. Totally given over to the light and the sun, Claude appeared ungainly, and contorted. His mouth was open, his "pupils dilated."[87] Rather than standing straight, Claude was "precariously balanced on his right leg, with his left leg bent and resting on a hillock."[88] The entire figure was thus cast in a position of taut immobility: head turned to the sun at left, limbs swerving and body flexing to press the weight on the right leg, the left leg raised and buckling.

The inspired painter stood on a heavy stone pedestal. Rather than a base of staid conventional columns or figurines, Rodin's pedestal projected an active, animated allegory: Apollo driving the chariot of the sun (Fig. 55). Apollo appeared in the center, his arm raised to "break through the clouds for a passage for the sun's rays."[89] Two horses flanked the god, galloping forward as if to propel themselves out of the stone. Both Apollo and his steeds were half-formed, half-concealed in stone. Only the upper part of Apollo was visible. The horses thrust outward in the front of the pedestal, their necks, shoulders, and legs detached from the stone. The horses' hindquarters were only outlined in the two adjoining sides of the pedestal, fused with the stone without three-dimensional tangibility.

The taut immobility of the statue of Claude above contrasted sharply with the agitated force and furious energy embodied in the pedestal. Yet both parts of the monument were contorted and asymmetrical. The rearing horse on Apollo's right strained its neck and shoulders upward in extreme distension. Mouth open and nostrils flaring, this horse twisted to the right to follow the furious charge. The horse on Apollo's left writhed similarly, its mouth also open and its nostrils distended, straining to race off center to the right.

In explaining his intentions, Rodin explicitly attached his Claude monument to the rococo revival and to the ensemble of rococo design in Nancy. In the text describing his project Rodin stated that "the preoccupation of this project has been to personify, in the most tangible manner possible, the genius of the painter of light, by means of a composition in harmony with the Louis XV style of the capital of Lorraine."[90]

The eighteenth-century derivation of Rodin's project was evident in several elements of the bronze model Rodin made for the monument in 1889. The leafy wreath that encircled the base of the statue above the pedestal was a typically eighteenth-century detail. Moreover, at the back of the pedestal, just below the statue, a familiar sign of rococo heritage appeared: a cartouche surrounded by fanning shell forms. Resting on it was a crown (Pl. 10). The crown and cartouche had appeared together in the late seventeenth- and eighteenth-century versions of the royal banner *Fluctuat nec mergitur,* resurrected by the Third Republic. And a raised cartouche and crown bedecked the splendid gates at Nancy, which guarded the entrance to the park where the statue was to be situated (see Pl. 5). Indeed, each of the three rococo sculptures in the place Stanislas—Neptune and the sea goddesses—was framed by a gilded iron gate and a central ornament: a large fanning escutcheon graced with gilded crowns. Rodin's attachment of the cartouche and crown at the back of his sculpture may have been an explicit reference to these rococo pendants on the Lamour gates, "a composition in harmony with the Louis XV style of the capital of Lorraine."[91]

The most visible debt to eighteenth-century precedent, however, was in the allegory of Rodin's pedestal, Apollo and the chariot of the sun. Quivering movement and dramatic agitation characterized the international baroque style. In its French variant, the rococo, horses caught in stone in the midst of forceful galloping were a favored subject. The fountain at Versailles featured two animated horses rising out of the water, frozen in a moment of action. And stone stallions writhed atop the *grandes écuries* of Chantilly, a paradigmatic rococo monument. An even closer parallel to the horses on Rodin's pedestal was an open-mouthed charging horse that half emerged from the water's depths in Guibal's 1752 statue of Neptune and the sea goddesses at the gateway to the Pépinière garden in Nancy (see Pl. 6). This horse turned toward Neptune; Rodin's chargers turned away from Apollo, inattentive to all but their own frenzied force.

More important than any of these precedents was a 1735 bas-relief by Robert Le Lorrain, to which Rodin's pedestal bore striking affinities. Le Lorrain had carved his horses of Apollo in the stone wall of the courtyard of the Hôtel de Rohan-Soubise in Paris. Le Lorrain's rearing horses broke through an array of clouds, their heads twisting, their nostrils distended. In the center Apollo appeared, holding a shell-shaped trough for one of the stallions (Fig. 56).

In his own representation Rodin repeated Le Lorrain's device of revealing only parts of the horses, obscuring other parts. Moreover, one of Rodin's horses and his Apollo, with one arm raised (Fig. 57), looked like similar figures at the right of Le Lorrain's panel (see Fig. 56). And Rodin repeated Le Lorrain's technique of carving the stone into rounded, rolling masses to simulate clouds, pierced by long beams that resemble the rays of the sun (see Figs. 56, 57).

Between the submission of the bronze model and the unveiling of the stone and bronze monument in Nancy in 1892, Rodin modified his plan for the statue, tempering its eighteenth-century associations while strengthening its contemporary forms and meaning. For example, he eliminated from the final work the leafy wreath around the base of the statue as well as the cartouche and crown at the back of the pedestal, which he replaced with simpler, smaller ornaments and an inscription thanking the committee from Nancy for the commission. The bronze statue of Claude Lorrain remained largely the same; and the representation of Apollo and the sun chariot in the stone pedestal still evoked rococo equestrian sculpture and still echoed Robert Le Lorrain's bas-relief (Fig. 58).

Yet Rodin's stone base diverged in an important way from Le Lorrain's work, which, despite its character of movement and animation, celebrated the harmonious

Fig. 56. The Horses of the Sun, by Robert Le Lorrain, 1735. In the courtyard of the Hôtel de Rohan-Soubise, Paris. Photograph by Roger-Viollet.

Fig. 57. Frontal view of base, bronze model for the *Monument to Claude Lorrain,* by Auguste Rodin, 1889. The Rodin Museum, Philadelphia.

Fig. 58. Monument to Claude Lorrain, by Auguste Rodin, 1892. Final version, Nancy, France. Photograph by Bulloz.

interaction between man and animal. The central figure of the relief offers water to a horse, which turns toward him and drinks tamely. Rodin's horses, in contrast, are wild, unbridled, frenzied. Their impetuous force is accentuated by their projection outward from a stone pedestal. Le Lorrain's horses are less intrusive; they emerge from, but remain largely embedded in, the stone face of the bas-relief. Rodin's pedestal thrusts the horses outward, and the part of their bodies that does emerge from the stone is propelled out with furious energy. Unharnessed by their Apollo, Rodin's horses, unlike Le Lorrain's, have no master; they writhe, strain, rear, and swerve of their own volition.

At the unveiling ceremony, Rodin's monument set off both hostile criticism and impassioned defense. Among his official defenders were the president of the Third Republic Sadi Carnot, who personally complimented the artist, and Léon Bourgeois, minister of public instruction and beaux-arts, who offered a celebratory speech at the inauguration in Nancy.[92] One target of criticism was the pedestal; the representation in it of volatile movement defied the traditional function of a base—to offer a resting place and a support for a statue. Rodin's composition was "a paradox," an "audacity" "that consists of having a whole monument rest on two horses that run, carried away in a mad race."[93] And the horses themselves seemed incomplete and insubstantial. The fragmentary character of the legs and hooves and the fusion of the hindquarters in the two adjoining panels were singled out for attack. A commentator in the *Lorraine-artiste* summarized the objections to the pedestal:

> "It must be completed," people say . . . Rodin must redo the pedestal, free the horses' legs to make them look like *real* legs, soften the tautness of these necks that are not, so it seems, gracious necks; he must comb the manes, still the shuddering nostrils, attenuate this inordinate fury, this fury *without measure,* and finally give the general appearance of his piece tact and prudence.[94]

If the pedestal drew fire, the bronze figure of Claude Lorrain was nonetheless the main target of both critics and defenders. Gawky, ungainly, and unidealized, Rodin's *Claude* defied the convention of glorifying a revered artist. Rodin's reasons for representing Claude as he did related to his goals of physical and psychological realism. He strove to render accurately Claude's physique and facial character, which he had studied carefully in portraits, busts, and engravings available in Paris, Tours, and Versailles. John Tancock has suggested that Rodin also used as a model a man who physically resembled his subject, a practice he replicated when he began to prepare the Balzac statue in 1891. Rodin found the resemblance to Claude in another painter, Charles François Marchal. Rodin's quest for physiognomic veracity was also evident as he "studied the figure of Claude in the nude before proceeding to the clothed figure."[95]

Rodin's meticulous research on Claude's appearance and his studies of a man resembling Claude underscore his interest in physical accuracy. Yet the figure of Claude also resulted from Rodin's quest for psychological truth and its physical manifestations. Rodin's Claude was not simply an exercise in physical realism but an attempt to represent in bronze the inner state of creativity and inspiration. His goal was

to *personify, in the most tangible manner possible, the genius* of the painter of light.
. . . My Claude Lorrain has found . . . a splendid sunrise. The broad orange
light bathes his face, intoxicates his heart, provokes his hand armed with a palette. . . . So I have a living Claude Lorrain, instead of a sheet of paper more or
less covered with black strokes. As regards the soul, the thought, the genius of
Claude, I had his pictures, in which he has put the sun and himself.[96]

Rodin was interested in concretizing, in plastic form, the "genius" of the painter, his
internal state. If Rodin studied likenesses to capture Claude's physical appearance, he
immersed himself in Claude's works to penetrate his "soul" and "thought."

For Rodin, the rendering of Claude's genius had a very specific and "tangible
manner," linked inextricably with the figure's physical contortion, irregularity, and
imbalance. Rodin chose to represent Claude not in a calm, frontal pose but engaged
in the act of creation, precariously poised in the inspirational moment before apply-
ing brush to canvas. This state of inspiration found its physical embodiment in torsion, in the awkward bending and swerving of the legs, in taut immobility. If
Rodin's goal had been only physical realism, he would have executed an accurate
sculptural likeness of Claude Lorrain; to achieve psychological realism, however,
Rodin ultimately subordinated his scrupulous observations of Claude's physical appearance to his vision of Claude's psychological state—his "genius," his "thought,"
and his "soul," all elements of his creative inspiration. In the final representation of
Claude inner and outer truth were indivisible: Rodin's image, resonant with the
themes of fin-de-siècle French *psychologie nouvelle,* cast artistic labor as the union of
psychological strain and physical pain.

In his rendering of an anxious, ungainly Claude Lorrain, Rodin captured on the
surface of the flesh the signs of the internal activity of the nervous system. Rodin's
conception of the correspondence between internal pressure and external tension was
informed by Charcot's neuropsychiatry, which, as we have seen earlier, was articulated in artistic representations and visual morphologies. During Charcot's long tenure as a clinician and teacher, Rodin frequented the Ecole de Médecine, where he
studied osteology, myology, and neurology.[97] According to his biographer Cladel,
this exposure to medical anatomy "stimulated Rodin's gift for penetrating the
depths" and invested his sculpture with the "distinctive quality of reproducing on
the surface of the human form the constitutive elements of its interior structure."[98]
Rodin's own statement on his work as a sculptor resonated with a specific and clinical
understanding of the relation between physical and psychological distension: "The
sculpture of antiquity sought the logic of the human body; I seek its psychology."[99]
Although we do not know if Rodin ever attended Charcot's Salpêtrière lecture-
demonstrations, he may have been included in the circle of artists that Charcot
cultivated for his evening salons. Rodin's invitation to the wedding of Charcot's
stepdaughter in 1888 confirms such a personal association.[100] The lessons Rodin absorbed from Charcot and his medical neurology were similar to those Edmond de
Goncourt and Emile Gallé had learned from the *psychologie nouvelle.* Whereas Doctor

Charcot isolated physical curvature as the index of psychopathology, however, Rodin conceived bodily deformation as an element of modern artistic intelligence.

Many art lovers would have preferred to see Claude represented with a less ungainly and distraught countenance. Despite the acclaim of the president and the minister of beaux-arts, some officials and journalists in Nancy attacked Rodin's image as one of physical and mental imbalance. A senator from Lorraine reminded the citizens of Nancy that Rodin's sculpture was inaugurated as part of the Festivals of the Union of Gymnastic Societies. What had the image of a slight, deformed, twisting, and "pock-marked" painter to do with an event designed to instill the love of physical agility, harmony, and muscular strength? In Nancy, rife with campaigns to avenge the lost provinces, gymnastics was inseparable from nationalism, the fostering of bodily power among young anti-German recruits. Critics in Nancy saw in Rodin's figure the threat of degeneration:

> We doubt the historical characterization of the hero, especially the appropriateness of the posture; we consider the stance to be melancholic . . . [We] see in it the legacy of generations deprived of gymnastics. In effect, this work is illegible, unbalanced, sick art, a product that seeks bizarre movements and injures our innate sense of the beautiful. For is not the clearest goal of art . . . the satisfaction of our noblest instincts, in choosing from Nature harmonious, simple, and beautiful poses, like those unsurpassed models offered us by antique sculpture? . . . In short, we find this statue a bad one![101]

Many writers and artists joined the official unveiling committee in rallying to Rodin's defense. Although they agreed that the figure defied conventional standards of beauty, they celebrated rather than derogated this departure; the harmonic valences of classical poses had been sacrificed to a new and higher truth.

One theme uniting the partisans of Rodin's *Claude* was liberation—the healthy progress of artistic tradition through individual freedom and the expansion of personality. A second theme also emerged: the expression of inner truth. This inner truth differed from an affirmation of artistic personality, a derivative of Romantic individualism. Its new meaning unfolded from the discovery of the inner world by medical psychologists: a febrile world of palpitating nerves. Rodin's allies in Nancy, Victor Prouvé and Emile Gallé in particular, drew upon this discovery in their statements about the physical and psychological costs of artistic creativity.

Victor Prouvé embraced Rodin's *Claude Lorrain* as an image of physical form governed by psychological processes. Prouvé's understanding of the psyche derived in part from his exposure to ideas of the unconscious circulating among intellectuals in Nancy and in part from his own connection to Doctor Bernheim. Prouvé construed the movement, convulsion, and contortion of Rodin's *Claude* not as the traces of degeneration but as the external signs of the internal vibrations of the nervous system, whose activities were intensified during artistic creation. Prouvé characterized Rodin's work as visualizing a state of tension in immobility. The fate of modern psy-

chological beings, according to Prouvé, was agonistic; even when they were stationary, the inner world worked relentlessly in them:

> For Rodin, a being is never inert but is passion ridden, full of dreams and mo-
> tion, racked by neurosis. . . . For him, the reproduction of a gesture or a form
> should not be the result of a servile whim or a petrified model but should
> spring from the sensation of displacement in movement. The shriveled muscles
> swell and ripple, and the observing eye follows the shuddering flesh from its
> energized contractions and tautness to its ample smooth and still slackness.
> Such an observation provokes an inner commotion, like the straightening of a
> bow that has just been released.[102]

Assuming that the mind was susceptible to suggestion, Prouvé argued that the pal-
pability of nervous tension on the surface of Rodin's *Claude* triggered a corresponding state of "inner commotion" in the viewer.

At the time he wrote this commentary on Rodin's statue, Prouvé was preparing to
paint a portrait of Emile Gallé, whom he depicted in a physical and psychological
state similar to that of Rodin's Claude Lorrain; Gallé, like Rodin's *Claude,* was caught
in the process of artistic creation, at the moment immediately preceding the application of his etching tool to glass (see Pl. 9). Both Gallé and Claude were turned away
from the spectator, their gazes absorbed, intense, fixed. As we have seen, Prouvé's
presentation of Gallé's sensory insulation resembled that of a hypnotic trance, with
Gallé yielding to the "depths of the dark layers" of his unconscious that were released. His nervous, electrified fingers in the portrait provided the physical expression of this interior action. The tension in immobility that Prouvé emphasized as a
feature of Rodin's *Claude Lorrain* captured a similar correlative of outer bodily dis-
placement and inner nervous mobility.

Emile Gallé himself interpreted Rodin's monument in the light of new psychological discoveries, echoing Prouvé in finding the statue unlike the harmonic, static sculpture of the past that was intended to please. Rodin's purpose was to offer a vision:
"moral and psychological truth"—searing, penetrating, and profound.[103] Prouvé
had described the viewer's response to the monument as an "internal commotion,"
"like the violent straightening of a bow that has just been released." Gallé characterized the sculpture similarly, as a work "that cuts us to the quick"; a "ferocious appa-
rition that imposes itself on our interior eye."[104]

In 1892 Gallé wrote a long defense of Rodin's *Claude* for the *Lorraine-artiste,* entitled "Expressive Art and the Statue of Claude Lorrain." In it he differentiated two
artistic traditions, two artistic truths: decorative art and expressive art. In constructing
this antinomy, Gallé formulated the essential distinction between the late nineteenth-
century craft artists and the rococo tradition in which they were all immersed. He
contrasted the embellishment of the surface with the revelation of the depths.

In the first part of his article, Gallé elaborated the difference between inner truth
and outer beauty. Attacked by critics for its "imperfection" and "deformation,"
Rodin's *Claude* represented to Gallé an integral "vital harmony," where the laws of

physical beauty were subordinated to a higher aesthetic standard: inner movement and striving.[105] The laws of vital harmony diverged from those of "plastic beauty." Such beauty caressed the senses through graceful line and perfection of form, whereas vital harmony revealed moral and psychological dilemmas through evocative, expressive form, often marked by the rupture of line and the departure from physical symmetry.

Gallé initially defined two traditions, placing Rodin's work in the tradition of expressive art, along with the work of such masters as Leonardo, Michelangelo, Berlioz, Beethoven, and Delacroix.[106] But Gallé differentiated Rodin from these other artists of the expressive tradition. If artists such as Michelangelo, Beethoven, and Rodin were united in their quest for the turbulent "human personality," Rodin alone tinctured this quest with neuropsychiatric categories. Rodin's *Claude* was not a general image of the "human condition" but a specific fin-de-siècle statement of the union of psychological strain and physical pain.

Rodin's sculptural portrait of Claude Lorrain captured the anxious concentration of artistic inspiration. The physical contortion, gaping mouth, and riveted eyes accurately reflected the artist's surrender to and absorption in the radiant spectacle he hoped to render. Awkwardness and asymmetry were appropriate for conveying Claude's arduous inner process; he was studying and would attempt to fix an intangible and immaterial force—light:

> On top [of the monument]: the scantiness, gauntness, and tension of a being on the lookout, lying in wait almost tragically as the stenographer of the transient things unfolding between heaven and earth—the bewildered awkwardness of a body racked by the labors of a persistent idea. . . . This effigy presents a mind less illuminated by the morning light than by its inner genius, a genius suffused with interior light. Its face is haunted by an unshakable, fixed thought. The figure is . . . contorted, hesitant, . . . its right shoulder curved, its coat on the ground, its forearm poised and ready for the magisterial act.[107]

An elegant, composed, and "decorative" Claude, linear and symmetrical, would betray the meaning of Claude's endeavor Claude's "inner genius" "palpitated," writhed, and twisted through his bodily form, visible to the spectator. His was a body rent, riven, and driven by intellectual labor—"racked by the labors of a persistent idea." The anxious, gawky tension of Claude's body was in direct proportion to the breadth and passion of the artist's quest; his slight frame was stretched and compressed by the magnitude of his inner vision:

> A battle of opposed feelings—the intense desire to seize the light, fear and virile bravery, liveliness and anxious meditation, all this inner lighting—assuredly Claude's soul is emanating through the face and eyes. . . . We have here a voluntary break from the decorative grace of the line. M. Rodin wanted to register the physical and spiritual pain, the immense effort through which Claude conquered the secrets of his luminous palette. Rodin's work is an eloquent an-

tithesis. It transcribes a mind's daring range as it pushes a timid body toward the conquest of a radiant ideal. The physical tension opposed to this ecstatic vision, this double effort, had to be expressed in a tangible way by the sculptor. A gymnast who triumphs would hide his effort beneath his smile and his gracious surface execution. . . . M. Rodin translates the intellectual labor and physical pain of his hero for us by this visible sign—his break with those lines that please the crowd. . . . He has hoisted up the gaunt Champagne peasant onto his vast dream.[108]

For Rodin himself, the monument to Claude Lorrain was not only a representation of "intellectual labor and physical pain" in general, but a statement about artistic creativity in particular. Indeed, in 1892 Rodin's *Claude Lorrain* stood as a pendant sculpture to a work still in progress in that same year, *The Gates of Hell*. In 1892 *The Gates of Hell* shared the fate that marked the Claude statue. The monument to Claude had begun as a composition anchored in the rococo revival but had emerged as a monument infused with the *psychologie nouvelle*. Similarly, *The Gates of Hell* had originally been commissioned as a gateway to the proposed decorative arts museum in 1880, during the revivalist phase of the Central Union's craft program. Yet as his project progressed, Rodin divested the *Gates* of its overt historical model and transformed it into an unprecedented modernist ensemble that resonated with psychological meaning specific to the French fin de siècle. The *Monument to Claude Lorrain* and *The Gates of Hell* resembled one another, embodying complementary visions of the creative process. *The Gates of Hell,* with its tympanum figure the Thinker-Poet, represented literary creation; *Claude Lorrain,* visual art. In each case, literary and visual, the artistic process emerged as an image of the union of psychological strain and physical pain. In each case, Rodin divided the artistic process into two parts—one instinctual and unharnessed, the other conscious and form giving.

When Rodin began the *Gates* in 1881, he projected two massive bronze doors: the initial design derived from historical and literary prototypes, the format from Ghiberti's fifteenth-century *Gates of Paradise,* and the multiple figures from Dante's epic poem, *The Inferno.*[109] By 1889 when Rodin exhibited studies for the *Gates* at the Exposition Monet-Rodin, the composition had been radically altered. The two main groups originally fashioned on either side of the portals, Francesca and Paolo on the right and Ugolino on the left, lost their recognizable outline and became fused in a turbulent mass of writhing half-formed bodies and fluid matter (Fig. 59). The tympanum figure also changed. In the original model, Rodin placed a figure to represent Dante above the portals in the center of a tympanum. Dante was to tower over, brood on, and survey the objects of his literary creation visualized below. By 1889 Rodin had renamed this figure simply "The Thinker; The Poet."[110] Rodin's friend and admirer Gustave Geffroy commented on Rodin's lifting both the portals and the tympanum figure out of the realm of literary and anecdotal detail to make them part of a general statement on suffering, vice, passion, and thought:

Fig. 59. The Gates of Hell, by Auguste Rodin, 1880–1917. Musée Rodin, Paris.
Photograph by Bulloz.

On the whole, *The Gates of Hell* was not sculpted as an illustration of Dante's poem. The time and place have been eliminated, and only general characters and human forms have been retained. . . . *The Gates of Hell* gathers, in one animated act, the instincts, fatalities, desires, and despairs of all that cries out and moans in man. It is a collection of those aspects of human kind that remain unchanged, regardless of nationality or time.[111]

While Geffroy was eager to establish the universal, timeless, and synthetic character of the *Gates,* other critics in 1889 emphasized the particularly modern themes the work embodied. Emile Michelet commented that "Rodin makes matter writhe beneath the impulse of the modern spirit."[112] Octave Mirbeau associated the *Gates* with the insatiable appetites of modern life, which provide no fulfillment: "Rodin forces matter to writhe with sadness and voluptuousness; he has also been able to force it to cry the supreme suffering of modern negation."[113]

What was the "impulse of the modern spirit," the "suffering of modern negation" embodied in *The Gates of Hell?* A specific and explicit feature of the unprecedented modernity of Rodin's hell emerged in the discussions of the Thinker-Poet by 1889. The new sources of modern hell lay in thought and creativity. The particular type of suffering attributed to the Thinker-Poet bound him to the suffering attributed to the other artist represented by Rodin in 1892: Claude Lorrain.

The physical pose of the Thinker-Poet was marked by tautly strained immobility. The crossover gesture of right elbow on left knee created tension and imbalance. This was the pose of a man at rest who was the antithesis of calm, relaxed, and immobile—the Thinker's body and his physical features revealed on their surfaces the agitation and activity within (Fig. 60). Many of the writers who celebrated Rodin's *Gates of Hell* emphasized the specifically psychological attributes of the Thinker-Poet. The columnist d'Auray discussed the figure's rigid concentration as the physical emanation of the strain of thought: "Above, at the summit . . . the Artist, the poet, the creator is crouching, head in hands, pressing his brain to the limit; all of his being is gathered in an attitude of meditation and of dreaming. . . . He is not leaning in repose, but overcome, is suffering, martyred by his own vision, by his intimate thought."[114] Roger Marx explained that Rodin's Thinker represented the shift from outer to inner reality as the ground of existence; the Thinker, insulated from the world, attended only to his own "interior demons."[115] Gustave Geffroy, the same critic who introduced the readers of the *Revue des arts décoratifs* to the psychological aestheticism of the Goncourts' house, characterized Rodin as the "veritable and great historian of this century of neurosis."[116] Although he interpreted the *Gates* in 1889 as a vision of humanity in general, Gustave Geffroy also suggested that it represented the suffering peculiar to fin-de-siècle psychological man. The seated, brooding poet was "a man of action at rest," "his alert, anxious face prey to the contractions of a fixed idea" (Fig. 61).[117] The poet Rilke later echoed d'Auray's description when he remarked how the Thinker's entire physical being was driven by the force of thought: "He sits absorbed and silent, heavy with thought; with all the strength of an acting

Fig. 60. The Gates of Hell, by Auguste Rodin, 1880–1917. Tympanum and upper section of the doors, with the Thinker.

Fig. 61. The Thinker, by Auguste Rodin. Musée Rodin, Paris. Photograph by Bulloz.

man he thinks. His whole body has become head and all the blood in his veins has become brain."[118]

Rodin himself identified the relation between internal psychological strain and the external physical form of his figure. He characterized the external torsion as a manifestation of the internal process—thinking and creating:

> What makes my *Thinker* think is that he thinks not only with his brain, with his knitted brow, his distended nostrils, and compressed lips, but with every muscle of his arms, back, and legs, with his clenched fist and gripping toes. . . . I conceived a thinker, a naked man, seated upon a rock, his feet drawn under him, his fist against his teeth, he dreams. The fertile thought slowly elaborates itself within his brain. He is no longer dreamer, he is creator.[119]

The position, physical features, and inner state of the Thinker-Poet had striking affinities with those of *Claude Lorrain*. In 1889 Rodin "conceived a thinker" and a "creator" in the same figure, "as the fertile thought slowly elaborates itself within his brain." Similarly, Claude Lorrain, a painter, was represented in the process of contemplation and inspiration, the moments preceding action. Rodin's Thinker-Poet was inactive but not at rest; Claude Lorrain, though immobile, was anxious and taut. Rodin depicted both artists as absorbed by and riveted on an idea. In each case, arduous concentration and inspiration were marked by physical strain and tension. The Thinker-Poet writhed and strained inside and out: "He thinks . . . with his brain, . . . his distended nostrils," stated Rodin, and "with every muscle of his arms, back, and legs, with his clenched fist and gripping toes." The Thinker-Poet held an imbalanced and pressing physical pose, right elbow on left knee. In describing the figure as "anxious," "prey to the contractions of a fixed idea," Geffroy used the French word *crispation* for "contraction" (it means "shriveling, or undulation"), thus pointing perhaps to the physical condition resulting from the struggle for the idea. Victor Prouvé, using similar terminology, described the "*crispations passionnées*" of the muscles, nerves, and limbs in *Claude Lorrain*: "For Rodin, a being is never inert but is passion ridden, full of dreams and motion; racked by neurosis. . . . Shriveled muscles swell and ripple and the observing eye follows this shuddering flesh from its energized contractions to its ample slackness."[120] Gallé's characterization of the anxious concentration and physical contortion of *Claude Lorrain* provided a mirror image to the taut contemplation and distended compression of the Thinker-Poet: "The scantiness, the gauntness, the tension of a being on the lookout . . . the bewildered awkwardness of a body racked by the labor of a fixed idea."[121] The strenuous quest of "a body racked by the labor of a fixed idea" was an exact analogue to that of the Thinker-Poet, "alert," and "prey to the contractions of a fixed idea."

If the union of physical pain and psychological strain characterized both the Thinker-Poet of *The Gates of Hell* and the painter in the statue *Claude Lorrain*, another feature also joined the two Rodin sculptures, extending their meaning as artifacts of fin-de-siècle French psychology. Both were concerned with the creative process and its psychophysical costs; moreover, in each the nature of the creative process was signified in the relation between the figure in the upper half and the lower half of his respective sculpture. In each monument the lower portion represented furious action and continuous motion, a striking contrast to the tense immobility of the figures above. And in each case, Thinker-Poet and *Claude,* the division between upper figure and lower forms expressed the dual structure of artistic creation: intuitional unconscious release, on the one hand, and, on the other, the stringent boundaries necessary to canalize limitless inspiration into artistic form.

The relation between thought and instinct, conscious order and unconscious dissolution, in Rodin's *Gates of Hell* was suggested by a friend and admirer of Rodin's, Maurice Rollinat. Although little known today, Rollinat was a celebrated figure in the Parisian avant-garde between 1875 and 1895. A poet and musician, he mesmerized audiences at the Club des Hydropathes and then at the Chat Noir with incantatory songs drawn from Baudelaire's *Fleurs du mal.*[122] Rollinat published his own books of poems after 1877, the most important of which were *Les Névroses* (1883) and *L'Abîme* (1886). Contemporaries identified him as a pivotal figure in the transition between literary realism and the new Symbolist consciousness of metaphysical evocation and self-revelation.[123]

Rodin and Rollinat became close friends sometime after 1877. Although it is difficult to document the precise date of their meeting, the two artists frequented the same Parisian circles by the early 1880s, among them those of Léon Cladel and Edmond de Goncourt.[124] Contemporary accounts describe Rodin and Rollinat as members of a small group of artistic confreres, including Gustave Geffroy, Claude Monet, Octave Uzanne, Eugène Carrière, Alphonse Daudet, Roger Marx, and Octave Mirbeau.[125] Geffroy, Rodin's defender among the critics, publicized Rollinat's literary contributions in celebratory articles on *Les Névroses* in 1883. Testimonials in the Paris Rodin archive indicate that Rollinat recited his verses to the sculptor and quote Rodin praising Rollinat, whom he "loved as a brother," for possessing a "pure artist's soul."[126] Rollinat sent Rodin an autographed copy of his book of poems *L'Abîme* with warm regards and statements of admiration.[127] Rodin reciprocated by sending drawings to Rollinat of sculptural groups inspired by his poems, one of which, *Le Déséspoir,* was completed in 1890.[128] Contemporary memoirs also chronicle how during the early stages of their friendship Rodin promised Rollinat that he would prepare the poet's portrait. At this time, Rollinat was already a Parisian sensation, whereas Rodin was struggling for financial security and recognition by the critics.[129] The bust Rodin finally made of Rollinat in 1906 was a memorial; the destinies of the two artists had been reversed. Rollinat died in relative obscurity in the French countryside, while Rodin had become the premier sculptor of France.[130]

Rollinat and Rodin shared many ideas and were united in a preoccupation with the spiritual sufferings of modern man. Rollinat, steeped in Catholicism and in the religious ideas of sin, lust, and guilt, wrote poems about death, putrefaction, and hell. Rodin was equally immersed in religious concepts of suffering and hell through his early ardent Catholicism. His devout family sent him to a religious school as an adolescent, the Ecole des Frères de la Doctrine Chrétienne. After the death of his beloved sister, Maria, a nun, in 1862, Rodin spent a year in a monastery, the Society of the Blessed Sacrament.[131] Both Rodin and Rollinat experienced a fundamental loss of faith in early adulthood, and the identity of each as an artist was inextricably tied to the problematic implications of the loss of religious certainty.[132]

Rollinat's books of poems unfolded as modern versions of the Last Judgment. *Les Névroses* began and ended with funeral epitaphs; *L'Abîme* ended with a grotesque *Requiescat in pace*. Dance of Death troupes devils, and skeletons peopled his poems, relentlessly enticing their victims into the final abyss.[133] Rollinat's Catholic universe, however, was filled with secular and contemporary meaning: psychological suffering and neurosis. The hell fires that "burn, burn, burn," according to Rollinat, haunted men for their modern "egoism," which had unprecedented arenas for appetite and acquisitiveness but no set of absolute truths for moral guidance.[134] A second source of modern hell lay in thought and self-consciousness. *Les Névroses* announced a new torment to which modern man was fated, torment from which there was no possibility of spiritual salvation or absolution. For the demons and hellfires of the medieval world were now internalized; the death troupe danced within the individual psyche rather than on a communitarian stage:

> All of man's inner being, with a ragged sigh,
> Tells the solitary night of its anguish.[135]

Rollinat's contemporaries characterized his literary world as that of a modern, inverted, Dante. One commentator noted that where Dante's hell had lain beneath the earth, Rollinat's was above ground.[136] Judith Cladel described Rollinat's poems as chronicling the journey through "the innumerable circles of a hell enclosed in man's consciousness."[137]

Rollinat explicitly defined "man's inner being" and inner demons in the language of medical psychology. Classified after diagnosis as a cachexia neurasthenic, Rollinat construed modern hell as introspection and neurotic tension.[138] The poems of *Les Névroses* and *L'Abîme* invoked a gamut of psychoneurotic disturbances and clinically defined cerebral states, such as psychic automatism, divided consciousness, amnesia, ataxia, and hysterical paralysis.[139] One of Rollinat's poems, entitled "La Céphalagie," described the severe headaches he suffered during his literary work:

> Torture invented by Satan,
> Red-hot pincers of hell,
> That grip the palpitating brain.[140]

Rollinat's depiction of painful mental conditions transposed a religious legacy of the seven deadly sins into their clinical and psychiatric equivalents. Thus he contributed a powerful secularizing impulse to prior religious conceptions of suffering. Like Doctor Charcot, Rollinat redefined religious experience as a medical phenomenon.

But unlike the doctor, Rollinat attributed psychopathological traits to all individuals, who he presumed were equally susceptible to the powerful force and ravages of the unconscious.

Among the poems Rollinat sent to Rodin were those that treated the process of thought and artistic creation. These poems shed light on Rodin's treatment of thought and the creative process in the Thinker-Poet and *Claude Lorrain*. The poems are particularly revealing of the struggle between instinct and thought in the creative process, which Rodin transposed into sculptural form in the dual structure of his two monuments.[141]

For Rollinat artistic creation was a painful process, an interminable battle between the ideal and the real. Art "is the pursuit of the eternal sphinx, the groping of physical beings for the dream and the ideal."[142] The artist, the seeker of "form and idea," sought the intangible; his anchorage in real existence was constantly unmoored in the flight to the ideal world:

> The poet, forgetting he is flesh and bone,
> Depraves his spirit for an impossible dream;
> And with ecstasy in his eye and the chimera behind him
> Flies to the final pit like a bullet to its target.[143]

In aspiring to capture the world of the dream, the artist cultivated a mode of being on the edge of reason. Rollinat presented the artist as precariously poised between reality and illusion, as teetering on the brink of unreason. His home was a tenebrous world, that no-man's-land where "illusion collides with reality and certainty dissolves into mystery."[144] While tapping the dream was the prerequisite for art, the creator was fated to find the "torch of his reason" threatened with extinction by the "spectral forces of madness" to which he was irresistibly drawn.[145]

Given the powerful solvent of the unconscious, the artist was locked in continuous combat to reassert order and control. The molding of "forms and ideas" required a rigorous withdrawal from the instinctual abyss, a strenuous, dessicating process.

In the poem "The Artist," sent to Rodin, Rollinat portrayed this combat between the creator and instinct:

> Forms and Ideas
> Dry him up
> For they drain his destiny
> Always present, never evaded.
> . . . .
> Vainly, like the libertine
> Does he pursue his corroded fibers
> And he watches for the clandestine step
> Of the slow death as it reaches him
> In spite of his dessicated marrow

He remains hunter and hunted
Of these intangible shadows.

. . . .

One day perhaps you may want
To return to your pure instinct
But your veins will have been emptied
By Forms and Ideas.[146]

The push and pull between "pure instinct" and "Ideas" experienced by the artist was a feature of all thought, according to Rollinat. In the poem "Thought," the second entry in the book sent to Rodin, Rollinat analyzed the heavy burden inflicted on modern man by his self-consciousness and his expanded desires. In Rollinat's poem, thought was a cunning, corrosive agent, an "intimate sphinx." In an image of graphic inner tension, Rollinat described thought as an iron bolt that drove through and pinned down the soul and the spirit:

Over soul and spirit it spreads
Its ulcerous lime
Then bolts them in
To crush them in its shackles
And to ferociously drive
Its wounding holes through and through.[147]

The poem "Thought" commented on the battle between instinct and thought. Rollinat ended by portraying thought graphically and metaphorically, as a lofty toll collector, or gatekeeper:

We think we drown in wine
That monster hellish or divine,
For which our backbone again gives of itself
In vain
Heaven would be so soothing,
The body so pure, love so white
And the grave so free of worry
Without Thought!

. . . .

But let us drink without end! Let us act!
Pointless battle! We think!
Our flesh shudders for all
This duress
And in spite of our obstinate will
To exist physically
We fall back into the torment
Of this embrace.

. . . .

> Justice and Truth
> That lead us to light,
> It casts aside,
> And we embark
> For blackness and uncertainty
> Before this lofty gatekeeper
> That lets instinct pass through
> Only with its stamp.
>
> . . . .
>
> It wears down through obsessions,
> Mystifications,
> Through the rancor and the suction
> Of its wounding censure.[148]

Rodin's *Gates of Hell* offers striking visual parallels to Rollinat's poetic rendering of the struggle between instinct and thought, illusion and reality, unconscious immersion and conscious control. Rodin divided his composition into two parts: a strong vertical thrust of the doors and a horizontal tympanum above them. The Thinker-Poet occupied, in tense imbalance, the central place in the tympanum, positioned in a space at its edge, sitting on a rock that protruded outward from it, creating a slight overhang (Pl. 11). His physical pose—back bent, body leaning forward, in crossover fashion, with right elbow on left knee—made him seem delicately poised between the two zones: he was too far forward to be firmly attached to the horizontal shelf further inside the tympanum, and he was visibly hovering over the vertical arena beneath him.[149] Rodin emphasized this ambiguous disposition by disrupting the boundaries between the two sculptural zones in places near the central figure. To the right of the Thinker-Poet, Rodin captured a man clambering upward from the doors, his left arm raised into the tympanum space, his upper body writhing across the underside of the shelf. The man, struggling to propel himself into the tympanum, was caught in a back flip, moments before he would crash into the vortex from which he emerged. Rodin further dislodged the boundary between the two areas by representing a number of figures to the left of the Thinker-Poet as spilling out of the recesses of the tympanum shelf onto its edges and into its corners.

The two-part structure of Rodin's composition and the tenuous boundaries between the parts evoked Rollinat's literary vision of the interplay of conscious and unconscious elements in artistic creation and intellectual work. The vertical zone of the gates themselves, erupting with enveloping bodies in swirling motion, encompassed Rollinat's world of the dream and of instinct: fluid, dynamic, and unbounded ("*sans trêve*"). The horizontal shelf of the tympanum, with its massive central figure the Thinker-Poet, resembled Rollinat's realm of censorship and constraint. Echoing Rollinat's poet, Rodin presented his Thinker-Poet as physically poised at the edge of the two worlds; he inhabited the ambiguous zone between dream and reality, the spectral no-man's-land where "certainty dissolves into mystery." And like Rollinat's poet, Rodin's figure tottered on the brink of unreason; he was depicted with "a chimera behind him"—a horned monster appeared at his back left—and the intense fixity of his concentration recalled the "ecstasy" in the eye of Rollinat's poet as he might fly "to the final pit." Rodin's Thinker-Poet, like Rollinat's poet, was drawn to the tenebrous abyss while straining to resist it. Rodin presented his Thinker-Poet as engaged in a strenuous battle with the instinctual and the unconscious, a process in which the dream was transformed into art through restraint and repression.

Modern scholars have characterized Rodin's Thinker-Poet as a judge, contemplating the ceaseless striving and suffering of his fellow men and women.[150] Rather than detaching the Thinker-Poet from the underworld of hell surrounding him, Rollinat's poems suggest that the central tympanum figure and the portals were indivisible parts of the modern psyche. It is significant that Rodin, "a notorious night worker," "hoped to have the gates lighted from below" and viewed as a "nocturnal illumination."[151] Night for Rodin and his art nouveau associates was the time of the dream, when the rush of unconscious images were released as a "sublime tyranny that takes away your reason."[152] Hippolyte Bernheim had invoked judgment in discussing the weakness of consciousness during the nocturnal dream state, noting that at this time the powers of judgment slackened, only to be reasserted upon awakening.[153] Rodin described his Thinker-Poet as caught in the moment of transition from dream to creation: "The fertile thought slowly elaborates itself within his brain. He is no longer dreamer, he is creator." The passage from dream to art required the distillation and compression of the tumultuous materials liberated in the dream. Rollinat depicted Thought as a gatekeeper, through whom all "instinct" must pass. Rodin's Thinker-Poet was not meditating *over* the human condition in general; he was mediating his own internal unconscious forces. The shackling, censoring, bolting powers of thought over instinct were embodied in the physical form of the Thinker-Poet, whose "whole body has become head," who presses "his brain to the limit," and who thinks with "distended nostrils" and "clenched fist and gripping toes."[154] Rodin's "lofty gatekeeper" surveys and waits at the point in the sculpture where the writhing bodies aim, with their clambering upward thrust; the unconscious forces below strive toward their "censor." This gatekeeper, like Rollinat's Thought, "lets instinct pass through only with its stamp." The result, for both Rollinat and Rodin, is that the unconscious, instinct, and abandon are never freed from the ingression of thought, while thought bears the suffering of restraint and repression.

Rodin repeated the relation between the elevated Thinker-Poet and the dream world seething below him in *The Gates of Hell* when he made his sculpture *Claude Lorrain* in Nancy. He transformed Dante into the Thinker between 1883 and 1889; his alterations of the Claude statue unfolded simultaneously. Rollinat's poems may have catalyzed the changes in both works, which emerged in 1889 and 1892, respectively, as general statements about the intellectual and artistic process. The Claude statue was marked by the "conflicting rhythms" of statue and base.[155] Above, the bronze figure of Claude is frozen in a position of taut immobility and contemplation (see Fig. 58). Below, exploding out of the stone, is the allegory of Apollo and the chariot of the sun. The horses, in "furious commotion," are caught in the midst of a frenzied gallop, their limbs and heads rearing off-right in violent agitation.

Guided by Rollinat's poems and the composition of *The Gates of Hell,* we may construe *Claude Lorrain,* like the Thinker-Poet, as hovering above the animated and turbulent forces within his own psyche. Thought and Poetry, according to Rollinat, involved a strenuous battle between instinct and consciousness; Rodin had evoked this struggle in the relation between the Thinker-Poet and the seething physical world beneath him along the portals. In the *Claude Lorrain* monument, this same struggle may have been rendered, more neatly divided than the *Gates,* into two distinct parts. The chariot of the sun was Rodin's representation of the unharnessed, volatile forces in Claude's instinctual world, the world of intuition where the artist sought the material for his "impossible dream." The painter above, Claude Lorrain, strained and absorbed, was caught, like the Thinker-Poet, at the moment when the "fertile thought elaborates" and moves from dream to creation. This process involved restraining, harnessing, and condensing the disorderly fury of the unconscious. Claude Lorrain, like the Thinker-Poet, was a "lofty gatekeeper." The physical torsion and awkward imbalance of Claude may have signaled the same arduous process as his analogue on *The Gates of Hell:*

> Let us act!
> Pointless battle! We think!
> Our flesh shudders for all
> This duress.[156]

Claude, as "lofty gatekeeper," "lets instinct pass through only with the stamp" of thought. *Psychologie nouvelle* infused the poet of *Les Névroses* and the sculptor of *Claude Lorrain.* Rodin's *Claude* and Thinker-Poet emerged as images freed from their historicist origins and resonant with the sufferings of modern hell.

*

The contributions of Emile Gallé and Auguste Rodin illuminate how two views of interiority flourished in the institutions of craft modernism in the 1890s. The first view emerged in the attitudes toward the works of Jean Dampt, Lucien Falize, and Albert Besnard, which I explored in the preceding chapter. This view characterized the interior as an organic refuge, a place of calm, protectiveness, charm, and harmony—what Roger Marx construed as providing reassurance and consolation amid the "agitation of modern life." The second view, exemplified by the works of Emile Gallé and Auguste Rodin, linked the organic interior to the exploration of the inner psychological world of nervous tension, suggestion, and indeterminacy, thereby transporting to the interior some of the problematic qualities experienced in the outer world: instability, ambiguity, and irritability.

Gallé's and Rodin's association of nature and neurology extended the paradox of the organic retreat discovered by their friends the Goncourts a generation earlier:

where the brothers created their rococo paradise as a shield against the invasion of the metropolis, the artists' psychological consciousness transformed their interiors into spaces pulsating with energy, stimulation, and agitation. Gallé, Rodin, and their sponsors among the critics carried this paradoxical mixture of organic integrity and nervous distortion into the mainstream of official Salon culture and Central Union craft initiative.

CHAPTER FOURTEEN

National Initiative to International Awakening: The Maison de l'Art Nouveau Bing

AT THE END of an article discussing the distinctively French unity of all the arts, Roger Marx proposed that the Third Republic initiate a centralized collaborative system of craft production, modeled on the collective workshop that had flourished under Lebrun in the Gobelins manufacture. Although the reformed official Salon provided a model for reintegrating the fine and applied arts, Marx suggested that more active government intervention was necessary to extend craft revitalization to a broader community of artisans. A "single manufacture encompassing all the arts" would allow a diversity of craft producers to function under a common stylistic direction.[1]

While Roger Marx lamented the lack of a single official workshop, Siegfried Bing decided to pursue his own program to integrate groups of artisans under a single, central, direction. If a new Lebrun did not arise under the tutelage of a modern Louis, private enterprise would provide a centralizing agent: the Maison de l'Art Nouveau. In 1895–1896, the reformed Salon and the Central Union continued their programs and exhibitions, but Bing's 1895 initiative temporarily shifted the momentum for craft modernism from public institutions to the private sector.

This chapter examines the origins, goals, and reception of Siegfried Bing's center for craft innovation. Both the personnel and themes of this center had been visible earlier in the reformed Salon and the Central Union programs. But Bing's Maison de l'Art Nouveau departed in one significant way from the efforts of the official craft coalition. Bing conceived it as an internationalist, rather than solely French, craft center.

Bing himself did not consider his plan for an international center of art nouveau as a break from his attachment to the official craft coalition, whose ethos was the promotion of French national supremacy. Indeed, he intended his plan as a natural extension of his official efforts and continued to share the assumptions of French national exceptionalism in the arts. He framed his international center partly to clarify and strengthen the different national variants of style and partly to help consolidate the distinctively "elegant" French idiom. But Bing's effort to establish international ties among the diverse creators of an art nouveau prompted a strong reaction against him that would lead him to modify his internationalism in favor of a recognizably French program at the 1900 exposition.

Siegfried Bing's decision to establish the Salon de l'Art Nouveau as a showcase for contemporary design represented a fundamental transformation of his long-term concentration on the arts and crafts of Japan. One catalyst for this reorientation was Bing's trip to the United States in 1894 and his enthusiasm for American innovations in the applied arts. I have discussed earlier how Bing's 1895 official report of his American visit mixed a chronicling of American achievements with a defense of French cultural endowments. Yet while he characterized American culture as garish and "parvenu" and even attributed some American design innovations to the influx of French artisans,[2] Bing could not mask his admiration for American ingenuity and creativity in the decorative arts. He applauded the "youthful vigor" and experimental initiative of Americans like Louis Comfort Tiffany and compared American progress with the "anemic debility" and "sluggishness" of French applied arts. Superior taste and the "glorious heritage" of France as the "teacher of all nations" could not conceal the present possibility of American ascendancy. One passage of Bing's report emphasized the contest between French atavism and American advance in the field of ceramics:

> It may well be that in this area . . . America will rapidly overtake us, given her energetic methods of tackling every problem. . . .
>
> How much more worthy, to be sure, are the painstaking, individual labors of our fine French artisans, . . . who have, as their only weapons, their inmost intuition of Beauty, their tenacious and passionate faith. In them we see the atavistic traces of our great artists of the past, whose concentrated passion seems out of place in our practical century. Everything has changed. For progress in the years to come, it is results, alas, not feelings, which count. The future belongs to those who can foresee it and whose only fear is delay.[3]

In America Bing discovered how to activate these "passionate," sensitive French artists. His report celebrated the "inventive minds" and crusading spirits of Tiffany, Coleman, and Lafarge. He called them "pioneers" and was convinced that "the greatness of the industrial arts in America stems from the indomitable energy of the bold men who created it."[4] Bing took his cue from the American entrepreneurial efforts to stimulate innovation in the applied arts, intimating his own new mission when he stated that "the spirit of initiative must be awakened and kept alive in the artisan's soul."[5] Bing was particularly impressed by Tiffany's creation of "a vast central workshop" integrating artisans from many branches of the arts, from furniture to glassware to silver and ceramics, and his coordination of their activities in a single stylistic direction.[6] Inspired by Tiffany, Bing transferred the American model to Paris. Rather than a producing, collaborative atelier like Tiffany's, however, Bing established an international exhibition center and boutique, where under a single roof and under a single director experiments in different branches of the applied arts were assembled, all offered for sale to the public.

Bing discovered in the New World that the regenerative potential of Japanese arts had yielded to other national centers of craft innovation. Until 1895, Bing, through his gallery-boutique, his journal *Le Japon artistique*, and his association with the Central Union, had been devoted to the applied arts of Japan, anchored in organic forms, as liberating examples for French artists shackled by historicism. During his trip to America, Bing realized that the vital centers of innovation were now in those countries that had begun to assimilate the Japanese example according to their own indigenous traditions. The "new spark" that Bing had hoped the Japanese example would generate in French crafts he now saw redirected to America and other nations.[7]

Bing's reorientation away from Japan was confirmed by his exposure to another center of craft innovation, Belgium. In 1895 Bing was introduced to Henry Van de Velde, who was in the midst of creating the first "built manifesto" of art nouveau. Van de Velde, following the example of his hero William Morris, had set about in 1894 to build a monument to the ideals of honesty and integrity in architecture and interior design. Inspired by Morris's Red House, Van de Velde sought to erect a personally designed total environment. His house in Uccle, near Brussels, was called the Bloemenwerf. Every element of the design, from door handles to wallpaper, from candelabra to chairs, assumed the same flowing linear shape and was adorned with the same patterned embellishment. Van de Velde's purpose was to fashion an ensemble in which all the components of both inner and outer design would form interdependent elements of a single spatial whole.[8] Built during the same years that Van de Velde formulated his "Déblaiement d'art" and "Prédication d'art," the Bloemenwerf was a testament to ethical and social principles. Underlying the fastidious attentiveness to the aesthetic coordination of the design was a moral ideal of sincerity and honesty. For Van de Velde, the interdependence of the spatial totality in the artistic microcosm expressed a model of harmony for the social macrocosm. The social implications of his spatial principles were evident in his theory, originally adopted from Charles Henry and the Neo-Impressionists, of the evocative and animating power of line. The linear force of his design was based on an assumed correlation between the direction of line and the triggering of emotional moods in the viewer. The harmonic direction and integration of the linear design in the Bloemenwerf were directed toward stimulating harmony and pleasure in the social order.[9]

Art historical accounts of Bing's meeting with Van de Velde do not indicate whether Bing understood or appreciated the social and ethical underpinnings of the Bloemenwerf design. Bing's own testimony omits any mention of Van de Velde's social principles and the politicized Brussels environment.[10] What is clear is that the convergence, in a short span, of the American and the Belgian examples catapulted Bing toward his organization of an international center of new design. From America Bing absorbed the lesson of applied arts transformed by the Japonist example and the model of Tiffany's workshop, coordinating different branches of artisanal production under a single roof. In Belgium Bing internalized what seemed to him the first example of a totally designed interior environment, where each piece contributed to a single ensemble. The Maison de l'Art Nouveau Bing was thus erected on the dual foundation of American crafts and Belgian interior space.

Following the revelations of America and Belgium, Bing proceeded to reorganize his Japanese art shop/gallery to make way for the new and vital sources of craft innovation. In 1895 he transferred his diverse Oriental objets d'art to one corner and commissioned the French architect Louis Bonnier to open up the space of the building adjoining his shop to install examples of international experiments in modern design. Bing retained the Japanese arts in an area whose entry faced the rue Chauchat. The contiguous space was a two-story house transformed by Bonnier along the rue de Provence. The adjoining buildings together were named La Maison de l'Art Nouveau Bing.[11] The converging spaces expressed the meeting, under one man's initiative, of the plural centers of design innovation. The catalyst for a modern style provided by Japan was now to be joined to the examples of other national initiatives. Together, Bing hoped, they would light the spark for a quintessentially French version of modern design.

To fill the new Maison de l'Art Nouveau, Bing solicited entries from diverse artists in many media. His primary purpose was to integrate the artists and their creations into suites; to this end he transformed his gallery. Repudiating the eclectic and cluttered installations packed with objects from different historical periods, he composed total ensembles of "elegance" and "perfect homogeneity" in which every element expressed the integral unity of nature.[12] The new style, appropriate to the needs and aspirations of modern life, was realized as a model private environment where the supple and curvaceous forms of nature offered an oasis of intimate pleasure in the midst of the urban artifice. The comfort, luxury, and refinement that Bing proposed as the essence of modern design had a special resonance: the *hôtel* on the rue de Provence was originally designed in the mid-eighteenth century, a product of the first French "new art," the rococo, which celebrated intimacy, organicism, and elegance as the components of a "modern" style.[13]

Bing inserted into the rococo frame international elements that departed from the nationalist basis of the French craft movement in which he had participated. The republican art administrators and their political patrons, as well as the affiliates of the Central Union, had appealed to nature as the source of solidarity in both style and society; Bing's appeal to nature was cast as a binding net for French and non-French creators. Artists from England, Belgium, Holland, America, Germany, and France were commissioned to design a total organic ensemble.[14]

Behind the diversity of contributors was the reigning ideal of the unity of the arts, a proclamation of the fusion and equal value of all the different media. The international participants in the Maison de l'Art Nouveau included painters, engravers, sculptors, ceramicists, fabric designers, jewelers, furniture makers, bookbinders, and iron forgers. Bing's goal was to reintegrate the pure and applied arts by assembling these various media of art and craft for display on an equal basis. Some artists themselves practiced this unity of the arts by their simultaneous involvement in different media. The painter Théo van Rysselberghe, for example, designed a mantlepiece, covered with colored tiles, for a dining room, one of a suite of model rooms.

And the painters Vuillard, Toulouse-Lautrec, Bonnard, Ranson, and Ibels made their debuts in interior decor by designing a series of stained glass windows, executed by Tiffany and installed in the Maison Bing. Vuillard also created an entire set of porcelain dinnerware, which was displayed on the table in model dining room.[15] Thus the ideal of the unity and equality of all the arts was realized both in the inclusion of various arts and crafts and by the practice of different media by single artists.

Bing pursued a second goal in organizing the Maison de l'Art Nouveau: the ideal of the ensemble. He exhibited some objects in separate vitrines to display recent trends in ceramics, stained glass, and sculpture. But his primary aspiration was to integrate all the arts in the space of a totality, in which the components of individual rooms would correspond one to another, as an unfolding of interdependent elements of a single design whole. Although the model rooms were executed by different artists favoring a variety of materials, they were coordinated by their common dependence on nature and their liberation from historical styles.

Bing commissioned seven rooms, of which six were completed for the inaugural exhibition. Henry Van de Velde received the largest commission, for a suite of three rooms. The first was a dining room, with the mantlepiece by van Rysselberghe and a stained glass panel by the Nabi painter Paul Ranson. Van de Velde executed the entire room in rich wood, adorned with curving copper ornaments. The chairs, shelves, and table were all shaped with the same linear force that moved across the walls.[16]

Van de Velde's two other rooms encapsulated the theme of elegant cultivation that marked Bing's domestic model. One was a *cabinet de l'amateur,* a separate chamber for a collector to house and enjoy his treasures, a room many of Bing's Japonist clients delighted in having in their homes. And the very year that Bing installed Van de Velde's *cabinet de l'amateur* in the Maison de l'Art Nouveau, the Central Union of the Decorative Arts announced a competition for a model *cabinet de l'amateur* to house the entries of its members at the 1900 exhibition.[17] Van de Velde's cabinet was an intimate chamber, with rich wood walls and alcoves for sitting and viewing. The design of the floral friezes along the walls was matched by that of a patterned curtain, behind which would appear the *amateur's* collection.[18] These matching designs were prepared by a Parisian fabric designer, a M. Issac, whose work typically deemphasized mechanical means. For one contemporary commentator, "the liberty and vitality of the artist" in Issac's work replaced the "cold perfection of the machine."[19]

The third of Van de Velde's commissions was a *fumoir,* a room for smoking and after-dinner male conversation, designed in what came to be called the yachting style because all the elements in the room—wooden walls, chairs, tables, and mantle, emerged in a single linear flow. No division marked the table as separate from the wooden wall; places to sit were also part of it, outward protrusions from the flat, molded boundary of the room. Another Belgian, Georges Lemmen, assisted Van de Velde by creating wall hangings, a design for a rug, and windows adorned with the same arabesque linear patterning that danced along the wood surfaces.[20]

Bing commissioned three other rooms, which were marked by similar design integrity and organic adornment. One was a boudoir featuring painting on silk by the English artist Charles Condor.[21] A second was a rotunda salon with walls and ceiling painted by the muralist Albert Besnard.[22] At the time of Bing's commission, Besnard was already a celebrated decorative painter and a vaunted representative of French modernist craft reform in the Salon. In a small room bathed in light and glowing with soft pastel colors, Besnard painted large panels with alpine scenes. The walls of the room were shrouded in visions of mountains and pines—a perpetually sunlit universe. The vaporous, delicate colorism of Besnard's Salon murals also appeared in the room he painted for Bing, on whose ceiling he depicted "aerial figures" that one critic described as "clouds in the form of goddesses."[23] A recently published photograph reveals that Besnard represented a circle of eight dancing young women, locking arms in a joyous swirl of movement. In the center of the circle another female appeared, propelling downward from the sky in a dazzling spiral of light and twisting energy. Caught in a back flip with face forward, the central figure of Besnard's ceiling at the Maison Bing resembled closely the central figure of Besnard's triptych *Life Is Born from Death* at the Sorbonne (see Fig. 49). In the charge of bright light and the chain of curving motion featured in the ceiling, Besnard transported the transformist ideals of the unity of being and the continuum of matter to the Maison de l'Art Nouveau Bing.

Besnard, who described himself as "drunk with the glories of nature,"[24] may have painted into the Maison Bing an evocation of his own domestic environment and his personal quest for elegant insulating interiors. A close friend of his, Frantz Jourdain, described the "dream of [Besnard's] life":

> to live in a house where splendid doors would open without a sound. Soft rugs would stifle the noise of footsteps; thin curtains would muffle the sounds of outdoors. All of life would pass, enveloped voluptuously in the calm warmth of the *foyer*—far from the bustle of the street that one forgot, close to an art that rocked you in a cradle of delicate intoxication.[25]

The last of Bing's model rooms was a bedroom designed by the Nabi artist Maurice Denis, whose main contribution was to execute a frieze, consisting of seven painted panels, entitled *Love and the Life of Woman*.[26] Denis represented woman's life in a passage from youth to maturity as an uninterrupted organic cycle of familial devotion and protection. Although no reproductions of the frieze exist, Gustave Geffroy's review suggests the tone and theme of the panels: "Denis has painted all the sweet figures of young girls, women, mothers, as represented in scenes of betrothals, marriages, visits to a new mother, in supple lines and attenuated colors, they match the walls with a soft light."[27]

All of the French artists who contributed elements of applied arts and interior decor to the Maison Bing had participated and exhibited their work in the reformed Salon. Besnard executed his murals specifically for Bing, but they differed in neither

LE SALON DU CHAMP-DE-MARS (1895) — LES VITRAUX

Fig. 62. Stained glass window designs by the Nabis, exhibited at the Salon of the Champ–de–Mars, 1895. *Revue des arts décoratifs,* 1895.

style nor subject from work for which he was already known in the Salon. Bing had commissioned the Nabi painters, also known as the intimists, to design stained glass in late 1894; the finished works, executed by Tiffany, were exhibited in the spring Salon of 1895, prior to their installation in the Maison de l'Art Nouveau. The themes of women and nature so central in the modern crafts shown and affirmed in the Salon were also central to the Nabi works commissioned by Bing. Ranson, for example, depicted a harvest, Roussel, a garden, Bonnard, maternity, Vuillard, chestnuts (Fig. 62).[28]

The continuity between the reformed Salon and the Maison Bing was further evident in the entries of other French artists, such as Dampt, Carrière, Rodin, and Gallé. Dampt, heroized in the Salon by Roger Marx and Frantz Jourdain, exhibited plaster models of the same sculpted wood bed that had won acclaim in the Salon. The stages of life Dampt depicted on the bed frame paralleled Denis's cycle of the ages of woman in the Maison Bing model bedroom. Eugène Carrière, a painter and draftsman, had exhibited his monochromes, vaporous images of mothers and children, in the Salon since 1884. He contributed three works to the Maison Bing. Rodin, a major Salon figure, contributed a small marble statuette and a bronze head of John the Baptist. This same head reappeared along the side left portal of *The Gates of Hell* (see Fig. 72). Finally, Emile Gallé exhibited fragile glass vases in the Maison Bing, similar to those that had won him renown since the 1891 Salon.[29]

In the work of Besnard, Gallé, Rodin, Dampt, the Nabis, and Carrière, all the visual themes and the ideational core had been clearly defined before the advent of the Maison de l'Art Nouveau Bing. Nature, women, aristocratic tradition, and psychological transformation had all been identified, by both artists and critics, before the 1895 experiment. These very themes and images were displayed within the center of French official culture, and affirmed by critics of official standing such as Louis de Fourcaud and Roger Marx.[30]

Despite the continuity between the Salon and the Maison Bing—and even though the French artists represented in his group were established as the representatives of a psychologically charged, organic, and feminine craft modernism—the public and the critics bitterly rejected Bing and his French artistic affiliates in 1895. The reasons for this hostility derived mainly from political and nationalist considerations rather than from aesthetic preferences, for many of the stylistic and theoretical dimensions of the French art nouveau had been identified and celebrated in the center of a resilient official culture before the inception of Art Nouveau Bing. Bing himself, until 1895, had been championed as an ally of those in official circles who wanted to revitalize French crafts. But when Bing departed from his sponsorship of a distant, exotic model for French design—when he moved away from Japonism—he was suddenly perceived as breaking the rules on which the official movement for craft regeneration operated. By introducing international ties between French artists and those from Belgium, England, Germany, the United States, and Holland and by displaying their works together in the center of Paris, Bing had unwittingly reconstituted before the eyes of the public the menacing revelation of 1889—the possibility that France would be overtaken in luxury craft production by her international rivals. The coalition of politicians, art administrators, and the Central Union of the Decorative Arts had crystallized precisely because of the perception of that international danger in 1889. In 1895 Bing assembled the reality of non-French creative initiatives in art crafts and thus resurrected the fear of international competition and beleaguerment, triggering a defensive reaction against him and his project.

*

The day after the opening of the show, Arsène Alexandre, art critic for *Figaro,* published a scathing attack on the Bing initiative. Alexandre was an expert on the French decorative arts and a friend and ally of those administrators promoting a modern style for French crafts in the 1890s. He worked closely with Roger Marx and compiled a massive history of the French decorative arts. Until 1895, he approved of Bing, calling him a discreet and expert carrier of "one of the most celebrated cradles of Japonism."[31] When Oriental Japonism turned into European cosmopolitanism, however, Alexandre lashed out against Bing as an agent of foreign pathology in art.

Alexandre's review praised some of the French elements in the Maison Bing; Besnard's ceiling, for example, was "ravishing," Ranson's painted wall panels "simple and skilled," and Vuillard's panels "harmonious and discreet." Alexandre also noted the "fine" "authentic cast-iron ramp from the eighteenth century," a vestige of the original *hôtel* of Bing's gallery, perceiving it as an ironic contrast to the ugliness of the objects it encircled.[32]

Even if Besnard, Ranson, and Vuillard were praiseworthy in their own right, their association with non-French artists led Alexandre to denigrate the whole Maison Bing. Contiguous to Ranson's panels, for example, were "mahogany woodworks, encrusted with larvae of copper, executed by English craftsmen, under the direction of a Belgian."[33] Van de Velde's smoking room was filled with "furnishings that grope for form and are unformed, with wall coverings composed of enormous arabesques that enter your head and swirl about."[34] The central message of the review was clear:

> All this is confused, incoherent, almost unhealthy. It all smacks of the vicious Englishman, the Jewess addicted to morphine, or the Belgian spiv, or a good mixture of these three poisons. Ah! If only I could now see even pastiches of a Riesener or a Jacob, or even the tame diversions of M. de Montesquiou!
>
> I left exhausted, sick, exasperated, my nerves on edge and my head full of dancing nightmares.[35]

Alexandre concluded with a qualification that revealed the international invasion, not the quest for the new, as the reason for his negative reaction. Indeed, one of Alexandre's strongest attacks on Art Nouveau Bing was that it sidetracked French artists into foreign emulation. The Salon, union, and government efforts of the 1890s had facilitated the discovery of a quintessentially French *style moderne;* Bing's cosmopolitan assemblage produced a setback for French artisanal innovation. For in reacting against the Maison de l'Art Nouveau, one was forced into being against modernism, which Alexandre was not: "It pains me that in having to reject this new, false, art, I am forced to appear as if I am the partisan of the old, traditional art." Alexandre warned young French craft innovators not to be "duped" by foreign emulation.[36]

While Alexandre's article caused "considerable stir,"[37] another critic registered his reaction against Bing's Art Nouveau in his private journal. Edmond de Goncourt, who had relied on Siegfried Bing for over fifteen years as he developed his extraordinary collection of Japanese and Chinese objets d'art, strongly disapproved of Bing's new turn. Goncourt's repudiation of the art nouveau forms, like Alexandre's, was indivisible from his nationalist stance. At the core of his attack was the idea of the foreign incursion.

On December 30, 1895, Goncourt recounted his visit to the Maison Bing and assessed its contents. Art historians' accounts of art nouveau usually note that Edmond coined the phrase "yachting style" and characterized Bing's display as "a delirium of ugliness." These formal judgments, however, were bound tightly to his fear that foreigners would overrun French culture. Only the entire passage can situate Edmond de Goncourt's comments and clarify his role in the critical discourse on Art Nouveau in 1895:

> At the Bing Exhibition. . . . What! our country, heir to the coquettish and curving furniture of eighteenth-century languor, is now menaced by this hard and angular stuff, which appears to have been made for crude cave and lake dwellers? Will France be condemned to these windows . . . borrowed from ship's portholes, ... to these small tables akin to the sinks in decrepit dentists' offices? . . . And will the Parisian really sleep in a bedroom lacking all taste, on a mattress poised as if on a tomb? Are we to be *denationalized,* conquered morally in a conquest worse than real war . . . ? Is this a time when there is no longer any place in France except for Anglo-Saxon or Dutch furniture? No! This cannot be the new furniture of France! No! No![38]

It was no accident that Goncourt invoked the "coquettish" and "curving furniture" of the eighteenth century as the standard against which to measure the harsh, angular furniture of the English and Belgian participants in the Maison de l'Art Nouveau. That the nationalist issue shaped Goncourt's overall aesthetic judgment is confirmed by his continuing to collect, both before and after the exhibition of the Maison de l'Art Nouveau Bing, the work of several French innovators in the applied arts who exhibited in the Bing group. If the Goncourts adored the eighteenth century, they could nonetheless affirm a style in accord with contemporary life. Edmond, for example, commissioned Emile Gallé to create a jeweled glass goblet for him and welcomed Gallé to his home for visits and discussions of the art of gardening.[39] Gallé, in turn, praised Edmond as the mentor of French applied artists and as a primary agent of craft revitalization.[40] The Goncourts also praised Eugène Carrière, the painter and draftsman, whom Edmond saw both as a successor to La Tour, a mid-eighteenth-century pastelist whom Carrière had indeed studied at the Musée de Saint-Quentin, and as a particularly "modern" artist, in fact, "*the* painter of modern maternity."[41] Finally, the Goncourts esteemed Rodin, whose statuette *Minotaure,* inscribed to Edmond, found its niche in the modern art gallery on the top floor of the Maison d'Auteuil.[42] Thus it was not the style or forms of art by Gallé, Rodin, or Carrière that either Alexandre or Edmond de Goncourt objected to; it was the collaboration of French artists with their European counterparts.

Yet another assertion of nationalism over style in criticism of the Maison Bing was printed in the *Revue des arts décoratifs,* whose editor, Victor Champier, had sought in the 1890s a quintessentially French modern style for the luxury crafts and an interior style in accord with "our self." Champier himself was not as virulent or as rigidly antagonistic to the Bing experiment as either Alexandre or Goncourt. He respected Bing and agreed in principle, as one of "the partisans of art nouveau," with Bing's efforts.[43] But he felt Bing had erred in embracing an international circle of contributors; Bing's cosmopolitanism would breed snobbery:

> Snobbism has intervened now in our cause, . . . troubling many minds. . . . It may lead to a compromise of the goal for which we have all been working for years. . . . What is certain is that Bing, by choosing foreign furniture, Belgian and others, by proclaiming cosmopolitanism from his doors, . . . has diminished the enthusiasm of those collectors who hitherto had been most inclined to favor a new art.[44]

Along with Champier's mild review, the *Revue des arts décoratifs* published a more aggressive attack on the Maison Bing by a contemporary furniture designer, Charles Genuys. Like Alexandre, Champier, and to some extent Edmond de Goncourt, Genuys advocated modernism, what he called art nouveau.[45] Acknowledging that "our French art is sick, depleted by a century of sterile imitations,"[46] Genuys hoped for a French modern style rooted in the forms of French nature and adapted to modern needs and uses. He criticized the Maison Bing in the rhetoric Marx, de Fourcaud, and Champier used in assessing modern crafts because he assumed that modern styles had to accord with national temperaments and "the character of our race."

Genuys's article was entitled, boldly, "A propos de l'art nouveau, soyons français!" The first part aggressively negated what he had seen at the Maison de l'Art Nouveau. "Let us be French!" cried Genuys; "let us not allow this invasion of English and Belgian art!" French crafts needed to be revitalized, but "we cannot violate our Latin and Gaulish nature by capitulating to the Saxons." Reminding his readers of the grandeur of the French cultural tradition, Genuys urged French designers not to compromise their heritage or undermine their potential cultural supremacy by emulating foreign innovators.[47]

Besides invoking former French cultural grandeur and attacking the capitulation to foreign arts, Genuys proposed a nationalist artistic theory. He explained that he did not reject Belgian, English, or other non-French designs as such; they were appropriate and acceptable in their own national contexts. But their migration to

France was illogical, defying the natural bases of artistic creation, especially in interior design, which had to be rooted in the spirit and uses of a national culture:

> Always, in fact, we are inferior to the English as Englishmen, to the Belgians as Belgians, to the Germans as Germans. It is not that the artists of these countries are insincere; they are true to their races, to their countries, and to themselves. And we would be dishonest to imitate them in our country, so different from theirs. This sense of art flows from the race.[48]

At the end of his article Genuys proclaimed the need for an art nouveau—"new, modern, and French." Its basis was to be French nature and the peculiarly French temperament, mediated by the glorious cultural traditions of the past. Genuys stated plainly, like Alexandre, that his repudiation of the Maison Bing was not to be interpreted as a regressive attack on modernity and innovation; he urged artists *not* to "turn back" to imitating past styles, but to forge ahead in the quest for a French modern style. Genuys invoked the eighteenth century, not as a model to be copied but as an inspiration to contemporary artisans, whom he urged to create not *what* their ancestors had made, but in their spirit.[49]

Paradoxically, Bing accepted the very ideas about artistic nationalism and French primacy that critics marshaled against him. His international enterprise did not eradicate his deep identification with the French nation and its cultural gifts. Facing the critics in 1896, he responded by explicating his intentions and defending his project. Though that project was international in scope, its aim was to facilitate a truly French art nouveau. He conceived it as an extension of, rather than as a break from, the ideals he had shared with the official craft coalition during the 1880s and 1890s.[50]

In characterizing the term "art nouveau," Bing distinguished its inclusive, experimental features from its coherence as a style. "L'Art Nouveau was the name of a movement, not a style,"[51] and the character of that "movement" in 1895 was ecumenical, open-ended, and diverse. Bing's purpose was simple; he wanted to create a haven for innovation, to provide a center for all types of artists who quested for liberation from historicism:

> L'Art Nouveau, at the time of its creation, did not aspire in any way to the honor of becoming a generic term. It was simply the name of an establishment opened as a meeting ground for all ardent young spirits anxious to manifest the modernness of their tendencies, and open to all lovers of art who desired to see the workings of the hitherto unrevealed forces of our day. Thus the term was nothing but a title, a name, if you like a sign, incapable of expressing in the two words composing it the idea which called it forth, the aim to which it was tended.[52]

Bing defended his Maison de l'Art Nouveau in French nationalist terms, claiming that his international openness was meant to galvanize a particularly French style. This argument was a direct extension of Bing's attitude toward Japanese arts, which, until the revelation of American and Belgian innovations, had symbolized to Bing the best agent for the revitalization and reintegration of French art and craft. Always on the lookout for the new, in accord with the "law of perpetual metamorphosis,"[53] Bing shifted his enthusiasm from Oriental to Belgian design, transferring his idea of the "catalyst" from Japan to Belgium. He did not propose that French artisans imitate or emulate Belgian design, but he hoped Belgian work would encourage French artists to define their own national stylistic idiom:

> To Belgium belongs in all justice the honor of having first devised truly modern formulas for the interior decoration of European dwellings. . . . The cradle of this species of art was, therefore, Belgium, the country belonging to the Flemish race, whose tranquil and positive mind demanded an art of austere character adapted to patriarchal customs: hostile to the principles of the light fancy which willingly takes inspiration from the slender grace of the flower. If through an apparent failure in logic, France served as the stage for the appearance of an art so little French in essence, it was because at that time, . . . there was as yet nothing beside it; no conception sufficiently mature to serve the projected uprisal *which had as its first aim to sound the awakening call,* while waiting to give later an impetus and aim more conformable to the national spirit.[54]

Bing's ideas resonated clearly with those of his critics. Genuys too had tied the austere, linear art of Belgium to both climate and the cast of the national mind; so too Bing distinguished French floral, feminine grace from Belgian structural severity. In discussing the relation between national character and artistic creation in Germany, Holland, Russia, England, and America, Bing revealed his absolute conviction of national differentiation in the emergence of a modern style.[55]

Although Belgium and America had taken the lead in craft art and interior design, Bing offered to the French artisans an artistic center where they could recover their primacy as the bearers of elegance and grace in style. Not only did he delineate the peculiar quality of a French return to nature as the source of an integral design, but he reaffirmed the core ideal of the Central Union and the government craft coalition: to pursue innovation within the framework of national tradition. In 1895 Bing had called for a renewal of the "spirit which animated" French artisans in the past.[56] He reiterated this ideal in his explication of the meaning of his Art Nouveau:

> It is evident that a return to divine Nature, always fresh and new in her counsels, can solely and incessantly restore failing inspiration.[57]

> The aim of l'Art Nouveau would be indicated more clearly by the denomination: *Le Renouveau dans l'Art*—the Revival of Art . . . according to the following program: *Thoroughly impregnate oneself anew with the old French tradition; try to pick up the thread of that tradition, with all its grace, elegance, logic, and purity, and give it new developments, just as if the thread had not been broken for nearly a century; strive to realize what our distant predecessors would do if they were alive today—that is, enrich the old patrimony with a spirit of modernness,* bearing in mind the eternal law which ordains that everything which fails to keep progressing is doomed to perish.[58]

Renouveau rather than *nouveau:* to immerse oneself in the French tradition; to "enrich the old patrimony with the spirit of modernness"; each of these ideas resonated not only with those Bing had articulated during his association with the craft movement but also with those of his official French colleagues. Roger Marx had proclaimed the law of "invent or perish," mediated by the "distinguishing features of the French race." Louis de Fourcaud had argued that the logic of the French tradition demanded revitalization and an artistic "successive evolution." Despite his internationalist inclinations and his advocacy of "a universal empire of Beauty,"[59] Siegfried Bing remained steadfast in his attachment to his adopted home and to its tradition and culture. The wandering Jew, international art dealer, and Maecenas was also a recipient of the French Legion of Honor and an affiliate of both the Central Union and the government craft coalition.[60] When the nationalist weapon was wielded against him, Bing pleaded his own nationalist credentials in theory, and then, in practice, he transformed his "cosmopolitan" experiments.

Besides defending his project, Bing responded to its critics by modifying it. In the years following the 1896 exhibition, Bing embarked on his own campaign to facilitate a distinctively French version of modern design. He had "sounded the awakening" to France by exhibiting the design innovations of Belgium and America; now he would turn to fostering the creation of design "conformable to the French national spirit." By 1898 Bing had organized his own workshops to produce furniture and interior ensembles that would resonate with French traditions, particularly those of the eighteenth century. Purified of most international elements and contracted into an intimate model pavilion, Bing's Maison de l'Art Nouveau reappeared at the 1900 exposition, to the enthusiastic acclaim of art critics and the public.

CHAPTER FIFTEEN

Conclusion: The 1900 Paris Exhibition

THE PARIS EXHIBITION of 1889 had inaugurated a modern style of technological innovation and revealed the possibility of creating cultural monuments with the new materials of industrial production. The crafts, though by no means absent, were subordinated to the colossal presence of what was called the art nouveau of iron and glass.

A very different conception and configuration of the modern style emerged in 1900. The elaborately worked decorative arts, enclosed in their iron and glass frames in 1889, were externalized; they conquered the surface and substance of the exhibition. Now the new materials of iron and glass were shielded from view, overlaid with sculpted stone, ceramic, and plaster facades. The 1900 fair glorified an art nouveau of interior decoration, charged with contemporary organic, feminine, and psychological meanings, while evoking distinctively French design traditions.

This chapter analyzes the 1900 exhibition as the culmination of the modernist ideals of the official craft movement. These ideals, as they were defined by Victor Champier, Georges Berger, Louis de Fourcaud, and Roger Marx, were rococo inspiration, feminization, and psychological expression, unified by particularly French organic forms. At the Paris Exhibition of 1900, all of these elements crystallized not only in Bing's Pavilion of Art Nouveau, but in a wide-ranging celebration of a new French modern style. Bing's pavilion was an essential part of that celebration, but not all of it. Art historians tend to isolate Bing's contribution to the fair as they isolate his 1895 experiment from the broader official craft movement in France. But the model house Bing designed for the 1900 exhibition marked the reattachment of his project to the official movement for craft renewal in which he had already participated. Like the other constituents of craft modernism at the fair, it was a variation on the general theme: feminine, organic, nationalist, and psychological modernism in 1900.

Although the exhibition was an apotheosis of the craft modern style, it also recapitulated the essential tension within the craft movement. The two types of interiority that had surfaced in the arts of the reformed Salon and the Central Union exhibits of the 1890s reappeared at the 1900 fair. Modern comfort, intimacy, and organic integration marked one type; modern nervousness, indeterminacy, and psychological agitation marked the other. In 1900 both shaped the character of artistic modernism, glorified as the essence of France as the century turned.

Bing's 1900 Pavilion

In his pavilion for the 1900 fair, Bing reaffirmed, in a specifically national version, the principles that had guided his 1895 project: the integration of art and craft, the collaboration between artists and artisans, the creation of interior ensembles that unfolded as interdependent elements of a single design whole, composed from the vocabulary of nature. The 1900 exhibit was a model home with six fully decorated rooms. Each was marked by the artistic rendering of every surface, from walls and rugs to ceiling corners and bedposts.[1]

Bing's model home of 1900 differed in two significant ways from his similar project of 1895. First, responding to the vehement nationalist criticism of the first Maison de l'Art Nouveau, Bing returned to the basic principles of the official French craft movement. He organized the 1900 pavilion as a project to be clearly in accordance with French traditions, especially the stylistic precedent of the eighteenth century. Second, Bing entered the 1900 fair in a new guise: although he continued his activities as an art dealer, after 1898 he concentrated on establishing and directing his own craft workshops. Bing's 1900 exhibit represented the work of these luxury ateliers, which promoted a new design inspired by the French patrimony. Furniture and jewelry were the major crafts produced directly under his supervision, but Bing also contracted with other companies for tapestries, rugs, and wall coverings custom ordered to match the other components of the interiors.[2] In 1895 Bing had acted as an impresario and promoter, assembling objects from different countries to show the multiple possibilities for a new interior ensemble. In 1900 Bing, as artistic director, selected one of these possibilities for the public—only French designs were represented, and the interior style of the model modern home was conceived as distinctively French, derived from specifically French sources.

Bing commissioned three artists to design the model home, urging them to express their individual temperaments while seeking a graceful organic whole. Edward Colonna, an architect turned furniture maker and jeweler, designed a salon and music room, whose rich citrus wood furnishings were inlaid with colored marquetry; the walls were hung with pastel fabric, and the rugs repeated the floral shapes that had been incised into the wood furniture. Eugène Gaillard, a sculptor who had turned to furniture, designed a dining room and a bedroom, with carpets, leaded glass, fabrics, and painted murals (Fig. 63). Finally, Georges de Feure, a painter, engraver, and lithographer, tried his hand at the boudoir and a *cabinet de toilette* with silk tapestries and gilded screens (Fig. 64). Each of the three artists was closely observed by Bing in the design stages; each subscribed to the principle of "a united effort, a collective will in which all are impelled to the same goal."[3] In some instances, this goal was realized by one artist adding to the room created by another, as when de Feure provided bedposts and silk embroidered curtains for Gaillard's bedroom.[4]

The critics celebrated Bing's Maison de l'Art Nouveau in 1900, identifying it as an embodiment of quintessentially French modern design. *Modern* was defined by crit-

Eugène GAILLARD

CHAMBRE A COUCHER exposée au Pavillon de l' "Art Nouveau". Bing en 1900.

Fig. 63. Bedroom by Eugène Gaillard for the Pavillon de l'Art Nouveau Bing in 1900. Courtesy of the Bibliothèque Nationale, Paris.

Georges de FEURE

BOUDOIR, exposé au Pavillon de l' "Art Nouveau". Bing en 1900.

Fig. 64. Boudoir by Georges de Feure for the Pavillon de l'Art Nouveau Bing in 1900. Courtesy of the Bibliothèque Nationale, Paris.

ics as the evocation and transformation of the eighteenth century, the first French modern style of organic craft integration. One critic described the model rooms in Bing's dwelling:

> The minutely wrought metal follows almost voluptuously the moldings and panels of furniture of a solid elegance; their lines suggest, without actually imitating, the finest models of the eighteenth century. . . . The furniture is soft to the touch, like silk, and has the shimmering hues of sumptuous damasks; the finish of the details, the preciosity of the chased copper, like so many jewels, make each item a collector's piece, a rare object, and—a delightful thing—it all blends into the whole. . . . This return of gilding in the "New Art" . . . is a revelation. . . . On the walls, in dream-like rosettes, the same dawn and twilight shades, of which de Feure seems to have discovered the secret, adorn the shimmering waters of a lake.[5]

Voluptuous elegance; soothing and soft slender shapes; dreamlike flora, and gilded settees—all evoke the eighteenth century while offering a nineteenth-century version of enveloping interior retreat.

Another critic, echoing this one, glorified the feminine organic refuge of the truly French art nouveau. Gabriel Mourey, the writer and art critic, had been hostile to the Maison Bing of 1895 as a foreign invasion.[6] He had urged Bing then to "produce a work truly French which would be a genuine expression of the sensibility of our race and not an adaptation of foreign principles."[7] In 1900 Mourey was an absolute enthusiast of the Bing pavilion, seeing in it the "perfect example" of such a "truly French" work.[8] Mourey too identified the Maison Bing of 1900 as a contemporary transposition of the modernity of the eighteenth-century goût nouveau—organic, feminine, and interiorizing. Mourey applauded Bing's purification of internationalism and the crystallization of quintessentially French design. "Rather than succumbing to international seduction," Mourey stated, "we are animated now by a lofty goal; we are wary of external influences and have reattached ourselves to the true sources of French national style."[9]

Mourey characterized the Bing pavilion as "a source of French inspiration," a resuscitation of the "treasures of grace, elegance and delicacy bequeathed to us by the eighteenth century." Bing's products had the merit and distinction of being "modern and original in our period in the same way that the furnishings for the Trianon were in theirs."[10]

Thus the critics complimented Bing for achieving a modern style inspired by, but not imitative of, the glorious phases of French design history. His pavilion, however, carried the "mark of the era" in ways that its critical champions did not explain. Paradoxically, the "quintessentially French" style that critics celebrated in Bing's art nouveau was the creation of artists who were not all native French. Colonna, for example, had been born in Cologne, had trained as an architect in Brussels, and had moved to the United States in 1882. He lived in Paris after 1897, when Bing hired him. Colonna's versatility enabled him to design furniture that clearly evoked the French eighteenth-century forms; Bing charged him "to eschew the bulky, box-like forms of British and Belgian furniture and instead to apply a modern decorative vocabulary to the light, graceful forms of Louis XV."[11] Georges de Feure had been born in Holland, though he had trained and lived in France for most of his life. He had been clearly integrated into the French craft movement when Bing commissioned him in 1898; de Feure had exhibited his work at the reformed Salon in 1893 and 1894. He was preoccupied with women and with the theme of the *femme-fleur* that was central to modern organic craftsmen.[12] Bing characterized him as Dutch by birth, though he noted how this origin was "hidden under a thick layer of French varnish."[13]

The "truly French" and "distinctively contemporary" character of the Bing pavilion was also carried in the new psychological themes of the intimate dwelling. Critics applauding it spoke generally of the "dream-like qualities" of the rooms;[14] Mourey called its foundations "stones of memories," "evocative motifs of thoughts and dreams."[15] Bing himself linked the interior to two psychological concepts. On the one hand, "art in an enclosed space" was to supply "peace for the eye and the nerves," and the interior itself was "a refuge from the feverish haste of modern existence."[16] On the other hand, the interior refuge was a dynamic, vital place where the dream world was released. The "lavish interior," Bing noted, is a site where the "mysterious gleam of a luminous wall emerges from the shadows, magical in its harmonies, whose appearance stimulates the imagination and transports it to enchanted dreams."[17] This idea that the interior could be at once a domain of tranquility for overwrought nerves and an arena for nervous stimulation surfaced in other places at the 1900 exhibition.

The Entryway: The Parisienne Replaces the Tour Eiffel as Art Nouveau

In 1889 the plan of the Paris Exposition had been compared to a "cathedral," whose steeple was the Eiffel Tower and whose cruciform construction was embodied in the Dome of the French Nation and in the Gallery of Machines behind it.[18] In 1900 both guidebooks and critics likened the fair to a vast pulsating "organism," lacking the linear regularity of 1889 in a vitalist force "where everything moves."[19] Lamenting the denuded and lifeless carcass of the wrought-iron Eiffel Tower in 1889, Robert de la Sizeranne had called for an "Ezekial" as master builder for 1900: breathe life into the dry iron bones, he thundered.[20] In 1900 his imperative was realized; the exhibition was an organism: "The 1900 Exposition envelops its disparate parts in an ensemble that can be accused of everything except lifelessness; life seethes in this immense reservoir of energy."[21]

A new entryway set the vitalist tone of the exhibition, replacing the Eiffel Tower as the "main attraction." The central focus of the 1900 exhibition was the Esplanade des Invalides and Champs-Elysées, newly unified by the Pont Alexandre III, which was completed for the fair. Two palaces reserved for the arts were included in the

Fig. 65. The Porte Binet, 1900, entry to Paris Exhibition. Photograph by Roger-Viollet.

plans for the new bridge: the Grand and Petit Palais. As a monumental entryway to
the palace ensemble, a bejeweled and mosaic-covered arch was erected, atop which
rose a tower to woman—*La Parisienne.* The statue was characterized as "an 'art
nouveau,' supple and vital."[22]

The Porte Binet, as the entryway was called, after the architect who designed it,
consisted of two slender minarets, framing the arch on which the *Parisienne* perched,
and a dome with arches at either side (Fig. 65). The high arch and two side arches of
the dome together composed a haunchlike structure much like the base of the Eiffel
Tower. But the dome, the female figure, and the extravagant ornamental wrap of the
arches offered a striking contrast to the open and interlaced character of the iron
monument.

In its surfaces the Porte Binet embodied the multiple themes of the 1900 art nouveau. Along the walls that joined the minarets to the main arch, the sculptor Guillot
carved, in high relief, a frieze of workers, representing the contributors to the fair.
Guillot's laborers were artisans, carrying the tools of their wood, iron, ceramic, and
rural traditional trades. The *Frieze of Labor* was a procession, a Panathenaea to soli-

darity based on unity in diversity: "A long train of workers unfolds in close ranks: day laborers, bakers, masons, carpenters, carrying their tools and the fruits of their labors. This is the symbol of an entire nation contributing to the common good."[23] The theme of political solidarity was reiterated in the *Fluctuat nec mergitur* device, and its ship projected out of the tip of the highest arch. The *Parisienne* atop the arch herself wore as a headdress the crown of the *Fluctuat* emblem. Thus the "corporations" of workers to whom the solidarists turned were chiseled along the base of the Porte Binet, while the allegory of the ship of state charting a fluid course amid the winds of change, an allegory of royal and imperial origins, crowned the monument.

Craft labor as the essence of solidarist unity in diversity was one theme of the Porte Binet; the splendid decoration of its massive dome and arches carried out another. Binet was an architect who symbolized the liberation from classical and historical styles touted at the Academy and the reintegration of architecture and decoration, art and craft. Binet's commission for the 1900 fair was made possible by the same institutional adaptiveness that characterized the official sponsorship of craft modernism.

Born in Chaumont-sur-Yonne in 1866, Binet entered the Ecole des Beaux-Arts for architectural training in 1882. Despite his high achievements, he turned away from the classical world of Italy he had studied there; rather than explore Rome, Binet traveled to Sicily, Tunisia, Algeria, and Spain, where he was "swept away" by the ornamentalism and color of Moorish architecture.[24] The Porte Binet was a fantastic mélange of the Oriental splendors he had observed in his travels: the framing minarets derived from those he saw during his *séjour* in the French colonies; the ornamentation—the most startling element of the *porte's* design—testified to the splendors of Moorish palaces.

An elaborate layer of ceramic and jeweled ornamentation enveloped the minarets, dome, and three arches of the Porte Binet. A team of luxury artisans helped Binet with this splendid decorative wrap. His own role was not that of a distant master builder, for he had personal experience in craft design, including vases for the Sèvres porcelain works and tapestries for the Gobelins.[25] The radiant overlay on the *porte* mingled "shimmering stones," "glistening silver and gold pieces," and multicolored enamel and ceramic patterns like fanciful rockwork.[26] Crystal cabochons studded the dome, minarets, and arches, sparkling in sunlight and blazing at night with thousands of miniature electric lights.

This exotic Orientalism of decorative surfaces did not derive wholly from the fantasies of a votary of southern civilizations. The presence of a very modern form of organic science directly informed the architect's ornamental plan, for Binet, like Besnard and Gallé, endorsed metamorphic evolutionism:

> For years it has been Binet's passion to frequent the Museum, to bury himself in an enthusiastic study of both living and inorganic bodies; he has read the admirable *Philosophy of Palaeontology* by Gaudry: he has observed the laws of *transformism* and has noted how, with the lower beings, the natural kingdoms

converge and intermingle; finally, and most importantly, he has met Haeckel and discovered what an unfathomable treasure of forms nature has given to art.[27]

Indeed one can recognize "the vertebrae of the dinosaur in the porch, the cells of the beehive in the dome and the madrepores in the pinnacles."[28] Binet's own notebooks explicitly linked the formal structure of his designs to the shapes and structures of lower life forms, whose characteristics he had studied in paleontological and zoological sources.[29]

The scientific character of Binet's ornamentation extended beyond the identification of particular paleontological elements. Because the essence of transformism was the unity of being and the continuum of matter, which joined human and other forms of being in a single metamorphic flow, it was perhaps no accident that the Porte Binet culminated architecturally in a large statue of a woman. In Besnard's panels *Life Is Born from Death,* woman was fused with rock and ocean and spawned the world from the milky fluid of her breasts. Given Binet's explicit immersion in transformist theory, the *Parisienne* atop the traces of other forms of being may have represented a similar linkage of woman to the unity of matter and its eruptive force.

Whatever the relation of the statue of woman to transformist theory, commentators on the exhibition linked her particular appearance to the specifically decorative scheme of the architecture. *La Parisienne* was no timeless goddess or clearly allegorical figure but appeared as the triumph of modern decoration (Fig. 66). Like the dome and arches of the Porte Binet, the statue was elaborately decorated. The great couturier Paquin designed a special costume for her, consisting of a long dress, with a layered bodice gathered tightly at the waist, and over it a long cloak with a standing collar. In her regal garb she looked like a queen, and indeed her crown was shaped like the prow of the ship, emblem of *Fluctuat nec mergitur* and the city of Paris. Yet this was an unprecedented figure, portrayed in contemporary dress and having little historical reference. The relation between the sculpture and its base was highly resonant. One commentator applauded "the unexpected originality, the pretty notion of getting rid of Venus, Mercury and Apollo and of replacing the mythological rubbish with a modern woman, *the* modern woman; of evoking in the low-relief of the base, the concept of the operative, the manual worker, too often forgotten in our century."[30] The commentator does not mention, however, that the frieze focused on a particular kind of worker, the artisan, whose products were intended to nourish the very types of elaborate decoration encasing the surfaces of the *porte* and the body of *La Parisienne.* Taken together, the frieze of work along the base, the complex community of luxury craftsmen contributing to the *porte,* and the sculpture of La Parisienne signified in one monument the triumph of the decorative arts and the decorative woman as the target of the artisans. The elegant, feminizing interior of Bing's Pavillon de l'Art Nouveau found a magnified image in Binet's entryway, where woman as objet d'art and her role as inspirer of the craftsman found such striking architectural expression.

Fig. 66. La Parisienne, 1900.

Those who called the Porte Binet and *La Parisienne* "an 'art nouveau,' supple and vital," referred to the glorification of "the architect as decorator and colorist," working in collaboration with teams of skilled craftsmen, "sculptors, ceramicists, and draftsmen."[31] This art nouveau was also explicitly linked to an organicization and feminization of technology, similar to the transformation of the *grand goût* into *la grâce* in the mid-eighteenth century: "The monumental Porte will prepare . . . the triumph of this decorative architecture, whose greatest apostle is Monsieur Binet. Boldly breaking with classical tradition, this architecture happily attempts to soften the rigid forms of antique art with the needs of modern taste."[32]

The theme of the supple, decorative art nouveau and its eighteenth-century heritage continued in the major elements of the exhibition behind the colossal Porte Binet: the Grand and Petit Palais, the two major permanent edifices constructed for the 1900 fair. The architect who designed them compared his plan to that of the twin Trianon Palaces at Versailles, and commentators on the exhibition noted the similarity.[33] Rococo forms emerged repeatedly along the surfaces of the twin palaces. The sculpture crowning the Grand Palais, *The Triumph of Apollo* that appeared to be racing off its unsteady pedestal, evoked the fiery charge of the horses atop the *grandes écuries* at Chantilly, though this time with the writhing and torment of Rodin's *Claude Lorrain* base. Rococo flourishes were also evident in the huge fanning shells on the Grand Palais and in the pink marble colonnade of the Petit Palais, inspired by the interior courtyard of the Grand Trianon.[34] The scrollwork on the massive gate of the Petit Palais (Pl. 12) was as delicate and serpentine as that of Jean Lamour's mid-eighteenth-century gates (see Pl. 5).

Both the Grand and Petit Palais were created as temples of art, integrating the fine and the applied arts. Behind the massive stone columns of the Grand Palais a gilded frieze of polychrome faience depicted the "great epochs of art" and named the great artists of France, including Boucher and Fragonard: the eighteenth century thus took its place in the patrimony.[35]

The revivalist elements of the two palaces did not mean that modernity had been banished. Rather, as in the story of craft renovation, the emphasis was on the evolution of a modern idiom from the crucible of the French tradition. On the facades of both palaces was the republican symbol of continuity and change, *Fluctuat nec mergitur*. Albert Besnard was commissioned to decorate the vast ceilings of the Petit Palais. In a majestic marble vestibule, he painted the ship in the waves and the *Fluctuat* banderole in the exact center of the ceiling. In the adjacent hall, Besnard illustrated his version of the organicist, feminine Republic—not the stalwart classical Marianne of 1889 but a fashionable and playful figure (Pl. 13). Besnard painted a young woman in a Phrygian cap—the emblem of the Republic since the 1880s—wrapped in diaphanous red veils that revealed her body beneath. Besnard's representation of her, flying through the air with her red veils around her wings, indicated that the "red" political associations of her cap were no longer to be feared: the cap itself was part of her depoliticized decorative outfit.

The melding of eighteenth-century *patrimoine* and late nineteenth-century modern style was extended in the contents of the two palaces. The exhibition at the Petit Palais included an unprecedented array of rococo furniture, clocks, and other sumptuous artifacts. Commentators noted that this extraordinary exhibition provided the final impetus to the official institutionalization of the eighteenth-century unity of the arts, for its success convinced Henri Roujon, the director of the beaux-arts, and Emile Molinier, a curator at the Louvre, of the need to create a permanent museum of French furniture.[36]

Other elements of the fair besides the palaces, with their splendid display of the applied arts, their architecture, and their decoration, expressed the ideals of the official craft movement. The entire Esplanade des Invalides and Champs-Elysées sections of the fair were devoted to the arts, specifically to home furnishings and "the arts and crafts of the universe."[37] Included here were the first major exhibitions of "the decoration of public buildings" and elaborate pavilions for the major national craft manufactures—Gobelins, Sèvres, and Beauvais.[38]

The pavilion of the Central Union of the Decorative Arts echoed the themes of the organic, feminine, and interiorizing art nouveau that resounded throughout the fair. And the same transfiguration of eighteenth-century elegance by nineteenth-century meaning crystallized in this pavilion, which stood as a pendant to the Maison de l'Art Nouveau Bing in the affirmation of a particularly French modern style.

In accord with the elitist craft modernism central to its new program of the 1890s, the Central Union of the Decorative Arts proposed that its pavilion for the 1900 exhibition would embody a new type of "collector's chamber."[39] The collector's chamber was originally the realm of erudition and acquisition of aristocratic collectors; we have already seen one of its nineteenth-century transformations in the 1895 Maison de l'Art Nouveau, where a M. Issac decorated the model collector's chamber. In the original proposal for the 1900 fair, the Central Union called for a "collector's chamber" that would contain "truly modern" works, divested of historicist imitations, whose artifacts would express the new imperative "Let us be of our own time."[40]

The union plan as realized in 1900 was a pavilion consisting of three rooms, designed as integral ensembles. Each room was dedicated to one of three materials: wood, ceramics, or iron.[41] The union pavilion in 1900 recapitulated the theme of the union's earlier exhibitions dedicated to the materials of the decorative arts and stressed the same purpose: "the exploitation in decoration of the essential qualities of the materials."[42]

The union rooms were designed as interdependent elements of a single stylistic whole, mirroring the principles of Art Nouveau Bing. Each room derived its vocabulary of forms from the surface and structure of nature. Georges Hoentschell, a member of the Central Union, designed the Wood Room, which included contributions by Gallé, Besnard, Prouvé, Majorelle, and Dampt. Hoentschell was a collector and decorator whose vases and stoneware had been exhibited at the National Society of Beaux-Arts during the 1890s. As a collector, he specialized in the eighteenth-century rococo and conceived of the Wood Room as a variation on the eighteenth-century *folie,* a type of structure created for amusement in the mid-eighteenth century.[43] Hoentschell's room, which stands today in its original form as part of the Musée des Arts Décoratifs in Paris, was an integrated ensemble that reflected the forms of nature in its carved ceiling panels and the interlacing trellises of the walls. The carved wood evoked both the roots, trunk, and leaves of trees and delicately gnarled nerves. Plant forms appeared in the pattern of the textured cloth wall coverings. Hoentschell continued the ensemble character of the Wood Room in wood display cases, built into the wood walls in a single linear flow.

Nerves and plants were echoed throughout the room in works by Gallé, Majorelle, and Besnard. Gallé, who wrote on this occasion that he was attempting to emulate the "life-lines, the physiological characteristics of flora and fauna," their "muscles and nerves,"[44] provided a multiplicity of vases and "modern furniture" in wood carved to resemble dragonflies and hemlock. Majorelle designed a carved and inlaid marquetry piano, on whose surface was an inscription and a painted image. A colleague of Gallé's from Nancy, Majorelle chose to depict sleep and dreams on his piano. The agent of both was woman, who appeared on the piano upon a cloud, whispering softly to her child and caressing him. Here was a transposition of Gallé's dicta that modern decoration should "caress us and respond to our inner vibrations," should release us to the realm of the dream.[45]

The painter Albert Besnard added his pictorial version of eighteenth-century traditions and nineteenth-century transformations to the union's modern *folie.* On the wall, between the climbing plant-nerves, Besnard painted a large mural, *Island of Contentment.* In subject and form the mural evoked Watteau's *Disembarkment from Cythera,* and in the mural, as in Watteau's painting, it was unclear whether the parties were coming to or going from the island *fête champêtre.*[46] Besnard's evocations of the eighteenth century, however, did not belie his contemporary vision, for the women on his garden isle sported chignons, and his jarringly bright colors were appropriate to their time: critics linked the sharp tones of his reds, for example, to the electrifying color scheme of artificial lighting and to the expression of a ubiquitous "modern nervousness."[47]

A similar convergence of rococo decoration and modernist invention emerged in another room of the union's pavilion adjoining the three devoted to the decorative potential of iron, wood, and ceramic. This room was dedicated to the union's proposed ally and inspiration for organicized and domesticated art nouveau—women. Recapitulating the series of its exhibitions of the arts of woman in the 1890s, the union displayed here the work of its women members. Among the contributors were the aristocratic contingent, the countesses and duchesses of former shows, as well as the illustrious bourgeoises, such as Madame Charcot and her daughter, Madame Waldeck-Rousseau.[48] The glassware of Emile Gallé also found its way into this room. The meeting of Gallé's neurological vases and the furniture of Madame Charcot thus symbolically linked the receptor of Charcot's theories with the wife of the clinician–interior decorator.

The union's message of craft interiority, feminization, and organicism culminated in a small wood sculpture by Jean Dampt, displayed prominently in the Wood Room. On a slender wooden stand was a diminutive box, like a large jewelry case, with fleurs-de-lis on its surface. It opened to reveal a seated statuette of ivory, wood, and iron, materials similar to those used by Dampt for the *Fairy Mélusine* of 1895. The work was called *Domestic Bliss,* its seated figure a young woman in long robes, with two flowers bedecking her chignon (Pl. 14). On her lap she held a cat, in her hands a scepter. On the top of her throne was a wooden crown in whose surface were incised two lilies. Here was a secular Madonna, the queen of the home and the goddess of the decorative arts. *Domestic Bliss,* in her decorative setting and appearance, provided an interior analogue to the queen *Parisienne:* the two statues embodied the French art nouveau in its two aspects, public and private—official and Central Union.

The Central Union's legacy of female interiority, rococo tradition, and psychological consciousness was consolidated after the 1900 fair. By 1896, the union had given up its effort to acquire the site of the former Cour des Comptes for a decorative arts museum. Union administrators settled on establishing the museum as an extension of the Louvre, to be installed in a wing of the Pavillon de Marsan. The new Musée des Arts Décoratifs opened its doors in 1905. Arranged as a historical progression of the applied arts from the medieval to the modern period, the new museum's holdings were richest in the eighteenth century, reflecting the preferences of their donors. The union's art nouveau pavilion of 1900 was transferred directly to the museum, where the ensemble created by Besnard, Dampt, Gallé, Prouvé, Majorelle, and other modern decorative artists was completely reassembled. These artists' variants of rococo inspiration and psychological exploration furnished a permanent record of the Central Union's art nouveau, still on view today.[49]

The feminine and psychological themes of craft modernism in 1900 were brought together with their complex sources at the fair itself. The *femme nouvelle,* against whom, in part, union affiliates mobilized their ideal decorative craftswomen of the home, was represented in a second International Feminist Congress that met on the fairgrounds. The suggestible, imagistic consciousness of the *psychologie nouvelle* also made an appearance. A congress on the new psychology held at the 1900 fair partly resolved the decade-long debate between supporters of Bernheim's school in Nancy and the Salpêtrière in Paris in favor of Bernheim. By the time of Charcot's death in 1893, the core of his theories—the tripartite stages of hysteria and the belief that only psychopathological patients could be hypnotized—had been discredited. Charcot's own late work even acknowledged the role of unconscious *idées-forces* in human behavior, which he explored in his last book, *La Foi qui guérit* (Faith healing).[50] At the 1900 exhibition's Psychology Congress, Bernheim discussed the power of universal suggestibility, and he tried to defuse fears that the febrile, imagistic receptivity of the mind would entail the dethronement of rational discourse and rational behavior.[51] A disciple of Charcot's, the philosopher Théodule Ribot, provided the Parisian school with an explanation of how the new irrational tendencies could be accommodated by positivist intellection. Despite Charcot's having uncovered all the elements of volatile unreason, in 1900 many French psychic explorers remained bound to their

Cartesian grid. Ribot's book *The Creative Imagination,* published in 1901, offered a potent variation on the Enlightenment theme of the melding of *raison* and *esprit* in a single mind. Ribot acknowledged the presence and power of the unconscious and of suggestibility, which he associated with the "creative imagination," characterizing it as visual, "diffluent," and fluid. Alongside this "diffluent" segment of the mind was a logical, sequential one of linear rationality. Rather than replace it or overturn it, Ribot affirmed that the diffluent and discursive arenas of mind coexisted in a dynamic complementarity.[52]

Despite the themes of containment and accommodation in the emergence of French modernism in 1900, the exhibition expressed the unstable, volatile compound of which the art nouveau was composed. Three artistic examples illustrate how an eruptive nonrational world exploded the boundaries of rococo precedent and physiological psychology. The characteristics of this nonrational world visible in 1900—mobility, simultaneity, indeterminacy, and the metamorphic fluidity of the unconscious—are essential parts of twentieth-century modernity.

At first glance, the changes effected in the iron-and-glass Gallery of Machines between 1889 and 1900 seemed to signify the triumph of rococo ornamentalism over technological monumentalism. In 1889 the Gallery of Machines was the dramatic partner to the thousand-foot Eiffel Tower. Entering the fair through this "arch of triumph to science and industry,"[53] spectators were presented with a vast horizontal iron-and-glass shed, which displayed the industrial products and advanced machineries of all nations. The French contributions to this gallery—artisanal wares in elaborate wood and velvet cases—existed in spatial tension with the airy iron-and-glass frame surrounding them. This same tension between public and private space reappeared in the Eiffel Tower itself, in the juxtaposition of Eiffel's wood and velvet private room at the top of the tower and the open and interlaced iron webbing of the whole structure enveloping it.[54]

In 1900 the iron and glass shed of the 1889 Gallery of Machines was covered. Superimposed over the stark, denuded facade of the gallery was a sprawling plaster and ceramic rococo envelope, called the Château d'Eau (Fig. 67). Directly "inspired by the style Louis XV,"[55] the Château d'Eau was a mass of solids and voids from which water rushed out of a central source. From the top layer of the château unfurled a scroll studded with thousands of multicolored lights. The main body of the château was a vast low-lying structure with numerous bays; in its center was a cavernous grottoed inset designed to resemble a dolphin's open mouth.[56] Out of this scooped-out shell spouted water, flowing down along many layers of terraced rockwork. The model for this set of terraced fountains was clearly the eighteenth century; drawings by Pineau for the Peterhof fountains show striking formal similarities.[57] Particularly prominent reminders of the exuberant irregularities of rococo organicism were the scrolled shapes of the plaster and ceramic, the interplay of scooped-out rockwork and overlaid shell forms, and the gigantic farming cartouche atop the building, framing the banner of the Republic, with its R and F.

Despite the overt evocation of eighteenth-century organic ornamentalism, the

Fig. 67. The Château d'Eau, 1900 Paris Exhibition. Photograph by Roger-Viollet.

Château d'Eau was not an archaistic reconstruction. Indeed, like other examples of rococo revivalism, this building joined eighteenth-century forms to distinctively modern content: in this case, electricity. The 1889 fair had already exploited the wonders of electricity in its nightly spectacle of colored light on the Eiffel Tower and the Central Dome of the French Nation. In 1900 electricity played center stage, more so than in 1889, largely because of the construction of a separate pavilion, the Palais de l'Electricité, as a testament to its powers. The Château d'Eau, with its elaborate and continuously flowing streams, was the complex facade for this Palace of Electricity. The waters washing down the grottoes were powered by electrical generators inside.

Although we can discuss electricity only briefly here, it is important to note that its centrality in 1900 implied certain perceptions about the instability and fluidity of the world, a theme related to the vitalist organicism of the fair. The electrical underpinnings of the exhibition—a form of magic or energy that could not be seen or rendered tangible—nourished a sense of seething, unbounded, and immaterial power: "Life seethes in this immense reservoir of energy . . . a too violent magnificence." [58]

The Palace of Electricity contains the living, active soul of the Exhibition, providing the whole of this colossal organism with movement and light. . . . Without electricity the Exhibition is merely an inert mass devoid of the slightest breath of life. In the Palace of Electricity, indeed, is manufactured all the energy necessary for the lighting of the Exhibition. . . . From the basement of the Palace, leading in all directions, run miles and miles of wire transmitting power and light, along the walls, winding underground and crossing the Seine. . . . The magic fluid pours forth: everything is immediately illuminated, everything moves. . . . The soul of the Palace brings Light and Life.[59]

The wires could be traced, but the energy running through them could be perceived only in its results. This sense of a new reality as a "magic fluid," of energy as a continuum and totality, harbored a corresponding sense of the indeterminate limits and boundaries of time and space that would be left to Bergson and Proust to explore fully.

The convergence of fluid energy and woman was also realized at the fair, breaking the defining frames of both the *femme nouvelle* and the ideal of the decorative female artisan envisioned to contain her. Close to the Maison de l'Art Nouveau Bing was a second small pavilion, the Loïe Fuller Theater, designed in the art nouveau style by the young architect Henri Sauvage. In many ways, Loïe Fuller, who performed a dance of veils, embodied the ideals of art nouveau; she danced to personify a butterfly, a huge flower, and a mobile iridescent decoration:

Woman-flower, woman-bird, woman-butterfly, the themes of metamorphosis which characterized the work in precious metals, the jewelry and glass of Art Nouveau were all found in the sinuous dancing of Loïe Fuller, evocator of a "vegetation of fantasy and impassioned love, which brings together, in one symbol, nature and being, which illumines the frail substance of a flower with a woman's smile."[60]

Despite the "romantic biologism," as some have called it, of Loïe Fuller, and her embodiment of the ideals of art nouveau, the dancing veils of woman also expressed two unprecedented phenomena. First, Loïe Fuller's dance incorporated a new advanced technology: electricity. Indeed, her dance depended on the streaking of the veils with colored electric lights, which she designed herself, "taking on the role of the engineer."[61] The fluid, dynamic dance was made possible by the energy and simultaneous effects of electricity; as an explorer of "artificial vibrations and light waves," Loïe Fuller summarized an image of "life in inanimate matter."[62] Second, Loïe Fuller's dance was explicitly linked to the form and meaning of *psychologie nouvelle*. Indeed, as she explained in her memoirs, she conceived her dance as an extension of the psychological trance that followed suggestion. Originally an actress, she was playing the part of a young woman in the process of being "healed" by a hypnotist-doctor. One day, during rehearsal, she put on a dress recently given her by a beau from India, a dress with long flowing diaphanous veils. She improvised an acting out of the dream state initiated by the doctor's hypnosis: this was the origin of the veil dance.[63] Loïe Fuller's contribution to the 1900 fair was thus a daily demonstration of ideodynamism. She offered the public a new kind of psychological theater, replacing Charcot's spectacle of female hysteria with a feminine aesthetic vision embodying unconscious forces. Fuller transformed the images released by the hypnotic trance into direct, irregular movements, which she expressed automatically, without conscious mediation. The veil dance articulated in physical motion the experience of ideodynamism that had also facilitated Emile Gallé's artistic creativity.

The centrality of psychology, mobility, and simultaneity to Emile Gallé and Auguste Rodin provides a final indication of the eruption of new ideas from the containing frames of the 1900 fair. Emile Gallé's statements on the occasion of the exhibition summarized a contradictory conception of art as organic restoration, national affirmation, and psychiatric exploration. In a commentary on the 1900 fair, Gallé praised the "distinctively French" qualities of the new decorative arts featured at the Central Union pavilion.[64] He also characterized the "lessons of the applied arts" as providing "an atmosphere of tranquility," "a sanctuary," and an "amphitheater of refuge" "very much needed to calm our nerves."[65] In another text of 1900, Gallé identified the craftsman as a "sower," whose harvest would form an organic buffer against the "poisonous, artificial atmosphere" of the modern "age of industrialization."[66] Yet like the Goncourts, Rodin, and Bing, Gallé attributed dynamic energy and suggestibility to that organic refuge. Visual objects in the room acted as hypnotic agents releasing unconscious forces and stimulating the dream. The psychological being assumed to inhabit the interior transformed the soothing "amphitheater of refuge" into an unstable field of vibration and fluidity (Pl. 15).

Gallé provided the clearest statement of the role of the irrational in the modern interior in a speech entitled "Symbolic Decor," delivered in May 1900. While paying homage to the traditions of Jean Lamour and the "design preferences of our ancestors," he proposed a new model of artistic creation that tapped unconscious sources. "Every work of art springs from the rich ambiance of the artist's dreams," Gallé explained, and is independent of his conscious deliberations. The artist's concentration stimulates a spontaneous "cogitation of the spirit," which in turn releases dream images.[67] The images could be beneficent or menacing—what Gallé described as either magical fantasies or dark forebodings. Gallé went on to discuss the impact of art on the viewer in terms of the relationship between artistic symbolism and suggestion. He identified the "synthetic" quality of the symbol, defining it as an "abstract figuration" with suggestive power.[68] As "evocative form," the symbol derived its impact from its direct and autonomous appeal to the unconscious; it effected in the viewer, by "emotional contagion," the same state of feeling experienced by the artist. The visual symbol condensed and stimulated multiple ideas; it offered a center of "piqued attention" and the instant point of entry to the rich associative world of the unconscious.[69]

Gallé's conception of the origin and impact of art confirmed two central tenets of the new psychology, each of which played formative roles in the twentieth-century redefinition of consciousness. First, his understanding of the power of his art affirmed Bernheim's notion of imagistic thinking, of the mind's newfound ability to "translate ideas into images." Gallé, for whom the artistic process closely resembled the clinical state of ideodynamism, proposed in 1900 the ideodynamic quality of visual symbolism—that images were converted into ideas automatically and without mediation. In Gallé's text, Bernheim's doctrine of suggestion as the "transformation of ideas into images" emerged like this: "In the decor of a vase, as in medals, statues, and painting . . . it is always the translation, the evocation of an idea by an image." [70] Second, Gallé's ideas corresponded to Henri Bergson's notion of the special role of the visual as a point of entry to the unconscious. We have noted earlier how Bergson, on the basis of the new medical psychology, had evolved a theory of the artist replacing the hypnotist as the agent of direct access to the unconscious. He argued in the 1889 *Données* that the formal qualities of art captured the beholder by an irresistible "contagion" and provoked, without conscious mediation, an emotional state matching that of the artist. Emile Gallé's 1900 assertion that visual symbolism acted as "abstract" "evocative form" to create in the viewer, through an "emotional contagion," a state corresponding to that of the artist reaffirmed Bergson's dynamic philosophy of consciousness. Each set of ideas, Gallé's and Bergson's, was facilitated by the revelations of the new psychology, whose legacy nurtured both the concepts of abstract, nonfigurative language in art and of fluid, nondiscursive mental operations.

The art and ideas of Auguste Rodin in 1900 pointed even more forcefully toward the future. Rodin, who had pressed his craft training and his knowledge of aesthetic traditions into the service of unparalleled visions of particular psychological processes, at the 1900 fair confirmed and extended these tendencies, with important implications for the reconceptualization of modern consciousness.

Rodin's separate pavilion at the exhibition won him great acclaim among the critics and a spate of wealthy international patrons. Three of the numerous examples of his work displayed there merit a brief description: first, a small statuette, dedicated to Edmond de Goncourt, a *Nymph and Satyr*,[71] showed Rodin's extension of the rococo heritage; second, a plaster model for a colossal tower, originally designed as a possible monument for the 1900 fair, was explicitly construed as a "Tower of Labor," an artistic negation of the menacing Eiffel Tower.[72] Spiraling upward, the Rodin tower would be of marble, and the spectator would be greeted at each level with a series of plaques to admire. The tower expressed the triumph of art over work. On the base of the tower Rodin represented the laborers to whom the structure was dedicated: divers, miners, diggers, and craftsmen similar to those on the Porte Binet. As the structure rose, the subject changed from the material to the spiritual, from work to art. On the top of the tower was a second symbolic group, a beneficent angel blessing a male figure, the Poet.

In the Tower of Labor Rodin celebrated art and the spirit, ideals that he promoted as the direct antitheses to the invasive technics of modern life. In his writings, Rodin criticized his age "as one of engineers and manufacturers, not artists." [73] He lamented that "science" and "mechanics" tended to "replace the work of the human mind with the work of a machine," yielding "the death of art." [74] Modern life, for Rodin,

Fig. 68. The Gates of Hell, by Auguste Rodin, 1880–1917. Plaster version shown at 1900 Paris Exhibition. Musée Rodin, Paris. Photograph by Bulloz.

meant "turmoil and constant hurry" and the reign of "ugliness," where "everything is manufactured hastily and without grace by stupid machines."[75] The vitality of art, in contrast, depended on the artist's "contemplative" immersion in the "mystery of nature," whose "unity in complexity" restored the primacy of "thinking and dreaming" in the creator.[76]

As the artist in solitude "penetrated" the "profound organism"[77] of nature and the self, however, he did not discover a sanctuary of harmony, wholeness, and tranquility. Rodin's understanding of "thinking and dreaming"[78] in the artistic process incorporated many of the qualities he found so disturbing in the outer world of industrial modernity. Turmoil, pressure, and turbulence in the psyche resurfaced as unavoidable components of the creative process. I have discussed earlier how Rodin expressed nervous tension and the condensation of unconscious eruptions in his sculptural forms of the 1890s. In 1900 Rodin amplified this psychiatric vision, and reaffirmed Maurice Rollinat as one source of it in his revised version of *The Gates of Hell*.

A massive plaster model of *The Gates of Hell* dominated Rodin's pavilion at the 1900 fair (Fig. 68). While largely similar to models of the *Gates* exhibited previously, the 1900 plaster version included an important addition.[79] Along the base of the sculpture, Rodin inserted two reliefs as inside panels to the door jambs, on the left a seated female nude, identified as a figure of Eve, and on the right a kneeling, bearded male figure, whose resemblance to Rodin has led scholars to identify it as a self-portrait (Fig. 69).[80] The way Rodin represented himself was significant. His left arm was poised on his head, and his knitted brow and downward gaze suggested the process of concentration and "cogitation."[81] Cupped in the artist's right hand was a small female figure, which embodied an "offspring of his imagination."[82] Art historians have not commented on a third element of the self-portrait—a partial head appearing above the figure of Rodin, in the exact vertical plane over the artist's left arm. The head was covered by a close-fitting cap, with the face not clearly identifiable, as it appeared to merge with the door. In 1886 Rodin had executed another figure with a similar close-fitting cap, entitled *La Pensée* (Fig. 70). In that sculpture a woman's face and cap-covered head loomed out of a solid block of bronze. Only the head of that woman's body was visible, with part of the chin and neck locked into the mass. The fragment of a head above Rodin's self-portrait in *The Gates of Hell* closely resembled *La Pensée*. In addition to the cap over the head, the lower half of the face contained the outline of a nose whose shape suggested the finely chiseled nose of *La Pensée*.

Visual strategies as well as intellectual tendencies suggest why *La Pensée* could plausibly reappear as part of the self-portrait group Rodin added to the *Gates*. For example, Rodin often experimented with his own repertoire of free-standing sculptures by repeating them in smaller versions among the multiple figures on the *Gates*.[83] Moreover, by evoking *La Pensée*, Rodin paid a final personal tribute to Maurice Rollinat, whose neuropsychiatric understanding of tension in the thought process deeply affected the form and composition of the *Gates*. *La Pensée*, the title of

Fig. 69. The Gates of Hell, by Auguste Rodin, 1880–1917. Right door jamb, relief of Rodin's self-portrait, with small figure in his right hand, and capped figure over his head. The Stanford University Museum of Art, Gift of B. Gerald Cantor. Photograph by William L. Schaeffer © 1986.

Rodin's bronze figure of 1886, was also the title of a poem in Rollinat's book *L'Abîme,* published in 1886 and given by the author to Rodin.[84] Rodin's representation of "Thought" offered a close visual equivalent to Rollinat's literary version. The same poem that envisioned thought as "a lofty gatekeeper," "a censor," "who lets instinct pass through only with its stamp," also emphasized the paralytic and dessicating powers of thought: its restrictions and repressions vitiated the will to act and undermined erotic pleasure. In imagining these qualities, Rollinat described thought as acting like a "block of ice, freezing our resolve," and as "spreading an ulcerous lime across the spirit."[85] A final image projected thought as sealing the soul in its cement and then bolting its captive to iron screws, which it repeatedly hammered in.[86] Rodin's 1886 figure, *La Pensée,* was graphically presented as a head frozen in place in a block of bronze. The head was caught in the metal, and the rest of the body appeared, as in Rollinat's poem, to be trapped and sealed in a solid mass. Rodin transposed into sculptural form Rollinat's literary rendering of thought as a brake on the instinctual and the compressive force of its continual obstructions.

As we have seen, in developing *The Gates of Hell* before 1900, Rodin had already testified to the formative influence of Maurice Rollinat. The physical tension visible in the Thinker-Poet and the relation between this elevated cogitating figure and the libidinal frenzy driving the bodies beneath resonated with Rollinat's distinctive representations of intrapsychic struggles (see pp. 261–268). In adding the self-portrait group at the base of the 1900 *Gates,* Rodin offered a personalized and microscopic version of the themes he had generalized earlier in the larger structure of the monu-

Fig. 70. La Pensée, by Auguste Rodin, 1886–1889 Bronze. Courtesy of the Rodin Museum, Philadelphia. Gift of Jules E. Mastbaum.

ment. The self-portrait group visualized Rodin, like the Thinker-Poet, as engaged in the process of concentration. To his right sprang an active nude female figure, whose contorted form and cascading pose resembled the tumbled gymnastic disposition of many of the figures on the doors. This figure, cupped in the artist's hand and emerging from one side of his head, embodied the inner release of unconscious forces and unbounded erotic desire. Above the other side of Rodin's head, over the knitted brow immersed in thought, hovered the fragment of *La Pensée,* the emblem of the censorious and restrictive elements inherent in creativity. The capped head of *La Pensée* could have fit exactly into the hollow beside the artist's head. In the contrast between the mobile nude in Rodin's hand and *La Pensée*'s rigid stillness, Rodin formalized the interior struggle between unconscious turbulence and the repressive force necessary to transform the dream into art.

The interpretation of Rodin's 1900 self-portrait group as a recapitulation of the neuropsychiatric themes in Rollinat's poetry has one final evidentiary base. In an unconventional fashion, Rodin had attached yet another head of a man, an "anguished head framed by large leaves,"[87] to the outside of the right door (Fig. 71). The head was placed on a horizontal plane exactly parallel to the head of the Thinker-Poet, beyond the right entablature and tympanum. This head was also disposed diagonally above the self-portrait group along the right door jamb. According to Albert Elsen, it would have been recognizable as "the severed head of John the Baptist," which Rodin had previously done in bronze and marble.[88] This same head was also the model for a male head in a monument Rodin later created as a memorial to Maurice Rollinat. Both the statements of some of his friends and a comparison to contemporary portraits suggest a striking resemblance to Rollinat (Figs. 72, 73).[89] Perhaps the male head on the outside of the *Gates* was not Saint John but a contemporary psychological sufferer, Maurice Rollinat. The spatial relation between the male head and the Thinker-Poet, on the one hand, and the same head and the artist's self-portrait with *La Pensée,* on the other, suggests that Rodin may have created a triangular tribute to Maurice Rollinat. If, as Albert Elsen has noted, the self-portrait at the base of the *Gates* was a fitting way for Rodin to "sign" his work,[90] the signature may have a more complex character. Rodin's "signature" self-portrait operated as one element of the field of interaction between Rollinat himself, visualized above, Rodin himself, depicted below, and the products of their dual imaginations—the representations of the dynamic, clinical, and agonistic neuropsychiatry of creativity. Rodin's 1900 model inscribed *two* signatures in *The Gates of Hell,* his own and Rollinat's, and his additions to the *Gates* consolidated his debt to Rollinat's uniquely fin-de-siècle vision.

If Rodin's *Gates of Hell* expressed the specificity of late nineteenth-century French literary and psychological themes, his work also captured one of the broader historically significant themes of the European fin de siècle: the reaction against positivism and the emergence of a new way of knowing the world, based on the primacy of the self and its irrational components. I have emphasized throughout this book the distinctiveness of each national setting, and the effects of different political contexts and intellectual traditions in shaping the form and meaning of this new consciousness, as

Fig. 71. The Gates of Hell, by Auguste Rodin, 1880–1917. Right door with tympanum Thinker and man's head at side. The Stanford University Museum of Art, gift of B. Gerald Cantor. Photograph by William L. Schaeffer © 1986.

well as the degree to which it threatened Enlightenment rationalism. Yet I would like here to relate my analysis to the more general emergence outside of France of a new epistemology that ultimately identifies the fin de siècle as one crucible of our own modernity.

In the works of three philosophers among those credited with formulating the new fin-de-siècle consciousness—Henri Bergson, Georg Simmel, and Sigmund Freud—there are correspondences to Rodin's art nouveau. Simmel explicitly invoked Rodin's work as the symbol of precisely such an unprecedented modern spirit. Bergson's and Freud's convergence with Rodin's art derives from their underlying assumptions and from the literary strategies they employed in their texts on dreams.

In early 1901 Henri Bergson presented a lecture entitled "The Dream" to the Institut Général Psychologique. In it he discussed the mechanism of the dream and the role of memory in the dream process. Bergson described the dream as an interior visualization composed of a multitude of images released with "vertiginous rapidity" during the sleep state. The dream was like a "cinematic panorama," in which

Fig. 72. Head of Saint John the Baptist, by Auguste Rodin, c. 1887. Plaster. Courtesy of the National Gallery of Art, Washington, D.C., Gift of Mrs. John W. Simpson.

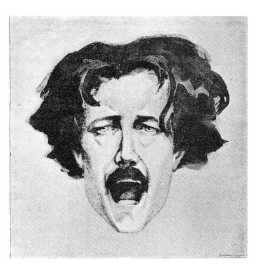

Fig. 73. Maurice Rollinat, by Georges Bethune. *La Revue universelle,* 1903.

events that would consciously be recognized as discrete were compressed simultaneously into a single field.[91] Bergson devoted most of his lecture to isolating the different roles of unconscious memories in the dream state and in the waking state, characterizing the pressures of these memories in the dream state in a way strikingly similar to Rodin's visualization of intrapsychic struggle.

Bergson relied heavily on pictorial definitions, descriptions, and metaphors. The rich and ever-present storehouse of memory, for example, was a "solidary whole" in the form of a pyramid. At its tip were the memories that impinged directly on an activity or event in the waking state; these memories configured a discrete "scene illuminated by consciousness." At the base of the pyramid, beneath the memories related to a specific act, were "thousands and thousands of others," a dynamic repository of "invisible phantoms." These memories inhabited the most obscure regions of "the depths":

> Shrouded in darkness, the memory phantoms aspire toward the light. Yet they do not attempt to ascend to it; they know it is impossible and that my self, a busy and active being, has other things to do besides attend to them. But suppose I am relieved of pressing action and memory no longer concentrates on a single focus. Suppose, in other words, that I go to sleep. Suddenly all these immobile memories, sensing that I have removed the obstacle, that I have lifted the trap door that kept them in the subterranean recesses of consciousness, set themselves in motion. They rise up, they agitate, they perform, in the night of the unconscious, an immense dance of death. And all together they race toward the gate that has just opened up.[92]

Bergson's discussion of the memory phantoms in the dream state could have been a description of the agitated spectral figures assembled on the doors of Rodin's *Gates of Hell*. Rodin's "tenebrous" intertwined corporeal forms closely resemble what Bergson called the "indistinct," dematerialized "contours" of the memory phantoms.[93] The sudden release of multiple phantoms and their clambering upward toward the door in Bergson's image recalled the vigorous upward movement of Rodin's panoply of figures inhabiting the obscure regions of the depths. Rodin hoped the full drama of his spectral figures would be heightened by nocturnal viewing and illumination, suggesting their association with the Bergsonian "night of the unconscious." It is worth remembering that contemporary commentators on the *Gates* compared parts of the sculpture to a dance of death, which also appeared in Bergson's rendition.[94] Yet the dance of death, in both Rodin and Bergson, functioned not as a medieval enactment of the meeting of the living and the damned but as a formulation of a modern psyche driven by the interplay of conscious and unconscious forces.

Bergson's memory phantoms did not succeed in their collective attempt to pass through the gate. "Of this multitude who are called up" only a few will obtain passage.[95] By a process resembling censorship and condensation, the vague, immaterial unconscious memories pressing for entry were distilled. When the waking state resumed, only a small number had been granted entry.[96] As Bergson described it, this phase of compression and restricted passage recapitulated Rodin's and Rollinat's representations of the censorship succeeding unconscious release. In his lecture, Bergson posed the question, "Of the multitude of those called up, who will become the elect?" The answer was provided by an agency Bergson did not name, which might plausibly assume the role of the judge, weighing and choosing the select few from among the mass. Like the judge in Rodin's and Rollinat's visions, the agency appointing the elect in Bergson's text inverted the medieval judge's role in the *théâtre mundi*. Rather than protect the sacred few from the grasp of the devil, the psychological censor funneled some unconscious fragments into the condenser of consciousness. Bergson's distilling agent faced with a rush of unconscious forces evoked the Thinker-Poet on Rodin's *Gates* and Thought in Rollinat's poem. Bergson's imagery of high and low, release and repression, tumult and election re-created the two artists' illuminations of the way that the mind "lets instinct pass through only with its stamp."

Bergson concluded his 1901 lecture with a directive to his colleagues. "The principal task of psychology in the coming century," he claimed, was "to explore the unconscious, to work in the subterranean of the mind with especially appropriate methods." This task, he noted, would yield discoveries "as important as those of the physical and natural sciences in preceding centuries."[97] Auguste Rodin and Maurice Rollinat had already set themselves to this task, mobilizing the "especially appropriate methods" of artistic form to explore the unconscious. Bergson confirmed some of their revelations, pressing them into the service of a new theory of mind and attitude toward reality.

Gateways, doorkeepers, spatial divisions between unconscious percolation and conscious condensation—these images were central to the most radical redefinition of the mind proposed by Sigmund Freud. In *The Interpretation of Dreams*, Freud quoted Schiller's representation of creative work as the slackening of the constraint usually imposed by intellect upon the imagination. In normal mental operations the intellect acted as a "judge," selecting and sifting among ideas through the agency of its "watchers at the gates." In creative minds, these "watchers are withdrawn"; "the ideas rush in pell-mell" without prior adjudication.[98] In his succeeding discussion, Freud transposed Schiller's description of the special qualities of the creative mind into a psychological theory of the operations of all minds during the state of sleep. Replacing the categories of intellect and imagination with censorship and the unconscious, Freud envisioned "two thought-constructing agencies" whose roles were reversed during sleep:

> In our mental apparatus there are two thought-constructing agencies of which the second enjoys the privilege of having free access to consciousness for its products, whereas the activity of the first is in itself unconscious and can only reach consciousness by way of the second. On the frontier between the two agencies, where the first passes over to the second, there is a censorship, which only allows what is agreeable to it to pass through and holds back everything else. According to our definition, then, what is rejected by the censorship is a state of repression. Under certain circumstances, of which the state of sleep is one, the relation between the strength of the two agencies is modified in such a way that what is repressed can no longer be held back. In the state of sleep this

probably occurs owing to a relaxation of the censorship; when this happens it becomes possible for what has hitherto been repressed to make a path for itself to consciousness. Since, however, the censorship is never completely eliminated but merely reduced, the repressed material must submit to certain alterations which mitigate its offensive features. What becomes conscious in such cases is a compromise between the intentions of one agency and the demands of another. Repression—relaxation of the censorship—the formation of a compromise—this is the fundamental pattern for the generation . . . of dreams.[99]

Freud's conception of the interaction of censorship and the unconscious was certainly informed by some distinctive features of his Judaic, German Enlightenment, and Romantic legacies. And his preoccupation with repression also resonated with the firsthand experience of particular obstructions to freedom confronting a Jewish liberal in fin-de-siècle Vienna.[100] But his vision also corresponded to the new ideas of the mind expressed by his French counterpart, Bergson, and Bergson's artistic anticipators. Indeed Freud's pattern of "repression—relaxation of the censorship—the formation of a compromise" corresponded exactly to the stages of nocturnal consciousness represented by Rodin and Rollinat.

The convergence of Freud and Rodin extended beyond their common reliance on the image of the struggle between divided mental zones. A more fundamental connection existed, that suggests yet another way Rodin's *Gates of Hell* symbolized some of the unparalleled features of twentieth-century consciousness. Rodin's mode of representation—his use of a new non-narrative visual language—bore a striking affinity to the new nondiscursive, metamorphic logic that Freud defined as the essence of the psychological mental style.

In *The Interpretation of Dreams,* Freud embarked on a *voyage intérieur* to "stir up hell" by a bold encounter with the "unconscious activities of the mind" and "repressed instinctual impulses."[101] In chronicling his discoveries about the unconscious, Freud, like Bergson, relied heavily on visual language and images. He identified four qualities of the unconscious, each of which implied what he called a "mode of representation" significantly different from the expected rules of linear, objective description. First, dreams assumed the form of "a pictorial situation," "a series of pictures."[102] Second, they embodied a "composite picture," in which a plurality of separate events or themes coexisted in a dynamic totality, "a conceptual group."[103] Third, the "intricate structure" of the dream was marked by simultaneity and juxtaposition; dream elements are not an additive accretion of individual units but "stand in manifold logical relations to one another: they represent foreground and background, conditions, digressions, and illustrations, chains of evidence and counterarguments. Each train of thought is almost invariably accompanied by its contradictory counterargument."[104] Finally, rather than a one-to-one causal progression, the dream incorporated an associative net, where each dream element

is, in the strictest sense of the word, representative of all the disparate material in the content of the dream. . . . Just as connections lead from each element of the dream to several dream thoughts, so as a rule a single dream thought is represented by more than one dream element; the threads of association do not simply converge from the dream thoughts to the dream content, they cross and interweave with each other many times over in the course of their journey.[105]

All of these qualities of the dream contributed to Freud's major proposition—that the unconscious possessed its own complex logic and order, penetrable only by discarding the tools of positivist intellection. Discursive reasoning, confronting the unconscious, could only retreat from what it would consider a "wild" "disordered heap of disconnected fragments."[106] Yet the psychic explorer accepting the principles of interdependence, association, and the simultaneity of "either-*and*" rather than one-dimensional "either-or" could begin to render what Freud called the special "intelligibility" and "representability" of the unconscious.[107]

Many of the distinctive "modes of representation" preferred by Freud's unconscious were similar to Auguste Rodin's unconventional visual language. Art historians credit Rodin with transforming the nature of sculptural representation, moving from the objective description of the world observed to a subjective expression of inner states. Albert Elsen identified three features of *The Gates of Hell* that symbolize the emergence of this modernist artistic form and logic. First, Rodin broke with the tradition of sequential literary narrative in sculpture. Rather than present a legible progression of "historiated relief panels," Rodin created a generalized field of movement. Second, Rodin's art defied the rules of stable symmetry, which hinged on anatomical accuracy, unity of scale, and a clear indication of a single perspective point organizing all parts of the composition. Rodin's *Gates* featured irregular spacing, fragments of bodies, and a continually shifting "roving perspective," resembling the "plural points of view of a constant voyager."[108] Finally, Rodin's *Gates of Hell* inverted the relation between sculpture and architecture. Rather than subordinate the decorative components to the architectural frame, the *Gates* dissolved limits and boundaries, eliminating enclosure and "straight continuous edges." As Elsen noted,

> Rodin made sculptural extensions of moldings, as in the sides of the tympanum, and he simply attached sculpture to the frame. When architecture did establish a field for reliefs, figures would cling to, push off from, or overlap its borders contrary to the rules that required the framing features be adhered to and kept clear. . . . Seen in three-quarter view, the whole portal projects forward and backward. . . . The compositional coherence . . . depends upon our ability to read the work as a totality—seeing and sensing everything at once rather than sequentially.[109]

Rodin's departure from the rules of linear description in sculpture is analogous to the unconscious mental activities Freud attributed to the dream. *The Gates of Hell,* like Freud's dream work, embodied a "composite picture" in which multiple events and themes interacted in a dynamic totality. The intricate structure of the *Gates,* like Freud's dream, featured simultaneity and juxtaposition. Rather than a stable set of

narrative sequences, Rodin's figures "stand in manifold logical relations to one another: they represent foreground and background, conditions, digressions, and illustrations, chains of evidence and counterarguments." And like Freud's dream elements, Rodin's composition was marked by an associative net where each of the
elements "cross and interweave with each other many times over in the course of
their journey."

The critics in Rodin's own time who relied on the conventions of academic sculpture could not apprehend the form and meaning of his work and reacted to it, like
Freud's positivist, as a "wild" "disordered heap of disconnected fragments." Yet
many of Rodin's contemporaries, including some members of the official circles of
craft renovation, recognized that the sculpture implied a new form of artistic representation and, by extension, a new mode of consciousness. In 1900 commentators perceived the work as an apotheosis of the "ultramodern self," "the nervous
enigma." [110] They also analyzed the *Gates* as an example of a new "school of movement," [111] as "cerebral life materialized and transfigured in stone, marble, and
bronze." [112]

Mobility, indeterminacy, and the inversion from outer to inner reality—these essential features of a new model of mind were in fact explicitly related to Rodin's art
by the philosopher Georg Simmel. In 1901 in an essay entitled "Rodin's Work as an
Expression of the Modern Spirit," Simmel argued that Rodin's art concretized new
assumptions of the self and the nature of reality. Simmel discussed reality as a continuum in Rodin's work; what was construed as real changed constantly according to
the shifting and plural viewpoints of an unstable self. Contrasting Rodin's mobile
figures with Michelangelo's, Simmel explained that the two artists' worldviews differed fundamentally. Movement in Michelangelo's world expressed an "oscillation
between varying states of being—between faith and incredulity, courage and weakness, melancholy and ecstasy"—each of which was indentifiable and fixed. The
movement driving Rodin's figures was interminable, divested of the coordinates of
departure and resolution: "This modern *transmutabilita* is a continual sliding without
fixed poses of resolution and lacking all landmarks. It is a simultaneity of yes and no
more than an alteration between yes and no." [113] Simmel here echoed Freud's understanding of the associative net of "either-*and*" rather than the logical progression of
"either-or."

Simmel joined his assessment of Rodin's mobile figures to a conception of the primacy of the psychological self, "the tendency to live and interpret the world according to the reactions of our inner life." Simmel explained the revelatory significance
of Rodin's work in this summary statement

> By inventing a new flexibility of joints, giving surfaces a new tone and vibra-
> tion, suggesting in a new way the contact of two bodies or parts of the same
> body, using a new distribution of light by means of clashing, conflicting, or
> corresponding planes, Rodin has given to the human figure a new mobility
> that reveals the inner life of man, his feelings, thoughts, and personal vicissi-

tudes more completely than was ever possible before. . . . What characterizes the modern age is the tendency to live and interpret the world according to the reactions of our inner life, the dissolution of solid content in the fluid of the perfectly insubstantial soul, whose only forms can be forms of movement.[114]

Thus, the 1900 fair crystallized, in artistic expression and official celebration, a particularly French modernist form and meaning. The exhibition offered the culmination of a decade of searching for a French craft art nouveau, which resonated with eighteenth-century heritage and late nineteenth-century discoveries. Yet contained within this organic, psychological modern style were the seeds of a broader twentieth-century metamorphic consciousness.

NOTES

Short forms of titles are given for some books and periodicals cited in the notes. Full titles are listed in the Bibliography.

Introduction

1. S. Tschudi Madsen, *Art Nouveau* (New York: McGraw-Hill, 1967); Peter Selz and Mildred Constantine, eds., *Art Nouveau: Art and Design at the Turn of the Century* (New York: Museum of Modern Art, 1975).

2. E. Monod, *L'Exposition universelle de 1889* (Paris: Dentu, 1890), 1:34–40; Debora Silverman, "The Paris Exhibition of 1889: Architecture and the Crisis of Individualism," *Oppositions* 8 (Spring 1977): 71–78. A new study by Miriam R. Levin examines in detail the development of a liberal republican ideology of art in the 1880s as the expression of technological rationalism, scientific synthesis, and secular community solidification. See *Republican Art and Ideology in Late Nineteenth-Century France* (Ann Arbor, Mich.: UMI Research Press, 1986).

3. Silverman, "Exhibition of 1889," p. 88

4. Quoted in Joseph Harriss, *The Tallest Tower: Eiffel and the Belle Epoque* (Boston: Houghton Mifflin, 1975), p. 14. See also Jacques Morlaine, *La Tour Eiffel inconnue* (Paris: Hachette, 1971), pp. 10–14.

5. Quoted in Harriss, *Tallest Tower,* p. 10.

6. Melchior de Vogüé, "A travers l'Exposition," *Revue des deux mondes* 94 (1889): 201.

7. Ibid., p. 197.

8. Ibid., pp. 190–199.

9. Quoted in Harriss, *Tallest Tower,* pp. 24–25.

10. Quoted in ibid., p. 25.

11. Quoted in ibid., p. 25. Commissioner Edouard Lockroy made similar statements about the tower. See Monod, *L'Exposition universelle de 1889,* 1:17, 27.

12. Quoted in Silverman, "Exhibition of 1889," p. 77.

13. Picard, quoted in Harriss, *Tallest Tower,* p. 20.

14. Lockroy, quoted in Monod, *L'Exposition universelle de 1889,* vol. 1, pp. xxv–xxvii; see also Levin, *Republican Art and Ideology,* pp. 40–45. Translations from French sources are my own unless otherwise stated.

15. Jacques Desroches, "La Porte monumentale de l'Exposition," *Revue illustré de l'Exposition universelle de 1900* (June 25, 1900): 127.

16. De Vogüé, statement of 1901 quoted in Roger Marx, *L'Art social* (Paris: Fasquelle, 1913), p. 290. On the change in de Vogüé's thinking between the fairs, see also his article "La Défunte Exposition," *Revue des deux mondes* 162 (1900): 394–395.

17. Alfred Picard, *Exposition universelle internationale de 1900 à Paris: Rapport général, administratif, et technique* (Paris: Imprimerie nationale, 1903), 1:50–66, and *Le Bilan d'un siècle, 1801–1900* (Paris: Imprimerie nationale, 1906), pp. 350–355.

18. Georges Berger, "Rapport de M. Georges Berger," *Revue des arts décoratifs* 12 (1891–1892): 360–361. This report and Berger's role in the 1890s art nouveau will be discussed more fully in later chapters.

19. Roger Marx, "L'Exposition universelle de 1889," *L'Architecture* 111 (1890): 362.

20. Roger Marx, *La Loïe Fuller: Estampes modelées par Pierre Roche* (Evreux: Charles Hérissey, 1904), pp. 21–24 (a commentary on Loïe Fuller's performances at the 1900 exhibition).

21. See Eugène Hénard, *Exposition universelle de 1889: Le Palais des Machines, notice sur l'édifice et sur la marché des travaux* (Paris, 1891), p. 1.

22. Peter M. Wolf, *Eugène Hénard and the Beginning of Urbanism in Paris, 1900–1914* (The Hague: International Federation for Housing and Planning–Centre de Recherche d'Urbanisme, 1968), p. 33.

23. Emile Zola, *The Masterpiece (L'Oeuvre)* (Ann Arbor: University of Michigan Press, 1968), p. 138.

24. Zola, quoted in Frantz Jourdain, "Que pensez-vous de l'architecture moderne?" *Revue des arts décoratifs* 16 (1896): 95.

25. Zola, quoted in "Souvenirs des Goncourts," *La Revue encyclopédique* no. 153 (August 8, 1896): 552.

26. See, for example, the discussion of Ruskin in Roger Marx, *L'Art social,* pp. 169–172, 9–13, 29; Emile Gallé, *Ecrits pour l'art* (Paris: Laurens, 1908), pp. 194–199; the statements on the English model in S. Bing, "Wohin treiben wir?" *Dekorative Kunst* 1 (1898): 1–3; and Jean Lahor, *William Morris et le mouvement nouveau de l'art décoratif* (Geneva: Charles Eggmann, 1897), and *L'Art Nouveau: Son histoire, l'art nouveau étranger à l'Exposition, l'art nouveau au point de vue social* (Paris: Lemerre, 1901), pp. 84–104. Lahor argues for the inversion of Morris's ideas from a democratizing art "*par* le peuple" to a paternalist art "*pour* le peuple."

27. Lahor, *L'Art nouveau,* esp. pp. 1–26, 18–19, 53–69, 88; Victor Champier, "Les Arts décoratifs de l'Angleterre jugés par un français," *Revue des arts décoratifs* 14 (1893–1894): 249–259; Roger Marx, "La Renaissance des arts décoratifs," *Les Arts* 1 (January 1902): 38; Marx, *L'Art social,* esp. pp. 171–172.

28. In this regard, the work of the architect Hector Guimard has a history separate and different from the one I am recovering here. Guimard was not part of the institutional network of art nouveau luxury crafts in the 1890s, nor was he associated with Art Nouveau Bing. He shares neither the rococo revivalist nor neuropsychiatric dimensions of the decorative arts group. Guimard worked on his own and his stylistic evolution is somewhat idiosyncratic. His architecture was modeled explicitly on that of the Belgian innovator Victor Horta, which sets him apart from the primary interests and traditions of the craft art nouveau. For Guimard, see, for example, David Dunster, ed., *Hector Guimard, Architectural Monographs 2* (London: Rizzoli, 1978). For art historians' concentration on French art nouveau as interior decoration, see Gabriel P. Weisberg, *Art Nouveau Bing: Paris Style 1900* (New York: Abrams, 1986); and Nancy J. Troy, "Toward a Redefinition of Tradition in French Design, 1895–1914," *Design Issues* 1 (Fall 1984): 53–69.

29. The historian Eugen Weber's *France, Fin de Siècle* (Cambridge, Mass.: Harvard University Press, 1986), supports the meliorist interpretation. Weber acknowledges the theme of cultural crisis in the period but attributes it to the restricted realm of elite perception and misperception. He studies closely the changes that bettered the quality of life among the ordinary French: in fashion, transportation, electricity, and mass entertainment. Susanna Barrows and Robert Nye argue against the notion of the effervescent *Belle Epoque*. Barrows proposes that France in the 1890s "was as beleaguered as it was belle," and she demonstrates a mentality of beleaguerment in the intellectuals she studies. Robert Nye explores the paradox of material improvement in late nineteenth-century French life amid what he calls the experience of "a

national anxiety crisis." He identifies a number of factors—population decline, fear of the German Empire, and the weakening myth of France as a "Grande Nation"—that contributed to contemporary minimizations of material improvement. See Susanna Barrows, *Distorting Mirrors: Visions of the Crowd in Late Nineteenth-Century France* (New Haven, Conn.: Yale University Press, 1981), esp. chap. 1 and conclusion; and Robert A. Nye, *Crime, Madness, and Politics in Modern France: The Medical Model of National Decline* (Princeton, N.J.: Princeton University Press, 1984), esp. chap. 5, pp. 132–140.

30. Studies of the other fin-de-siècle avant-gardes in their distinctive national contexts are beginning to emerge. The historian Peter Paret is particularly interested in establishing a typology of European secessions and in identifying their general and unique characteristics. See his *Berlin Secession: Modernism and Its Enemies in Imperial Germany* (Cambridge, Mass.: Harvard University Press, 1980), esp. pp. 1–5; 29–37. Carl E. Schorske's analysis of the Vienna Secession is also suggestive for comparative issues; see his *Fin-de-Siècle Vienna: Politics and Culture* (New York: Knopf, 1980), esp. p. xxvii and chap. 5. On Belgium, see Jane Block, *Les XX and Belgian Avant-Gardism, 1868–94* (Ann Arbor, Mich.: UMI Research Press, 1981); and Susan M. Canning, "A History and Critical Review of the Salons of Les Vingt, 1884–1893" (Ph.D. diss., Pennsylvania State University, 1980). On Munich, see Maria Makela, "The Munich Secession" (Ph.D. diss., Stanford University, 1985).

31. The quoted phrase was used by Louis Vauxcelles, "L'Oeuvre de Gaston La Touche," *Les Arts* 7 (July 1908): 10.

32. H. Stuart Hughes, *Consciousness and Society: The Reorientation of European Social Thought, 1890–1930* (New York: Vintage Books, 1958).

33. Schorske, *Fin-de-Siècle Vienna,* esp. pp. xxvi–xxvii, 3–7.

Chapter One

1. Ch. Le Goffic, "Les Frères de Goncourt," *La Grande Encyclopédie* (Paris: Lamirault, c. 1898), 18:1190–1191; Roger L. Williams, *The Horror of Life* (Chicago: University of Chicago Press, 1980), pp. 63–65.

2. F. W. J. Hemmings, *Culture and Society in France, 1848–1898* (New York: Scribner, 1971), pp. 185–190.

3. Edmond de Goncourt and Jules de Goncourt, *La Révolution dans les moeurs* (Paris: Dentu, 1854); see also Jerrold Seigel, *Bohemian Paris: Culture, Politics, and the Boundaries of Bourgeois Life, 1830–1930* (New York: Viking Press, 1986), pp. 157–180.

4. Carol Duncan, *The Pursuit of Pleasure: The Rococo Revival in French Romantic Art* (New York: Garland, 1976), pp. 55–57. According to Duncan, the *fêtes galantes* of the eighteenth century were revived at court largely because of Madame de Berry, who organized balls "consciously designed to recall the fêtes of Louis XV." The Restoration rococo revival was also extended by the returning aristocrats, who decorated and partied à la Louis XV in the Faubourg Saint-Germain to reassert their power (Duncan, p. 56).

5. Charles Henry, *Mémoires inédits de Charles-Nicolas Cochin sur le Comte de Caylus, Bouchardon, les Slodtz* (Paris: Librairie de la Société de l'art français, 1880), pp. 6–7.

6. Ibid.; Duncan, *Pursuit of Pleasure,* pp. 34–38, 64–84.

7. Louis Hautecoeur, *Histoire de l'architecture classique en France* (Paris: Picard, 1957). 7: 290–292, 412. See also Duncan, *Pursuit of Pleasure,* pp. 95–101. Eighteenth-century elegance and feminization melded into a celebration of contemporaneity in, for example, Gautier's cult of women and fashion, evinced in his participation in the journal *La Mode,* rife with illustrations by Gavarni.

8. Henry, *Mémoires inédits,* pp. 7–8. See also "Arsène Houssaye," in G. Vapereau, *Dictionnaire universel des contemporains* (Paris: Hachette, 1893), pp. 807–808; Duncan, *Pursuit of Pleasure,* pp. 34–102.

9. Hautecoeur, *Histoire de l'architecture,* 7:265–270. A painting of Eugénie in the court dress of Marie Antoinette is now in the Metropolitan Museum of Art.

10. E. Williamson, *Les Meubles d'art du Mobilier National: Choix des plus belles pièces conservées au Garde-Meuble* (Paris: Baudry, c. 1900), p. 7; Hautecoeur, *Histoire de l'architecture,* pp. 265–270. Williamson and Hautecoeur explain how Eugénie redecorated the Tuileries Palace and Saint-Cloud with the furniture and tapestries originally created for Marie Antoinette in the Petit Trianon at Versailles.

11. See Philadelphia Museum of Art, *The Second Empire, 1852–1870: Art in France under Napoleon III* (Philadelphia: Philadelphia Museum of Art, 1978), pp. 74–203.

12. Ibid.; see the examples pictured on pp. 87 and 88 (decorative panels) and 110 and 111 (writing table and mirrored wardrobe).

13. F. Trawinski, "Musée du Louvre," *La Grande Encyclopédie* (Paris: Lamirault, c. 1898), 22:694–699; Michael Fried, "Manet's Sources: Aspects of His Art," *Artforum* 7 (March 1968): 28–82.

14. Fried, "Manet's Sources," pp. 45, 71. The exhibit was held in 1860.

15. The Goncourts' books on mid-eighteenth-century art included *Les Saint-Aubin* (1859), *Watteau* (1860), *Proud'hon* (1861), *Boucher* (1862), *Chardin* (1863), *Fragonard* (1865), *Deboucourt* (1866), *La Tour* (1867), *Les Vignettistes* (1868). All of these were later published together as *L'Art du XVIIIe siècle.*

16. Elaborate descriptions of these eighteenth-century rococo and Oriental artifacts are contained in Edmond de Goncourt, *La Maison d'un artiste,* 2 vols. (Paris: Charpentier, 1881).

17. The *préambule* to *La Maison d'un artiste,* 1:1–4 describes the house as a fortress of aristocratic retreat.

18. Quoted in T. J. Clark, "The Bar at the Folies-Bergère," in *The Wolf and the Lamb: Popular Culture in France from the Old Regime to the Twentieth Century,* ed. J. Beauroy and M. Bertrand (Saratoga, Calif.: Anma Libri, 1976), p. 247.

19. Edmond de Goncourt, *La Maison d'un artiste,* 1:15–16.

20. Ibid., p. 1.

21. Ibid., p. 188.

22. Ibid., 2:200.

23. *La Grande Larousse encyclopédique* (Paris: Larousse, 1963), s.v. "Arts décoratifs."

24. Guillaume Janneau, *Les Styles du meuble français* (Paris: Presses universitaires de France, 1972), pp. 18–19.

25. Monica Burckhardt, *Mobilier Régence, Louis XV* (Paris: Charles Massin, n.d.), pp. 7–8.

26. Art historical accounts of this period emphasize that the naturist, decorative, and intimate paintings beginning with Watteau and extending to Boucher and Fragonard were accepted by and celebrated in a liberalized Academy. See Arnold Hauser, *The Social History of Art,* Vol. 3, *Rococo, Classicism, and Romanticism* (New York: Vintage Books, 1951), pp. 25–36; Hugh Honour, *Neo-Classicism* (Middlesex, England: Penguin Books, 1968), pp. 25–36; Michael Levey, *Rococo to Revolution: Major Trends in Eighteenth-Century Painting* (London: Thames & Hudson, 1966), pp. 13–58; and W. Kalnein and Michael Levey, *Art and Architecture of the Eighteenth Century in France* (Middlesex, England: Penguin Books, 1972), pp. 4–86. For a more intricate and compelling discussion of the debates about art in the Academy and in other circles, see the splendid book by Thomas Crow, *Painters and Public Life in Eighteenth-Century Paris* (New Haven, Conn.: Yale University Press, 1985).

27. Detailed discussions of the rococo artists' craft backgrounds and interior decorations may be found in Kalnein and Levey, *Art and Architecture,* pp. 4–182, 202–297.

28. Ibid., pp. 83–106.

29. Edmond de Goncourt, *La Maison d'un artiste*, 1:292–295.

30. Ibid., 2:186–187.

31. Kalnein and Levey, *Art and Architecture*, pp. 201–202, 270–271. They quote from an architectural treatise of 1721 by the architect Blondel, who defines the *style moderne* as the movement toward intimacy and organic adornment in architecture. Another originator of the mid-eighteenth-century rococo style, the ornamental sculptor Nicolas Pineau, also called the intimate ensembles with their furniture and ornaments patterned after the forms of nature the *style moderne* and *goût nouveau*. Pineau is cited in Léon Deshairs, *Dessins originaux des maîtres décoratifs* (Paris: Longuet, c. 1900), pp. 12, 20–21, 22–24, 27. See also the extensive documentation of contemporary discussions and definitions of the rococo as *style moderne* and *genre pittoresque* in Fiske Kimball, *The Creation of the Rococo Decorative Style* (1943; reprint New York: Dover, 1980), esp. pp. 106–225.

32. Edmond de Goncourt and Jules de Goncourt, *Révolution dans les moeurs*, n.p.

33. Ibid.

34. Quoted in Levey, *Rococo to Revolution*, p. 121.

35. Quoted in Edmond de Goncourt and Jules de Goncourt, *French Eighteenth Century Painters*, trans. Robin Ironside (New York: Phaidon, 1948), p. 55.

36. Edmond de Goncourt, *La Maison d'un artiste*, 2:99–100; see also Kalnein and Levey, *Art and Architecture*, pp. 201–297; and Kimball *Rococo Style*, pp. 106–222.

37. See Edmond's description in *La Maison d'un artiste*, 2:99–100. Kalnein and Levey also discuss the invention of the small apartment in *Art and Architecture*, pp. 218–230, as does Kimball, in *Rococo Style*, pp. 106–222. The *petit appartement* made its way into Versailles, and during the 1720s the *ornemanistes* Oppenordt and Pineau, among others, created private chambers within the vast open palace.

38. Edmond de Goncourt, *La Maison d'un artiste*, 1:290–292; 2:109. Pompadour took lessons from Boucher, and some of her engravings are listed in Edmond's collection.

39. Ibid., 1:188, 319–322; 2:99–100.

40. Ibid., 1:318–320; see also the excellent discussion of the new, feminine, definition of interior space and its expression in the new arsenal of furniture in Janneau, *Les Styles du meuble français*, pp. 29–57; and Burckhardt, *Mobilier Régence, Louis XV*, pp. 9–77.

41. Edmond de Goncourt, *La Maison d'un artiste*, 1:14–190; Kalnein and Levey, *Art and Architecture*, pp. 202–260; Honour, *Neo-Classicism*, pp. 17–26; and Kimball, *Rococo Style*, pp. 106–222.

42. A good example of this interpenetration and integration of all pieces in the ensemble may be found in the description and illustration of Edmond's grand salon, in *La Maison d'un artiste*, 1:181–192.

43. Ibid., 1:325, and 319–327 on fashion.

44. Ibid., 1:319–320.

45. Ibid., 1:2, 343–349; 2:350–359. Elsewhere Edmond notes that he possessed Marie Antoinette's *secrétaire* and the bed of the princesse de Lamballe.

46. Ibid., 1:2–18, 188–192, 215–226; 2:278–296, 346.

47. Ibid., 1:199–218, 12–17.

48. Ibid., 1:3–16, 182–195, 215–218, 234–240. Typical of this emphasis on creativity and inspiration was Edmond's discussion of a Japanese sword buckle, molded of iron: "travail de fer d'une imagination merveilleusement créatrice" (1:218).

Signatures affixed to eighteenth-century craft objects were not testaments to the individual creative genius of their makers but marked the "corporate self" of the producer, the regulation of the guild to which the artisan belonged. Eighteenth-century applied arts that were signed also bore stamps related to royal taxes and inventories. The Goncourts elided these facts in the service of their Romantic criteria of individual imagination. For eighteenth-century signatures and their meanings for applied arts see, for example, Burckhardt, *Mobilier Régence, Louis XV,* pp. 33–40, 58–75; and Robert Wark, *French Decorative Arts in the Huntington Collection* (San Marino, Calif.: Huntington Library, 1979), pp. ix–xxv, 1–59. Wark reminds us how many artisans involved in craft production did not sign their names to a product, for example, the sculptors of ornamental metal who provided decorative flourishes for wood furniture.

49. Edmond de Goncourt, *La Maison d'un artiste,* 2:273.

50. Ibid., 2:227, 231, 256–257, 260–261, 273–275. On p. 257 Edmond compared the delicacy of the porcelain to a *"gouache translucide."*

51. Edmond de Goncourt, *La Maison d'un artiste,* quoted in *Collection des Goncourts: Arts de l'Extrême-Orient* (Paris: May & Metteroz, 1897), p. 99.

52. *La Maison d'un artiste,* 1:5–6, 10–11.

53. Erich Auerbach, *Mimesis: The Representation of Reality in Western Literature* (Princeton, N.J.: Princeton University Press, 1973), pp. 493–506.

54. See the discussion of the Goncourts' literary modernism in Paul Bourget, *Nouveaux essais de psychologie contemporaine* (Paris: Lemerre, 1883), pp. 137–198; Roger Marx, *préface* to Edmond de Goncourt and Jules de Goncourt, *Etudes d'art: Le Salon de 1852, la peinture à l'Exposition de 1855* (Paris: Librairie des Bibliophiles, 1893), pp. 211–214. Bourget's discussion is particularly compelling on the centrality of visual language in the Goncourts' style.

55. Roger Marx, "L'Art et les Goncourts," *La Lorraine-artiste* 14 (1896): 275–276; Paul Verlaine, "Edmond de Goncourt," in *La Lorraine-artiste* 14 (1896): 279; Roger Marx, *préface* to Goncourt, *Etudes d'art,* pp. 211–213; "Les Goncourts," in *Larousse du XXe siècle* (Paris: Larousse, c. 1912), 3:820. The author here noted the "vocabulaire et le style nouveau" of the Goncourts, and that "ce sont avant tout des impressionistes"; "leur prose est souple, pittoresque."

56. Bourget, *Nouveaux essais de psychologie contemporaine,* pp. 139–157.

57. Bourget quoted passages from *La Maison d'un artiste* to illustrate the way that Edmond aestheticized and complicated the visual character of his eighteenth-century objects (*Nouveaux essais de psychologie contemporaine,* pp. 143–144, 151–152).

58. Edmond de Goncourt and Jules de Goncourt, *Journal, mémoires de la vie littéraire* (Paris: Fasquelle & Flammarion, 1956), 3:354–355, entry for June 9, 1884 (hereafter cited as *Journal des Goncourts*).

59. Ibid.

60. Ibid., 3:307–308, entry for January 23, 1884.

61. Edmond de Goncourt, *La Maison d'un artiste,* 1:25–27.

62. Edmond de Goncourt and Jules de Goncourt, *Révolution dans les moeurs,* n.p. The ruin of men by bourgeois women and the demonic power of women's sexual and social ambitions were the themes of three of the brothers' novels (*Charles Démailly, Renée Mauperin,* and *Germinie Lacerteux*), according to Roger Williams, *The Horror of Life,* pp. 70–85. See also Jerrold Seigel's discussion of women and bourgeois society in the Goncourts' novels, in *Bohemian Paris,* pp. 157–180.

63. Williams, *The Horror of Life,* pp. 63–109.

64. Williams cites a passage from Jules's diaries that celebrates his life with Edmond as a "complete marriage of the entire moral being" and as "love, without the carnal side" (*The Horror of Life,* p. 66). Seigel offers a penetrating psychological portrait of the two brothers' fusion of selves in *Bohemian Paris,* pp. 173–180.

65. Cited in Williams, *The Horror of Life,* pp. 87–90.

66. Edmond de Goncourt, *La Maison d'un artiste,* 1:12–13, 18–19, 181–184.

67. Ibid., 1:4–355; 2:197–200.

68. Ibid., 1:2–3.

69. Williams, *The Horror of Life*, pp. 91–94. The details of Charcot's clinical work as well as the diffusion of his ideas across a range of high and low French culture will be discussed in chapter 5.

70. See *Journal des Goncourts*, 2:1267, October 31, 1878.

71. Ibid., 3:21, May 26, 1879.

72. Ibid., 3:164, April 11, 1882; 3:252–253, April 26, 1883.

73. Edmond comments on Charcot's treatment of Alphonse Daudet in the *Journal des Goncourts*, 3:171, May 14, 1882; 3:442–443, April 1, 1885; 3:493, October 7, 1885; 3:911, January 27, 1889; and 3:929, February 25, 1889.

74. Edmond's early entries concerning Charcot are respectful; later he developed a strong personal dislike of the doctor, partly because Charcot booed at one of his plays and partly because there had been a scandal involving the Daudet and Charcot families. Alphonse's son, Léon, was to marry Charcot's daughter but married Jeanne Hugo instead. As a result, Charcot blocked Léon's medical career. For these incidents, see the *Journal des Goncourts*, 3:1040–1041, September 23, 1889; 4:16–17, January 15, 1891; 4:146, September 22, 1891; and 4:612–613, July 9, 1894. Some time before the end of 1888, Edmond declined an invitation to dine at the Charcots—because of fatigue, he claimed. Later he learned from Madame Burty that his refusal had infuriated Madame Charcot, who may have turned the doctor against his play. The dinner invitation is recounted in the *Journal des Goncourts*, 3:1275, December 5, 1890. Despite Edmond's personal antipathy toward Charcot in this later period, the *Journal* offers ample evidence that Edmond had absorbed Charcot's ideas and practices. After 1885 he even compared some of the high-strung society women he knew to the "hysterics of the Salpêtrière," suggesting that he may have attended the Salpêtrière demonstrations: see the *Journal des Goncourts*, 3:626, December 30, 1885, and 3:961, April 17, 1889. Further evidence of Charcot's influence on both Edmond and Jules de Goncourt appears in a fascinating article by a Charcot colleague at the Salpêtrière, A. De Monzie. De Monzie situates the brothers in an important group of writers of a new "école psychiatrique" derived from Charcot's writings and teaching. De Monzie states that the brothers "apparentent étroitement au doctrinaire de la Salpêtrière." See A. De Monzie, "Eloge de Charcot," *Revue neurologique* 1, no. 6 (1925): 1159–1162. I am grateful to Professor Toby Gelfand for helping me to clarify precisely the relation between the Goncourts and Charcot.

75. Edmond de Goncourt, quoted in Harry Levin, *The Gates of Horn: A Study of Five French Realists* (New York: Oxford University Press, 1966), pp. 376–377. Significantly, Levin cites Edmond's statement about being an "écrivain des nerfs" for its direct impact on Proust's style and substance. For one example of Edmond's stating that "j'ai écrit avec mes nerfs," see the *Journal des Goncourts*, 3:877, December 19, 1888.

76. Paul Hartenberg explained that "surmenage cérébral" and nervous irritation were the infallible marks of the Goncourts' temperament, traits that Edmond defined as those of an "aristocratie intellectuelle." See Hartenberg, "Le Tempérament d'Edmond de Goncourt," *La Lorraine-artiste* 14 (1896): 289–293. See also Bourget's important discussion in *Nouveaux essais de psychologie contemporaine*, pp. 137–196, which includes an analysis of the Goncourts' self-conscious cultivation of neurasthenia as the basis for modern artistic production.

77. Quoted in Bourget, *Nouveaux essais de psychologie contemporaine*, pp. 152–168; the quotation is on page 168; Hartenberg, "Le Tempérament," p. 292, also quotes Edmond concerning the pathological bases of modern literature. Edmond's comments on the clinical and literary interest of his own mental tension are in the *Journal des Goncourts*, 2:1142, July 31, 1876.

78. A. de Monzie, "Eloge de Charcot," p. 1161. De Monzie credits this case file to Edmond de Goncourt's familiarity with Charcot.

79. *Journal des Goncourts*, 3:885, December 24, 1888.

80. Quoted in Williams, *The Horror of Life*, p. 63.

81. Edmond de Goncourt and Jules de Goncourt, *Idées et sensations,* quoted in "Souvenirs des Goncourts," *La Revue encyclopédique* no. 153 (August 8, 1896): 550–551.

82. See, for example, Edmond de Goncourt, *La Maison d'un artiste,* 1:12–192. Bourget's essay on the Goncourts also points out the neuropathological effects of the eighteenth-century collection and Edmond's description of them. See Bourget, *Nouveaux essais de psychologie contemporaine,* pp. 136–167.

83. Edmond de Goncourt, *La Maison d'un artiste,* 2:349. See also the entry in the *Journal des Goncourts,* 4:911, January 25, 1896, about working in a state of "éréthisme cérébral, où votre cervelle travaille . . . bouillonne, surchauffée."

84. Bourget, *Nouveaux essais de psychologie contemporaine,* pp. 145–152; the quotation is on p. 151.

85. Ibid.; Roger Marx, "Les Goncourts collectionneurs," in *Collection des Goncourts: Dessins, aquarelles, et pastels du XVIIIe siècle, Catalogue du vente* (Paris: May & Metteroz, 1897), pp. i–xiii.

Chapter Two

1. Arthur Meyer, *Ce que mes yeux ont vu* (Paris: Plon, 1911), pp. 31, 33.

2. Quoted in Theodore Zeldin, *France, 1848–1945,* vol. 1, *Ambition, Love, and Politics* (Oxford: Clarendon Press, 1973), p. 655.

3. On the widespread economic problems of the 1880s, both rural and urban, see Jacques Néré, *La Crise industrielle de 1882 et le mouvement boulangiste* (Paris: Sorbonne, 1959); Charles Mayet, *La Crise industrielle: L'Ameublement* (Paris: Dentu, 1883); and Philip Nord, *Paris Shopkeepers and the Politics of Resentment* (Princeton, N.J.: Princeton University Press, 1986).

4. Jean-Marie Mayeur, *Les Débuts de la IIIe République, 1871–1898* (Paris: Seuil, 1973), p. 233.

5. R. D. Anderson, *France, 1870–1914: Politics and Society* (London: Routledge & Kegan Paul, 1977), pp. 166–167; Frederick H. Seager, *The Boulanger Affair: Political Crossroads of France, 1886–1889* (Ithaca, N.Y.: Cornell University Press, 1969), pp. 5–104; C. Stewart Doty, *From Cultural Rebellion to Counterrevolution: The Politics of Maurice Barres* (Athens: Ohio University Press, 1976), pp. 36–70.

6. I base my view of the politics of the 1890s on three historical works that offer a phaseology of 1889–1898 and subordinate the incipient Dreyfus affair to a more fundamental process of this decade: the restructuring and resolidification of the Third Republic and the realignment of political forces. Each work dates the political significance of the Dreyfus affair from January of 1898. These works are Anderson, *France, 1870–1914,* esp. pp. 5–29; Jean-Marie Mayeur, *Les Débuts de la IIIe République,* esp. pp. 193–228; and Pierre Sorlin, *Waldeck-Rousseau* (Paris: Colin, 1966), esp. pp. 354–365. A new book by Sanford Elwitt, which I received too late to incorporate fully into my analysis, also supports this interpretation of French politics in the 1890s. See *The Third Republic Defended: Bourgeois Reform in France, 1880–1914* (Baton Rouge: Louisiana State University Press, 1986).

7. The long and remarkable history of the royal seal and Haussmann's addition of the *Fluctuat* motto as the emblem of the empire is described in A. de Coetlogon and L. M. Tisserand, *Histoire générale de Paris, collection de documents publiée sous les auspices de l'édilité parisienne, Les armoiries de la ville de Paris, sceaux, emblèmes, couleurs, devises, livrées et cérémonies publiques,* vol. I (Paris: Imprimerie nationale, 1874), pp. 98–99, 155–164, 189–192. See also Fig. 16.

8. Mayeur, *Les Débuts de la IIIe République,* pp. 207–211; Sorlin, *Waldeck-Rousseau,* pp. 354–356.

9. Sorlin, *Waldeck-Rousseau,* p. 354.

10. Mayeur, *Les Débuts de la IIIe République*, p. 207. During the Freycinet ministry of 1886 the plans for a thousand-foot iron tower as the monumental gateway to the Paris Exhibition of 1889 were proposed and ratified. See Charles Braibant *Histoire de la Tour Eiffel* (Paris: Plon, 1964), pp. 25–29.

11. Mayeur, *Les Débuts de la IIIe République*, pp. 207, 211; Sorlin, *Waldeck-Rousseau*, pp. 354–355. Poincaré, for example, was born in 1861 and was elected to the Chamber of Deputies from the Meurthe-Moselle department of the Lorraine in 1883, at the age of twenty-two. In 1894 Poincaré was appointed minister of public instruction and beaux-arts, at age thirty-three. Poincaré's best friend, Léon Barthou, appointed minister of the interior at age thirty-two, served with him in this Dupuy cabinet. Poincaré and Barthou were referred to in the Parisian press as "*les deux gosses*" ("the two kids") (Jean Vartier, *Histoire de notre Lorraine* [Paris: Editions France-Empire, 1973], pp. 306–311).

12. Quoted in Mayeur, *Les Débuts de la IIIe République*, p. 211.

13. Paul Deschanel coined the term *progressisme* after the electoral victory of the moderates in 1893. According to Mayeur, in *Les Débuts de la IIIe République* (p. 211), these politicians "vont donner un *style nouveau* à l'opportunisme discrédité, en imposant le terme de 'progressisme.'" Sorlin indicates "le centre . . . remplace le terme d'opportunisme, trop décrié, par celui du 'progressisme'" (*Waldeck-Rousseau*, p. 355).

14. Zeldin, *France, 1848–1945*, p. 645; Anderson, *France, 1870–1914*, pp. 5–21.

15. Anderson, *France, 1870–1914*, p. 15: "The 1889 election was the last in which the question of the regime was a real issue, and the bulk of the Right gave up hope of reversing the verdict of 1877." See also the discussion of the turning point of 1889 in John McManners, *Church and State in France, 1870–1914* (New York: Harper & Row, 1972), pp. 64–65; Alexander Sedgwick, *The Third French Republic, 1870–1914* (New York: Thomas Y. Crowell, 1968), p. 52; and Zeldin, *France, 1848–1945*, p. 645, who characterizes the period after 1889 as a decade when "monarchy was no longer a practical possibility. The nobles and notables who had attached themselves to it needed to find a new outlet for their ambitions."

16. Zeldin, *France, 1848–1945*, pp. 645–646; Anderson, *France, 1870–1914*, p. 15.

17. Mayeur, *Les Débuts de la IIIe République*, pp. 193–217; Anderson, *France, 1890–1914*, p. 15; Sorlin, *Waldeck-Rousseau*, pp. 354–365; Georges Picot, "La Lutte contre le socialisme," *Revue des deux mondes* 132 (1895): 591–621.

18. Quoted in Sorlin, *Waldeck-Rousseau*, p. 355.

19. Susanna Barrows explores the pattern of elite misperception of the threat of social radicalism in the 1890s and its impact on the development of crowd theory by Gabriel Tarde and Gustave Le Bon in *Distorting Mirrors: Visions of the Crowd in Late Nineteenth-Century France* (New Haven, Conn.: Yale University Press, 1981), esp. pp. 18–42.

20. In 1893 there were 634 strikes, which involved more than 120,000 workers (Michael Curtis, *Three against the Third Republic: Sorel, Barrès, Maurras* [Princeton, N.J.: Princeton University Press, 1959], p. 19). See also Barrows, *Distorting Mirrors*, pp. 18–23.

21. Sorlin, *Waldeck-Rousseau*, p. 359; Anderson, *France, 1870–1914*, p. 125; Barrows, *Distorting Mirrors*, pp. 25–30.

22. Sorlin, *Waldeck-Rousseau*, p. 355; see also Anderson, *France, 1870–1914*, pp. 125–126, 168.

23. Mayeur, *Les Débuts de la IIIe République*, p. 181. In 1898, membership in the Parti Ouvrier reached sixteen thousand. Although the figure is small relative to total population, one of the factors contributing to the misperception of socialist strength was its concentration in particular regions and locales, corresponding to the small number of highly visible areas where heavy industry was concentrated. Recent work has suggested the significance of socialism at the local level, where it mushroomed in the 1890s. See Joan Scott, "Social History and the History of Socialism: French Socialist Municipalities in the 1890's," *Mouvement social*

no. 111 (April–June 1980): 145–153. Socialism among the electorate expanded from 1893, when 160,000 voted for socialist candidates in the election that had socialist contenders for the first time, to 1898, when 295,000 voted, or 2 percent of the total population (Mayeur, *Les Débuts*).

24. Sorlin, *Waldeck-Rousseau*, pp. 356–357.

25. Ibid.

26. George Woodcock, *Anarchism: A History of Libertarian Ideas and Movement* (New York: Meridian Books, 1962), pp. 319–320; James Joll, *The Anarchists* (New York: Grosset & Dunlap, 1964), pp. 197–198; Mayeur, *Les Débuts de la IIIe République*, pp. 181, 188–192.

27. The republicans responded to the rash of violence by ratifying a series of extremely harsh laws restricting press statements and associations, which socialists perceived as a pretext for an attack on all forms of counter-republicanism (Mayeur, *Les Débuts de la IIIe République*, p. 212; Anderson, *France, 1870–1914*, p. 125; Eugenia Herbert, *The Artist and Social Reform: France and Belgium, 1885–1898* [New Haven, Conn.: Yale University Press, 1961], pp. 118–123).

28. John McManners, *Church and State in France*, pp. 81–93.

29. Quoted in Mayeur, *Les Débuts de la IIIe République*, p. 212; Sedgwick, *The Third French Republic*, pp. 56–57. On Spuller's evolution from Gambettist anticlerical to antisocialist Catholic reconciler see the article by R. S., "Eugène Spuller," in *La Grande Encyclopédie* (Paris: Lamirault, c. 1897) 30:418.

30. Sorlin, *Waldeck-Rousseau*, p. 362; see also McManners, *Church and State in France*, pp. 75–80; Sedgwick, *The Third French Republic*, pp. 52–56; and David Shapiro, "The *Ralliement* in the Politics of the 1890's," in *The Right in France, 1890–1919*, St. Antony's Papers no. 13 (Oxford: Oxford University Press, 1962), esp. pp. 29–33.

31. For details of the unfolding of the alliance see Meyer, *Ce que mes yeux ont vu*, pp. 109–115; Anderson, *France, 1870–1914*, pp. 146–148; and Sedgwick, *The Third French Republic*, pp. 102–103; and chapter 9 of this book.

32. Anderson, *France, 1870–1914*, pp. 98, 95–97; Zeldin, *France, 1848–1945*, p. 659.

33. J.E.S. Hayward, "The Official Social Philosophy of the French Third Republic: Léon Bourgeois and Solidarism," *International Review of Social History* 6 (1961): 19, 20–48. Zeldin, *France, 1848–1945*, describes solidarity as "the most talked about ideal of the nineties and the first decade of the twentieth century" (p. 654). Karen Offen includes a useful characterization of solidarism in relation to republican sexual politics in her article "Depopulation, Nationalism, and Feminism in Fin-de-Siècle France," *American Historical Review* 89 (1984): 664–666. A valuable book by Judith F. Stone examines the origins and long-term impact of solidarism in republican politics: *The Search for Social Peace: Reform Legislation in France, 1890–1914* (Albany: State University of New York Press, 1985).

34. Zeldin, *France, 1848–1945*, p. 656.

35. Both Fouillée and Durkheim relied heavily on the French zoologist Milne-Edwards for their understanding of cellular interdependence. See Zeldin, *France, 1848–1945*, pp. 654–656.

36. Anderson, *France, 1870–1914*, p. 89, isolates the liberal legacy of the French Revolution as one of "negative freedom." Zeldin rightly argues that two more fundamental issues underlay the search by liberals such as Fouillée, Durkheim, and Léon Bourgeois for a scientifically legitimated anti-egoist theory. The first was a new attitude toward the French Revolution, which was indicted as excessively atomistic. The second was a deeper search for a new morality as a binding power for desiccated liberal rationalism. See Zeldin, *France, 1848–1945*, pp. 654–656.

37. Léon Bourgeois, *Solidarité* (Paris: Colin, 1896).

38. The phrases are those of Adolphe Retté, the Symbolist poet, in 1894, after the Emile Henry bombing of the Chamber of Deputies, in "Floréal," *La Plume* no. 123 (June 1–15, 1894): 229–230.

39. Durkheim's *Suicide* (1897), quoted in James Joll, *Europe since 1870: An International History* (New York: Harper & Row, 1973), p. 135

40. Quoted in Zeldin, *France, 1848–1945*, pp. 655, 657.

41. Quoted in Anderson, *France, 1870–1914*, p. 96. Solidarist theory propounded a variety of measures for state social welfare programs including progressive taxation, old-age pensions, public assistance, and unemployment insurance. It did not propose a doctrine of equality but sought to offset the inequalities of inherited wealth and social background. See the comprehensive discussion of these policy issues in Stone, *Search for Social Peace*, esp. chaps. 5 and 6.

42. Zeldin characterizes solidarism as envisioning "society as a giant mutual insurance company, which helped the disadvantaged, but left man free to make his own way once he had paid his premiums" (*France, 1848–1945*, p. 658). Solidarism may also be usefully understood as a secularized version of the major conceptual positions offered in the *Rerum Novarum*. As we have seen earlier, the papal encyclical argued that all men were not born equal, but it was the duty of the state to offset social injustices on behalf of the poor, and that more fortunate citizens owed, from birth, a debt to society.

43. Anderson, *France, 1870–1914*, pp. 17–18; McManners, *Church and State in France*, p. 78; Sedgwick, *The Third French Republic*, pp. 55–56; and Sorlin, *Waldeck-Rousseau*, pp. 354–365.

44. Zeldin, *France, 1848–1945*, pp. 654, 660–667.

45. Quoted in Anderson, *France, 1870–1914*, p. 18; McManners, *Church and State in France*, p. 78.

Chapter Three

1. The phrase is that of the French economic historian Crouzet, quoted in Jean Mayeur, *Les Débuts de la IIIe République, 1871–1898* (Paris: Seuil, 1973), p. 64.

2. Ibid.

3. Jacques Néré, "The French Republic" in *The New Cambridge Modern History*, vol. 11, *Material Progress and World-Wide Problems, 1878–1898* (Cambridge: Cambridge University Press, 1962), p. 308; Mayeur, *Les Débuts de la IIIe République*, p. 64.

4. Néré, "The French Republic," p. 308. See also Pierre Sorlin, *La Société française*, vol. 1, *1840–1914* (Paris: Arthaud, 1969), pp. 161–167.

5. Néré, "The French Republic," p. 307.

6. Quoted in Theodore Zeldin, *France, 1848–1945*, vol. 1, *Ambition, Love, and Politics* (Oxford: Clarendon Press, 1973), pp. 650–651. See also pp. 649–654. Méline explicated his theories in the 1905 publication *Le Retour à la terre et la surproduction industrielle*.

7. Biographical information on Berger is contained in G. Vapereau, *Dictionnaire universel des contemporains*, vol. 1 (Paris: Hachette, 1893), p. 156. For Berger and the 1889 exhibition, see E. Monod, *L'Exposition universelle de 1889* (Paris: Dentu, 1890), vols. 1–4, especially 1:i–xxxi; *Catalogue général officiel de l'Exposition universelle de 1889* (Lille: Imprimerie L. Danel, 1889); and Georges Berger, *Exposition universelle internationale de 1889* (Paris: Imprimerie de Chaix, 1889).

8. "Rapport de M. Georges Berger," *Revue des arts décoratifs* 12 (1891–1892): 360–361.

9. Pierre Du Maroussem, *La Question ouvrière*, vol. 2, *Ébénistes du Faubourg Saint-Antoine* (Paris: Arthur Rousseau, 1892), p. 169.

10. Antonin Proust summarizes and comments on these reports in his *Commission d'en-*

quête sur la situation des ouvriers et des industries d'art (Paris: Quantin, 1883), pp. 1–40; Antonin Proust, *Le Salon de 1891* (Paris: Bussod, Valadon, 1891), pp. 52–96; and Victor Champier, *Catalogue illustré de l'Union centrale des arts décoratifs* (Paris: Librairie d'art L. Baschet, 1884), pp. 9–18.

11. Pierre Du Maroussem, *La Question ouvrière*, 2:167, 169.

12. Ibid., pp. 167, 181. The volume of imports into the Parisian market in particular during this period increased dramatically, from 642,000 in 1873 to 2,342,000 in 1889.

13. Ibid., p. 168.

14. Louis Comfort Tiffany's displays in 1889 drew particular attention among the French commentators, among them Roger Marx, *La Décoration et l'art industriel à l'Exposition universelle de 1889* (Paris: Librairies-imprimeries réunies, 1890), pp. 2–60.

15. Henri Béraldi, "Les Bibliophiles et la décoration de la reliure: créateurs et vénérants," *Revue des arts décoratifs* 12 (1891–1892): 133. See also Louis de Fourcaud's assessment of the 1889 displays in "A propos de la réorganisation de la manufacture de Sèvres," *Revue des arts décoratifs* 12 (1891–1892): 164–165; and Edmond Plauchut, "La Rivalité des industries d'art en Europe," *Revue des deux mondes* 105 (1891): 630–643.

16. Berger, "Rapport de M. Berger," pp. 360–361, 366.

17. Marius Vachon, *Les Musées et les écoles d'art industrielle en Europe* (Paris: Imprimerie nationale, 1890). See also Henry Havard and Marius Vachon, *Les Manufactures nationales: Les Gobelins, la Savonnerie, Sèvres, Beauvais* (Paris: G. Decaux, 1889).

18. When Méline stepped down from his position as Prime Minister in 1898, he applauded Vachon's efforts. See Vachon's introduction to his *Pour la défense de nos industries d'art* (Paris: Lahure, 1899), p. iii.

19. At the conclusion of his 1888 mission, Vachon had proclaimed, "After seeing what I have seen abroad, I declare loudly, with the consciousness of fulfilling a patriotic duty, that today the organization of our artistic and industrial education is a work of national defense of the same importance as the organization of our Army" (in Marius Vachon, *Some Industrial Art Schools and Their Lessons for the United States* [Washington, D.C., Government Printing Office, 1923] p. 43).

20. Vachon, quoted in Edmond Plauchut, "La Rivalité des industries d'art en Europe," p. 643.

21. Ibid., p. 644.

22. Pierre Du Maroussem gives the best account of this relation between the exporting of luxury items and deference to French culture (*La Question ouvrière*, 2:176).

23. Quoted in Edmond Plauchut, "La Rivalité des industries d'art en Europe," pp. 642–643.

24. Synthetic historical description and analysis of the French craft sector in the mid and late nineteenth century is difficult to come by. The most useful general treatment I have consulted is Jeanne Gaillard, *Paris, La Ville, 1852–1870: L'Urbanisme parisien à l'heure de Haussmann: Des provinciaux aux vocations parisiennes* (Paris: Champion, 1977). T. J. Clark provides an excellent summary and extension of Gaillard's findings in *The Painting of Modern Life: Paris in the Art of Manet and His Followers* (New York: Knopf, 1985), chap. 1. Philip Nord offers the essential account of commercial change and the Parisian trades in the fin de siècle in *Paris Shopkeepers and the Politics of Resentment* (Princeton, N.J.: Princeton University Press, 1986).

25. Pierre Du Maroussem, *La Question ouvrière* (Paris: Arthur Rousseau), vol. 1, *Charpentiers de Paris, compagnons et indépendants* (1891); vol. 2, *Ebénistes du Faubourg Saint-Antoine: Grands magasins, "Sweating system"* (1892); vol. 3, *Le Jouet parisien: Grands magasins, "Sweating-system"* (1893); vol. 4, *Halles centrales de Paris et le commerce de l'alimentation* (1894).

26. Du Maroussem, *La Question ouvrière*, 1:11–46; 2:48.

27. Du Maroussem, *La Question ouvrière*, 2:134–135.

28. Specialists in social and labor history treat Du Maroussem as a reliable source. See, for example, the recent treatment of the late nineteenth-century Parisian cabinetmakers by Lee Shai Weissbach, who depends on Du Maroussem's account, in "Artisanal Response to Artistic Decline: The Cabinetmakers of Paris in the Era of Industrialization," *Journal of Social History* 16, no. 2 (Winter 1982): 67–83.

29. Du Maroussem, 2:47–49.

30. Ibid., 2:129, 47–48.

31. Ibid., 2:130, 52.

32. Ibid., 2:49, 129–152.

33. Ibid., 2:130, 132.

34. Ibid., 2:135–138, 46. The *trôleur* often worked twelve to fourteen days to complete one product. Du Maroussem presents an intricate account of the working methods, costs, and surroundings of the *trôleur* (2:139–143).

35. Ibid., 2:134–135.

36. Ibid., 2:92–93, 47–48.

37. Ibid., 2:46, 48. See also pp. 92–111 for a detailed account of the atelier structure and working procedures.

38. Ibid., 2:46, 93–94.

39. Ibid., 2:188–198, 209–234, 277–279.

40. Ibid., 2:102–114, 130–137.

41. Ibid., 2:213, 228–229, 230.

42. Ibid., 2:241–256.

43. Ibid., 2:50, 75.

44. The continuity of craft traditions enabled one atelier of the *haut luxe* to reconstruct, from the original design plans and with identical techniques, an authentic Louis XV bureau, according to Du Maroussem (2:50). The establishments of *haut luxe* production in the 1890s included the Maison Lemoine, one of whose prize craftsmen, Père Seguin, had worked for fifty-two years like his father before him; other centers were the Maisons Damon, Roux, Janselme, Dasson, Chévry, Krieger, and Allard (Du Maroussem, *La Question ouvrière*, 2:49–64, 74, 210–211).

45. Ibid., 2:46, 50–92, esp. 60–63.

46. "Sauf dans les ateliers de haut luxe, où les ouvriers doivent savoir construire et construisent toute espèce de meuble, le métier est divisé en spécialités" (Du Maroussem, *La Question ouvrière*, 2:64; see also 65–67).

47. This presentation is replicated beautifully in *Métiers disparus, édition comportant 70 planches avec notes explicatives, tirées de l'Encyclopédie Diderot* (Paris: Baudouin Editeur, 1978).

48. These procedures included, according to Du Maroussem's invocation of the *Art du Menuisier* by Roubo of 1772, those of wood *découpeurs* and *sculpteurs,* followed by a series of elaborate finishing and adornment procedures that included work by *bronziers, ciseleurs, monteurs* and *ouvriers en pierres fines* for incrustation in "*écaille teinte, étain, ivoire* and *ébène*" (Du Maroussem, *La Question ouvrière*, 2:39–40).

49. Ibid., 2:60–66.

50. Ibid., 2:59–60, 208–209. Du Maroussem visited one of the *haut luxe* ateliers to examine the mechanized part of the production process firsthand.

51. Du Maroussem noted that the *haut luxe* houses sometimes even rented out their machines to *petits patrons*. Yet even if they could benefit from the time-saving devices offered by mechanical power for certain parts of the work process, the *petits patrons* were locked into a production of a single specialized item for the *grand magasin* supply contract. The genuine benefits of machine power were obtained only if the initial, mechanically-executed, cutting and shaping procedures were followed by an extensive and highly varied set of finishing pro-

cesses, a system limited to the realm of *haut luxe* production. The use of advanced technology in the *haut luxe* sector freed the fine craftsmen to focus on the arts of embellishment, whereas the *petit patron* who rented a machine was merely trying to meet a pressured production schedule for a multitude of the same items (Du Maroussem, *La Question ouvrière,* 2:196–200, 59–69, 208–222).

52. Ibid., 2:242–243, 263. See also Weissbach, "Artisanal Response," pp. 67–83.

53. Du Maroussem, *La Question ouvrière,* 2:262.

54. Roger Marx, *L'Art social* (Paris: Fasquelle, 1913), p. 52.

Chapter Four

1. Georges Valbert, "L'Age des machines," *Revue des deux mondes* 93 (1889): 667.

2. Karen Offen, "Depopulation, Nationalism, and Feminism in Fin-de-Siècle France," *American Historical Review* 89 (1984): 654.

3. Ibid., p. 655.

4. "Les Femmes et les féministes," special issue of *La Revue encyclopédique* no. 168 (November 28, 1896): 825–895, 910–913; Jean Rabaut, *Histoire des féminismes français* (Paris: Stock, 1978), pp. 207–242.

5. Rabaut, *Histoire des féminismes français,* pp. 207–242; Steven C. Hause and Anne R. Kenney, "The Limits of Suffragist Behavior: Legalism and Militancy in France, 1876–1922," *American Historical Review* 86 (1981): 781–788, 793–799, 801–806.

6. Offen, "Depopulation, Nationalism, and Feminism," p. 654; see also Offen, "The Second Sex and the Baccalauréat in Republican France, 1880–1924," *French Historical Studies* 13 (1983): 252–296.

7. Offen, "Depopulation, Nationalism, and Feminism," pp. 667–673; Hause and Kenney, "The Limits of Suffragist Behavior," pp. 781–806.

8. Maria Chéliga, "L'Evolution du féminisme," *La Revue encyclopédique* no. 168 (November 28, 1896): 825; Rabaut, *Histoire des féminismes français,* pp. 207–242.

9. Chéliga, "L'Evolution du féminisme," p. 912; Rabaut, *Histoire des féminismes français,* pp. 207–242; Offen, "Depopulation, Nationalism, and Feminism," pp. 648–676.

10. Pierre Sorlin, *Waldeck-Rousseau,* (Paris: Colin, 1966), pp. 358–362; Rabaut, *Histoire des féminismes français,* p. 190. The exaggerated fear of feminism and the conflation of feminism and socialism among conservative social theorists are explored by Susanna Barrows in *Distorting Mirrors: Visions of the Crowd in Late Nineteenth-Century France* (New Haven, Conn.: Yale University Press, 1981), pp. 43–60, 149, 165.

11. Sée, quoted in Rabaut, *Histoire des féminismes français,* pp. 182–183.

12. Ibid. See also Offen, "The Second Sex," pp. 252–261.

13. Offen, "The Second Sex," p. 261.

14. Barrows, *Distorting Mirrors,* pp. 55–56.

15. Françoise Mayeur, *L'Enseignement secondaire des jeunes filles sous la IIIe République* (Paris: Presses de la Fondation nationale des sciences politiques, 1977), pp. 9–69, 106–149, 151–171, 439–444, and *L'Education des filles en France au XIXe siècle* (Paris: Hachette, 1979), pp. 138–168; Barrows, *Distorting Mirrors,* pp. 54–55.

16. Armand Lanoux, *Amours 1900* (Paris: Hachette, 1961), pp. 106–123, 133–140; Rabaut, *Histoire des féminismes français,* pp. 182–183, 240.

17. Jean Mayeur, *Les Débuts de la IIIe République, 1871–1898* (Paris: Seuil, 1973), pp. 55–56; Richard D. Mandel, *Paris 1900: The Great World's Fair* (Toronto: University of Toronto Press, 1967), p. 28.

18. Alexander Sedgwick, *The Third French Republic, 1870–1914* (New York: Thomas Y. Crowell, 1968), p. 22.

19. Quoted in Mandel. *Paris 1900,* p. 145.

20. "F," "La Femme nouvelle," *La Revue* 18 (1896): 125.

21. Works defending female domesticity and maternity in the 1890s include Alfred Fouil-lée, "La Psychologie des sexes et ses fondements physiologiques," *Revue des deux mondes* 119 (1893): 397–429; H. Thulié, *La Femme au XXe siècle* (Paris: Calmann-Lévy, 1892); Octave Uzanne, *La Femme à Paris, nos contemporaines* (Paris: Quantin, 1894), pp. 153–159.

22. The *Revue des deux mondes* ran a series beginning in 1889, that surveyed the condition of women in different countries to gauge the universality of female destiny in the home. The first of these articles argued that even in America, the *"nouveau monde"* par excellence, the sexual division of labor was preeminent. See M. C. de Varigny, "La Femme aux Etats-Unis: L'Amour et le mariage," *Revue des deux mondes* 92 (1889): 350–375, and 93 (1889): 432–464. The avant-garde journal *La Plume* devoted its issue of September 15, 1895, to "Le Féminisme et le bon sens," an attack on the *femme nouvelle.*

23. In 1890, the journal *La Revue* initiated a separate rubric in its synoptic tables for *Le Féminisme,* articles relating to the *femme nouvelle* controversies. These are listed exhaustively in the *Table générale des travaux publiés par les revues, 1890–1902* (Paris: Bureau de la Revue, 1902), pp. 122–136. Among these articles were Paul Margueritte and Victor Margueritte, "Mariage et divorce: Enquête," *La Revue* 35 (1900): 449–462, and 36 (1901): 485–497; and Jules Simon, "Il faut rester femme," *La Revue* 18 (1896): 135–141. In 1896, *La Revue encyclopédique* devoted an entire issue to discussions, pro and con, of feminism, the *femme nouvelle,* divorce, and women's education: "Les Femmes et les féministes," *La Revue encyclopédique* no. 168 (November 28, 1896): 825–923.

24. Women cyclists wore *culottes,* short pants that defied fashion codes for female dress. Posters of the period show a woman cyclist in culottes raising her bicycle with muscular arms, as bewildered male spectators observe her. Cartoons in *Le Charivari* show policemen harassing women cyclists for wearing pants. See Paul Ducatel, *La Belle Époque, 1891–1910: Vue à travers l'imagerie populaire et la presse satirique* (Paris: Grassin, 1973), 3:38.

25. Alfred Robida, *Le XXe siècle: La Vie électrique* (Paris: Librairie illustrée, 1893).

26. Georges Valbert, "L'Age des machines," 686–697.

27. Camille Mauclair, "La Femme devant les peintres modernes," *La Nouvelle Revue,* 2d ser., 1 (1899): 190–213.

28. Ibid., pp. 212–213.

29. Marius-Ary Leblond, "Les Peintres de la femme nouvelle," *La Revue* 39 (1901): 275–276, 289–290.

30. Ibid., pp. 278, 283.

31. Ibid., p. 285.

32. Uzanne divided his time between writing books about the eighteenth-century traditions of feminine display and promoting Symbolist aestheticism. He sponsored a club and journal for modern bibliophiles, where he celebrated the cult of artifice and withdrawal into a world of refined "art for art's sake." He delineated these ideas, mingling eighteenth-century traditions of collecting with nineteenth-century goals of self-fashioning, in *L'Art et l'idée: Revue contemporaine du dilettantisme littéraire et de la curiosité,* publiée par Octave Uzanne, 2 vols., 1891–1892, esp. 1:1–3.

33. Octave Uzanne, *La Femme à Paris, nos contemporaines,* pp. 8–9, 12–13.

34. Ibid., pp. 153–178.

35. Ibid., pp. 9, 319, 320–321.

36. Quoted in "Causerie littéraire: M. Octave Uzanne," *La Grande Dame* 1 (1893): 61–62.

37. Octave Uzanne, "Le Paravent," *La Grande Dame* 1 (1893): 177–178.

38. Octave Uzanne, "Coquetteries féminines," *La Grande Dame* 1 (1893): 75, and "Le Paravent," p. 178.

39. Octave Uzanne, "Le Paravent," p. 181 and "Causerie littéraire," p. 62.

40. Octave Uzanne, "Coquetteries féminines," pp. 75–76, 77–78.

41. John Rewald, *Post-Impressionism from Van Gogh to Gauguin,* 2d ed. (Garden City, N.Y.: Doubleday, 1962), pp. 98–148; Eugenia Herbert, *The Artist and Social Reform: France and Belgium, 1885–1898* (New Haven, Conn.: Yale University Press, 1961), pp. 59–179.

42. *La Plume,* numéro spéciale, *L'Aristocratie* no. 124, (June 15–30, 1894): 246–262; Rémy de Gourmont, "Sur la hiérarchie intellectuelle," *La Plume* no. 124, (June 15–30, 1894): 251–254.

43. Victor Jozé, "Le Féminisme et le bon sens," *La Plume* no. 154, (September 15–30, 1895): 391–392.

44. Ibid.

45. On the virulent antifeminism of Tarde and Le Bon, see Barrows, *Distorting Mirrors,* pp. 43–193. My analysis of republican responses to the "woman question" in the 1890s has benefited from Karen Offen's recent articles "Depopulation, Nationalism, and Feminism" and "The Second Sex."

46. R. S., "Jules Simon," *La Grande Encyclopédie,* 30:46–47; Jules Simon, "Il faut rester femme"; *La Revue de famille,* edited by Simon, 1888–1893; "Jules Simon: *La Femme au XXe siècle,*" *L'Illustration* no. 2542 (November 14, 1891): p. 396; Philip A. Bertocci, *Jules Simon: Republican Anticlericalism and Cultural Politics in France, 1848–1886* (Columbia: University of Missouri Press, 1978).

47. Jules Simon, "Il faut rester femme," pp. 134–137, 140–141.

48. Offen, "The Second Sex," p. 258.

49. Offen, "Depopulation, Nationalism, and Feminism," pp. 657–667; Alfred Fouillée, "La Psychologie des sexes et ses fondaments physiologiques," pp. 327–429.

Chapter Five

1. Georges Valbert, "L'Age des Machines," *Revue des deux mondes* 93 (1889): 692–693, 694, 696–697.

2. Jules Héricourt, "L'Activité inconsciente de l'esprit," *Revue scientifique* 44 (1889): 257–268; quoted in Henri F. Ellenberger, *The Discovery of the Unconscious: The History and Evolution of Dynamic Psychiatry* (New York: Basic Books, 1970), pp. 314–315.

3. Ellenberger, *Discovery of the Unconscious,* pp. 759, 340.

4. The writings of Pierre Janet were particularly important in establishing this consensus. See the discussion in Ellenberger, *Discovery of the Unconscious,* pp. 358–374, and Janet's influential early works, "Les Actes inconscients et le dédoublement de la personnalité pendant le somnambulisme provoqué," *Revue philosophique* 22 (1886): 577–592, and *L'Automatisme psychologique* (Paris: Alcan, 1889).

5. Quoted in Ellenberger, *Discovery of the Unconscious,* pp. 314–315.

6. The term used by H. Stuart Hughes, *Consciousness and Society: The Reorientation of European Social Thought, 1890–1930* (New York: Vintage Books, 1958), p. 33.

7. I have drawn my discussion of the Symbolists' formal innovations and their inversion of reality from the surface to the depths from the writings of Edward Engelberg, *The Symbolist Poem* (New York: Dutton, 1967), pp. 17–46; C. M. Bowra, *The Heritage of Symbolism* (New York: Macmillan, 1947), pp. 2–12; Edmund Wilson, *Axel's Castle* (New York: Scribner, 1931), pp. 8–27; Eugenia Herbert, *The Artist and Social Reform: France and Belgium, 1885–1898* (New Haven, Conn.: Yale University Press, 1961), pp. 59–86; John Rewald, *Post-Impressionism from Van Gogh to Gauguin,* 2d ed. (Garden City, N.Y.: Doubleday, 1962), pp. 142–158; Robert Goldwater, "Symbolic Form: Symbolic Content," in *Problems of the Nineteenth and Twentieth Centuries, Studies in Western Art, Acts of the International Congress of the*

History of Art 4 (1963): 111–121. Kahn's Manifesto, which I quote here, is reprinted in Rewald, *Post-Impressionism,* pp. 134–135.

8. Letter from Huysmans to Edmond de Goncourt, cited in Bibliothèque Nationale, *Joris-Karl Huysmans: Du naturalisme au satanisme et à Dieu,* Catalogue de l'exposition (Paris: Bibliothèque Nationale, 1979), p. 33. Huysmans was a regular member of Edmond's weekly salons. See Edmond de Goncourt and Jules de Goncourt, *Journal, Mémoires de la vie littéraire* (Paris: Fasquelle & Flammarion, 1956), 3:111, 142–143, 163, 345, 354–355, 452, 732; 4:37, 61–62, 73, 464, 467, 553, 693, 902 (hereafter cited as *Journal des Goncourts*). Other essential information on the relation of Huysmans to Edmond de Goncourt is contained in the Bibliothèque Nationale catalogue noted above, pp. 30–33, 131–137.

9. De Montesquiou's visits to the Goncourts are described in the *Journal des Goncourts,* 3:179, 357, 603, 1189–1190; 4:115–117, 249–251, 275–279, 380–381, 580–581, 594–597, 756, 800–810, 900, 1010. De Montesquiou wrote volumes of Symbolist poetry in the 1890s, executed in the new free verse, among them *Les Chauves-souris* (1893), *Les Hortensias bleus* (1896), and *Le Chef des odeurs suaves* (1893). Many of the poems in these volumes recorded personal visions stimulated by objets d'art and interior space. De Montesquiou dedicated some of the poems to Edmond de Goncourt, testifying to his discovery of a new union between the literary cult of artifice and the aesthetic coordination of private space.

The manuscript collection of the Bibliothèque Nationale has a remarkable archive of all of de Montesquiou's interior design plans, instructions, and written intentions under *Comte Robert de Montesquiou-Fezensac: Sa vie et ses demeures,* Mss. n.a. fr. 15037–15380. See especially the photographs in "L'Appartement de Robert de Montesquiou, Le Quai d'Orsay" (Ms. 15037), and "L'Appartement de Robert de Montesquiou, La rue Franklin" (Mss. 15038–15039). Drawings, collages, pastels, chinoiseries, furniture designs, and designs for applied art objects are also assembled: "Documents iconographiques" (Mss. n.a. fr. 15349–15380).

10. De Montesquiou's conception of the interior as evocative psychological form emerges most clearly in his essay "Le Mobilier libre," in *Roseaux pensants* (Paris: Charpentier, 1897), pp. 159, 163–164, 165–166.

11. Throughout *Remembrance of Things Past,* Proust articulated a new definition of interior space, not as a characteristic of historical eras but as an index of personal memories. The following passages from *Within a Budding Grove* (New York: Vintage Books, 1970) illustrate:

> Our frail self is the one habitable place, the sole means of realization. . . . That composite, heterogeneous room has kept in my memory a cohesion, a unity, an individual charm . . . alive and stamped with the imprint of a living personality; for we alone can, by our belief that they have an existence of their own, give to certain of the things we see a soul that they afterwards keep, which they develop in our minds. . . . The things in my room . . . were merely extensions of myself. (pp. 83, 178, 237)

Proust's conception of the equivalence between interior space and the psychological interior flowed directly from the two elements of the inner world discovered by the Goncourts, which marked the specifically French version of Proust's "plumbing the depths of the individual personality": first, the self as a chamber of febrile nerves and, second, the taxing, visual force of objects in a room. The interaction between the nervous mechanism of the self, the room as an extension of the self, and the objects in the room as animating forces converged in Proust's discussion of moving from Paris to Balbec in *Within a Budding Grove,* pp. 178–182.

12. Edmond de Goncourt, *La Maison d'un artiste* (Paris: Charpentier, nouvelle ed., 1904; first published 1881), 2:202–204.

13. Proust, *Swann's Way* (New York: Vintage Books, 1970), pp. 10, 240; *Within a Budding Grove,* pp. 83, 178.

14. Alfred Fouillée used the term in "Les Grandes Conclusions de la psychologie contemporaine—la conscience et ses transformations," *Revue des deux mondes* 107 (1891): 814.

15. Huysmans explicitly acknowledged Axenfeld's book as a source. Des Esseintes is presented as a victim of neurosis, which Huysmans studied scrupulously in the medical text: "Je me suis gêné, tout au long du livre, à être parfaitement exact. J'ai pas à pas suivi les livres de Bouchut et d'Axenfeld sur la névrose." Huysmans later called his book *A rebours* "mon hobereau névrosé." Both statements are cited in Bibliothèque Nationale, *Joris-Karl Huysmans,* pp. 32–33.

16. The first exploration of the affinities between Symbolist theory and psychological research was Filiz Eda Burhan, "Vision and Visionaries: Nineteenth-Century Psychological Theory, the Occult Sciences, and the Formation of the Symbolist Aesthetic in France," Ph.D. diss., Princeton University, 1979. Burhan concentrated on the connections between idealist philosophy, psychology, and the emerging abstract ideas of the Nabis painters Emile Bernard, Paul Gauguin, Maurice Denis, and Paul Sérusier and their critical defenders Charles Morice, Albert Aurier, and Téodor de Wyzewa.

17. The words are those of Jules Bois, "Les Guérisons par la pensée," *La Revue* 35 (1900): 29:

> Dans nos chambres mentales il n'y a pas seulement des locataires honorables et de bonne compagnie, mais aussi des visiteurs étranges, . . . des impressions troublées et morbides; ils passent sur le théâtre intérieur qu'est le cerveau, comme des fântomes dans les maisons hantées. Les plus forts ont connu ces étranges malfaisants et des envahisseurs.

18. Georges Guillain, *J.-M. Charcot: His Life, His Work* [1955], trans. Pearce Bailey (New York: Paul Hoeber, 1959). See also Jan Goldstein, "The Hysteria Diagnosis and the Politics of Anticlericalism in Late Nineteenth-Century France," *Journal of Modern History* 54 (1982): 222–235, on the role of triumphalist, opportunist republicanism as the precondition for Charcot's selection and success.

19. Guillain, *J.-M. Charcot,* pp. 97–132, esp. 118–125. A popular discussion of some of the therapeutic techniques appeared in *L'Illustration* no. 2404 (March 23, 1889): 231.

20. Quoted in "Souvenirs des Goncourts," *La Revue encyclopédique* no. 153 (August 8, 1896): 546.

21. Quoted in "Souvenirs des Goncourts," p. 552.

22. On the application of medical ideas to national problems, see Robert A. Nye, *Crime, Madness, and Politics in Modern France: The Medical Model of National Decline* (Princeton, N.J.: Princeton University Press, 1984). Nye's study emphasizes the medicalization of social policy and criminology in the fin de siècle. He includes a compelling and original discussion of the role of neurasthenia in the development of Emile Durkheim's social theory. I limit my own discussion to noting the widespread contemporary linkage of neurasthenia to the city as Charcot and his followers publicized the ideas and affected a new cultural understanding of interiorization.

23. George Frederick Drinka, *The Birth of Neurosis: Myth, Malady, and the Victorians* (New York: Simon & Schuster, 1984), pp. 184–197, 210–217. Drinka, noting the Catholic legacy of original sin, proposes that different religious traditions account for this difference in American and French attitudes toward neurasthenia. I believe there are broader political and cultural reasons for this difference as well.

24. Max Nordau cites a series of articles by Richet called "Dans cent ans," in his *Degeneration* (1895; reprint New York: Howard Fertig, 1968), pp. 38–39.

25. Charles Richet, *Le Surmenage mental dans la civilisation moderne* (Paris: Alcan, 1890).

26. Fernand Levillain, *La Neurasthénie,* avec une préface du Professeur Charcot (Paris: A. Maloire, 1891).

27. Ibid., pp. 17–36.

28. J. Rengade, "Le Nouveau Traitement de l'ataxie à la Salpêtrière," *L'Illustration* no. 2204 (March 23, 1889): 231–232.

29. *La Grande Dame* interspersed discussions of "Névroses féminines" and the "Névroses et couleurs" among columns devoted to "Couture," "L'Annuaire de châteaux," "Grands Mariages," "Portraits de grandes dames," and "Grandes Résidences." The new knowledge of nervous pathologies and urban *surmenagement* infiltrated this center of fashionable *mondanité*. See especially Doctor Foveau de Courmelles, "Ce que dit le Docteur—Névroses et couleurs," *La Grande Dame* 4 (1896), supplément, pp. 9, 11.

30. Octave Uzanne, *La Femme à Paris, nos contemporaines* (Paris: Quantin, 1894), pp. 6, 9.

31. Charles Ténib, "Psychologie," *La Plume* no. 130 (September 15, 1894): 369–370. In that same journal a second writer, Adolphe Retté, expressed in an article entitled "Floréal" the nervous overtaxing of urban life: "La sottise urbaine, certains jours, distille un si mordant vinaigre sur les nerfs agacés, . . . qu'on rêve . . . d'oases perdues, . . . loin . . . de la civilisation parisienne" (no. 123 [June 1, 1894]: 229).

32. Doctor de Fleury, "La Tristesse et son traitement," *La Revue* 18 (1896): 422. An astonishing number and range of articles relating to the psychology and neurology of urban degeneration and *surmenagement* are registered in the useful index of periodicals compiled by *La Revue: Table générale des travaux publiés par les revues, 1890–1902* (Paris: Bureau de la Revue, 1902), s.v. "Psychologie." This index covers the period from 1888 to 1901.

33. See, for example, the many articles by Alfred Fouillée, including "Dégénérescence: Le Passé et le présent de notre race," *Revue des deux mondes* 131 (1895): 793–824, and "Psychologie de l'esprit français," *Revue des deux mondes* 138 (1896): 58–88. See also Robert Nye, *Crime, Madness, and Politics,* pp. 132–265.

34. Nordau's psychopathology melded what he had learned from Charcot with the theories of Doctor Cesare Lombroso, the Turin psychologist who formulated the relations between nervous degeneration and criminality. Information on Nordau's biography and motives may be found in George Mosse's introduction to Nordau's *Degeneration,* pp. xv–xxiv, and in Drinka, *Birth of Neurosis,* pp. 243–258.

35. Raymond Rudorff, *The Belle Epoque: Paris in the Nineties* (New York: Saturday Review Press, 1972), p. 206.

36. Nordau, *Degeneration,* pp. 15–16.

37. Ibid., pp. 3, 20.

38. Ibid., especially pp. 35–37, 39, 42.

39. Ibid., pp. 42–43.

40. Fouillée, "Dégénérescence," pp. 812, 815, 818–819.

41. Guillain, *J.-M. Charcot,* pp. 133–146, 165–169; Goldstein, "Hysteria Diagnosis," pp. 214–220.

42. Guillain, *J.-M. Charcot,* pp. 133–146, 165–169; Goldstein, "Hysteria Diagnosis," pp. 214–220; Susanna Barrows, *Distorting Mirrors: Visions of the Crowd in Late Nineteenth-Century France* (New Haven, Conn.: Yale University Press, 1981), p. 121. In my own research on Charcot and hypnotism, I found two contemporary sources particularly illuminating: E. Boirac, "La Suggestion," *La Grande Encyclopédie* (Paris: Lamirault, 1902), 30:662–664; and Alfred Binet, "Le Problème hypnotique," in *Etudes de psychologie expérimentale* (Paris: Doin, 1888), pp. 279–298.

43. See the Charcot lecture cited in Ellenberger, *Discovery of the Unconscious,* p. 149; and Binet, "Le Problème hypnotique," p. 281. A good description of the stages of hysterical hypnosis may be found in Boirac, "La Suggestion," pp. 662–664.

44. Georges Guignon and Sophie Woltke, "De l'influence des excitations sensitives et sensorielles dans les phases cataleptique et somnambulique du grand hypnotisme," *Nouvelle Iconographie de la Salpêtrière* 4 (1891): 78, 81.

45. The Symbolists' quest for a direct emotional response to visual form is described in

Rewald, *Post-Impressionism,* pp. 148–188, and, in the artists' own words, in *Impressionism and Post-Impressionism: Sources and Documents, 1874–1904,* ed. Linda Nochlin (Englewood Cliffs, N.J.: Prentice-Hall, 1966), pp. 107–203. I discuss the psychophysical basis of color response embraced by the Neo-Impressionists in my unpublished MS "The Quest for Harmony: Neo-Impressionism and Anarchism in France, 1885–1900," pt. 1, chap. 2.

46. Jean-Martin Charcot and Paul Richer, *Les Démoniaques dans l'art* (Paris: Delahaye & Lecrosnier, 1887), p. 92.

47. Guinon and Woltke, "De l'influence des excitations sensitives," p. 87. Elsewhere in the essay the authors describe such imagistic projection as "les tableaux qui défilent devant les yeux du malade" (p. 79).

48. Charcot and Richer, *Les Démoniaques dans l'art,* pp. 92, 102.

49. In my discussion of Bernheim and Liébault I draw upon Jean Vartier, *Histoire de notre Lorraine* (Paris: Editions France-Empire, 1973), pp. 336–345. For other accounts, see Ellenberger, *Discovery of the Unconscious,* pp. 85–89; Barrows, *Distorting Mirrors,* p. 120; and Drinka, *Birth of Neurosis,* pp. 138–143.

50. Boirac, "La Suggestion," pp. 662–663; Hippolyte Bernheim, *De la suggestion dans l'état hypnotique et dans l'état de veille* (Paris: Doin, 1884).

51. Vartier, *Histoire de notre Lorraine,* pp. 341–342. Vartier recounts Bernheim's discovery that patients acted upon suggestion over a month after their sessions with him.

52. Quoted in Vartier, *Histoire de notre Lorraine,* p. 343.

53. Hippolyte Bernheim, *De la suggestion dans l'état hypnotique, Response à Paul Janet* (Paris: Doin, 1884), pp. 5–6, 7, 10, 14.

54. Quoted in Vartier, *Histoire de notre Lorraine,* p. 343.

55. Hippolyte Bernheim, *De la suggestion dans l'état hypnotique et dans l'état de veille* (Paris: Doin, 1884), pp. 89–90.

56. Hippolyte Bernheim, *Suggestive Therapeutics: A Treatise on the Nature and Uses of Hypnotism* [1884], trans. Christian Herter, M.D. (New York: Putnam, 1887), pp. 28, 125, 129, 130, 137–139, 184. Henri Ellenberger first identified the importance of ideodynamism in the work of Charcot, Liébault, and Bernheim in *Discovery of the Unconscious,* esp. pp. 148–151, 760.

57. Bernheim, *Suggestive Therapeutics,* pp. 96, 99, 100, 103. The entire discussion, from pp. 95–104, is fascinating.

58. Ibid., pp. 103–104.

59. Ibid., p. x.

60. Ibid., p. 125.

61. The words are those of Charcot's associate Paul Richer, *Etudes cliniques sur la grande hystérie ou hystéro-épilepsie* (Paris: Delahaye & Lecrosnier, 1881), p. 730.

62. Bernheim, *Suggestive Therapeutics,* pp. 183–184.

63. Ellenberger, *Discovery of the Unconscious,* pp. 758, 163; Barrows, *Distorting Mirrors,* p. 123.

64. Tribute to Charcot by the Symbolist critic Téodor de Wyzewa, published in *Le Figaro* in 1893, quoted in Ellenberger, *Discovery of the Unconscious,* p. 99. Ellenberger's book contains an encyclopedic list of the literary works inspired by the Charcot-Bernheim hypnosis debates, though he does not discuss any in detail (pp. 99–100, 164–167, 758–759). His book offers a point of departure for more analytic treatments of the artistic community's selective assimilation of the lessons of the Salpêtrière. Essential information about the Salpêtrière audience, its literary representatives, and Charcot's influence on literature may be found in Guillain, *J.-M. Charcot,* pp. 174–175; Axel Munthe, *The Story of San Michele* (New York: Dutton, 1930), pp. 296–322; A. de Monzie, "Eloge de Charcot," *Revue neurologique* 1, no. 6 (1925): 1159–1162; Elisabeth Roudinesco, *La Bataille de cent ans: Histoire de la psychanalyse en France,* vol. 1,

1885–1939 (Paris: Ramsay, 1982), esp. pp. 51–86; and J. L. Signoret, "Variété historique: 'Une Leçon clinique à la Salpêtrière (1887)' par André Brouillet," *Revue neurologique* 139 (1983): 687–701.

65. Cited in Ellenberger, *Discovery of the Unconscious,* p. 165; see also Roudinesco's discussion of de Maupassant, *La Bataille,* pp. 76–84. Guilain prints a letter written by Charcot's friend and traveling companion of 1893, René Vallery-Radot, documenting Charcot's reaction to de Maupassant's psychiatrically inspired stories (*Charcot,* p. 72); Charcot called them "the work of a sick man."

66. Ellenberger, *Discovery of the Unconscious,* pp. 165–166. Other examples of the incorporation of Charcotian ideas into literary works are noted in De Monzie, "Eloge de Charcot," pp. 1159–1162; Signoret, "Une Leçon à la Salpêtrière," pp. 697–701; and Barrows, *Distorting Mirrors,* p. 122.

67. Charles Epheyre, "Soeur Marthe," *Revue des deux mondes* 93 (1889): 384–431. Richet wrote a novel, *Possession* (1887), under the same pseudonym, evoking the horrors of a suicide committed by a character with a somnambulic double personality.

68. Binet and de Lorde called their project *le théâtre épouvante* and *le théâtre de la peur.* Their best-known production was an exposé of Charcot's despotic practices, *Une Leçon à la Salpêtrière,* which was performed at the Grand Guignol in 1908. The play represented the women patients, in alliance with the young medical interns, rebelling against the master doctor. De Lorde's psychiatric play *La Dormeuse* was performed at the Théâtre de l'Odéon in February 1901, and his *L'Homme mystérieux* at the Théâtre Sarah Bernhardt in November 1910. The only scholar, to my knowledge, who has mentioned the expression by the clinicians Binet and Richet of new neuropsychiatric themes in literary and theatrical representations is Jacqueline Carroy-Thirard, "Hystérie, théâtre, littérature au XIXe siècle," *Psychanalyse à l'université* 7 (1982): 299–317. Particularly suggestive for future study are the themes of oedipal rebellion and secret identities: these successful colleagues of Charcot's may have chosen to explore in literature some of the perplexing implications of the new discoveries of the mind that were excluded from the domain of medical practice. Binet's theatrical work is powered by anger and terror, and his portrait of Charcot in the *Leçon* play is devastating. This play should be compared with the literary attack on Charcot published earlier by a medical student "defector," Léon Daudet, *Les Morticoles* (1894). On Daudet, see Toby Gelfand, "Medical Nemesis, Paris, 1894: Léon Daudet's 'Les Morticoles,'" *Bulletin of the History of Medicine* 60 (1986): 155–176.

69. Alfred Robida, *Le XIXe Siècle* (Paris: Decaux, 1888), pp. 159–174. The story involved a mischievous nephew, who took revenge on his aging stingy uncle by hypnotizing him. Once the uncle was in the state of somnambulic receptivity, the nephew was able to ask him about his indolent youth. The uncle remembered nothing upon waking from his "nap."

70. Paul Bonnetain, "Maternité," *L'Illustration* no. 2397 (February 2, 1889): 94–95.

71. Caran D'Ache, "Nouveautés pour étrennes: Revue comique de 1889," *L'Illustration* no. 2440 (November 30, 1889): 473–476.

72. From an article by Philippe Daryl, "La Suggestion et la personnalité humaine," *Le Temps* no. 8970 (November 21, 1885): 3, cited in Robert G. Hillman, "A Scientific Study of Mystery: The Role of the Medical and Popular Press in the Nancy-Salpêtrière Controversy on Hypnotism," *Bulletin of the History of Medicine* 39 (1965): 163–182. Hillman notes how the ideas of the new psychiatry were spread by the press. The index of the middle-brow journal *La Revue,* not used by Hillman, also illustrates the diffusion of ideas, listing hundreds of articles devoted to hypnosis, suggestion, and dreams between 1888 and 1902. See *Table générale des travaux publiés par les revues, 1880–1902,* under "Psychologie."

73. James Joll refers in passing to the link between Bergson and neuropsychiatry in *Europe since 1870: An International History* (New York: Harper & Row, 1973). Henri Ellenberger also

mentions Bergson's involvement with mental medicine, specifying his knowledge of local hypnotists and hypnosis. Close examination of Bergson's writings does indeed indicate that his theories of fluidity and imagistic thought processes were informed by the new psychiatric research. Ellenberger also discovered that Bergson wrote an early article on the mechanism of hypnosis and an interior visual language: "De la simulation inconsciente dans l'état d'hypno-tisme," *Revue philosophique* 22 (1886): 525–531. Only more research can establish the precise impact of neuropsychiatry on Bergson's conceptions of the irrational, of creativity, and of the unconscious. I have attempted a beginning here.

74. Bergson uses the term *imprinting* in his *Essai sur les données immédiates de la conscience* [1889], 8th ed. (Paris: Alcan, 1911), p. 12.

75. Ibid., pp. 11–14.

76. Ibid., esp. pp. 11–12, 14.

77. Ibid., pp. 13–14.

78. Ibid., pp. 11–14.

79. Fouillée reported on the discoveries and debates of the new psychology every month after 1883. His many articles devoted to psychology are enumerated in the *Revue des deux mondes: Table générale* (Paris: Bureaux des deux mondes, 1904), vols. 1–3, 1883–1904.

80. Alfred Fouillée, "Le Physique et le mental à propos de l'hypnotisme," *Revue des deux mondes* 105 (1891): 429–461; "Les Grandes Conclusions de la psychologie contemporaine—la conscience et ses transformations," *Revue des deux mondes* 107 (1891): 788–816.

81. Fouillée, "Les Grandes Conclusions," p. 815.

82. Fouillée, "Le Physique et le mental," pp. 433–434.

83. Ibid., pp. 431, 461.

84. Fouillée, "Les Grandes Conclusions," pp. 798–799.

85. Ibid., p. 798. Fouillée uses the same language and image of subterranean psychic theater in "Le Physique et le mental," p. 440.

86. Fouillée, "Le Physique et le mental," p. 446; see also 431.

87. Ibid., p. 445: "Les phénomènes hypnotiques prouvent précisément que des images toutes cérébrales peuvent être projetées sous forme d'objets réels."

88. Ibid., pp. 431, 442.

89. "Nothing is worse for a people than the autosuggestion of its own disintegration. By repeating to itself that it is going to fall, a people makes itself dizzy and induces the fall" (Al-fred Fouillée, "Dégénérescence," pp. 793, 795).

90. Fouillée, "Les Grandes Conclusions," pp. 811–813.

91. Ibid., p. 814.

92. Ibid., p. 816.

93. Ibid., pp. 814–815.

94. Ibid., p. 815.

95. Ibid. Fouillée was only one of many political and social thinkers to be directly influ-enced by the new psychology. Books by both Susanna Barrows and Robert Nye isolate the way that antirepublican theorists, in particular Gustave Le Bon, channeled medical suggest-ibility into a new doctrine of the crowd. See Barrows, *Distorting Mirrors,* and Robert A. Nye, *The Origins of Crowd Psychology: Gustave Le Bon and the Crisis of Mass Democracy in the Third Republic* (London: Sage, 1975). I have concentrated on Fouillée because I am most concerned with the way that republicans incorporated the new irrationalism into their doctrine of liber-alism, which paralleled the similar efforts of visual and decorative artists sponsored by the state.

96. A. Souques, "Charcot intime," *La Presse médicale* no. 42 (May 27, 1925): 697.

97. The discussion that follows is based on an extraordinary contemporary account of the role of art in Charcot's medical and personal activities: Henri Meige, *Charcot-artiste* (Paris:

Masson, 1925); and Gustave Goetschy, "Les Femmes du monde artistes—Madame Charcot," *Revue des arts décoratifs* 20 (1900): 41–51. Meige was a student of Charcot's and later professor at the Ecole des Beaux-Arts. According to Charcot's biographer Guillain (*J.-M. Charcot,* p. 21), Meige's text was originally written "several years after Charcot's death" in 1893. The 1925 published version that I consulted is available at the Paris Bibliothèque Nationale.

Another scholar has explored the role of the visual in Charcot's medicine, emphasizing issues different from those I explore here. See Georges Didi-Huberman, *L'Invention de l'hystérie: Charcot et l'iconographie photographique de la Salpêtrière* (Paris: Editions Macula, 1982), and his "Charcot, l'histoire, et l'art," postface to J.-M. Charcot and Paul Richer, *Les Démoniaques dans l'art, suivi de la 'Foi qui guérit,'* ed. Pierre Fédida and Georges Didi-Huberman (Paris: Editions Macula, 1984), pp. 125–182. This essay appeared after my own chapter had been drafted.

98. Meige, *Charcot-artiste,* pp. 7–9.

99. Ibid., pp. 8–9.

100. Recounted in Meige, *Charcot-artiste,* p. 8.

101. Ibid., pp. 7, 15. Scuques states the same idea in "Charcot intime," p. 697.

102. *Sigmund Freud: His Life in Pictures and Words,* ed. Ernst Freud (New York: Harcourt Brace Jovanovich, 1978), pp. 114–124.

103. Meige, *Charcot-artiste,* pp. 10–15. See also the description of Charcot's teaching methods in Guillain, *J.-M. Charcot,* p. 55.

104. Paul Richer and J.-M. Charcot, "Note sur l'anatomie morphologique de la région lombaire: Sillon lombaire médian," in *Nouvelle Iconographie de la Salpêtrière* 1 (1888): 13, 14–15.

105. Cited in Ernst Freud, *Sigmund Freud,* p. 117:

He was not a reflective man, not a thinker: he had the nature of an artist—he was, as he himself said, a "*visuel,*" a man who sees. Here is what he himself told us about his method of working. He used to look again and again at the things he did not understand, to deepen his impression of them day by day, till suddenly an understanding of them dawned upon him. . . . He might be heard to say that the greatest satisfaction a man could have was to see something new—that is to recognize it as new; and he remarked again and again on the difficulty and value of this kind of "seeing."

See also the description of Charcot's clinical "visual scrutiny" by his students A. Souques and Henri Meige in Guillain, *J.-M.Charcot,* p. 52. William J. McGrath analyzes the impact of Charcot's visual focus on the development of Freud's "architecture of hysteria" in *Freud's Discovery of Psychoanalysis: The Politics of Hysteria* (Ithaca, N.Y.: Cornell University Press, 1986), esp. pp. 152–194. See also Roudinesco's apt contrast between the Charcotian eye and the Freudian ear in *La Bataille,* pp. 21–49.

106. Paul Richer, Giles de la Tourette, Albert Londe, "Avertissement," *Nouvelle Iconographie de la Salpêtrière* 1 (1888): ii. For another interpretation of the Salpêtrière iconographic practices, see Didi-Huberman, *L'Invention de l'hystérie.*

107. Meige, *Charcot-artiste,* pp. 13–14.

108. J.-M. Charcot and Paul Richer, "Le Mascaron grotesque de l'Eglise Santa Maria Formosa, à Venise, et l'hémispasme glosso-labie hystérique," *Nouvelle Iconographie de la Salpêtrière* 1 (1888): 87–88, 92.

109. J.-M. Charcot and Paul Richer, "Sur un lepreux d'Albrecht Dürer," *Nouvelle Iconographie de la Salpêtrière* 1 (1888): 43–44.

110. Charcot and Richer, *Les Démoniaques dans l'art,* pp. 91–105.

111. The term appears in Charcot and Richer, *Les Démoniaques dans l'art,* p. 102; the illustrated depictions of hysterical physical contortions are on pp. 91–105.

112. Goldstein, "Hysteria Diagnosis," pp. 209–239.

113. Meige describes the photographic laboratory, museum, sculpture studio, and Charcot's office in *Charcot-artiste,* pp. 11–15. See also the description of the office in Souques, "Charcot intime," p. 696.

114. J.-M. Charcot and Paul Richer, *Les Difformes et les malades dans l'art* (Paris: Lecrosnier & Babé, 1889), p. v.

115. Ibid., p. ii.

116. Ibid., p. v: "L'art n'a rien à redouter de ce contrôle qui, lorsqu'il est exercé par l'artiste lui-même sur ses propres oeuvres, devient une force nouvelle."

117. Souques, "Charcot intime," p. 694.

118. Guillain, *J.-M. Charcot,* p. 24.

119. From J.-M. Charcot, "Leçon d'ouverture," *Oeuvres completes,* vol. 3, cited in English in Guillain, *J.-M. Charcot,* p. 139 ([*sic*] in English text).

120. I am thinking here of such drawings as *The Deluge,* a striking contrast to da Vinci's meticulous scientific drawings of anatomy and machinery.

121. The words are those of Henry Meige, quoted in Guillain, *J.-M. Charcot,* p. 23.

122. Among the many contemporaries who likened Charcot to Napoléon—a self-styled resemblance arising from Charcot's own idolization of the man—were Léon Daudet, *Devant la douleur: Souvenirs des milieux littéraires, politiques, artistiques, et médicaux de 1880 à 1905* (Paris: Nouvelle librairie critique, 1915), p. 5; and Souques, "Charcot intime," p. 693.

123. Pierre Marie, "Discours prononcé à l'Académie de Médecine le 26 mai 1925, à l'occasion du centenaire de Charcot," *Revue neurologique* 1, no. 6 (1925): 731–745.

124. Daudet, *Devant la douleur,* pp. 13–14.

125. Meige, *Charcot-artiste,* pp. 11–12.

126. From the accounts of Souques and Meige, cited in Guillain, *J.-M. Charcot,* p. 5.

127. Meige, *Charcot-artiste,* quoted in English in Guillain, *J.-M. Charcot,* pp. 22–23. Didi-Huberman, who located the original drawing, discovered that some of the notes Charcot wrote on the drawing had been censored because of their explicitly sexual meanings ("Charcot, l'histoire, et l'art," pp. 178–180).

128. J.-M. Charcot, "Le Scotome scintillant," *Oeuvres complètes,* vol. 3, cited in Didi-Huberman, *L'Invention de l'hystérie,* appendix 15, p. 283; Charcot's drawing of the zigzag schema is on p. 132.

129. The words are those of Henry Meige, *Charcot-artiste,* pp. 17, 10.

130. See Guillain, *J.-M. Charcot,* pp. 12–13; Pierre de Roux, *L'Hôtel Amelot et l'Hôtel Varengeville, Faubourg Saint-Germain* (Paris: Bank of Algeria, 1947), pp. 5–44. The rococo architect Jacques Gabriel built the original residence in 1704 (de Roux, pp. 5–6).

131. On Charcot's salons, see Guillain, *J.-M. Charcot,* pp. 32–33; Roudinesco, *La Bataille,* p. 37; and Freud's account, in *The Letters of Sigmund Freud,* ed. Ernst Freud (New York: Basic Books, 1975), pp. 193–204.

132. Meige, *Charcot-artiste,* p. 23; Guillain, *J.-M. Charcot,* p. 22; Souques, "Charcot intime," p. 696.

133. *Letters of Sigmund Freud,* p. 194 (letter of January 20, 1886).

134. Meige, *Charcot-artiste,* pp. 20–21, 22.

135. Ibid., pp. 23–24; see also Souques, "Charcot intime," pp. 696–697; and Goetschy, "Madame Charcot," pp. 41–51.

136. Meige, *Charcot-artiste,* pp. 18, 20–23, 17.

137. Ibid., pp. 24–26.

138. Ibid., pp. 18, 20, 22.

139. Goetschy, "Madame Charcot," pp. 41, 42, 51.

140. Souques, "Charcot intime," p. 696; Guillain, *J.-M. Charcot,* p. 21.

141. See n. 134.

142. *Journal des Goncourts,* 3:932, March 8, 1889.

Chapter Six

1. Yolande Amic, "Les Débuts de l'U.C.A.D. et du Musée des Arts Décoratifs," *Cahiers de l'Union centrale des arts décoratifs* 1 (1978): 52. See also Victor Champier, *Catalogue illustré de l'Union centrale des arts décoratifs* (Paris: Librairie d'art L. Baschet, 1884), pp. 9–15.

2. Antonin Proust, *L'Art sous la République* (Paris: Charpentier, 1892), pp. 183–214.

3. Ibid.; see also Marius Vachon, *La Guerre artistique avec l'Allemagne: L'Organisation de la victoire* (Paris: Payot, 1916), pp. 153–154.

4. Proust, *L'Art sous la République,* pp. 212–214; Amic, "Les Débuts de l'U.C.A.D.," p. 52; *Dictionnaire universel du XIXe siècle,* IIe supplément, (Paris: Larousse, 1884), s.v. "Arts décoratifs," p. 355.

5. Victor Champier, "La Société de l'Union centrale des arts decoratifs: Son histoire, ses débuts, ses doctrines, l'influence qu'elle a exercée sur le goût public par ses concours et par ses expositions," *Revue des arts décoratifs* 4 (1883–1884) 74–75; Vachon, *La Guerre artistique,* p. 156.

6. Champier, "La Société de l'Union centrale," p. 72.

7. Quoted in Champier, *Catalogue illustré de l'Union centrale,* p. 12; see also Vachon, *La Guerre artistique,* p. 155, for full program quote, and the "Appel aux artistes" quoted in Amic, "Les Débuts de l'U.C.A.D.," p. 52.

8. Champier, *Catalogue illustré de l'Union centrale,* pp. 12–13.

9. Ibid., p. 13; Champier, "La Société de l'Union centrale," pp. 74–75.

10. Roger Marx, "La Renaissance des arts décoratifs," *Les Arts* 1 (January 1902): 36.

11. See, for example, the discussion of Charles Ephrussi and Gustave Dreyfus, in *Catalogue descriptif des dessins de décoration et d'ornement de maîtres anciens* (Paris: Chamerot, 1879), pp. ii–viii; and Emile Molinier, "Le Mobilier français au XVIIIe siècle dans les collections étrangères," *Les Arts* 1 (February 1902): 19–22.

12. Philippe de Chennevières, "Les Dessins du XVIIIe siècle de la collection des Goncourts," in *Collections des Goncourts: Dessins, aquarelles, et pastels du XVIIIe siècle, Catalogue du vente* (Paris: May & Metteroz, 1897), pp. xix–xxii. An excellent discussion of the "nouvelle génération des amateurs" that arose after 1850 is contained in Jules Guiffrey, "La Collection de M. Gustave Dreyfus," *Les Arts* 7 (January 1908): 4–8.

13. In *Collection Carle Dreyfus léguée aux Musées Nationaux au Musée des Arts Décoratifs* (Paris: Musées Nationaux, 1953), pp. iv, 26.

14. Victor Champier, *Catalogue illustré de l'Union centrale,* p. 14.

15. Victor Champier, "La Société de l'Union centrale," pp. 83–84.

16. Ibid., pp. 84–85.

17. *Dictionnaire universel du XIXe siècle,* s.v. "Arts décoratifs," p. 355.

18. Ibid.

19. Ibid.; see also Yolande Amic, "Les Débuts de l'U.C.A.D.," p. 52.

20. Amic, "Les Débuts de l'U.C.A.D.," p. 52.

21. Ibid., pp. 52–53.

22. The exposition's three catalogues reflected its three display sites: *Catalogue descriptif des dessins de décoration et d'ornement de maîtres anciens exposés à l'Ecole des Beaux-Arts, mai–juin 1879; Catalogue descriptif des dessins de décoration et d'ornement de maîtres anciens exposés au Musée des Arts*

Décoratifs en 1880 (Paris: Imprimerie de publications périodiques, 1880); *Le Musée du Louvre: Modèles d'art décoratif d'après les dessins originaux*, Notice par Victor Champier (Paris: Quantin, 1882).

23. De Chennevières, "Les Dessins du XVIIIe siècle," p. xxi.

24. Ibid.

25. De Chennevières, quoted in Champier, *Catalogue illustré de l'Union centrale*, p. 14.

26. See Victor Champier, "Charles-Philippe, Marquis de Chennevières-Pointel," *La Grande Encyclopédie* (Paris: Lamirault, c. 1897), 10:1077–1078; "Marquis Philippe de Chennevières" in Frits Lugt, *Les Marques de collections de dessin et d'estampes* (Amsterdam: Vereenigte Drukkerijen, 1921), pp. 382–383.

27. Lugt, *Marques de collections*, p. 383.

28. Edmond de Goncourt noted these royal applied arts in de Chennevières's collection in Edmond de Goncourt and Jules de Goncourt, *Journal, mémoires de la vie littéraire*, 4 vols. (Paris: Fasquelle & Flammarion, 1956), 1:249–250, entry for 16 June 1856 (hereafter cited as *Journal des Goncourts*).

29. "Marquis de Chennevières," in Lugt, *Marques de collections*, p. 383.

30. See the note on Edmond de Goncourt's participation in the commission and the list of other members in *Journal des Goncourts*, 2:1025–1026, 4 December 1874.

31. See Ministère de l'Instruction publique et des Beaux-Arts, *Inventaire générale des richesses d'art de la France*, vol. 2 (Paris: Plon, 1878), pp. 1–17.

32. In a circular reprinted at the beginning of the *Inventaire générale*, de Chennevières envisioned a national fraternity of "goût et savoir," composed of local "amateurs" (Paris: Plon, 1876), pp. ix–xii, xiii–xvi.

33. Ibid., p. xi.

34. "Marquis de Chennevières," in Lugt, *Marques de collections*, p. 384.

35. Ibid., p. 382.

36. Philippe de Chennevières, *préface* to Paul Ratouis de Limay, *Aignan-Thomas Désfriches, 1715–1800: Sa vie, son oeuvre, ses collections, sa correspondance* (Paris: Librairie H. Champion, 1907), pp. i–xxxiii.

37. Ibid., pp. iii–iv, xxiv–xxvi, 7–9, 38–39. Among the illustrious design practitioners in Désfriches's circle were the comte de Caylus, an honorary member of the Academy; Watelet, the receiver-general of finances for Orléans; Madame de Joli; the personal secretary to the prince de Condé; and the duc de Chabot, the nobleman who founded the *amateur* drawing school in the Faubourg Saint-Germain.

38. Ibid., pp. xxv–xxix.

39. Ibid., pp. vi–vii, xxv–xxviii. See also pp. 146–148, xx–xxi, where one of Désfriches's contemporary admirers says that his "dessins valent d'excellens tableaux."

40. Philippe de Chennevières, "Revue des arts décoratifs," *Revue des arts décoratifs* 1 (1880–1881): 3.

41. Philippe de Chennevières, introduction to *Catalogue descriptif des dessins de décoration et d'ornement de maîtres anciens exposés au Musée des Arts Décoratifs en 1880* (Paris: Imprimerie de publications périodiques, 1880), pp. v–vi, ix.

42. De Chennevières, "Les Dessins du XVIIIe siècle," p. xxi.

43. De Chennevières, introduction to *Catalogue descriptif*, p. i. See also de Chennevières, "Revue des arts décoratifs," pp. 1–4.

44. De Chennevières, introduction to *Catalogue descriptif*, pp. ii–iii, x; "Revue des arts décoratifs," p. 3.

45. De Chennevières, introduction to *Catalogue descriptif*, pp. viii–ix.

46. Ibid., p. x.

47. Ibid.

48. De Chennevières himself explained that he modeled his morning habits as an art conservator exactly on those of his aristocratic ancestors who served in the *parlements* (*préface* to de Limay, *Désfriches*, p. ii).

49. "Marquis de Chennevières," in Lugt, *Marques de collections*, pp. 382–383.

50. De Chennevières, "Les Dessins du XVIIIe siècle," p. xviii.

51. De Chennevières, cited in Lugt, *Marques de collections*, p. 384.

52. Ibid.

53. De Chennevières, "Revue des arts décoratifs," p. 3.

54. See Henri de Chennevières, "Jean-Nicolas Servandoni, peintre, architecte, ordonnateur des fêtes publiques," *Revue des arts décoratifs* 1 (1880–1881): 122–126, 170–177, 403–407, 429–436.

55. Paul Mantz, "Considérations générales sur l'ensemble des expositions organisées en 1880, par les soins de l'Union centrale," *Revue des arts décoratifs* 1 (1880–1881): 229–233, 284–302.

56. G. Vapereau, *Dictionnaire universel des contemporains* (Paris: Hachette, 1893), s.v. "Paul Mantz," p. 1050. Mantz is listed, along with his title in 1876, in the full account of the Inventaire Commission in Ministère de l'Instruction publique et des Beaux-Arts, *Inventaire générale*, p. xiii. Mantz's friendship with Edmond de Goncourt is chronicled in the *Journal des Goncourts*, vols. 1, 2. The friendship was sealed when the artist Bracquemond sent Mantz an engraving of Edmond de Goncourt surrounded by his eighteenth-century and Japanese objets d'art. The original version, signed by Bracquemond to Mantz, is now in the collection of the Palace of the Legion of Honor, San Francisco.

57. *Grand Larousse encyclopédique* (Paris: Larousse, 1963), s.v. "Jules Guiffrey"; see also the list of the Inventaire Commission in Ministère de l'Instruction publique et des Beaux-Arts, *Inventaire générale*, p. xiii.

58. Jules Guiffrey, "Notes sur l'orfèvrerie française, vaisselle d'argent, 1740–1753, Nollin, Ballin, et Le Brun," *Revue des arts décoratifs* 1 (1880–1881): 436–440.

59. Ibid. De Goncourt enumerated the plates and their use in different courses in describing the eighteenth-century art of cuisine in *La Maison d'un artiste* (Paris: Charpentier, 1881) 1:53–55.

60. *Dictionnaire universel du XIXe siècle*, s.v. "Arts décoratifs," p. 355; Victor Champier, *Catalogue illustré de l'Union centrale*, pp. 17–18.

61. The new membership list, after the 1882 fusion, is contained in Victor Champier, "La Société de l'Union centrale," pp. 85–86; see also Champier, *Catalogue illustré de l'Union centrale*, p. 18.

62. Proust, *L'Art sous la République*, pp. 102, 128–148.

63. Michael Fried, "Manet's Sources: Aspects of His Art," *Artforum* 7 (March 1968): 69, 71, nn. 30, 82. Manet painted a portrait of Antonin Proust, which he exhibited in the Salon of 1880.

64. The bronze bust of Proust was executed in 1884. It is included as an illustration in the Union centrale catalogue for the 1884 exhibition of "verre, terre, bois et pierre," in which Rodin displayed some of his ceramics (Champier, *Catalogue illustré de l'Union centrale*, p. 11).

65. Discussed in Proust, *L'Art sous la République*, pp. 115–121, 136–141.

66. Georges Guillain, *Jean-Martin Charcot: Sa vie, son oeuvre* (Paris: Masson, 1955), pp. 36–37.

67. Proust, criticizing the banal decorative arts, stated that it was the task of applied arts to "seduce us." In the face of their bad quality, "l'opinion finit par se désintéresser de ce qui devrait nous séduire" (Proust, *L'Art sous la République*, p. 161).

68. Antonin Proust, quoted in Louis de Fourcaud, "Rapport générale," *Revue des arts décoratifs* 5 (1884–1885): 231; Proust, *L'Art sous la République*, pp. 174, 181, 182.

69. The words of Champier, *Catalogue illustré de l'Union centrale,* p. 18. Proust was especially valuable to the Union centrale as he sat on the state budget committee for the beaux-arts.

70. Professor Kirk Varnedoe presented the post-Commune Tuileries Palace as a Piranesian ruin in a lecture at Princeton University in 1979. On the Cour des Comptes as the museum site, see Yolande Amic, "Les Débuts de l'U.C.A.D.," pp. 52–53.

71. Antonin Proust lobbied zealously for the museum in the Cour des Comptes, stating that "un palais nous faut" ("Discours: Distribution des récompenses," *Revue des arts décoratifs* 5 [1884–1885]: 478–479).

72. Amic, "Les Débuts de l'U.C.A.D.," pp. 53–54; Proust, *L'Art sous la République,* pp. 226–253.

73. Even as the *Revue des arts décoratifs* discussed eighteenth-century rococo style and accompanying visual images in the 1880s, eighteenth-century pattern books for decorators and applied artists were newly available. One such book, a folio reprinting large illustrations from the originals of Oppenordt, Meissonnier, and Pineau, was D. Guilmard, *Les Maîtres ornemanistes: Ecoles française, italienne, allemande, et pays-bas* (Paris: Plon, 1881).

74. Henri Thirion, "L'Oeuvre de Clodion," *Revue des arts décoratifs* 5 (1884–1885): 33–44.

75. Champier introduced Thirion's article on Clodion with the discussion of his soon-to-be-published book, "rempli de documents inédits," in *Revue des art décoratifs* 5:33.

76. Ibid., p. 34.

77. Ibid., pp. 34, 35–36, 42–43.

78. Ibid., p. 36.

79. Victor Champier, *Le Musée du Louvre,* p. 19.

80. Victor Champier, "La Collection d'orfèvrerie de M. Paul Eudel," *Revue des arts décoratifs* 4 (1883–1884): 306–311.

81. Ibid., p. 308.

82. Paul Mantz, "Les Meubles du XVIIIe siècle," 3 pts., *Revue des arts décoratifs* 4 (1883–1884): 313–325, 356–367, 377–389. The quotation here is from p. 387.

83. Ibid., pp. 313–314, 380.

84. Ibid., pp. 313, 380.

85. Ibid., p. 320. For another account of the feminization of the decorative arts during the eighteenth century and the centrality of aristocratic female practitioners, see Anthony Valabrègue, "Les Ornements de la femme: La Table à ouvrage et les outils de travail," *Revue des arts décoratifs* 4 (1883–1884): 326–337, 345–355, esp. 347.

86. See n. 24.

87. Mantz, "Les Meubles du XVIIIe siècle," p. 387.

88. Paul Mantz devoted attention to the eighteenth-century craze for Japanese and Chinese furniture, screens, and objets d'art in "Les Meubles du XVIIIe siècle," pp. 317–318, 379–384.

89. S. Bing, introduction to *Collection Philippe Burty: Objets d'art japonais et chinois qui seront vendus à Paris dans les Galeries Durand-Ruel* (Paris: Chamerot, 1891), pp. vi–vii, and introduction to *Exposition de la gravure japonaise à l'Ecole Nationale des Beaux-Arts à Paris, 25 avril–22 mai 1890* (Paris: Alcan-Lévy, 1890), pp. xi, xiii.

90. Gabriel P. Weisberg et al., *Japonisme: Japanese Influence on French Art, 1854–1910* (Cleveland: Cleveland Museum of Art, 1975), pp. 4–140.

91. See, for example, S. Bing, "Programme," *Le Japon artistique* 1 (1888): 2–9; Edmond de Goncourt, "Ecritoire de poche," *Le Japon artistique* 1 (1888): 68–74; Philippe Burty, "Les Sabres: 'Le Katana,'" *Le Japon artistique* 1 (1888): 119–130.

92. Bing, introduction to *Collection Burty,* p. vii.

93. Philippe Burty, "Conférence du Japon," *Revue des arts décoratifs* 5 (1884–1885): 388; *Journal des Goncourts,* 2:1194, July 27, 1877; 3:269, July 17, 1883.

94. Yolande Amic, "Les Débuts de l'U.C.A.D.," p. 52.

95. S. Bing, introduction to Union centrale des arts décoratifs, *Salon annuel des peintures japonaises,* 1e and 2e années (Paris: Pillet & Demoulin, 1883, 1884). Bing also provided notes and scholarly commentary on the entries.

96. Champier, *Catalogue illustré de l'Union centrale,* p. 165.

97. Ibid., pp. 31–40, 65–131.

98. See Champier, "L'Architecture japonaise: Les Temples," and "L'Architecture japonaise: Les Habitations," in *Le Japon artistique* 1 (1888): 25–32, 39–46; Burty, "Les Sabres: 'Le Katana'" and "Les Sabres: 'Le Wakizashi,'" *Le Japon artistique* 1 (1888): 119–130, 139–146; and Lucien Falize, "Travaux d'orfèvre," *Le Japon artistique* 1 (1888): 51–57. For Burty in particular the sword covers had moral and spiritual significance as the "soul" of their samurai bearer.

99. Bing, "Programme," *Le Japon artistique* 1 (1888): 2–3. Roger Marx analyzes the same difference between Far Eastern arts as playful curiosities and subjects of scholarly study in "Sur le rôle et l'influence des arts de l'Extrême-Orient et du Japon," *Le Japon artistique* 3 (1890): 142–146.

100. See the list of contributors incorporated into the frontispiece of *Le Japon artistique* 1 (1888). For another view of the magazine and its role in stimulating market prices for Oriental arts in France, see Gabriel P. Weisberg, *Art Nouveau Bing: Paris Style 1900* (New York: Abrams, 1986), pp. 25–28.

101. "Philippe Burty," in Lugt, *Marques de collections,* pp. 381–382. Some of Burty's own drawings and engravings may be found in *Collection Philippe Burty: Objets d'art japonais et chinois,* pp. 95, 167, 192, 200, 224, 240, 242, 250. Some of these same images were originally in Bing's *Le Japon artistique* 2 (1889).

102. "Burty," in Lugt, *Marques de collections,* pp. 381–382.

103. Burty, *Eaux-fortes de Jules de Goncourt* (Paris: Librairie d'art, 1876), pp. ii–xvi.

104. "Burty," in Lugt, *Marques de collections,* p. 382; Robert de Montesquiou-Fezensac, "Japonais d'Europe," *Roseaux pensants* (Paris: Charpentier, 1897), pp. 216–217.

105. The quality and breadth of Burty's collection may be traced in *Collection Burty,* with notes by Bing, pp. 1–253.

106. Guillain, *Jean-Martin Charcot,* pp. 36–37. Henri Meige mentions Burty as advisor to Charcot on collecting Oriental arts in *Charcot-artiste* (Paris: Masson, 1925), p. 34. Edmond de Goncourt recounted how he and the Charcots met at one of Burty's lectures at the Ecole des Beaux-Arts and assembled later that evening for drinks at the doctor's home. See the *Journal des Goncourts,* 3:21, May 26, 1879.

107. "Burty," in Lugt, *Marques de collections,* p. 382.

108. Philippe Burty, "La Potérie et la porcelaine de Japon," *Revue des arts décoratifs* 5 (1884–1885): 385–418.

109. Ibid., pp. 389–390, 395–398.

110. Ibid., p. 397.

111. Ibid., p. 392.

112. Ibid.

113. Ibid., p. 388.

114. Bing, "La Vie et l'oeuvre de Hok'sai," *Revue blanche* 14 (1896): 97.

115. Bing, introduction to *Salon annuel des peintures japonaises,* 1e année (Paris: Pillet & Demoulin, 1883), p. 5.

116. Ibid.

117. Bing, introduction to *Salon annuel des peintures japonaises,* 2e année (Paris: Pillet & Demoulin, 1884), pp. 3–4.

118. Gabriel P. Weisberg, "A Note on Bing's Early Years in France, 1854–1876," *Arts Magazine* 57, no. 5 (January 1983): 84–85; Weisberg, *Art Nouveau Bing,* pp. 12–16.

119. Gabriel Weisberg demonstrates Bing's extraordinary energy and ingenuity in developing a commercial art exchange between East and West, both in importing Orientalism to Europe and in creating a market for French products in Japan, in *Art Nouveau Bing,* esp. chap. 1.

120. The terms are those Bing used in his introduction to *Collection des Goncourts: Arts de l'Extrême-Orient* (Paris: May & Metteroz, 1897), p. ii. See also the quotation cited in n. 117 concerning French "hospitality" and "openness" to other cultural sources.

121. From the quotation cited in n. 117.

122. Bing speaks, for example, of the "charme de grâce et d'élégance, qui est la tradition de notre race" in his introduction to *Collection des Goncourts,* p. v. All through his writings Bing consistently discusses "nous les français."

123. Bing, "Programme," pp. 3–5.

124. Ibid., pp. 4–5.

125. Victor Champier, *Catalogue illustré de l'Union centrale,* p. 128.

126. "Faites comme les maîtres ont fait, ne refaites point ce qu'ils ont fait" (in Champier, *Catalogue illustré,* p. 163).

127. M. Du Cléuziou, "Les Origines de notre céramique nationale," *Revue des arts décoratifs* 5 (1884–1885): 364, 373.

128. Philippe Burty, "La Nouvelle Porcelaine de Sèvres," *Revue des arts décoratifs* 4 (1883–1884): 156.

129. Louis de Fourcaud, "Rapport général," *Revue des arts décoratifs* 5 (1884–1885): 263–266.

Chapter Seven

1. Alfred Fouillée, quoted in E. Goutière-Vernolle, "L'Art et le programme municipal," *La Lorraine-artiste* 10 (1892): 143–144.

2. The phrase is that of Roger Marx, quoted in Louis Hautecoeur, *préface* to *Catalogue des objets d'art moderne . . . faisant partie de la collection Roger Marx* (Paris: Manzi, Joyant, 1914), p. i.

3. Raymond Poincaré, "Discours à l'Union centrale," *Revue des arts décoratifs* 15 (1894–1895): 318–319.

4. Gustave Larroumet, "L'Art décoratif et les femmes," *Revue des arts décoratifs* 16 (1896): 102, 104, 105.

5. Roger Marx, "La Renaissance des arts décoratifs," *Les Arts* 1 (January 1902): 35–36, 38.

6. After Berger's appointment to the presidency of the Central Union, the union journal, the *Revue des arts décoratifs,* published accounts of the parliamentary debates over the arts budget. See, for example, Judex, "Chronique du mois: Le Budget des beaux-arts pour 1895," *Revue des arts décoratifs* 15 (1894–1895): 153–157.

7. Yolande Amic, "Les Débuts de l'U.C.A.D. et du Musée des Arts Décoratifs," *Cahiers de l'Union centrale des arts décoratifs* 1 (1978): 53.

8. Edmond de Goncourt and Jules de Goncourt, *Journal, mémoires de la vie littéraire* (Paris: Fasquelle & Flammarion, 1956), 4:751, March 1, 1895; see also 4:510, January 26, 1894 (hereafter cited as *Journal des Goncourts*).

9. See the text of Poincaré's speech to Edmond de Goncourt, reprinted in *Journal des Goncourts,* 4:752; full text, 4:750–752. See also the "Discours prononcé par M. Raymond Poincaré, ministre de l'Instruction publique et des Beaux-Arts, le premier mars 1895, au banquet offert à Edmond de Goncourt," *La Lorraine-artiste* 14 (1896): 278–279. At the banquet, Poincaré spoke before Georges Clemenceau, the politician, Edmond's longtime friend, who dubbed Edmond the "Chevalier de Marie-Antoinette." In *Journal des Goncourts,* 4:752.

10. In this speech, Poincaré used the idea of hypnosis to describe the pathological fixa-

tion on the repetition of past styles: "Nous ne devons pas vivre hypnotisés sur le cadavre des siècles défunts."

11. Antonin Proust, *L'Art sous la République* (Paris: Charpentier, 1892), pp. 147–148.

12. In *Le Congrès des arts décoratifs, tenu à l'Ecole Nationale des Beaux-Arts du 18 au 30 mai 1894, comptes-rendus sténographiques* (Paris: Lahure, 1894), pp. 22–456; speeches on pp. 4–15, 28–33.

13. In "Discours de M. Spuller," *Congrès des arts décoratifs*, pp. 15–27; quotations from pp. 18, 26.

14. Victor Champier, "A propos de la réorganisation de la manufacture de Sèvres," *Revue des arts décoratifs* 12 (1891–1892): 164–170.

15. Ibid., pp. 165–170.

16. The *pâte tendre* had been rediscovered as early as 1884, when some of its representatives were featured as the "*porcelaine nouvelle*" in the *Revue des arts décoratifs* 5 (1884–1885). The Bourgeois directive made this reissuing state policy.

17. Victor Champier, "Les Arts décoratifs et le budget des beaux-arts en 1895," *Revue des arts décoratifs* 15 (1894–1895): 296.

18. Judex, "Chronique du mois," *Revue des arts décoratifs* 16 (1896): 398.

19. Discussed in Eugenia Herbert, *The Artist and Social Reform: France and Belgium, 1885–1898* (New Haven, Conn.: Yale University Press, 1961), pp. 16–20.

20. See Fernand Pelloutier, "Les Conditions du travail et de la vie ouvrière en France," *Société nouvelle* 12 (1894): 433–458, 566–580, 690–706. In 1894 this Belgian journal also published Morris's own writings as "L'Art du peuple," 12:32–47.

21. The *Journal de Débats* of October 18, 1896, registered a debate on issues sparked by two studies by a M. Leclerc on English culture, education, and the industrial arts. A deputy named Colin spoke about William Morris and the impact of his Morris and Company, of which Leclerc had written. Deputy Colin celebrated Morris's impact as a reformer of taste, urging the French to follow Morris's example by promoting provincial craft associations. This appropriation of Morris in official channels is discussed by Gabriel Mourey in "William Morris," *Revue encyclopédique* no. 167 (November 21, 1896): 805–810. Mourey, whose own treatment of Morris in this essay is also marked by selective interpretation, presented Morris as an aesthete, rather than a revolutionary, calling him "un *gentleman* dans le sens le plus large et le plus noble de ce mot" (p. 807). Mourey wrote a book on English painting and arts and crafts, *Passé le Détroit*, which together with the writings of Robert de la Sizeranne and Marcel Proust between 1890 and 1900 promotes some aspects of English craft culture and design while depoliticizing and aestheticizing the ideas of Ruskin and Morris.

22. Bourgeois, quoted in Judex, "Chronique du mois," *Revue des arts décoratifs* 16 (1896): 398.

23. Waldeck-Rousseau is listed as a lawyer for the Central Union, among others on a *conseil judiciaire,* in Union centrale des arts décoratifs, *Exposition des arts de la femme, guide livret illustré* (Paris: A. Warmont, 1895), p. 13.

24. Pierre Sorlin, *Waldeck-Rousseau* (Paris: Colin, 1966), pp. 288–299, 345–364, 461–480; Theodore Zeldin, *France, 1848–1948,* vol. 1, *Ambition, Love, and Politics* (Oxford: Clarendon Press, 1973), pp. 671–675.

25. G. W., "Pour le centenaire de Roger Marx," *Gazette des beaux-arts* 54 (1959), supplément, pp. 1–3; "Roger Marx," in Frits Lugt, *Les Marques de collections de dessin et d'estampes* (Amsterdam: Vereenigte Drukkerijen, 1921), p. 417.

26. Roger Marx, "La Villa moderne," in *L'Art social* (Paris: Fasquelle, 1913), pp. 193–194.

27. Claude Roger-Marx, "Roger Marx," *Evidences* 12, no. 88 (March–April 1961): 34–35; Arsène Alexandre, préface to *Catalogues des tableaux, pastels, dessins, aquarelles, sculptures faisant partie de la collection Roger Marx* (Paris: Manzi, Joyant, 1914), pp. 1–10; Louis Hautecoeur, pré-

face to *Catalogue des objets d'art moderne . . faisant partie de la collection Roger Marx* (Paris: Manzi, Joyant, 1914), pp. i–iv.

28. Roger Marx, "La Renaissance des arts décoratifs," p. 38.

29. M. Tx., "Gustave Larroumet," *La Grande Encyclopédie* (Paris: Lamirault, c. 1898), 21:973–974. Larroumet had been director of beaux-arts between 1888 and 1890 and was appointed honorary director of the beaux-arts in 1896. His appointment as professor of modern literature at the Sorbonne began in 1891.

30. Gustave Larroumet, *Le XVIIIe siècle et la critique contemporaine* (Paris: Administration des deux revues, 1891), pp. 25–26.

31. "Bulletin de l'Union centrale des arts décoratifs," *Revue des arts décoratifs* 17 (1897): 128.

32. Larroumet, *Le XVIIIe siècle,* p. 13.

33. Ibid., pp. 27–28, 13.

34. The words of Georges Berger, president of the Central Union after 1889. In Berger, "Bulletin de l'Union centrale des arts décoratifs, note de M. Georges Berger," *Revue des arts décoratifs* 16 (1896): 276; and the words used to describe Jules Jacquemart, whose son participated in the founding of the eighteenth-century decorative arts museum, the Musée Jacquemart-André. In Frits Lugt, *Marques de collections,* p. 251.

35. This personnel is traceable through the articles in the *Revue des arts décoratifs* 12–20 (1891–1900) and through Central Union membership lists and lists of consulting committees such as V. C., "La Commission consultative nommée par le Conseil d'administration de l'Union centrale," *Revue des arts décoratifs* 15 (1894–1895): 319, and "Bulletin de la Société: Exposition des Arts de la Femme," *Revue des arts décoratifs* 12 (1891–1892): 251–256; *Congrès des arts décoratifs,* pp. 693–718; *Exposition des arts de la femme, guide livret illustré,* pp. 11–15.

36. *La Grande Larousse encyclopédique* (Paris: Larousse, 1963), s.v. "Gaston Migeon."

37. André Michel, *Les Artistes célèbres: François Boucher* (Paris: Librairie J. Rouam, 1886), pp. 6, 4–7.

38. André Michel, "Du bon usage des oeuvres d'art," *Les Arts* 1 (January 1902): 1–2. This article, inaugurating the journal, proposed a new role for the *amateur.* Michel was a curator at the Louvre and sat on the Union centrale's "Commission consultative."

39. See Avertissement des editeurs, in Henry Havard, *L'Art dans la maison* [1884], 4th ed. (Paris: Rouvèyre, 1891), pp. v–vi. Havard's book included explications of the splendid applied arts and design activities of Mesdames de Pompadour, de Genlis, and du Barry, and of the princesse de Condé. Havard also described and illustrated King Louis XVI's artisanal works as a locksmith and key molder. These accounts were based on hitherto unavailable archival sources and memoirs from the eighteenth century. See *L'Art dans la maison,* esp. pp. 9–30, and Havard's *L'Art et le confort dans la vie moderne: Le Bon Vieux Temps* (Paris: Flammarion, 1904).

40. Listed in *Exposition des arts de la femme, guide livret illustré,* pp. 11–15.

Chapter Eight

1. Notes 1–3 are based on my calculations at the Bibliothèque Nationale in Paris, using their chronological "Catalogue des matières" under the rubrics Louis XIV, Louis XV, and Louis XVI. Although these calculations are rough, both the increase in book titles on these subjects and the chronology of their appearance are significant.

2. Listed on the title page to S. Rocheblave, *Louis de Fourcaud et le mouvement artistique en France de 1875 à 1914* (Paris: Les Belles-Lettres, 1926) as *Essai sur le Comte de Caylus* (Paris: Hachette, 1889), and *Les Cochin,* (Paris: Librairie d'art, 1893).

3. Roger Portalis et Henri Béraldi, *Les Graveurs du XVIIIe siècle* (Paris: Damascène Morgond & Charles Fatout, 1880), p. xi. Portalis also wrote articles on Fragonard, originally published as "La Collection Walferdin et ses Fragonards," *Gazette des beaux-arts* 21 (1880): 297–332. These were expanded into a full monograph in 1889: *Honoré Fragonard: Sa vie et son oeuvre* (Paris: J. Rothschild, 1889).

4. D. Guilmard, *Les Maîtres ornemanistes: Ecoles française, italienne, allemande, et pays-bas* (Paris: Plon, 1881).

5. Nicolas Pineau, *Nouveaux dessins* (Paris Rouvèyre, 1889).

6. Th. Biais, *Nicolas Pineau* (Paris: Société des Bibliophiles français, 1892).

7. Léon Deshairs, *Dessins originaux des maîtres décoratifs* (Paris: Longuet, c. 1900), pp. 5–10.

8. A report of 1896 noted the preeminence of eighteenth-century drawings and documents in the Central Union's library holdings. The eighteenth century also figured prominently in donations and acquisitions for the Musée des Arts Décoratifs. See Yolande Amic, "Les Débuts de l'U.C.A.D. et du Musée des Arts Décoratifs," *Cahiers de l'Union centrale des arts décoratifs* 1 (1978): 52–54. See also R. K., "Les Arts décoratifs," a description of the museum's holdings, in *Les Arts* 1 (June 1902): 30. The primacy of eighteenth-century gifts and acquisitions in both the union library and the museum may be traced, year to year, in the column "Dons et acquisitions" included in the "Bulletin du mois" of the *Revue des arts décoratifs* 12–20 (1891–1900).

9. On de Nolhac, see *La Grande Encyclopédie*, s.v. "Pierre de Nolhac," 24:1180. *La Reine Marie-Antoinette* (Paris: Bossud, Valadon, 1890) cost one hundred francs.

10. Advertisement on the back cover of Antonin Proust, *Le Salon de 1891* (Paris: Bossud, Valadon, 1891).

11. On Spuller's promotion of the restoration of Versailles, see Antonin Proust, *L'Art sous la République* (Paris: Charpentier, 1892), pp. 147–148. De Nolhac's appointment as curator of Versailles is noted in *La Grande Encyclopédie*, s.v. "Pierre de Nolhac."

12. Unsigned review, "Un Livre de M. Pierre de Nolhac sur J. M. Nattier," *Les Arts* 3 (November 1904): 2–3.

13. Gaston Migeon, "Les Accroissements des musées: Musée du Louvre," *Les Arts* 1 (January 1902): 15; F. Trawinski, "Musée du Louvre," *La Grande Encyclopédie*, 22:695.

14. See Ernest Daudet, *Le Duc d'Aumale, 1822–1897* (Paris: Plon, 1898), pp. 351–364, 454–456; Institut de France, *Le Musée Condé de Chantilly* (Chantilly: Editions Horarius, 1978), pp. 5–11.

15. Institut de France, *Le Musée Condé de Chantilly*, pp. 5–9, 23. Good illustrations of the Huet ensembles and *singerie* in the château de Chantilly may be found in Pierre Verlet, *The Eighteenth Century in France: Society, Decoration, Furniture* (Rutland, Vt.: Charles Tuttle, 1967).

16. Institut de France, *Le Musée Condé de Chantilly*, pp. 8–10.

17. Ibid.; see also "Duc d'Aumale," in Frits Lugt, *Marques de collections de dessin et d'estampes* (Amsterdam: Vereenigte Drukkerijen, 1921), p. 518.

18. Daudet, *Le Duc d'Aumale*, pp. 351–357, 454–456; "Duc d'Aumale," in Lugt, *Marques de collections*, p. 518.

19. Quoted in Daudet, *Le Duc d'Aumale*, pp. 357, 364, 455–456.

20. Roger Marx, *La Décoration et l'art industriel à l'Exposition universelle de 1889* (Paris: Librairies-imprimeries réunies, 1890), pp. 21–35, and accompanying plates illustrating the ramp. The same ramp was cited and reproduced in the *Revue des arts décoratifs* 12 (1891–1892) as a model of craft renovation.

21. Philippe Garner, *Emile Gallé* (London: Academy, 1976), p. 126.

22. The paintings in the collection are listed in Institut de France, *Le Musée Condé de Chantilly*, pp. 24–31.

23. The duc's book collection included Edmond and Jules de Goncourt's *L'Art du XVIIIe siècle*; Alfred de Champeaux's *Le Meuble*; Louis Gonse's *L'Art japonais*; *La Collection Philippe*

Burty; G. Bourcaud's *Dessins, gouaches, estampes, et tableaux du XVIIIe siècle;* E. Williamson's *Les meubles d'art du Mobilier National;* and Paul Mantz's *La peinture française.* These books remain today on the shelves where the duc placed them, adjacent to the Hunt Gallery in the *petit château.*

24. On Labrouste and the Bibliothèque Nationale, see Philadelphia Museum of Art, *The Second Empire, 1852–1870: Art in France under Napoleon III* (Philadelphia: Philadelphia Museum of Art, 1970), pp. 35–38, 53–56. A comprehensive account of Labrouste and iron architecture may be found in Louis Hautecoeur, *L'Histoire de l'architecture classique en France* (Paris: Picard, 1957), 7:119–136. Additional information on Labrouste is contained in David Van Zanten, "Architectural Composition at the Ecole des Beaux-Arts from Charles Percier to Charles Garnier," and Neil Levine, "The Romantic Idea of Architectural Legibility: Henri Labrouste and the Neo-Grec," both in *The Architecture of the Ecole des Beaux-Arts,* ed. Arthur Drexler (New York: Museum of Modern Art, 1977), pp. 111–324 and 325–416, respectively.

25. Hautecoeur, *Histoire de l'architecture,* pp. 119–121; Philadelphia Museum of Art, *The Second Empire,* pp. 35–36.

26. De Champeaux's scholarly identifications of the consoles and vases in the de Cotte ensembles are discussed in Jean Babelon, *Le Cabinet du Roi; ou, le Salon Louis XV de la Bibliothèque Nationale* (Paris: G. Vanoeust, 1927), p. 37.

27. Bapst's manuscript collections listing the de Cotte furnishings for the rococo Bibliothèque Nationale are discussed in Babelon, *Le Cabinet du Roi,* p. 36.

28. Henri Bouchot, "Les Derniers Travaux de décoration exécutés à la Bibliothèque Nationale," *Revue des arts décoratifs* 12 (1891–1892): 91–97.

29. Paul Mantz, quoted in Bouchot, "Les Derniers Travaux," p. 94.

30. Bouchot, "Les Derniers Travaux," p. 95. Bouchot's indictment of the iron shed of Labrouste and his celebration of the rococo restoration were commensurate with his scholarly interests and personal affinities. An archivist and writer, Bouchot specialized in two areas of mid-eighteenth-century decorative arts: the career of François Boucher, and the delicate craft of painted miniatures. A contributor to the *Revue des arts décoratifs* and a member of the administrative council of the Central Union, Bouchot was also a member of the Institut de France.

31. Ibid.

32. Ibid., p. 97.

33. A key element in the public discussion of and outcry against the Eiffel Tower was the standardization of its design and its prefabrication. The engineer Eiffel planned the project in its entirety, down to the placement of every one of its twelve thousand iron rivets. Assembly took eighteen months, compared with the seven-year period needed to build Sacré-Coeur. The public attributed menacing qualities to the tower, calling it a "bolted metal column," an "odious pole of trade and industry," and the "American Babylon of the future," partly because the tower itself subverted the relation between architect and builder. Eiffel left to the construction teams only mechanical and finishing tasks: hammering in iron rivets and hauling prefabricated wrought-iron parts. The distant and omniscient engineer suggests the silent office in Bouchot's contrast of rococo renovation teams of the fin de siècle with the design process of precisely engineered construction projects. For public outcries against both the standardized, technological menace of the tower and Eiffel himself, see Joseph Harriss, *The Tallest Tower* (Boston: Houghton Mifflin, 1975), pp. 19–24; and Charles Braibant, *Histoire de la Tour Eiffel* (Paris: Plon, 1964).

34. Quoted in Debora Silverman, "The Paris Exhibition of 1889: Architecture and the Crisis of Individualism," *Oppositions* 8 (Spring 1977): 77.

35. F. Trawinski, "Musée du Louvre," *La Grande Encyclopédie,* 22:695–697; Georges Poisson, *Les Musées en France* (Paris: Presses universitaires de France, 1965), pp. 18, 30–31. A running contemporary account of the additions to the new Département des Objets d'art is

contained in the special column of the journal *Les Arts*, "Les Accroissements des musées: Musée du Louvre" 1–7 (1902–1908). Two other contemporary sources document the collections of the Département des Objets d'art during its early years: Carle Dreyfus, *Musée du Louvre: Les Objets d'art du XVIIIe siècle* (Paris: Editions Morancé, 1923); J. J. Marquet de Vasselot, *Musée du Louvre: La Céramique chinoise de l'époque de K'ang-Hi à nos jours, 1662–1911* (Paris: Editions Morancé, 1921).

36. Carle Dreyfus, *Musée du Louvre: Le Mobilier français, époques de Louis XIV et de Louis XV* (Paris: Editions Morancé, 1923), p. 5; Gaston Migeon, "Les Accroissements des musées: Musée du Louvre, Département des Objets d'art du Moyen Age, de la Renaissance, et des temps modernes," *Les Arts*, 7 (April 1908): 10–15; Gustave Babin, "Le Musée du Mobilier français au Louvre," *L'Illustration* no. 3039 (May 25, 1901): 343.

37. Migeon, "Les Accroissements des musées: Musée du Louvre," *Les Arts* 1 (January 1902): 15.

38. The budget increase went into effect after 1890; the decree for a separate "*caisse des musées*" for the Louvre became law on April 16, 1895. See Migeon, "Les Accroissements des musées: Musée du Louvre," *Les Arts* 1 (January 1902): 15; F. Trawinski, "Musée du Louvre," p. 695.

39. Trawinski, "Musée du Louvre," pp. 694–696.

40. Empress Eugénie did renew interest in late eighteenth-century furniture by using rococo and Louis XVI pieces for her own rooms. The essential point here is that the Second Empire rococo revival was a personal campaign of hers to deepen the associations between the court and luxury of Napoléon III and those of Louis XV and Louis XVI. The Third Republic presented the eighteenth-century arts differently: as part of a newly defined national tradition and heritage. The caprice of personal, imperial taste was transposed into a durable national *patrimoine*.

41. Edmond Williamson, *Les Meubles d'art du Mobilier National: Choix des plus belles pièces conservées au Garde-Meuble* (Paris: Baudry, c. 1897), esp. p. 3; Gaston Migeon, "Meubles que le Musée du Louvre pourrait recueillir," *Les Arts* 7 (May 1908): 30; "Les Accroissements des musées: Musée du Louvre," *Les Arts* 7 (April 1908): 10–15; and Emile Molinier, "Le Mobilier français au XVIIIe siècle dans les collections étrangères," *Les Arts* 1 (January 1902): 19–22.

42. Migeon, "Les Accroissements des musées: Musée du Louvre," *Les Arts* 7 (April 1908): 10–11.

43. Williamson, *Les Meubles d'art du Mobilier National*, pp. i–vii. Williamson is emphatic about the character of the political radicals of the French Revolutionary government as cultural custodians of Old Regime applied arts.

44. Ibid. See also Migeon, "Les Accroissements des musées: Musée du Louvre," *Les Arts* 7 (April 1908): 10–11.

45. Migeon, "Les Accroissements des musées: Musée du Louvre," *Les Arts* 7 (April 1908): 10–11; Molinier, "Le Mobilier français."

46. *Union centrale des arts décoratifs, Exposition rétrospective de 1882: Les Arts du métal* (Paris: Quantin, 1882), with comments by E. Williamson, "Objets appartenant au service du Mobilier National"; *Union centrale des arts décoratifs, Exposition rétrospective de 1884* (Paris: Quantin, 1884).

47. Gaston Migeon's family were descendants of the Migeon royal furniture suppliers to the court of Louis XV and Madame de Pompadour. Migeon's ancestor Pierre Migeon (1710–1758) created luxurious small-scale furnishings for Madame de Pompadour in the lacquer, rosewood, almondwood and acacia woods favored by the royal courtesan. As assistant curator in the Louvre department of applied arts, Migeon catalogued objects and searched for rococo artifacts in private collections. One of the magnificent tables fashioned by his ancestor Pierre was donated to the Louvre, the famous *bureau* of Vergennes. See Migeon, "La collection

Baron Schlichting," *Les Arts* 1 (July 1902): 6–16, and "Les Accroissements des musées: Musée du Louvre," *Les Arts* 7 (April 1908): 10–15. See also *La Grande Larousse encyclopédique,* s.v. "Migeon."

Emile Molinier, trained at the Ecole de Chartres, specialized in scholarly writing on eighteenth-century furniture, enamels, and bronzework. He continually defended the fragile miniature applied arts of the eighteenth century, such as the small boxes and screens typical of the period, as "equal to the most beautiful painting and sculptures." See his *Musée du Louvre: Le Mobilier français du XVIIe et du XVIIIe siècles* (Paris: Vanoeust, 1901), and "Le Mobilier français." Migeon and Molinier are listed as jury members for the Central Union exhibitions after 1891, in *Revue des arts décoratifs* 12–18 (1891–1898).

Carle Dreyfus grew up amid erudition and connoisseurship; his father, Gustave Dreyfus, was a well-known Parisian collector and founding member of the Central Union of the Decorative Arts. At the age of nineteen the son began a career of scholarship in and curatorship of the applied arts in the new institutions of the Louvre. He continued his father's passion for collecting objets d'art, specializing in the applied arts of the eighteenth century, and maintained his father's ties to the Central Union, which later bore fruit: through his long friendship with the de Commando family, Carle Dreyfus convinced Isaac de Commando to donate the eighteenth-century ensembles in his home to the Central Union, a donation that led subsequently to the creation of the Musée Nissim de Commando as an annex to the Musée des Arts Décoratifs.

48. See Carle Dreyfus, *Musée du Louvre: Le Mobilier français,* p. 9; Migeon, "Meubles que le Louvre pourrait recueillir," pp. 28–32.

49. Migeon, "Les Accroissements des musées: Musée du Louvre," *Les Arts* 7 (April 1908): 13.

50. Ibid.

51. Roujon collaborated closely with Léon Bourgeois, the solidarist prime minister. The curators' relations with Roujon are discussed in Gaston Migeon, "Les Accroissements des musées: Musée du Louvre," *Les Arts* 7 (April 1908): 11, and "Meubles que le Louvre pourrait recueillir," pp. 29–30. See also Gustave Babin, "Le Musée du Mobilier français au Louvre," p. 343. Roujon's writings on seventeenth- and eighteenth-century architecture and interior design include *Les Grandes Eaux de Versailles* (Paris: Dunon & Pinat, 1907) and *Les Dames d'autrefois* (1910). Roujon was elected to the Académie des Beaux-Arts in 1899 and to the Académie française in 1911.

52. Migeon, "Les Accroissements des musées: Musée du Louvre," *Les Arts* 7 (April 1908): 14.

53. Clemenceau was allowed to keep a magnificent rococo *bureau* as his personal desk. This furnishing was depicted in contemporary prints as the arena of confrontation between Clemenceau and the representative of the vociferous striking southern winegrowers of 1907–1908.

54. Lists of acquisitions are included in Migeon, "Les Accroissements des musées: Musée du Louvre," *Les Arts* 7 (April 1908): 13–15, and "Meubles que le Louvre pourrait recueillir," p. 32; Molinier, "Le Mobilier français," p. 22. A complete list of holdings acquired through 1912 is contained in Carle Dreyfus, *Musée du Louvre: Catalogue sommaire du Mobilier et des objets d'art du XVIIe et XVIIIe siècles* (Paris: Manzi, 1913).

55. Migeon, "Les Accroissements des musées: Musée du Louvre," *Les Arts* 7 (April 1908): 11.

56. Migeon, "Meubles que le Louvre pourrait recueillir," pp. 30–31. Elsewhere Migeon suggested that contemporary artisans should learn a crucial lesson from their eighteenth-century ancestors: the rococo was "considered *modern* in its time." The evolution of style was

an imperative, evinced by the continuous variation of style until the nineteenth century. See Migeon, "Meubles," p. 29.

57. Migeon, "Les Accroissements des musées: Musée du Louvre," *Les Arts* 7 (April 1908): 11.

58. Ibid.

59. The most notorious of these foreign collections was that of Robert Wallace, which included furnishings originally belonging to Madame de Pompadour and the daughters of Louis XV.

60. Migeon, "Les Accroissements des musées: Musée du Louvre," *Les Arts* 7 (April 1908): 10–15, and "Meubles que le Louvre pourrait recueillir," pp. 28–32; Molinier, "Le Mobilier français"; Migeon, "La Collection Baron Schlichting."

61. Migeon, "Les Accroissements des musées: Musée du Louvre," *Les Arts* 7 (April 1908): 11.

62. Ibid.

63. Ibid.

64. Ibid.

65. Louis de Fourcaud, "Les Arts décoratifs au Salon de 1892: Champs-Elysées et Champ-de-Mars," *Revue des arts décoratifs* 12 (1891–1892): 329–330.

Chapter Nine

1. Arthur Meyer, *Ce que mes yeux ont vu* (Paris: Plon, 1911), pp. 109–115; Raymond D. Anderson, *France, 1870–1914: Politics and Society* (London: Routledge & Kegan Paul, 1977), pp. 146–148; Alexander Sedgwick, *The Third French Republic, 1870–1914* (New York: Thomas Y. Crowell, 1968), pp. 102–103.

2. Meyer, *Ce que mes yeux ont vu*, pp. 109–115; Anderson, *France, 1870–1914*, pp. 146–148; Sedgwick, *The Third French Republic*, pp. 102–103

3. Information on the building of the Peterhof Palace by Leblond is contained in M. Normand, "A Saint-Pétersbourg et à Peterhof," *L'Illustration* no. 2843 (August 21, 1897): 148. Pineau's contributions to the Peterhof may be found in Léon Deshairs, *Dessins originaux des maîtres décoratifs* (Paris: Longuet, c. 1900), pp. 5–7. Falconet's most famous contribution in Russia remained the equestrian sculpture of Peter the Great. The statue was reproduced in French magazines during the Franco-Russian alliance, for example, in *La Grande Encyclopédie*, vol. 16 (1896), as an advertisement on the back cover that promoted orders for prints of the statue. The entire plan of the Peterhof Palace and photographs of the rococo decorative schemes in its *appartements* were reproduced in *L'Illustration* no. 2844 (August 28, 1897): 168–169, upon the occasion of President Félix Faure's visit to Russia.

4. At the height of his popularity, in 1769, Boucher was nominated honorary associate of the Académie Impériale de Russie et de Saint-Pétersbourg. See *François Boucher: A Loan Exhibit for the Benefit of the New York Botanical Gardens, November 12–December 19, 1980* (New York: Wildenstein, 1980), p. 32. On Clodion's Russian connection in the eighteenth century see Henri Thirion, "L'Oeuvre de Clodion," *Revue des arts décoratifs* 5 (1884–1885): 38–39.

5. Deshairs, *Dessins originaux*, p. 5; *Catalogue descriptif des dessins de décoration et d'ornement de maîtres anciens exposés au Musée des Arts Décoratifs en 1880* (Paris: Imprimerie de publications périodiques, 1880), pp. 107–108.

6. *Catalogue descriptif*, pp. 107–108.

7. Henri Thirion, "L'Oeuvre de Clodion," pp. 38–39.

8. André Michel, *Les Artistes célèbres: François Boucher* (Paris: Librairie Rouam, 1886).

9. *Oeuvres de Nicolas Pineau, Recueil des oeuvres de Nicolas Pineau, sculpteur et graveur de la cour du régent* (Paris: Librairie des Beaux-Arts appliqués à l'Industrie, 1889).

10. Th. Biais, *Nicolas Pineau* (Paris: Société de bibliophiles français, 1892).

11. The passage of Pineau's works from French to Russian hands and then back again is described in Deshairs, *Dessins originaux,* p. 6. Deshairs mentions that the Musée des Arts Décoratifs was also able to buy Pineau drawings from the sale of the collection of the baron Pichon in 1897.

12. Georges Guillain, *Jean-Martin Charcot: Sa vie, son oeuvre* (Paris: Masson, 1955), pp. 36–37.

13. Ibid., p. 30.

14. Ibid.

15. Judex, "Chroniques et nouvelles du mois: L'Exposition française de Moscou," *Revue des arts décoratifs* 12 (1891–1892): 313.

16. The Pineau escutcheons and decorative ensembles featuring the Russian double-headed eagle are illustrated in Deshairs, *Dessins originaux,* plates 95 and 97.

17. Judex, "L'Exposition française de Moscou," p. 313.

18. Ibid.

19. An excellent description of the reconstruction in Nancy by the duc Stanislas is found in Roland Clément and Pierre Simonin, *L'Ensemble architectural de Stanislas* (Nancy: Librairie des arts Nancy, 1966), pp. 3–46.

20. Roger Marx, *L'Art social* (Paris: Fasquelle, 1913), pp. 137–138.

21. Gallé's close scrutiny of Lamour's gates and his transformation of Lamour's gilded foliage into his own glass vase decoration in 1884 are commented on by Louis de Fourcaud, "Rapport général," *Revue des arts décoratifs* 5 (1884–1885): 260–261. In chapter 13 I will examine in detail Gallé's participation in the Central Union in the 1880s and his development of an art nouveau in the 1890s.

22. Marx, *L'Art social,* p. 141. Roger Marx stated that Gallé's workshop was transformed into an "atelier enfiévré de patriotisme."

23. Quoted in Marx, *L'Art social,* pp. 138–139.

24. Quoted in Marx, *L'Art social,* p. 140.

25. Victor Champier, "Souhaits d'artistes: A propos de la réception des souverains russes," *Revue des arts décoratifs* 16 (1896): 341.

26. Ibid., p. 342–343.

27. Roger Marx, *L'Art social,* pp. 259–260. Originally published as "Le décor de la rue et les fêtes franco-russes" in October 1896.

28. Champier, "Souhaits d'artistes," pp. 343–344.

29. The decorated train station and shields are reproduced in *L'Illustration* no. 2798 (October 10, 1896): 285.

30. The vase by Gallé and Falize and the medallion by Chaplain are illustrated in Champier, "Souhaits d'artistes," pp. 345, 347.

31. The Sèvres statuette of Catherine II and the jewelry box are reproduced in Champier, "Souhaits d'artistes," pp. 346–347.

32. Hénard, cited in Peter M. Wolf, *Eugène Hénard and the Beginning of Urbanism in Paris, 1900–1914* (The Hague: International Federation for Housing and Planning–Centre de Recherche d'Urbanisme, 1968), p. 27.

33. The project for the 1900 esplanade and monuments is reproduced in Wolf, *Eugène Hénard,* p. 33, with the quotation on the same page.

34. The two hammers and their devices were described and illustrated in "La Pose de la première pierre du Pont Alexandre III," *L'Illustration* no. 2798 (October 10, 1896): 290.

35. The trowel and its visual symbolism are explained and illustrated in "La Pose de la première pierre," p. 290.

Chapter Ten

1. William Morris, *News from Nowhere,* in *Three Works by William Morris* (New York: International Publishers, 1968), pp. 181–401.

2. Jules Destrée, "Art et socialisme: Arts dans la vie courante," in *Jules Destrée: Tous ses visages, toute sa vie,* ed. Pierre Bourgeois (Brussels: Editions Labor, 1963), pp. 97–103. In contrast to Morris, Destrée based his vision on art as an *agent* of social transformation. If Morris believed that art erupted only after basic wants were satisfied and only after all other changes were effected, Destrée and the Belgian radicals construed art as a revolutionary tool that would promote change before and during revolution and would occupy a central place in the new society. I believe these differences derive from different religious traditions.

3. Carl E. Schorske, *Fin-de-Siècle Vienna: Politics and Culture* (New York: Knopf, 1980), pp. 237, 275. The quotation is from p. 275, n. 35.

4. Ibid., pp. 238–239.

5. Ibid., pp. 236–238; the quotation is from p. 236.

6. Quoted in Schorske, *Fin-de-Siècle Vienna,* p. 237. See also Michel Pollak, *Vienne 1900* (Paris: Gallimard, 1984), pp. 111, 138–139.

7. Schorske, *Fin-de-Siècle Vienna,* p. 236.

8. The words of Roger Marx, quoted in Louis Hautecoeur, *préface* to *Catalogue des objets d'art moderne* (Paris: Manzi, Joyant, 1914), p. ii.

9. Judex, "Roger Marx: La Réforme de la monnaie," *Revue des arts décoratifs* 12 (1891–1892): 312.

10. Portions of these articles are reprinted in Judex, "Roger Marx," pp. 312–313; and in Roger Marx, *L'Art social* (Paris: Fasquelle, 1913), pp. 95–99.

11. Marx, *L'Art social,* p. 104.

12. Ibid., p. 95.

13. Ibid., pp. 96, 99.

14. Roger Marx, *La Décoration et l'art industriel à l'Exposition universelle de 1889* (Paris: Librairies-imprimeries réunies, 1890), p. 60.

15. Roger Marx, "La Renaissance des arts décoratifs," *Les Arts* 1 (January 1902): 35, 38.

16. Roger Marx, *L'Art social,* pp. 96–97, 98.

17. Roger Marx, "La Renaissance des arts décoratifs," p. 38.

18. Roger Marx, quoted in Judex, "La Réforme de la monnaie," p. 312.

19. Roger Marx, "La Renaissance des arts décoratifs," p. 38.

20. Judex, "La Réforme de la monnaie," p. 312.

21. Judex, "L'Initiative d'une nouvelle monnaie," *Revue des arts décoratifs* 15 (1894–1895): 568.

22. Biographical information on Paul Doumer and his connection with Roger Marx is from R. Renoult, "Paul Doumer," *La Grande Encyclopédie* (Paris: Larousse, c. 1896), p. 1022; and Louis Hautecoeur, *préface* to *Catalogue des objets d'art moderne,* p. iv.

23. Cited in Judex, "L'Initiative d'une nouvelle monnaie," p. 568.

24. Maurice Agulhon, *Marianne into Battle: Republican Imagery and Symbolism in France, 1789–1880* (New York: Cambridge University Press, 1981), pp. 87–189, examples on pp. 163, 173.

25. Ibid., pp. 188–189.

26. See the discussion in T. J. Clark, *The Absolute Bourgeois: Artists and Politics in France, 1848–1851* (Greenwich, Conn.: New York Graphic Society, 1973), pp. 72–98; and Linda Nochlin, *Realism* (Middlesex, England: Penguin Books, 1971), pp. 111–122.

27. Roger Marx, *L'Art social,* pp. 266–267, 49–50.

28. The metaphor of artistic renewal as a tree with sturdy roots bearing new fruit is used by Camille Mauclair to characterize the French craft movement as a whole. See Camille Mauclair, "La Réforme de l'art décoratif en France," *La Nouvelle Revue* 98 (1896): 746.

29. S. Bing, *La Culture artistique en Amérique* (Evreux: Imprimerie de Charles Hérissey, 1895), pp. 87, 82.

30. See the discussion on pp. 126–132.

31. The members of the organizing committee are listed after the frontispiece of the catalogue *Exposition de la gravure japonaise à l'Ecole Nationale des Beaux-Arts* (Paris: Alcan-Lévy, 1890).

32. *Exposition de la gravure japonaise,* pp. 1–52.

33. See the "Table chronologique des principaux artistes figurant dans l'exposition" and the subsequent four phases in *Exposition de la gravure japonaise.*

34. Splendid reproductions of these and other images are contained in the exhibition catalogue. Many of them are marked "Extrait de la revue mensuelle *Le Japon artistique,*" the magazine published by Bing between 1888 and 1890.

35. S. Bing, *Exposition de la gravure japonaise,* p. 16.

36. S. Bing, introduction to *Exposition de la gravure japonaise,* esp. pp. xviii–xxiv.

37. Ibid., p. xxi.

38. Ibid., p. xxii.

39. Ibid., pp. xxiii–xxiv.

40. Bing described his mission and findings in the dedication to Directeur Roujon, following the title page of *La Culture artistique en Amérique.* Robert Koch notes that the exact dates of Bing's visit to the United States are not known; he believes Bing came to the United States in 1892. Gabriel Weisberg identifies the date of the trip as 1894 and describes Bing's business ventures in America. See Robert Koch, introduction, to S. Bing, *Artistic America, Tiffany Glass, and Art Nouveau,* trans. Benita Eisler (Cambridge: MIT Press, 1970), pp. 2–3; and Gabriel P. Weisberg, *Art Nouveau Bing: Paris Style 1900* (New York: Abrams, 1986), pp. 47–50.

41. Bing, *La Culture artistique en Amérique,* p. 74.

42. Ibid., p. 81.

43. See the discussion above, pp. 130–131.

44. Bing, *La Culture artistique en Amérique,* p. 77.

45. Ibid., pp. 111, 113.

46. Ibid., p. 113.

47. Ibid., p. 81.

48. Ibid., p. 77.

49. Bing commented on "la grâce et l'élégance—qui est la tradition de notre race" in a written eulogy to Edmond de Goncourt. See S. Bing, "Les Arts de l'Extrême-Orient dans la collection des Goncourts," in *Collection des Goncourts: Arts de l'Extrême-Orient* (Paris: May & Metteroz, 1897), p. v. In the 1895 report Bing also noted "les qualités de grâce et de finesse natives" (*La Culture artistique en Amérique,* p. 98).

50. Roger Marx, *La Décoration et l'art industriel à l'Exposition universelle de 1889,* p. 60.

51. Bing, *La Culture artistique en Amérique,* p. 108.

52. Roger Marx, "La Renaissance des arts décoratifs," pp. 35, 38. In another text, Roger Marx provided a more succinct statement of his credo of modernity and tradition: "Préparer l'avenir en reliant le présent au passé" (quoted in D. Loys, *préface* to *Catalogue des estampes modernes composant la collection Roger Marx* [Paris: Baudoin, 1914], p. i).

53. Bing, *La Culture artistique en Amérique*, p. 111.

54. Ibid., pp. 90–91.

55. Ibid., pp. 95–96.

56. Ibid., pp. 108, 82.

57. Ibid., p. 113.

58. Some examples are to be found in Bing, *La Culture artistique en Amérique*, pp. 71, 75, 77, 78, 81, 95, 113.

59. Ibid., pp. 111–112.

60. Ibid., p. 77.

61. Ibid., p. 111.

Chapter Eleven

1. Victor Champier, "Notre nouveau programme," *Revue des arts décoratifs* 12 (1891–1892): 1–4.

2. Georges Berger, "Discours de M. Georges Berger, Bulletin de la Société," *Revue des arts décoratifs* 15 (1894–1895): 318.

3. For information on the planning of the exposition, see Lucien Falize, "Histoire d'une exposition ajournée," *Revue des arts décoratifs* 12 (1891–1892): 225–242; and the "Rapport de M. Georges Berger," *Revue des arts décoratifs* 12 (1891–1892): 355–359.

4. Responses to the Galerie des Machines are discussed in Debora Silverman, "The Paris Exhibition of 1889: Architecture and the Crisis of Individualism," *Oppositions* 8 (Spring 1977): 71–91.

5. "Rapport de M. Berger," p. 356.

6. Falize, "Histoire d'une exposition ajournée," p. 227.

7. Ibid., pp. 227, 228–229.

8. "Rapport de M. Berger," pp. 357–358. The plan adopted was that the union, with government subsidies, would cover the costs of building the museum under the title Musée des Arts Décoratifs. After a period of eleven years, the museum would be ceded to the government as the Musée *National* des Arts Décoratifs.

9. "Rapport de M. Berger," pp. 356–358.

10. Quoted in Falize, "Histoire d'une exposition ajournée," p. 242.

11. P. Plauszewski, "Un Salon de fleurs à l'exposition des arts de la femme," *Revue des arts décoratifs* 12 (1891–1892): 319–320.

12. Berger, "Discours de M. Georges Berger, Bulletin de la Société," p. 318.

13. Ibid., pp. 317–318.

14. Georges Berger, "Appel aux femmes françaises," *Revue des arts décoratifs* 16 (1896): 97–99.

15. "Bulletin de la Société: Exposition des arts de la femme, Classification," *Revue des arts décoratifs* 12 (1891–1892): 221–223.

16. The objects displayed in this section of the exhibit are described in Louis de Fourcaud, "Les Arts de la femme au Palais de l'Industrie," *La Grande Dame* 1 (1893): 25–26.

17. The full list of the scholars, collectors, Japonists, and union officials on the committee for the "Section rétrospective, travaux d'art féminins" is found in "Bulletin de la Société: Exposition des arts de la femme, Constitution des comités d'organisation," *Revue des arts décoratifs* 12 (1891–1892): 255–256.

18. See the catalogue, Palais de l'Industrie, *Exposition des arts de la femme: Histoire de la coiffure,* (Paris: Le Comité des Coiffeurs de Paris, Syndicat général des Coiffeurs de Dames,

1892); see also the statement of M. Brylinski, "Chambre syndicale de la couture et de la confection pour dames," *Revue des arts décoratifs* 12 (1891–1892): 222–223.

19. Victor Champier, "Bulletin: L'Exposition des arts de la femme," *Revue des arts décoratifs* 12 (1891–1892): 192.

20. Quoted in Champier, "Bulletin: L'Exposition des arts de la femme," p. 192.

21. "Exposition des arts de la femme, Classification," p. 222; "Exposition des arts de la femme, Constitution des comités d'organisation," pp. 252–254.

22. Louis de Fourcaud, "Les Arts de la femme au Palais de l'Industrie," p. 24.

23. Ibid., p. 25.

24. Ibid.

25. See the goals of the congress delineated in Victor Champier, "Le Prochain Congrès des arts décoratifs," *Revue des arts décoratifs* 14 (1893–1894): 210; and *Le Congrès des arts décoratifs, tenu à l'Ecole Nationale des Beaux-Arts du 18 au 30 mai 1894, comptes-rendus sténographiques* (Paris: Lahure, 1894).

26. Karen Offen, "Depopulation, Nationalism, and Feminism in Fin-de-Siècle France," *American Historical Review* 89 (1984): 655, n. 13.

27. Madame Pégard, "Mémoire," in *Congrès des arts décoratifs*, pp. 218–224, quotations on pp. 218, 221.

28. Ibid., p. 218.

29. Ibid., pp. 218–222.

30. Ibid., pp. 220–221, 223.

31. Ibid., p. 252.

32. Ibid., pp. 221–223, 236–237. Pégard was particularly concerned about the decline of native art industries, such as lace and embroidery, and the problem that mechanization and foreign imports posed to the production of the crafts in France.

33. Ibid., pp. 222–223.

34. Ibid., pp. 236–237, 252.

35. Ibid., pp. 223–224.

36. See the discussion in chapter 4.

37. Respondents to Pégard's report at the 1894 congress stated there would be no general discussion of gender inequalities—this was a set of issues outside the realm of the congress's concerns. See Pégard, "Mémoire," pp. 224–228.

38. See "Rapport de M. Berger," *Revue des arts décoratifs* 16 (1896): 157–160. The membership list is taken from *Exposition des arts de la femme, guide livret illustré, Musée des Arts Décoratifs, Palais de l'Industrie* (Paris: A. Warmont, 1895), p. 14.

39. See the stipulations outlined and the charter segments quoted in "Rapport de M. Berger," pp. 158–160.

40. Ibid., p. 159.

41. Ibid.

42. Siegfried, Uzès, and Schlumberger are identified as bourgeois feminists in Steven C. Hause and Anne R. Kenney, "The Limits of Suffragist Behavior: Legalism and Militancy in France, 1876–1922," *American Historical Review* 86 (1981): 781–799, 801–804; Jean Rabaut, *Histoire des féminismes français* (Paris: Stock, 1978), pp. 207–241; and Karen Offen, "The Second Sex and the Baccalauréat in Republican France, 1880–1924," *French Historical Studies* 13 (1983): 266.

43. De Fourcaud, "Les Arts de la femme au Palais de l'Industrie," p. 24.

44. Ibid., pp. 27–28.

45. Ibid., p. 28.

46. Georges Berger, "Appel aux femmes françaises," *Revue des arts décoratifs* 16 (1896): 97–99.

47. De Fourcaud, "Les Arts de la femme au Palais de l'Industrie," pp. 24, 27.

48. Berger, "Appel aux femmes françaises," pp. 97–98.

49. Ibid., p. 98.

50. Ibid.

51. Gustave Larroumet. "L'Art décoratif et les femmes," *Revue des arts décoratifs* 16 (1896): 100–101, 102.

52. Ibid., p. 101.

53. Ibid., pp. 102–103.

54. Ibid., p. 104.

55. Ibid., pp. 104–105; see also Judex, "Le Goût du moderne et les femmes," *Revue des arts décoratifs* 15 (1894–1895): 148–157.

56. Larroumet, "L'Art décoratif et les femmes," p. 105.

57. "Bulletin de la Société: IIe Exposition des arts de la femme," *Revue des arts décoratifs* 15 (1894–1895): 254–255.

58. Georges Berger, "Circulaire," in "Bulletin de la Société: IIe Exposition des arts de la femme," p. 255.

59. Ibid.

60. Berger, "Appel aux femmes françaises," pp. 98–99.

61. Information on female workers in the fashion and consumer trades may be found in Ernest Labrousse and Fernand Braudel, eds., *Histoire économique et sociale de la France*, vol. 4, *1880–1980*, pt. 1; *Enquête sur le travail à domicile dans l'industrie de la fleur artificielle* (Paris: Office du Travail, 1913); Charles Benoist, *Les Ouvrières à l'aiguille à Paris* (Paris: Alcan, 1905); Pierre Du Maroussem, *La Question ouvrière*, vol. 3, *Le Jouet parisien: Grands magasins, "Sweating-system"* (Paris, A. Rousseau, 1893); and Marilyn J. Boxer, "Women in Industrial Homework: The Flowermakers of Paris in the *Belle Epoque*," *French Historical Studies* 12 (1982): 401–423. Boxer is particularly informative on the internal divisions within the artificial flower-maker trade and the drudgery of the labor at all but the top tier of the craft.

62. *Exposition des arts de la femme, guide livret illustré*, pp. 6–7.

63. The entries and names of the illustrious "femmes du monde" contributors may be found in *Exposition, guide livret*, pp. 48–66. Among the participants were the princesse de Bibesco, Madame Charcot, Madame Waldeck-Rousseau, the comtesse Greffulhe, and the duchesse de Brissac.

64. Among the institutions represented in the exhibit were the Ecole Normale d'Enseignement du Dessin de M. Guérin and the Cours de Mlle Cavaillé-Coll. See the entries in *Exposition, guide livret*, pp. 32–45.

65. The associations represented included the Union comtoise des arts décoratifs de Besançon, the Association de l'aiguille, la Société de l'Adélphie, and an Orphélinat des arts (*Exposition, guide livret*, pp. 16–22).

66. Berger, "Discours de M. Georges Berger, Bulletin de la Société," p. 318.

Chapter Twelve

1. See Louis Hautecoeur, *Histoire de l'architecture classique en France*, vol. 7, *La Fin de l'architecture classique, 1848–1900* (Paris: Picard, 1957), pp. 293–297; Albert Boime, "The Teaching Reforms of 1863 and the Origins of Modernism in France," *Art Quarterly* 1 (Autumn 1977): 1–39.

2. Hautecoeur, *Histoire de l'architecture*, pp. 297–299. See also the information contained in the exhibition catalogue *"Equivoques": Peintures françaises du XIXe siècle* (Paris: Union centrale des arts décoratifs, 1973), pp. 19–20.

3. Camille Mauclair, "La Réforme de l'art décoratif en France," *La Nouvelle Revue* 98 (1896): 724–725; "*Equivoques,*" pp. 3–20.

4. Marius Vachon, "La Société des artistes français," in *La Guerre artistique avec l'Allemagne: L'Organisation de la victoire* (Paris: Payot, 1916): 165–169. A list of the original members in the new society is included in Jeffrey Tancock, *The Sculpture of Auguste Rodin: The Collection of the Rodin Museum in Philadelphia* (Philadelphia: Philadelphia Museum of Art, 1976), pp. 72–73.

5. Quoted in Edmond de Goncourt and Jules de Goncourt, *Journal, Mémoires de la vie littéraire* (Paris: Fasquelle & Flammarion, 1956), 3:1173 (hereafter cited as *Journal des Goncourts*). Vachon called the "secessionist" group "une association embourgeoisée, pleine d'académiciens et d'académisables," which welcomed the "protocole des visites presidentielles et ministerielles" (*La Guerre artistique,* p. 168).

6. Quoted in Juste Sévéran, "Les Objets d'art aux Salons des Champs-Elysées et du Champ-de-Mars," *La Grande Dame* 3 (1895): 249.

7. The problem of artistic property in the decorative arts was a subject of heated debate in the 1890s. At the Central Union's Decorative Arts Congress, sponsored jointly with the Ministry of Beaux-Arts, for example, the issue of property and signatures was a major item on the agenda, taking up one of the three days of the congress. This congress debated a new copyright law that would protect designers and specify the contributions of designers and artisans to the final product. See *Le Congrès des arts décoratifs, tenu à l'Ecole Nationale des Beaux-Arts du 18 au 30 mai 1894, comptes-rendus sténographiques* (Paris: Lahure, 1984).

8. Ironically, only a few artisans exhibiting applied arts at the reformed Salon were the creators of the whole product. Most provided designs for the objects and were aided in making them by groups of artisanal executants. In its statement about artistic "property" and "personal invention" the society seemed to privilege the initial process—inspiration and design—over material execution.

9. Sévéran, "Les Objets d'art," p. 249.

10. *Journal des Goncourts,* 4:249, entry for May 13, 1892.

11. Frantz Jourdain, "Les Objets d'art aux Salons de 1896," *La Grande Dame* 4 (1896): 221. Jourdain, an architect who later built the Samaritaine Department Store, was an important art critic during the 1890s. He designed the top floor of the Goncourts' house, the famous *Grenier* where the brothers held their weekly salon.

12. Jourdain, "Les Objets d'art," p. 221; see also the discussions of Watteau, Fragonard, and Boucher as the models for artists adorning objects for use, in Frantz Jourdain, *Propos d'un isolé en faveur de son temps* (Paris: E. Figière, n.d.); and Debora Silverman, "Frantz Jourdain: Rococo and Art Nouveau," in *Macmillan Encyclopedia of Architects* (New York: Macmillan, 1982). For another view of Jourdain, see Meredith Clausen, *Frantz Jourdain and the Samaritaine: Art Nouveau Theory and Criticism* (Leiden: E. J. Brill, 1987), which I received too late to incorporate into my analysis.

13. Jourdain, "Les Objets d'art," p. 222.

14. Among Mauclair's specialties were the works of Watteau, Fragonard, and Greuze (he wrote these artists' biographies) and the eighteenth-century arts of miniature painting on tiny snuff boxes, perfume holders, and lockets. Mauclair typified the mixture of eighteenth-century affirmation and aestheticism in French intellectual life. His eighteenth-century interests led directly to his deep immersion in such modern artists as Whistler, Carrière, Rodin, Besnard, and Verlaine.

15. Mauclair, "La Réforme de l'art décoratif en France," p. 739. This article clarifies the particularly French impetus to reunite the arts.

16. Ibid., p. 741.

17. Eugenia Herbert, *The Artist and Social Reform: France and Belgium, 1885–1898* (New Haven, Conn.: Yale University Press, 1961), pp. 156–158.

18. Ibid.; Donald Drew Egbert, *Social Radicalism and the Arts, Western Europe: A Cultural History from the French Revolution to 1968* (New York: Knopf, 1970), pp. 603–610; Jules Destrée, *Art et socialisme* (Brussels, 1896); Jules Destrée and Emile Vandervelde, *Le Socialisme en Belgique* (Paris, 1898).

19. The Nabis showed stained glass designs at the Salon of 1895; Gauguin exhibited ceramics at the Salon of 1891. See Victor Champier, "Les Arts fraternels au Salon du Champ-de-Mars," *Revue des arts décoratifs* 12 (1891–1892): 5–16.

20. Quoted in Victor Arwas, *Berthon and Grasset* (New York: Rizzoli, 1978), p. 53.

21. Quoted in Arwas, *Berthon and Grasset,* p. 53.

22. Quoted in Arwas, *Berthon and Grasset,* p. 53. Typical of the crossover between art nouveau and *société nouvelle* in the Belgian context was that art journals, such as *L'Art moderne,* published articles on social change while political journals, such as *Société nouvelle,* ran articles on art, including those by Henry Van de Velde.

23. Henry Van de Velde, "Déblaiement d'art," *Société nouvelle* 12 (April 1894): 444–456. See also the complementary piece, "Une Prédication d'art," *Société nouvelle* 13 (July–December 1895): 733–744.

24. Van de Velde, "Une Prédication d'art," pp. 743–744.

25. Van de Velde, "Déblaiement d'art," pp. 446–455.

26. See John Rewald, *Georges Seurat* (New York: Wittenborn, 1943), pp. 13–18; and Martha Ward, "The Eighth Exhibition, 1886: The Rhetoric of Independence and Innovation," in *The New Painting: Impressionism, 1874–1886* (San Francisco: The Fine Arts Museum of San Francisco, 1986), pp. 421–423.

27. Robert Herbert, *Neo-Impressionism* (New York: Guggenheim Foundation, 1968), pp. 14–15; Debora Silverman, "The Quest for Harmony: Neo-Impressionism and Anarchism," unpublished MS, 1975, chap. 2.

28. Paul Signac, "Impressionistes et révolutionnaires," *La Révolte,* June 13–19, 1891, quoted in *Impressionism and Post-Impressionism, 1874–1904,* ed. Linda Nochlin (Englewood Cliffs, N.J.: Prentice-Hall, 1966), p. 124.

29. Eugenia Herbert, *The Artist and Social Reform,* pp. 180–192, 99–131.

30. Signac, quoted in Nochlin, *Impressionism and Post-Impressionism, 1874–1904,* p. 125.

31. Kahn, quoted in Herbert, *The Artist and Social Reform,* p. 133.

32. Fénéon, quoted in Herbert, *The Artist and Social Reform,* p. 133.

33. The letter from Signac is included in Van Gogh's collected letters, quoted here from John Rewald, *Post-Impressionism from Van Gogh to Gauguin* 2d ed. (Garden City, N.Y.: Doubleday, 1962), p. 139.

34. Victor Champier, "Notre nouveau programme," *Revue des arts décoratifs* 12 (1891–1892): 2.

35. Ibid.

36. Champier, "Les Arts fraternels," pp. 5–16.

37. Paul Mantz was a scholarly architect of the rococo revival in the Central Union who wrote on eighteenth-century furniture (see chapter 6). Mantz was also a friend of Edmond de Goncourt and a government arts administrator.

38. Champier, "Les Arts fraternels," pp. 9–10. A similar argument, identifying the "liberty" and "equality" of all the arts under the Old Regime and the destruction of the "republic of all the arts" by the French Revolution, is presented by another Central Union writer, Louis de Fourcaud, in "Les Arts décoratifs au Salon de 1892: Champs-Elysées et Champ-de-Mars," *Revue des arts décoratifs* 12 (1891–1892): 324–328, 385–388.

39. Champier, "Les Arts fraternels," p. 10.

40. Ibid., p. 16.

41. Ibid.

42. Champier, "Notre nouveau programme," p. 3.

43. Victor Champier, "Chroniques et nouvelles du mois," *Revue des arts décoratifs* 12 (1891–1892): 400.

44. Ibid.

45. Victor Champier, "L'Habitation moderne: Hôtel de Madame Salomon de Rothschild, l'ancienne Folie-Beaujon et la maison de Balzac," *Revue des arts décoratifs* 12 (1891–1892): 65.

46. Ibid., pp. 66–67.

47. Ibid.

48. Ibid., pp. 70–75.

49. Ibid., p. 75.

50. Geffroy (1855–1926) was a member of Clemenceau's staff at the newspaper *La Justice*. His defense of modern art in all its forms was compiled in *La Vie artistique,* an eight-volume work written between 1892 and 1903. Not only Japonism, Impressionism, and art nouveau but also the eighteenth century played a major role in the first three volumes. The foreword was written by Edmond de Goncourt, who lauded Geffroy's artistic tastes and his sensitive "*langue picturale.*" Geffroy realized his lifelong promotion of the arts when he was appointed director of the Gobelins tapestry manufacture in 1902. There he was able to commission modern decorative artists like Chéret and Besnard for state service. See the Bibliothèque Nationale catalogue, *Gustave Geffroy et l'art moderne* (Paris: Bibliothèque Nationale, 1957).

51. Gustave Geffroy, "L'Habitation moderne, II: La Maison des Goncourts," *Revue des arts décoratifs* 12 (1891–1892): 147. (Quotation from Edmond de Goncourt, *Maison d'un artiste.*)

52. Geffroy, "L'Habitation moderne," p. 146.

53. Ibid., p. 151.

54. See Claude Roger-Marx, "Roger Marx," *Evidences* 12, no. 88 (March–April 1961): 34–38 (written by Roger Marx's son, with fragments of letters from various artists to his father); G. W., "Pour le centenaire de Roger Marx," *Gazette des beaux-arts* 54, no. 1088 (September 1959), supplément, pp. 1–3; Loys D., *préface* to *Catalogue des estampes modernes composant la collection Roger Marx* (Paris: Baudoin, 1914), pp. 1–7; and Arsène Alexandre, *préface* to *Catalogue des tableaux, pastels, dessins, aquarelles, sculptures faisant partie de la collection Roger Marx* (Paris: Manzi, Joyant, 1914), pp. 1–10. The two catalogues chronicle the breadth of Roger Marx's personal collection of modern artists.

55. G. W., "Pour le centenaire de Roger Marx," pp. 1–2.

56. The pivotal role of art administrators like Roger Marx has not received sufficient scholarly attention. Marx's mediative role may be compared, though political circumstances differed, with that of Tschudi in Germany, analyzed by Peter Paret in "The Tschudi Affair," *Journal of Modern History* 53 (1981): 589–618.

57. G. W., "Pour le centenaire de Roger Marx," pp. 1–3; "Roger Marx" entry in Frits Lugt, *Les Marques de collections de dessins et d'estampes* (Amsterdam: Vereenigte Drukkerijen, 1921), p. 417. One example of his direct mediation occurred during the planning of the 1900 exposition, when Roger Marx personally persuaded Monet, Pissarro, and Renoir to display their works. Originally none of these artists had wanted to participate in an official celebration such as the fair. The exchange of letters between Marx and these artists is reprinted in Claude Roger-Marx, "Roger Marx," pp. 34–37.

58. Mauclair, "La Réforme de l'art décoratif en France," p. 737.

59. Ibid., pp. 725–739; Alexandre, *préface* to *Catalogue des tableaux,* pp. 1–9; Loys D., *préface* to *Catalogue des estampes modernes,* pp. 1–8; Louis Hautecoeur, *préface* to *Catalogue des objets d'art moderne . . . faisant partie de la collection Roger Marx* (Paris: Manzi, Joyant, 1914),

pp. i–iv. See also the way that Victor Champier cites from Roger Marx's articles in Champier, "Les Arts fraternels," pp. 5–6.

60. Alexandre, *préface* to *Catalogue des tableaux*, pp. 6–7; Mauclair, "La Réforme de l'art décoratif," pp. 725, 736–737.

61. Claude Roger-Marx, "Roger Marx," p. 36; G. W., "Pour le centenaire de Roger Marx," pp. 1–3.

62. Claude Roger-Marx, "Roger Marx," pp. 34–37; Roger Marx, "Les Arts à l'Exposition universelle de 1900," *Gazette des beaux-arts* 24 (1900): 397–421, 563–576.

63. Anatole France, *préface* to Roger Marx, *L'Art social* (Paris: Fasquelle, 1913), pp. viii, xi, vii.

64. Van de Velde, "Une Prédication d'art," p. 744.

65. Roger Marx, *L'Art social*, pp. xi, 69, 82, 114, 166–169, 207–208.

66. Ibid. Other examples of art as consolation are found in Roger Marx's statement about the soothing and withdrawing impulses in collecting prints: "Il y en a peu qui surent goûter aussi profondément le plaisir de la belle épreuve. Emanation spontanée, immédiate du génie de l'artiste, l'estampe requiert d'être accueillie, goûtée un peu à la manière d'une confidence, dans l'intimité du calme avec la dévotion du silence" (quoted in "Roger Marx," entry in Lugt, *Marques de collections*, p. 417).

67. "Roger Marx" entry in *Marques de collections*, p. 417.

68. Roger Marx, "Les Goncourts et l'art: Etude de leur esthétique et des aquarelles de Jules de Goncourt," *Gazette des beaux-arts* 17 (1897): 159–163, 238–248, 402–416; Roger Marx, "L'Art et les Goncourts," *La Lorraine-artiste* 14 (1896): 275–276; Roger Marx, "Souvenirs des Goncourts," *Revue encyclopédique* no. 155 (August 22, 1896): 545–555.

69. Edmond de Goncourt and Jules de Goncourt, *Etudes d'art: Le Salon de 1852, la peinture à l'Exposition de 1855*, préface de Roger Marx (Paris: Librairie des Bibliophiles, 1893), pp. i–xix.

70. Roger Marx, "Les Goncourts collectionneurs," in *Collection des Goncourts: Dessins, aquarelles, et pastels du XVIIIe siècle, Catalogue du vente* (Paris: May & Metteroz, 1897), p. xiv. See also Marx's affirmation of the Goncourts' eighteenth-century rediscovery in his *préface* to Goncourt, *Etudes d'art*, pp. iii–xvii.

71. Marx, "Les Goncourts collectionneurs," pp. ix–xvi, and *préface* to Goncourt, *Etudes d'art*, pp. i–xix. In these essays Marx emphasized the anguish and torment that accompanied the insatiable need of the brothers de Goncourt for aesthetic stimulation, in both their art collecting and their writing. Marx's assessment of this psychological cost is among the most penetrating. Marx also clarifies the new design principle behind the Maison d'Auteuil: that of aesthetic, personal, and psychological spatial integration rather than historical eclecticism.

72. In Roger Marx, *L'Art social*, p. 88.

73. Ibid., p. 22.

74. Ibid., pp. 162–163, 165, 179, 205.

75. Ibid., pp. 193–194.

76. Roger Marx, "La Renaissance des arts décoratifs," *Les Arts* 1 (January 1902): 38.

77. Marx, quoted in Loys D., *préface* to *Catalogue des estampes modernes*, p. 5; see also Roger Marx, *L'Art social*, p. 36.

78. Roger Marx, "Le Salon au Champ-de-Mars," *Revue encyclopédique* no. 138 (April 25, 1896): 286–287.

79. Roger Marx, "Jean Dampt, Maître des arts," *La Grande Dame* 4 (1896): 90.

80. Ibid., p. 92.

81. Ibid., pp. 91, 93.

82. Ibid., p. 92.

83. Edmond repeatedly invoked the notion of the "caress" of the artisan on the "skin" of his diminutive, usually female, objects in describing such rococo masters as Falconet and

Meissonnier. It is revealing that Roger Marx also used the language of seduction in describing the decorative arts; he explained the sexual meaning of the Goncourts' attitude toward their objets d'art in "Les Goncourts collectionneurs," pp. ix–xvi.

84. Roger Marx, "Jean Dampt," pp. 94–95.

85. Ibid., p. 94.

86. Ibid., pp. 90, 96.

87. Emmanuel Bénézit, *Dictionnaire critique et documentaire des peintres, sculpteurs, dessina- teurs, et graveurs* (Paris: Girund, 1976), 7:434; Roger Marx, *The Painter Albert Besnard: A Biog- raphy with Original Etchings and Illustrations after His Pictures* (Paris: Hennuyer, 1893), pp. 2–10.

88. Marx, *The Painter Besnard,* pp. 17–22. See also Camille Mauclair's analysis of Bes- nard's bridging of the innovative world of Impressionism with the Academy: "M. Besnard s'est trouvé, lui esprit classique et français . . . presque à la limite extrême du classicisme et de l'impressionnisme pour en donner *une conciliation imprévue et merveilleuse*" ("L'Art décoratif d'Albert Besnard," *La Nouvelle Revue* 33 [1900]: 255–256).

89. Roger Marx, *The Painter Besnard,* pp. 18, 22, 6, 17, 20.

90. Ibid., pp. 16–17.

91. Ibid. See also pp. 18–21 for more of Roger Marx's descriptions of the shimmering effects of colored light in Besnard's technique.

92. Roger Marx, "La Vie naît de la mort d'Albert Besnard," *Revue encyclopédique* no. 146 (June 20, 1896): 434–435.

93. Ibid.

94. Carl E. Schorske, *Fin-de-Siècle Vienna: Politics and Culture* (New York: Knopf, 1980), pp. 226–277.

Chapter Thirteen

1. See the discussion of the Lamour gates in chapter 9.

2. Françoise-Thérèse Charpentier, *Emile Gallé* (Nancy: Université de Nancy, 1978), pp. 11–16, and "La Clientèle étrangère de Gallé," in *Stil und Überlieferung in der Kunst des Abendlandes, Akten des 21. Internationalen Kongresses für Kunstgeschichte in Bonn 1964,* Band I, *Epochen Europäischer Kunst* (Berlin: Mann, 1967), pp. 256–258.

3. Emile Gallé, *Ecrits pour l'art* (Paris: Laurens, 1908), p. 239; Charpentier, *Emile Gallé,* pp. 15–17.

4. Charpentier, *Emile Gallé,* pp. 15–34; Philippe Garner, *Emile Gallé* (London: Academy, 1978), pp. 15–28.

5. Garner, *Emile Gallé,* pp. 19–20; Charpentier, *Emile Gallé,* pp. 18–21.

6. S. Tschui Madsen, *Art Nouveau* (New York: McGraw-Hill, 1967), p. 59.

7. Louis de Fourcaud, "Rapport général de l'Exposition de 1884," *Revue des arts décoratifs* 5 (1884–1885): 260–261.

8. Gallé's scientific studies of plant life are amply recorded in his technical articles on bot- any, included in *Ecrits pour l'art,* pp. 1–112. See also Roger Marx, "Emile Gallé," in *L'Art social* (Paris: Fasquelle, 1913), pp. 124–126. Gallé became president of the Nancy Horticul- tural Society and the editor of their journal.

9. Garner, *Emile Gallé,* p. 50; Charpentier, *Emile Gallé,* p. 29; Gallé, *Ecrits pour l'art,* pp. 46–88. On the gates of his factory, Gallé inscribed his motto celebrating the soil of France: "Our roots are in the depths of the forest / Among the mosses, amidst the water" (in Gallé, *Ecrits pour l'art,* p. 133).

10. Gallé, *Ecrits pour l'art,* pp. 150, 346.

11. Ibid., pp. 352, 154, 153, 150, 183.

12. Ibid., pp. 212–216.

13. Ibid., p. 77.

14. Ibid., pp. 81, 202.

15. Ibid., pp. 316–317, 324, 337.

16. Ibid., pp. 219–220.

17. Ibid., pp. 210–236.

18. Ibid., p. 216; quoted in Charpentier, Emile Gallé, p. 112.

19. Gallé, Ecrits pour l'art, pp. 152, 129.

20. Emile Gallé, "Les Verreries de M. Emile Gallé au Salon du Champ-de-Mars," Revue des arts décoratifs 12 (1891–1892): 335.

21. Ibid., p. 334.

22. Reproduced in the Corning Museum of Glass, Emile Gallé: Dreams into Glass (Corning, N.Y., 1984), p. 169.

23. See the correspondence between de Montesquiou and Gallé in the manuscript collection of the Bibliothèque Nationale, Nafr. 15266, "Comte Robert de Montesquiou-Fezensac: Sa vie et ses demeures," pp. 12–46, 80–88, 152, 164, 171; and Nafr. 15039, "La rue Franklin," pp. 6–24.

24. Ibid., Nafr. 15039, in press clipping on the dresser (L'Eclair, May 7, 1892), n.p.

25. Ibid. (La Cocarde, May 7, 1892; L'Eclair, April 25, 1892), n.p.

26. Ibid. (Le Monde musical, June 30, 1892), n.p.

27. Depicted in a portefeuille entitled "Mobilier, Salon du Champ-de-Mars, 1892," Revue des arts décoratifs 12 (1891–1892).

28. Emile Gallé, "La Table aux herbes potagères," Revue des arts décoratifs 12 (1891–1892): 381, 383.

29. Gallé, Ecrits pour l'art, p. 176.

30. Ibid., pp. 165, 173.

31. Ibid., p. 184.

32. Ibid., p. 201.

33. Henri de Moncel, "Un Discours de M. Bernheim," La Lorraine-artiste 10 (1892): 731–734; quotations from 731 and 732.

34. Henri de Moncel, "Vers l'inconscient," La Lorraine-artiste 10 (1892): 674–676.

35. Jacques Turbin, "Hypnotisme," La Lorraine-artiste 10 (1892): 407–408.

36. A. G., "La Divinité de l'inconscient," La Lorraine-artiste 10 (1892): 697.

37. See chapter 5.

38. Gallé, Ecrits pour l'art, p. 91.

39. Reported in "Victor Prouvé," La Lorraine-artiste 14 (1896): 236.

40. Gallé, Ecrits pour l'art, p. 350, translated in Corning Museum, Emile Gallé, p. 188.

41. Ibid.

42. Ibid.

43. Gallé, Ecrits pour l'art, p. 351, translated in Corning Museum, Emile Gallé, p. 189.

44. Gallé, Ecrits pour l'art, pp. 148–149, translated in Corning Museum, Emile Gallé, p. 49. This commentary originally appeared in La Revue encyclopédique, May 15, 1893.

45. Gallé, Ecrits pour l'art, pp. 149–150, translated in Corning Museum, Emile Gallé, p. 49.

46. See chapter 5.

47. Hippolyte Bernheim, Suggestive Therapeutics: A Treatise on the Nature and Uses of Hypnotism [1884], trans. Christian A. Herter, M.D. (New York: Putnam, 1887), pp. x, 45–46, 96–104, 130–131.

48. Ibid.; see also chapter 5.

49. Gallé, Ecrits pour l'art, p. 75.

50. Ibid., p. 198.

51. Victor Champier, "Les Arts fraternels au Salon du Champ-de-Mars," *Revue des arts décoratifs* 12 (1891–1892): 14.

52. Victor Champier, introduction to "Les Verreries de M. Emile Gallé au Salon du Champ-de-Mars," p. 332.

53. See S. Rocheblave, *Louis de Fourcaud et le mouvement artistique en France de 1875 à 1914* (Paris: Les Belles-Lettres, 1926); and Louis de Fourcaud, "Les Arts décoratifs au Salon de 1892: Champs-Elysées et Champ-de-Mars," *Revue des arts décoratifs* 12 (1891–1892), pp. 324–328, 385–388.

54. Louis de Fourcaud, *Emile Gallé* (Paris: Librairie d'art ancien et moderne, 1903), p. 6.

55. Ibid., p. 30.

56. Ibid., pp. 6–7, 8.

57. Edmond de Goncourt, quoted in Gustave Geffroy, "L'Habitation moderne, II: La Maison des Goncourts," *Revue des arts décoratifs* 12 (1891–1892): 147.

58. De Fourcaud, *Emile Gallé*, p. 13. De Fourcaud immediately went on to join Gallé's physical state, "nerveux au suprême," with his impatience to "traduire un afflux d'idées emergés toutes ensembles," as if the physical state expressed the continuous and insatiable creativity.

59. Ibid., p. 30.

60. Louis de Fourcaud, "Les Arts décoratifs aux Salons de 1894," *Revue des arts décoratifs* 15 (1894–1895): 2.

61. Ibid.

62. Ibid.

63. Roger Marx, *L'Art social*, p. 148.

64. Ibid., pp. 117, 116, 122.

65. Roger Marx, *La Décoration et l'art industriel à l'Exposition universelle de 1889* (Paris: Librairies-imprimeries réunies, 1890), p. 52.

66. Marx, *L'Art social*, pp. 126–128.

67. Marx, *La Decoration à l'Exposition de 1889*, pp. 26, 54–55, 59.

68. Marx, *L'Art social*, pp. 134, 149.

69. Ibid., p. 116.

70. Roger Marx, preface to Edmond de Goncourt and Jules de Goncourt, *Etudes d'art: Le Salon de 1852, la peinture à l'Exposition de 1855* (Paris: Librairie de Bibliophiles, 1893), p. xiii.

71. Roger Marx, "Les Goncourts collectionneurs," in *Collections des Goncourts: Dessins, aquarelles, et pastels du XVIIIe siècle* (Paris: May & Metteroz, 1897), p. xv.

72. Gallé, quoted in Marx, *L'Art social*, p. 128.

73. Ibid., p. 114.

74. Details about the commission may be found in Judith Cladel, *Auguste Rodin: Sa vie glorieuse et inconnue* (Paris: Grasset, 1936), pp. 136–138; and Albert E. Elsen, *"The Gates of Hell" by Auguste Rodin* (Stanford, Calif.: Stanford University Press, 1985), pp. 3–11.

75. Auguste Rodin, *Rodin: The Man and His Art, with Leaves from His Notebooks*, comp. Judith Cladel and trans. S. K. Star (New York: Century, 1918), p. 116.

76. Ibid., p. 247.

77. Rodin, quoted in Ionel Jianou, *Rodin* (Paris: Arted, Editions d'art, 1979), p. 34; see also pp. 30–35.

78. Cladel, *Auguste Rodin*, pp. 82–83, 128–129; Rodin, *Notebooks*, p. 115.

79. Jianou, *Rodin*, pp. 48–49; Cladel, *Auguste Rodin*, pp. 130–131. The rococo designs for the Sèvres ceramics are reproduced in the rare volume of Roger Marx, *Rodin céramiste* (Paris: Société de propagation des livres d'art, 1907). The *Revue des arts décoratifs* also featured illustrations of several of Rodin's Sèvres figurines. See, for example, one included in Victor Cham-

pier, "Les Arts fraternels au Salon du Champ-de-Mars," *Revue des arts décoratifs* 12 (1891–1892): 7, and again on 295.

80. Rodin, *Notebooks,* pp. 246–247, 115.

81. Ibid., pp. 126–129 ("Scattered Thoughts on Flowers"). Rodin's development from rococo caprice to dynamic organicism depended, to be sure, on a number of different influences, not all of which can be discussed here The most important is the Italianate influence, particularly of Michelangelo, which is amply examined in the scholarly literature beginning with Albert Elsen's classic studies. My purpose is to highlight aspects of Rodin's development, underemphasized in the literature, that converge with the development of official modernism: his anchorage in eighteenth-century traditions of drawing and modeling, his nationalist naturism, and his neuropsychiatric conceptions.

82. Rodin, *Notebooks,* pp. 211–212.

83. Descriptions of the 1892 fête at Nancy during which the statue was unveiled may be found in Jean Vartier, *La Vie quotidienne en Lorraine au XIXe siècle* (Paris: Hachette, 1973), pp. 214–224.

84. Jeffrey Tancock, *The Sculpture of Auguste Rodin: The Collections of the Rodin Museum, Philadelphia* (Philadelphia: Philadelphia Museum of Art, 1976), p. 403; Cladel, *Auguste Rodin,* pp. 167–168.

85. Albert E. Elsen, *Rodin* (New York: Museum of Modern Art, 1963), pp. 208–209.

86. Tancock, *Sculpture of Auguste Rodin,* pp. 72–73

87. Description of Judex, "M. Carnot à Nancy: Le Statue de M. Rodin," *Revue des arts décoratifs* 12 (1891–1892): 402.

88. Tancock, *Sculpture of Auguste Rodin,* p. 404.

89. Judex, "M. Carnot à Nancy," p. 402.

90. Quoted in Tancock, *Sculpture of Auguste Rodin,* p. 403.

91. Ibid. This analysis of the rococo elements is based on my examination of the model in the Rodin Museum, Philadelphia.

92. Judex, "M. Carnot à Nancy," p. 402.

93. N. Pierson, "Le Monument de Rodin,' *La Lorraine-artiste* 10 (1892): 250–251.

94. E. Goutière-Vernolle, "La Statue de Claude Lorrain," *La Lorraine-artiste* 10 (1892): 385.

95. Tancock, *Sculpture of Auguste Rodin,* p. 404.

96. Rodin, quoted in Tancock, *Sculpture of Auguste Rodin,* pp. 402–403 (emphasis mine).

97. Cladel, *Auguste Rodin,* p. 86.

98. Ibid.

99. Quoted in Elsen, *Rodin,* p. 57.

100. Charcot file at the Rodin Archive, Musée Rodin, Paris. Frederic Grunfeld notes in his *Rodin: A Biography* (New York: Henry Holt & Co., 1987, p. 145) that Rodin was a regular guest at the Saturday evening dinners at the home of Charcot's stepdaughter, Madame Liouville, throughout the 1880s. The wedding invitation of 1888 (when the widowed stepdaughter remarried, becoming the wife of Réné Waldeck-Rousseau) thus indicates a long-term association between Rodin and the Charcot family.

101. Critics in Nancy, quoted in Emile Gallé. "L'Art expressif et la statue de Claude Gelée, par M. Rodin," *La Lorraine-artiste* 10 (1892): 534.

102. Victor Prouvé, quoted in Jules Rey, "La Statue de Claude Gelée," *La Lorraine-artiste* 10 (1892): 477–478.

103. Gallé, "L'Art expressif et la statue de Claude Gelée," p. 537.

104. Ibid., pp. 535, 537.

105. Ibid., pp. 534–538.

106. Ibid., p. 536.

107. Ibid., pp. 536–537.

108. Ibid., pp. 537, 538.

109. Tancock, *Sculpture of Auguste Rodin,* pp. 90–92, 111–112; Elsen, *Rodin,* pp. 35–40; Elsen, *"The Gates of Hell,"* pp. 35–55.

110. Tancock, *Sculpture of Auguste Rodin,* p. 111. The figure was exhibited at the Monet-Rodin show in 1889 and listed in the catalogue of the show as no. 27—"Le Penseur; Le Poète." See Galerie Georges Petit, *Exposition Claude Monet, A. Rodin* (Paris: Imprimerie de l'art, 1889), p. 88. Albert Elsen found a letter referring to the sculpture as the Thinker as early as 1884. See Elsen, *"The Gates of Hell,"* pp. 152–153, and n. 9, p. 253.

111. Gustave Geffroy, "A. Rodin," in Galerie Georges Petit, *Exposition Claude Monet, A. Rodin,* pp. 68–69, 56–57.

112. Quoted in Daniel Rosenfeld, "Rodin's Carved Sculpture," in *Rodin Rediscovered,* ed. Albert E. Elsen (Washington, D.C.: National Gallery of Art, 1982), p. 88.

113. Quoted in Rosenfeld, "Rodin's Carved Sculpture," p. 88.

114. Quoted in Albert E. Elsen, *Rodin's Thinker and the Dilemmas of Modern Public Sculpture* (New Haven, Conn.: Yale University Press, 1985), p. 61.

115. Roger Marx, "Souvenirs sur Auguste Rodin," included in the MS file labeled "Auguste Rodin: Letters, Essays, Criticisms," Philadelphia Museum of Art, Rodin Museum Archives, manuscript M392sPr, p. 7, n.d.

116. Gustave Geffroy, "L'Imaginaire," *Le Figaro,* August 29, 1893, included in Philadelphia Museum of Art, Rodin Museum Archives, "French Newspaper Clippings, 1866–1917," R692f.

117. Geffroy, "A. Rodin," pp. 58–59.

118. Quoted in Elsen, *Rodin's Thinker,* p. 64.

119. Rodin, quoted in Tancock, *Sculpture of Auguste Rodin,* pp. 112, 111.

120. Victor Prouvé, quoted in Rey, "La Statue de Claude Gelée," pp. 477–478.

121. Gallé, "L'Art expressif et la statue de Claude Gelée," p. 536.

122. Emile Vinchon, *L'Oeuvre littéraire de Maurice Rollinat* (Issoudun: Labourer, 1927); Jerrold Seigel, *Bohemian Paris: Culture, Politics, and the Boundaries of Bourgeois Life, 1830–1930* (New York: Viking Press, 1986), pp. 231–234.

123. Judith Cladel, "Maurice Rollinat," *Portraits d'hier* no. 32 (June 15, 1910): 3–29; Gustave Geffroy, "Maurice Rollinat: Poète des Névroses" [1883], in *Notes d'un journaliste* (Paris: Bibliothèque Charpentier, 1887), pp. 278–292; Marie Krysinska, "Les Cénacles artistiques et littéraires, autour de Maurice Rollinat," *La Revue* (August 15, 1904): 477–491.

124. Cladel, *Auguste Rodin,* pp. 31–32; Cladel, "Maurice Rollinat," pp. 3–29.

125. Georges Elie-Berthet, "Chez les autres," *Le Gil Blas,* November 3, 1903, n.p.; Gustave Kahn, "Les Poètes, Maurice Rollinat," *La Revue blanche* (August 1, 1896): 537–538. These and other accounts of witnesses are included in the Rollinat file at the Paris Musée Rodin archive.

126. Marcel Adam, "Rodin et Rollinat," 1906, unidentified article in Rollinat file at the Paris Musée Rodin archive; and two articles, also in the Rollinat file, one clipped from *Le Radical,* August 24, 1906, the other from *L'Art et les artistes,* July 1906, pp. 170–171.

127. Reported in *Exposition Rodin et les écrivains de son temps: Sculptures, dessins, lettres, et livres du fonds Rodin* (Paris: Musée Rodin, 1976), p. 125. The autographed copy of the book was displayed as part of this exhibition.

128. The letters from Rollinat to Rodin acknowledging receipt of drawings and plaster reliefs are in the Rollinat file at the Paris Musée Rodin; *Exposition Rodin et les écrivains de son temps,* p. 125. Georges Grappe dates the *Déséspoir* from 1890 in his *Catalogue du Musée Rodin: Essai de classement chronologique des oeuvres d'Auguste Rodin* (Paris: Musée Rodin, 1944), p. 84.

129. Adam, "Rodin et Rollinat," n.p.

130. On the memorial, see the numerous articles in the Rollinat file at the Paris Musée Rodin.

131. Tancock, *Sculpture of Auguste Rodin*, pp. 60–62; Cladel, *Auguste Rodin*, pp. 68–72.

132. Cladel, "Maurice Rollinat," p. 22.

133. See, for example, "Villanelle du diable," "Ballade du cadavre," "L'Enfer," and "Mademoiselle Squelette," in *Les Névroses* (Paris: L. Marétheux, 1883).

134. Maurice Rollinat, "L'Egoisme," in *L'Abîme* (Paris: Charpentier, 1886), pp. 31–33.

135. Quoted in Vinchon, *L'Oeuvre littéraire de Maurice Rollinat*, p. 107.

136. Gustave Geffroy, "Maurice Rollinat," *La Revue universelle* 3, no. 99 (1903): 618.

137. Cladel, "Maurice Rollinat," p. 12.

138. Clipping of November 10, 1906, in Rollinat file at the Paris Musée Rodin.

139. See, for example, the poems "La Folie" and "L'Angoisse" in *Les Névroses*, pp. 319, 363–364; "L'Ingratitude," "L'Epée de Damocles," "L'Automate," and "Le Spectre" in *L'Abîme*, pp. 262–270, 206–213, and 84–85. Judith Cladel mentions ataxia and paralysis in "Maurice Rollinat," p. 6.

140. Rollinat, "La Céphalagie," in *Les Névroses*, pp. 300–301.

141. Following the discoveries of Albert Elsen, scholars assume Charles Baudelaire, along with Dante, is the key literary source for Rodin's *Gates of Hell*. Elsen demonstrates convincingly that Baudelaire exerted a powerful influence on Rodin, particularly as the sculptor executed drawings for an edition of *Fleurs du mal*. But Rollinat, a devoted follower of Baudelaire and a close friend and exact contemporary of Rodin's, is nonetheless a key new source for understanding the genesis, development, and meaning of Rodin's work. Rollinat appropriated Baudelaire's general theme of the irremediable conflict between passion and guilt, desire and suffering, and infused it with particular clinical and psychiatric meaning. This aspect of Rollinat's work caught the interest of Rodin, who from his days as a student had been intrigued by trends in medical neurology. My analysis suggests that specific poems by Rollinat on the artistic and intellectual process offer a new way to understand the dual structure and meaning of Rodin's *Gates of Hell* and *Monument to Claude Lorrain*. The poems point to a hitherto unnoticed correspondence between the two sculptures. Scholars have not previously compared *The Gates of Hell* to *Claude Lorrain*, nor have they assessed the role of Rollinat's poems in the development of these works.

142. Rollinat, quoted in Emile Vinchon, *La Philosophie de Maurice Rollinat* (Paris: Jouve, 1929), p. 60.

143. From the poem "Le Gouffre" ("the abyss" or "pit"), in Rollinat, *Les Névroses*, p. 348.

144. Ibid., p. 347.

145. From the poem "L'Angoisse," in Rollinat, *Les Névroses*, p. 364.

146. From the poem "L'Artiste," in Rollinat, *L'Abîme*, pp. 177, 178, 179.

147. From the poem "La Pensée," in Rollinat, *L'Abîme*, p. 8.

148. Ibid., pp. 9, 10, 11, 12.

149. Albert Elsen reminds us, in a masterful visual tour of the *Gates*, that the Thinker is to be viewed from below, so that his protrusion from the shelf is clearly visible to the spectator (*"The Gates of Hell,"* pp. 161–221, and *Rodin's Thinker*, pp. 66–71). Rodin's contemporaries also noted the precarious position of the Thinker and its projection forward from the shelf. See the article from *Art et Décoration* cited in Jacques de Caso and Patricia B. Sanders, *Rodin's Sculpture: A Critical Study of the Spreckels Collection*, California Palace of the Legion of Honor (Rutland, Vt.: Charles Tuttle, 1977), p. 137.

150. See Tancock, *Sculpture of Auguste Rodin*, p. 112; and Elsen, *Rodin*, p. 53, *"The Gates of Hell,"* pp. 211–212, 227, 243, and *Rodin's Thinker*, p. 66.

151. From the testimony of Judith Cladel, reported to Albert Elsen, in Elsen, *"The Gates of Hell,"* pp. 111–112.

152. From the poem, "La Divinité de l'inconscient," in *La Lorraine-artiste* 10 (1892): 697; see p. 236.

153. Bernheim, *Suggestive Therapeutics*, pp. x, 129–131, 134–136, 140–142.

154. The words of Rilke, d'Auray, and Rodin, cited in nn. 118, 114, 119.

155. Tancock, *Sculpture of Auguste Rodin,* p. 403.

156. Rollinat, "La Pensée," in *L'Abîme,* p. 10.

Chapter Fourteen

1. Roger Marx, *L'Art social* (Paris: Fasquelle, 1913), pp. 22–24.

2. S. Bing, *Artistic America, Tiffany Glass, and Art Nouveau,* trans. Benita Eisler, with an introduction by Robert Koch (Cambridge, Mass.: MIT Press, 1970), p. 168: "Among the foreign artists who had successfully worked in American silver, the most numerous, and by far the most talented, came from France. But it is not this industry alone which the French have helped to establish in America. When one investigates the field of American industrial design, one finds significant traces of our national genius at its base."

3. Ibid., pp. 170, 177.

4. Ibid., p. 164.

5. Ibid., pp. 130, 132.

6. Ibid., p. 146.

7. S. Bing, Introduction to Union centrale des arts décoratifs, *Salon annuel des peintures japonaises,* 2e année (Paris: Pillet & Demoulin, 1884), pp. 2–3.

8. *Art Nouveau: Art and Design at the Turn of the Century,* ed. Peter Selz and Mildred Constantine (New York: Museum of Modern Art, 1975), pp. 95–97, 8; Henry Van de Velde, "Memoirs, 1891–1901," *The Architectural Record* 112 (September 1952): 144–145; A. Hammacher, *Le Monde de Henry Van de Velde* (Paris, 1967), pp. 25–88, 112–114.

9. Van de Velde's immersion in Neo-Impressionist theory of evocative, rhythmic line is noted in S. Tschudi Madsen, *Art Nouveau* (New York: McGraw-Hill, 1967), pp. 51, 53–55, 99, 203–204, 209; and in Hammacher, *Le Monde de Henry Van de Velde,* pp. 71–72. Van de Velde comments on the psychophysical impact of his theory of line in his introduction to *Le Style moderne: Contribution de la France,* (Paris: Librairie des Arts décoratifs, 1925), n.p., where he identifies the "ornementation structo-linéaire" "dynamographique." Dynamogeny and inhibition were the psychophysical qualities attributed by Van de Velde and the Neo-Impressionists to the visual arts. The social implications of this theory and their application to the Bloemenwerf have not, to my knowledge, been explored.

10. The new study of Bing by the art historian Gabriel Weisberg suggests that he was influenced by a second Brussels center of art nouveau, the Maison d'Art housed in Edmond Picard's Hôtel de la Toison d'Or. Picard's residence provided the opportunity for the Brussels avant-garde members of Les XX, which included Henry Van de Velde, to exhibit art works from many different media as a single integral environment, modeled on the Gesamtkunstwerk. As I noted in chapter 12, Picard and the members of Les XX explicitly related their artistic innovations to political radicalism, stimulated partly by the volatile character of Belgian politics in the 1880s and 1890s. Weisberg does not indicate whether Bing responded to the social and political goals underlying the Picard art nouveau initiative, but he notes a fundamental and revealing difference between the Maison Picard and the Maison Bing: Picard's Maison did *not* offer any works for sale but rather created an exhibition space and social center for the entire Brussels avant-garde. Bing's establishment was created as an exhibition center cum boutique-gallery—all items were for sale, and the selection criteria were determined partly by commercial imperatives. (For example, Bing could not include works by artists who were represented by other art dealers or galleries.) See Gabriel P. Weisberg, *Art Nouveau Bing: Paris Style 1900* (New York: Abrams, 1986), p. 56, and n. 11, p. 273. Thus Picard's center expressed the ideals of an oppositionist culture, for whom the integration of

all the arts implied the return of harmony to society and the individual; Bing divested the Brussels art nouveau of its social idealism, transposing the Gesamtkunstwerk into an aesthetic model for making beautiful houses for the refined and elegant consumer.

11. Louis Bonnier was a successful architect trained at the Ecole des Beaux-Arts, who was experimenting, at the time of the Bing commission, with new building materials such as terra-cotta tiling. Gabriel Weisberg indicates that Bing may have selected Bonnier as a result of their common association with Japonism. Bonnier, a collector of Japanese prints, was a client of Bing's. For this information, as well as a detailed discussion of the design and execution of Bonnier's renovations, see Weisberg, *Art Nouveau Bing*, pp. 57–65.

12. Bing, quoted in Weisberg, *Art Nouveau Bing*, p. 56.

13. Bernard Marrey and Paul Chemetov, *Architectures: Paris, 1848–1914* (Paris: ICOMOS, 1972), p. 89.

14. The complete list of contributors is included in *Salon de l'art nouveau, premier catalogue, Hôtel S. Bing, 26 décembre 1895* (Paris: Chamerot & Renouard, 1896), n.p. See also Weisberg, *Art Nouveau Bing*, pp. 52–95.

15. The Vuillard dinnerware has been rediscovered by Weisberg and is reproduced in *Art Nouveau Bing*, pp. 94–95.

16. Described in Th. L., "L'Art nouveau," *La Grande Dame* 4 (1896): 64.

17. "Jugement du premier concours pour l'Exposition de 1900: Un Cabinet de l'amateur, *Revue des arts décoratifs* 15 (1894–1895): 416.

18. Th. L., "L'Art nouveau," p. 63.

19. Ibid.

20. Ibid., p. 64.

21. Weisberg, *Art Nouveau Bing*, p. 66.

22. Th. L., "L'Art nouveau," p. 62.

23. Ibid.

24. Quoted in Frantz Jourdain, "Albert Besnard," in *De choses et d'autres* (Paris: H. Simonis Empis, 1902), p. 38.

25. Ibid., pp. 37–38. Jourdain (p. 38) compared Besnard to Des Esseintes and described Besnard's home as a place where art offered "ses hypnotisantes hallucinations."

26. The furniture was executed by Eugène Pinte, after designs by Denis. Weisberg demonstrates that Bing originally wanted Denis to decorate the bedroom with furniture by Emile Gallé, but Denis did not cooperate and the plan was abandoned, at great financial cost to Bing (*Art Nouveau Bing*, p. 67).

27. Geffroy, quoted in Weisberg, *Art Nouveau Bing*, p. 274.

28. "Le Salon du Champ-de-Mars," *Revue des arts décoratifs* 15 (1894–1895): 420. See also comments on the stained glass at the Salon of 1895 in Gerstle Mack, *Toulouse-Lautrec* (New York: Knopf, 1953), p. 218, with quotations from the critics. On the original Bing commission of the Nabis, see Weisberg, *Art Nouveau Bing*, pp. 49–50.

29. The entries of Dampt, Carrière, Rodin, and Gallé are listed in Bing, *Salon de l'art nouveau*, n.p.

30. Even the physical arrangement of the applied arts in the Maison Bing resembled the disposition of objets d'art in the Salon. Photographs of the gallery at the entrance to the Maison Bing show an array of mahogany vitrines, in which ceramics and glass were displayed. Between the display cases were various sculptures and circular velvet sofas for the spectators. The overall impression of this entryway was that of a typical Salon at the Champ-de-Mars. Photographs of the Salons of the National Society of the Beaux-Arts illustrate similar displays, from the cases for the decorative arts to the accompanying sculptures and sofas. The primary difference between the Maison Bing and the Salons was Bing's concentration, beyond the entryway, on the coordinated ensembles of the model rooms.

31. Arsène Alexandre, "L'Art nouveau," from *Le Figaro,* December 28, 1895, reprinted in Victor Champier, "Les Expositions de l'art nouveau," *Revue des arts décoratifs* 16 (1896): 4.

32. Alexandre, "L'Art nouveau," in Champier, "Les Expositions," p. 5.

33. Ibid.

34. Ibid.

35. Ibid.

36. Ibid.

37. Champier, "Les Expositions de l'art nouveau," p. 5.

38. Edmond de Goncourt and Jules de Goncourt, *Journal, mémoires de la vie littéraire,* 4 vols. (Fasquelle & Flammarion, 1956), 4:893–894, entry for December 30, 1895, emphasis in original (hereafter cited as *Journal des Goncourts*).

39. Philippe Garner, *Emile Gallé,* (London: Academy, 1976), pp. 110, 120.

40. Emile Gallé, "Les Goncourts et les métiers d'art," *La Lorraine-artiste* 14 (1896): 266–274.

41. *Journal des Goncourts,* 4:270, June 20, 1895; 5:259, May 23, 1892; 5:85, May 4, 1891.

42. Count Robert de Montesquiou-Fezensac reported that he bought the inscribed statuette by Rodin from the Goncourt collection after Edmond's death. See Montesquiou-Fezensac, "Rodin," in *Les Maîtres-artistes,* numéro spécial consacré à Auguste Rodin no. 8 (October 15, 1903): 262–263. In another regard, there was a striking affinity between the Maison de l'Art Nouveau Bing and the Goncourts' Maison d'un Artiste. Photographs of the Maison Bing show how a large bronze Japanese crane was suspended from the glass dome on the top floor of the gallery, beneath which various modern prints were displayed. The mélange of Japanese and contemporary art also typified the Goncourts' third-floor *Grenier.* Photos of the Goncourts' house reveal the same Japanese crane in their garden, while their *Grenier,* built by the modern architect Frantz Jourdain, was marked by the same diffused light and mélange of modern prints and Japonism featured at the Maison Bing. Edmond had the *Grenier* renovated by Jourdain precisely to have a space in which to highlight modern arts, distinct from the rococo collections occupying the bottom two floors.

43. Champier, "Les Expositions de l'art nouveau," p. 3.

44. Ibid., p. 4.

45. Charles Genuys, "A Propos de l'art nouveau, soyons français!" *Revue des arts décoratifs* 17 (1897): 1.

46. Ibid.

47. Ibid., pp. 1, 2, 3, 5.

48. Ibid. pp. 2, 3.

49. Ibid., pp. 5–6.

50. Documents recording Bing's intentions in the exact year of the art nouveau inaugural exhibition are scarce; I therefore rely, as do other scholars, on two articles Bing wrote in 1902 and 1903, where he explained the origins and meaning of the 1895 exhibit.

51. Bing, "L'Art Nouveau," in *Artistic America,* p. 227. (The article was originally published in *The Craftsman* 5, no. 1 [October 1903]: 1–15).

52. Bing, "L'Art Nouveau," in *Artistic America,* p. 216. This article, with the same title as the article cited in n. 51, was originally published in *The Architectural Record* 12 (1902): 281–285.

53. Bing, *Artistic America,* p. 185.

54. Bing, "L'Art Nouveau" [1903], in *Artistic America,* pp. 237–238 (emphasis mine).

55. See ibid., pp. 236–251.

56. "Egaler le génie qui leur donna naissance," in Bing, *Artistic America,* p. 127.

57. Bing, "L'Art Nouveau" [1903], p. 241.

58. Bing, "L'Art Nouveau" [1902], pp. 216, 222 (emphasis mine).

59. Bing, *Artistic America,* p. 188.

60. Robert Koch, introduction to *Artistic America,* p. 1, notes that Bing received the Légion d'honneur in 1890.

Chapter Fifteen

1. Gabriel Mourey, "L'Art nouveau de M. Bing à l'Exposition universelle," *Revue des arts décoratifs* 20 (1900): 257; Gabriel P. Weisberg, *Art Nouveau Bing: Paris Style 1900* (New York: Abrams, 1986), pp. 163–169.

2. Gabriel P. Weisberg, "S. Bing's Craftsmen Workshops: A Location and Importance Revealed," *Source* 3, no. 1 (Fall 1983): 42–48; Weisberg, *Art Nouveau Bing,* pp. 142–157, 163–169.

3. G. M. Jacques, 1900, quoted in Franco Borsi and Ezio Godoli, *Paris 1900* (New York: Rizzoli, 1977), p. 39.

4. Philippe Julien, *The Triumph of Art Nouveau: Paris Exhibition of 1900* (New York: Larousse, 1978), p. 117.

5. Jean Lorrain, 1900, quoted in Julien, *The Triumph of Art Nouveau,* pp. 116–117.

6. Martin Eidelberg, "The Life and Work of E. Colonna," pt. 2: "Paris and L'Art Nouveau," *Decorative Arts Society Newsletter* 7, no. 2 (June 1981): 3.

7. Mourey, quoted in Borsi and Godoli, *Paris 1900,* p. 39.

8. Mourey, quoted in Eidelberg, "Colonna," p. 3.

9. Mourey, "L'Art nouveau à l'Exposition universelle," p. 265.

10. Gabriel Mourey, "L'Art nouveau de M. Bing à l'Exposition universelle," deuxième article, *Revue des arts décoratifs* 20 (1900): 280, 283. Weisberg, in *Art Nouveau Bing* (179, 191, 210), quotes other critics who echoed precisely this theme of Bing's 1900 art nouveau as, in the words of one, "a compromise between the 'new style' . . . on the one side and the favorite French style, rococo, on the other." The critic continued:

> No one can but admire the nimbleness with which these, Bing's new artists, have understood how to combine the new style elements with the thread of a rediscovered tradition. Some of the charm which used to surround noblemen's radicalism is to be found in their art. The art in l'Art Nouveau has, for the most part, a radical character; but it has found its ancestry. It clearly bears rococo's family character, and no heritage can be more advantageous for art in the eyes of a Frenchman. (p. 201)

11. Eidelberg, "Colonna," p. 3.

12. De Feure's many lithographs and paintings centered on the *femme-fleur* and the woman as decorative object, that is, as an integral aesthetic part of an interior decorative world. In 1895, de Feure was preparing a series of illustrations called Féminiflores, a series of women's figures symbolizing certain flowers. See Octave Uzanne, "On the Drawings of Georges de Feure," *The Craftsman* 1 (1899): 95–102.

13. Quoted in Weisberg, *Art Nouveau Bing,* p. 241.

14. Lorrain, 1900, quoted in Julien, *The Triumph of Art Nouveau,* p. 117.

15. Mourey, "L'Art nouveau à l'Exposition universelle," p. 257.

16. Quoted in Weisberg, *Art Nouveau Bing,* p. 148.

17. S. Bing, *Artistic America, Tiffany Glass, and Art Nouveau,* trans. Benita Eisler, with an introduction by Robert Koch (Cambridge, Mass.: MIT Press, 1970), p. 183. There is other evidence that Bing absorbed theories of suggestion and dreams triggered by images in rooms. In his catalogue to the collection of Philippe Burty, Bing describes the power of "*objets enchantés,*" which, in the "refuge" of the interior space, project a "*fluide magnétique*" into the

mind of the collector (introduction to *Collection Philippe Burty: Objets d'art japonais et chinois qui seront vendus à Paris dans les Galeries Durand-Ruel* [Paris: Chamerot, 1891] pp. vi–ix).

18. Joris-Karl Huysmans, "Le Fer," in *L'Art moderne / certains* (Paris: Union générale d'éditions, 1975), pp. 408–409.

19. Victor Champier, "Coup d'oeil d'ensemble," in *Les Industries d'art à l'Exposition universelle de 1900* (Paris: Bureaux de la Revue des arts décoratifs, 1902), 1:11. See also the comment of Melchior de Vogüé in Philippe Julien, *The Triumph of Art Nouveau,* pp. 56–57.

20. Robert de la Sizeranne, "L'Esthétique du fer," in *Les Questions esthétiques modernes* (Paris: Hachette, 1904), p. 43.

21. De Vogüé, quoted in Julien, *The Triumph of Art Nouveau,* pp. 56–57. See also Champier, "Coup d'oeil," pp. 10–11, for a discussion of the organic plan of 1900 as a "unity in diversity."

22. Jacques Desroches, "La Porte monumentale de l'Exposition," *Revue illustrée de l'Exposition universelle* (June 25, 1900): 127.

23. Ibid., p. 126.

24. Ibid., p. 127.

25. Ibid., p. 128.

26. Ibid., pp. 124–125.

27. Unidentified contemporary, quoted in Julien, *The Triumph of Art Nouveau,* p. 39.

28. Julien, *The Triumph of Art Nouveau,* p. 39.

29. See Réné Binet, *Esquisses décoratives par Réné Binet* (Paris: Librairie centrale des Beaux-Arts, n.d.), esp. pp. 1–14.

30. Frantz Jourdain, 1900, quoted in Borsi and Godoli, *Paris 1900,* p. 26.

31. Desroches, "La Porte monumentale de l'Exposition," pp. 127, 122.

32. Ibid., p. 121.

33. Julien, *The Triumph of Art Nouveau,* pp. 42–44; Peter M. Wolf, *Eugène Hénard and the Beginning of Urbanism in Paris, 1900–1914* (The Hague: International Federation for Housing and Planning–Centre de Recherche d'Urbanisme, 1968), pp. 33, 27.

34. Julien, *The Triumph of Art Nouveau,* p. 46. The explicit evocations of the eighteenth century also included elements of the Pont Alexandre III leading to and from the twin palaces. The lamps on the bridge were also explicitly rococo, as were the stone piers with their sculpted cartouches.

35. This account is based on my observation of the gilded faience frieze around the front of the building, where the names of the artists are visible.

36. Discussion of the rococo decorative arts and furniture in the two *palais* and their direct impact on the founding of the Musée du Mobilier Français may be found in Lady Dilke, *French Architects and Sculptors of the Eighteenth Century* (London: George Bell and Sons, 1900), pp. v–vi; and Gustave Babin, "Le Musée du Mobilier français au Louvre," *L'Illustration* no. 3039 (May 25, 1901): 343.

37. Quoted in Julien, *The Triumph of Art Nouveau,* pp. 42–44.

38. There are indications, among the planners and critics, that the new centrality of decoration in 1900 related to the need of each individual for a personalized environment, which in a city like Paris would have meant an apartment. Though I have come across this idea three times, once expressed by the planner Picard, it needs further study to demonstrate.

39. "Jugement du premier concours pour l'Exposition universelle de 1900: Un Cabinet de l'amateur," *Revue des arts décoratifs* 15 (1894–1895): 416.

40. Victor Champier, "Les Expositions de l'art nouveau," *Revue des arts décoratifs* 16 (1896): 6. On Issac's 1895 collector's chamber for the Maison Bing, see above, p. 274.

41. Borsi and Godoli, *Paris 1900,* p. 57; Emile Gallé, "Le Pavillon de l'Union centrale des arts décoratifs à l'Exposition universelle de 1900," in *Ecrits pour l'art* (Paris: Laurens, 1908), pp. 229–236.

42. Quoted in Borsi and Godoli, *Paris 1900*, p. 57.

43. Julien, *The Triumph of Art Nouveau*, p. 112. The inventory and photographs of Hoentschell's large collection of rococo decorative art may be found today in the Cabinet des Estampes at the Bibliothèque Nationale. Hoentschell was also a friend of the comte Robert de Montesquiou-Fezensac.

44. Emile Gallé, "Le Mobilier contemporain orné d'après la nature," *Revue des arts décoratifs* 20 (1900): 377.

45. Emile Gallé, "Les Goncourts et les métiers d'art," *La Lorraine-artiste* 14 (1896): 270.

46. One exhibition booklet even lists the title of Besnard's union mural as *Le Débarquement à Cythère*, in A. Quantin, *L'Exposition du siècle* (Paris: Le Monde moderne, 1900), p. 80.

47. See Camille Mauclair, "La Femme devant les peintres modernes," *La Nouvelle Revue*, 2d ser., 1 (1899): 210–211, and "Les Peintres de l'élégance nerveuse," *La Revue* 38 (1901): 24–25; Marius-Ary Leblond, "Les Peintres de la 'Femme Nouvelle,'" *La Revue* 39 (1901): 277.

48. The union women and their entries are listed in Emile Gallé, "Le Pavillon de l'Union centrale des arts décoratifs à l'Exposition universelle de 1900," *Revue des arts décoratifs* 20 (1900): 224–225.

49. On the collections of the Musée des Arts Décoratifs at the Louvre, see R. K., "Les Arts décoratifs au Pavillon de Marsan," *Les Arts* 1 (June 1902): 30.

50. Georges Guillain, *J.-M. Charcot: His Life, His Work*, trans. Pearse Bailey (New York: Paul Hoeber, 1959), pp. 177–179; George Frederick Drinka, *The Birth of Neurosis: Myth, Malady, and the Victorians* (New York: Simon & Schuster, 1984), pp. 276–278.

51. Hippolyte Bernheim, "La Doctrine de la suggestibilité et ses conséquences: Discours prononcé à l'ouverture des travaux de la Ve section du IXe Congrès international de psychologie," *La Revue* 34 (1900): 532–535.

52. Théodule Ribot, *Essai sur l'imagination créatrice* (Paris: Alcan, 1901).

53. Eiffel's words, quoted in Joseph Harriss, *The Tallest Tower: Eiffel and the Belle Epoque* (Boston: Houghton Mifflin, 1975), p. 19.

54. Debora L. Silverman, "The Paris Exhibition of 1889: Architecture and the Crisis of Individualism," *Oppositions* 8 (Spring 1977): 71–91.

55. Quantin, *L'Exposition du siècle*, p. 215.

56. Reported in Quantin, *L'Exposition du siècle*, p. 216.

57. See Léon Deshairs, *Dessins originaux des maîtres décoratifs* (Paris: Longuet, c. 1900).

58. De Vogüé, quoted in Julien, *The Triumph of Art Nouveau*, pp. 56–57.

59. From the 1900 Hachette Guide, quoted in Julien, *The Triumph of Art Nouveau*, pp. 82–83.

60. Roger Marx's statements of 1900, quoted in Borsi and Godoli, *Paris 1900*, p. 196.

61. Ibid.

62. Ibid., p. 197.

63. Loïe Fuller, *Fifteen Years of a Dancer's Life* (New York: Dance Publications, 1979), pp. 25–42. The doctor was "Doctor Quack, hypnotizing a young widow" and then inducing suggestion.

64. Gallé, "Le Pavillon de l'Union centrale des arts décoratifs à l'Exposition universelle de 1900," in *Ecrits pour l'art*, p. 232.

65. Ibid., pp. 232, 234.

66. Emile Gallé, "Le Décor symbolique," in *Ecrits pour l'art*, pp. 212, 226.

67. Ibid., pp. 213, 224, 211.

68. Ibid., pp. 215–216.

69. Ibid., pp. 217–218.

70. Ibid., p. 215.

71. Listed in the 1900 catalogue of Rodin's exhibition works, in *Exposition Rodin: L'Oeuvre de Rodin* (Paris: Imprimerie Dumoulin, 1900), pp. 5–6.

72. See the discussion and the quotation from Rodin about his tower as the antithesis of the Eiffel Tower in John Hunisak, "Rodin, Dalou, and the Monument to Labor," in *Art and the Ape of Nature: Studies in Honor of H. W. Janson,* ed. M. Barasch and L. Sandler (New York: Abrams, 1981), pp. 689–707.

73. Auguste Rodin, *Art: Conversations with Paul Gsell* [1911], trans. Jacques de Caso and Patricia B. Sanders (Berkeley: University of California Press, 1984), p. 4.

74. Auguste Rodin, *Rodin: The Man and His Art, with Leaves from His Notebook,* comp. Judith Cladel, trans. S. K. Star (New York: Century, 1918), p. 206.

75. Rodin, *Art: Conversations with Paul Gsell,* p. 5.

76. Ibid., p. 4. See also Auguste Rodin, "Art and Nature," in *Impressionism and Post-Impressionism: Sources and Documents, 1874–1904,* ed. Linda Nochlin (Englewood Cliffs, N.J.: Prentice-Hall, 1966), pp. 69–70.

77. Rodin, "Art and Nature."

78. Rodin, *Art: Conversations with Paul Gsell,* p. 4.

79. Although there is some debate about the exact dating of the addition to the *Gates,* I am following Albert Elsen's research and conclusion that the addition was in place by 1900 (*"The Gates of Hell" by Auguste Rodin* [Stanford, Calif.: Stanford University Press, 1985], pp. 138, 221 and 252, n. 5). Elsen discovered that the additions were visible in photographs taken of the doors in 1900, two of which he reproduces, on pp. 132, 137.

80. See the discussion of the current scholarship and Elsen's own assessment, in *"The Gates of Hell,"* p. 221.

81. Ibid.

82. Ibid., p. 207.

83. Ibid., p. 210.

84. Maurice Rollinat, "La Pensée," in *L'Abîme* (Paris: Charpentier, 1886), pp. 6–13.

85. Ibid., esp. pp. 6–12. For the earlier discussion of Thought as gatekeeper, see pp. 261–268.

86. Rollinat, "La Pensée," p. 8.

87. Elsen, *"The Gates of Hell,"* p. 210.

88. Ibid.

89. Albert E. Elsen, ed., *Rodin Rediscovered* (Washington, D.C.: National Gallery of Art, 1981), p. 130. Elsen notes how the poet's friends asserted the resemblance. I discovered a contemporary drawing (reproduced in my text) of Rollinat's portrait that strongly resembles the Rodin severed head of John. See Gustave Geffroy, "Maurcie Rollinat," *La Revue universelle* 3, no. 99 (1903): 626.

90. Elsen, *"The Gates of Hell,"* pp. 138, 221.

91. Henri Bergson, "Le Rêve," in *L'Energie spirituelle,* 161st ed. (Paris: Quadrige, Presses universitaires de France, 1982), pp. 85–109. His words are from p. 106.

92. Ibid., pp. 95–96.

93. Ibid., pp. 96–97.

94. See the critics cited in Elsen, *"The Gates of Hell,"* p. 151.

95. Bergson, "Le Rêve," p. 96.

96. Ibid., pp. 96–97.

97. Ibid., pp. 108–109.

98. Sigmund Freud, *The Interpretation of Dreams* (New York: Modern Library, 1950), p. 15.

99. This passage (on which I base the succeeding discussion) is from another of Freud's texts, *On Dreams* [1901] (New York: Norton, 1980), pp. 93–94.

100. See the analyses of Carl E. Schorske, *Fin-de-Siècle Vienna: Politics and Culture* (New York: Knopf, 1980), pp. 181–207; and William C. McGrath, *Freud's Discovery of Psychoanalysis: The Politics of Hysteria* (Ithaca, N.Y.: Cornell University Press, 1986).

101. Quoted in Schorske, *Fin-de-Siècle Vienna,* p. 200.

102. Freud, *On Dreams,* p. 61.

103. Ibid., pp. 47, 64.

104. Ibid., p. 62.

105. Ibid., pp. 49–50.

106. Ibid., pp. 77, 75.

107. Ibid., pp. 65, 61.

108. Elsen, *"The Gates of Hell,"* pp. 55, 53, 235, 241.

109. Ibid., pp. 240, 241.

110. Raymond Bouyer, "Rodin inconnu," in *Les Maîtres-artistes,* numéro spécial consacré à Auguste Rodin, no. 8 (October 15, 1903): 269.

111. Anatole France, "La Porte de l'enfer." in *Les Maîtres-artistes,* pp. 260–262.

112. Frantz Jourdain, in *Les Maîtres-artistes,* p. 292.

113. Georg Simmel, "L'Oeuvre de Rodin comme expression de l'esprit moderne" (1901), in *Mélanges philosophiques* (Paris: Alcan, n.d.), p. 135.

114. Ibid., pp. 131, 136.

SELECTED BIBLIOGRAPHY

Archival Sources

Bibliothèque Nationale. MSS n.a.fr. 15037–15380. "Comte Robert de Montesquiou-Fezensac: Sa vie et ses demeures."

Philadelphia Museum of Art. MS M329sPr. "Auguste Rodin: Letters, Essays, Criticisms." Rodin Museum Archives.

Princeton University Library. Am 18619. "The Cheruy Letters of Auguste Rodin."

Primary Sources

Béraldi, Henri. "Les Bibliophiles et la décoration de la reliure; créateurs et vénérants." *Revue des arts décoratifs* 12 (1891–1892): 129–133.

Berger, Georges. "Appel aux femmes françaises." *Revue des arts décoratifs* 16 (1896): 97–99.

———. *Exposition universelle internationale de 1889*. Paris: Imprimerie de Chaix, 1889.

———. "Rapport de M. Georges Berger." *Revue des arts décoratifs* 12 (1891–1892): 355–361.

Bergson, Henri. "De la simulation inconsciente dans l'état d'hypnotisme," *Revue philosophique* 22 (1886): 525–531.

———. *Essai sur les données immédiates de la conscience* [1889]. 8th ed. Paris: Alcan, 1911.

———. *Matter and Memory* [1896]. Translated by N. M. Paul and W. Scott Palmer. London: Allen & Unwin, 1911.

———. *Mélanges: Correspondances, pièces diverses, documents*. Paris, 1972.

———. "Le Rêve," in *L'Energie spirituelle*. 161st ed. (Paris: Quadrige, Presses universitaires de France, 1982), pp. 84–109.

Bernheim, Hippolyte. *De la suggestion dans l'état hypnotique et dans l'état de veille*. Paris: Doin, 1884. Translated by Christian A. Herter, M.D., under the title *Suggestive Therapeutics: A Treatise on the Nature and Uses of Hypnotism* (New York: Putnam, 1887).

———. *De la suggestion dans l'état hypnotique, Réponse à Paul Janet*. Paris: Doin, 1884.

———. *Hypnotisme, suggestion, psychothérapie*. Paris: Doin, 1891.

Biais, Th. *Nicolas Pineau*. Paris: Société des bibliophiles français, 1892.

Binet, Alfred. *Etudes de psychologie expérimentale: La vie psychique des microorganismes, l'intensité des images mentales, le problème hypnotique, notes sur l'écriture hystérique*. Paris: Doin, 1888.

———. *Le magnétisme animal*. Paris: Alcan, 1886.

———. *Questionnaire de psychologie adressé aux peintres*. Paris: Administration des deux revues, 1892.

———. *La Suggestibilité*. Paris: Bibliothèque de Pédagogie et de Psychologie, Schleicher Frères, 1900.

Bing, S[iegfried]. *Artistic America, Tiffany Glass, and Art Nouveau*. Translated by Benita Eisler, with an introduction by Robert Koch. Cambridge, Mass.: MIT Press, 1970.

———. "L'Art nouveau." *The Architectural Record* 12 (1902): 281–285.

————. "L'Art nouveau." *The Craftsman* 5, no. 1 (October 1903): 1–15.

————. "Les Arts de l'Extrême-Orient dans la collection des Goncourts." In *Collection des Goncourts: Arts de l'Extrême-Orient, objets d'art japonais et chinois, peintures, estampes. Catalogue du vente.* Paris: May & Metteroz, 1897.

————. *La Culture artistique en Amérique.* Evreux: Imprimerie de Charles Hérissey, 1895.

————. Introduction to *Collection Philippe Burty: Objets d'art japonais et chinois qui seront vendus à Paris dans les Galeries Durand-Ruel.* Paris: Chamerot, 1891.

————. Introduction to *Exposition de la gravure japonaise à l'Ecole Nationale des Beaux-Arts à Paris, 25 avril–22 mai 1890.* Paris: Alcan-Lévy, 1890.

————. Introduction to Union centrale des arts décoratifs, *Salon annuel des peintures japonaises,* 1e and 2e années. Paris: Pillet & Demoulin, 1883, 1884.

————. "Programme." *Le Japon artistique* 1 (1888): 2–9.

————. *Salon de l'art nouveau. Premier Catalogue, Hôtel S. Bing, 26 décembre 1895.* Paris: Chamerot & Renouard, 1896.

————. "La Vie et l'oeuvre de Hok'sai." *Revue blanche* 14 (1896): 97–101.

————. "Wohin treiben wir?" *Dekorative Kunst* 1 (1898): 1–3.

Blum, Jean. "La Philosophie de M. Bergson et la poésie symboliste." *Mercure de France* 63 (1906): 201–207.

Bouchot, Henri. "Les Derniers Travaux de décoration exécutés à la Bibliothèque Nationale." *Revue des arts décoratifs* 12 (1891–1892): 81–98.

————. "La Femme comme objet d'art." *Revue des arts décoratifs* 17 (1897): 46–55.

Bourget, Paul. *Nouveaux essais de psychologie contemporaine.* Paris: Lemerre, 1883.

————. "Psychologie féminine, à quarante ans." *La Grande Dame: Revue de l'élégance et des arts* 1 (1893): 129–135.

Burty, Philippe. *Eaux-Fortes de Jules de Goncourt.* Paris: Librairie d'art, 1876.

————. "La Nouvelle porcelaine de Sèvres." *Revue des arts décoratifs* 4 (1883–1884): 153–157.

————. "La Poterie et la porcelaine de Japon." *Revue des arts décoratifs* 5 (1884–1885): 385–418.

————. "Les Sabres: 'Le Katana.'" *Le Japon artistique* 1 (1888): 119–130.

Catalogue général officiel de l'Exposition universelle de 1889. Lille: Imprimerie L. Danel, 1889.

"Centenaire de Charcot en 1925. Toutes les allocutions prononcées aux cérémonies commémoratives par les savants français et étrangers." *Revue neurologique* 1, no. 6 (1925): 731–1192.

Champeaux, Alfred de. *Le Meuble.* Vol. 1. Paris: Quantin, 1885.

Champier, Victor. "L'Architecture japonaise: Les Habitations." *Le Japon artistique* 1 (1888): 39–46.

————. "L'Architecture japonaise: Les Temples." *Le Japon artistique* 1 (1888): 25–32.

————. "Les Arts fraternels au Salon du Champ-de-Mars." *Revue des arts décoratifs* 12 (1891–1892): 5–16.

————. "La Bijouterie et la joaillerie d'autrefois." *La Grande Dame: Revue de l'élégance et des arts* 1 (1893): 126–144.

————. "Les Cadeaux offerts à l'escadre russe." *Revue des arts décoratifs* 14 (1893–1894): 129–135.

————. *Catalogue illustré de l'Union centrale des arts décoratifs.* Paris: Librairie d'art L. Baschet, 1884.

————. "La Collection d'orfèvrerie de M. Paul Eudel," *Revue des arts décoratifs* 4 (1883–1884): 306–311.

————. "Exposition des arts de la femme." *Revue des arts décoratifs* 15 (1894–1895): 321–326, 473–477.

————. "Les Expositions de l'art nouveau." *Revue des arts décoratifs* 16 (1896): 1–7.

————. "L'Habitation moderne: Hôtel de Madame Salomon de Rothschild, l'ancienne Folie-Beaujon et la maison de Balzac." *Revue des arts décoratifs* 12 (1891–1892): 65–76.

———. *Les Industries d'art à l'Exposition universelle de 1900*. 2 vols. Paris: Bureau de la Revue des arts décoratifs, 1902.

———. *Le Musée du Louvre, modèles d'art décoratif d'après les dessins originaux*. Paris: Quantin, 1882.

———. "Notre nouveau programme." *Revue des arts décoratifs* 12 (1891–1892): 1–4.

———. "Parures de soirées." *La Grande Dame: Revue de l'élégance et des arts* 3 (1895): 113–118.

———. "La Société de l'Union centrale des arts décoratifs: Son histoire, ses débuts, ses doctrines, l'influence qu'elle a exercée sur le goût public par ses concours et par ses expositions." *Revue des arts décoratifs* 4 (1883–1884): 70–87.

———. "Souhaits d'artistes: A propos de la réception des souverains russes." *Revue des arts décoratifs* 16 (1896): 341–349.

———. "Les Verreries de M. Emile Gallé au Salon du Champ-de-Mars." *Revue des arts décoratifs* 12 (1891–1892): 332.

Charcot, Jean-Martin. *Clinical Lectures on Diseases of the Nervous System*. Vols. 1–3. Translated by Thomas Savill. London: The Sydenham Society, 1889.

Charcot, Jean-Martin, and Paul Richer. *Les Démoniaques dans l'art*. Paris: Delahaye & Lecrosnier, 1887.

———. *Les Difformes et les malades dans l'art*. Paris: Lecrosnier & Babé, 1889.

Chéliga, Maria. "Le Mouvement féministe en France. *Revue politique et parlementaire* 13 (1897): 271–284.

———. "L'Evolution du féminisme." *La Revue encyclopédique* no. 168 (November 28, 1896): 825–837.

Chennevières, Henri de. "Jean-Nicolas Servandoni, peintre, architecte, ordonnateur des fêtes publiques." *Revue des arts décoratifs* 1 (1880–1881): 122–126, 170–171, 403–407, 429–436.

Chennevières, Philippe de. "Les Dessins du XVIIIe siècle de la collection des Goncourts." In *Collections des Goncourts: Dessins, aquarelles, et pastels du XVIIIe siècle. Catalogue du vente*. Paris: May & Metteroz, 1897.

———. Introduction to *Catalogue descriptif des dessins de décoration et d'ornement de maîtres anciens exposés au Musée des Arts Décoratifs en 1880*. Paris: Imprimerie de publications périodiques, 1880.

———. Préface to *Inventaire générale des richesses d'art de la France*. Vol. 1. Paris: Plon, 1876.

———. Préface to Paul Ratouis de Limay. *Aignan-Thomas Désfriches, 1715–1800: Sa vie, son oeuvre, ses collections, sa correspondance, lettres du Duc de Chabot, de Cochin, Descamps, Mgr de Grimaldi, De Mirosmenil, Perronneau, Vernet, Watelet, Wille, etc*. Paris: Librairie H. Champion, 1907.

Cladel, Judith. *Auguste Rodin: Sa vie glorieuse et inconnue*. Paris: Grasset, 1936.

Clarétie, Jules. *L'Obsession: Moi et l'autre*. Paris, 1908.

Le Congrès des arts décoratifs, tenu à l'Ecole Nationale des Beaux-Arts du 18 au 30 mai 1894, comptes-rendus sténographiques. Paris: Lahure, 1894.

Couty, Edme. "L'Art dans la décoration de l'intérieur moderne." *La Grande Dame: Revue de l'élégance et des arts* 4 (1896): 19–24.

Daudet, Ernest. *Le Duc d'Aumale, 1822–1897*. Paris: Plon, 1898.

Daudet, Léon. *Devant la douleur: Souvenirs des milieux littéraires, politiques, artistiques, et médicaux de 1880 à 1905*. Paris: Nouvelle librairie critique, 1915.

———. *Les Morticoles*. Paris: Charpentier, 1894.

Deshairs, Léon. *Dessins originaux des maîtres décoratifs: Les Dessins du Musée et de la Bibliothèque des Arts Décoratifs, époque Louis XV, Nicolas et Dominique Pineau*. Paris: Longuet, c. 1900.

Desroches, Jacques. "La Porte monumentale de l'Exposition." *Revue illustrée de l'Exposition universelle de 1900*, June 25, 1900, 124–128.

Destrée, Jules. "Art et socialisme: Art dans la vie courante." In *Jules Destrée: Tous ses visages, toute sa vie*. Edited by Pierre Bourgeois. Brussels: Editions Labor, 1963.

Dreyfus, Carle. *Musée du Louvre: Le Mobilier français, époques de Louis XIV et de Louis XV*. Paris: Editions Morancé, 1923.

————. *Musée du Louvre: Les Objets d'art du XVIIIe siècle, époques de Louis XIV, Louis XV, et de Louis XVI*. Paris: Editions Morancé, 1923.

Du Maroussem, Pierre. *La Question ouvrière*. Vol. 1, *Charpentiers de Paris, compagnons et indépendants*. Paris: Arthur Rousseau, 1891.

————. *La Question ouvrière*. Vol. 2, *Ebénistes du Faubourg Saint-Antoine*. Paris: Arthur Rousseau, 1892.

————. *La Question ouvrière*. Vol. 3, *Le Jouet parisien: Grands magasins, "Sweating-system."* Paris: Arthur Rousseau, 1893.

Falize, Lucien. "Histoire d'une exposition ajournée." *Revue des arts décoratifs* 12 (1891–1892): 225–242.

————. "Travaux d'orfèvre." *Le Japon artistique* 1 (1888): 51–57.

Fouillée, Alfred. "Dégénérescence: Le Passé et le présent de notre race." *Revue des deux mondes* 131 (1895): 793–824.

————. "Les Grandes Conclusions de la psychologie contemporaine—la conscience et ses transformations." *Revue des deux mondes* 107 (1891): 788–816.

————. "Le Physique et le mental à propos de l'hypnotisme." *Revue des deux mondes* 105 (1891): 429–461.

————. "La Psychologie des sexes at ses fondements physiologiques." *Revue des deux mondes* 119 (1893): 397–429.

————. "Psychologie et l'esprit français." *Revue des deux mondes* 138 (1896): 58–88.

Fourcaud, Louis de. "Les Arts décoratifs au Salon de 1892: Champs-Elysées et Champ-de-Mars." *Revue des arts décoratifs* 12 (1891–1892): 321–332, 385–398.

————. "Les Arts décoratifs aux Salons." *Revue des arts décoratifs* 14 (1893–1894): 1–19; 340–351; 377–386.

————. "Les Arts décoratifs aux Salons de 1894." *Revue des arts décoratifs* 15 (1894–1895): 1–17.

————. "Les Arts décoratifs aux Salons de 1895." *Revue des arts décoratifs* 15 (1894–1895): 356–364; 385–398.

————. "Les Arts décoratifs exclus du Salon." *Revue des arts décoratifs* 12 (1891–1892): 293–297.

————. "Les Arts de la femme au Palais de l'Industrie." *La Grande Dame: Revue de l'élégance et des arts* 1 (1893): 19–29.

————. "Le Droit des arts décoratifs au Salon des Champs-Elysées." *Revue des arts décoratifs* 12 (1891–1892): 257–261.

————. *Emile Gallé*. Paris: Librairie d'art ancien et moderne, 1903.

Freud, Sigmund. *The Letters of Sigmund Freud*. Edited by Ernst Freud. New York: Basic Books, 1960.

————. *On Dreams* ([1901] New York: Norton, 1980).

Gallé, Emile. "L'art expressif et la statue de Claude Gelée, par M. Rodin." *La Lorraine-artiste* 10 (1892): 533–539.

————. "Le Baumier, épave." *La Plume: Littéraire, artistique, et sociale* no. 157 (November 1, 1895): 493.

————. *Ecrits pour l'art*. Paris: Laurens, 1908.

————. "Encore l'exposition de la plante: Réponse à M. Lucien Falize, maître-orfèvre-joaillier à Paris." *Revue des arts décoratifs* 12 (1891–1892): 377–380.

————. "Les Goncourts et les métiers d'art." *La Lorraine-artiste* 14 (1896): 266–274.

————. "Le Mobilier contemporain orné d'après la nature." *Revue des arts décoratifs* 20 (1900): 365–377.

————. "Le Pavillon de l'Union centrale des arts décoratifs à l'Exposition universelle de 1900." *Revue des arts décoratifs* 20 (1900): 217–224.

————. "La Table aux herbes potagères." *Revue des arts décoratifs* 12 (1891–1892): 381–383.

————. "Les Verreries de M. Émile Gallé au Salon du Champ-de-Mars." *Revue des arts décoratifs* 12 (1891–1892): 333–335.

Geffroy, Gustave. "A. Rodin." In Galerie Georges Petit, *Exposition Monet-Rodin*. Paris: Imprimerie de l'art, 1889.

————. "L'Habitation moderne, II: La Maison des Goncourts." *Revue des arts décoratifs* 12 (1891–1892): 146–151.

————. "Maurice Rollinat." *Revue universelle* 3, no. 99 (1903): 618–626.

————. "Maurice Rollinat: Poète des névroses" [1883]. In *Notes d'un journaliste*, pp. 278–292. Paris: Charpentier, 1887.

Genuys, Charles. "A propos de l'art nouveau, soyons français!" *Revue des arts décoratifs* 17 (1897): 1–7.

Godron, D. A. *Le Rôle politique des fleurs*. Nancy: Berger-Levrault, 1879.

Goetschy, Gustave. "Les Femmes du monde artistes—Madame Charcot." *Revue des arts décoratifs* 20 (1900): 41–51.

Goncourt, Edmond de. "Écritoire de Poche." *Le Japon artistique* 1 (1888): 68–74.

————. *La Maison d'un artiste*. 2 vols. Paris: Charpentier, 1881; nouvelle édition, Paris: Charpentier, 1904.

Goncourt, Edmond de, et Jules de Goncourt. *L'Art du XVIIIe siècle et autres textes sur l'art*. Textes réunis et présentés par J. P. Bouillon. Paris: Hermann, 1969.

————. *Etudes d'art: Le Salon de 1852, la peinture à l'Exposition de 1855*. Préface de Roger Marx. Paris: Librairie des Bibliophiles, 1893.

————. *Germinie Lacerteux*. Paris: Charpentier, 1865.

————. *Idées et sensations* [1866]. Paris: Charpentier, 1904.

————. *Journal, Mémoires de la vie littéraire*. Texte intégral établi et annoté par Robert Ricatte. 4 vols. Paris: Fasquelle & Flammarion, 1956.

————. *Madame de Pompadour*. Paris: Charpentier, 1878.

————. *Les Maîtresses de Louis XV*. Paris: Didot, 1860.

————. *Portraits intimes du XVIIIe siècle*. Paris: Dentu, 1857.

————. *Préfaces et manifestes littéraires*. Paris: Charpentier, 1888.

————. *La Révolution dans les moeurs: La Famille, le monde, la vieille femme, les jeunes gens, le mariage, les demoiselles à marier, les gens riches, les lettres et les arts, la pudeur sociale, le catholicisme*. Paris: Dentu, 1854.

Guiffrey, Jules. "Notes sur l'orfèvrerie française, vaisselle d'argent, 1740–1753, Nollin, Ballin, et Le Brun." *Revue des arts décoratifs* 1 (1880–1881): 436–440.

Guignon, Georges. "Charcot intime." *Paris médical*, May 12, 1925, 511–516.

Guilmard, D. *Les Maîtres ornemanistes: Ecoles française, italienne, allemande, et pays-bas, ouvrage renfermant le répertoire général des maîtres ornemanistes avec l'indication précise des pièces d'ornement qui se trouvent dans les collections publiques et particulières en France, en Belgique, etc.* Paris: Plon, 1881.

Hamlin, A.D.F. "L'Art Nouveau: Its Origin and Development." *The Craftsman* 3, no. 3 (1902): 129–143.

Hartenberg, Paul. "Le Tempérament d'Edmond de Goncourt." *La Lorraine-artiste* 14 (1896): 289–293.

Havard, Henry. *L'Art dans la maison* [1884]. 4th ed. Paris: Rouvèyre, 1891.

————. *L'Art et le confort dans la vie moderne: Le Bon Vieux Temps*. Paris: Flammarion, 1904.

Hénard, Eugène. *Exposition universelle de 1889: Le Palais des Machines, notice sur l'édifice et sur le marché des travaux*. Paris, 1891.

Henrivaux, Jules. "Emile Gallé." *L'Art décoratif* 7 (1905): 124–135.

Henry, Charles. *Mémoires inédits de Charles-Nicolas Cochin sur le Comte de Caylus, Bouchardon, les Slodtz.* Paris: Librairie de la Société de l'art français, 1880.

Héricourt, Jules. "L'Activité inconsciente de l'esprit." *Revue scientifique* 44 (1889): 257–268.

Huysmans, Joris-Karl. *Against the Grain.* New York: Dover, 1969.

———. *L'Art moderne / certains.* Paris: Union générale d'éditions, 1975.

Janet, Paul. "Une Chaire de psychologie expérimentale comparée au Collège de France." *Revue des deux mondes* 86 (1888): 518–549.

———. "J.-M. Charcot: Son oeuvre psychologique." *Revue philosophique* 39 (1895): 567–604.

Jourdain, Frantz. *De Choses et d'autres.* Paris: H. Simonis Empis, 1902.

———. "Les Objets d'art aux Salons de 1896." *La Grande Dame: Revue de l'élégance et des arts* 4 (1896): 220–226.

———. *Propos d'un isolé en faveur de son temps.* Paris: E. Figière, n.d.

———. "Que pensez-vous de l'architecture moderne?" *Revue des arts décoratifs* 16 (1896): 93–96.

Lahor, Jean [Henri Cazalis]. *L'Art nouveau: Son histoire, l'art nouveau étranger à l'exposition, l'art nouveau au point de vue social.* Paris: Lemerre, 1901.

———. *William Morris et le mouvement nouveau de l'art décoratif.* Geneva: Charles Eggmann, 1897.

Larroumet, Gustave. "L'Art décoratif et les femmes." *Revue des arts décoratifs* 16 (1896): 100–106.

———. *Le XVIIIe Siècle et la critique contemporaine: Leçon d'ouverture du cours de littérature française à la Faculté des lettres à Paris, 11 décembre 1891.* Paris: Administration des deux revues, 1891.

Leblond, Marius-Ary. "Les Peintres de la 'Femme Nouvelle.'" *La Revue: Ancienne revue des revues* 39 (1901): 274–290.

Le Bon, Gustave. "La Psychologie des femmes et les effets de leur education actuelle." *Revue scientifique* 46 (1890): 449–460.

Lefébure, Ernest. "De l'influence qui pourrait être exercée sur les industries d'art par les femmes." *Revue des arts décoratifs* 16 (1896): 106–112.

Levillain, Fernand. *La Neurasthénie.* Avec une préface du Professeur Charcot. Paris: A. Maloine, 1891.

Lugt, Frits. *Les Marques de collections de dessin et d'estampes.* Amsterdam: Vereenigte Drukkerijen, 1921.

Mantz, Paul. *Boucher, Lemoine, et Natoire.* Paris: Quantin, 1880.

———. "Considérations générales sur l'ensemble des expositions organisées en 1880, par les soins de l'Union centrale." *Revue des arts décoratifs* 1 (1880–1881): 229–233, 284–302.

———. "Les Meubles du XVIIIe siècle." 3 pts. *Revue des arts décoratifs* 4 (1883–1884): 313–325, 356–367, 377–389.

Margueritte, Paul, and Victor Margueritte. "Mariage et divorce: Enquête." *La Revue: Ancienne Revue des revues* 35 (1900): 449–462, and 36 (1901): 485–497.

Marx, Roger. *L'Art à Nancy en 1882.* Nancy: Wiener, 1883.

———. "L'Art et les Goncourts." *La Lorraine-artiste* 14 (1896): 275–276.

———. "Les Arts à l'Exposition universelle de 1900." *Gazette des beaux-arts* 24 (1900): 397–421, 563–576.

———. *L'art social.* Paris: Fasquelle, 1913.

———. *Auguste Rodin, céramiste.* Paris: Société de propagation des livres d'art, 1907.

———. *La Décoration et l'art industriel à l'Exposition universelle de 1889. Conférence faite au congrès de la Société centrale des architectes français, 17 juin 1890.* Paris: Librairies-imprimeries réunies, 1890.

————. *La Décoration et les industries d'art à l'Exposition universelle de 1900*. Paris: Delagrave, 1901.

————. "Emile Gallé: Psychologie de l'artiste et synthèse de l'oeuvre." *Art et décoration* 30 (1911): 231–252.

————. *Essais de rénovation ornementale: Une Villa moderne: La Salle de billiard*. Paris: Gazette des beaux-arts, 1902.

————. "Les Goncourts collectionneurs." In *Collection des Goncourts: Dessins, aquarelles, et pastels du XVIIIe siècle. Catalogue du vente*. Paris: May & Metteroz, 1897.

————. "Les Goncourts et l'art: Etude de leur esthétique et des aquarelles de Jules de Goncourt." *Gazette des beaux-arts* 17 (1897): 159–163, 238–248, 402–416.

————. "Jean Dampt, maître des arts." *La Grande Dame: Revue de l'élégance et des arts* 4 (1896): 90–96.

————. *La Loïe Fuller: Estampes modelées par Pierre Roche*. Evreux: Charles Hérissey, 1904.

————. *The Painter Albert Besnard: A Biography with Original Etchings and Illustrations after His Pictures*. Paris: Hennuyer, 1893.

————. *Les Pointes-Sèches de Rodin*. Paris: Gazette des beaux-arts, 1902.

————. "La Renaissance des arts décoratifs." *Les Arts. Revue mensuelle des musées, collections, expositions* 1 (January 1902): 34–39.

————. "Souvenirs des Goncourts." *La Revue encyclopédique* no. 155 (August 22, 1896): 545–555.

————. "Sur le rôle et l'influence des arts de l'Extrême-Orient et du Japon." *Le Japon artistique* 3 (1890): 141–149.

————. *Theodore Chasseriau et les peintures de la Cour des Comptes*. Paris: Grange-Batelaire, 1898.

————. "La Vie naît de la mort d'Albert Besnard." *La Revue encyclopédique* no. 146 (June 20, 1896): 434–435.

Mauclair, Camille. "La Femme devant les peintres modernes." *La Nouvelle Revue*, 2d ser., 1 (1899): 190–213.

————. *Fragonard*. Paris: Laurens, 1904.

————. *Histoire de la miniature féminine française*. Paris: Michel, 1925.

————. "Les Peintres de l'élégance nerveuse.' *La Revue: Ancienne revue des revues* 38 (1901): 15–29.

————. *Princes de l'esprit: Poe, Flaubert, Mallarmé, Villiers de l'Isle-Adam, etc.* Paris: Ollendorff, n.d.

————. "La Réaction nationaliste en art." *La Revue: Ancienne revue des revues* 54 (1905): 151–174.

————. "La Réforme de l'art décoratif en France." *La Nouvelle Revue* 98 (1896): 724–746.

Maupassant, Guy de. *Chroniques*. Vols. 1–3. Paris, 1980.

————. *Contes cruels et fantastiques*. Paris, 1976

————. *Le Horla*. Paris, 1976.

Mayet, Charles. *La Crise industrielle: L'Ameublement*. Paris: Dentu, 1883.

Meige, Henri. *Charcot-artiste*. Paris: Masson, 1925.

Meixmoron de Dombasle, Charles de. "Réponse du Président M. Ch. de Meixmoron de Dombasle au récipidaire M. Emile Gallé." *Mémoires de l'Académie de Stanislas*, pp. 1–25. Nancy, 1899 / 1900.

Meyer, Arthur. *Ce que mes yeux ont vu*. Paris: Plon, 1911.

Michel, André. *Les Artistes célèbres: François Boucher*. Paris: Librairie J. Rouam, 1886.

————. "Du bon usage des oeuvres d'art." *Les Arts: Revue mensuelle des musées, collections, expositions* 1 (January 1902): 1–2.

Migeon, Gaston. "Les Accroissements des musées: Musée du Louvre." *Les Arts: Revue mensuelle des museés, collections, expositions* 1 (January 1902): 15–18.

————. "Les Accroissements des musées: Musée du Louvre, Département des objets d'art du Moyen Age, de la Renaissance, et des temps modernes." *Les Arts: Revue mensuelle des musées, collections, expositions* 7 (April 1908): 10–15.

————. "Meubles que le Musée du Louvre pourrait recueillir." *Les Arts: Revue mensuelle des musées, collections, expositions* 7 (May 1908): 28–32.

Ministère de l'Instruction publique et des Beaux-Arts, *Inventaire générale des richesses d'art de la France.* Vols. 1 and 2. Paris: Plon, 1876, 1878.

Molinier, Emile. "Le Mobilier français du XVIIIe siècle dans les collections étrangères." *Les Arts: Revue mensuelle des musées, collections, expositions* 1 (January 1902): 19–22.

Moncel, Henri de. "Un Discours de M. Bernheim." *La Lorraine-artiste* 10 (1892): 731–732.

————. "Vers l'inconscient." *La Lorraine-artiste* 10 (1892): 674–676.

Monod, E. *L'Exposition universelle de 1889.* Paris: Dentu, 1890.

Montesquiou-Fezensac, Robert de. "Cette petite clef-ci, Emile Gallé." *La Plume: Littéraire, artistique, et sociale* no. 157 (November 1, 1895): 490.

————. *Les Chauves-souris: Deuxième Ouvrage carnival.* Paris: Richard, 1893.

————. *Le Chef des odeurs suaves: Floral Extrait.* Paris: Richard, 1893.

————. *Les Hortensias bleus.* Paris: Charpentier, 1896.

————. "Le Mobilier libre." In *Les Roseaux pensants.* Paris: Charpentier, 1897.

————. *Pays des Aromates: Commentaire descriptif d'une collection d'objets relatifs aux parfums suivi d'une nomenclature des pièces qui la composent.* Paris: Floury, 1900.

————. "Rodin." In *Les Maîtres-artistes.* Numéro spécial consacré à Auguste Rodin no. 8, October 15, 1903.

————. *Les Roseaux pensants.* Paris: Charpentier, 1897.

————. "Les Verres forgés d'Emile Gallé." In *Têtes d'expression.* Paris: Emile-Paul, 1904.

Monzie, A. de. "Eloge de Charcot." *Revue neurologique* 1, no. 6 (1925): 1159–1162.

Morand, Paul. *1900.* Paris: Flammarion, 1930.

Morris, William. "L'Art du peuple." *Société nouvelle* 12 (1894): 32–47.

————. *News from Nowhere.* In *Three Works by William Morris.* New York: International Publishers, 1968.

Mourey, Gabriel. "Anglaises et françaises, école du XVIIIe siècle." *L'Art et les artistes,* pp. 49–98. Numéro spécial, May 1909.

————. *Passé le détroit.* Paris, 1895.

————. "William Morris." *La Revue encyclopédique* no. 167 (November 21, 1896): 805–810.

Nénot, P. *La Nouvelle Sorbonne.* Paris: Colin, 1895.

Nocq, Henri. *Tendances nouvelles: Enquête sur l'évolution des industries d'art.* Paris: Floury, 1896.

Nordau, Max. *Degeneration.* 1895. Reprint. New York: Howard Fertig, 1968.

Oeuvres de Nicolas Pineau, recueil des oeuvres de Nicolas Pineau, sculpteur et graveur de la cour du Régent. Paris: Librairie des beaux-arts appliqués à l'industrie, 1889.

Pelloutier, Fernand. "Les Conditions du travail et de la vie ouvrière en France." *Société nouvelle* 12 (1894): 433–458, 566–580, 690–706.

Picard, Alfred. *Le Bilan d'un siècle, 1801–1900.* Paris: Imprimerie nationale, 1906.

————. *Exposition universelle internationale de 1900 à Paris: Rapport général, administratif, et technique.* 3 vols. Paris: Imprimerie nationale, 1903.

Pineau, Nicolas. *Nouveaux Dessins de plaques, consoles, torchères, et médaillers, nouveaux dessins de pieds de tables, de vases et de consoles de sculpture en bois, nouveaux dessins de lits, à l'usage des architectes et décorateurs, ébénistes, fabricants d'ornements pour appartements, estampeurs, sculpteurs, ornemanistes, fabricants de bronzes, etc.* Paris: Rouvèyre, 1889.

Plauchut, Edmond. "La Rivalité des industries d'art en Europe." *Revue des deux mondes* 105 (1891): 628–645.

Poincaré, Raymond. "Discours à l'Union centrale." *Revue des arts décoratifs* 15 (1894–1895): 318–319.

———. "Discours prononcé par M. Raymond Poincaré, Ministre de l'Instruction publique et des Beaux-Arts, le 1er Mars 1895, au Banquet offert à Edmond de Goncourt." *La Lorraine-artiste* 14 (1896): 278–279.

Portalis, Roger. "La Collection Walferdin et ses Fragonards." *Gazette des beaux-arts* 21 (1880): 297–332.

———. *Honoré Fragonard: Sa vie et son oeuvre.* Paris: J. Rothschild, 1889.

Portalis, Roger, and Henri Béraldi. *Les Graveurs au XVIIIe siècle.* Paris: Damascène Morgond & Charles Fatout, 1880.

Proust, Antonin. *L'Art sous la République.* Paris: Charpentier, 1892.

———. *Commission d'enquête sur la situation des ouvriers et des industries d'art.* Rapport de Monsieur Antonin Proust. Paris: Quantin, 1883.

———. "Discours: Distribution des récompenses." *Revue des arts décoratifs* 5 (1884–1885): 478–479.

———. *Le Salon de 1891.* Paris: Bussod, Valadon, 1891.

Proust, Marcel. *Remembrance of Things Past. Swann's Way.* New York: Vintage Books, 1970.

———. *Remembrance of Things Past. The Guermantes' Way.* New York: Vintage Books, 1970.

———. *Remembrance of Things Past. Within a Budding Grove.* New York: Vintage Books, 1970.

Rey, Jules. "La Statue de Claude Gelée." *La Lorraine-artiste* 10 (1892): 475–478.

Ribot, Théodule. *Essai sur l'imagination créatrice.* Paris: Alcan, 1900.

Richer, Paul. *L'Art et la médecine.* Paris: Gaultier. Magnier, n.d.

———. *Physiologie artistique de l'homme en mouvement.* Paris: Doin, 1895.

Richet, Charles. *Le Surmenage mental dans la civilisation moderne.* Paris: Alcan, 1890.

Richet, Charles [Charles Epheyre, pseud.]. *Possession.* Paris, 1887.

———. "Soeur Marthe." *Revue des deux mondes* 93 (1889): 384–431.

Robida, Alfred. *Le XIXe Siècle.* Paris: Decaux, 1888.

———. *Le XXe Siècle: La Vie électrique.* Paris: Librairie illustrée, 1893.

Rocheblave, S. *Louis de Fourcaud et le mouvement artistique en France de 1875 à 1914.* Paris: Les Belles-Lettres, 1926.

Rodin, Auguste. *Art: Conversations with Paul Gsell* [1911]. Translated by Jacques de Caso and Patricia B. Sanders. Berkeley: University of California Press, 1984.

———. *Rodin: The Man and His Art, with Leaves from His Notebook.* Compiled by Judith Cladel; translated by S. K. Star. New York: Century, 1918.

Roger-Marx, Claude. *La Gravure originale au XIXe siècle.* Paris: Somogy, 1962.

———. "Roger Marx." *Evidences* 12, no. 88 (March–April 1961): 34–38.

Rollinat, Maurice. *L'Abîme.* Paris: Charpentier, 1886.

———. *Les Névroses.* Paris: L. Marétheux, 1883.

Simon, Jules. *La Femme au XXe siècle.* Paris: Calmann-Lévy, 1892.

———. "Il faut rester femme." *La Revue: Ancienne Revue des revues* 18 (1896): 135–141.

Sizeranne, Robert de la. *Les Questions esthétiques modernes.* Paris: Hachette, 1904.

Soriau, Paul. *La Suggestion dans l'art.* Paris, 1893.

Souques, A. "Charcot intime." *La Presse médicale,* May 27, 1925, 693–698.

Ténib, Charles. "Le Nouvel Art décoratif et l'école Lorraine." *La Plume: Littéraire, artistique, et sociale* no. 157 (November 1, 1895): 481–486.

Thirion, Henri. "L'Oeuvre de Clodion." *Revue des arts décoratifs* 5 (1884–1885): 33–44.

Thulié, H. *La Femme: Essai de sociologie physiologique.* Paris: Delahaye & Lecrosnier, 1885.

Trawinski, F. "Musée du Louvre," *La Grande Encyclopédie,* 22:692–698. Paris: Lamirault, c. 1898.

Turbin, Jacques. "Hypnotisme." *La Lorraine-artiste* 10 (1892): 407–408.

Uzanne, Octave, ed. *L'Art et l'idée: Revue contemporaine du dilettantisme et de la curiosité.* 2 vols., 1891–1892.

———. "Coquetteries féminines." *La Grande Dame: Revue de l'élégance et des arts* 1 (1893): 75–79.

———. *La Femme à Paris, nos contemporaines.* Paris: Quantin, 1894.

———. "Le Paravent." *La Grande Dame: Revue de l'élégance et des arts* 1 (1893): 177–181.

Vachon, Marius. *L'Ancien Hôtel de Ville de Paris, 1533–1871.* Paris: Quantin, 1882.

———. *Le Château de Saint-Cloud, son incendie en 1870. Inventaire des oeuvres d'art détruites et sauvées.* Paris: Quantin, 1880.

———. *La Crise industrielle et artistique en France et en Europe.* Paris: Lahure, 1899.

———. *La Femme dans l'art, les protectrices des arts, les femmes artistes.* Paris: J. Rouam, 1893.

———. *La Guerre artistique avec l'Allemagne: L'Organisation de la victoire.* Paris: Payot, 1916.

———. *Les Musées et les écoles d'art industrielle en Europe.* Paris: Imprimerie nationale, 1890.

———. *Nos industries d'art en péril.* Paris: Baschet, 1882.

———. *Pour la défense de nos industries d'art: L'Instruction artistique des ouvriers en Allemagne, Angleterre, et en Autriche. Missions officielles d'enquête.* Paris: Lahure, 1899.

———. *Ruines de la Cour des Comptes au Palais d'Orsay, Frèsques de Théodore Chasseriau.* Album de vues photographiques suivies de découpages d'articles illustrés de Marius Vachon, Ary Renan, et Roger Marx. N.p., n.d.

———. *Some Industrial Art Schools and Their Lessons for the United States.* Extracts from the Studies Made for the French Government by Marius Vachon. Translated by Florence Levy. Washington, D.C.: Government Printing Office, 1923.

Valabrègue, Anthony. "Les Ornements de la femme: La Table à ouvrage et les outils de travail." *Revue des arts décoratifs* 4 (1883–1884): 1–12, 106–113, 326–337, 345–355.

Valbert, Georges. "L'Age des machines." *Revue des deux mondes* 93 (1889): 686–697.

Vapereau, G. *Dictionnaire universel des contemporains.* Paris: Hachette, 1893.

Varenne, Gaston. "La Pensée et l'art d'Emile Gallé." *Mercure de France* 86 (1910): 31–44.

Varigny, M. D. "La Femme aux Etats-Unis: L'Amour et le mariage." *Revue des deux mondes* 92 (1889): 350–375, 432–464.

Velde, Henry Van de. "Déblaiement d'art." *Société nouvelle* 12 (1894): 444–456.

———. "Memoirs, 1891–1901." *Architectural Record* 112 (1952): 144–155.

———. "Une Prédication d'art." *Société nouvelle* 13 (1895): 733–744.

Verlaine, Paul. "Edmond de Goncourt." *La Lorraine-artiste* 14 (1896): 279.

Vinchon, Emile. *L'Oeuvre littéraire de Maurice Rollinat.* Issoudun: Labourer, 1927.

———. *La Philosophie de Maurice Rollinat.* Paris: Jouve, 1929.

W. G. "Pour le centenaire de Roger Marx." *Gazette des beaux-arts* 54 (1959): supplément, 1–3.

Williamson, Edmond. *Les Meubles d'art du Mobilier National: Choix des plus belles pièces conservées au Garde-Meuble.* Paris: Baudry, c. 1900.

Wyzewa, Téodor de. "La Suggestion et le spiritisme." *Revue indépendante* 2 (1887): 201–223.

Zola, Emile. *The Masterpiece.* Ann Arbor: University of Michigan Press, 1968.

Periodicals

Les Arts: Revue mensuelle des musées, collections, expositions
Gazette des beaux-arts
La Grande Dame: Revue de l'élégance et des arts
L'Illustration
Le Japon artistique

La Lorraine-artiste
Nouvelle Iconographie de la Salpêtrière: Clinique des maladies du système nerveux
La Nouvelle Revue
La Plume: Littéraire, artistique, et sociale
La Revue: Ancienne revue des revues
Revue des arts décoratifs
Revue des deux mondes
La Revue encyclopédique
Société nouvelle

Contemporary Encyclopedias and Biographical Dictionaries

Bénézit, Emmanuel. *Dictionnaire critique et documentaire des peintres, dessinateurs, et graveurs.* Paris: Girund, 1976.
Dictionnaire universel du XIXe siècle. IIe supplément Paris: Larousse, 1884.
La France contemporaine: Album illustré biographique. Paris: Clément Deltour, 1904.
La Grande Encyclopédie. Paris: Lamirault, c. 1898.
Larousse du XXe siècle. Paris: Larousse, c. 1912.

Exhibition and Auction Catalogues

Art Nouveau France/Belgium. Houston: Rice University Press, 1976.
Bibliothèque Nationale. *Gustave Geffroy et l'art moderne.* Paris: Bibliothèque Nationale, 1957.
Bibliothèque Nationale. *Joris-Karl Huysmans: Du naturalisme au satanisme et à Dieu. Catalogue de l'exposition.* Paris: Bibliothèque Nationale, 1979.
The Brooklyn Museum. *Belgian Art, 1880–1914.* Brooklyn, N.Y.: Brooklyn Museum of Art, 1980.
Catalogue descriptif des dessins de décoration et d'ornement de maîtres anciens exposés à l'Ecole des Beaux-Arts, mai–juin 1879. Paris: Chamerot, 1879.
Catalogue descriptif des dessins de décoration et d'ornement de maîtres anciens exposés au Musée des Arts Décoratifs en 1880. Paris: Imprimerie de publications périodiques, 1880.
Catalogue des estampes modernes composant la collection Roger Marx. Paris: Baudoin, 1914.
Catalogue des objets d'art moderne: Porcelaines, grès, verres, cristaux, pâtes de verre, étains, émaux translucides, émaux cloisonnés faisant partie de la collection Roger Marx. Paris: Manzi, Joyant, 1914.
Catalogue des tableaux, pastels, dessins, aquarelles, sculptures faisant partie de la collection Roger Marx. Paris: Manzi, Joyant, 1914.
Collection Carle Dreyfus léguée aux Musées nationaux et au Musée des Arts Décoratifs, Exposition au Cabinet des Dessins du Musée du Louvre, avril–mai 1953. Paris: Musées nationaux, 1953.
Collection des Goncourts: Arts de l'Extrême-Orient, objets d'art japonais et chinois, peintures, estampes. Catalogue du vente. Paris: May & Metteroz, 1897.
Collection des Goncourts: Dessins, aquarelles, et pastels du XVIIIe siècle. Catalogue du vente. Paris: May & Metteroz, 1897.
Collection Philippe Burty: Objets d'art japonais et chinois qui seront vendus à Paris dans les Galeries Durand-Ruel. Paris: Chamerot, 1891.
Corning Museum of Glass. *Emile Gallé: Dreams into Glass.* Corning, N.Y., 1984.

"Equivoques": Peintures françaises du XIXe siècle. Paris: Union centrale des arts décoratifs, 1973.

Exposition de la gravure japonaise à l'Ecole Nationale des Beaux-Arts à Paris, 25 avril–22 mai 1890. Paris: Alcan-Lévy, 1890.

Exposition des arts de la femme, guide livret illustré, Musée des Arts Décoratifs, Palais de l'Industrie. Paris: A. Warmont, 1895.

Exposition Rodin et les écrivains de son temps: Sculptures, dessins, lettres, et livres du fonds Rodin. Paris: Musée Rodin, 1976.

François Boucher: A Loan Exhibit for the Benefit of the New York Botanical Gardens, November 12–December 19, 1980. New York: Wildenstein, 1980.

Galerie Georges Petit. *Exposition Claude Monet, A. Rodin.* Paris: Imprimerie de l'art, 1889.

Munich. Stadtsmuseum. *Nancy 1900—Jugendstil in Lotheringen zwischen Historismus und Art Deco, 1865–1930.* Mainz: Münchner Stadtsmuseum, 1980.

Musée des Arts Décoratifs, *Grands Ebénistes et menuisiers parisiens du XVIIIe siècle, 1740–1790.* Paris: Musée des Arts Décoratifs, 1957.

Le Musée du Louvre: Modèles d'art décoratif d'après les dessins originaux. Notice par Victor Champier. Paris: Quantin, 1882.

Office du tourisme de la ville de Nancy. *Nancy Architecture 1900.* Nancy: Imprimerie Star, 1976.

Palais de l'Industrie, *Exposition des arts de la femme: Histoire de la coiffure.* Préface de Marius Vachon. Paris: Le Comité des coiffeurs de Paris, Syndicat général des coiffeurs de dames, 1892.

Philadelphia Museum of Art. *The Second Empire, 1852–1870: Art in France under Napoleon III.* Philadelphia: Philadelphia Museum of Art, 1978.

Salon de l'art nouveau, Premier Catalogue, Hôtel S. Bing, 26 décembre 1895. Paris: Chamerot & Renouard, 1896.

Stanford University. *Rodin and Balzac.* Stanford, Calif.: Stanford University Press, 1973.

Union centrale des arts décoratifs. *Salon annuel des peintures japonaises.* Paris: Pillet & Demoulin, 1883.

Union centrale des arts décoratifs. *Salon annuel des peintures japonaises, 2e année.* Paris: Pillet & Demoulin, 1884.

Secondary Sources

Agulhon, Maurice. *Marianne into Battle: Republican Imagery and Symbolism in France, 1789–1880.* New York: Cambridge University Press, 1981.

Amic, Yolande. "Les Débuts de l'U.C.A.D. et du Musée des Arts Décoratifs." *Cahiers de l'Union centrale des arts décoratifs* 1 (1978): 51–55.

Anderson, Raymond D. *France, 1870–1914: Politics and Society.* London: Routledge & Kegan Paul, 1977.

Arquié-Bruley, Françoise. "Les Graveurs amateurs français au XVIIIe siècle." *Nouvelles de l'estampe* no. 50 (March–April 1980): 5–13.

Arwas, Victor. *Berthon and Grasset.* New York: Rizzoli, 1978.

Auerbach, Erich. *Mimesis: The Representation of Reality in Western Literature.* Princeton, N.J.: Princeton University Press, 1973.

Barrows, Susanna. *Distorting Mirrors: Visions of the Crowd in Late Nineteenth-Century France.* New Haven, Conn.: Yale University Press, 1981.

Baxandall, Michael. *The Limewood Sculptors of Renaissance Germany.* New Haven, Conn.: Yale University Press, 1980.

————. *Painting and Experience in Fifteenth Century Italy*. Oxford: Oxford University Press, 1972.

Benjamin, Walter. *Charles Baudelaire: Lyric Poet in the Era of High Capitalism*. London: New Left Books, 1973.

————. *Illuminations*. Edited by Hannah Arendt. New York: Schocken Books, 1969.

Bernier, Olivier. *The Eighteenth-Century Woman*. New York: Doubleday, 1981.

Bertocci, Philip A. *Jules Simon: Republican Anticlericalism and Politics in France, 1848–1886*. Columbia, Mo.: University of Missouri Press, 1978.

Billy, André. *L'Epoque 1900, 1885–1905*. Paris: Julles Taillandier, 1951.

Bloch-Dermant, Janine. *The Art of French Glass, 1860–1914*. New York: Vendome Press, 1980.

Block, Jane. *Les XX and Belgian Avant-Gardism, 1868–94*. Ann Arbor, Mich.: UMI Research Press, 1984.

Boime, Albert. *The Academy and French Painting*. 2d ed. New Haven, Conn.: Yale University Press, 1986.

————. "The Teaching Reforms of 1863 and the Origins of Modernism in France." *Art Quarterly* 1 (Autumn 1977): 1–39.

Bowra, C. M. *The Heritage of Symbolism*. New York: Macmillan, 1947.

Boxer, Marilyn J. "Women in Industrial Homework: The Flowermakers of Paris in the *Belle Epoque*." *French Historical Studies* 12 (1982): 401–423.

Braibant, Charles. *Histoire de la Tour Eiffel*. Paris: Plon, 1964.

Braudel, F., and Ernest Labrousse, eds. *Histoire économique et sociale de la France*. Vol. 4, *L'Ere industrielle et la société d'aujourd'hui, siècle 1880–1980*. Paris: Presses universitaires de France, 1980.

Burckhardt, Monica. *Mobilier Régence, Louis XV*. Paris: Charles Massin, n.d.

Carroy-Thirard, Jacqueline. "Hystérie, théâtre littérature au XIXe siècle." *Psychanalyse à l'université* 7 (1982): 299–317.

Champigneulle, Bernard. *Art Nouveau, Art 1900, Modern Style, Jugendstil*. Woodbury, N.Y.: Barron's, 1976.

————. *Rodin*. Paris: Somogy, 1980.

Charpentier, Françoise-Thérèse. *Emile Gallé*. Nancy: Université de Nancy, 1978.

Chastenet, Jacques. *Histoire de la IIIe république*. Vol. 2, *Triomphes et malaises*. Paris: Hachette, 1962.

Clark, T. J. *The Absolute Bourgeois: Artists and Politics in France, 1848–1851*. Greenwich, Conn.: New York Graphic Society, 1973.

————. *The Painting of Modern Life: Paris in the Art of Manet and His Followers*. New York: Knopf, 1984.

Clausen, Meredith L. *Frantz Jourdain and the Samaritaine: Art Nouveau Theory and Criticism*. Leiden: E. J. Brill, 1987.

Clément, Roland, and Pierre Simonin. *L'Ensemble architectural de Stanislas*. Nancy: Librairie des arts Nancy, 1966.

Crow, Thomas. *Painters and Public Life in Eighteenth-Century Paris*. New Haven, Conn.: Yale University Press, 1985.

Décaudin, Michel. *La Crise des valeurs symbolistes: Vingt ans de poésie française, 1895–1914*. Toulouse: Editions Privat, 1960.

Didi-Hubermann, Georges. *L'Invention de l'hystérie: Charcot et l'iconographie photographique de la Salpêtrière*. Paris: Editions Macula, 1982.

Digeon, Claude. *La Crise allemande de la pensée française, 1870–1914*. Paris: Presses universitaires de France, 1959.

Doty, C. Stewart. *From Cultural Rebellion to Counterrevolution: The Politics of Maurice Barrès*. Athens: Ohio University Press, 1976.

Drinka, George Frederick. *The Birth of Neurosis: Myth, Malady, and the Victorians.* New York: Simon & Schuster, 1984.

Ducatel, Paul. *La Belle Epoque, 1891–1910: Vue à travers l'imagerie populaire et la presse satirique.* Paris: Jean Grassin, 1973.

Duncan, Carol. *The Pursuit of Pleasure: The Rococo Revival in French Romantic Art.* New York: Garland, 1976.

Duroselle, J. B. *La France de la Belle Epoque: La France et les français.* Paris: Richelieu, 1972.

Ellenberger, Henri F. *The Discovery of the Unconscious: The History and Evolution of Dynamic Psychiatry.* New York: Basic Books, 1970.

Elsen, Albert E. *"The Gates of Hell" by Auguste Rodin.* Stanford, Calif.: Stanford University Press, 1985.

———. *Rodin.* New York: Museum of Modern Art, 1963.

———. *Rodin's Gates of Hell.* Minneapolis: University of Minnesota Press, 1960.

———. *Rodin's Thinker and the Dilemmas of Modern Public Sculpture.* New Haven, Conn.: Yale University Press, 1985.

———, ed. *Rodin Rediscovered.* Washington, D.C.: National Gallery of Art, 1981.

Engelberg, Edward. *The Symbolist Poem.* New York: Dutton, 1967.

Freud, Ernst. *Sigmund Freud: His Life in Pictures and Words.* New York: Harcourt Brace Jovanovich, 1978.

Garner, Philippe. *Emile Gallé.* London: Academy, 1976.

Gelfand, Toby. "Medical Nemesis, Paris, 1894: Léon Daudet's 'Les Morticoles.'" *Bulletin of the History of Medicine* 60 (1986): 155–176.

Goldstein, Jan. "The Hysteria Diagnosis and the Politics of Anticlericalism in Late Nineteenth-Century France." *Journal of Modern History* 54 (1982): 209–239.

Goldwater, Robert. *Symbolism.* New York: Harper & Row, 1979.

Grunfeld, Frederic V. *Rodin: A Biography.* New York: Henry Holt & Co., 1987.

Guillain, Georges. *Jean-Martin Charcot: Sa vie, son oeuvre.* Paris: Masson, 1955. Translated by Pearse Bailey, under the title *J.-M. Charcot: His Life, His Work.* New York: Paul Hoeber, 1959.

Hammacher, A. M. *Le Monde de Henry Van de Velde.* Paris: Hachette, 1967.

Harriss, Joseph. *The Tallest Tower: Eiffel and the Belle Epoque.* Boston: Houghton Mifflin, 1975.

Hause, Steven C., and Anne R. Kenney. "The Limits of Suffragist Behavior: Legalism and Militancy in France, 1876–1922." *American Historical Review* 86 (1981): 781–806.

Hautecoeur, Louis. *Histoire de l'architecture classique en France.* Vol. 7, *La Fin de l'architecture classique, 1848–1900.* Paris: Picard, 1957.

Hayward, J.E.S. "The Official Social Philosophy of the French Republic: Léon Bourgeois and Solidarism." *International Review of Social History* 6 (1961): 28–41.

———. "Solidarity: The Social History of an Idea in Nineteenth-Century France." *International Review of Social History* 4 (1959): 261–284.

Hemmings, F.W.J. *Culture and Society in France, 1848–1898.* New York: Scribner, 1971.

Herbert, Eugenia. *The Artist and Social Reform: France and Belgium, 1885–1898.* New Haven, Conn.: Yale University Press, 1961.

Hillman, Robert G. "A Scientific Study of Mystery: The Role of the Medical and Popular Press in the Nancy-Salpêtrière Controversy on Hypnotism." *Bulletin of the History of Medicine* 39 (1965): 163–182.

Hobsbawm, Erich, ed. *The Invention of Tradition.* New York: Cambridge University Press, 1983.

Holt, Elizabeth. "The Documentation of the Contribution of Three Mid-Nineteenth Century Exhibitions to the Popularization of Japanese Art." In *Art and the Ape of Nature:*

Studies in Honor of H. W. Janson, edited by M. Barasch and L. Sandler. New York: Abrams, 1981.

Honour, Hugh. *Neo-Classicism.* Middlesex, England: Penguin Books, 1968.

Hughes, H. Stuart. *Consciousness and Society: The Reorientation of European Social Thought, 1890–1930.* New York: Vintage Books, 1958.

Institut de France. *Le Musée Condé de Chantilly.* Chantilly: Editions Horarius, 1978.

Janneau, Guillaume. *Les Styles du meuble français.* Paris: Presses universitaires de France, 1972.

Jianou, Ionel. *Rodin.* Paris: Arted, Editions d'art, 1979.

Kalnein, W., and Michael Levey. *Art and Architecture of the Eighteenth Century in France.* Middlesex, England: Penguin Books, 1972.

Kimball, Fiske. *The Creation of the Rococo Decorative Style.* 1943. Reprint. New York: Dover, 1980.

Koch, Robert. "Art Nouveau Bing." *Gazette des beaux-arts* 53 (1959): 179–190.

Latham, Ian, ed. *Art Nouveau, Arts and Crafts, Modern Style, Secession.* Paris: Academy, 1980.

Levey, Michael. *Rococo to Revolution: Major Trends in Eighteenth-Century Painting.* London: Thames & Hudson, 1966.

Levin, Harry. *The Gates of Horn: A Study of Five French Realists.* New York: Oxford University Press, 1966.

Levin, Miriam R. *Republican Art and Ideology in Late Nineteenth-Century France.* Ann Arbor, Mich.: UMI Research Press, 1986.

McGrath, William C. *Freud's Discovery of Psychoanalysis: The Politics of Hysteria.* Ithaca, N.Y.: Cornell University Press, 1986.

McManners, John. *Church and State in France, 1870–1914.* New York: Harper & Row, 1972.

Madsen, S. Tschudi. *Art Nouveau.* New York: McGraw-Hill, 1967.

———. *Sources of Art Nouveau.* 1959. Reprint. New York: Da Capo, 1976.

Mainardi, Patricia. *Art and Politics of the Second Empire: The Universal Expositions of 1855 and 1867.* New Haven: Yale University Press, 1987.

Maitron, Jean. *Histoire du mouvement anarchiste en France, 1880–1914.* Paris: Société universitaire d'éditions et de librairie, 1955.

Mandel, Richard D. *Paris 1900: The Great World's Fair.* Toronto: University of Toronto Press, 1967.

Mannoni, Edith. *Mobilier 1900–1925.* Paris: Ch. Massin, n.d.

Marrey, Bernard, and Paul Chemetov. *Architectures: Paris, 1848–1914.* Paris: ICOMOS, 1972.

Masini, Laura Vinca. *Art Nouveau.* London: Thames & Hudson, 1984.

Mayer, Arno. *The Persistence of the Old Regime: Europe to the Great War.* New York: Pantheon, 1981.

Mayeur, Françoise. *L'Education des filles en France au XIXe siècle.* Paris: Hachette, 1979.

Mayeur, Jean. *Les Débuts de la IIIe République, 1871–1898.* Paris: Seuil, 1973.

Métiers disparus: Édition comportant 70 planches avec notes explicatives, tirées de l'Encyclopédie Diderot. Paris: Baudoin Editeur, 1978.

Morlaine, Jacques. *La Tour Eiffel inconnue.* Paris: Hachette, 1971.

Naylor, Gillian. *The Arts and Crafts Movement in England: A Study of its Sources, Ideals, and Influences on Design Theory.* Cambridge, Mass.: MIT Press, 1971.

Néré, Jacques. *La Crise industrielle de 1882 et le mouvement boulangiste.* Paris: Sorbonne, 1959.

Nipperdey, Thomas. "Nationalidee und Nationaldenkmal in Deutschland im 19. Jahrhundert." *Historische Zeitschrift* 206, no. 3 (1968): 529–585.

Nord, Philip. *Paris Shopkeepers and the Politics of Resentment.* Princeton, N.J.: Princeton University Press, 1986.

Nye, Robert A. *Crime, Madness, and Politics in Modern France: The Medical Model of National Decline.* Princeton, N.J.: Princeton University Press, 1984.

Offen, Karen. "Depopulation, Nationalism, and Feminism in Fin-de-Siècle France." *American Historical Review* 89 (1984): 648–676.

———. "The Second Sex and the Baccalauréat in Republican France, 1880–1924." *French Historical Studies* 13 (1983): 252–286.

Paret, Peter. *The Berlin Succession: Modernism and Its Enemies in Imperial Germany.* Cambridge, Mass.: Harvard University Press, 1980.

———. *"The Enemy Within"—Max Liebermann as President of the Prussian Academy of Arts.* Leo Baeck Memorial Lecture 28, 1984. New York: Leo Baeck Institute, 1984.

———. "The Tschudi Affair." *Journal of Modern History* 53 (1981): 589–618.

Paret, Peter, and Beth Irwin Lewis. "Art, Society, and Politics in Wilhelmine Germany." *Journal of Modern History* 57 (1985): 696–710.

Pevsner, Nicholas. *Pioneers of Modern Design from William Morris to Walter Gropius* [1936]. Middlesex, England: Penguin, 1975.

Pevsner, Nicholas, and J. M. Richards, eds. *The Anti-Rationalists: Art Nouveau Architecture and Design.* New York: Harper & Row, 1973.

Poggioli, Renato. *The Theory of the Avant-garde.* New York: Harper & Row, 1971.

Rabaut, Jean. *Histoire des féminismes français.* Paris: Stock, 1978.

Rewald, John. *Post-Impressionism from Van Gogh to Gauguin.* 2d ed. Garden City, N.Y.: Doubleday, 1962.

Roudinesco, Elisabeth. *La Bataille de cent ans: Histoire de la psychanalyse en France.* Vol. 1, *1885–1939.* Paris: Ramsay, 1982.

Russell, John. *Edouard Vuillard, 1868–1940.* London: Thames & Hudson, 1971.

Schorske, Carl E. *Fin-de-Siècle Vienna: Politics and Culture.* New York: Knopf, 1980.

Scott, Joan. *The Glassworkers of Carmaux.* Cambridge, Mass.: Harvard University Press, 1976.

Seager, H. *The Boulanger Affair: Political Crossroads of France, 1886–1889.* Ithaca, N.Y.: Cornell University Press, 1969.

Sedgwick, Alexander. *The Third French Republic, 1870–1914.* New York: Thomas Y. Crowell, 1968.

Seigel, Jerrold. *Bohemian Paris: Culture, Politics, and the Boundaries of Bourgeois Life, 1830–1930.* New York: Viking Press, 1986.

Selz, Peter, and Mildred Constantine, eds. *Art Nouveau: Art and Design at the Turn of the Century.* New York: Museum of Modern Art, 1975.

Signoret, J. L. "Variété historique: 'Une Leçon clinique à la Salpêtrière (1887)' par André Brouillet." *Revue neurologique* 139 (1983): 687–701.

Silverman, Debora. "Frantz Jourdain: Rococo and Art Nouveau." In *Macmillan Encyclopedia of Architects.* New York: Macmillan, 1982.

———. "J.-M. Charcot et Sigmund Freud," in *Vienne, 1880–1938: L'Apocalypse joyeuse,* 576–586. Paris: Editions du Centre Pompidou, 1986.

———. "The Paris Exhibition of 1889: Architecture and the Crisis of Individualism." *Oppositions* 8 (Spring 1977): 71–91.

Sorlin, Pierre. *La Société française.* Vol. 1, *1840–1914.* Paris: Arthaud, 1969.

———. *Waldeck-Rousseau.* Paris: Colin, 1966.

Stansky, Peter. *Redesigning the World: William Morris, the 1880's, and the Arts and Crafts.* Princeton, N.J.: Princeton University Press, 1984.

Sterner, Gabrielle. *Art Nouveau.* Woodbury, N.Y.: Barron's, 1982.

Stone, Judith F. *The Search for Social Peace: Reform Legislation in France, 1890–1914.* Albany: State University of New York Press, 1985.

Tancock, Jeffrey. *The Sculpture of Auguste Rodin: The Collection of the Rodin Museum, Philadelphia.* Philadelphia: Philadelphia Museum of Art, 1976.

Vaisse, Pierre. "La Querelle de la tapisserie au début de la IIIe République." *Revue de l'Art* 22 (1973): 66–82.

Vartier, Jean. *Histoire de notre Lorraine*. Paris: Editions France-Empire, 1973.

———. *La Vie quotidienne en Lorraine au XIXe siècle*. Paris: Hachette, 1973.

Verlet, Pierre. *The Eighteenth Century in France: Society, Decoration, Furniture*. Rutland, Vt.: Charles Tuttle, 1967.

———. *Styles, meubles, décors du Moyen Age à nos jours*. 2 vols. Paris: Larousse, 1972.

Waddell, Roberta. *The Art Nouveau Style*. New York: Dover, 1977.

Ward, Martha. "The Eighth Exhibition, 1886: The Rhetoric of Independence and Innovation." In *The New Painting: Impressionism, 1874–1886*, pp. 421–439. San Francisco: Fine Arts Museum of San Francisco, 1986.

Wark, Robert. *French Decorative Arts in the Huntington Collection*. San Marino, Calif.: Huntington Library, 1979.

Weber, Eugen. *France, Fin de Siècle*. Cambridge, Mass.: Harvard University Press, 1986.

Weisberg, Gabriel P. *Art Nouveau Bing: Paris Style 1900*. New York: Abrams, 1986.

———. "A Note on Bing's Early Years in France, 1854–1879." *Arts Magazine* 57, no. 5 (January 1983): 84–85.

———. "S. Bing's Craftsmen Workshops: A Location and Importance Revealed." *Source* 3, no. 1 (Fall 1983): 42–48.

———. "Samuel Bing, Patron of Art Nouveau." *Connoisseur* 172 (1969): 119–125, 294–299; 173 (1970): 61–68.

Weisberg, Gabriel P., Phillip Dennis Cate, Gerald Needham, Martin Eidelberg, and William R. Johnston. *Japonisme: Japanese Influence on French Art, 1854–1910*. Cleveland: Cleveland Museum of Art, 1975.

Weissbach, Lee Shai. "Artisanal Responses to Artistic Decline: The Cabinet-Makers of Paris in the Era of Industrialization." *Journal of Social History* 16, no. 2 (Winter 1982): 67–83.

Williams, Roger L. *The Horror of Life*. Chicago: University of Chicago Press, 1980.

Wilson, Edmund. *Axel's Castle*. New York: Scribner, 1931.

Wolf, Peter M. *Eugène Hénard and the Beginning of Urbanism in Paris, 1900–1914*. The Hague: International Federation for Housing and Planning–Centre de Recherches d'Urbanisme, 1968.

INDEX

*Plate 14 was inadvertently reversed
in printing.*

Designer: Sandy Drooker
Compositor: G & S Typesetters, Inc.
Text: 10/13 Bembo
Display: Bembo
Printer: Malloy Lithographing, Inc.
Binder: John H. Dekker & Sons